DESIGNING SYSTEMS AND PROCESSES FOR MANAGING DISPUTES

DESIGNING SYSTEMS AND PROCESSES FOR MANAGING DISPUTES

Second Edition

NANCY H. ROGERS
Moritz Chair in Alternative Dispute Resolution Emeritus
The Ohio State University Moritz College of Law

ROBERT C. BORDONE
Thaddeus R. Beal Clinical Professor of Law
Harvard Law School

FRANK E.A. SANDER
Late Bussey Professor of Law Emeritus
Harvard Law School

CRAIG A. McEWEN
Daniel B. Fayerweather Professor of Political Economy and Sociology Emeritus
Bowdoin College

Published by Wolters Kluwer in New York.

Wolters Kluwer Legal & Regulatory U.S. serves customers worldwide with CCH, Aspen Publishers, and Kluwer Law International products. (www.WKLegaledu.com)

Cover image: iStock/Kaligraf

To contact Customer Service, e-mail customer.service@wolterskluwer.com, call 1-800-234-1660, fax 1-800-901-9075, or mail correspondence to:

Wolters Kluwer
Attn: Order Department
PO Box 990
Frederick, MD 21705

Printed in the United States of America.

1 2 3 4 5 6 7 8 9 0

ISBN 978-1-4548-8082-0

Library of Congress Cataloging-in-Publication Data

Names: Rogers, Nancy H., author. | Bordone, Robert C., 1972- author. |
  Sander, Frank E.A., author. | Mcewen, Craig A., author.
Title: Designing systems and processes for managing disputes / Nancy H.
  Rogers, Moritz Chair in Alternative Dispute Resolution Emeritus, The Ohio
  State University Moritz College of Law; Robert C. Bordone, Thaddeus R.
  Beal Clinical Professor of Law, Harvard Law School; Frank E.A. Sander,
  Late Bussey Professor of Law Emeritus, Harvard Law School; Craig A.
  McEwen, Daniel B. Fayerweather Professor of Political Economy and
  Sociology Emeritus, Bowdoin College.
Description: Second edition. | New York : Wolters Kluwer, [2019] | Includes
  bibliographical references and index.
Identifiers: LCCN 2018048777 | ISBN 9781454880820
Subjects: LCSH: Dispute resolution (Law) | Dispute resolution (Law)—Social
  aspects.
Classification: LCC K2390 .R64 2019 | DDC 303.6/9—dc23
LC record available at https://lccn.loc.gov/2018048777

About Wolters Kluwer Legal & Regulatory U.S.

Wolters Kluwer Legal & Regulatory U.S. delivers expert content and solutions in the areas of law, corporate compliance, health compliance, reimbursement, and legal education. Its practical solutions help customers successfully navigate the demands of a changing environment to drive their daily activities, enhance decision quality and inspire confident outcomes.

Serving customers worldwide, its legal and regulatory portfolio includes products under the Aspen Publishers, CCH Incorporated, Kluwer Law International, ftwilliam.com and MediRegs names. They are regarded as exceptional and trusted resources for general legal and practice-specific knowledge, compliance and risk management, dynamic workflow solutions, and expert commentary.

In fond memory of
one of the most innovative and thoughtful designers,

Frank E.A. Sander,

and to the many individuals who take on the challenge
of designing or redesigning processes and systems
for managing and preventing disputes and who, in doing so,
make workplaces better, increase the effectiveness of organizations, and
improve the lives of individuals, communities, and nations.

Summary of Contents

Contents

Contents

Preface

We hope this book will aid in preparing and encouraging a new generation of individuals to bridge differences. In writing it, we have sought to equip readers who already have a basic knowledge of dispute resolution with the tools they will need to help build into organizations, institutions, companies, schools, and communities— within this nation and elsewhere—a fundamental "hard-wiring" for creative problem-solving and the dynamic management of conflict. It is our belief that tomorrow's professionals and leaders would do well to understand how to design dispute management processes and systems that:

- help identify and capture opportunities for mutual gains;
- build and enhance relationships between individuals, constituencies, and communities;
- advance the cause of justice;
- promote peace and reconciliation;
- support appropriate structural reform as indicated by advancing the rule of law, meeting the interests and the rights of less powerful stakeholders, or curing systemic deficiencies in currently prevailing dispute management practices; and
- adapt to changing times and needs of stakeholders.

Early in our discussions of this second edition, we lost our friend and co-author, Frank Sander. Frank participated in the visioning for this next edition, which adds a story of designers who used their expertise to help Sanford, Florida leaders and residents deal with an immediate crisis and then continue working on identifying and resolving long-term problems to bridge racial divisions. While working on this edition, we recalled Frank's voice urging us to take something out when we add something new. As a result, this new edition maintains the size of the first edition.

Responding to professors who wanted to teach their students facilitation skills, we re-vamped Chapter 15 to meet this need. New stories are scattered throughout the book, and a question has been added in Chapter 5 for professors who want to focus discussion on court dispute resolution programs. The appendix now has a quick review of mediation in addition to negotiation and arbitration, though readers new to the field should also read a dispute resolution textbook.

This edition maintains and updates the references to research and theory from the dispute resolution and law field as well as from political science, sociology, psychology, behavioral economics, and other related disciplines. It also includes valuable and creative examples of dispute management processes and systems. It incorporates our own experience as dispute systems designers in various contexts as well as insights and advice from many scholars and practitioners who have written about designing processes and systems.

The Teacher's Manual and course website direct professors to video and other resources related to these examples. It also directs faculty to the documentary "Endgame," which many instructors will find brings to life the example of Michael Young's secret meetings to design a process for the South African president and Nelson Mandela to negotiate an inclusive form of democratic governance for South Africa. This is one of the seven primary illustrations of DSD we discuss at length throughout the book.

In this book, we aspire to do more than simply synthesize theory, research, and practice. We also hope to expand upon past work. For example:

(1) The book underscores the importance of taking what we term "design initiative"—the decision to take a more proactive role in creating systems and processes to deal with current disputes or even latent and unaddressed conflict. In fact, rarely do clients approach designers with a request for a new process or system. Instead, would-be designers often find themselves asked to resolve a particular dispute, perhaps through mediation or litigation, and then recognize the possibility for a broader and more systemic reform of an organization's dispute resolution system. One inclined to take design initiative might then offer, for example, to help a community think more holistically how it might handle ongoing tensions related to racial, ethnic, or religious issues (Chapters 3, 5, and 8).

(2) The book also examines a broad set of contexts in which designers work. The over 200 design examples come from courts, organizations, churches, schools, and informal communities. We sample widely systems designed for a few individuals and those designed for entire nations because we believe that the breadth will help stimulate your creativity, raise aspirations, and challenge you to identify the core questions that arise across contexts as well as the need for uniquely tailored answers in different contexts.

(3) The book focuses on the opportunities and potential that designers have to help people enhance their relationships and improve their ability to manage ongoing differences between them. The approach that a designer takes in working with stakeholders can sow the seeds for this constructive approach or, alternatively, can sow the seeds for future dissension and discord. We examine the role that the designer has in enhancing relationships not only

within the design of the system or process, but also in the manner that the designer uses to build the system (Chapter 8).

(4) The book presents the challenges that designers face in managing competing interests in their design work, such as those of justice and reconciliation, or those of resolving the immediate dispute and achieving deeper change. Such dilemmas, if not dealt with carefully, can undermine the perceived legitimacy of a system over time. We discuss these dilemmas pervasively throughout the book (*see, e.g.*, Chapters 1, 2C, 3D, 4B5, 4E, 7B, 8, and 12C).

(5) Because this book is written with the idea of the lawyer-as-designer in mind, we suggest how a lawyer's expertise can be leveraged in design, particularly with respect to confidentiality and implementation, including the use of contracts before disputes arise and the pros and cons of changing laws as a means to implement a design (Chapters 7, 12, and 13).

(6) The book also introduces designers to some of the practical tools and skills helpful in design work (especially "practice notes" in Chapters 4D, 7C, and Chapters 14, 15).

(7) And the book offers an approach to evaluating whether a design is achieving the aims set for it (Chapter 14).

Many professionals working with others will find much of what is in these pages valuable. While imagining the audience for this book to be broad, we wrote it in a special way to accompany our own teaching in dispute systems design and in running a skills-based clinic on stakeholder assessment, dispute systems creation, implementation, and evaluation in a law school environment. We assume that the readers already understand dispute resolution practice and theory, but professors whose students are taking this as their first dispute resolution course can order a version of this book that incorporates chapters from some of the publisher's dispute resolution textbooks. We target this book toward those with a special interest in conceiving of their roles broadly as creative problem-solvers. Our notion of problem-solving includes the deployment of the law, but goes well beyond traditional legal reasoning or argument recognized by a court or a judge.

Our goal is to offer a systematic series of questions for the designer along with ideas on where to look for answers. We acknowledge that the answers will differ by context. Designing conflict management processes and systems is not a science. As Martin Luther King, Jr. pointed out, science has made the world a "neighborhood," but not a "brotherhood."[1] Bridging differences fits into the "brotherhood" portion— the non-science portion—of the task ahead. We hope to encourage creative

---

1. Martin Luther King, Jr., Remaining Awake Through a Great Revolution, https://kinginstitute.stanford.edu/king-papers/documents/remaining-awake-through-great-revolution

thinking, collaborative planning, and iterative implementation accompanied by careful assessment. For that endeavor, this book offers materials for the class discussions and individual student reflection.

N.H.R.
R.C.B.
C.A.M.

November 2018

Acknowledgments

We are grateful for the able research and/or editorial assistance provided by John Abbruzzese, Jason Blake, Charles Ellis, Jon Franz, Megan Fulcher, Janice Kwon, Nate Mealey, Courter Shimeall, Jonny Tan, and Elizabeth Keefe Ward, and in addition Barbara Peck's and Jon Franz's creative assistance in assembling and creating photos and video interviews. Some of our academic colleagues shared their insights in reaction to earlier drafts—Tobias Berkman, Chad Carr, Amy Cohen, Florrie Darwin, Steve Goldberg, Sheila Heen, Jeremy McClane, Carrie Menkel-Meadow, John Quigley, Tom Sander, Andrea Schneider, Stephan Sonnenberg, Doug Stone, Gillien Todd, and Rory Van Loo—and these insights contributed in important ways. Jenny Pursell, Carol Thomas, Allyson Hennelly, and Susan Edwards of the Ohio State University Moritz College of Law provided excellent word processing assistance, and Tracy Blanchard and Marilyn Uzuner of Harvard Law School provided helpful support and communication assistance. We thank Dean Alan Michaels at The Ohio State University Moritz College of Law and Dean Martha Minow of Harvard Law School for their encouragement and support of this project. We also thank June Casey of the Harvard Law School Library and Bruce Johnson, Sara Sampson, and Stephanie Ziegler of the Moritz Law Library for providing resources and support. We appreciate hours of help by those pioneers in dispute systems design who are featured in the book: Gary Slutkin, Tio Hardiman, and Candice Kane of Cure Violence; Michael Young who conducted the negotiations regarding South Africa; Rachel A. Wohl, Louis G. Gieszl, Cheryl Jamison, and Nick White of the Maryland Mediation and Conflict Resolution Office; Chief Judge Robert M. Bell of the Maryland Court of Appeals; Colin Rule of eBay; Howard Gadlin of the National Institutes of Health; Professor Jennifer Llewellyn of the Schulich School of Law, Dalhousie University in Halifax, Nova Scotia; collaborative law specialist Pauline Tesler, San Francisco; Andrew Thomas of the City of Sanford, Florida; Brazilian Federal Judge Bruno Augusto Santos Oliveira; and Justice Richard Goldstone of South Africa. Lynn Churchill and John Devins at Aspen/Wolters Kluwer and Kathy Langone, Andrew Blevins, and Renee Cote of The Froebe Group have provided helpful guidance. We want to express gratitude to our many students, for what they have taught us and for the ways in which they use their design talents to contribute to the lives of others. As always, we are thankful for our friends and families who gave us cheer along the way.

The authors gratefully acknowledge the permissions granted to reproduce the following materials:

Beckwith, Sandra (2011) Letter, later adapted as "District Court Mediation Programs: A View from the Bench," 26 *Ohio St. J. on Disp. Resol.* 357. Reprinted by permission.

Brazil, Wayne D. (2006) "Should Court-Sponsored ADR Survive?," 212 *Ohio St. J. on Disp. Resol.* 241. Reprinted by permission.

Cole, Sarah R., and Kristen M. Blankley (2012) "Arbitration Overview," adapted from chapter in Michael L. Moffitt and Robert C. Bordone eds. (2005) *The Handbook of Dispute Resolution* 381. Jossey-Bass. Reprinted by permission.

Cole, Sarah R. Nancy H. Rogers, Craig A. McEwen, James R. Coben, and Peter N. Thompson (2011-2012) *Mediation: Law, Policy, and Practice* (3rd ed.). West Publishing. Reprinted by permission.

Costantino, Cathy A. (2013) Untitled essay. Reprinted by permission.

eBay, Logo and slides. Copyright eBay. Reprinted by permission.

eBay, PayPal dispute form. Reprinted with permission.

Faleck, Diego (2013) Untitled essay. Reprinted by permission.

Goldberg, Stephen B., Frank E.A. Sander, Nancy H. Rogers, and Sarah R. Cole (2012) *Dispute Resolution: Negotiation, Mediation, Arbitration, and Other Processes* (6th ed.). Wolters Kluwer. Reprinted by permission.

Goldstone, Richard J. (2000) *For Humanity: Reflections of a War-Time Investigator.* Yale University Press. Reprinted by permission.

Harvey, Robert (2001) *The Fall of Apartheid: The Inside Story from Smuts to Mbeki.* Palgrave Macmillan. Reprinted by permission of Palgrave Macmillan.

Maryland Mediation and Conflict Resolution Office. "The Road to Success" and "Maps, ADR Programs Available in 2008 and 1998." Slides reprinted by permission.

Oliveira, Bruno Augusto Santos. Photo of Canastra National Park and account of the Canastra National Park process. Reprinted with permission.

Photo of Andrew Thomas and Norton Bonaparte. Reprinted with permission.

Photo of Divided Community Project. Copyright The Ohio State University Moritz College of Law. Reprinted with permission.

Photos of filming Cure Violence interrupter Ameena Matthews for the documentary "The Interrupters." Kartemquin Films/Aaron Wickenden. Reprinted with permission.

Photo of Nelson Mandela and P.W. de Klerk. Copyright Reuters. Reprinted by permission.

Photos of Tio Hardiman, Dr. Gary Slutkin, Chief Judge Robert Bell, Rachel Wohl, Jennifer Llewellyn, Colin Rule, Cathy Costantino, Diego Faleck, Oliver Quinn, PD Villarreal, and Howard Gadlin. Reprinted by permission.

Photo of University of Michigan Hospital. Copyright University of Michigan. Reprinted by permission.

Quinn, Oliver (2013) Untitled essay. Reprinted by permission.

Ury, William, Jeanne Brett, and Stephen Goldberg (1993) *Getting Disputes Resolved.* Reprinted by permission.

Villarreal, PD (2013) Untitled essay. Reprinted by permission.

Cure Violence logo. Reprinted by permission.

Stipanowich, Thomas J. (1998) "The Multi-Door Contract and Other Possibilities," 13 *Ohio St. J. on Dis. Resol.* 303. Reprinted by permission.

Uniform Mediation Act (2002). Copyright National Conference of Commissioners of Uniform State Laws. Reprinted with permission.

Washington Post (2010) "Health Care Summit Live Analysis." Reprinted by permission.

DESIGNING SYSTEMS AND PROCESSES FOR MANAGING DISPUTES

PART ONE

SETTING THE STAGE

CHAPTER 1

Introduction

A. DEFINITIONS: DESIGNING, PROCESSES, AND SYSTEMS

Colin Rule was running an online dispute resolution company in 2003 when eBay hired him to improve the resolution of disputes among the users of both eBay and PayPal. Over the years, Rule and his colleagues created a structure for eBay/PayPal users to negotiate differences. We think of what Rule did as *designing.* We refer to the structured negotiations and a new online jury trial that Rule established as new *processes.* Rule's coordinated series of processes formed what we call a dispute processing *system.*

In the 1980s, Michael Young, a British mining company executive, strove to find a way to end the racial oppression and violence he had witnessed in South Africa. He began building a secret process for reaching consensus on how to structure formal negotiations even before the government and the insurgents accepted his help. Young's negotiations on how to hold negotiations formed the foundation for the people of South Africa to achieve the change that they sought. We refer to the meetings that ultimately occurred between Nelson Mandela and the government as the *process* that Young and others created through a series of facilitated meetings. We call Young and Rule *designers.*

These two stories are examples of a more general phenomenon—the design of processes and of systems for preventing and managing disputes. Two people can deal with the disputes arising between them in a number of familiar ways. They can enter into negotiations, go to mediation, agree to arbitrate, litigate, try to overpower each other, or separate. In these common situations, people do not need a designer to create new processes or systems. But suppose people are dealing with many disputes arising from a massive and complex event (such as the September 11, 2001 attacks or the BP oil spill in the Gulf of Mexico in 2010). Or consider organizations, like hospitals, that deal with hundreds of unexpected medical outcomes and the scores of lawsuits that stem from these outcomes. Rather than dealing with these as isolated events, organizations could fruitfully develop systems for learning from, preventing, and responding to recurring disputes. Situations like these call for creative approaches—sometimes new processes or new systems to order existing processes. They present challenging domains for those who design processes or dispute processing systems.

Designing such processes and systems is what this book is all about. The designer might create just one process, as Young did regarding South Africa, or a series of coordinated processes for many disputes or potential disputes—a system—as Rule did at eBay. We use the term "design" with intention. A design is not random or arbitrary. By *design* we mean the intentional creation of a system or a process to achieve some end or set of goals.

This book covers what has become known in the past 30 years as "dispute systems design," but adds significantly to that work. Building on others' past contributions, the book broadens the scope beyond intra-organizational conflicts and conflicts between people with continuing relationships. Two books in particular popularized "dispute system design" and suggested frameworks for those who do it. Though we draw heavily on their insights, these books took a somewhat more limited view than we take in this book. They examined systems for persons who would be interacting frequently over time, almost always within the context of an organization, institution, or industry. William Ury, Jeanne Brett, and Stephen Goldberg's *Getting Disputes Resolved: Designing Systems to Cut the Costs of Conflict* examined employment disputes in coal mines and offered broad design concepts that could guide designs in other settings (pp. 106-110). Catherine Costantino and Christina Sickles Merchant based their book, *Designing Conflict Management Systems,* on their work within government agencies and other organizations, providing practical ways to work collaboratively with these organizations to create and implement new dispute resolution systems (pp. 391-393). These seminal books stimulated a rich array of design scholarship (*see* Collected References, pp. 430-451).[1]

Perhaps emboldened by this growing body of scholarship, dispute resolution experts have turned increasingly to designing new systems and new processes, sometimes on their own and often with others whose expertise may not be primarily in dispute resolution. What kinds of knowledge, skills, and training do the individuals who do design work possess? Because systematic thinking about design has only emerged in the last 30+ years and because each situation

---

1. *See also* the annotated bibliography on conflict management systems design, edited by Melissa Zarda, at http://www.mediationworks.com/mti/certconf/bib-systems.htm.

presents different challenges, there is as of yet no established professional path for undertaking this work. That is partially what makes this work so exciting and satisfying.

There is also no final list of required competencies or an agreed-upon knowledge base to qualify one to be a designer. However, during the past quarter-century, there has emerged a set of basic skills that most agree are helpful for those who would aspire to be designers on occasion or as a career. Typically, individuals who have some general background in conflict resolution and who also possess a healthy amount of creativity and imagination as well as group facilitation skills will be most likely to succeed in this work (*see* Appendix A for the autobiographies of four individuals who currently do design work). Active listening, curiosity, effective assertion, and self-reflection aid designers in their work. Designers benefit from sound judgment to guide decisions about when and how to become involved and what viewpoints and expertise ought to be represented among stakeholders, as well as when to take a more neutral stance.[2] They often possess an openness to interdisciplinary thinking and have some exposure to basic research in social- and cognitive-psychology, sociology, economics, neuroscience, and game theory. The most successful designers also make close studies of past design efforts by looking for repeating patterns and noting the elements of success and failure. In the chapters that follow we recount several of these stories.

Because the presenting problems vary so widely, and the settings in which they arise range so far and wide, it is difficult to come up with many useful generalizations. For example, normally the designer goes to work after the presenting problem has arisen. But sometimes a designer or design team works proactively (as, for example, when the client is a newly established company or organization) or correctively (when an existing community or organization's present way of handling disputes has proven ineffective or unsatisfactory).

Despite these differences, designers take certain basic steps in most situations:

1. *Taking design initiative:* They find a way to assist, using their design expertise. They become engaged in designing because they are retained as designers, they expand the scope of the work they are already doing (such as a lawyer representing a company on employment-related litigation but suggesting a new internal disputing system, or a mediator asked to assist on one dispute but offering broader ideas), or they take

---

2. The authors are grateful to Michael Young, whom you will meet in the story of the South African negotiations in Chapter 2, who pointed out this characteristic. Young took an active role in deciding to enter, select the participants, and set the initial agenda and then let the participants guide the agenda. He notes the importance of neutrality by the designer "and, as far as possible, the suspension of one's own value judgments" (email to authors, September 3, 2012). *See* the dilemmas concerning a designer's role discussed in Chapters 3, 4.B, 8 and elsewhere in the book.

the initiative to become involved (for example, Michael Young in South Africa). We call this proactive entry or role broadening "design initiative" (Chapter 3).

2. *Assessing or diagnosing*[3] *the current situation:* They identify those who may have a stake in the outcome, including those directly involved, affected by the conflict, or important to the success of a new design. Using this *stakeholder* list, they investigate stakeholders' interests and the extent to which these interests are met or not met by the current dispute processes and systems. They learn as well about the context—anything pertinent to modifying the system and making it work (Chapter 4).

3. *Creating processes and systems:* They convene a design process that will permit the interested parties to voice their concerns (reflecting the basic conflict resolution principle that any proposal emerging from the active participation of all interested parties is more likely to succeed) and they work with these interested parties to build a process or system (Chapters 5-10).

4. *Implementing the design:* They implement a system, with robust feedback loops that keep the system dynamic and responsive to changes in the needs of the organization, situation, context, or external environment (Chapters 11-14).

The first of the four steps just mentioned—taking design initiative—may seem unusual for lawyers who imagine assuming professional obligations only after clients retain or employ them. But designing often begins differently. While individuals, organizations, or government agencies sometimes ask a designer to assist, most have never thought to do so; they may not even recognize the term "designer" in this context. And, if the designer already is engaged as a lawyer or employee, these entities may not expect a proposed process or system as novel as a designer might suggest.

In most of the stories in this book, the results could not have been achieved had the designer simply waited for those involved to ask for this type of assistance. These varied examples and the broad but often unrecognized need for systemic intervention highlight the need and opportunity not only for design skills but also frequently for some level of assertiveness.

In this book, we will urge you to consider being proactive—what we call taking "design initiative"—when your expertise can make a positive difference. At some point, you may be the best person to help your own community find a way to deal more productively and fairly with a conflict that has produced a bitter divide. Within your organization or your legal practice, you may see clearly how conflict management could be improved.

Put another way, ours is a world that provides limitless opportunities for wise and considered design of processes and systems to prevent and deal with disputes.

---

3. This book uses "assessing" and "diagnosing" interchangeably.

We hope that the ideas and examples in this book inspire you to take design initiative. We also hope that when you do so, the materials and structure of this book described in the next section will have prepared you to assist ably and thoughtfully.

B. AN OWNER'S GUIDE TO THIS BOOK

You are the primary target for this book if you are a student with a background in dispute resolution and interested in making design a part of your future work and community involvement. If you fit this description and this is not your first dispute resolution course, skip to subsection 2 below.

1. For those new to dispute resolution

We noted that a designer makes principal use of the basic dispute resolution processes—negotiation, mediation, and adjudication—as well as of some of the variants of these processes and the hybrids that they have spawned. Ours is not a dispute resolution textbook, but as a designer, you should read one in addition to this text (*see* chapter-end references).

2. Learning what steps to take

The book parts and the chapters within each part provide an outline of design steps. A box like the one on the left will remind you occasionally where a chapter fits in the overall design process. Chapter 2 begins the widest portion of the funnel approach of the book with an overview of the entire process. The funnel narrows somewhat as The Planning Process, Part Two, examines in more depth how to take design initiative (Chapter 3), conduct an assessment of the current situation (Chapter 4), and create or choose a process or system that fits the situation (Chapter 5).

Key Planning Issues in More Detail, Part Three, is the narrowest portion of the funnel, examining special design problems in detail—how to select, engage, and prepare participants in the newly designed process (Chapter 6); balance openness and transparency with concerns for confidentiality and privacy (Chapter 7); design a system to take into account the desires to do more than resolve a dispute such as the efforts to prevent recurrence, address deeper change, allow people to be heard, and provide justice (Chapter 8); improve relationships among the

---

DESIGNING STEPS

1. Design initiative
2. Basic planning steps
- Assessing stakeholders, their goals and interests, and contexts
- Creating processes and systems
3. Key planning issues (that may arise throughout the planning)
- Planning how to select, engage, and prepare intervenors and parties
- Determining the extent of confidentiality and openness in the process
- Dealing with desires for change, justice, accountability, understanding, safety, reconciliation
- Enhancing relationships
- Incorporating technology
4. Implementing and institutionalizing the system or process
- Implementing
- Using contracts
- Using law
- Evaluating, revising

people involved in conflict (Chapter 9); and incorporate technology (Chapter 10). Part Four focuses on implementing, including employing informal means such as education and persuasion (Chapter 11) or formal means like contracts (Chapter 12) or law (Chapter 13) and ideas for evaluating the implementation and success of a design (Chapter 14).

One drawback of this structure is that it suggests that designing is a linear activity; it is not. Instead, designers may have to loop back to do a deeper assessment or to reconsider plans (e.g., how open or how confidential?) in light of information discovered later in the design process. We try to mitigate this structural shortcoming in the next chapter—Chapter 2—by first giving you an overview of some of the ways that designers work, replete with many examples, before you embark on an in-depth examination of each part of the design process.

3. Tapping into accumulated experience; searching for ideas

When designers come to a situation, it can be helpful to consider:

a. Stories of designs that have worked or failed in comparable contexts,
b. Empirical evidence of what works and what does not,
c. Theoretical work that examines many accounts and suggests common themes, and
d. Your own life experiences.

To ease your reading, we mark some of these resources for easy reference.

a. Stories
We shade the stories of designs that we cover in some depth. As you will see, some of these designers succeeded more than others in achieving the goals for the new design.

The Community Relations Service intervention without invitation: Public policy and other community-wide mediations often fail because at least one key stakeholder refuses to come to the table.

As you read these stories, consider what lessons you might draw from them. Because seven of these stories will be referenced throughout the book, we mark the repeating stories with an icon, so that you will know to remember them especially:

Cure Violence: In 2000, Dr. Gary Slutkin took the initiative to test a new model for violence prevention by creating a nonprofit called Cease Fire Chicago—now named Cure Violence. He drew from his experience with the World Health Organization in preventing the spread of disease to develop ways to interrupt the spread of violence in high-crime Chicago neighborhoods. The central technique was to employ street-wise interrupters to intervene to prevent retaliatory violence and defuse high-conflict situations. After starting small with one neighborhood, Cure Violence now operates programs in about a dozen U.S. cities, as well as other countries, including Mexico, Honduras, Trinidad, and South Africa.

Chapter 2 introduces each of these seven primary stories.

b. Empirical research

You can find extended discussions of empirical work by looking for text marked like this:

> *Psychology professor Tom Tyler:* "What makes a procedure fair in the eyes of the public? Four factors dominate evaluations of procedural justice.
> • "First, people want the opportunity to state their cases to the authorities. . . ."

c. Theoretical work

Scholars sift through the stories and research to suggest over-arching theory for designers. When these are extended discussions, we box them as in this example:

> *Robert D. Putnam and Lewis M. Feldstein:* "[A]nalysts find it helpful to distinguish between 'bonding social capital' (ties that link individuals or groups with much in common) and 'bridging social capital' (ties that link individuals or groups across a greater social distance). Both kind of connections are valuable to us as individuals, but bridging is especially important. . . ."

d. Your own experience

As you become a designer, you will draw on what you have learned throughout your life—especially what you know about conflict and its resolution, justice, culture, organizations and how they work, interacting with people effectively, law, and leadership. The designers you will read about in this book often deliberately deepened their knowledge in these aspects of designing. Consider doing the same and use this book as the beginning of that journey.

4. Designer practice notes

Designers spend much of their time interviewing, facilitating group discussions, and interacting with clients and other key players. Chapter 15, Facilitation and Related Skills for Designers, in Part V, provides ideas and resources for those who want to improve design skills. To augment this chapter, we include "Practice Notes" throughout the book. Look for these marked like the following:

Practice Notes: Interest Mapping

Once a designer has surveyed all of the stakeholders, the designer can organize that information by creating a chart or "map" depicting each stakeholder, their interests, and the intensity of those interests so that they can be accounted for in the creation of any process.

---

5. Questions and exercises

The chapter-end questions and exercises sometimes ask you to speculate or brainstorm based on only a few facts. We want to ask you many questions and yet spare you from a time-consuming review of detailed fact patterns as you apply what you have read and practice your creativity. Naturally, designers conduct research and analysis before advising a real client, but you can still do thoughtful analysis based on a brief factual prompt.

Your instructor may assign the chapter-end exercises about the fictional Tallahoya University as a way to challenge you to apply what you have learned. These exercises place you in a familiar, though imaginary, setting—a university that encounters some of the problems you might have observed as a student—so that you will probably understand the dynamics of a conflict and the context despite the lack of detailed description. Because the exercise continues throughout the book, you may occasionally have to refresh your memory of the facts by re-reading the first exercise at the end of Chapter 2.

6. Using the book as a reference tool

If you are looking for information for a paper or class project before it is assigned, try checking the following:

a. the table of contents; then turn to the end of these chapters and read the succinct synopsis in a section entitled "Thoughts Going Forward" to decide whether it would be helpful to read further;

b. chapter-end references and collected references at the end of the book;

c. appendix references for those who want to learn more about:

　i. careers of designers (Appendix A);

      ii. arbitration (an overview by Sarah Cole and Kristen Blankley, Appendix B);

      iii. a primer about mediation and the mediation process (Appendix C);

      iv. a primer for teaching stakeholders about negotiation and consensus building (Appendix D);

      v. the Uniform Mediation Act, adopted by eleven states and the District of Columbia (Appendix E); and

  d. the course page for this book, http://aspenlawschool.com/books/managing_disputes/, with a link to a guide to researching in the dispute resolution field.

  e. a video documentary called "Endgame," on the secret South African negotiations referenced in this book, which may be available from your instructor, library, or on Amazon Prime.

THOUGHTS GOING FORWARD

Once you know how to work collaboratively to design a new process or system of processes, you may be surprised by the opportunities you will then recognize to bring about an improvement in the ways that people, organizations, communities, courts, and governments manage their conflicts. This book will offer some structure—a series of steps or questions—plus grist for your decision-making in the form of stories, empirical work, and theory. It will add practice tips and ask you to reflect on justice and policy. To this, you add your own experiences and research, building on this foundation throughout your career. As a designer, you frequently will need to take "design initiative" because people may find it hard to step back to see the potential value of doing things differently and, if they do, may not realize that they might secure process or system design assistance. Ultimately, what you contribute as a designer may improve the quality of life—sometimes even save lives—and represent the most personally rewarding contributions of your career.

BIBLIOGRAPHY AND REFERENCES

BRUNET, Edward, Charles B. CRAVER, and Ellen E. DEASON (2016) *Alternative Dispute Resolution: The Advocate's Perspective* (5th ed.). New York: LexisNexis.

COSTANTINO, Cathy A., and Christina Sickles MERCHANT (1995) *Designing Conflict Management Systems*. San Francisco: Jossey-Bass.

FOLBERG, Jay, Dwight GOLANN, Thomas J. STIPANOWICH, and Lisa KLOPPENBERG (2016) *Resolving Disputes: Theory, Practice, and Law* (3rd ed.). New York: Wolters Kluwer.

FOLGER, Joseph P., Marshall Scott POOLE, and Randall K. STUTMAN (2012) *Working Through Conflict: Strategies for Relationships, Groups, and Organizations* (7th ed.). London: Pearson.

GOLDBERG, Stephen B., Frank E.A. SANDER, Nancy H. ROGERS, and Sarah R. COLE (2012) *Dispute Resolution: Negotiation, Mediation, Arbitration, and Other Processes* (6th ed.). New York: Wolters Kluwer.

GOLDBERG, Stephen B. et al. (2017) *How Mediation Works: Theory, Research, and Practice.* Bingley, UK: Emerald Press.

"Symposium: Leveraging on Disruption" (2017) 13 *U. St. Thomas L.J.* 159.

MENKEL-MEADOW, Carrie J., Lela P. LOVE, Andrea K. SCHNEIDER, and Jean R. STERNLIGHT (2010) *Dispute Resolution: Beyond the Adversarial Model* (2d ed.). New York: Aspen.

MOFFITT, Michael, and Robert BORDONE eds. (2005) *Handbook of Dispute Resolution.* San Francisco: Jossey-Bass.

MOFFITT, Michael, and Andrea Kupfer SCHNEIDER (2014) *Examples & Explanations: Dispute Resolution* (3rd ed.). New York: Wolters Kluwer.

RISKIN, Leonard L., James E. WESTBROOK, Chris GUTHRIE, Timothy J. HEINSZ, Richard C. REUBEN, Jennifer K. ROBBENNOLT, and Nancy WELCH (2009) *Dispute Resolution and Lawyers* (4th ed.). St. Paul: West (also published in an abridged 5th ed. in 2014).

SLAIKEU, Karl A., and Ralph H. HASSON (1998) *Controlling the Costs of Conflict: How to Design a System for Your Organization.* San Francisco: Jossey-Bass.

STITT, Allan J. (1998) *Alternative Dispute Resolution for Organizations: How to Design a System for Effective Conflict Resolution.* Toronto: John Wiley & Sons Canada.

"Symposium: Honoring the Contributions of Christina Merchant to the Field of Conflict Resolution" (2015) 33 *Conflict Resol. Q.* S1, Winter.

WARE, Stephen J. (2016) *Principles of Alternative Dispute Resolution.* St. Paul: West.

URY, William, Jeanne BRETT, and Stephen GOLDBERG (1988) *Getting Disputes Resolved: Designing Systems to Cut the Costs of Conflict.* San Francisco: Jossey-Bass; Cambridge: Harvard Program on Negotiation, http://www.pon.harvard.edu/shop/getting-disputes-resolveddesigning-systems-to-cut-the-costs-of-conflict/.

Overview of the Design Process

In this chapter, we offer an overview of what designers do. By the end of the chapter, you will have a rough sense of the steps in a design process (Section A); where designers find ideas (Section B); and how they work collaboratively with those affected by their work (Section C). In later chapters, we will assume that you have in mind this bigger picture as we examine in more depth each stage in the design process.

We also introduce here seven stories that illustrate the design steps and the innovative and collaborative nature of design work. Like the court opinions that pepper law textbooks, these stories make the issues more vivid and allow the class to have a joint reference. As later chapters examine narrow aspects of design in more depth, they will augment these stories with pertinent details.[1] So, as you read, keep the stories in mind, and we will remind you with the photos or symbols you see below.

South Africa: Just a few years before Nelson Mandela assumed the Presidency of South Africa in 1994, such a peaceful transition to full-suffrage democracy in South Africa seemed beyond reach. Mandela was in prison and the South African government had declared the primary insurgent organization, the African National Congress (ANC), to be an illegal terrorist organization. Its

---

1. We omit footnotes, for the most part, to promote readability of these stories, but note our sources in Appendix F.

Nelson Mandela (right) as he became the President of South Africa, clasping the hand of his predecessor, F.W. de Klerk.

officers were outside the country or in prison. The government had announced a firm position—no negotiations with the ANC until violence by insurgents stopped. The government nonetheless continued using violence to enforce its own racially repressive policies. In the face of what seemed to be poor odds, Michael Young designed an extraordinary process that ultimately set the stage for these two antagonistic parties to come together for formal negotiations. Young's talks led the government to lift the ban on the ANC, free Mandela from prison, and begin formal negotiations for a peaceful transition to majority rule.

Sanford, Florida: Opposing demonstrations sometimes reached 25,000 in Sanford's community of 55,000 in 2012-2013, sparked by public announcements regarding whether to arrest, prosecute, and convict the neighborhood watch volunteer who killed Trayvon Martin, an African-American teenager, as he walked home with a snack from a convenience store.[2] Thanks to Andrew Thomas, a senior city project manager, and the city manager, both trained mediators, the city immediately called for help from mediators within the U.S. Justice Department. With this help and with Thomas coordinating process design, Sanford was one of a few cities facing major civil unrest that had collaborative processes quickly in place to deal with the immediate issues. Sanford emerged from months of unrest without arrests or violence. Even more unusual, Thomas helped the city initiate processes that have continued over the years to deal with other causes of ethnic and racial conflict, including those that had simmered in that community for over a century.

Cure Violence: In 2000, Dr. Gary Slutkin took the initiative to test a new model for violence prevention by creating a nonprofit called Cease Fire Chicago—now named Cure Violence. He drew from his experience with the World Health Organization in preventing the spread of disease to develop ways to interrupt the spread of violence in high-crime Chicago neighborhoods. The central technique was to employ street-wise interrupters to intervene to prevent retaliatory

---

2. Nancy H. Rogers, *When Conflicts Polarize Communities: Designing Localized Offices That Intervene Collaboratively,* 30 Ohio St. J. on Disp. Resol. 173 (2015) (some of the material on Sanford is quoted or paraphrased from this article).

violence and defuse high-conflict situations. After starting small with one neighborhood, Cure Violence now operates programs in about a dozen U.S. cities, as well as other countries, including Mexico, Honduras, Trinidad, and South Africa.

 eBay: Online purchases on eBay result in millions of disputes with relatively low dollar amounts in controversy. When Colin Rule became Director of Online Dispute Resolution at eBay/PayPal in 2003, the dispute resolution system in place was not meeting either buyers' or sellers' needs. Rule re-structured the interactions between buyer and seller to encourage effective negotiations and reduce reliance on mediation and arbitration, and he invented an innovative new system for handling online disputes that arose on eBay.

 National Institutes of Health (NIH): In each of the prior examples, the designer began work when conflict had already surfaced. But a designer working within an organization has the opportunity to build systems that both create the best atmosphere for preventing escalation and deal with conflicts that do emerge. Howard Gadlin exemplifies such a designer. Gadlin worked within the National Institutes of Health, often called simply "NIH," a government agency focused primarily on medical research. Construing his role as "ombuds"[3] broadly, he sought to prevent and resolve disputes and to encourage a working atmosphere in which conflicts among research collaborators and members of scientific research teams are managed effectively.

Truth and
Reconciliation
Commission of Canada

The "Indian Residential Schools": Imagine being asked to design processes and systems for survivors of residential schools when for over a century thousands of children had been removed from their homes to these government-supported institutions. Once there, the religious staff entrusted with their care had allowed them instead to be neglected and abused. As more members of the general public learned about this, many people wanted the government to respond swiftly. Though this story could be about at least three governments, we focus here on Canada, where the government's first alternative processes were widely criticized. Law professor Jennifer Llewellyn then worked as part of a group including Aboriginal representatives and churches to create a novel series of processes that earned broad support.

---

3. Ombuds (or ombudsmen or ombudspersons) investigate informally and try to resolve complaints regarding the government or, within an organization, regarding the organization's administration. Ombuds often also mediate and make recommendations for change when they notice patterns of complaints and sometimes take the initiative to act as dispute systems designers for the organizations they serve.

Maryland courts: Two remarkable individuals—the Chief Judge of the Maryland Court of Appeals (the equivalent of Chief Justice of a state supreme court) Robert M. Bell, and Rachel Wohl, the Director of the Mediation and Conflict Resolution Office—decided to offer more access to mediation for citizens of Maryland. They succeeded. The design process they chose involved citizens throughout the state in collaborative planning.

Chief Judge Robert M. Bell and Rachel Wohl

In these seven stories, the designers ask similar questions as they work with stakeholders to assess, create processes and systems, and implement, though they answer the questions differently. We turn now to the common threads in all seven stories—the design steps and the types of questions they asked.

A. STEPS IN THE DESIGN PROCESS

We refer to four roughly sequential steps:

1. taking design initiative,
2. assessing or diagnosing[4] the current situation,
3. creating systems and processes, and
4. implementing the design, including evaluation and process or system modification.

The real sequence, though, turns out to be much more complicated; it is not linear. A more realistic series of steps might be: assess and analyze the problem and context; plan; take design initiative and become engaged; discover new stakeholders who should be involved; re-analyze, re-plan in collaboration with stakeholders; implement a pilot program; gather and analyze some evidence about how well it works; assess, modify, or implement more widely; re-assess, redesign, and evaluate systematically; perhaps institutionalize and secure a change in law (*see* Potapchuk and Crocker, 1999). Though implementation is listed toward the end, the best designers have one eye on implementation issues (such as finding resources, building support for the idea, and starting thoughtful data collection) right from the start and try to reduce implementation problems with the first steps they take. Realizing that they will later evaluate success, they

---

4. "Assessing" and "diagnosing" are common terms for the same stage in the designing process. *See, e.g.,* Ury et al., 1988:20 (using diagnosis); Costantino and Merchant, 1996:96 (using assessment).

also are attentive to gathering information along the way about how the implementation is going "on the ground" and how people and organizations respond.

1. Taking design initiative

The designers we are studying did not hang out a "Designer for Hire" shingle and then wait for clients. They took the initiative. In the first of our stories, the antagonists seemed unlikely to initiate negotiations. Nonetheless, the prospective designer could envision a means to overcome the barriers to holding talks. First, though, he had to create a role for himself; those involved in the conflict did not ask him for assistance until he had already worked for some months. As you read this segment of the story, consider how and why Michael Young took "design initiative."

Setting the stage to end South Africa's apartheid: In the mid-1980s, the Afrikaner-dominated South African government was engaged in a power struggle with most of its people. The government had excluded 90 percent of the South African people from the enjoyment of key rights because of their race, a policy known as "apartheid." ("Apartheid" means separation but referred to government policies to impose, brutally if necessary, racial superiority of whites. "Afrikaners" were persons of Dutch descent.) By 1985, insurgents[5] opposed to the apartheid regime were throwing grenades or planting bombs several times a month, and police had killed and jailed hundreds of demonstrators.

1985 was also the year Michael Young decided to become involved in the conflict. Young was no stranger to process design in the face of civil unrest and violence. He had intervened in volatile situations in Northern Ireland and elsewhere a few years earlier when he worked for the British government. Now he was an executive with a British mining company that had interests in South Africa. Asked later why he began inviting key people to negotiations when no one could imagine a consensus-based process succeeding, Young responded, "[T]o anyone with half an eye, it was clear that the existing South Africa regime could only end in tears" (PBS, 2009).

In designing a process that would eventually lead to the design of formal negotiations between the government in South Africa and the African National Congress (ANC), Young took into account the reasons why a typical negotiation or mediation process could not succeed in South Africa. First, Young recognized that neither the government nor the ANC wanted the public to know that they were willing to negotiate.[6] To deal with that problem during the planning negotiations, Young sought out people who were sufficiently connected to decision-makers

---

5. There were a number of insurgent groups, making it difficult for Young to select appropriate negotiators, as discussed further on pp. 58-60, 147-148.

6. For more on the reluctance to negotiate, *see* p. 419.

on all sides that they could predict what the decision-makers would find accept-able, but who were sufficiently inconspicuous that they could sneak away from their workplaces unnoticed for meetings (Harvey, 2001:ix, 126-127, 130). Over the course of two years, Young met with people who might fit these criteria. Some welcomed his initiative; others flatly refused. By 1987, Young had persuaded enough of these individuals to become involved that he called the first meeting.

There was another major hurdle: the government had banned the ANC; it was an illegal organization in South Africa, and security forces would arrest its leaders if they entered South Africa. Young addressed this barrier by hosting the meetings that included ANC members at a rural mansion retreat in England.

Using this retreat also increased the secrecy of the meetings. Young knew that secrecy was an essential design feature for yet other reasons. First, the negotiators would be in danger if anyone learned that they were meeting with the other side. Second, absent secrecy, the negotiators would need to show a particular public face to constituents, complicating and prolonging the con-sensus-building process.

The ongoing violence created yet another barrier—the difficulty of focusing on a future that involved shared governance in the midst of bitterness and fear. To surmount this barrier, Young had to find negotiators who cared deeply enough about the future to engage despite the rancor.

Later, Young listed the following as essential elements for his consensus-building process:

- sponsorship by a private company not a direct party to the negotiations
- secrecy
- party choice of agenda items
- involvement of persons who cared about the long term, who were not the most visible leaders, and who genuinely represented their constituents (Young, 2009).

Each element responds to one of the barriers mentioned above or to one of the implementation issues: the need for resources to hold the talks and the need to let the parties know that success rested with them.

As secret negotiations to plan the official negotiations progressed and the situation changed in South Africa, Young encountered new obstacles. For example, the government began parallel secret negotiations with the admired ANC principal, Nelson Mandela, imprisoned by the government, hoping to take advantage of Mandela's lack of communication with those outside to secure a better deal with him. Those involved with Young's process did not learn of these parallel negotiations until well into their own discussions and managed to get word to Mandela so that neither set of negotiations would undermine the other. Young's flexibility in dealing with these problems that arose throughout the negotiations became another essential element of that process.

In 1990, after three years of meetings in England, the South African govern-ment secretly accepted the negotiators' terms of agreement on how to hold official negotiations to end apartheid. The government then released Nelson Mandela from prison and lifted the ban on the ANC. From their meeting site in England, Young and the negotiators watched with deep emotion the live, televised reports of Mandela walking free after 27 years in prison (*see* http://news.bbc.co.uk/2/hi/7499429.stm).

The subsequent official negotiations between Mandela and the government ultimately led to the transition of power to a democratic government and the creation of a Truth and Reconciliation Commission to deal with the past transgressions and plan for peace (Harvey, 2001). The ANC's lead negotiator from the secret talks, Thabo Mbeki, succeeded Nelson Mandela as the second post-apartheid President of South Africa. Mbeki appointed his Afrikaner counterpart in Young's talks, Willie Esterhuyse, as his advisor.

OFTEN-MENTIONED FIGURES IN THE SECRET TALKS

INDIRECT INVOLVEMENT	DIRECT INVOLVEMENT
Oliver Tambo, ANC Executive	Thabo Mbeki, ANC Executive Committee
Nelson Mandela, best known ANC member (in prison)	Tony Trew, ANC constitutional adviser Aziz Pahad, ANC Executive Committee
PW Botha, President (1984-1989)	Professor Willie Esterhuyse
FW de Klerk, President (1989-1994)	Professor Sampie Terre Blanche
Neil Barnard, Director General, National Intelligence Service	W. de Klerk, brother of cabinet member who became President

---

Michael Young used his experience with volatile situations elsewhere to assess the situation in South Africa and build a process to surmount barriers to agreement. Persuading people to work with him took months. Then he had to maintain progress in order to retain their involvement and interest in working with him (*see* pp. 147-148). Clearly, taking design initiative was a crucial and especially challenging step in this process.

In taking design initiative, Young risked rejection, but a joint agreement to invite a designer would have been unlikely. And because Young took initiative, the process succeeded; his involvement averted significant violence.

As you read the examples throughout the book (generally less dramatic than Young's), you will see that designers succeed using varying levels of proactive entry, and that designing by invitation is not necessarily the only or even, at times, the best approach (*see* Chapter 3).

2. Assessing or diagnosing the current situation

One could examine Michael Young's work not only as an example of taking design initiative, but also as modeling the importance of conducting a careful assessment or diagnosis (using these terms interchangeably) before creating the process. From the start, it was obvious that the process would need to build consensus. But careful assessment was key to fine-tuning the process—who would participate, whether they would meet in person, where they would meet, what would be done about publicity, what would be on the agenda, what role would Young himself take, and so forth.

In other contexts, even the general nature of the process—whether it is to build consensus or adjudicate, for example—is in doubt. Designers tend to ask a series of questions to assess the current circumstances that generate and sustain conflict and that may assist in its resolution as a prerequisite to determining whether designing a new process or system would better fit the varied interests. They might begin with questions like the following:

- What are the problems to be addressed—in what ways are the current processes or systems deficient in meeting needs?
- What might be the deeper or systemic causes of the problems (e.g., management strategies, ethnic tensions)?
- Who will be affected by and who could help implement a new design? (We refer to those people whom a conflict affects or who could affect implementation as "stakeholders.")
- How should a designer decide who is or is not a stakeholder?
- What are the stakeholders' expressed goals?
- What unexpressed interests should be considered likely goals as well? How could one determine the accuracy of the guesses on these unexpressed interests?
- How does the current process or system (if there is one) fall short of meeting these goals and interests?

Because the likely direction of the design may add stakeholders and implicate more aspects of the context, the assessment also anticipates the next two stages—creating the process or system and implementing. That involves questions such as:

- What other approaches might better meet the varied stakeholders' interests, deal with the deeper or systemic causes, and be feasible, given the context and constraints?
- What will be broadly regarded as legitimate and fair over time?
- What barriers might exist to implementing changes?

As you read the next account, consider how Andrew Thomas might have answered some of the questions above.

 An ongoing assessment in Sanford, Florida: In 2011, Norton N. Bonaparte, Jr. became Sanford's city manager, and he noticed divisions among Sanford residents and the alienation of some residents from their government. Bonaparte brought Andrew Thomas, who had been hired by his predecessor to coordinate community block grants, into the city manager's office to assist with community projects in addition to his prior duties. Thomas had moved to Florida after his retirement, having mediated hundreds of conflicts and directed the Rochester, New York Center for Dispute Settlement for 26 years. Before becoming a city staff member, Thomas had consulted with the Sanford police department, holding workshops, focus groups, and dialogue sessions. With that background, Thomas began listening to community concerns and placed a high priority on building a trusting relationship with law enforcement. Some residents expressed anger because they believed that Sanford had not invested in the predominately African-American parts of the community. Thomas also learned that many African-American residents of Sanford thought the police did not respond quickly if a person of color complained about a violent crime.

In 2012, the anger and distrust erupted into angry street protests when residents learned that the Sanford police did not immediately arrest George Zimmerman, the man who had shot Trayvon Martin. Later, after prosecutors charged Zimmerman, some city officials spoke optimistically about moving past what they viewed as responses to a single incident, but Thomas had a different view as the result of his earlier assessment and experience.

Thomas's first designs were based on his earlier assessment—before the Trayvon Martin shooting—including his review of homicides in Sanford from 2007 through 2012. Recognizing a lack of trust in city government, Thomas worked with the U.S. Department of Justice Community Relations Service (CRS) mediators to form a group of interfaith clergy from various Sanford neighborhoods and schedule regular meetings to discuss the wide variety of viewpoints held by various parts of the community. Called "Sanford Pastors Connecting," these clergy could help Thomas in his assessment of the issues, and they also could be communicators who would be more trusted by some residents than city officials. In fact, later on CRS mediators arranged seats for Sanford Pastors Connecting at the Zimmerman trial, so that they could send out trusted firsthand accounts to parishioners to counteract inaccurate rumors.

At about the same time, the city asked the U.S. Department of Justice Civil Rights Division to investigate the Sanford Police Department's actions regarding the Trayvon Martin case. The Justice Department staff declined, explaining that the evidence of a single incident was insufficient to constitute a pattern or practice of misconduct, which was required for them to investigate. Thomas then began work on a process for dealing with residents' issues with the police. He asked Department of Justice mediators to identify effective and credible leaders from various communities within the city. He chose from this list an advisory committee (referred to as the "Blue Ribbon Panel") to review the police department. A former judge respected in the legal and business community and the chair of Sanford Pastors Connecting became co-chairs of the advisory committee. The police department periodically reported back to the city manager and city commission (council) as it made changes in response to the advisory group's report. For the first time in memory, in 2013 a representative group of

Andrew Thomas and Sanford City Manager Norton Bonaparte. Photo courtesy of Divided Community Project, The Ohio State University Moritz College of Law.

residents participated in the recruitment process for a new police chief.

Because of the resources provided by outside mediators, Thomas could focus on short-term and long-term issues at the same time. Thomas worked with city officials to develop joint goals that would guide communications, police reactions, and process design. Their goals, informed by the early assessment, were to understand concerns, be open to positive change, proceed with inclusion in decision-making that would make all segments of the community feel valued and accepted, and focus on improving stressed areas of the community.

Consistent with these goals, mediators arranged to meet outsiders as they arrived, helped them to get city permits, and facilitated safe places for them to demonstrate, even arranging transportation for those who might otherwise have been unable to attend a vigil. The city's approach and training for local leaders allowed even rival demonstrations to proceed without any arrests or violence. Thomas and these mediators worked with local residents to develop protocols for dealing with outside groups more intent on confrontation with each other and with local groups. For example, when an outside group marched onto the stage to grab a microphone, the local participants knew what their protocol indicated: they yielded the stage to avoid a confrontation.

As demonstrations occurred periodically for a couple of years, Thomas continued his assessment of the community's issues and his design of processes to deal with them. Community concerns included housing for low-income elderly and disabled residents, and infrastructure issues such as sidewalks, streetlights, and open ditches. At first, residents did not believe that city officials were responsive, especially in neighborhoods with high percentages of African-American residents. The police chief and other city department heads agreed to attend periodic neighborhood meetings, facilitated by City Commissioners and the city manager. After meetings, city officials reported back to that community on any actions taken in response to neighborhood concerns. City officials were able to announce new youth employment programs and training for youth in nonviolent approaches, for example. This process—high-level listening and response—was still in place five years after the Trayvon Martin shooting.

Both the assessment and the implementation of processes in Sanford depended initially on identifying the right leaders who understood concerns of various stakeholders and who would be credible with them. Sanford was fortunate to have an influx of federal mediators who could talk with community members and quickly identify these effective leaders—who sometimes were not the persons who claimed to be leaders or even the officers of key organizations. In time, Thomas supplemented this leader approach with direct conversations with residents.

Determining stakeholders' goals is challenging, as the Sanford story illustrates. For one thing, individuals and organizations are not accustomed to identifying goals for resolving conflict. And when they do identify their goals, these goals might conflict with one another or might shift over time. As a result, it may help to examine the broader interests that give rise to the goals. For this purpose, one might think of the goals as negotiating interests. Roger Fisher, William Ury, and Bruce Patton remind us of the difficulty in separating negotiating positions (here is what I/we want) from interests (why we want what we want). For example, one set of South African negotiators might have "wanted" to avoid discussion of moving to a democracy based on universal suffrage while the ANC saw universal suffrage as essential. The government-leaning group's underlying interest in avoiding that discussion might not be the prevention of universal suffrage, however, but rather protecting the safety, language, and culture of minority group members after transition to majority rule. A designer can be attentive to this distinction between positions and interests in sifting through stakeholders' goals. In this instance, for example, it meant setting an agenda that would address underlying interests—preserving the safety, language, and culture of the minority group members—while also taking up the issues of universal suffrage.

The stakeholders' lack of clarity about their own goals and interests and their failure to parse out short-term versus long-term goals can sometimes lead them to pursue a dispute resolution process not well suited to their needs. For example, initial anger over an injury or set of perceived wrongs, such as a medical error, may lead individuals to seek adjudication even though, over time, they realize their more important interests could have been met with a different approach. Or a public interest group, fearing delay with the court system, may pursue a more expeditious yet private forum only to realize that these processes failed to respond to important interests of public transparency.

DESIGNING STEPS

1. Design initiative
2. Basic planning steps
   - **Assessing stakeholders, their goals and interests, and contexts**
   - **Creating processes and systems**
3. Key planning issues (that may arise throughout the planning)
   - Planning how to select, engage, and prepare intervenors and parties
   - Determining the extent of confidentiality and openness in the process
   - Dealing with desires for change, justice, accountability, understanding, safety, reconciliation
   - Enhancing relationships
   - Incorporating technology
4. Implementing and institutionalizing the system or process
   - Implementing
   - Using contracts
   - Using law
   - Evaluating, revising

The challenge becomes reading between the lines of these goal statements and discerning the underlying interests (*see* pp. 73-78). Designers must persistently deploy skills of artful listening and questioning if they want to help stakeholders understand their own interests better while also building trust with them (*see* Chapter 15 for more discussion of these skills). To translate goals into interests, designers can also draw upon the rich bank of empirical research related to people in conflict, reflect on stories like those in this chapter, and consider design theory.

Using existing research: Psychologists study what they call "procedural justice"—what people in conflict tend to value as part of a process for dealing with disputes (*see* p. 74). Designers may use the procedural justice research to temper their interpretations of a stakeholder's perceptions (perhaps uninformed) about the "best" process. The research suggests that for many disputants being heard, being treated with respect, and working with a trusted and unbiased third party will likely be highly valued, even if stakeholders do not articulate these process goals (Tyler, 1989:831). Studying this research reduces the chances of miscalculating and learning only later that the stakeholders regretted their choices.

The procedural justice literature is just one example of research that assists in reading between the lines to determine interests. Many fields of study offer research pertinent to designers. In this book, we draw most heavily from sociology, social psychology, and economics. But political scientists and others also offer valuable evidence and commentary. Research currently being conducted in neuroscience and decision-making, for example, can offer lessons to designers about how to best build systems and processes that work and that persuade stakeholders to use them and see them as legitimate (Sunstein, 2011:1349; Birke, 2010:477). You can develop your talents as a designer by studying the research from these additional fields.

Using design experience: Studying past design experience, like studying social science research, provides insights on what matters to people in conflict over time. For example, Cure Violence Chicago's evolving design combined the experiences of Gary Slutkin with the World Health Organization's efforts at epidemic control and the organization's Chicago director Tio Hardiman's experience "on the streets" and with others who mediated gang conflict. Thus, while others viewed the Chicago violence as a social and law enforcement problem, Cure Violence's designers first saw it as a health problem, and then also as unresolved disputes, the latter insight leading to the use of street mediators to help resolve some of these disputes before they escalated to violence.

Personal experience implementing new designs can also help designers understand how people will react over time. In the next story, Colin Rule, a conflict resolution expert hired by eBay and its subsidiary, PayPal, drew on his previous online dispute resolution experience to understand how people view online processes. Consider what actions Rule took to determine whether his ideas actually met the interests of those involved and fit the context.

eBay: eBay realized that it needed a dispute resolution process for its users just weeks after it opened its doors in 1995. eBay's rationale was that people would use eBay more often if they had confidence that their disputes would be well handled. Within a few years, eBay had contracted with an online mediation provider that deployed hundreds of mediators to help resolve disputes online.

When Colin Rule became eBay's and PayPal's online dispute resolution director in 2003, he wanted instead to build dispute resolution into the core processes of their websites. For one thing, parties often had disputes over small amounts, and they balked at paying a filing fee to retain a professional dispute resolver over a $25 or $50 disagreement. Rule suggested to management that it made sense for eBay to cover dispute resolution costs as a worthwhile business expense, and the company agreed.

Next, Rule had a hunch, based on his past experiences, that parties arguing over small amounts would rather have a quick decision than an exhaustive process aimed at delivering perfectly fair decisions in every case, and he gathered data that confirmed his hunch. In order to speed up the process, Rule developed software for managing the initial phases of disputes, tailored the software to fit each particular kind of dispute, and offered self-help tools to aid direct negotiation.

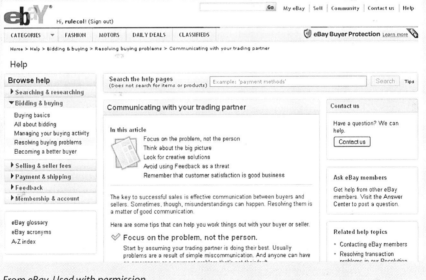

From eBay. Used with permission.

Rule also put in place preventive techniques, such as collecting detailed information on the number of times customers returned merchandise and presenting that information prominently to buyers at the point of purchase. This significantly decreased the volume of disputes associated with item returns and replacements.

Knowing the importance of language from his experience as a mediator (on "framing" and labeling, *see* Korobkin, 2006:305-306, 308-316, 320), Rule modified the language that eBay used in its communications with disputants in an attempt to lessen the likelihood of escalation. For example, eBay replaced the "fraud alert" process with the "item not received" process. "Non-paying bidder" or "deadbeat buyer" reports became "unpaid items." Rule noticed that users began using more problem-solving-focused language in their negotiations with each other after he introduced the new phrases.

eBay continued these and other changes because its in-depth internal analysis showed that user satisfaction increased after their introduction. As eBay reduced customer service contacts, user retention and loyalty improved as a result of the new processes (Rule, 2008:8-10).

Notice that Rule did not rely exclusively on his extensive past experience as a mediator and dispute resolution systems administrator. Instead, he instituted the changes on a trial basis; he gathered data systematically to learn how users reacted, ready to change the practices again to achieve a closer fit with stakeholders' interests.

You will learn more about diagnosis in Chapter 4, but even now you can see how tentative assessments must be, and the importance of gathering information and data about how things are going and continuing to reassess throughout the planning and implementation processes.

3. Creating processes and systems

As noted above, designers consider empirical evidence and factor in their own experience as they are invited in or take design initiative and conduct an assessment. In the same vein, they draw on these resources as they create a process and/or system. At the process- and system-building stage, as well as in earlier ones, designers can also consult a growing body of theory.

Scholars offer theories regarding what people want and will consider fair over time from a dispute resolution process or system. Take the issue of when to create a process that reconciles interests, as did Young and Rule in the stories above. Does the following seminal design theory (discussed more thoroughly in Chapter 5) accurately describe what should be weighed in making that determination?

"In their book, *Getting Disputes Resolved*, . . . William Ury, Jeanne Brett, and Stephen Goldberg assert that in seeking to resolve a dispute, negotiators can focus on interests (the things they want or care about), rights (independent standards with perceived legitimacy, such as law or contract), or power (the capacity to force someone to do something he would not otherwise do). They recognize that the dynamic of the negotiation may require a negotiator to move from one focus to another during a negotiation, but contend that an interest-based approach is preferable, both because it has the greatest likelihood of leading to a mutually advantageous agreement and because it imposes the fewest relational and financial costs" (Goldberg et al., 2012:15).

Further, Ury, Brett, and Goldberg contend that not just during negotiations but in dispute system design among persons with continuing relationships designers should privilege interest-based processes over rights-based ones (arbitration, litigation) and rights-based ones over power-based ones (voting, striking). In the design setting, just as in the negotiation context, they argue that interest-based approaches are generally less costly, with "costs" broadly defined to include effects on transaction expenses, stakeholders' satisfaction with the outcome, relationships, and recurrence of the dispute. Thus, they suggest making the more costly processes the backup processes to an interest-based one (Ury, Brett, and Goldberg, 1988:4).

As these authors point out, their analysis may resonate in many contexts but not all. Think about their theory as it pertains to a context very different from those that they considered—street violence in Chicago.

Cure Violence: Dr. Slutkin drew upon his experience in and evidence from disease control efforts to approach urban violence in an unconventional way—as primarily a public health problem like a contagious disease. His early process design mirrored that used in public health—employing outreach workers to help young people change their thinking about violence and relying heavily on public education and neighborhood involvement to heighten community disapproval of violence. In theory, this would lead to changes in behavior and norms. Although effective in stemming the spread of diseases such as tuberculosis, cholera, and AIDS, this approach to process did not work as well in preventing violence because the outreach workers had little credibility on the streets.

Then Tio Hardiman, later Director of Cease Fire Chicago, proposed a different process that recognized the centrality of disputes to the spread of violence. He proposed getting workers with their own histories of gang engagement and violence to use their networks to identify and then interrupt interpersonal and gang-related disputes. Hardiman thought a mediation-like process could help young people recognize that their interests could be met by choices other than retaliation and violence, despite their sense that society had left them few good choices. He further believed that these young men and women had the resilience to resist the violent street life, if guided by someone who modeled the choice of a different path.

Slutkin and Hardiman discussed this idea with groups essential to the initiative's success, such as police, neighbors, faith communities, and public officials. With their blessing—sometimes skeptical—Cease Fire Chicago began to select, train, supervise, and support former gang members to become interrupters and to deploy them to engage one on one with shooting victims, friends, and relatives to discourage retaliation.[7] They also used their contacts to intervene in other situations where conflict seemed likely, such as cases of insults and of competition in street-level businesses.

A key to the workers' success was building relationships of trust with high-risk individuals in neighborhoods and working regularly with them to find alternatives to violence. The workers also developed caseloads to help young men and women deal with substance abuse, build work skills, find jobs, and leave gangs. Cease Fire Chicago collaborated with community groups and leaders, using every available venue to help them drive home the message that violence was unacceptable and that alternatives to violent responses to conflict were possible.

The early work of violence interrupters in the West Garfield Park demonstrated that this approach could work to help some gang leaders and potential shooters find nonviolent ways to manage their anger while protecting their reputations. The incidence of retaliatory shootings dropped markedly, and overall shootings decreased by two-thirds in the first year of operation. A subsequent formal evaluation found that six of the seven Cease Fire Chicago neighborhoods became safer (Skogan et al., 2008). Impressed with this success, health departments and nonprofit groups in 25 other cities in the United States have adopted aspects of the organization's approach (renamed Cure Violence in 2008), as have groups in seven other nations ranging from England to South Africa to Honduras. Later evaluations in new sites have largely replicated the themes of the Chicago results.

Interrupters Kobe Williams and Eddie Bocanegra with Tio Hardiman (right). Photo courtesy of Kartemquin Films.

In setting up a violence-interruption program, Slutkin and Hardiman were addressing a problem in the status quo—too much violence. It was plausible to assume that the varied stakeholders—including police, neighbors, faith communities, public officials, gang leaders, and community members—shared a strong interest in reducing violence. The challenge for interrupters was to help individuals and groups in conflict to give priority to that interest as compared to others, such as protecting a reputation.

---

7. A documentary on this process, "The Interrupters," was released in 2011. *See* http://www.pbs.org/wgbh/pages/frontline/interrupters/.

This design of an interest-based process to reduce violent retaliation on city streets should help you consider the contexts and conditions in which you find Ury, Brett, and Goldberg's analysis to be sound and those in which you believe a different approach might be better as you read the examples in this text, work on your own design contexts, and look to examples in the world. In Chapters 5 and 8, you will learn to augment Ury, Brett, and Goldberg's theory, which comes from the field of dispute resolution, with other theories—those relating to the yearning for "justice" or "safety," for example. Often these theorists are from other fields, such as deliberative democracy (*see* Gastil and Levine, 2005:14-16), comparative dispute resolution (Cohen and Deason, 2006:23-24), restorative justice and transitional justice (*see* Chapter 8), and leadership, as well (*see* Cohen, 2008). The theories sift through experience to provide insights that can help to guide a designer.

If one outlines Cure Violence's steps, they resemble the list below of typical steps in a design process, though not neatly, as designing in real life involves combined activity and re-tracing steps to modify the plans.

4. Implementing the design

The newly designed system may remain on the shelf unless the designer also assists in planning its implementation and does so from the start. A key implementation challenge is anticipating and addressing resistance to the suggested changes (Chapter 11). Designers recount cautionary tales about times that they failed to identify at the outset who might resist and undermine the design after it was implemented and therefore did not plan well enough to avoid that problem. For example, judges in a local court may develop a new mediation system, but the court clerks might find the new scheduling responsibilities arising from court referrals to be burdensome. The clerks might then slow down the scheduling of mediations. If, instead, the designer includes a clerk's office representative in the planning process, the clerk's needs may become part of the plan, the clerk may feel some ownership of the new program, and the likelihood of resistance from the clerk's office might decrease.

The next story focuses on implementation. Like eBay's Rule, Howard Gadlin used his position to design processes for managing disputes. Gadlin still encountered resistance when he began to do so, even though he was hired as ombuds at the National Institutes of Health (NIH) explicitly to implement a new dispute resolution system. Note how he prepared for that resistance at the start and dealt with it further after it arose.

DESIGNING STEPS

1. Design initiative
2. Basic planning steps
- Assessing stakeholders, their goals and interests, and contexts
- Creating processes and systems
3. Key planning issues (that may arise throughout the planning)
- Planning how to select, engage, and prepare intervenors and parties
- Determining the extent of confidentiality and openness in the process
- Dealing with desires for change, justice, accountability, understanding, safety, reconciliation
- Enhancing relationships
- Incorporating technology
4. **Implementing and institutionalizing the system or process**
- **Implementing**
- **Using contracts**
- **Using law**
- **Evaluating, revising**

The National Institutes of Health Ombuds: The National Institutes of Health (NIH) established an ombuds office in 1999 to build a more collaborative workplace atmosphere and finely tune over time the internal processes for managing employee disputes. NIH is a federal research agency with a $31 billion budget and about 20,000 employees, half of whom are engaged in scientific research. One reason for establishing the ombuds office was to focus on reducing or resolving disputes among collaborating scientists. Modern science relies on teams of scientists working closely together. Without effective teamwork among scientists, major scientific breakthroughs might not happen. But tensions are inherent in teams led by one or more scientists who won competitive grant support for their work (principal investigators). Their teams typically included postdoctoral fellows, graduate students, and laboratory technicians. Conflicts over mentorship quality, perceived favoritism, choice of scientific methods and data interpretation, authorship priority, and work ethic and style can easily disrupt the scientific enterprise. By establishing an ombuds, NIH administrators wanted to facilitate a preventive and active design role to help scientists learn how to work effectively in teams and to anticipate and resolve conflicts on their own.

Former NIH Ombuds Howard Gadlin

NIH administrators were thus embracing a more recent trend to broaden the role of the ombuds (Sturm and Gadlin, 2007). Historically, ombuds (also called ombudsmen) acted as intermediaries between citizens and their government. As they helped people resolve complaints informally, the ombuds observed patterns of disputes and became a source of recommendations for improved governance. Private organizations and public agencies began to employ "organizational" ombuds during the 1970s and 1980s to perform not only this historical function within the organizations but also to act as process and system designers. The goal was to work with individuals within an organization to build their capacity to deal effectively with conflict. Organizations employed this approach with the hope that it would reduce the likelihood that conflicts would occur or become acute and would require costly dispute resolution procedures.

As Howard Gadlin arrived in 1999 and began mediating individual disputes among collaborating scientists, Gadlin wondered what sort of systems might resolve them earlier or avert them altogether. Listening to a conference presentation about partnering agreements used in the building trades,[8] Gadlin

---

8. In partnering agreements, those involved in a construction project discuss likely issues and establish regular meetings at which to discuss these before they become disputes. They also identify in advance the processes they will use to resolve disputes. *See* Thomas J. Stipanowich, *Beyond Arbitration: Innovation and Evolution in the United States Construction Industry,* 31 WAKE FOREST L. REV. 65 (1996).

recognized that the construction parties in an ongoing project had dispute system interests that resembled the interests of collaborating scientists.

Gadlin adapted the construction partnering agreements for use among collaborating scientists and shared the draft with an NIH stakeholder group. By encouraging these scientists to draft partnering agreements, Gadlin sought to help them consider, at the beginning of their collaboration, how they would resolve potentially disruptive issues that might arise between them. He listed for their discussion and agreement the kinds of issues that could provoke conflict—such as how co-authored articles would be published, who could conduct derivative research, and who would appear on the news if they made a major discovery.

Implementing this new idea was not easy. The stakeholder group of supervisors and others rejected the idea, saying that scientists would never negotiate a complex contract like his prototype.

Incorporating this new information, Gadlin returned to the group with a modified proposal. He reconfigured the contract into a simple list of questions and included a place to agree in advance to mediate or arbitrate if a dispute arose.[9]

The stakeholders were still skeptical that scientists would use the question list with a mediation/arbitration clause, but now they were supportive of his idea. Unit supervisors created opportunities for Gadlin to present his plan to NIH scientists and included a unit on what they began to call the "prenuptial" agreement as part of new employee orientation.

Over time, NIH scientists increasingly used the Gadlin "prenuptial" agreements. Based on the NIH's success, universities have adapted the NIH "prenuptials" for faculty collaborations (Sturm and Gadlin, 2007:2122, 33-39).

Gadlin continued developing new systems to strengthen interactions and resolve disputes. He interviewed scientists whose collaborations were most successful, distilled success principles, taught these principles, listened to suggestions to augment them, and released a collaboration workbook for scientists.[10] He also worked with several executive officers to pilot a new employee grievance system. Gadlin's staff regularly attends the dispute resolution sessions, interviews those involved or affected, and suggests changes.

Gadlin not only used the implementation phase to overcome unexpected resistance but also took advantage of that phase to test ideas and modify them. He adapted ideas from varied contexts and experimented, not always achieving success in the first instance. Other designers find value in Gadlin's approach of anticipating and planning for the unexpected but also cultivating and embracing

---

9. The list of questions for collaborating scientists is discussed in more detail on p. 284.

10. The workbook contents are discussed on pp. 121-122.

humility. Like Gadlin's first attempt at a contract to structure collaborating scientists' relationships, a dispute resolution process or system may hit bumps in the road. For example, a designer may recommend that courts use mediation to decrease litigation. But lawyers who know that a court will schedule mediation shortly after filing may postpone settlement talks until after they sue. As a result, court filings may increase rather than decrease. That sends the designer back to the drawing board.

Recognizing that surprises may be in store, the designers may begin with a pilot (Chapter 11), and then evaluate the results before counseling expansion (Chapter 14). They may also locate resources, take a small program to scale, weave it into the fabric of society and its institutions (Chapter 11), make it part of contracts (Chapter 12), and even, in some circumstances, seek a new statute or rule so that the program will be successful and fair (Chapter 13).

B. DRAWING FROM OTHER CONTEXTS, BUT WITH CAUTION

Parties in conflict often find themselves so embedded in their own situation that they fail to look outside their own immediate context for ideas on how to change the disputing patterns and systems—even when these existing patterns and systems do not achieve their goals. You, like the designers discussed earlier in this chapter, can use your own experiences, empirical research evidence, and scholarly design theory. Once designers have surveyed their own experience and the relevant research and theory, they often look to successful dispute resolution systems in other contexts from which they can draw lessons and analogies. As noted above, for example, Howard Gadlin studied partnering agreements from the construction industry and adapted them for use by collaborating National Institutes of Health scientists (pp. 30-31).

But suppose that you have little time to assess the shortcomings of the current situation before suggesting a tentative solution. You may feel pressure to adapt a successful process for a similar problem from elsewhere. While sometimes this is the only practical option, designing a system "on the fly" or simply importing the experience of one context into another is fraught with risk, especially if there is no opportunity to gain input or launch a pilot version first.

In the example below, the government instituted a common dispute resolution approach in the aftermath of a major problem but soon learned that the new processes did not meet the aspirations of those involved. The government then funded a group of stakeholders and experts to propose new processes.

Truth and
Reconciliation
Commission of Canada

Processes in the aftermath of the Indian Residential Schools of Canada: In 2004, the Assembly of First Nations, a national political organization for the Aboriginal groups in Canada, invited dispute resolution and restorative justice scholar Jennifer Llewellyn to join a task force that would propose new procedures to the Canadian government and church representatives. These new procedures might replace those the government put in place in 1998 to deal with the aftermath of the "Indian Residential Schools." To this task force of legal experts and representatives of former residential school students and Aboriginal communities, Llewellyn suggested that the new process could be crafted to fit the interests—theirs as well as other stakeholders'—and context. Though the group would decide what processes fit best, Llewellyn encouraged the group to consider processes used throughout the world but also to feel free to modify them or to create a new process or system.

The background of this design work was a tragic chapter of Canada's history that continues to affect hundreds of thousands of Canadians. From 1883 until the 1990s, the Canadian government funded residential schools, often operated by churches, to "assimilate Aboriginal people forcibly into the Canadian mainstream by eliminating parental and community involvement in the intellectual, cultural, and spiritual development of Aboriginal children" (Truth and Reconciliation Commission of Canada, 2012a:1). Over time, there were about 140 such schools.

As related in 2012 by the Truth and Reconciliation Commission of Canada: "[P]eople spoke of parents having to send children off to residential school against their will, . . . of tearful farewells at train stations, shorelines, and in school parlours, of children crying throughout the entire flight to school, and of cold and impersonal receptions given to children on arrival. . . .

"Traditional, and often highly valued, clothing and footwear, handmade by loving mothers and grandmothers, were taken from them and never seen again. Long hair, often in traditional braids that reflected sacred beliefs, was sheared off. . . . Children lost their identity as their names were changed—or simply replaced with a number. . . . In the words of countless students, it was a frightening, degrading, and humiliating experience.

"Former students described how they came from loving families and were cast into loveless institutions. . . . Brothers and sisters were separated from each other within the schools, and often were punished for hugging or simply waving at one another.

"Food was strange, spoiled and rotten in many cases, poorly prepared, and often in short supply. . . . For many, little in the classroom related to their lives. The only Aboriginal people they could recall from their history books were savages and heathen, responsible for the deaths of priests. [T]he spiritual practices of their parents and ancestors were belittled and ridiculed. . . .

"The Commission heard of discipline crossing into abuse: of boys being beaten like men, of girls being whipped for running away, of children being forced to beat other children, sometimes their own brothers and sisters, . . . of being sexually abused within days of arriving at residential school. In some cases, they were abused by staff; in others, by older students. . . .

"The Commission was told of children who died of disease, of children who killed themselves, of mysterious and unexplained death. Many students who came to school speaking no English lost the right to express themselves. Students repeatedly told the Commission of being punished for speaking their traditional languages. . . . It was clear that not only language was lost: it was voice. . . . If they were abused, the only people they could complain to were abusers. . . .

"Survivors described what happened after they left the schools. People no longer felt connected to their parents or their families. . . . Some people still find themselves reliving the moments of their victimization. . . . People spoke of how the residential school left them hardened . . . they had not been given the skills needed to keep their families together. They had difficulty in showing love. . . . People spoke of incredible anger, the damage it did to them and caused them to inflict on others. The abused often became abusers: husbands, wives, parents, children all fell victim" (Truth and Reconciliation Commission of Canada, 2012a:1, 4-6).

When more members of the general public learned of this story in the late 1980s, prosecutors began investigating and prosecuting some former residential school staff, but there were few prosecutions. More significantly, survivors of the schools began suing the government and churches. The last schools were closed in the early 1990s. In 1996 the government-sponsored blue ribbon commission on the Aboriginal condition (the "Royal Commission on Aboriginal Peoples") issued a report setting out the abuses of the residential schools. In 1998, the Canadian Minister for Indian Affairs and Northern Development acknowledged the government's role in the schools and expressed regret for students who suffered physical or sexual abuse. The government also committed $350 million for "healing" for former students who suffered physical or sexual abuse, though the Aboriginal Healing Foundation, charged to administer the fund, took a more holistic approach.

Then, the government also implemented an optional claims process after a few exploratory discussions with Aboriginal representatives and a pilot program. The government did not engage in the collaborative design process or the evaluations of pilot programs described in this chapter. Called the "ADR" process, the claims process had simpler procedures than courts, though the procedures resembled the adversary process. The government authorized the ADR process to issue the types of tort recoveries available through litigation. The ADR process used an award schedule that tied claims payments to likely court recoveries within the claimant's province (Jung, 2009a:6-7).

The government's response was typical of what other governments have done as the public learned of large-scale abuses—for child abuse for children in government-funded, church-run institutions in Ireland and Australia, for example (Savage and Smith, 2003; http://www.ccypcg.qld.gov.au/pdf/genesis/forde-govtresp.pdf). But residential school survivors and the broader Aboriginal communities reacted negatively to it. A few years later, thousands of claimants still preferred the courts to the government's new claims process, and the Assembly of First Nations issued a "scathing critique" of the alternative process as unfair as well as failing to fit the problems that included non-physical harm to the survivors and the damage to the entire communities, including their cultures, the people involved, and their aspirations (Jung, 2009a:7-8; *see also* Regan, 2010:122-130).

The government then funded the new design task force through the Assembly of First Nations. Task force members talked about the inadequacy of the courts or the government-created tort-based claims process in fulfilling the needs of stakeholders. First, the harms that mattered most to survivors were often not the bodily harm for which both systems offered compensation. They recommended that the government and churches create a "common experience" payment for all survivors of the system, reflecting the forced removal from families, destruction of culture and language, harsh conditions, and dehumanization. This payment would be based on the number of years of attendance at a residential school and would be in addition to recovery for sexual abuse or assaults (Regan, 2010:111-124). Second, the claimants frequently had not learned to read during their time in the residential schools and could not complete the technically worded claim forms. They were offended by the trial-like requests for evidence.

Third, the task force members recognized that the survivors as well as their families and communities sought more than monetary compensation, apologies, and a report. About 80,000 former students were still alive and suffering from their ordeals in the residential schools, as were some of their parents and children and the wider communities affected by them after their return. In addition to the compensation, the former students sought, as recounted later by the Truth and Reconciliation Commission:

- Help in gaining assistance with emotional issues, including ways to do this in parts of the country that lacked professional services, and with parenting skills that would reflect their traditions and values.
- Respect. "People are angry at being told they should simply 'get over it.' For them, the memories remain, the pain remains" (Truth and Reconciliation Commission of Canada, 2012a:7).
- Control over their children's education.
- Investment in restoring their languages and traditions, which they believed were endangered by the residential school system.

- Assurance that the story of the residential schools would be told broadly, including in Canadian history textbooks used throughout the nation (Truth and Reconciliation Commission of Canada, 2012a:6-8).

> "The road we travel is equal in importance to the destination we seek. There are no shortcuts. When it comes to truth and reconciliation, we are all forced to go the distance."
>
> —Justice Murray Sinclair, Chair of the Truth and Reconciliation Commission of Canada (2010, in 2012a:1)

In what Llewellyn described as a generous spirit, they also sought opportunities for reconciliation. She also noted their preference for procedures that fit their traditions.

What the task force proposed, and what ultimately formed the basis for the agreement established among all the parties to the pending class actions, broke new ground: the new claims tribunal (with a fund of $1.9 billion), grants to help with treatment and research ($225 million), and a new federal agency that would award funds for commemorative activities ($20 million for commemoration) and act as a truth and reconciliation commission[11] for five years ($60 million for operations). The Truth and Reconciliation Commission of Canada was to "reveal the complete story of Canada's residential school system, and lead the way to respect through reconciliation . . . for the child taken, for the parent left behind" (Truth and Reconciliation Commission of Canada, 2012a:2). The courts approved the 2006 settlement agreement in 2007. Though not required by the settlement, the parties hoped that the Prime Minister would apologize, and he did.[12]

The story of copying an ADR process in 1998 illustrates the limitations of skipping two design steps—assessment and collaborative process/system creation—even if others (in this case two other governments) have used that same process. By reinserting the assessment and process/system creation step in 2004-2006 through the funding of the Assembly of First Nations' task force,

---

11. Chapter 8 discusses the distinct nature of Canada's Truth and Reconciliation Commission when compared to such commissions in about forty other nations.

12. In 2008, Prime Minister Stephen Harper issued an apology at the House of Commons, with Aboriginal leaders and former students in attendance. "In his statement, the prime minister recognized that the primary purpose of the schools was to remove children from their homes and families in order to assimilate them better into the dominant culture. Harper said, 'These objectives were based on the assumption Aboriginal cultures and spiritual beliefs were inferior and unequal. Indeed, some sought, as it was infamously said, "to kill the Indian in the child." Today, we recognize that this policy of assimilation was wrong, has caused great harm, and has no place in our country'" (Truth and Reconciliation Commission of Canada, 2012b:80-81). The churches and House of Commons had issued apologies earlier.

the government hit a responsive chord. The claims tribunal compensated about 10 percent of the Aboriginal population of Canada, and relatively few claimants exercised their right to opt out of the claims process (Jung, 2009a:11, 14). The Assembly of First Nations leader, Chief Phil Fontaine, himself a school survivor, supported the new processes. Many of those who wanted more than compensation have participated in the Truth and Reconciliation processes. The Truth and Reconciliation Commission issued a six-volume report and 94 "calls to action" in 2015. While some Canadians continue to debate the success of the new processes, others note the educational value for future generations of Canadians (Capitaine and Vanthune, 2017; Costa, 2016; Jung, 2009a:2; James, 2012:182-184; *see* Chapter 8; Menkel-Meadow, 2014). Many Canadians deeply engaged with the Truth and Reconciliation Commission and appreciated the opportunities it provided. For example, at a 2010 Commission event, 10,000 people attended each day; one group of residential school survivors and their families walked 1,200 kilometers to demonstrate their commitment. At a 2011 event, 550 residential school survivors told their stories to Commission members. Over a hundred local families opened their homes to the 1,000 survivors who came by car, bus, boat, and plane (Truth and Reconciliation Commission of Canada, 2012a:18-20).

A dispute management system that was successful elsewhere may fail to thrive in a new time, a new institution, a new social context. Still, studying these other initiatives often provides a starting point, to be followed by a new assessment and process/system creation. Llewellyn thus urged her colleagues in the Canadian design process to consider truth and reconciliation commissions and other processes used elsewhere in the world as "illustrations" but not necessarily "answers" for the Canadian situation. The limitations on using these ideas from other contexts, though, is yet another reason for a designer to operate modestly and in collaboration with stakeholders who will be affected by the design, as well as to operate with thoroughness, curiosity, and a deep commitment to listening.

C. DESIGNING COLLABORATIVELY

No matter the step in design, designers say that they pay attention to what the stakeholders say they want, what their underlying needs may be, and why they have not achieved these goals in the current context (Ury et al., 1988). They then identify the features of a system and the kinds of processes that can help them achieve their goals. At times, designers may need to work with stakeholders in an educational capacity to expose them to different dispute resolution options, help them attain a clearer view of their own goals, and assist them in gaining a new perspective on their problems. This can be challenging as parties in a dispute are often locked into their own perspectives. Chapters 3 and 5 discuss in more detail some of the challenges that designers face when working on behalf of clients and other stakeholders to help design a dispute resolution system.

As the planning proceeds, the parties may raise goals or identify interests that they did not think to express before. Sometimes, the pilot implementation of a forum or system demonstrates that the new approach would not improve the status quo. For example, an insurance company began a pilot program in which the company offered to pay for a private mediator if a complainant agreed to mediate before suing it. After a brief period of success, attorneys for claimants began routinely to demand at least the amount of the mediator's fee ("You will have to pay it anyway if I ask for mediation before suing.") in cases that the company viewed as lacking merit. The company preferred the status quo to that new situation and terminated the pilot program.

How early in the process should designers involve other stakeholders as co-planners? The next story illustrates how bringing stakeholders into a collaborative design process from the outset can improve the designer's ability to identify stakeholders' interests and implement the resulting designs (Costantino and Merchant, 1996).

Maryland Mediation and Conflict Resolution Office: Rachel Wohl was a litigator for the Maryland Attorney General's Office when she participated in her first mediation. Wohl had low expectations for the mediation, and was surprised by how much it helped the parties to overcome their differences. She decided to learn more about dispute resolution and to look for opportunities to use it in new contexts. After some years, she proposed to Robert M. Bell, the Chief Judge of the Maryland Court of Appeals (Maryland's highest court), that he develop a new dispute resolution plan for Maryland. The plan would expand dispute resolution in the courts and also extend its use beyond the courts into arenas like education, government, and business. Wohl offered to leave her job as head of a nonprofit to help implement the plan.

Chief Judge Bell accepted Wohl's proposal. He also agreed with Wohl's idea to "use dispute resolution to plan for dispute resolution"—in other words, to make sure that the planning process itself incorporated the types of collaborative approaches that Wohl sought to implement. Ultimately, Chief Judge Bell appointed 40 persons, representing a variety of stake-holders, to a planning commission and engaged hundreds of others in advising them. He chaired the commission and provided staff and funding. Nationally renowned experts donated their time to provide commission members with background information on dispute resolution and systems design.

Photo by Jonathan Franz

The commission worked collaboratively with both Wohl and her deputy director, Lou Gieszl, to develop a plan to "advance appropriate use of ADR statewide and to improve the way in which we, as a society, manage conflict." Within 18 months, the commission recommended a number of possible initiatives. The scope of their recommendations extended beyond the courts; they recommended reforms for schools, universities, government, businesses, and communities. To help implement the action plan, Chief Judge Bell turned the commission into a staff office—the Mediation and Conflict Resolution Office (MACRO). MACRO received half a million dollars in public funds to award in grants in its first year of operations.

A decade later, Marylanders had more dispute resolution options, particularly for mediation, than before, and they were using them. In addition, MACRO had developed software that permitted ongoing assessment of program quality at no cost to the individual programs. Chief Judge Bell appointed an advisory board that included representatives from key stakeholder groups, and that advised a permanent staff of designers at MACRO.

Rachel Wohl

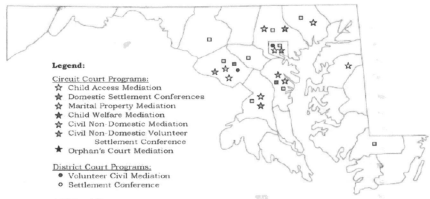

ADR Programs Available in 1998

Legend:

Circuit Court Programs:
☆ Child Access Mediation
★ Domestic Settlement Conferences
☆ Marital Property Mediation
★ Child Welfare Mediation
☆ Civil Non-Domestic Mediation
☆ Civil Non-Domestic Volunteer
    Settlement Conference
★ Orphan's Court Mediation

District Court Programs:
● Volunteer Civil Mediation
○ Settlement Conference

Additional Programs:
■ State's Attorneys' Office Mediation
□ Community Mediation
■ Juvenile Justice and Other ADR

For program-by-program detailed maps, see www.marylandmacro.org

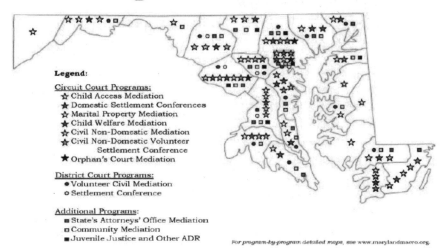

ADR Programs Available in 2008

Legend:

Circuit Court Programs:
☆ Child Access Mediation
★ Domestic Settlement Conferences
☆ Marital Property Mediation
★ Child Welfare Mediation
☆ Civil Non-Domestic Mediation
★ Civil Non-Domestic Volunteer
    Settlement Conference
★ Orphan's Court Mediation

District Court Programs:
● Volunteer Civil Mediation
○ Settlement Conference

Additional Programs:
■ State's Attorneys' Office Mediation
□ Community Mediation
■ Juvenile Justice and Other ADR

For program-by-program detailed maps, see www.marylandmacro.org.

The months of collaborative planning may have enabled the rapid growth in mediation programs that followed the release of the Maryland report. Certainly, the collaborative process increased the chances that the planners understood the interests of those affected and could take them into account in the planning. Those working with the Maryland program also credit the collaborative process for generating trust of the program among the courts, bar, and mediators. That trust, in turn, has helped the Maryland program institute additional reforms discussed later in this book.

Collaborative designers may also uncover conflicting interests, raising the issue of whom the designer serves. How should the designer respond to a client who seeks an uneven playing field? For example, a corporate client may encourage a designer to work with it to create a system that decreases the ability of aggrieved employees to sue the company. The client might accomplish that by using an employment agreement containing a clause that requires employees to mediate before filing suit and to split the mediation expenses equally with the employer. Because the employees may not be able to afford half of the mediator's fee, such a clause would effectively block most from pursuing their claims. Or, a court may tell a designer that it wants its mediators to tell judges about uncooperative negotiators even though experience indicates that some mediators will take advantage of this authority to pressure parties to settle (*see* p. 176). Should designers in these contexts accept their clients' wishes at the expense of others' interests?

In this and other ways, the conflicting interests that emerge in assessing a situation can create dilemmas for the designer. Some designers begin by advising clients that dispute systems work well in the long term only if they take into account the highest priority goals of all stakeholders and fit prevailing norms about what is fair. Suppose that a client resists this advice. How should the designers proceed? Should they resign (Menkel-Meadow, 2009; *see also* p. 81)? Simply follow the clients' request (*see* pp. 78-83)? These dilemmas can carry high stakes, and these stakes are complicated by the fact that there are currently no professional ethics requirements for designers and no agreed upon professional body monitoring the work of designers. You can even see these dilemmas in situations beyond this book—for example, a nation, bitterly splintered after widespread violence, wants to choose "peace over justice" (*see* Zartman and Kremenyuk, 2005). Should a designer refuse to help unless a nation gives high priority to the international community's demands that the perpetrators of violence be prosecuted (Chapter 8)? Chapter 4.B.5 provides diagnostic questions for you to reflect upon as you consider some of the challenging professional and ethical choices you may face in your role as a designer.

THOUGHTS GOING FORWARD

The stories in this chapter serve as a reminder that designing is both hard and consequential work. Designers often arrive after the failure of more established conflict systems. And they are not always successful in improving the existing systems. The examples of how Canada first responded in the aftermath of Indian Residential Schools illustrates the problems incurred when skipping a careful inquiry about the fit of a proposed design with the present context, stakeholder interests, and broader demands for change and justice, while Canada's second response shows the advantages of undertaking such an inquiry. By doing exceptional design work, the designers in some of the stories helped to bring about remarkable changes, sometimes saving lives and often improving the quality of life.

As you think about the stories from this chapter, you may begin to see a pattern in the thinking of the successful designers. The designers assessed or evaluated the situation—some quickly; others over years—and then began to imagine a feasible process or system that would work better in resolving one or many conflicts and perhaps in preventing others. They also took design initiative to become involved or to broaden and define their involvement. They then worked with stakeholders to develop processes more closely suited to their varied interests and context. They dealt thoughtfully with dilemmas, such as competing confidentiality interests and desires for reconciliation and accountability. They tended to stay on for the implementation. We move now to examine elements of this pattern—design initiative, assessment, process creation, implementation, evaluation, and analysis—in more depth.

QUESTIONS

2.1 A group of business lawyers has a request for your design group. In your state, a project like a wind farm or oil drilling operation must secure approvals to operate on a particular site from one or more of about ten state agencies that have jurisdiction over siting requests under various circumstances. These ten agencies include, for example, the state power siting board and the state environmental protection agency. The lawyers describe to you a recent incident in which a company that had filed for a site approval with a state agency did not learn that it had filed with the wrong agency until a hearing was held a year later. This is the tip of the iceberg, they say. None of these siting agencies convenes an informal process in advance of a hearing, and hearings are often delayed by crowded dockets. In the view of these lawyers, the lack of informal procedures has created a hostile environment for businesses in the state. They ask, "Could you help us persuade the state to design a better way of handling the approval process and the subsequent conflicts that might emerge from them? This is killing business in our state." Make a list of issues that your design group should discuss before responding to this request.

2.2   A staff member for your state supreme court asked for your advice about whether or not to have a manual written for the state trial court judges on implementing mediation programs. The staff member explains, "Eight trial courts in our state now have such mediation programs. I can point you to the best three. What I have in mind is for the manual to profile these three court mediation programs. It should include details, like local court rules and press releases, so that other courts can just select one of the three approaches and implement it. The justices would like to see court mediation programs proliferate. They also want the programs to be successful in settling cases early in ways that increase satisfaction with the courts and are consistent with justice system values. I hope that the courts that have not yet adopted a mediation program will do so, and do so successfully, if we give them a 'how-to' manual." What would you advise the staff member about pursuing this idea and why?

2.3   With the number of homeless people exceeding available shelter capacity, your city proposed rehabilitating a shuttered factory to create another homeless shelter. The factory site has the advantage of being in a residential neighborhood. As a result, the location would also be appropriate for later modification to provide longer term housing if the city decided to do so. Some fiscally conservative political groups oppose the city expenditure for this project as costly and unnecessary. Legal services lawyers point out that the city could give grants that would help people avoid eviction, and therefore homelessness, for a fraction of the cost. Residents living near the factory have joined to hire a lawyer to stop or slow down the approval of zoning variances and construction permits. Cold weather will arrive in four months, threatening a humanitarian crisis if the controversy is not soon resolved, and the neighbors, in particular, could slow down the work well beyond that time. The mayor turns to your design group to help bring about consensus on what the city should do. What issues should the group discuss before responding to the mayor?

Exercise 2.1   *The design team at Tallahoya University:* Your enrollment in this class has landed you an interview for the new dispute resolution systems design team at Tallahoya University (TU), a 20,000-student, private university in the City of Tallahoya. TU's in-house counsel suggested employing designers because TU faces several challenging issues.

TU's counsel warned that you will be asked at the interview to give your preliminary thinking about new designs for these matters. "Don't worry," the counsel added, "if we hire you, you will have much more information before you recommend a design. Plus, you will have completed your dispute systems design course by then. To get a sense of your talents and creativity, we just want to know your initial thoughts about processes that might help deal with these issues. I know that your class has already studied seven innovative forum or systems designs. Why don't you just compare TU's situations with what has been done elsewhere and suggest what else you would need to know to decide whether this would be a good solution for TU?"

Here are TU's most pressing issues:

a. TU just announced its plans to substitute "Fighting Wolves" as its mascot in place of the "Fighting Braves," the mascot used for the last century. Before the change, many had argued that the use of the traditional mascot and its depiction showed insensitivity to Native Americans, but now a number of TU constituencies resist giving up the century of traditions associated with the current mascot.

b. TU wants to increase its four-year graduation rate for undergraduates. A recent survey indicates that a number of students attend part time so that they can work, leading to delayed graduation and additional indebtedness. Although the students can secure student loans to cover tuition, rent, and food, many work to maintain a car so that they can commute to apartments in the City of Tallahoya suburbs. Students tend to move out of university dormitories after their sophomore year. There are apartments just east of campus, but these juniors and seniors do not consider these nearby apartments more than three blocks from campus to be in a safe enough area, so they live primarily on the eastern fringe of campus or in the suburbs. In addition, these apartments on the eastern fringe of campus increasingly have unwanted additional roommates, like rats and bed bugs, and the landlords often do not return deposits. The best landlords have left the area because the students who have rented their apartments often trash the apartments and leave without paying the last month's rent. So, more and more students rent suburban apartments, buy cars, get jobs, reduce their credit hours, and delay graduation.

c. TU has an anti-discrimination policy that includes religious discrimination. It was rarely invoked until the last couple of years when the university began attracting more international students, staff, and faculty. The university routes religious discrimination complaints through existing procedures. For example, claims against faculty go through the regular procedures that can lead to dismissing even tenured faculty, but faculty members are rarely terminated. Claims against staff go to the supervisor, and supervisor reactions have varied. Claims against students go through the student misconduct procedures, with peer judges. Complainants tend not to pursue any complaints at all after learning about TU's procedures, though a few retain attorneys and sue TU.

d. TU's Board of Trustees developed a policy last year of protecting its intellectual property while also helping developing nations have access to its expertise. The Board was surprised by the controversy that arose as the policy was applied. To name one example, those companies supporting TU faculty research to develop high-performing seeds want an unbending contractual obligation for the farmers using the seeds—all would be prohibited from gathering the seeds at harvest and re-using them. The seed research will not be feasible without outside grants from these companies. In a similar vein, pharmaceutical companies that support medical research will terminate research funding if TU's policy means that the products developed based on the TU research will be distributed at below-U.S.-market prices in developing nations. They fear that drugs distributed in developing nations will leak back into developed nations, destroying the profit prospects for their products. These controversies divide even those within the university. Faculty collaborators sometimes argue bitterly over whether to accept outside funding under these circumstances. Students have started to refuse to work on projects that they think will provide huge windfalls to companies and to TU and its faculty while denying the benefits to persons in poor and developing countries.

e. TU has embarked on a 50-year expansion of its sprawling university campus, this time impinging on properties west of campus that are next to or across the street from upscale residential properties (student-occupied apartments tend to be east of campus). TU contracted with a business to purchase the properties, hiding from the community the fact that TU would be the eventual owner and would demolish existing residential buildings. The families living west of campus expressed outrage when they learned of the deception and the plans. The construction and then the new uses will add noise and traffic and draw upon city services such as fire and police. The sight lines for these residential areas will change as well. TU has no processes planned to deal with the likely future "town/gown" conflicts.

BIBLIOGRAPHY AND REFERENCES

BENNETT, L. Michelle, Howard GADLIN, and Samantha LEVINE-FINLEY (2010) *Collaboration & Team Science: A Field Guide.* Bethesda, MD: National Institutes of Health.

BINGHAM, Lisa Blomgren (2008) "Designing Justice: Legal Institutions and Other Systems for Managing Conflict," 24 *Ohio St. J. on Disp. Resol.* 1.

BIRKE, Richard (2010) "Neuroscience and Settlement: An Examination of Scientific Innovations and Practical Applications," 25 *Ohio St. J. on Disp. Resol.* 477.

BRADY, Rory (undated, approximately 2002) *Report to the Government on the Review of the Laffoy Commission* (unpublished Irish government document).

CAPITAINE, Brieg, and Karine VANTHUYNE eds. (2017) *Power Through Testimony: Reframing Residential Schools in the Age of Reconciliation.* Vancouver: UBC Press.

CARR, Alan, Barbara DOOLEY, Mark FITZPATRICK, Edel FLANAGAN, Roisin FLANAGAN-HOWARD, Kevin TIERNEY, Megan WHITE, Margaret DALY, and Jonathan EGAN (2010) "Adult Adjustment of Survivors of Institutional Child Abuse in Ireland," 34 *Child Abuse & Neglect* 477.

COHEN, Amy J. (2008) "Negotiation, Meet New Governance: Interests, Skills, and Selves," 32 *Law & Soc. Inquiry* 503.

COHEN, Amy J., and Ellen E. DEASON (2006) "Comparative Considerations: Towards the Global Transfer of Ideas on Dispute System Design," 12 (3) *Disp. Resol.* 23.

COLL, Bryan (2009) "Why Ireland Is Running Out of Priests," *Time Magazine*, Dec. 3, *available at* http://www.time.com/time/world/article/0,8599,1942665,00.html.

COSTANTINO, Cathy A., and Christina Sickles MERCHANT (1996) *Designing Conflict Management Systems*. San Francisco: Jossey-Bass.

DE COSTA, Ravi (2016) "Discursive Institutions in Non-Transitional Societies: The Truth and Reconciliation Commission of Canada," 38(2) *Int'l Pol. Sci. Rev. 185.*

FADER, Hallie (2008) "Designing the Forum to Fit the Fuss: Dispute System Design for the State Trial Courts," 13 *Harv. Negot. L. Rev.* 481.

FEINBERG, Kenneth R. (2005) *What Is Life Worth?* New York: Public Affairs.

FISHER, Roger, William URY, and Bruce PATTON (1991) *Getting to Yes: Negotiating Agreement Without Giving In* (2d ed.). New York: Penguin Group.

GASTIL, John, and Peter LEVINE eds. (2005) *The Deliberative Democracy Handbook: Strategies for Effective Civic Engagement in the 21st Century*. San Francisco: Jossey-Bass.

GOLDBERG, Stephen B., Frank E.A. SANDER, Nancy H. ROGERS, and Sarah R. COLE (2012) *Dispute Resolution: Negotiation, Mediation, Arbitration, and Other Processes* (6th ed.). New York: Wolters Kluwer.

HARVEY, Robert (2001) *The Fall of Apartheid: The Inside Story from Smuts to Mbeki*. New York: Palgrave Macmillan.

JAMES, Matt (2012) "A Carnival of Truth? Knowledge, Ignorance and the Canadian Truth and Reconciliation Commission," 6 *Int'l J. Transitional Just.* 182.

JUNG, Courtney (2009a) "Transitional Justice for Indigenous People in a Non-Transitional Society," *ICTJ Research Brief*, www.ictj.org.

JUNG, Courtney (2009b) "Canada and the Legacy of the Indian Residential Schools: Transitional Justice for Indigenous People in a Non-Transitional Society," http://ssrn.com/abstract+1374950.

KOROBKIN, Russell B. (2006) "Psychological Impediments to Mediation Success: Theory and Practice," 21 *Ohio St. J. on Disp. Resol.* 281.

LANDE, John (2002) "Using Dispute System Design Methods to Promote Good-Faith Participation in Court-Connected Mediation Programs," 50 *UCLA L. Rev.* 69.

LLEWELLYN, Jennifer J. (2002) "Dealing with the Legacy of Native Residential School Abuse in Canada: Litigation, ADR, and Restorative Justice," 52 *U. Toronto L.J.* 253.

LLEWELLYN, Jennifer (2008) "Bridging the Gap Between Truth and Reconciliation: Restorative Justice and the Indian Residential School Truth and Reconciliation Commission," in M. Brant-Castellano, L. Archibald, M. DeGagne eds., *From Truth to Reconciliation: Transforming the Legacy of Residential Schools* 183. Ottawa: Aboriginal Healing Foundation.

MAYER, Bernard (2000) *The Dynamics of Conflict Resolution: A Practitioner's Guide*. San Francisco: Jossey-Bass.

MENKEL-MEADOW, Carrie (2009) "Are There Systemic Ethics Issues in Dispute System Design? And What We Should [Not] Do About It: Lessons from International and Domestic Fronts," 14 *Harv. Negot. L. Rev.* 195.

MENKEL-MEADOW, Carrie (2014) "Unsettling the Lawyers: Other Forms of Justice in Indigenous Claims of Expropriation, Abuse, and Injustice," 64 *U. Toronto L.J.* 620.

POTAPCHUK, William R., and Jarle CROCKER (1999) "Implementing Consensus-Based Agreements," in Lawrence Susskind, Sarah McKearnan, and Jennifer Thomas-Larmer eds., *The Consensus Building Handbook* 527. Thousand Oaks, CA: Sage Publications.

PBS, (2009) Interview with Michael Young, *available at* https://www.youtube.com/watch?v=8-_EP8VI78E (last visited Aug. 15, 2018).

REGAN, Paulette (2010) *Unsettling the Settler Within: Indian Residential Schools, Truth Telling, and Reconciliation in Canada.* Vancouver: UBC Press.

RULE, Colin (2008) "Making Peace on eBay: Resolving Disputes in the World's Largest Marketplace," *ACResolution*, Fall 8.

SAVAGE, Robert J., and James M. SMITH (2003) "Sexual Abuse and the Irish Church: Crisis and Responses," in Boston College, The Church in the 21st Century: Occasional Paper #8.

SCHNEIDER, Andrea Kupfer, and Natalie C. FLEURY (2011) "There's No Place Like Home: Applying Dispute Systems Design Theory to Create a Foreclosure Mediation System," 11 *Nev. L.J.* 368.

SKOGAN, Wesley G. et al. (2008) *Executive Summary, Evaluation of Cease Fire-Chicago* (Northwestern University), *available at* www.northwestern.edu/ipr/publications/ceasefire .html.

SLAIKEU, Karl A., and Ralph H. HASSON (1998) *Controlling the Costs of Conflict: How to Design a System for Your Organization.* San Francisco: Jossey-Bass.

STITT, Allan J. (1998) *Alternative Dispute Resolution for Organizations: How to Design a System for Effective Conflict Resolution.* Toronto: John Wiley & Sons.

STURM, Susan, and Howard GADLIN (2007) "Conflict Resolution and Systemic Change," 2007 *J. Disp. Resol.* 1.

SUNSTEIN, Cass R. (2011) "Empirically Informed Regulation" 78 *U. Chi. L. Rev.* 1349.

SUSSKIND, Lawrence, Sarah McKEARNAN, and Jennifer THOMAS-LARMER eds. (1999) *The Consensus Building Handbook: A Comprehensive Guide to Reaching Agreement.* Thousand Oaks, CA: Sage Publications.

TESLER, Pauline H. (2007) *Collaborative Law: Achieving Effective Resolution Without Litigation* (2d ed.). Chicago: ABA.

TRUTH AND RECONCILIATION COMMISSION OF CANADA (2012a) *Interim Report.* Winnipeg, Manitoba: TRC of Canada.

TRUTH AND RECONCILIATION COMMISSION OF CANADA (2012b) *Canada, Aboriginal Peoples, and Residential Schools: They Came for the Children.* Winnipeg, Manitoba: TRC of Canada.

TRUTH AND RECONCILIATION COMMISSION OF CANADA (2015) *Honouring the Truth, Reconciling for the Future: Summary of the Final Report of the Truth and Reconciliation Commission of Canada.* Winnipeg, Manitoba: TRC of Canada.

TYLER, Tom R. (1989) "The Psychology of Procedural Justice: A Test of the Group-Value Model," 57 *J. Personality and Social Psych.* 830.

URY, William, Jeanne M. BRETT, and Stephen B. GOLDBERG (1988) *Getting Disputes Resolved: Designing Systems to Cut the Costs of Conflict.* San Francisco: Jossey-Bass; Harvard Program on Negotiation, http://www.pon.harvard.edu/shop/getting-disputes-resolveddesigning-systems-to-cut-the-costs-of-conflict/.

WELSH, Nancy, and David B. LIPSKY (2013) "'Moving the Ball Forward' in Consumer and Employment Dispute Resolution: What Can Planning, Talking, Listening and Breaking Bread Together Accomplish?," 19 (3) *Disp. Resol. Mag.* 14.

YOUNG, Michael (2009) "The South African Talks: A Template for Peace," Huffington Post, Oct. 20, at http://www.huffingtonpost.com/michael-young/the-south-african-talks-a_b_327316.html.

ZARTMAN, I. William, and Victor KREMENYUK eds. (2005) *Peace Versus Justice: Negotiating Forward- and Backward-Looking Outcomes.* Lanham, MD: Rowman & Littlefield Publishers, Inc.

PART TWO

THE PLANNING PROCESS

The next three chapters focus in more detail on three parts of planning—taking design initiative (Chapter 3), assessment or diagnosis (Chapter 4), and process and system creation (Chapter 5). In application, these concepts overlap. These concepts also implicate issues discussed in more detail in Part Three, such as confidentiality; implementation issues covered in Part Four; and matters we have called "skills"—the focus of Part Five.

Taking Design Initiative and Clarifying Roles

This chapter addresses the first step in designing—establishing and clarifying your role as a designer. You might take that first step in a number of ways: offering to help conflicting groups within your community develop a process for working through their differences productively; suggesting new ways for a corporate client to resolve matters prior to litigation though the client retained you only to defend litigation; offering ideas to improve the management of conflict in your workplace; responding to an international agency's request to redesign a conflict resolution process. Whatever the circumstance, you are likely to play an active role in intervening or redefining your role. We call this taking "design initiative." After reading this chapter, you should have a better understanding of when and how you might take design initiative and what role issues—both conceptual and practical—you should think about at the start.

The chapter is organized to respond to the following questions:

- Might there be a better process or system—one that will improve the situation for those involved—and can it be implemented (Section A)?
- If so, who should be involved in the design (Section B)?
- What are the most effective ways to gain acceptance as a designer (Section C)?
- How should you define your role conceptually (Section D)?
- How do you negotiate the operational parts of the role—resources, time-frame, etc. (Section E)?

A. IDENTIFYING A PROBLEM OR OPPORTUNITY AND ENVISIONING A BETTER WAY

DESIGNING STEPS

1. **Design initiative**
2. Basic planning steps
- Assessing stakeholders, their goals and interests, and contexts
- Creating processes and systems
3. Key planning issues (that may arise throughout the planning)
- Planning how to select, engage and prepare intervenors and parties
- Determining the extent of confidentiality and openness in the process
- Dealing with desires for change, justice, accountability, understanding, safety, reconciliation
- Enhancing relationships
- Incorporating technology
4. Implementing and institutionalizing the system or process
- Implementing
- Using contracts
- Using law
- Evaluating, revising

The first question is whether there is a problem with the current approach to managing conflict or whether there might be an opportunity to handle conflict more effectively as it arises. Put negatively, it would be inadvisable to take design initiative or to accept an invitation to assist if no feasible new disputing process or system would fit stakeholders' interests better and work more effectively than the existing one. For this reason, designers may devote considerable time to answering the questions posed in the remainder of this book before they assume responsibility for design work.

One could fashion this initial analysis a number of ways depending on the context. For a public policy dispute, for example, a designer might assess the political environment before deciding whether to suggest a collaborative approach to a conflict between municipalities, developers, and others involving city incorporation, zoning, and other jurisdictional matters. Such an examination might ascertain "whether the issues are likely to be negotiable (or whether there may be significant barriers or a lack of ripeness for intervention at a particular moment); whether the stakeholders are identifiable, reasonably empowered, and have some interdependence; and whether parties are pursuing political strategies that would make it difficult for them to enter negotiations" (Laue et al., 1988:15). In another context, designers might ask instead whether there will be resources for the newly designed system to work; whether an organization or the law could be changed in a particular way; whether key parties could be required to participate; and more. These are illustrative questions only; the next two chapters will examine assessment and process creation in more detail.

At this design initiative stage, the problem analysis and ideas to improve conflict management will be tentative. As Peter Woodrow and Christopher Moore counsel designers, "Hold all conclusions and assumptions lightly; be prepared for surprises and abrupt changes. Develop an attitude of informed humility, with the awareness that there is much you do not know" (2002:89). This initial assessment helps a designer determine whether it would be productive for someone to take design initiative, though it is still too tentative to share with others.

If the answer is "no," it might be helpful to lay out the reasons why. For example, are necessary parties missing? Are there insufficient resources—financial or otherwise? Are there powerful inertia forces in place or major power imbalances that would block change? Or is the situation or conflict not yet ripe to motivate stakeholders? Reasons like these might not preclude a design initiative but might invite an analysis of how a designer could assist in creating conditions for a design process to succeed. If, on the other hand, the reason for a "no" answer is simply related to a well-functioning current system or a better system that cannot be implemented as a practical matter, the designer might conserve resources and search for another context in which to assist.

If the answer is "yes," the next step is to imagine what you might be able to provide as a designer and whether you might step forward to become more involved.

B.   DECIDING TO BECOME INVOLVED

Michael Young, the mediator in the South African matter, posited that you decide whether or not to become personally involved by determining whether you have something to offer because of experience, personality, resources, ability to generate trust, and resolve (PBS, 2009). We examine in turn (1) added value and (2) resolve.

1.   Whether you would add value

Once you have a sense of the path that a designing project might take, you can do a self-assessment. Do you have the qualities needed to succeed? Should you recommend another designer who has the requisite qualities? You might begin by considering how Rachel Wohl's background and situation contributed to her success in taking design initiative in Maryland.

Maryland courts program: Chief Judge Robert Bell was not in the market for a designer when Rachel Wohl asked to meet with him. It was Wohl who proposed that he begin a dispute resolution initiative in Maryland. And it was Wohl who offered to help design it. Chief Judge Bell first engaged Wohl as a consultant and then, after working with her for some months, as a court staff member.

Wohl brought to her role as a designer her newly acquired knowledge of dispute resolution as well as experience as a Maryland assistant attorney general and as a nonprofit administrator in the legal arena who had worked collaboratively with volunteers. Though she was not as well known as Chief Judge Bell, people scattered throughout the bar and courts knew and respected Wohl.

As you consider Wohl's situation, you can see the fit between her background and this project within the Maryland legal community. She had dispute resolution expertise. Chief Judge Bell could easily inquire about her among people he knew and learn about her values. She had collaborative leadership experience.

Though not all likely stakeholders knew Wohl, they all knew Chief Judge Bell. He could make certain that key stakeholders began interacting with Wohl.

Contrast the Maryland situation, where many individuals might have been able to work with Judge Bell to take design initiative, with the design initiative Michael Young took in South Africa, where relatively few individuals could have succeeded in initiating a process.

Intervening to organize talks to negotiate formal talks in South Africa: Michael Young, a British business executive, initiated the talks among South Africans. He began listening to people who might know how to guide South African toward negotiations. One conversation with a leader of the African National Congress led to a general request to get conversations going. But, in general, Young had to persuade people to become and remain involved.

Young had experience in intervening to resolve conflicts amid violence in Northern Ireland, Portugal, and Spain. He learned then how a government reacts to internal violence and what is necessary to bring people together, as well as how to judge whom to work with, how to secure cooperation, and how to build processes to deliver effective collective action. His bias, as an employee of a British mining company, was obvious to the parties and not seen to be in conflict with what they wanted to achieve—a peaceful transition that left the vital economy intact.[1] His company was willing to pay his salary and the considerable expenses of negotiation (and when his company dissolved, he was devoted enough to the project to find donations to continue). He was both an experienced and talented mediator and a modest person who could allow the negotiating parties to control the negotiations as soon as they were able to do so. He had the courage to operate in a situation that was not safe. Young's relative invisibility may have also contributed to his success.

As you think about Michael Young's work, you can see the arguments that those intervening outside their own communities and in volatile situations should clear a higher bar before taking design initiative than should insiders like Wohl. Not all persons do this self-assessment well, according to groups that regularly work in Africa to build consensus, and persons without the right qualities sometimes make things worse (Diamond, 2002:32,34; Lederach,

---

1. In later meetings, another conflict of interest emerged—Young's company preferred a post-transition capitalistic economy; some of the ANC members preferred a command economy such as some in African liberation movements supported or a mixed economy. These differences, though discussed, would ultimately be resolved through later official decisions rather than Young's talks on how to conduct the official talks. (When Mbeki became President, he adopted a mixed economy model.) Also, by the time this issue was on the agenda for the Young's talks, his mining company had dissolved. Michael Young, [Minutes of the Mells Park Conference February 9-12, 1990] (1990); Michael Young, [Minutes of the Mells Park Conference June 28-July 1, 1990] (1990).

2002:xiv-xv). Making things worse, of course, has dire consequences in the midst of violence. And it often has serious negative costs even when not in the shadow of violence.

If, in contrast to Michael Young and Rachel Wohl, your background and situation do not make you an optimal designer for a particular situation ripe for design, you might consider taking on the role of finding, persuading to become involved, and preparing the right persons. For example, Fordham law professors Jacqueline Nolan-Haley and John Feerick could envision using interest-based processes to build trust and relationships between Catholics and Protestants in Northern Ireland in 1998. That year the antagonists in the Northern Ireland "Troubles" had reached political resolution through the Good Friday Agreement and its subsequent overwhelming approval by the electorate. As a dispute resolution scholar, Nolan-Haley knew the importance of having designers with local ties to the places where interactions between Protestants and Catholics might occur. She and University of Ulster professor Seamus Dunn hand-picked 21 persons in Northern Ireland to become the design group. They included a school principal, magistrate, police official, fair employment commission member—people situated to understand the context and to implement designs. They also selected persons who might work together—who could surmount the "avoidance and violence" aspects of sectarianism (Dunn and Nolan-Haley, 1999:1388). Securing a grant, Dunn and Nolan-Haley persuaded these persons to attend two seminars in Ulster and then to take two weeks of dispute resolution classes (including visits to mediation programs) at Fordham. Returning to Northern Ireland, these 21 became a design group of sorts and have implemented a series of interest-based projects (Dunn and Nolan-Haley, 1999:1382-1388). Nolan-Haley and Dunn thus limited their roles as designers to preparation, consultation with, and encouragement of those who ultimately designed the processes.

In these examples and many others, the self-assessment involves determining whether there is a match between designer and context, particularly in terms of:

- experiences that help you understand the situation and exercise appropriate skills,
- ability to generate trust,
- willingness to take risks and commit the time,
- knowledge regarding dispute resolution,
- resources,
- contacts,
- absence of or acceptance of (as in the case of Michael Young's company) conflicts of interest,
- willingness to listen, and
- often humility (*see generally* Lederach and Jenner, 2002:315-318; Warfield, 1996: 156-157).

2.   Whether you would be willing to do it

While the last section ended with a caution about entering when not sufficiently well suited to be the designer, we begin this section with the other side of that coin—encouragement to take design initiative when you have an idea that would improve conflict management and you will add value by dint of your qualities, experience, and situation. In fact, to appreciate the significance of Wohl's and Young's willingness to take design initiative, you might begin by answering the counter-factual question: What would have occurred if instead of taking initiative these designers had waited to be invited in or been content with a more narrow role? The answer might include: less expansion of mediation in Maryland courts, agencies, and schools and more months of violence in South Africa. It then becomes apparent what would have been lost absent the right person stepping forward to offer assistance, to begin assisting, or to promote the recruitment of a more experienced person to take up the design project.

To avoid missing the right opportunities, you may have to deal with your personal reluctance to intervene in a conflict or potential conflict ("This is not my problem."). By analogy to mediation, many mediators are reluctant to enter "uninvited" (Murray, 1984:573), and some mediators seem unwilling even to broaden the scope of mediation discussions beyond what the parties' attorneys raise as issues (Relis, 2007:474-475; Welsh, 2001:25). At the same time, successful civil rights mediators, for example, have developed a willingness and skill in entering conflict situations (*see* p. 160; Salem, 1982:91).

If you are a law student, you may be a product not only of your personal tendencies, but also of professional conditioning. Scholars contend that lawyers increasingly answer only the questions put to them by clients. While acknowledging the worth of the lawyer's role as zealous advocate for a client, these scholars lament lawyers' diminished use of the broader "public spirited" or "wise counselor" role for attorneys who might challenge clients to think of the problem differently or might take on a proactive role within the community or nation (Glendon, 1994:35-39; Kronman, 1993: *but see* Galanter, 1996:561; Wilkins, 1994:466). Whether or not these scholars conclude accurately that the lawyers they profiled were prevalent years ago and now are scarcer, they describe a broader role for lawyers that gives them permission to suggest that clients consider their problems more holistically (*see* Brown and Dauer, 1978:xix). A lawyer who only answers client questions is not likely to take the creative and active role played by a designer.

For this reason, those advocating a design-type of role for lawyers commonly counsel them to resist an increased narrowing of the lawyer's role—what Leonard Riskin calls the "lawyer's philosophical map" that shows only a legalistic terrain (Riskin, 1982:43-48). Dispute resolution advocate James Henry urges lawyers "to do a better job of defining ourselves and articulating to the public our larger role of counseling, crafting and problem solving. . . ." (2001:49). Former American Bar Association President Jerome Shestak argues that the legal profession should "minister [to] the body politic or society" (2001:57), meaning that lawyers should engage in reconciling conflict, even "helping to harmonize a community threatened by divisiveness" (id.). Dispute resolution scholar Carrie Menkel-Meadow describes a problem-solving lawyer as "[f]ocused not just on 'winning' the case, but on meeting the needs of multiple sets of parties and affected third parties, and on looking for substantive solutions that will require marshaling new resources, drafting new regulations, creating new institutions . . . and implementing and enforcing new plans" (2002:1773; *see also* Welsh, 2008). A lawyer who takes design initiative necessarily takes a broad view of a lawyer's role.

Even if you have settled that you would find the design project rewarding personally such that you are willing to invest time and even take risks (as in Michael Young's entry into the volatile South African situation), you will also want to assess whether you have the support and understanding of professional colleagues and relatives whose work or whose lives your decision may affect. Brazilian judge Bruno Augusto Santos Oliveira recognized these issues once he decided to take design initiative regarding issues underlying litigation that had been pending for 30 years and had held up creation of a federal park. Before announcing his design initiative, Judge Oliveira secured the help of a fellow judge and the support of his appellate court and the national association of judges. He also took his family on a vacation in the breathtakingly beautiful area designated for the long-delayed park (for the results of Judge Oliveira's work, *see* Chapter 8).

You are not alone if you or others in your design team are reticent to take design initiative even if your sober assessment leads you to believe that you could add value. When you overcome the reticence, and the situation is right, the next issue is how to do it.

C. GAINING ACCEPTANCE

Two factors play a central role in whether stakeholders, sponsors, or clients will welcome a designer:

1. stakeholder perceptions that they could gain if they changed the processes or systems they use for disputing, and
2. trust that the designer has the ability to help (*cf.* Laue et al., 1988:19).

A few techniques seem to help especially.

Listening and learning with humility: In the initial exchange with a contact, a designer can best assess the situation by asking questions and listening carefully. The initial interest in talking with a designer might stem from a particular problem or series of problems, and it is the designer who perceives this as an opportunity to resolve even broader issues. For example, a large nationwide trucking company realized in the early 2000s that it was incurring huge legal fees adjudicating claims made by those injured or killed when they were involved in accidents with the company's trucks, and so sought to develop a more empathetic and cost-efficient way to handle such claims. The designer wondered whether the company should develop a means to handle these situations before they ripened into claims against the company. Or suppose that the Recruitment and Retention Committee of a large Chicago law firm notices a trend: the firm excels at recruiting diverse lawyers at the entry level, but has trouble retaining the same diverse talent for more than two or three years after they start. A partner at the firm might guess that the problem is related to latent conflict and take design initiative.

Even when ideas come quickly to mind, someone tempted to take on the role of designer should continue to probe and learn at this early stage. Designers who presume that they understand interests and goals or who are quick to propose a set of solutions are prone to find themselves in trouble with a client down the road, even if their substantive answers end up being correct. Conversely, stakeholders' and clients' trust will grow when a designer takes a keen interest in shaping new processes or systems to better meet their interests, as the story below illustrates.

Truth and
Reconciliation
Commission of Canada

Processes in the aftermath of the Indian Residential Schools: In Professor Frank Sander's law school dispute resolution class, Jennifer Llewellyn wrote a paper critiquing the Canadian government's first set of processes for dealing with the aftermath of the Indian Residential Schools. The topic was a good fit for Llewellyn. As a teenager she had been involved in her church's national council when it issued an apology to First Nations, and she had worked in South Africa's Truth and Reconciliation Commission before enrolling at Harvard Law School for an LL.M. Prior to the LL.M. class, Llewellyn had also co-authored a paper on restorative justice (*see* pp. 111-112) for the Law Commission of Canada, urging these ideas as a broader conception of justice. Later she turned her law school paper into a law review article (Llewellyn, 2002), and that article led to an invitation to present a paper at a scholarly conference on the Indian Residential Schools.

At the conference, survivors of the Residential Schools rose to give unscheduled remarks about their experiences and what they were now seeking. Moved by their comments, Llewellyn set aside her prepared talk and responded directly to the interests they had expressed.

In 2004, the Assembly of First Nations put together a special task force to propose new processes for dealing with the aftermath of the Indian Residential Schools and asked Llewellyn to join. She saw her role as putting the stakeholders on the task force in a decision-making capacity, while listening carefully to their interests,

Jennifer Llewellyn

sharing with them information about processes used elsewhere, and helping them to consider and interpret the potential of these models in light of the nature of the harms and of the values and needs of the stakeholders. Llewellyn said later, "It was about more than a similar fit in terms of interests. It was about assessing existing experiences and models in light of what we wanted and needed to do and the way in which we thought about what had happened and needed to happen next" (Appendix F).

That task force proposed the series of processes that Canada adopted (pp. 33-36). Llewellyn describes her service on the task force as one of the most rewarding experiences in her career.

Educating with empathy: At the same time that a designer listens, asks questions, and learns, that designer can use the initial entry and contracting phase of an engagement to educate the client and stakeholders. What an individual or organization initially wants might be a swift resolution to a presenting problem—representation in litigation or bringing peace back to a community where a racially motivated crime has caused backlash and violence, for example. Reasonable as this may sound, designers may realize that the presenting problem is a symptom of a deeper organizational or structural issue and that a more comprehensive approach might lead to a more suitable system going forward. Still, other individuals might view as an alarmist the designer who points out the merit of a more comprehensive process design, a risk that Andrew Thomas took into account in devising a way to take design initiative.

 Persuading city colleagues that creating new processes might help in Sanford, Florida: Remember that Andrew Thomas was hired as a community block grant administrator, not a designer, when he recognized that a series of processes might need to be created to help Sanford resolve differences brought to the fore by the aftermath of the Trayvon Martin shooting. Some city colleagues thought that once prosecution began, and order was restored, the city could move on to other matters. Thomas warned them that he expected long-term local reactions that would not be limited to the initial official reactions to this shooting. Having worked in polarized situations before, Thomas also predicted that media and national groups of various kinds would arrive within days and would assert additional demands and raise additional viewpoints. City Manager Bonaparte, a mediator himself, placed Thomas in charge of coordinating local resources with the team of U.S. Justice Department Community Relations Service mediators who were flying in from around the country.

Knowing from experience that counterparts in other cities might be more persuasive than a local colleague, Thomas gave each key city official the name and contact information for someone with the same position in a city in which a local incident had grown quickly into one with national visibility. Once they had talked with someone in their own position elsewhere, Thomas's colleagues were eager to forge a collaborative approach to a broader range of issues and to circumstances that would challenge even a large city, let alone one of 55,000.

Particularly when counterparts with experience are not available, educating a client about the contents of this book—what design is and why it might lead to a more comprehensive and robust way to define the problem—can be helpful, though complicated to accomplish effectively. It requires empathy, tact, and skill. If instead the designers educate arrogantly, that person or persons may feel bullied or frightened—both feelings that may make them less cooperative. At the same time, designers who avoid the topic or fail to explain forcefully enough may agree to work on a design project that will frustrate both designers and clients because they may create a process or system that does not address the underlying issues which may be causing the presenting problem.

Even at an early stage of conversation with a potential client, designers educate with an eye to potential resistance. For example, a client may wonder about how much time and money such a design process might take, or a client may be excited about the prospect of systemic change but certain that supervisors or organizational leadership will balk at such suggestions. Listening carefully and responding with stories of success can make a difference for a client. At the same time, designers need to buffer their idealism with practicality as well.

Building relationships: Stakeholders, sponsors, and clients may not trust the designer enough to "sign on" to a design effort at an initial meeting. And it may take longer than a meeting to build their confidence that their interests would be served by a new process or system. Consider the reluctance to become involved and Michael Young's persistence in building relationships as he as he put together the talks to agree on formal negotiations for a government transition in South Africa.

Engaging reluctant groups in the talks on talks in South Africa: The leadership of the African National Congress (ANC) responded to Michael Young's inquiry in 1986, a year after Young began his efforts. Young caught up with the ANC officers after he heard them speak to a group of British business representatives. Young introduced himself and asked if he could help. ANC head Oliver Tambo responded positively, saying that the ANC would like to open communications with the South African government. The government had announced its refusal to talk with the ANC until it abandoned violence. And the ANC feared entering into negotiations with a government representative who might then imprison the ANC representatives, as the South African government had classified the ANC as an illegal organization. Also, among ANC supporters, some viewed negotiations as an appeasement strategy, and they would undermine any ANC attempts to talk.

Young followed up on this initial request and the ANC sent representatives to his first meeting in 1987. It was not, though, until the second of Young's meetings that the ANC sent a senior executive, Thabo Mbeki. Young purposely made the development of the right climate the goal of that first meeting, and he prepared the agenda with open-ended opportunities to discuss history, and he planned social breaks. He even prepared the environment, situating participants from each side so that they would run into each other informally and asking the hotel staff to practice the pronunciation of participants' names. The ANC leadership apparently sensed that Young had created the right atmosphere and that the government had an interest in secret talks with the ANC. Taking the participation risks now seemed worth the gamble.

Nelson Mandela (right) as he became the President of South Africa, clasping the hand of his predecessor, F.W. de Klerk. Reuters photo.

Young's relationship with the South African government developed even more slowly. Professor Willie Esterhuyse was one of the first from the Afrikaner community to join the talks, but Esterhuyse was not a direct government representative; in fact, he opposed apartheid openly. The government connection grew when Neil Barnard, South Africa's Director General of the National Intelligence Service, asked Esterhuyse to brief him after each session. As the negotiating parties began finding areas of commonality, Barnard sought permission to send a direct representative to the talks and the participants agreed to allow it, but Barnard changed his mind. Direct involvement would increase the risks that government involvement would leak out, leading to embarrassment and political use of that information by hardliners opposed to negotiating with insurgents.

Consistent links to principals would be crucial, but the relationships that made those links changed because of events external to the talks. In the midst of the talks, F.W. de Klerk succeeded P.W. Botha as President, and de Klerk curtailed Barnard's (the intelligence director's) inside track to his office (*see* chart on p. 19). The negotiators had anticipated this. In advance of de Klerk taking office, Young briefed de Klerk's brother on the progress in the talks, and the brother began participating. As de Klerk took office and the talks began leading to a conclusion welcomed by the President, his brother started representing what the President would do.

Throughout, Young appreciated the role of momentum in sustaining the participants' involvement and talked separately with participants between sessions to prepare for bilateral meetings that would allow progress. At the second bilateral meeting in 1988, Young asked participants for their ideas for creating

momentum toward change. The government side surprised the ANC participants by letting them know that the government, through these attending
individuals, would talk without the ANC ordering a moratorium in violence as
long as the government's indirect involvement remained confidential. The ANC
representatives offered to help prevent discord if and when the government
released Nelson Mandela from prison. At the third meeting, the ANC set out
guidelines for a new constitution that the government side found, after some
questions and suggestions, to be more to their liking than they had expected;
it seemed probable that direct negotiations between the ANC and government would succeed. By 1989, the government representatives could say that
a release of Nelson Mandela and other key ANC prisoners was likely as was the
end of the ban against insurgent groups like the ANC. The ANC side responded
that the ANC would call a moratorium on violence when this occurred. The
participants had made progress steadily toward the implementation of this
tentative agreement in 1990 and none of the parties left the negotiating table
even when word of the secret talks leaked out and placed them in political and
physical danger. In February 1990, they watched Mandela's release from prison
and President de Klerk's announcement that the ANC was no longer banned
and that the direct negotiations would begin.

Throughout the talks, Young recognized that full involvement of the ANC,
government, and other interested organizations was not always feasible,
and that even partial involvement in the talks could be useful. Thus, he listened to and kept informed the chairman of the Broederbond, the Afrikaner
organization that might influence the selection of the next President. The
Broederbond chairman seemed to fear that direct involvement by attending
Young's meetings would leak out and would be used by hardliners to block
his re-election.

Young also used indirect engagement to lead to direct participation by
key stakeholders. For example, the Dutch Reformed Church, another influential organization in the Afrikaner community, declined involvement initially.
After Young apprised a representative of the church of the progress made in
the talks, the church sent a representative in 1989, about three years after talks
began. Toward the end, Young scheduled dinners with other stakeholders, such
as South African business leaders, to educate them on the matters under discussion and to ask for their input.

Young's careful tending of the relationships necessary to get agreement on
initiating official talks to end apartheid illustrates some common themes for
those who take design initiative and commit the time to listen, educate, and
build relationships:

- People who initially express reticence may agree to involvement when
  they sense the project moving toward satisfaction of their interests.

- Involving people trusted by key stakeholders (e.g., the grudging respect the Director General of the National Intelligence Agency had for Esterhuyse) can lead to that stakeholder's trust and indirect involvement.
- A designer sometimes succeeds without direct participation by stakeholders if the designer stays in touch with them and makes certain that those involved take their interests into account.

Young's approach to building relationships translates into other contexts as well. In the story below, an ombuds expected that he would not be accepted in his role until he had established relationships with his new colleagues, and he seized opportunities to do that.

National Institutes of Health's new ombuds: Howard Gadlin had reached only his second day as the NIH's first ombuds when the NIH Director asked if he would handle the aftermath of a tragedy—an employee had committed suicide in her car in the NIH parking lot the previous day. Having served as an ombuds for the University of California at Los Angeles, Gadlin understood that the key question was not whether the director's request fell within his role (it did not fit the typical ombuds role) or whether he had sufficient authority to get help (he had no authority), but rather whether he could facilitate a helpful response without compromising his effectiveness as ombuds. Answering "yes" to the latter question, Gadlin began talking with those responsible for the division where the deceased employee worked, recognizing the special burden they would be carrying. He next spoke with those who had expertise in counseling employees, working his way through the organization to find out who was affected or could help to develop a plan to deal with the aftermath. Once that was done, he brought together some of the people he now knew had a role to play in the future or had special abilities that would be useful. He broadened their task to helping with an employee who might be violent or was violent, whether the violence was suicidal or directed toward others. That new group proposed an ongoing program that could be put in place with a supervisor's phone call about a potentially violent or violent employee, with the designated staff member prepared to give the caller the resources and advice needed to plan quickly a sound course of action.

Now that he understood how the organization worked, knew some sensitive and trusted individuals within it, and had gained recognition as a collaborative innovator, Gadlin began developing dispute management systems for NIH more broadly.

As the NIH and South African accounts demonstrate, a person taking design initiative in a bitterly divided community or with an organizational client can expect to devote energy to building a variety of kinds of relationships over time.

In sum, gaining acceptance entails listening, educating, spending time outside meetings to increase the chances that participants sense progress during their time together, keeping people informed about progress, building trust with people trusted by others, maintaining flexibility about types of involvement, and allowing people to join throughout the project.

D. DEFINING THE DESIGNER'S ROLE ON A CONCEPTUAL LEVEL

Designers assume a role that is novel to most of the people with whom they will be dealing, a circumstance that heightens the importance of coming to agreement with those involved about the parameters of the designer's role in a given situation. In this section, we flag some of the issues, though we will deal with them in more detail in Chapter 4.B.5.

Innovative nature and breadth: Designers are often first introduced to a situation in order to execute a more traditional task (e.g., "Would you draft an arbitration clause?" or, "Help facilitate this meeting between the angry parishioners and the pastor."). The designer must then re-define the role, if warranted.

Changing the anticipated role at the National Institutes of Health: Howard Gadlin initially served as a consultant to NIH executives about their plan to hire someone who could set up an arbitration and mediation system—essentially to take an "off the shelf" dispute resolution system and implement it at NIH. Gadlin advocated instead for the creation of an NIH ombuds office. The ombuds then could tailor a design to the needs of those at NIH and adapt it on an ongoing basis. Ultimately, NIH hired him for the ombuds role. Even after being hired, though, Gadlin sometimes had to secure his own involvement in a particular design initiative. As discussed in the example immediately above, he began by working on a non-design project, realizing as a result of previous ombuds experience that the designer must always build and re-build credibility and acceptance. He even secured agreement that he could work with supervisors about the climate that they created for dealing with conflict, something they did not realize would fall within his role.

In this example, Gadlin considered it important to be seen as an innovator in the conflict area, not just the administrator of a process, and to create a healthy conflict environment in advance, not simply react to disputes that arose. He did that by promoting an understanding of a broader role, both in initial conversations and those subsequent to his hiring.

Stakeholder priorities: It helps to have agreement on what the designer will do when stakeholder interests conflict. Michael Young defined his role as setting the appropriate conditions for negotiators who could then predict the reactions of the two key contending forces in South Africa. Like a mediator, Young played no favorites when their agendas clashed.

Loyalties: The person contracting or paying for the designer's work may expect loyalty, defined as generally coming down on the side of the person paying the bill, when there are differences about design choices. This expectation of loyalty is natural but can pose serious challenges as a designer begins working and engages with other stakeholders who may view the paying client with suspicion or distrust. These dilemmas become more complex if the designer has been hired in another professional capacity. For example, if an attorney is expanding a role from advocate for a client to systems designer (perhaps suggesting that the client consider an internal disputing system for the client's organization rather than just defending each employee claim against the client organization), legal ethics rules may constrain the role and loyalties of the designer and even any agreement to modify those roles. The attorney-designer may nonetheless help a client understand that meeting others' interests will serve the client's interests over time.

If instead the designer enters without that expectation of representing a legal client, more leeway is possible. Public policy designers, for example, often initially consider stakeholders to be "sponsors," who may provide some resources but are not owed a duty of loyalty such as the duty owed by attorney to client.

At the initial stage of an engagement, designers should consider carefully what, if any, fiduciary duty may be owed to a client. The designers might then consider having an open conversation to negotiate or renegotiate the terms of an engagement to ensure that the retaining client has a firm grasp of the role and approach that the designers will take in their work. At times, a designer might even suggest that a second client be officially added to a retainer agreement as a way of signaling to the larger set of community stakeholders that the design process will be different from what they might expect. For example, in the early 2000s Latino leaders in a major American city approached a team of designers to get assistance on how to design processes for building consensus in the law enforcement community regarding the approach to criminal justice issues in minority communities. Aware that having the Latino organization be the main client might stifle its ability to be effective, the design team suggested that the mayor be added as a client. This could then signal to all stakeholders that the design process would be legitimate, fair, and balanced.

Duties to the larger public: A single client or a coalition of stakeholders may accept designer assistance but wish to take the design in a direction that might hurt the rights of others or lack legitimacy with the larger public. If designers can predict these dilemmas, they may provide themselves more leeway in responding by defining their role clearly at the beginning of the engagement.

These dilemmas are not easily resolved. We present them here to get them on your mental checklist, and we will examine them in more depth in the next chapter (Chapter 4.B.5). Your preparation of a checklist of questions in advance

of accepting an engagement as a designer can help. It will increase the likelihood that you will minimize ethical and moral quandaries that might arise as
you balance your expertise as a designer with the wishes or preferences of a particular stakeholder who might also be footing the bill or sponsoring your work.

E. SECURING AGREEMENT ON THE DETAILS

With a basic understanding of roles at a conceptual level, designers might next discuss the mandate, scope, time frame, and estimated costs for their work. Designers
and clients alike—anxious to begin the substantive work—may be prone to skip
this stage or, alternatively, may have inaccurate and mismatched assumptions
about the work that will follow, the time it may take, or the roles that designer and
client will play in the engagement. A client negotiation is not always feasible before
taking initiative, of course. Michael Young could only talk with his employer before
taking initiative in South Africa, for example. When practical, though, working out
these important details explicitly and upfront can help make the ensuing work
more efficient and productive. The more aligned a designer is with the client about
the goals of the work, its scope, and what is needed to make the project successful,
the fewer roadblocks that designer is likely to face along the way.

You can prepare for conversations about time frame, mandate, and costs
in the same way you might prepare for any negotiation. Presumably, you will
want to do thorough, high quality work in a professional and ethical way. As
you will learn as you read later chapters, this often means conducting a careful
stakeholder assessment followed by analysis, design, pilot, and implementation
phases that all include a variety of stakeholders. In order to do this, you might
contract with the client for some or all of the following:

- a budget for hiring sufficient professional and support staff;
- permission to and assistance in accessing stakeholders, including organizational leaders;
- access to information, often sensitive or confidential, that the organization may not want to share with an outsider;
- permission to interview and approach a set of individuals whom the client
  may prefer you to avoid either because the client perceives them as the
  "opposition," as lacking in power (i.e., unnecessary to achieve at least their
  most pressing short-term goals), or as possible spoilers or holdouts; and
- use of physical space for meetings, staff resources for photocopying and
  organizing meetings, etc.

When a client approaches you as a designer, the person might not have given
much consideration to the role that you will need to play in order to ensure the
success of the project. Upon hearing of these needs, clients are apt to quickly
say, "Yes, yes . . ." or find reasons why the design team's assessment of what they
need for a successful project is not necessary in this instance.

To increase the likelihood of a successful engagement, designers can approach these conversations in a spirit of negotiation and openness. Suppose the contact is already a client, and not just one of several sponsors. Simply caving in to the client's wishes at this early stage might set the stage for unwanted challenges later. At the same time, designers may want to avoid a "take-it-or-leave-it" approach as well. After all, clients typically have a better understanding of their own organization than does an outsider and, on many occasions, time and resources are genuinely limited. In such situations, designers apply their professional judgment to assess whether they can ethically and professionally do their work with the limits imposed by a client. Some diagnostic questions that a designer might use in making this decision can include:

- Do the persons with whom I am working directly have sufficient standing and clout within the organization to connect me to the resources, stakeholders, and information I need to be successful?
- Are the clients or contacts prepared to make themselves available to answer questions and be responsive to needs in a timely way as they arise?
- Are the clients or contacts genuinely open to the professional experience and skills I have to bring or are they looking for an outside "imprimatur" to bless an already-determined course of action?

THOUGHTS GOING FORWARD

Taking design initiative begins with imagining a better conflict resolution path that is feasible to implement. Next comes a sober self-assessment—"Am I the right person for this work?" "If so, am I willing and able to devote myself to the task?" When you insert yourself, broaden an existing role, or are asked to take on the designer role, you will commit yourself to listening, educating, building relationships, and dealing with the dilemmas posed by competing interests and broader justice concerns. You will also want to be certain that you and those involved share a common view of your role—both conceptually and practically. Even if you do not yourself take the initiative as a designer, you may become an advocate for a design initiative to be led by someone else when you see a need that others miss (Laue et al., 1988:13).

QUESTIONS

3.1 Colin Rule (eBay) and Howard Gadlin (NIH) were designers by vocation. Designing a forum or disputing system was a logical extension of a role for Andrew Thomas (Sanford, Florida) and Maryland Court of Appeals Chief Judge Bell. But Michael Young (South Africa) had no role that called for him to design a process to move South Africans to formal negotiations about adopting universal suffrage. Imagine yourself taking on a mantle like Michael Young's in the future, perhaps to help your community deal with a conflict regarding resource allocation or your employer to resolve conflicts arising from recent budget cuts and layoffs. Or imagine trying to expand a role as Gadlin, Rule, and Hardiman did—also a risky venture. What additional expertise and skill would you want to have first? What risks would you incur in stepping forward to propose or to begin to establish a process or system in the context you have imagined? Would there be rewards for you that would make it worthwhile for you to take such risks? Michael Young was asked similar questions and responds at https://www.youtube.com/watch?v=8-_EP8VI78E. When we asked Andrew Thomas about what became five years of work in Sanford, Florida, he responded that it was rewarding to bring value to the table and to help a community to make a difference.

3.2   We mentioned that the designers in this book probably had not heard of the term "designer." It is even more unlikely that others would recognize that they needed to retain a designer or know what you meant if you suggested that you could act as a designer for them. Imagine a problem in which you might intervene as a designer. How could you explain your role in the example you identified?

Exercise 3.1   *Taking design initiative at Tallahoya University:* University Counsel just forwarded an email from the University's Provost: "Pam, I met last week with a group of agricultural extension officers with affiliated faculty status with the university. They say that Dutch immigrants have purchased farms in the northeast part of the state and have set up huge dairy operations that threaten to put other dairy farms out of business. The community's antagonism toward the Dutch dairy farmers and their families plays out in schools, community programs, police operations, and more. As I listened, I remembered that you have a new intern with dispute resolution expertise and thought that this would be an opportunity for the University to make a contribution to the broader community. I told the extension officers that your intern might go there and help resolve the divisive issues that are plaguing this community. Rattan."

As the intern who is the subject of this email, what do you imagine might be the rough outlines of a dispute management process or system that could help this community? Do you have the background and time to design and implement a process or system for this community? If not, who might be able to? Would they need preparation, as did the design group in Northern Ireland discussed in this chapter? What first steps would you take to secure trust for those who might become the designers for the community?

BIBLIOGRAPHY AND REFERENCES

AVRUCH, Kevin (2002) "What Do I Need to Know About Culture? A Researcher Says . . . ," in John Paul Lederach and Janice Moomaw Jenner eds., *A Handbook of International Peacebuilding: Into the Eye of the Storm* 75. San Francisco: Jossey-Bass.

BROWN, Louis M., and Edward A. DAUER (1978) *Planning by Lawyers: Materials on a Nonadversarial Legal Process.* New York: Foundation Press.

COSTANTINO, Cathy A., and Christina Sickles MERCHANT (1996) *Designing Conflict Management Systems.* San Francisco: Jossey-Bass.

COSTANTINO, Cathy A. (2009) "Second Generation Organizational Conflict Management Systems Design: A Practitioner's Perspective on Emerging Issues," 14 *Harv. Negot. L. Rev.* 81.

DIAMOND, Louise (2002) "Who Else Is Working There?," in John Paul Lederach and Janice Moomaw Jenner eds., *A Handbook of International Peacebuilding: Into the Eye of the Storm* 25. San Francisco: Jossey-Bass.

DUNN, Seamus, and Jacqueline NOLAN-HALEY (1999) "Conflict in Northern Ireland After the Good Friday Agreement," 22 *Fordham Int'l L.J.* 1372.

FAURE, Guy Oliver (2011) "Practice Note: Informal Mediation in China," 29:1 *Conflict Resol. Q.* 85.

FORESTER, John (2009) *Dealing with Differences: Dramas of Mediating Public Disputes.* Oxford, UK: Oxford University Press.

GALANTER, Marc (1996) "Lawyers in the Mist: The Golden Age of Legal Nostalgia," 100 *Dick. L. Rev.* 549.

GLENDON, Mary Ann (1994) *A Nation Under Lawyers: How the Crisis in the Legal Profession Is Transforming American Society.* Cambridge, MA: Harvard University Press.

GOLDEN, Jim, H. Abigail MOY, and Adam LYONS (2008) "The Negotiation Counsel Model: An Empathic Model for Settling Catastrophic Personal Injury Cases," 13 *Harv. Negot. L. Rev.* 211.

HENRY, James F. (2001) "Lawyers as Agents of Change," in Russ Bleemer, Cynthia Blustein, Susan Scott, and Rosemarie Yu eds., *Into the 21st Century: Thought Pieces on Lawyering, Problem Solving and ADR* 49. New York: CPR Institute for Dispute Resolution.

KRONMAN, Anthony T. (1993) *The Lost Lawyer: Failing Ideals of the Legal Profession.* Cambridge, MA: The Belknap Press of Harvard University Press.

KUTTNER, Ran (2011) "Conflict Specialists as Leaders: Revisiting the Role of the Conflict Specialist from a Leadership Perspective," 29(2) *Conflict Resol. Q.* 103.

LAUE, James H., Sharon BURDE, William POTAPCHUK, and Miranda SALKOFF (1988) "Getting to the Table in Policy Conflicts," 1988 (20) *Conflict Resol. Q.* 6.

LEDERACH, John Paul (2002) "Where Do I Fit In?," in John Paul Lederach and Janice Moomaw Jenner eds., *A Handbook of International Peacebuilding: Into the Eye of the Storm* 37. San Francisco: Jossey-Bass.

LEDERACH, John Paul, and Janice Moomaw JENNER (2002) "So What Have We Learned?," in John Paul Lederach and Janice Moomaw Jenner eds., *A Handbook of International Peacebuilding: Into the Eye of the Storm* 315. San Francisco: Jossey-Bass.

LLEWELLYN, Jennifer J. (2002) "Dealing with the Legacy of Native Residential School Abuse in Canada: Litigation, ADR, and Restorative Justice," 52 *U. Toronto L.J.* 253.

LLEWELLYN, Jennifer (2008) "Bridging the Gap Between Truth and Reconciliation: Restorative Justice and the Indian Residential School Truth and Reconciliation Commission," in M. Brant-Castellano, L. Archibald, and M. DeGagne eds., *From Truth to Reconciliation: Transforming the Legacy of Residential Schools* 183. Ottawa: Aboriginal Healing Foundation.

MENKEL-MEADOW, Carrie (2001) "Lawyering, Dispute Resolution, Problem Solving and Creativity for the 21st Century," in Russ Bleemer, Cynthia Blustein, Susan Scott, and Rosemarie Yu eds., *Into the 21st Century: Thought Pieces on Lawyering, Problem Solving and ADR* 52. New York: CPR Institute for Dispute Resolution.

MENKEL-MEADOW, Carrie (2002) "Practicing 'In the Interests of Justice' in the Twenty-First Century: Pursuing Peace and Justice," 70 *Fordham L. Rev.* 1761.

MURRAY, John S. (1984) "Third Party Intervention: Successful Entry for the Uninvited," 48 *Alb. L. Rev.* 573.

NELSON, Dorothy (2001) "ADR in the New Era," in Russ Bleemer, Cynthia Blustein, Susan Scott, and Rosemarie Yu eds., *Into the 21st Century: Thought Pieces on Lawyering, Problem Solving and ADR* 65. New York: CPR Institute for Dispute Resolution.

PBS (2009) Interview with Michael Young, *available at* https://www.youtube.com/watch?v=8-_EP8VI78E (last visited Aug. 15, 2018).

RELIS, Tamara (2007) "Consequences of Power," 12 *Harv. Negot. L. Rev.* 445.

RENO, Janet (2001) "The Federal Government and Appropriate Dispute Resolution: Promoting Problem Solving and Peacemaking as Enduring Values in Our Society," in Russ Bleemer, Cynthia Blustein, Susan Scott, and Rosemarie Yu eds., *Into the 21st Century: Thought Pieces on Lawyering, Problem Solving and ADR* 16. New York: CPR Institute for Dispute Resolution.

RISKIN, Leonard (1982) "Mediation and Lawyers," 43 *Ohio St. L.J.* 29.

SALEM, Richard A. (1982) "Community Dispute Resolution Through Outside Intervention," 8(2-3) *Peace & Change* 91.

SHESTACK, Jerome J. (2001) "Civility, Mediation and Civitas," in Russ Bleemer, Cynthia Blustein, Susan Scott, and Rosemarie Yu eds., *Into the 21st Century: Thought Pieces on Lawyering, Problem Solving and ADR* 56. New York: CPR Institute for Dispute Resolution.

WARFIELD, Wallace (1996) "Building Consensus for Racial Harmony in American Cities: Case Model Approach," 1996 *J. Disp. Resol.* 151.

WELSH, Nancy A. (2001) "The Thinning Vision of Self-Determination in Court-Connected Mediation: The Inevitable Price of Institutionalization?," 6 *Harv. Negot. L. Rev.* 1.

WELSH, Nancy A. (2008) "Looking Down the Road Less Traveled: Challenges to Persuading the Legal Profession to Define Problems More Humanistically," 2008 *J. Disp. Resol.* 45.

WILKINS, David B. (1994) "Book Review: Practical Wisdom for Practicing Lawyers: Separating Ideals from Ideology in Legal Ethics," 108 *Harv. L. Rev.* 458.

WILLIAMS, Sue K. (2002) "Who Is Calling?," in John Paul Lederach and Janice Moomaw Jenner eds., *A Handbook of International Peacebuilding: Into the Eye of the Storm* 3. San Francisco: Jossey-Bass.

WOODROW, Peter, and Christopher MOORE (2002) "What Do I Need to Know About Culture? Practitioners Suggest . . . ," in John Paul Lederach and Janice Moomaw Jenner eds., *A Handbook of International Peacebuilding: Into the Eye of the Storm* 89. San Francisco: Jossey-Bass.

CHAPTER 4

Diagnosing or Assessing Stakeholders, Goals and Interests, and Contexts

Designing begins with a careful diagnosis or assessment of the current situation. This phase has sometimes been called a conflict assessment, an issues assessment, a conflict analysis, or a stakeholder analysis. A first level of diagnosis precedes the decision to become involved as a designer. One can analogize to a physician looking quickly at the patient visually, before a more thorough check of vital signs. The designer might conduct this initial "once-over" prior to agreeing to help, as discussed in Chapter 3. Afterward, however, a deeper diagnosis or assessment provides the basis for determining whether there may be a way to move forward constructively to create or modify dispute management processes and systems, the topic of the next chapter. In this chapter, you will learn how to identify and better understand the stakeholders (those who will be affected by a new design or play a role in its success), their goals and interests, and the relationships among them. You will also learn how to investigate the context, including relationship dynamics, customary practices, and political considerations.

DESIGNING STEPS

1. Design initiative
2. Basic planning steps
- **Assessing stakeholders, their goals and interests, and contexts**
- Creating processes and systems
3. Key planning issues (that may arise throughout the planning)
- Planning how to select, engage and prepare intervenors and parties
- Determining the extent of confidentiality and openness in the process
- Dealing with desires for change, justice, accountability, understanding, safety, reconciliation
- Enhancing relationships
- Incorporating technology
4. Implementing and institutionalizing the system or process
- Implementing
- Using contracts
- Using law
- Evaluating, revising

The chapter is organized to answer the following diagnosis and assessment questions:

- Who are the stakeholders (Section A)?
- What are the stakeholders' goals and underlying interests (Section B)?
- What about the context matters for the design and its implementation (Section C)?
- What cultures, customary practices, and organizational structures are important parts of the context (Section D)?
- What research tools might be used to answer these questions (Section E)?

A. IDENTIFYING STAKEHOLDERS

The first step of an assessment or diagnosis is making an initial estimate of who the stakeholders might be in a given context. The segment that follows illustrates the importance of persistence during this time-consuming part of the design process.

 MACRO MARYLAND JUDICIARY Mediation and Conflict Resolution Office

Maryland courts' use of a consensus-building approach to systems design: Maryland's dramatically successful expansion of mediation—from 26 to 135 programs in the first decade—began with three months of phone calls. Soon after beginning work for Chief Judge Bell, Rachel Wohl started calling her contacts as former assistant attorney general and executive director of a nonprofit. Wohl had in mind a rough script for the calls: "Chief Judge Bell has hired me to help him create an ADR commission to advance dispute resolution broadly throughout the state. He wants to expand the use of mediation and related processes—when it makes sense—in the courts but also in neighborhoods, business, state and local governments, schools, and criminal and juvenile outreach efforts. Please fill me in about the conflict resolution scene, politics, and players in Maryland. What do you think that his planning commission should do? What should it not do? Who are the people who need to be on that commission? Whom else should I talk with?" (Appendix F). Three months of asking questions and listening.

Wohl found that most people tried to discourage her. Among those who did not understand the process of mediation, some were opposed to the court beginning a dispute resolution initiative. Mediators understood the process and goals but were fearful that the Chief Judge's initiative would instead slow things down and that non-mediators would capture the planning process. Wohl heard often, "We have tried this before." Nearly all were cynical about whether the process would be collaborative and whether commissions do any good. But, they talked with her anyway and gave her names of those who should be involved.

Photo by Jonathan Franz

Wohl whittled her stakeholder list down to 110 people—leaders in the courts, state and local government, legislature, criminal justice and juvenile programs, bar, mediation community, academia, community, and business. She included influential cynics and opponents of the dispute resolution commission on the list.

Chief Judge Bell invited 40 from Wohl's list to be members of the commission, and Wohl placed many of the remainder on working committees, which kept them involved in, and supportive of, the commission's work. Chief Judge Bell told them that he would attend meetings as chair. Despite the frequent cynicism about forming a commission, only one person declined the invitation from the Chief Judge of Maryland's highest court.

This stakeholder group moved quickly, issuing their consensus plan within two years after Wohl was hired. In the decade that followed, the commission was modified into an advisory board, with its membership and committees continuing to reflect business, schools, community, and other sectors. Wohl's staff became the Mediation and Conflict Resolution Office (MACRO), an agency that reported to the Chief Judge but served the state's broader interests. With support from many sectors, MACRO has at times enjoyed substantial state and private sector support, distributing nearly $2 million annually in grants to mediation and other conflict resolution programs that deal with issues of mediator quality, assessment, and public education.

What led the Maryland designers to decide that the key stakeholders were "leaders in the courts, state and local government, legislature, criminal justice and juvenile programs, bar, mediation community, academia, community, and business"? Which stakeholders, if any, might have been left out? What are the risks of leaving out important stakeholders, whether intentionally or by overlooking someone or an organization? Obviously, this expansive list includes those who could help both in planning and implementation. In other contexts, some of the questions a designer may ask to determine who the stakeholders are include:

- Who cares about the problem?
- Who is affected either by the problem/conflict or by a potential solution to it?
- Who must be part of any resolution?
- Who has expertise that will help to create or assess proposals?
- Who will ultimately provide the resources?

- Who will approve the new process?
- Who will implement the new process or system?
- Who will be persuasive with the decision-makers?
- Who might effectively oppose implementation (preceding questions suggested by Howard Gadlin, interview, 2011)?
- Who will have similar disputes in the future?
- Who was "involved in designing previous dispute resolution processes" (Stitt, 1998:28)?

The exercise of discretion in deciding who is a legitimate stakeholder raises important questions for the designer:

- Who must be "on board" to get a process designed and implemented?
- Who must be included to ensure the sustainability of the system?
- Who must be included to ensure that justice is achieved and all voices are represented and heard, including the voices of those who may not have access to power or influence in the current system?
- How does one achieve inclusivity and comprehensiveness without making the process inefficient, unduly burdensome, or unworkable?
- How does one deal with those who are in fact stakeholders but are acting as hold-outs or spoilers to scuttle a deal?

These questions overlap with the first list, but the redundancy can be helpful in triggering thoughts about stakeholders to add. An alternative way to stimulate thought about stakeholders is to identify every person or group that will be important regarding each issue of the design. For example, you might use the following chapters of this book as a checklist for questions:

- Who will care about the process chosen and whose opinion will determine its legitimacy (Chapter 5)?
- Whose participation as a party, attorney for a party, intervenor, or convener is essential to the success of the new process (Chapter 6)?
- Who will care about the confidentiality or openness of the process (Chapter 7)?
- If some or many define the disputes primarily as raising issues of deterrence, future security, justice, accountability, being heard, improving public understanding of what occurred, or reconciliation, who can represent these perspectives appropriately (Chapter 8)?
- Who can preserve, enhance, or destroy relationships among the people involved in the process (Chapter 9)?
- Who might add expertise or resources for the use of technology (Chapter 10)?
- Who will be involved in implementation because they can effectively resist the changes or might be invested in existing processes or patterns of dispute management, lead the change, have resources, sponsor a pilot, or provide publicity (Chapter 11)?

- Who might be parties to needed contracts (Chapter 12)?
- Who can help secure useful or necessary changes in law (Chapter 13)?
- Who will evaluate the project's success (Chapter 14)?

The process of identifying stakeholders does not end after an initial inquiry. After learning stakeholders' goals and understanding more about the context, a designer may need to add, subtract, or modify the list of stakeholders. When that happens, though, the latecomers may feel less invested, and therefore less willing to help, than those involved "from the beginning." For this reason, being comprehensive and thoughtful about identifying stakeholders upfront represents a worthy investment.

Clients may complicate the task of consulting all stakeholders near the beginning of the design process if they do not recognize its importance. In one design project of the Ohio State University Design Workshop, a client requested that the designers present a tentative proposal to the client's advisory committee before consulting other stakeholders. "The committee members would be offended," the client explained, "if they heard about this project indirectly." The design group followed the client's admonition to keep the project quiet only to discover that the client had invited one of the project's key stakeholders to the advisory committee meeting because of an agenda item to be considered right after presentation of the tentative design proposal. That key stakeholder was furious about not being consulted prior to presentation of even a tentative proposal, thus complicating implementation of the plans. This cautionary tale underscores the importance of bringing the client on board about the stakeholder consultation strategy.

B. IDENTIFYING GOALS AND INTERESTS

1. Discerning interests after hearing goals

The designers profiled in this book often devoted considerable energy to researching the stakeholders' goals and interests, and the priorities among them. The Maryland courts' Rachel Wohl spent three months on this, and Michael Young devoted over a year to assessment before convening the first meeting of the South African negotiators. In this section, you will learn why designers do not simply accept the stakeholders' first response at face value. (Note that this inquiry is broader than simply looking at the interests of the parties to a particular dispute; it also involves, in the Maryland planning, for example, judges, bar officials, legislators, business leaders, and others.)

Though research enhances a designer's ability to identify stakeholder interests, there will still be surprises. Designers who make a list of goals at the first interview may learn later that the stakeholders' interests differ from the goals initially expressed. For example, judges in a municipal court may first express a desire to save as much time and money as feasible. When the designers discuss with judges the use of a local community mediation center, however, that suggestion prompts the judges to add another goal—that the local lawyers embrace the mediation program immediately. That newly expressed goal leads to the initial use of lawyer-mediators selected by the court. As they discuss implementation of a lawyer-mediator model, the judges learn that the use of lawyers to mediate may necessitate training, and this may reduce overall cost savings. Still, the judges favor the lawyer-mediator model, and the designer learns that the judges have elevated the goal of garnering bar support for the program over the goal of saving as much money as possible and also above the goal of gaining support from the nonlawyer mediators in the community. The designer then understands more about the priorities among the judges' goals.

2. The parties' process interests

When process or system design takes place in the context of a dispute, the interests of the disputants matter, though they are virtually never the only stakeholders. In many cases, though, a designer's system or process design work is done for prospective conflicts, not current ones. Because people are not accustomed to identifying what their dispute resolution–related goals will be if they are involved in future litigation, arbitration, or even stalemate, designers become avid readers of research on people's reactions to litigation and other processes.

Research suggests that individuals care a great deal about the dispute resolution process and not just about the results they reach through it. Individuals may respond favorably to adjudicative as well as consensus-based or facilitative dispute resolution processes. Of course, one would expect the parties to care about efficiency—time, effort, and costs, but their concerns about fairness have surprised some. What tends to matter in terms of fairness perceptions is that the process affords them an opportunity to be heard, that the process be deemed even-handed and respectful, and that the process be viewed as trustworthy. Social scientists have documented this point in a variety of contexts, as synthesized by a "procedural justice" scholar:

Psychology professor Tom Tyler: "What makes a procedure fair in the eyes of the public? Four factors dominate evaluations of procedural justice.
- "First, people want the opportunity to state their cases to the authorities.
- "Second, people expect neutrality of the authority's decision-making process.
- "People also value the quality of their interpersonal treatment by the authorities, that is, whether they feel they are being treated with dignity and respect by legal authorities.
- "Finally, people focus on cues that communicate information about the intentions and character of the legal authorities with whom they are dealing—trustworthiness" (Tyler, 2009:187-188).

Procedural justice research findings from many settings in the United States and elsewhere in the world provide robust evidence that the dimensions Tyler summarizes play a fundamental role in the way that individuals experience authority and conflict resolution.

Stakeholders who are not parties may still have an interest in being involved, even if they do not articulate this interest as a goal. Once the Truth and Reconciliation Commission of Canada began listening to former Residential Schools students, parents of former students wanted to participate. They had suffered loss if their children were taken from them. For many, the children never returned. Some children were lost or died, and the schools did not tell their parents. In response to the parents, the Commission began the Missing Children and Unmarked Graves Project. The Commission wrote:

> "We were reminded afresh that all this happened to little children who had no control over their lives and whose parents found themselves powerless to prevent their children from being taken from them. People came to the Commission in openness and honesty, seeking to be faithful to what had happened to them. For many people, it was an act of tremendous courage even to appear before the Commission. Some people were so overwhelmed by grief and emotion that they could not complete their statements. In other cases, the pain was so intense that it was necessary to halt the proceedings and simply hold hands. These Canadians have been carrying a tremendous burden of pain for years. Finally, they are starting to be heard. Their messages will play a crucial role in shaping the Truth and Reconciliation Commission's final report" (Truth and Reconciliation Commission of Canada, 2012a:6-7, 17).

3. Short-term and long-term interests

Social science research can help a designer understand typical ways that parties or stakeholders may make errors in articulating their own interests. One typical error is to fail to distinguish short-term and long-term interests. Researchers have documented patterns in the ways that people's goals about process change over time (Cole et al., 2011-2012:§3:8). For example, disputants tend not to realize ahead of time that they may be ready to move on once they have had a chance to voice concerns and be heard through some kind of process (*but see* Chapter 8 for a different situation, particularly after violence).

These researchers work primarily in the context of legal disputes, but their findings there have implications beyond just legal disputes. Imagine, for example, the lost opportunity if Cure Violence had accepted at face value the gang members' defiant statements that revenge was the only option despite the reality that many individuals and groups were able to move on without violence once they were part of the violence interrupters' process. Or imagine if Sanford's city manager had simply denied or accepted any of the demands on the police department made by residents and outside groups. Instead, through the efforts of the city manager and Andrew Thomas, city officials read the demands as expressing an interest in understanding and then being involved in changing police practices. Sanford formed a search committee for a new police chief that included persons respected within a wide variety of community groups. It also formed a broadly representative group to review police procedures, make recommendations, which the city manager and city commission used to monitor progress. The assessment of underlying interests rather than of only demands resulted in processes that were satisfying both to the residents and city officials, as they could find common interests in change and could develop a basis for increasing trust.

Designers can also use past experience to anticipate what a stakeholder might ultimately want. Mediator Bill Drake recalls that a group of people in South Africa asked for a process to discuss racial differences. Drake and colleagues surmised that the underlying interest was improving relations between people of different races but were cognizant of the research about the effects of particular types of cross-race contacts (discussed in Chapter 9). They drew on this research to suggest instead a process in which persons of different races worked together to solve a common problem. The suggested process was implemented and as a byproduct had the desired effect of reducing racial tensions.

Given the importance of assessing interests, designers may adopt more systematic means of taking them into account. The next subsection examines one such method, interest mapping.

Practice Notes: Interest Mapping

Once a designer has surveyed all of the stakeholders, the designer can organize that information by creating a chart or "map" depicting each stakeholder, their interests, and the intensity of those interests so that they can be accounted for in the creation of any process or system design (Elliott, 1999:219-220). Creating a visual "stakeholder interest map" gives voice to each stakeholder's concerns and enables the design team to understand more clearly the ways in which the parties' interests and concerns may be shared, may differ, or may overlap. For example, one design group lists interests by stakeholder; then gives each interest a color depending on whether the interest:

- Is shared by all stakeholders,

- Is not shared by all but does not conflict with other stakeholders' interests,
- Conflicts with interests of other stakeholders, or
- Might conflict with interests of other stakeholders.

Through this "interest mapping," the designers have a quick reference tool for identifying shared interests as well as those that might be accommodated without eroding support. They then can begin work on accommodating interests that conflict or might conflict.

Dispute systems design students conducting an assessment of an urban neighborhood in conflict over a proposed high-rise development created the following documents as part of their stakeholder/interest mapping for their client:

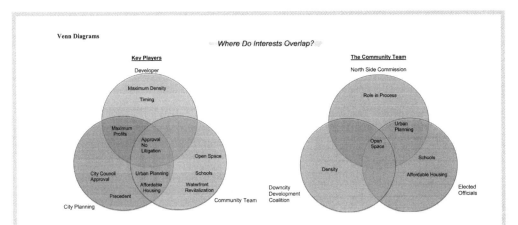

In an entirely different context, designers working through the Harvard Law School Negotiation and Mediation Clinical Program were invited by the Town of Nantucket, Massachusetts to help them design a more effective set of processes for conducting negotiations between the various unions in the town, the town manager, and the board of selectmen. After the designers conducted an exhaustive assessment, interviewing dozens of stakeholders, conducting polls, and holding several focus groups, they produced this stakeholder map for the client.[1]

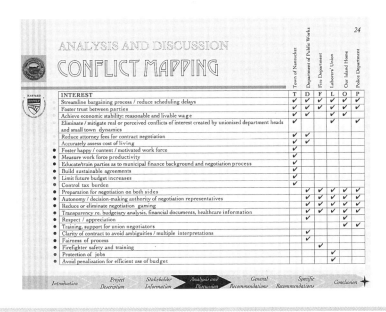

----

1. The conflict map is an exact reproduction of the one produced for the client and is used with the client's permission. The map captures interests of the stakeholders as they represented them in interviews that the design team conducted during the process. As you review the list, what surprises do you see? To what extent might those surprises be related to shortcomings of the designers in doing a thorough assessment that might have probed beyond stated positions to underlying interests? How else might surprises or inconsistencies be explained?

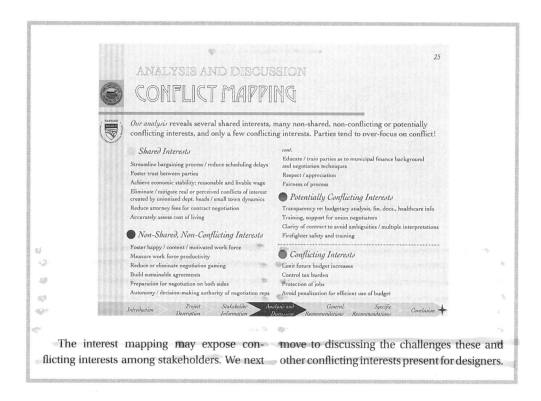

The interest mapping may expose conflicting interests among stakeholders. We next move to discussing the challenges these and other conflicting interests present for designers.

4. Designer's dilemma: conflicts among stakeholders' interests

As mentioned briefly in Chapter 3, clients may approach you in hopes of setting up a new forum or dispute resolution system that leans the client's way—"My company is being hit by too many employee-initiated lawsuits. Can you think of a process that will block some of them?" You may be successful in persuading the client that the new process will not meet the client's desires over time unless that process also meets the primary interests of other stakeholders and helps to identify and prevent the organizational problems that generate so many lawsuits. You can add that the broader community's sense of justice also affects the satisfaction of the individuals within it and the broader community's respect for the results—an uneven playing field is an unstable one. But, if you fail to dissuade the client or the client prefers the gain, even if short-term, you face a dilemma. Do you design the uneven playing field, ignore the directives of the client and design a more power-equalizing system, resign as designer, or take some other action?

Suppose instead that a client asks you to suggest what is "just" or "fair" — "What is the right way to distribute compensation to persons victimized while they were children in the care of government institutions run by religious orders (pp. 33-36)?" This task creates yet another dilemma. Should you respond based on the designer's view of justice or fairness if those in the broader community hold a different view?

Sometimes the resolution of a conflict affects society as a whole—the United Nations Compensation Commission for claims arising from the Iraqi invasion of Kuwait in 1990 awarded over $40 billion. Such massive fund distributions can affect political and economic structures. Should it matter who is requesting design advice? Should the designer factor in personal political views about how societies should be structured (*see* Cohen, 2009:63-64)?

No codes of ethics bind designers specifically, though some professional codes, like those for attorneys, may limit what designers are able to do depending on the circumstances under which they are originally retained (*see also* Chapter 3 regarding personal values). Ultimately, you have to decide whether to accept the client and the job, and how to resolve these dilemmas.

To get a flavor of this, imagine that you were working for Congress and asked to draft the statute providing a government claims facility for families of those killed in the September 11, 2001 terrorist attacks, along with provisions that made it difficult to recover against the airlines or World Trade Center instead. Would you have based the claims facility claim payments in part on economic damages, as Congress mandated in its enacting legislation? Special Master Feinberg noted that this statutory provision "almost guaranteed that the families of a stockbroker or bond trader who died on September 11 would receive more public money than the survivors of a firefighter, soldier, or dishwasher. . . . I knew it would anger 9/11 families, who would demand to know why the life of their wife or daughter was worth less than their next door neighbor's" (Feinberg, 2005:34). At the same time, the tort-based definition of damages resembled the recovery that the claimants might have achieved (if they received any recovery) in the courts absent the statute. What other possible standards might exist for determining the amounts of the awards in the 9/11 situation? What are the pros and cons of these different approaches?

In deciding what other possibilities you might consider, you may find yourself trying to compare the claims facility to something besides a court. After all, if the courts would meet the stakeholders' needs, including protecting the airlines against insolvency (2005:16-22, 182-188), why would the government supplement the courts with a claims facility? Should the 9/11 claims facility resemble those created by Canada for claims by institutionalized children (pp. 33-36)? If the U.S. government decided to create a claims facility again after a terrible event, should it require that the facility give the same amount to each claimant, as did the U.S. government in 1988 when it decided to pay $20,000 to each of the Japanese Americans detained by the U.S. government during World War II? What considerations guide your answer to these questions?

In the excerpts below, four scholars suggest approaches that designers might take in designs like these where interests and contexts differ, and the designer plays a role in deciding which to weigh most heavily. The first suggests a process for inviting a *composite view* ("rough justice") on whether the process is just—seeking counsel broadly from those whose sense of legitimacy matters and then taking that into account. The second takes a value-based, *aspirational goals* approach, focused on the designer's decision-making. The third limits the advice to a particular process—truth commissions in nations transitioning from internal fighting—and suggests attention to *competing goals.* The fourth, a market-based approach, proposes a *rating system* for employment and consumer arbitration pursuant to a pre-dispute clause, creating a system for potential users to trust or not trust a particular arbitration provider.

---

1. Using a "rough justice" concept: Law professor Francis E. McGovern points out that what people will later view to be legitimate and just in a claims facility varies a great deal. Nearly always, he notes, these tribunals provide simplified processes to distribute compensation. Thus, these tribunals cannot, if they are shortened or simplified, provide all of the protections offered by the judicial process. They might, for example, accept affidavits in place of live testimony, when a court would not. McGovern labels the concept of identifying what simplified process will be viewed as legitimate and just, as one of seeking a broader sense of what represents "rough justice" for that situation.

When removing some protections or procedures that a court would typically provide, the designers should not assume that they would always remove the same protections, he explains. The context will make protections important in one instance but not in another. To illustrate—one cannot simply replicate the process used for a United Nations tribunal after Iraq invaded Kuwait in 1990 and expect that it will be well received for the claims facility related to the 9/11 attacks in the United States. For one thing, the U.S. government—not the terrorist attackers—was paying the 9/11 claims while the invading regime paid in the U.N. tribunal. The differences continue—the U.N. as compared to a single government, the numbers and complexities of claims, the resources to administer, the importance of speed, the cultural and political acceptability of valuing claims in particular ways, and more. Thus, it should not be surprising that the 9/11 claims process simplified judicial process in ways that were distinct from the ways that the U.N. Iraq/Kuwait claims tribunal simplified process. The public might view both, though, as legitimate and fair—as providing "rough justice" for the pertinent situations.

How can a designer predict in advance what the stakeholders and, when material, the public will view as legitimate and fair in a simplified process? McGovern urges designers to look for a common view of what procedural protections should be retained in the following way: articulate the "rough justice" concept of a proposed tribunal—in other words, what part of judicial process is retained and what not and why. The designer may synthesize the political and procedural background and use that tentative synthesis of "rough justice" to elicit reactions.

In sum, claims tribunals sacrifice some procedural protections provided by courts because it is not feasible to provide them consistent with other constraints such as cost, timing, and volume. As articulated by McGovern, these tribunals leave unaddressed many important needs that those seeking compensation might value

---

with respect to the management of differences, opting instead to focus almost exclusively on resolving the issue of compensation. Still, McGovern asserts, people sometimes view these tribunals as legitimate and fair and perhaps sufficient in some contexts. He suggests the "rough justice" articulation, combined with elicited feedback and research on reactions to past tribunals, as a way to predict more accurately in advance whether that will be the case (McGovern, 2009:171-185, 188-189).

2. Aspirational goals: Law professor Carrie Menkel-Meadow suggests the following principles for the "well-meaning process designer," though she does not advocate creating a binding code of ethics for designers:

"1. Do no harm—do not make the parties worse off than they were before you were hired [including not incurring costs without benefits].

"2. Do not become a 'tool' of a client or organization or government that wants to use process design to achieve inappropriate or illegitimate ends [such as 'deterring rightful complaints'].

"3. Be sure that the end users . . . have had input into the design. . . .

"4. Attempt to ensure that any process you design can actually accomplish what it was designed to do. Take some responsibility for implementation and evaluation.

"5. Know what participants' legal rights are. . . .

"6. Be sure, as much as you can, that a system of dispute resolution does not systematically discriminate against or harm particular individuals.

"7. Be prepared and be competent. Learn about particular organizations, cultures, groups, and histories before embarking on a design project.

"8. Consider whether processes should include multiple choices, menus, gateways or tiers. . . .

"9. Ensure that any process designed can be adequately explained to and understood by its users.

"10. Suggest that any system designed should be evaluated and revised as conditions change" (Menkel-Meadow, 2009:229-230).

3. A competing goals checklist: Canadian lawyer Mark Freeman, who studied the effectiveness of truth commissions in two dozen nations, noted the following key aspects of effective truth commissions:

- "independence,
- "impartiality,
- "accountability,
- "competence,
- "nondiscrimination,
- "transparency,
- "proportionality,
- "dignity,
- "accessibility,
- "good faith."

At the same time, Freeman pointed out that the following procedural goals sometimes competed with accomplishing this first list of goals:

- "efficiency,
- "flexibility,
- "victim-centeredness,
- "accuracy,
- "comprehensiveness."

Another competing goal was feasibility in the context, given:

- "time pressure,
- "limited human and financial resources,
- "excessive caseload,
- "security concerns." (Freeman, 2006:132).

4. A ratings system: Law professor Thomas Stipanowich suggests a user rating system for employment and consumer arbitration providers—an approach that is reputation-based like McGovern's "rough justice" approach but more suggestive of specific criteria, more measurement-oriented (with its scale) than Freeman's, and more externally focused than Menkel-Meadow's checklist for the designer. Stipanowich draws on protocols developed by those in the arbitration field for his list but introduces the idea of user feedback. Under his system, users would be asked to rate the arbitration program on a 1 to 5 scale (terrible to very good) by the criteria listed below and the program's rating would be publicly available (Stipanowich, 2012:1031):

Meaningful Consent, Clarity, and Transparency

- Meaningful consent to arbitrate
- Adequate notice and disclosure
- Clear guidance for program users ("roadmap") and access to helpline
- Ease of court oversight
- Published program statistics

Independent and Balanced Administration

- Independent and impartial administration
- Balanced input in rules and policies

Quality and Suitability of Arbitrators

- Balanced input in roster of arbitrators
- Diversity
- Experience and training
- Disclosure and challenge mechanism
- Ethics standards and complaint mechanism

Fair Hearing

- Reasonable costs and fees
- Legal counsel
- Reasonable hearing location
- Access to information and discovery
- Limitations period
- Expeditious process
- Availability of class action

Fair Outcomes (Awards and Remedies)

- Access to remedies available in court
- Publication of reasoned awards
- Outcomes

C. EXAMINING THE CONTEXT

The assessment involves more than just talking to stakeholders and gauging interests. Because dispute resolution forums exist within broader institutional, organizational, or geopolitical environments, a design team can understand what to do only by assessing the broader context in which the conflict situation exists. The "context" includes:

- the numbers of disputes,
- available resources,
- leadership,
- history,
- religion,
- culture,
- language,
- demographics,
- economics,
- role of law and lawyers,
- organizational and power structure,
- currently prevailing dispute resolution institutions or practices,
- available leadership, and
- pretty much everything pertinent to the design that is not the identification of stakeholders and their goals and interests (Burgess and Burgess, 2002:62-63; Mitchell, 2002:57; Ury et al., 1988:24-40; Costantino and Merchant, 1996:100-106; Susskind and Thomas-Larmer, 1999:109-119).

In this section, we examine context in an organizational and then an international setting.

Imagining an assessment at eBay: An assessment of the context might begin with a single dispute, what we might call the "presenting problem." Take the eBay merchant unhappy with a buyer posting a comment about his product. Why did the buyer post the comment? Why is the merchant upset? Are others affected by this dispute? How are the buyer, merchant and others handling it now? What are the results? Who pays what amounts for the processing? How long does it take? To what degree is the current dispute handling process meeting their interests? To what degree not?

That first set of inquiries relates to a set of disputants. The designers might next move to assess a broader set of transactions on eBay. What other kinds of disputes occur? How do these get managed or resolved? What are the resources, skills, motivation of stakeholders—customers, sellers, eBay—to participate effectively in various processes? What is the broader environment like? The overriding legal regime? Likelihood of enforcement?

If the focus is on establishing a system, not just a single dispute resolution process, how many other disputes are like this one? The designer may try to aggregate other comment-posting disputes into distinct patterns as well. Are cross-border comment-posting disputes distinct from those within one nation? Does the amount in controversy affect the dispute profile?

Who beyond the immediate parties sees problems with the way that eBay comment-posting disputes are resolved? Who benefits from the system? Who has suggested change? How were the suggestions greeted? What are the resources for modifying the system and operating a new system? Does the issue vary depending on the nation in which it occurs?

Even in this organizational setting, the assessment quickly moves to the context beyond the organization, including the national settings in which the disputes arise. That was even more the case for Michael Young's intervention in South Africa. In fact, while he held about nine meetings between 1985 and 1990, he spent much of the rest of his time in an ongoing assessment of the context.

Key context factors for the talks to begin talks in South Africa: Michael Young emphasizes in his speeches that one cannot understand the choices of persons to join the talks nor the importance of discussions within the talks without understanding the history of South Africa. That history explained the Afrikaners' (persons of Dutch descent) hatred of the British, for example. Other key aspects of context included power struggles within the South African government and insurgent groups, the Cold War, and political events around the world. The elections in the United States, United Kingdom, and then West Germany affected the international economic sanctions on South Africa, and the list goes on. At one point, Young sought to meet with Britain's Prime Minister Margaret Thatcher to seek help in removing a roadblock to the talks—in other words, to modify the context. At another point, it became important to find out whether South Africa was removing its troops from Namibia, as it had agreed to do in the Geneva Protocol, because rumors that too many troops remained there fueled an ANC concern that the government would not keep any agreement reached about the transition to a full-suffrage government. Young believes that he could not have succeeded without this constant attention to the broader context in which his process fit.

We turn now to examine in more depth customary practices, organizational and community structures, and culture—significant parts of the context for a design.

D. CULTURES, ORGANIZATIONAL STRUCTURES, AND CUSTOMARY PRACTICES AS CRUCIAL FEATURES OF CONTEXT

One aspect of assessing context is gaining a sense of how people typically act in a community, organization, or profession/occupation. Some of this customary practice might also be called culture. Designers do not have to take on the complicated task of defining culture to recognize that they will err if they assume that the individuals and groups they work with will view conflicts and their management in the same way the designers do. As sociologist Calvin Morrill learned in studying 13 private corporations, "local customs of conflict management shape the possibilities of dispute processing that individuals imagine when they begin to make sense of a grievance and think about how to pursue it" (1995:217).

These same organizations, communities, and professions also have social structures, with some division of labor, hierarchy of prestige, official rules, systems of reward, and unevenly distributed power and resources. A systems design that works well in one social or cultural context may fail in others because practices, beliefs, perceptions, and experiences of the world differ or because structures of power, rules, and reward vary. Designers need not be experts in culture or group practices or in organizational analysis to know that a system that works well in a nonprofit might fail in a publicly traded company because of the different ways in which the people in that organization understand incentives and experience, relate to, and manage conflict.

Differences in the way groups of people engage with conflict also occur because of national, racial, ethnic, religious, socioeconomic, organizational, educational, and professional differences, to name just a few. Customary negotiation and adjudicative practices not only differ across nations but also within them. American lawyers, for example, have tendencies to negotiate in patterns that are distinct from their clients' negotiation approaches (pp. 150-151). Lawyers tend to focus more than their clients on the parts of the dispute with legal remedies (Riskin, 1982:29; Relis, 2009:232; Menkel-Meadow, 1997:1) and have professional training, rules of conduct, and incentives that encourage this approach. To pull an example from an organizational context, employees in some organizations may talk through their differences while those in another may rely more on avoidance. Because of reward structures, employees in some organizations are unlikely to bring bad news and problems to the attention of superiors. Small communities also display different practices in dealing with differences. One might expect, for example, to encounter more tendencies to discuss differences in a group setting with an aim toward broad consensus within a Quaker community than within a Roman Catholic community, which might be more apt to resolve such issues by referring to hierarchal norms of authority.

Designers' assessments can take these differences into account by being attentive to people's patterns of practice and the ways organizations operate and by resisting imposing their own worldviews on the context in which they are working. Having recognized local practices and organization, designers

- modify the forum or system to accommodate local patterns of practice or organizational structure, particularly when they and their client have neither authority nor resources to significantly alter incentives, rules, laws and structures; and/or
- try to modify the local practices, culture, and structure through the design (*see* Chapter 11).

In the example that follows, consider how eBay did some of each.

eBay and culture: Suppose people from various cultures have only one dispute resolution system available—will they be able to adjust and use that system effectively? eBay's Colin Rule has observed that a new online culture can emerge to dictate appropriate behavior in the merged system. On eBay, users from all over the world have established new behavioral norms that enable participants to communicate across the users' own face-to-face negotiating cultures. For example, users around the world now understand that it is impolite to use ALL CAPS in online communications, as that is interpreted as shouting. In fact, Rule believes that newcomers to online communities often experience a form of culture shock as they acclimatize to the new norms of the community they are joining.[2]

Still, Rule occasionally encountered regional cultural differences that intruded on online interactions. For example, some Italian eBay users found the interest-based negotiation coaching provided in eBay's Help system (*see* p. 25) to be patronizing, the sort of thing "a teacher would tell students in kindergarten." So

---

2. For a different viewpoint on culture and online dispute resolution, see Mary E. Hiscock, Cross-Border Online Consumer Dispute Resolution, 4(1) *Contemp. Asia Arb. J.* 1, 11 (2011).

eBay colleagues in Italy re-packaged that content specifically for Italian users "more along the lines of 'insider tips' and 'best practices' from experienced and successful sellers," as Rule recalled it. As another example, many Asian purchasers did not trust a system that charged their credit card and paid the seller before the merchandise arrived. When eBay began to escrow the funds until the buyers received the merchandise and indicated they were satisfied, Asian buyers increased their use of eBay. A similar escrow-based payment option in North America generated much buyer frustration, and eventually was shut down due to lack of use.

As eBay expands to other regions and international markets, the global rules of eBay's online dispute resolution system will be presented to new users, who will have to learn to adapt to and abide by them. However, if the system is to remain effective over the long haul, designers will undoubtedly need to adapt on occasion to regional cultural norms so as to ensure the system's continued relevance.

1. Acknowledging customary practice in the design

Designers develop their own checklists of questions about customary practices, because they recognize that they place the success of the design at risk if they fail to take these practices into account. Two designers who work extensively on dispute management systems within organizations suggest a checklist to tease out the nature of these local conflict management customs and the structures that may support them:

> "Does the organization avoid conflict? Deny it? Fight it? Control it? Is conflict seen as a sign of failure? How does the organization make decisions: is it risk-aversive, decision-avoiding, hierarchical? What is the attitude toward change? What would the typical response be to a suggestion for change in dispute resolution practices?" (Costantino and Merchant, 1996:98).

A process may "drift" (*see* Chapter 11.B) from meeting the originators' intent and toward being consistent with customary practices or an organization's reward system, if the designer does not anticipate this pull. Thus, for example, a court mediation program designed to encompass all of the parties' issues may develop the narrow focus on legal issues that dominates among lawyers (Relis, 2009:232; Riskin and Walsh, 2008:868). Or a school system that measures school and classroom performance by average test scores of enrolled students may continue to expel "problem students" (many of whom test poorly) rather than put into practice a restorative justice system (*see* pp. 111-112) designed to reintegrate those students into the school. What might a designer do to keep these sorts of "drift" from occurring or to minimize their effects?

Both research and experience tell us that imbedded practices and norms can change in response to modified structures, rules, and incentives. Designers may find themselves in a position to propose, plan, and advocate for such modifications by showing how crucial they are to successful implementation of a new design.

2. Using the design to change customary practices

Designers may be understandably modest about making claims that a process will change customary practices. To illustrate, designers may hope to improve one aspect of customary practice—the disputing patterns. They might want, for example, to improve habits of parental communications following divorce, for the sake of the children, or wish that they could reduce the violent patterns of resolving conflict in Chicago neighborhoods (pp. 27-28). In another context, administrators of a military college where hazing is a time-honored practice that fosters both in-group solidarity and inter-group conflict may want to transform the cultural norm of students for many reasons: desire to make the campus more welcoming, new anti-hazing legislation, or concerns about the short-term and long-term well-being of students exposed to hazing.

Assessing whether and to what extent a design team can influence or change the pattern or ways which individuals or an organization process and manage conflict is among a designer's most important challenges. Dogged attempts to transform a deeply ingrained set of norms, and expectations can simply lead to frustration and failure. At the same time, when the institutional norms and approaches to conflict are fundamentally unhealthy and a major reason for long-term conflict, simply resigning oneself to the status quo can be equally self-defeating.

For example, designers asked to help a Roman Catholic Church set up a dispute resolution system in the wake of the priest-abuse crisis in the early 2000s thought it essential to the goal of preventing future occurrences to change the institutional decision-making norms regarding reporting abuse allegations. At the same time, they believed that they would find themselves fighting a losing battle if they sought to reconfigure all decision-making norms in the Catholic Church. The challenge for the designer, then, is to determine which aspects of customary practice can be leveraged to improve a dispute resolution system, which must necessarily change in order to transform dysfunction to function, and which norms are likely to persist despite best efforts to change them.

Research occasionally documents that customary practices changed in the wake of a new disputing system in concert with changes in rules, organizational structures, or incentives. For example, a team of social scientists discovered that family lawyers in Maine, where all disputed child custody issues were sent to mediation, were more likely than New Hampshire family lawyers, where that rarely occurred, to take a broader, more long-term view of their clients' interests (McEwen et al., 1994:177-179). This and other research suggests that changing structures (e.g., introducing new procedures such as mandatory mediation) or creating rules requiring new accountability and openness (e.g., submitting to a court all information about finances of a divorcing couple) can help to reshape entrenched practices of the communities of divorce lawyers (*see* Chapter 13; Sunstein, 2012:1350).

So too can changing incentives result in shifts in customary practices, as researchers discovered in studying varying ways that large companies handled disputes with other businesses. When management set a goal of early settlement (knowing that this reduced costs), a company substantially altered the internal "culture of disputing," including in a division known for its "tough guy" culture (McEwen, 1998:19). The corporation did so by changing incentives as well as processes and structures. It tracked prominently how quickly disputes were resolved and celebrated reductions in time to resolution. It altered the way costs of inside and outside counsel were allocated and made those a part of a disputing manager's costs—not of corporate overhead—along with the costs of settlement. It introduced an intensive early case assessment process. It required completion of an ADR Case Evaluation Worksheet before outside counsel could be hired for more extended work. And it included independent advisors from another division of the company in assessing disputes so that broader corporate interests would be paramount rather than the more parochial and personal concerns of the manager involved in the dispute. Through the combination of these and other changes in incentives, processes, and structures, the company significantly altered its "disputing culture," increased the use of mediation and negotiated settlement, preserved many business relationships, and reduced costs (McEwen, 1998:18-19).

Changes in the law can also lead to changes in culture (though often they do not, as discussed in Chapter 13). For example, smoking in bars in New York and many other cities was commonplace in the early 2000s. When New York City banned smoking in bars in 2003, many doubted whether such a ban could work or even be enforced. Today, smoking in a New York City bar would be considered rude and culturally anachronistic. In the short span of a decade, what seemed to be deeply embedded in New York City bar culture completely disappeared.

In sum, designers may include the goal of changing customary practice but recognize that they may find it difficult to achieve success without also being able to alter aspects of incentives, organizational and community structures, and rules or laws.

E. ASSESSMENT TOOLS

Designers and design teams deploy a number of information-gathering methods during an assessment, as was evident in the stories reported in this and the last chapter. Tio Hardiman gathered much information by observation and by listening to people's stories through his work in high-violence Chicago neighborhoods, for example. Michael Young had to use methods consistent with the secret nature of his intervention. But, designers often have the opportunity to conduct a more focused and formal assessment. Common methods of information gathering in that setting include:

- interviews,
- focus groups,
- surveys,
- direct observation, and
- library and other outside research.

As you contemplate more systematic collection of information during the assessment process, try also to think ahead to later evaluation of the design and its impact (*see* Chapter 14). Data collected in the assessment phase can usefully serve as a point of comparison to data collected later in order to learn what changed as a result of the design implementation. For example, establishing in the assessment phase how disputes are perceived, what kinds there are, how frequent they are, and how they are currently managed will enable you to collect comparable data later, thus enabling clear before-after comparisons.

Most designers lack training in how to conduct high-quality empirical research, including the kind of detailed direct observation that an anthropologist or ethnographer might undertake. Expecting that a designer possesses expertise in using all of the above tools would result in far fewer designers than there are design needs. We offer practice notes below for designers who have the opportunity to do the research but lack the empirical research background.

Practice Notes: Research for an Assessment

Designers will be able to elicit more accurate information if they are armed with a basic awareness of the most commonly used assessment tools, when and where they might be used, how to best use a tool, and whether they can reasonably perform the work or need to look to outside experts for assistance. For example, in implementing the 9/11 Victim Compensation Fund, Special Master Ken Feinberg had neither the expertise nor the time to perform the actuarial analysis required for the efficient functioning of the system. As a result, he looked to experts at PricewaterhouseCoopers for this work.

Below we provide basic information about some of the most important assessment tools for designers in a typical consulting capacity, and we encourage designers to seek out the additional expertise they may need in any given project.

1. Interviews: In some law school design clinics, virtually every assessment entails at least some interviews with important stakeholders. Interviews provide a window through which design teams can learn about the interests of key stakeholders, the context and history of the situation, the possible barriers to agreement, and the emotions, perceptions, and relationships of the parties. Even when there are media accounts or ample written materials that divulge information about a given conflict or organizational design context, key informant interviews provide a degree of nuance and a depth of understanding that are indispensable for a design team. More than the other information-gathering methods above, interviews allow a designer to get a rich, qualitative understanding of the context as seen by a stakeholder. Because interviews also help to build rapport—a sense of trust and a relationship with the interviewee—in-person interviews seem more effective in securing information than phone interviews. In-person interviews allow the designer to observe facial reactions and emotional behavior that provide clues to good follow-up questions. (Interviews in a stakeholder assessment that run 30 to 45 minutes seem to yield essential information while fitting into the time busy people are willing to set aside.)

In some contexts where only small numbers of parties need a process design, it may be possible to conduct an interview with every single stakeholder. This is rarely the case, however. In most system design processes, there are simply too many stakeholders to make interviewing all of them workable. As a result, design teams must think strategically about how many interviews to conduct and who should receive one. This exercise of judgment should not be taken lightly. Questions to ask in making these decisions include:

- How much time does the design team have to make recommendations or issue the stakeholder assessment?
- Does the list of interviewees include a representative from every known stakeholder group?
- Are there influential others, perhaps connected to the situation but not directly involved, who ought to be offered an interview as a move to keep them engaged and to win their support of the broader design process?
- Has the design team left some time to interview at least a few additional others in case the first round of interviews indicate that they missed some key players?

Successful interviewing requires both careful planning and in-the-moment flexibility. In advance of the interview, designers create interview protocols. An *interview protocol* is a list of prepared questions or topics that you as a designer intend to pose to your interviewees. These questions should be designed to elicit thoughtful responses from interviewees about:

a. the context and/or the conflict itself,
b. the interviewee's interest,
c. the interviewee's notion of a "good outcome" or success, and
d. the interviewee's perception of other key stakeholders and their interests and concerns.

Successful interviewing requires probing—that is following up questions to understand and ask for elaboration of responses. Sometimes interviewees give general answers (e.g., "Group X distrusts us"). You can then probe for examples that may help contextualize and deepen understanding of perceptions and experiences. The protocols—the list of topics or questions that you begin with—thus are only a starting point for an interview.

Stakeholders who are involved in an assessment—whether because they are being interviewed, are part of a focus group, or are asked to take a poll or survey—often ask questions that designers should have answers to before beginning the process. Some commonly asked questions are:

- Will this interview remain confidential?
- Will I get to see the final work product you are producing?
- Who else will get to see the final work product?
- Will I have a chance to edit or correct any information that is inaccurate or wrong?

Answers to these questions help stakeholders decide not only *whether* they want to participate in a design process but also *how* they will participate—the degree to which they will be frank with you in their answers.

A design team may find itself listening to stakeholders who are angry, fed up, and frustrated. The interview may be the first time that a stakeholder has felt that anyone has been willing to listen to her story. As a result, first-time designers may be trapped in endless interviews, listening to what they might characterize as long diatribes and accusations. In such situations, there are a number of errors to avoid: First, though tempting as a way to build affiliation and trust, it is necessary to avoid agreeing with a stakeholder about the merits of her story; otherwise the designer may distort the answers and be quoted in ways that alienate other stakeholders. Second, when a stakeholder seems intransigent and unmovable, it is important to remain calm and use the information to dig past the settled "position" to the underlying interest. This will entail patient active listening, a skill discussed in some detail later (pp. 366-369), as well as an ability to reframe and be persistent in questioning. Next, though new designers are often afraid to interrupt and move the interview forward, skillful interviewing sometimes requires interrupting and pressing a stakeholder on to other topics.

If two members of a design team conduct an interview, one can conduct the interview while the other takes notes. Of course, concerns about cost or the dynamics of outnumbering the interviewee may weigh against using two interviewers. When designers conduct interviews on their own, it is often more important to focus on interacting with the stakeholder than it is on taking detailed notes. "At the end of each interview, the interviewee should be asked if there is anything more he or she would like to add. . . . A written summary of the highlights of the interview should be sent to each participant, to be certain that nothing has been misunderstood" (Susskind and Thomas-Larmer, 1999:115). If tempted to digitally record an interview, think first about whether it will inhibit frankness in the conversation. Think also about whether digital transcription will be feasible, and, if transcription must be done manually, the time that transcription takes—at least two to three hours for every hour of recording (for more detailed information on how to conduct interviews, see Weiss, 1994; Susskind and Thomas-Larmer, 1999). Rather than recording, an interviewer could take time immediately after completing an interview to fill in notes while the experience is fresh.

2. Focus groups: Focus groups are structured group interviews that serve multiple purposes. They encourage interaction among group members in a way that elicits a better understanding of a conflict situation or an organizational context. Design teams decide to use focus groups when there are too many stakeholders to interview individually. But they also use focus groups to allow group members to react to each other, to produce rich qualitative data, and to allow the designer to test ideas or hypotheses.

In planning for a focus group, a designer considers first who should be invited and for what purpose. The designer also must decide on the format of the focus group: how long, how many questions, how many individuals, whether to record the session, have someone take notes, use flipcharts, etc. Focus groups can vary in size, but most are between six and twelve participants because this allows them to participate more than once, and even interact, within the timeframe of about an hour. The facilitator then understands their views in more depth, and they feel more engaged.

Designers also face a choice of whether to create homogeneous or heterogeneous groups. Participants in homogeneous groups are often more comfortable and open to discussing sensitive topics. For example, a homogeneous group of Catholic priest abuse victims would encourage a degree of openness that could not be achieved with members of the Catholic clergy present. At the same time, having heterogeneous focus groups permits a designer to observe the interplay between victims' advocates and the Catholic hierarchy.

To increase the likelihood of a valuable focus group session, the moderator should set a positive tone and be well versed in skills of group facilitation (*see* Chapter 15). The moderator suggests ground rules of behavior, encourages introductions, and promotes a healthy and generous dialogue. The moderator should also be attentive to managing time and encouraging participation from all group members.

At times, participants may adopt unproductive roles or even act disruptively. Individuals who are deeply embedded in an institutional culture may resent the presence of outsiders and may take on the role of "expert" in a focus group. Others may act in ways that are hostile either to the moderator or to fellow group members. There are many strategies for effectively handling such participants, and it is important that designers who are not well equipped in facilitation skills either get the proper training to run them or engage those who have that training to run these groups on their behalf. If two persons facilitate a focus group, one can moderate and be attentive to the group's needs, and the other can record notes (either on a flipchart or in a notebook or laptop) while watching the time.

When developing questions for a focus group, experts suggest following two general principles: "The first suggests that the questions be ordered from the more general to the more specific. . . . Second, questions should be ordered by the relative importance of the research agenda. Thus, the questions of greatest importance should be placed early,

near the top of the guide, whereas those of lesser significance should be placed near the end" (Stewart et al., 2007:61).

As with interviewing, outside resources provide valuable guidance for running focus groups (*see generally* Morgan, 1996 and Stewart et al., 2007; *see* Herzig and Chasin, 2006 regarding designing and running focus groups for individuals who may be in conflict with each other).

3. Surveys: Designers turn to surveys or polls when they seek to gather information from large groups of stakeholders and when neither interviews nor focus groups can work. It is easy to put together a shoddy survey; it is difficult to design, conduct, and analyze a survey that will provide reliable information.

As with all information gathering, designers improve the reliability of information by considering the kind of information they hope to collect, the resources at their disposal, and the target audience of a survey. This will help drive decisions about whether the survey should be conducted via traditional "snail mail," the internet, the telephone, or in face-to-face interviews. It will also help determine whether the survey should consist primarily of open-ended or close-ended questions, whether to use a scale that permits rankings of feelings on a scale (e.g., 1. Absolutely disagree to 5. Absolutely agree), whether to allow ranking of choices, etc.

The online survey may not be the most effective or efficient approach. Online surveys frequently have low response rates, and the designer can have little control over who on the other end of the survey actually responds. Most important, however, stakeholder groups may not have access to the internet or computers—or email addresses may not be available for some stakeholder groups. For example, if you are working for a large U.S.-based retailer to help it design a dispute resolution system for factories in some part of the developing world, creating an online worker survey will be unsuccessful because few of the assembly line workers in such a facility have access to internet or computers at home. For these reasons, survey designers think carefully about the target audience and how best to reach them.

On the other hand, an advantage of online surveys conducted through commercial sites such as SurveyMonkey or Qualtrics is that the software provides summaries and modest statistical analysis of the data, reducing considerably the time and energy devoted to coding and entering and summarizing data derived from a mail survey. Such surveys work best when sent to clearly defined email lists of people with a brief note explaining the importance of responding. Follow-ups to the list to remind people to respond can help to increase survey response rates.

When designing the survey itself, a designer can employ open-ended, close-ended, and multiple-choice questions variously for different ends. Open-ended questions provide designers with explanations that can be helpful. They are also more likely to capture strong opinions and emotions. However, many times those taking a survey feel burdened by open-ended questions and prefer multiple-choice or close-ended ones.

Close-ended questions can be especially useful when trying to persuade a client or a supervisor who may value empirical findings over anecdotal experience in decision-making. There are many kinds of close-ended survey questions. Some require a single choice among many; others ask for a rank-ordering; still others ask a stakeholder to answer along a continuum from "strongly agree" to "strongly disagree." Therefore, think carefully about the kind of information you want to learn as a result of the survey and then what kind of question will best elicit that information.

The questions themselves should not be leading (Would you prefer to have more participation in the organization—yes or no?)

or "double-barreled" (Are you satisfied with the way management treats you *and* with your benefits?). Take care in the choice of words. Emotion-charged words may shape responses, for example. The sequence of questions can also affect responses. For example, usually "easier" questions should come first to build comfort. Earlier questions can influence answers to later questions, a factor that must be taken into account in sequencing them.

Surveys implicate client relations. A client may insist on signing off on the survey before it is distributed. In addition, designers may need the help of the client to disseminate the survey. Consequently, as designers create a survey, they should be working contemporaneously with a client to determine how and when the survey will get distributed. In order to increase the likelihood of honest responses from those surveyed, designers may want to assure those who take the survey that they will remain anonymous. That can easily be done through survey tools such as Qualtrics or SurveyMonkey, but cannot work if the respondent returns a survey using an email address. (If the client is a public entity, the law may require disclosure, a particular problem if the data are identifiable by case or party. In a highly litigious situation or one related to a criminal investigation, partisans or prosecutors may seek electronic discovery, even if the software aggregates results, to secure individual survey responses through formal discovery or investigation (*see* Chapter 7; pp. 180-186).)

Design teams commonly like to conduct more surveys than they have the time or resources to do. The survey work done in design projects may not satisfy a Ph.D. candidate in a sociology department. That said, designers can still improve the accuracy of results by being aware of possible errors in survey research related to inadequate sample size, non-response errors, and coverage errors. A non-response error occurs, for example, when a significant number of people who do not respond possess a similar characteristic. Since they are non-responsive, that characteristic and any resulting needs of that group simply do not get captured as a result of the survey.

In putting together a survey, designers should be aware of four cornerstones:

- "drawing a large enough sample of respondents, randomly, so that sampling error is kept to an acceptable level;
- "selecting a sample of people in such a way that virtually all members of the population in which we are interested have an equal (or sometimes known) chance of being selected, thus, limiting coverage error;
- "writing questions and arranging them in a questionnaire in ways that help avoid measurement error; and
- "obtaining a response rate high enough to lessen concern about nonresponse error" (Salant and Dillman, 1994:216).

4. Direct observation: A designer can find out through observation how parties interact with each other and about the "climate" within various units, departments, stakeholder groups, and individuals. For example, if a design team is helping a large urban school district in creating an integrated conflict management system, it could learn much by observing parent-teacher association meetings and sitting in on negotiations between the school board and the teachers' union. Direct observation thus is a powerful tool for the designer. It does not produce the kind of quantitative data that polls do, but it can provide rich insights on important relationships and organizational or system dynamics.

The presence of an observer and interactions with those observed can affect the accuracy of observations. Designers may try to minimize those effects but should be realistic. They already know that their very involvement

in the design project has disrupted the status quo. At the same time, observers can reduce their impact by sitting in the back of the room, dressing similarly to those who are actually involved in the session, and in other ways being as unobtrusive as possible.

As an assessment tool, direct observation helps a designer get a deeper understanding of the inner workings of an organization or conflict system. But direct observation can also be time consuming, so being thoughtful about when to use this assessment tool matters. For example, if the representatives for countries who are party to an international treaty are coming together for a biannual meeting and the designers are considering ways to improve the treaty, they can use their time efficiently if they send members of the design team to the biannual meeting. First, informal conversations and interviews will be possible; second, observing the interactions among stakeholders will yield lots of information; and third, this may be one of the few times when so many stakeholders are in a single place, creating an economy of scale and a wise use of limited resources. If, on the other hand, designing a dispute resolution system to help a Catholic archdiocese better manage conflict within parishes, sending design team members to observe the monthly meetings of several hundred parish council meetings is unlikely to be as rich a source of information as interviews, surveys, and focus groups.

Key informant interviews can help supplement or replace direct observation. Not only is observation time consuming, but observers rarely have access to all parts of a complex organization or of a community. By strategically selecting knowledgeable insiders (perhaps insiders without a stake in the design process), a design team can ask them to describe how the organization or community works and who some of the key actors are. Of course, informants, like observers, have biases that one must account for, but drawing from their experience can widen and deepen understanding of the context for disputing system design.

5. *Available data:* An assessment would be incomplete without some combination of interviews, focus groups, surveys, and direct observation. But designers also use more readily available data sources for assessment as well. These include research in libraries, newspaper accounts, statistical archives (such as the census), organizational reports and records, and online resources. In addition, depending on the context, a client may be able to provide internal data about an organization, a conflict setting, or dilemma. If a designer is doing an assessment for Howard Gadlin at the National Institutes of Health, Gadlin's office itself is a rich source of information. It can provide demographic data about the number of employees at NIH, their tenure, age, and gender. That office may also be able to provide statistical information about the number of EEOC complaints and how they are resolved. Earlier reports by consultants or internal studies may have been done that provide historical context and strengthen the framework for building a rich picture of an organization. This information helps designers understand the context, challenges, and opportunities with greater clarity.

The availability and reliability of outside resources vary widely across contexts. If a designer is working in a developing country to design a dispute resolution system to assist a local community with land disputes, there may be little statistical data or information relating to the community itself. In a case like this, it may be helpful to look for best practices in analogous situations.

At other times, the volume of data available through other sources such as client records, the library, newspaper archives, or web may be simply overwhelming. For example, a designer tasked with creating a system for Assistant U.S. Attorneys to make more frequent use of dispute resolution processes in their work may be given information about hundreds of thousands of cases handled by the U.S. Department of Justice. In a case like this, design teams need to be able to decipher what information is helpful and what needs to be put aside as distracting to the design task at hand. In your haste, you do not want to miss an important piece of information that would inform your design process; at the same time, it is neither advisable nor reasonable at times to read every piece of information that might be available on a given project. As in so many cases in design work, these are judgment calls, and you will get better at making them by seeking counsel from more experienced designers and gaining that experience yourself.

THOUGHTS GOING FORWARD

In this chapter, you have been challenged to deepen and broaden the ways that you think about assessing the problem that a disputing system design might solve and the environment in which you are working. This chapter also has helped acquaint you with some of the questions and skills necessary to carry out assessment work successfully. With these tools and a broadened perspective, your counsel on a new design is more likely to fit the context and interests of the people affected and to engage them in the process as early as possible. Ask questions in a variety of ways to generate as complete a list of stakeholders as feasible. Listen to stakeholders' goals and probe for underlying interests. As you do so, factor in what you have learned about the social science literature on human behavior, other comparable experience, and theories about disputing behavior. Investigate the context using a variety of research methods as well as what you learn about analogous designs and theories about conflict resolution. Recognize that the context includes people's customary practices, including national, regional, and local cultures and the social structures of organizations, groups, and communities. The assessment often challenges you to make key decisions that raise questions about your broader responsibilities. Consider legitimacy, fairness, and effects on the broader community as well as feasibility and the dilemmas these pose for you. Reflect on how you will handle competing interests among stakeholders, including your client.

QUESTIONS

4.1 What departments of eBay (e.g., customer support, marketing/sales, finance, human resources, mergers and acquisitions, product management, technology, safety, facilities, legal affairs) might be key stakeholders in terms of eBay resolution center director Colin Rule's proposal to substitute negotiation software for most of the human mediators (pp. 25-26)? Why?

4.2 Research suggests that attorneys sometimes act like separate stakeholders in disputes involving represented parties, and their interests may differ from their clients' (Relis, 2009:232). What distinct interests might attorneys and clients have in the following situations:

a. A plaintiff in a medical malpractice case whose lawyer will be paid on a contingent fee basis?
b. Five hundred clients of a lawyer in a toxic tort case?
c. A plaintiff in an employment civil rights case whose attorney will be paid, if at all, by attorney's fees imposed by a court or provided as part of the settlement by the defendant?

4.3 What do you imagine might be the underlying interests for the following stated goals? How would you go about finding out whether your guess is accurate?

a. A university administrator says, "If you start a mediation program on this campus, it must not mediate between faculty and their students."
b. A plaintiff's attorney says, "I will support creation of a claims facility for people harmed by the contaminated meat only if the claims facility offers all of the fairness guarantees of court process."
c. A divorce mediator says, "The court's divorce mediation program should exclude lawyers from the mediation sessions."
d. A member of a parish in the midst of conflict says, "Under no circumstances will I agree to participating in any trainings or trust-building exercises."

4.4 In developing an internal dispute resolution system for the National Institutes of Health employees (pp. 30-31), what are some practical ways to ascertain what people will want over time?

4.5 A Maryland domestic relations court asks you to design a mediation program. The local court's chief judge explains to you that the program will be continued, once started, only if it reduces the case backlog and alleviates the judges' oppressive workload. Make a checklist of what you will do before deciding whether to accept this job. Keep in mind that experienced designers counsel that such a decision be made as early as possible (Carpenter and Kennedy, 2001:74, 94-95).

4.6 Designers sometimes bring their own professional preferences to the situation, perhaps favoring consensus-based or mediation solutions because they are mediators (*see* Mayer, 2004:29-31). If an oil company asks you to plan a two-week-from-claim-to-decision binding arbitration process for claims following an oil spill, what might you do if you got into design work because you prefer consensus-based solutions like mediation?

4.7 Suggest a research plan for the assessment that precedes planning for a process to handle claims arising when a silo explodes, flooding a town with corn, destroying houses, cars, and crops, and injuring 50 people.

4.8 Imagine that the state Department of Transportation has adopted a new plan to identify near accidents that occur in the state railway industry. The goal of the new protocol is to transform the culture from one of denying the occurrence of such close calls to one encouraging their reporting so that the agency can learn from them and develop strategies to reduce their incidence in the future. Aware that the new protocol will result in occasional conflicts, you have been asked to conduct an assessment of the situation for the Department of Transportation. Suggest a research plan. What obstacles might you face given the stated goals of the new protocol?

4.9 You have been tasked with conducting an assessment prior to a design project for a small town (population 10,000) in conflict with its five service unions (fire, police, school, service workers, and sanitation). In addition to yourself, there are three more full-time members on your team. You will need to issue a report within three months. What assessment tools might you deploy and for what purposes? What might be challenges you would face in using these tools? How might you address these?

4.10 A candidate running for the role of comptroller in a major U.S. city has asked you to do an assessment of the way the current comptroller conducts audits, suggesting that the current audit process is adversarial, contentious, and costly to city taxpayers. The candidate wants to propose a more cooperative and integrative approach to conducting these audits. What challenges might you expect to face in the assessment part of your project?

4.11 Most organizations and people are not accustomed to using a designer. Suppose a corporate counsel hired you to help develop new methods for the company's 400 in-house attorneys to handle disputes. The attorneys think they are doing things as they should and are not used to having a consultant review their approaches. How would you begin your work, given the existing practices and attitudes?

4.12 Law professor Nienke Grossman suggests that common elements in treaty-created international adjudicatory tribunals also reflect what scholars think would make them legitimate—that is, that people and states believe that they should accept the tribunal's authority because it has earned that trust (Grossman, 2009:115). These elements include a perception that:

- "[T]he tribunal is fair and unbiased—a perception linked to its procedures and decision-makers."
- The tribunal is "interpreting and applying norms consistent with what states believe the law is or should be," and
- "Transparency and other democratic institutional norms" (Grossman, 2009:121-122, 160).

How does Grossman's approach to legitimacy for treaty-created international adjudicatory tribunals resemble and differ from the other approaches to legitimacy and fairness discussed in Chapter 4.B.5?

Exercise 4.1 *The design team at Tallahoya University:* Counsel for Tallahoya just called to say that you landed the job on the university's dispute management design team. Congratulations! Though the full-time position begins after you graduate, she has arranged for you to begin now on a part-time basis. "Your first assignment will be to do an assessment of one of the five issues I mentioned before your initial interview," she explained (pp. 42-44). "The assessment can include your current thinking about stakeholders, goals, interests, problems, and context, as well as your questions and work plan to be ready for the formal assessment in a few months."

BIBLIOGRAPHY AND REFERENCES

AMIR, Yehuda (1998) "Contact Hypothesis in Ethnic Relations," in Eugene Weiner ed., *The Handbook of Interethnic Coexistence* 162. NY: Continuum.

AVRUCH, Kevin (1998) *Culture and Conflict Resolution.* Washington, DC: United States Institute of Peace Press.

BINGHAM, Lisa B. (2008) "Designing Justice: Legal Institutions and Other Systems for Managing Conflict," 14 *Ohio St. J. on Disp. Resol.* 1.

BINGHAM, Lisa B. (2003) *Mediation at Work: Transforming Workplace Conflict at the United States Postal Service.* Bloomington, IN: Human Capital Management Series, IBM Center for the Business of Government.

BINGHAM, Lisa B. (2004) "Employment Dispute Resolution: The Case for Mediation," 22 *Conflict Resol. Q.* 145.

BRETT, Jeanne M. (2007) *Negotiating Globally: How to Negotiate Deals, Resolve Disputes, and Make Decisions Across Cultural Boundaries* (2d ed.). San Francisco: John Wiley and Sons, Inc.

BURGESS, Heidi, and Guy BURGESS (2002) "How Do I Get Good Information in a Short Time?," in John Paul Lederach and Janice Moomaw Jenner, eds. (2002) *A Handbook of International Peacekeeping: Into the Eye of the Storm* 59. San Francisco: Jossey-Bass.

BUSH, Robert A. Baruch, and Joseph P. FOLGER (2005) *The Promise of Mediation* (2d ed.). San Francisco: Jossey-Bass.

CARPENTER, Susan L., and W.J.D. KENNEDY (2001) *Managing Public Disputes.* San Francisco: Jossey-Bass.

CHEW, Pat K. (2001) *The Conflict and Culture Reader.* New York: New York University Press.

COHEN, Amy J. (2009) "Dispute Systems Design, Neoliberalism, and the Problem of Scale," 14 *Harv. Negot. L. Rev.* 51.

COLE, Sarah R., Nancy H. ROGERS, Craig A. McEWEN, James R. COBEN, and Peter N. THOMPSON (2017-2018) *Mediation: Law, Policy, Practice* (3rd ed.). Minneapolis: West.

COSTANTINO, Cathy A., and Christina Sickles MERCHANT (1996) *Designing Conflict Management Systems.* San Francisco: Jossey-Bass.

ELLIOTT, Michael L. Poirier (1999) "The Role of Facilitators, Mediators, and Other Consensus Building Practitioners," in Lawrence Susskind, Sarah McKearnan, and Jennifer Thomas-Larmer eds., *The Consensus Building Handbook* 199. Thousand Oaks, CA: Sage Publications.

FEINBERG, Kenneth R. (2005) *What Is Life Worth?* New York: Public Affairs.

FISHER, Roger, and Daniel SHAPIRO (2005) *Beyond Reason: Using Emotions as You Negotiate.* New York: Viking.

FREEMAN, Mark (2006) *Truth Commissions and Procedural Fairness.* Cambridge: Cambridge University Press.

GELFAND, Michele J., and Jeanne M. BRETT (2004) *The Handbook of Negotiation and Culture.* Stanford: Stanford Business Books.

GROSSMAN, Nienke (2009) "Legitimacy and International Adjudicative Bodies," 41 *Geo. Wash. Int'l L. Rev.* 107.

HERZIG, Maggie, and Laura CHASIN (2006) *Fostering Dialogue Across Divides.* Watertown, MA: Public Conversations Project.

LANDE, John (2008) "Practical Insights from an Empirical Study of Cooperative Lawyers in Wisconsin," 2008 *J. Disp. Resol.* 203.

LEBARON, Michelle (2003) *Bridging Cultural Conflicts: A New Approach for a Changing World.* San Francisco: John Wiley and Sons, Inc.

LEDERACH, John Paul (1995) *Preparing for Peace: Conflict Transformation Across Cultures.* Syracuse: Syracuse University Press.

LEDERACH, John Paul, and Janice Moomaw JENNER (2001) *A Handbook of International Peacekeeping: Into the Eye of the Storm.* San Francisco: Jossey-Bass.

LEIGHNINGER, Matt (2006) *The Next Form of Democracy: How Expert Rule Is Giving Way to Shared Governance . . . and Why Politics Will Never Be the Same.* Nashville: Vanderbilt University Press.

LLEWELLYN, Jennifer J. (2002) "Dealing with the Legacy of Native Residential School Abuse in Canada: Litigation, ADR, and Restorative Justice," 52 *U. Toronto L.J.* 253.

LLEWELLYN, Jennifer (2008) "Bridging the Gap Between Truth and Reconciliation: Restorative Justice and the Indian Residential School Truth and Reconciliation Commission," in M. Brant-Castellano, L. Archibald, and M. DeGagne eds., *From Truth to Reconciliation: Transforming the Legacy of Residential Schools* 183. Ottawa: Aboriginal Healing Foundation.

MAYER, Bernard S. (2004) *Beyond Neutrality: Confronting the Crisis in* Conflict *Resolution.* San Francisco: Jossey-Bass.

McEWEN, Craig A. (1998) "Managing Corporate Disputing: Overcoming Barriers to the Effective Use of Mediation for Reducing the Cost and Time of Litigation," 14 *Ohio St. J. on Disp. Resol.* 1.

McEWEN, Craig A., Richard MAIMAN, and Lynn MATHER (1994) "Lawyers, Mediation, and the Management of Divorce Practice," 28 *Law & Soc'y* 249.

McGOVERN, Francis E. (2009) "Dispute System Design: The United Nations Compensation Commission," 14 *Harv. Negot. L. Rev.* 171.

MENKEL-MEADOW, Carrie (1991) "Pursuing Settlement in an Adversary Culture: A Tale of Innovation Co-opted or 'the Law of ADR,'" 19 *Fla. St. U. L. Rev.* 1.

MENKEL-MEADOW, Carrie (2009) "Are There Systemic Ethics Issues in Dispute System Design? And What We Should [Not] Do About It: Lessons from International and Domestic Fronts," 14 *Harv. Negot. L. Rev.* 195.

MITCHELL, Christopher (2002) "How Much Do I Need to Know?," in John Paul Lederach and Janice Moomaw Jenner eds., *A Handbook of International Peacekeeping: Into the Eye of the Storm* 49. San Francisco: Jossey-Bass.

MORGAN, David (1996) *Focus Groups as Qualitative Research* (2d ed.). Thousand Oaks, CA: Sage Publications.

MORRILL, Calvin (1995) *The Executive Way: Conflict Resolution in Corporations.* Chicago: University of Chicago Press.

PARK, William W. (2010) "Arbitrators and Accuracy," 1 *J. Int'l Disp. Settlement* 25.

RELIS, Tamara (2009) *Perceptions in Litigation and Mediation: Lawyers, Defendants, Plaintiffs, and Gendered Parties.* Cambridge: Cambridge University Press.

RISKIN, Leonard (1982) "Mediation and Lawyers," 43 *Ohio St. L.J.* 29.

RISKIN, Leonard, and Nancy A. WELSH (2008) "Is That All There Is?: 'The Problem' in Court-Oriented Mediation," 15 *Geo. Mason L. Rev.* 863.

SALANT, Priscilla and Don DILLMAN (1994) *How to Conduct Your Own Survey.* San Francisco: John Wiley and Sons.

SILKENAT, James R., Jeffrey M. ARESTY, and Jacqueline KLOSEK eds., *The ABA Guide to International Business Negotiations: A Comparison of Cross-Cultural Issues and Successful Approaches* (3rd ed.). Chicago: ABA.

STEWART, David W., Prem N. SHAMDASANI, and Dennis W. ROOK (2007) *Focus Groups: Theory and Practice* (2d ed.). Thousand Oaks, CA: Sage Publications.

STIPANOWICH, Thomas (2012) "The Arbitration Fairness Index: Using a Public Rating System to Skirt the Legal Logjam and Promote Fairer and More Effective Arbitration of Employment and Consumer Disputes," 60 *Kan. L. Rev.* 985.

SUNSTEIN, Cass R. (2012) "Empirically Informed Regulation," 78 *U. Chi. L. Rev.* 1349.

SUSSKIND, Lawrence, and Jennifer THOMAS-LARMER (1999) "Conducting a Conflict Assessment," in Lawrence Susskind, Sarah McKearnan, and Jennifer Thomas-Larmer eds., *The Consensus Building Handbook* 99. Thousand Oaks, CA: Sage Publications.

STITT, Allan J. (1998) *Alternative Dispute Resolution for Organizations: How to Design a System for Effective Conflict Resolution.* Toronto: John Wiley and Sons.

TYLER, Tom (2009) "Governing Pluralistic Societies," 72 *Law & Contemp. Probs.* 187 (Spring).

URY, William, Jeanne BRETT, and Stephen B. GOLDBERG (1988) *Getting Disputes Resolved: Designing Systems to Cut the Costs of Conflict.* San Francisco: Jossey-Bass; Cambridge: Harvard Program on Negotiation, http://www.pon.harvard.edu/shop/getting-disputes-resolveddesigning-systems-to-cut-the-costs-of-conflict/.

URY, William (1999) *Getting to Peace: Transforming Conflict at Home, at Work, and in the World.* New York: Viking Penguin.

WEISS, Robert S. (1994) *Learning from Strangers: The Art and Method of Qualitative Interview Studies.* New York: Free Press.

WELSH, Nancy A., and Barbara GRAY (2002) "Searching for a Sense of Control: The Challenge Presented by Community Conflicts over Concentrated Animal Feeding Operations," 10 *Penn St. Envtl. L. Rev.* 295.

CHAPTER 5

Creating Dispute Management Processes and Systems

Choosing, adapting, and inventing new processes and systems may be the most creative phase of designing. Just as "creative" is one aspect of this phase of designing, "fit" is another. The new process or system succeeds when it *fits* the context and stakeholders' interests. To emphasize both aspects, some call this phase of designing "fitting the forum to the fuss," a termed coined by Maurice Rosenberg (Sander and Goldberg, 1994:67) and explained by Frank Sander and Stephen Goldberg as it relates to a single dispute:

> "In addressing the problem of 'fitting the forum to the fuss,' we have suggested two lines of inquiry [regarding the disputants' interests]: What are the disputants' goals in making a forum choice? And, if the disputants are amenable to settlement, what are the obstacles to settlement, and in what forum might they be overcome? . . .
>
> "When the decision regarding an appropriate dispute resolution procedure is made from a public perspective, the second question is similar to the kind of analysis an attorney should give to any client; the first question, however, is more complex. Initially, court personnel or public agencies making a recommendation regarding appropriate procedures for resolving a dispute must consider the goals of all parties to the dispute. Furthermore, they must consider the public interest in that dispute. While a private settlement may serve the interests of all parties to the dispute, the public interest may lie in public adjudication (e.g., because

of a need for judicial interpretation of a newly enacted statute). . . ." (Sander and Goldberg, 1994:66, 50).

In this view, the disputants' interests and the public's interests sometimes overlap; other times, they may not. By broadening this analysis to include consideration of stakeholders' views (not just the parties') and designing new processes and systems, designers can increase consideration of both public and private interests through a broad definition of stakeholders and a collaborative approach to the process and system creation. Though this stakeholder approach will help, designers still sometimes have to face whether they will personally intervene on behalf of public interests (*see* pp. 79-83, 110-113).

The themes of this chapter thus include:

- being *creative* in designing systems and processes,
- analyzing the *fit* between system/process and context and stakeholder interests and goals,
- taking account of *private-public* interests, and
- *collaborating* with stakeholders in design.

Reading this chapter, you will gain a sense of the innovative ways in which designers have tailored processes and systems to the situation, the philosophical debates about what might be non-party stakeholders' and public interests implicit in those choices, pitfalls to avoid when combining processes, and benefits of collaborating with stakeholders during this phase of designing.

Of course, the phrase "fitting the forum to the fuss" oversimplifies. For one thing, one process does not simply substitute for another. In particular, a process dependent on agreement such as negotiation often occurs in the context of continuing power contests or potential adjudication. Processes that involve adjudication (such as arbitration or litigation) or power contests (like strikes and voting) can provide default approaches to handling disputes if the processes designed to reconcile interests do not result in agreement.

As a further complication, rarely do designers begin with a clean slate. Instead, when they introduce new processes, they do so in the context of existing approaches. By the time the designer arrives on the scene, people already have options available that become part of the context that designers must take into account. For example, disgruntled National Institutes of Health employees might first file Equal Employment Opportunity Commission complaints to adjudicate rights if they have no ombuds process (pp. 125-126). Youths in a Cure Violence neighborhood might bully or kill in response to a disagreement (pp. 27-28). Sanford, Florida residents can demonstrate and block traffic (pp. 20-22). In many situations, then, the designer helps to create processes within the context of existing informal or formal modes of handling conflict.

"Fuss" also overly narrows the scope of work. Designers design preventive practices that work ahead of the "fuss," such as those cultivating the right kind of climate for people to deal constructively with disputes and solve problems when

```
┌─────────────────────────────────────┐
│  DESIGNING STEPS                     │
│                                      │
│  1. Design initiative                │
│  2. Basic planning steps             │
│  • Assessing stakeholders, their     │
│    goals and interests, and contexts │
│  • Creating processes and systems    │
│  3. Key planning issues (that may    │
│    arise throughout the planning)    │
│  • Planning how to select, engage,   │
│    and prepare intervenors and       │
│    parties                           │
│  • Determining the extent of con-    │
│    fidentiality and openness in the  │
│    process                           │
│  • Dealing with desires for change,  │
│    justice, accountability, under-   │
│    standing, safety, reconciliation  │
│  • Enhancing relationships           │
│  • Incorporating technology          │
│  4. Implementing and institutional-  │
│    izing the system or process       │
│  • Implementing                      │
│  • Using contracts                   │
│  • Using law                         │
│  • Evaluating, revising              │
└─────────────────────────────────────┘
```

they arise. At other times, designers' goals involve tackling the deeper causes that give rise to disputes and problems.

This chapter deals with the basic concepts and practice regarding this broader view of creating processes and systems. Chapters 6 through 10 treat in more detail several challenging features of process and system creation. Chapter 6 covers how to select, engage, and educate those who will be participants (including those who will be intervenors) in the new processes and systems. Chapter 7 discusses the tough choices about how open or confidential the process should be. Chapter 8 exposes you to designing in the midst of situations in which resolution of individual damage claims may be a small part of what stakeholders seek in a process—situations like the aftermath of the Canadian Indian Residential Schools (pp. 33-36). People in such situations may also seek accountability, restitution, a chance to tell their stories, an opportunity to persuade the general public of a need for basic societal change, a feeling that they will be safe from similar harms in the future, reconciliation, and more. Designing a system to meet these multiple, varied interests requires skill, tenacity, and a deep understanding of a growing conceptual and practical literature. Chapter 9 focuses on creating processes and systems that strengthen relationships, and Chapter 10 on deploying various technologies within the processes and systems.

Several questions provide the organization for this chapter:

- What basic design theory should be taken into account in creating new processes and systems (Section A)?
- How can designers use the assessment or diagnosis (Chapter 4) plus design theory to improve the fit between the process or system and the situation (Section B)?
- What are the advantages and challenges of working collaboratively with stakeholders in this phase of designing (Section C)?

A. DESIGN CONCEPTS

Scholars have synthesized experience in ways that assist in creating processes and systems. Most theoretical writings apply, however, to only a portion of the design work covered by this book. In the first excerpt, Ury, Brett, and Goldberg, as noted in Chapter 2, examine what best serves parties' interests regarding a dispute resolution system when the parties will have an ongoing relationship (Goldberg et al., 2012:483). They point out why beginning with a process that focuses on resolving the disputants' interests often fits best with their goals.

W. Ury, J. Brett, and S. Goldberg, *Getting Disputes Resolved*

Jossey-Bass (1988); Program on Negotiation at Harvard Law School
3-19 (1993)

THREE APPROACHES TO RESOLVING DISPUTES: INTERESTS, RIGHTS, AND POWER

A dispute begins when one person (or organization) makes a claim or demand on another who rejects it. The claim may arise from a perceived injury or from a need or aspiration. . . . To resolve a dispute means to turn opposed positions—the claim and its rejection—into a single outcome.

In a dispute, people have certain interests at stake. Moreover, certain relevant standards or rights exist as guideposts toward a fair outcome. In addition, a certain balance of power exists between the parties. Interests, rights, and power then are three basic elements of any dispute. In resolving a dispute, the parties may choose to focus their attention on one or more of these basic factors. They may seek to (1) reconcile their underlying interests, (2) determine who is right, and/or (3) determine who is more powerful.

Reconciling Interests

Interests are needs, desires, concerns, fears—the things one cares about or wants. They underlie people's positions—the tangible items they say they want. [Spouses] quarrel about whether to spend money for a new car. [One spouse's] underlying interest may not be the money or the car but the desire to impress his friends; the [other's] interest may be transportation. The director of sales for an electronics company gets into a dispute with the director of manufacturing over the number of TV models to produce. The director of sales wants to produce more models. Her interest is in selling TV sets; more models mean more choice for consumers and hence increased sales. The director of manufacturing wants to produce fewer models. His interest is in decreasing manufacturing costs; more models mean higher costs.

Reconciling such interests is not easy. It involves probing for deep-seated concerns, devising creative solutions, and making trade-offs and concessions where interests are opposed. The most common procedure for doing this is negotiation, the act of back-and-forth communication intended to reach agreement. . . . Another interests- based procedure is mediation, in which a third party assists the disputants in reaching agreement.

By no means do all negotiations (or mediations) focus on reconciling interests. Some negotiations focus on determining who is right, such as when two lawyers argue about whose case has the greater merit. Other negotiations focus on determining who is more powerful, such as when quarreling neighbors or nations exchange threats and counter threats. Often negotiations involve a mix of all three—some attempts to satisfy interests, some discussion of rights, and some references to relative power. Negotiations that focus primarily on interests we call "interests-based," in contrast to "rights-based" and "power-based" negotiations. Another term for interests-based negotiation is problem-solving negotiation, so called because it involves treating a dispute as a mutual problem to be solved by the parties. . . .

Determining Who Is Right

Another way to resolve disputes is to rely on some independent standard with perceived legitimacy or fairness to determine who is right. As a shorthand for such independent standards, we use the term rights. Some rights are formalized in law or contract. Other rights are socially accepted standards of behavior, such as reciprocity, precedent, equality, and seniority. . . .

Rights are rarely clear. There are often different—and sometimes contradictory—standards that apply. Reaching agreement on rights, where the outcome will determine who gets what, can often be difficult, frequently leading the parties to turn to a third party to determine who is right. The prototypical rights procedure is adjudication (court or arbitration), in which disputants present evidence and arguments to a neutral third party who has the power to hand down a binding decision. . . .

Determining Who Is More Powerful

A third way to resolve a dispute is on the basis of power. We define power, somewhat narrowly, as the ability to coerce someone to do something he would not otherwise do. Exercising power typically means imposing costs on the other side or threatening to do so. . . .

Determining who is the more powerful party without a decisive and potentially destructive power contest is difficult because power is ultimately a matter of perceptions. Despite objective indicators of power, such as financial resources, parties' perceptions of their own and each other's power often do not coincide. Moreover, each side's perception of the other's power may fail to take into account the possibility that the other will invest greater resources in the contest than expected out of fear that a change in the perceived distribution of power will affect the outcomes of future disputes.

Interrelationship Among Interests, Rights, and Power

The relationship among interests, rights, and power can be pictured as a circle within a circle within a circle (as in Figure 1 on page 108). The innermost circle represents interests; the middle, rights; and the outer, power. The reconciliation of interests takes place within the context of the parties' rights and power.

The likely outcome of a dispute if taken to court or to a strike, for instance, helps define the bargaining range within which a resolution can be found. Similarly, the determination of rights takes place within the context of power. One party, for instance, may win a judgment in court, but unless the judgment can be enforced, the dispute will continue. Thus, in the process of resolving a dispute, the focus may shift from interests to rights to power and back again.

Lumping It and Avoidance

Not all disputes end with a resolution. Often one or more parties simply decide to withdraw from the dispute. Withdrawal takes two forms. One party may decide to "lump it," dropping her claim or giving in to the other's claim because she believes pursuing the dispute is not in her interest, or because she concludes she does not have the power to resolve it to her satisfaction. . . . A second form of withdrawal is avoidance. One party (or both) may decide to withdraw from the relationship, or at least to curtail it significantly. Examples of avoidance include quitting the organization, divorce, leaving the neighborhood, and staying out of the other person's way. . . .

WHICH APPROACH IS "BEST"?

Interests Versus Rights or Power. A focus on interests can resolve the problem underlying the dispute more effectively than can a focus on rights or power. An

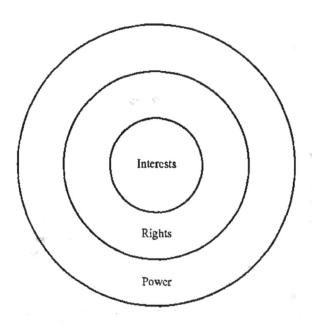

Figure 1.   Interrelationships Among Interests, Rights, and Power

example is a grievance filed against a mine foreman for doing work that contractually only a miner is authorized to do. Often the real problem is something else—a miner who feels unfairly assigned to an unpleasant task may file a grievance to strike back at his foreman. Clearly, focusing on what the contract says about foremen working will not deal with this underlying problem. Nor will striking to protest foremen working. But if the foreman and miner can negotiate about the miner's future work tasks, the dispute may be resolved to the satisfaction of both.

Just as an interests-based approach can help uncover hidden problems, it can help the parties identify which issues are of greater concern to one than to the other. By trading off issues of lesser concern for those of greater concern, both parties can gain from the resolution of the dispute. Consider, for example, a union and employer negotiating over two issues: additional vacation time and flexibility of work assignments. Although the union does not like the idea of assignment flexibility, its clear priority is additional vacation. Although the employer does not like the idea of additional vacation, it cares more about gaining flexibility in assigning work. An agreement that gives the union the vacation days it seeks and the employer flexibility in making work assignments would likely be satisfactory to both. Such joint gain is more likely to be realized if the parties focus on each side's interests. Focusing on who is right, as in litigation, or on who is more powerful, as in a strike, usually leaves at least one party perceiving itself as the loser.

Reconciling interests thus tends to generate a higher level of mutual satisfaction with outcomes than determining rights or power. If the parties are more satisfied, their relationship benefits, and the dispute is less likely to recur. Determining who is right or who is more powerful, with the emphasis on winning and losing, typically makes the relationship more adversarial and strained. Moreover, the loser frequently does not give up, but appeals to a higher court or plots revenge. To be sure, reconciling interests can sometimes take a long time, especially when there are many parties to the dispute. Generally, however, these costs pale in comparison with the transaction costs of rights and power contests such as trials, hostile corporate takeovers, or wars.

In sum, focusing on interests, compared to focusing on rights or power, tends to produce higher satisfaction with outcomes, better working relationships and less recurrence, and may also incur lower transaction costs. As a rough generalization, then, an interests approach is less costly than a rights or power approach.

■ ■ ■

In other writing, these authors note the importance of preventive approaches, including prior consultation and making changes based on learning about problems from earlier disputes. They also assert that their generally preferred focus on interests can be not only a starting place for a system, but also can be placed later in the process, after the disputants have a better understanding of their alternatives to agreement. They say, "Build in 'loop-backs' to negotiation" (Goldberg et al., 1991:52).

In contrast to Ury, Brett, and Goldberg's focus in this excerpt on the *disputants' interests*, others write about the *public interests* in process or system creation. One point of contention in the first set of quotes below is whether the choice of process further disadvantages those already disadvantaged in society. Both of these commentators assume that the default process, if the disputants do not settle, will be litigation, and, in fact, will be within that small fraction of cases in litigation that reach trial, whereas Ury, Brett, and Goldberg note that the alternative to settlement might also be a strike, arbitration, or something else.

Law professor Richard Delgado: "In some settings, persons feel free to act in prejudiced fashion; in others, they do not. The principal feature that suppresses prejudice is the certainty that prejudice, if displayed, will be remarked and punished—that it will not be tolerated but will result in active condemnation. . . . The formalities of court trial are calculated to check prejudice. The trappings of formality—the flags, black robes, the rituals—remind the participants that trials are occasions on which the higher values of the American Creed are to preponderate, rather than the less noble values we embrace during times of intimacy. Equality of status is sought to be preserved—each party is represented by a lawyer and has a prescribed time and manner of speaking. Counsel direct their arguments not toward each other but toward a neutral judge or jury.

Adjudication avoids the unstructured, unchecked, low-visibility types of interaction that, according to social scientists, foster prejudice. . . . When ADR cannot avoid dealing with sharply contested claims, its structureless setting and absence of formal rules increase the likelihood of an outcome colored by prejudice, with the result that the haves once again come out ahead" (Delgado, 1988:153-154).

Former legal services lawyer, now law professor, William Simon: "Formal systems tend to be more difficult for people without special training or experience to participate in. [The formal] procedures can also subvert conflict and induce acquiescence. They can do so by convincing the disadvantaged that their losses are the result of a fair contest . . . , by making disadvantaged litigants feel incompetent and by making litigants feel dependent on professional helpers" (Simon, 1985:386, 388).

Simon and Delgado disagree on the implications of litigation and settlement processes for disadvantaged parties, but both assume that one chooses between litigation and a process designed to encourage settlement. In the excerpts that follow the authors also assume that litigation is the backdrop, but Judge Weinstein contemplates litigation and settlement working together. These quotations focus on the "public good" provided by litigation.

> *U.S. District Judge Jack B. Weinstein:* "[I]n some cases full litigation of claims should be encouraged to avoid settlements that hide critical facts or substantive developments from the public, precluding (1) adequate compensation to those who were not aware of their rights or injuries and (2) necessary institutional and legal reform. In other instances, reasonably prompt settlement is desirable and can be achieved without a significant number of trials or summary dispositions. In still other cases, some trials and summary judgments are useful in creating an appropriate framework for settlement of most claims. . . . Settlements may be even more desirable in the mass commercial age in which we now live. Unsettled disputes about harms to large numbers of people across geographic and demographic lines, caused by large entities, present risks of social breakdowns without fair, timely, and efficient resolution. Time-consuming adjudication results in excessive transaction costs and unnecessary stress on individuals, families, local and national economies, and government service networks. If we persist in trying each dispute as if it were a unique horse-and-buggy collision at a muddy intersection in nineteenth-century Cairo, Illinois, businesses may be unfairly saddled with continuing litigations while individuals claiming harm may be left almost indefinitely adrift" (Weinstein, 2009:1266-1267).

> *Law professor Owen M. Fiss:* "Justice is a public good, objectively conceived, and is not reducible to the maximization of the satisfaction of the preferences of the contestants, which, in any event, are a function of the deplorable character of the options available to them. The contestants are simply making the best of an imperfect world and the unfortunate situation in which they find themselves. There is no reason to believe that their bargained-for agreement is an instantiation of justice or will, as a general matter, lead to justice" (Fiss, 2009:1277).

Yet another line of commentary views adjudication less as an alternative to settlement and more as an inadequate process for people in some situations. The commentators argue that a process should be tailored to the needs of people most affected, even if that means having two processes, such as prosecution and post-conviction victim-offender mediation. When related to *criminal* cases, some of this theoretical work is called restorative justice.

> *Sociologist Mark Umbreit and colleagues:* "Instead of viewing the state as the primary victim in criminal acts and placing victims, offenders, and the community in passive roles, restorative justice recognizes crime as being directed against

individual people. It is grounded in the belief that those most affected by crime should have the opportunity to become actively involved in resolving the conflict. Repairing harm and restoring losses, allowing offenders to take direct responsibility for their actions, and assisting victims to move beyond vulnerability towards some degree of closure stand in sharp contrast to the values and practices of the conventional criminal justice system with its focus on past criminal behavior through ever-increasing levels of punishment" (Umbreit et al., 2005:255; *see also* Zehr, 2002).

Commentary on the inadequacy of litigation as the sole process for *civil* cases takes a broader view of justice. This commentary, which will be discussed in Chapter 8, lists stakeholders' interests that cannot be achieved through litigation, or even through settlement based on likely litigation outcomes.

Law professor Jennifer Llewellyn (referencing the aftermath of Canada's Indian Residential Schools, pp. 33-35): "Settling abuse claims is only one (and, in some cases, a minor part) of what the parties seek. The abuse suffered by residential school students was the result of a relationship of inequality, oppression, and disrespect between the Canadian government, its citizens, the churches, and Aboriginal peoples. The restoration of this relationship to one of mutual concern, respect, and dignity is what victims seek first and foremost, and any process must have this as its goal or it will not resolve the conflict between the parties and may, in fact, make it worse" (Llewellyn, 2002:28, as quoted in Regan, 2010:123).

A further line of commentary assumes that disputes relate to larger societal issues. As Bernard Mayer characterizes these commentators who would prefer to let the disputes fester and prompt political action rather than be channeled into dispute management processes or systems, "Those who represent people or causes that are apparently in a less powerful societal position view conflict resolution as a means of preventing serious organizing, dissipating dissent through a show of dialogue, and focusing people on the potential for minor concessions rather than on the essence of exploitation" (Mayer, 2004:44; *see* Nader, 1993; Amy Cohen, 2009).

In partial response to this critique, law professor Susan Sturm and Howard Gadlin of the National Institutes of Health point out the role of ombuds and others who can promote structural changes by identifying patterns in intraorganizational disputes as a way to locate their root causes and then convey the results (with identifying information about individual disputants omitted) to decision-makers who can institute change (Sturm and Gadlin, 2007:25-27). In the same vein, state attorneys general mediate individual consumer complaints but their mediators aggregate their cases and notify staff attorneys where to focus their litigation and law reform efforts in response to patterns of problematic conduct by businesses. Dispute resolution scholars Robert A. Baruch Bush and Joseph P. Folger make a similar point regarding mediation—that "party-driven" mediation can help parties achieve issues of social justice if that matters to them (2012:49).

Using another line of reasoning that deals with part of the societal issues critique, Mara Schoeny, a former post-violence facilitator, and Wallace Warfield, a former civil rights mediator, explained that mediators focused on ferreting out the "root causes" and improving decision-making in the negotiations could, as a result, contribute to racial justice (Schoeny and Warfield, 2000:266; Warfield, 1996:153-154). The proponents of truth and reconciliation commissions make a similar point—that these commissions, discussed in Chapter 8, can educate the general public about abuses that occurred in the past and on the need to make structural and systemic changes to prevent their re-occurrence.

As you think about these and other perspectives, it will help you recognize some of the less obvious private and public interests and the ways that various types of processes and systems can serve them. The scholars' arguments seem not to meet in large part because their assumed contexts differ and because they take narrow or broad views of the possibilities and realities of alternative processes. Each commentator speaks to only a portion of the contexts covered by this book. Nonetheless, together they remind you that you ought to analyze each situation and whether:

- it involves only private or also public interests;
- the disputes are on the way to litigation (and if so how likely a trial actually is) as default or if the default is something different, such as a strike or violence;
- the disputes might form a basis for structural or societal change if left without effective dispute management processes or systems;
- criminal activity is involved;
- the parties will be engaged in ongoing relationships; and
- the stakeholders seek something beyond a remedy that a court might order.

This analysis can make you more thoughtful as you include stakeholders who can represent these viewpoints and more generally work with stakeholders to create processes and systems for managing disputes.

B. PROCESS AND SYSTEM INNOVATION, ADAPTATION, CHOICE, AND SEQUENCING

Your thoughtfulness and creativity can lead to breakthroughs in the creation, adaptation, choice, and sequencing of processes and systems. This section samples this innovative work—dividing the examples by the goals that the designer is trying to achieve.

1. Seeking ways to overcome barriers to reaching agreement

As Sander and Goldberg note, if stakeholders want a consensus-building process, a major design task is to identify the barriers to reaching agreement and to think of processes or systems that help surmount them (*see* pp. 103-104; Appendix D for a list of common barriers). The designer in each example below created a process to improve results by adding structure to negotiations that helped to overcome the predictable barriers to agreement. In this first story, think about what was done to overcome barriers and focus in particular on the importance of the agreement that the collaborative lawyer will resign if the case goes to litigation.

Collaborative law: Divorcing parents sometimes separate relatively amicably, only to be drawn into escalating anger and bitterness as their lawyers negotiate and litigate. This common situation brings to life the research discussed in Appendix D, especially the negotiation barriers created by:

- legalization of the dispute;
- festering feelings that interfere with rational planning;
- attorney-client tension;
- attorneys' strategic protection of litigation information; and
- fixed pie bias (*see* Appendix D).

Minneapolis lawyer Stuart Webb devised, through trial and error, a negotiation structure that helps surmount these barriers. He persuaded some of his family law colleagues to identify cases in which both lawyers and both parties would agree to try his new structure—collaborative law. Lawyers and clients agreeing to use collaborative law in a case replace their cagey, lawyer-to-lawyer positional bargaining with four-way negotiations that include the parties; focus on the parties' interests, not just the legal definition of the issues; freely exchange relevant data; steer clients away from blaming; and invent options that fit both parties' interests (*see* Appendix D).

To give the lawyers an incentive structure consistent with this negotiation approach, Webb persuaded the collaborative lawyers to sign an understanding with their clients that the collaborative lawyers would resign as counsel if they failed to reach agreement; the parties had to hire new counsel if they decided to litigate their differences. To join the collaborative law group, the lawyers also had to take classes to become skilled at interest-based negotiation and agree to use that approach.

Years later, San Francisco lawyer Pauline Tesler added another aspect of the design—rather than dueling experts, the negotiating teams together would hire the needed financial, child psychology, or other experts who would participate in the problem-solving process. Parties coping with strong emotions could have mental health professionals who would serve as coaches, helping them to deal with emotional swings during negotiations.

Collaborative lawyers screen clients carefully, noting that this approach works for only a portion of cases. For that portion, lawyers report that they achieve more positive results for the clients who agree to a collaborative approach than they can achieve under traditional negotiation and litigation—the collaborative law parties more often reach agreement (87 percent in one study), leave the children in uncertainty for a shorter time, maintain privacy, work through emotions, achieve workable parenting plans, and build a better relationship as they parent after divorce (*see* Schwab, 2004:375 n.111 (empirical results) and *see generally* Tesler, 2007; Webb and Ousky, 2006; Mosten, 2009; Schepard: 2010).

Groups of family lawyers in at least 38 U.S. states and abroad have adopted collaborative law as part of their practices.[1] In most cities, the vast majority of family law disputes are resolved in traditional ways, making it difficult to assess empirically the overall results of using collaborative law in terms of post-judgment relations between parties. But in Medicine Hat, a Canadian city of 61,000, all family lawyers joined the local practice collaborative, making it possible to observe dramatic changes in post-judgment behavior by divorcing couples. Within a few years after the family lawyers began their collaborative practices, the court in Medicine Hat reduced the staff dealing with post-judgment motions because divorced couples filed so many fewer motions (Tesler, 2010).[2]

In sum, the collaborative lawyers augmented their system with creative ways to avoid additional barriers—such as emotionalism and fixed pie bias—not just the barriers created by the lawyers' litigation focus. In the story below, the innovation in negotiations aimed to overcome barriers in:

- framing how the parties viewed the dispute (*see, e.g.,* Korobkin, 2006:305-306, 308-316, 320);
- organizing negotiations effectively;
- understanding techniques to resolve disputes;
- finding negotiation approaches that were productive of settlement;
- dealing with those seeking to delay; and
- helping negotiators be realistic about their alternatives to settling.

---

 eBay's structured negotiations: eBay offers structured negotiation to the millions of users each year who have an issue regarding an eBay purchase. If you visit the "Resolution Center" site (now http://resolutioncenter.ebay.com/), you can view specific help content for each of the parties and a thorough

---

1. The National Conference of Commissioners on Uniform State Laws adopted a uniform law to clarify some of the legal issues related to collaborative law. *See* http://uniformlaws.org. The ABA issued an advisory ethics opinion approving the use of an agreement to secure new counsel if the parties do not settle (ABA Ethics Opinion 07-447 (2007).

2. Interview with Pauline Tesler, Sept. 29, 2010.

description of the process. The instructions suggest, for example, some words to use (to improve how the issues are framed); they also set up, through questions, a workable agenda (avoiding disorganization); instruct on negotiation approaches (helping ineffective negotiators); review possible options others have used to resolve similar disputes (helping to find approaches productive of settlement); set time limits; and provide information on alternatives to resolving the issue (helping parties determine their alternatives to settling). The site also provides a small incentive (return of a fee) to sellers who resolve by returning the purchase price.

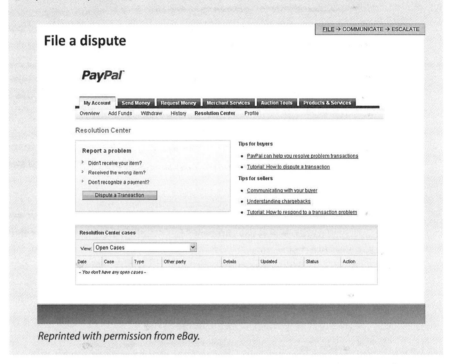

Reprinted with permission from eBay.

In a Chicago neighborhood where Cure Violence works with highest-risk youths and has developed a system in which it selects and trains former gang members to intervene as "violence interrupters" to avert violence, one of the barriers to reducing violence might be emotions—fear, anger, and more. In the context of this barrier, the interrupters use approaches designed to cool the high emotions that interfere with rational thinking. Like Rule's approaches, the interrupters' techniques also help individuals reframe their conflicts. Another barrier might be the failure to talk; the interrupters make communications feasible even though disputants believe that they are "past talking." These practices help to surmount barriers to reaching agreement, or at least to de-escalating the dispute.

A Cure Violence interruption, a fictional account by Tio Hardiman though not atypical of interrupter mediations: Tio Hardiman received a call from a policeman about the officer's teenage son, George. George, said the father, had just entered their house, grabbed a gun, and left. The father did not want to call the police on his own son but called Hardiman because he feared that George was on his way to see Sue. Sue was the mother of George's three-month-old son and recently broke up with George, who took it badly.

Hardiman called two of Cure Violence's trained mediators, or violence interrupters. The father's instincts had been on the mark—when the interrupters arrived at Sue's house, George was outside shouting that he wanted to see his baby or he would shoot. The interrupters, who were from the neighborhood, managed to persuade George to talk with them.

George began by muttering that life was not worth it. With prodding from one of the mediators, George eventually explained that Sue's new boyfriend, Sam, had pulled a gun on George when George went to the house earlier that day to see his three-month-old son. Sam told George he would shoot unless George stayed away. "It's not right," George said. "That's my baby. I can't take it."

Over time, the interrupters managed to get George to agree that it was over with his girlfriend, but that there would be ways to arrange to see his baby. As George calmed down, one of the interrupters knocked on the door of Sue's apartment to bring her into the discussion.

Sam opened the door, but with a gun in his pants. Sam's first reaction was, "Tell him to go. Sue is my girl now." Eventually, one interrupter persuaded Sam to come outside to talk.

The other interrupter began talking with Sue. Would she come out and tell George that she did not want to see him anymore but that George could see his son? Sue flatly refused to leave the house.

The interrupter returned to George. After working one on one with George and Sam separately, the two interrupters persuaded Sam to apologize for threatening George, and George to apologize for bringing a gun.

With things cooled down, one interrupter stayed to talk with Sam and the other with George about the "virus" infecting the neighborhood that led them each to resort to a gun. George readily agreed. He had let down his family and was ashamed; he knew that he should not have responded by getting a gun. Sam, though, was a gang member and saw violence as more central to his life. His father had served a prison term and both brothers were in prison. Cure Violence assigned a caseworker to keep working with Sam. Six months later, while Sam refused Cure Violence's offer to find him work, he has stayed in touch and has not re-offended.

These Cure Violence mediators dealt not only with the immediate dispute about relationships but also with the "virus" that led the parties to resort to guns and with social conditions breeding the virus, like unemployment. To deal with the antipathy that each individual had for the other, the Cure Violence media-tors engaged in shuttle diplomacy. To de-escalate emotions, they engineered apologies. Barriers changed; they worked as a team with George and then indi-vidually, doing shuttle mediation with Sue and Sam, and adapted to changing circumstances as the conflict unfolded before them. Knowing that the climate of the neighborhood represented barriers to lasting resolution, they continued to work with George, hoping to reinforce and strengthen anti-violence norms.

2. Seeking ways to reduce expenses and time

Over the centuries people have modified arbitration in ways they think better fit the goals of the disputing parties and broader stakeholders (*see on arbitration generally* Appendix B and Chapter 12). But the last few decades have spawned a particularly intense period of innovation in hearing processes throughout the world, especially because of cross-border disputes over matters as small as the purchase of a coffee pot or an online comment made about it by a purchaser.

eBay's Community Court pilot: eBay leaders knew from the start that a trust-worthy market was key to its success. At the same time, they recognized that adopting the arbitration processes developed for commercial transactions would not serve its users well. Cross-border commercial contracts often contain agreements to resolve disputes first through conciliation (a word that some-times refers to a fact-finding process but is used in this context interchangeably with mediation) and, failing settlement in conciliation, through arbitration. These clauses reflect the commercial parties' preferences to settle if feasible but, if unsuccessful, to arbitrate rather than litigate in foreign courts. The parties can agree on the place and the applicable law, and courts in nearly all nations will summarily enforce arbitration awards. But the costs of international com-mercial arbitration exceed the amount at issue in eBay disputes (median about $75), as would seeking judicial enforcement of an arbitration award.

eBay wanted a process that users would find fair and practical—one that would be used often. Over time, eBay's asynchronous, online negotiation-arbitration process became second nature for users, and it grew to be so efficient that eBay could offer it free to users, eliminating another barrier to par-ticipation in its processes.

eBay also developed its own enforcement processes. This was possible both because eBay managed the flow of money between the parties via its PayPal subsidiary and because eBay could restrict or remove users from the platform at any time. Colin Rule, eBay's first Director of Online Dispute Resolution, continu-ally monitored user reactions and modified the process over time.

Giving thought about how to further increase the efficiency and accuracy of adjudicative processes, Colin Rule heard a talk on consumer confidence and the "wisdom of the crowd." It was a concept, he thought, that was consistent with public confidence in the jury system in face-to-face contexts. He began developing an online, asynchronous jury trial, which he called eBay's Community Court.

In that process, disputants used an asynchronous method of submitting evidence and arguments online, responding to each other's submissions on their own schedules. Volunteer jurors, divided evenly between buyers and sellers, viewed the record and voted individually, also on their own schedule.

After market testing, the Community Court team selected India as the first place to implement the "jury trial" process in part because India is a common law nation, and adversarial trials fit Indian traditions.

Provided by eBay. Reprinted with permission.

Thousands of Indian users participated in Community Court processes for such disputes, and eBay followed the verdict of the 21 jurors—removing the negative user comment if the jury voted for that to occur. Based on research and monitoring, eBay over time strengthened its processes to protect against fraud and to improve the quality of jurors by weeding out jurors who did not provide timely votes or routinely departed from the majority view. Users and eBay found the Community Court to be inexpensive, easy to use, and quick.

A world-wide, online small claims tribunal? Hundreds of millions of cross-border consumer disputes occur each year—not just on eBay. Because consumers could not afford to litigate abroad, Brazil and Canada suggested to the Organization of American States that these small claims be resolved in the consumer's national courts, regardless of the forum designated in the sales agreement. In 2009, the United States proposed an online forum instead (Rule et al., 2010:228-332). An online forum met the interests of a number of nations, with the result that the United Nations Commission on International

Trade Law (UNCITRAL) later that year began a drafting process for a world-wide online court for disputes under a to-be-determined value.

eBay's Colin Rule was one of the consultants to the U.S. State Department, and the U.S. proposal resembles eBay's process with initiation and negotiation handled entirely by software followed by an arbitration that might first, at the arbitrator's discretion, include conciliation. Every participating nation would agree to enforce awards in that nation's jurisdiction. The parties would not be compelled to use the process; it would be voluntary for the seller to opt in, and each case would be initiated by the buyer. Drafters would have to resolve the thorny issue of whose substantive and arbitration law applies, or leave that to the parties' agreement (see Brand, 2012). Realistically, though, consumers have little other recourse for small disputes. The existence of such a system could benefit vendors by encouraging buyers to purchase more from merchants who have opted into the voluntary scheme. Ultimately, the United Nations provided a framework for online dispute resolution. http://www.uncitral.org/uncitral/en/uncitral_texts/online_dispute_resolution.html.

In each example, the designer helped stakeholders create new processes that improved existing processes by reducing transaction costs and time but were aimed also at preserving the essence of what the stakeholders valued in the existing processes.

3. Seeking to create processes that will operate in advance of disputes

Designers who are adept at identifying barriers to effective negotiations may work on reducing the barriers in advance of a dispute. For example, Cure Violence Chicago bussed rival gang members to meetings and social events to help them establish ways to work with each other. It anticipated inter-gang disputes, and this helped reduce barriers to communication and to preventing hostilities from escalating.

In a similar vein, designers endeavor to develop systems that give stakeholders the skills to identify and manage conflict in its early stages, before it escalates and imposes high costs on individuals within the organization and on the organization itself. The U.S. Transportation Security Administration fit this description when its designers trained employees to teach other employees constructive ways to discuss differences. The organization has tens of thousands of employees scattered at airports throughout the nation, and so it trained conflict coaches at major locations to help their colleagues consider their objectives in a conflict and effective options for resolving it. TSA also trained leaders to support expression of differences. Deborah Katz, who led TSA's "collaborative strategies," said to leaders, "You have a choice. You can be the first to know or the last to know what is going on in your organization. It depends on whether you have created an environment in which issues and concerns can be raised with confidence that they will be received respectfully and responsibly" (Cohen, 2009a:88). The overall goal was a broad one: to improve "cultural norms and everyday practices that go to the heart of how people treat each other, manage their differences, solve problems, and make decisions" (Cohen, 2009a:87).

In these situations, designers anticipate barriers to agreement and try to overcome them in advance of the barrier occurring, as with the educational program described below.

The National Institutes of Health collaboration "field guide": Howard Gadlin and his NIH colleagues decided that a set of "best practices" for collaborating scientists might help "prevent, reduce, or mitigate conflict" (Bennett et al., 2010:iii). They studied effective and ineffective collaborations and wrote a "field guide" for "collaboration and team science." In the guide, they suggest productive ways to lead group research, select researchers, build and retain trust, talk about science, discuss interpersonal differences, share recognition, and hold meetings. Consistent with the "upstream" approach, they include for each matter early indications that the atmosphere is positive as well as early warning signs. Warning signs for interpersonal conflict, for example, include: "Team members, including the team leader are unaware of interpersonal conflict(s) within the team; do not listen to concerns, engage in mediation between colleagues, or seek out other third-party resources to serve as neutral intervenors; are unaware of or avoid acknowledging other team members' motivations and needs or the 'deeper' meaning behind the conflict; fail to listen carefully to team discussion; interpret conflict as unhealthy when it is actually constructive. . . ." (Bennett et al., 2010:43).

The preventive initiative included cautionary tales for supervisors such as the following story about how the lack of an effective dispute management system can lead to a regrettable outcome—the loss of a talented scientist on an important project.

National Institutes of Health—the costs of no effective design: "Dr. Lewis, a team leader who recently assembled a new research group to address a thorny scientific issue, announces that she wants everyone to focus their energies on research and that she does not want to be bothered with petty personal disputes that arise among participants. 'I expect you to work out among yourselves whatever differences may arise,' she explains in her introductory discussion with every person who joins the team. After an initial period of harmonious interaction among members of the group, two postdoctoral students with different supervisors begin to quarrel about access to the electron microscope and other

---

team resources. Unable to resolve their differences, the two soon begin to have disagreements about cleaning the shared equipment after use and the usage and purchase of reagents. The tension between the two begins to affect negatively the overall group dynamic and functioning until one of the postdoctoral students approaches Dr. Lewis to inform her that he is leaving the team" (Gadlin et al., 2010:42).

Here are two other examples of preventive work:

- Designers create "safe space" forums where parties can raise difficult or contentious issues that need to be faced but are often avoided. For example, a designer—anticipating conflict over governmental budget priorities—might set up a series of "educational forums" at a local university months in advance of the budget negotiations and then invite legislators from both parties to participate in closed-door brainstorming after the session. The goal of such sessions would be to identify shared interests and engage in facilitated joint brainstorming at a time when public officials can speak away from the public glare of negotiations that occur right before a looming end-of-fiscal-year deadline.
- A U.S. Justice Department's Community Relations Service mediator facilitated agreement on a venue and format for the 1965 civil rights march from Selma to Montgomery that would make marchers less vulnerable to violent attack (Bass, 1993:239-242).

Chapter 9 covers in more depth those proactive or preventive design features—like the NIH "field guide" instructions—that can make relationships more constructive and thus prevent or resolve conflict.

4. Seeking more than a resolution of a dispute

People may not always seek resolution of disputes, or resolution may be a small part of what they want. They may want the truth told, their suffering noted, the general public educated, political or economic change, reconciliation, accountability, and more. Chapter 8 examines what designers, working with stakeholders, have done to respond to these broader concerns.

The 2007 Canadian Indian Residential Schools Settlement Agreement (pp. 33-36) represents an example of an innovative plan to deal with broader interests than resolution of individual claims for damages. It created new processes, including a truth and reconciliation commission, left in place some existing processes, and permitted all of the processes to proceed simultaneously. The settlement contemplated that prosecutions would proceed to the extent feasible; recoveries for school survivors would be broader than would be accorded through tort remedies; the larger public would learn about the perseverance and suffering of the Aboriginal children, their families, and communities; some consensus would be reached about how to deal more justly with the Aboriginal peoples in the future; and the work would begin to lay the foundations for some level of reconciliation. In the next example, Sanford officials broadened the issues that were the focus of their processes because of their goals to regain trust in government and reduce division among residents.

 Sanford, Florida: Designing processes to deal with disputes that occurred a century ago: Demonstrators originally focused their demands on police practices in the aftermath of the Trayvon Martin shooting, but later they broadened them. Residents of west Sanford, an area that was once the historically African-American town of Goldsboro, still resented efforts by Sanford and Florida a century ago to dissolve Goldsboro's incorporation, over the objection of Goldsboro residents, so that Sanford could take over the area. At the time of the Trayvon Martin shooting, west Sanford residents were still angry that Sanford renamed for white individuals the streets that had been originally named to honor African-American founders of Goldsboro. Many of these residents believed that Sanford officials had discriminated over time in provision of services to the former Goldsboro area. Sanford officials began to ask when resident demands would end and pointed out that they were not even alive, let alone public officials, when these events occurred. Andrew Thomas reminded them that their goal was not solely to resolve the concerns raised by the Trayvon Martin shooting but also to increase trust in the city and decrease racial division. While current public officials were not responsible for those past decisions, Thomas pointed out, they did have the authority to work with residents to deal with current resentments and distrust. After designing and participating in a planning process that included west Sanford residents, Sanford agreed to reverse the century-old decision to rename the Goldsboro streets and re-developed the primary business area.

The courts have also found reasons to innovate in efforts to reach beyond the immediate dispute. Some have diverted selected cases to less traditional adjudication processes, often called "problem-solving" or "community" courts (*see, e.g.,* Berman and Feinblatt, 2005; Nolan, 2001). These courts stem from a kind of "root cause analysis" that recognizes that both individual and community problem identification and solving can prevent future criminal activity and improve community life.

Once the defendant consents to the pre-trial diversion, instead of adjudicating guilt or innocence, the problem-solving court determines a course of treatment for drug addiction or mental health problems or a course of action regarding domestic violence, for example. Defendants return to the traditional process if they do not complete the requirements they consent to. In addition, by tracking patterns of law violation in local communities and involving members of the local community in planning and problem-solving, these courts may initiate community change—for example, the cleaning up of vacant lots where drug users congregate. This design uses more traditional rights-based adjudication as the fall-back process and opens up opportunities both for community collaboration and for individual efforts at change.

The problem-solving courts illustrate a common challenge for those modifying adjudication from the traditional models—with each change in adjudication, designers encounter new issues to resolve. For example, the judges in problem-solving courts discovered that they had to become personally involved in assuring the quality of the community treatment resources but encountered ethical obstacles to doing so that had to be resolved.

Chapter 8 examines a variety of attempts to deal with more than the presenting issue, where the stakeholders seek or the situation warrants greater depth. These include televised discussions, hearings that allow people to talk about what they think is important even if not legally relevant, re-focusing of mediation beyond legal issues, and more.

5. Seeking to create a system that sequences a variety of processes

Designers often create a set of processes: for example, mediation and, if it fails to result in agreement, then arbitration or litigation. Or community court defendants can agree to undertake treatment and counseling or face trial and criminal penalty. Alternatively, designers may combine the processes: for example, the Truth and Reconciliation Commission of Canada made findings and recommendations based on hearings but it also worked to promote reconciliation and to commemorate the past (pp. 33-36). These are what this book calls dispute processing "systems" as opposed to single processes.

While these approaches of creating progressions or combining processes permit the designer to achieve a close fit with interests and context, the results also raise challenging issues. Processes that appear responsive to the stakeholders' interests and the context when considered separately may produce unexpected results when the processes are combined and placed in progression.

Order: Some scholars suggest that, in general, beginning with consensual processes and then moving to adjudication and low-cost power-based processes in the design of an integrated system, often with loop backs from adjudication or power contests to consensual processes (Ury et al., 1988; Sander and Rozdeiczer, 2006; Sander and Goldberg, 1994:59). But there are exceptions. There may be compelling reasons for starting with an interest-based approach in some situations and with some form of adjudication in others. The designer needs to consider many factors in determining how to sequence the processes within the system. These include:

- fit with the interests of the stakeholders involved;
- public considerations of justice, accountability, precedent, deterrence, inequality (*see* Chapter 8); and
- feasibility in a given context.

Timing: Like order, timing has been studied empirically most often for settlement processes conducted against the background of litigation. Psychologist Roselle Wissler used research to identify some "sweet spots" in terms of scheduling court mediation. Settlement rates for mediation held shortly after the litigation starts, just as discovery has begun, are as high as those just before trial. The mediation settlement rates decrease when the mediation takes place while motions to dismiss or for summary judgment are pending. The parties save on transaction expenses when they settle earlier (Wissler, 2002:677-678; *see also* Lande, 2008:132).

Judges in these courts report that, despite this research, attorneys often seek delays in mediation so that they can first complete discovery and have more information to assess the settlement value. Thus, the conventional wisdom among attorneys that negotiation must await completion of discovery conflicts with the research results. Some judges reacted to the Wissler research by pressing for earlier scheduling of mediation, despite initial reluctance by counsel, reasoning that they could save the clients time and expense by doing so (2002:677-678). Wissler's research does not cover pre-suit mediation, but some small claims court mediation programs report higher settlement rates for pre-filing mediation than mediation held after filing and before the trial (Wissler, 2004:1-2).

Order and timing considered together: Outside the mediation-litigation or mediation-arbitration context, there is little empirical work to guide the designer on order and timing. Consider how order and timing affected success in the segments that follow, both in what occurred before the new design and after.

 The National Institutes of Health personnel grievance system: When ombuds Howard Gadlin arrived at the NIH, he noticed that employees sometimes converted their grievances into an equal opportunity employment format and filed with the Equal Employment Opportunity Commission (EEOC) even when the complaint did not start as a charge of discrimination. Once an employee had formally accused another of discrimination, Gadlin found the dispute more difficult to resolve through informal mediation, and the formal adjudications through the EEOC were provoking internal tensions.

Gadlin and his colleagues asked NIH employees why they filed with the EEOC and learned that the NIH's internal process for non-EEO complaints began with a complaint first to the employee's supervisor and then to the supervisor's supervisor before the employee could take advantage of any other internal processes. The employee, however, often was complaining *about* the supervisor—the processes were not ordered in a way that worked for employees. Also, the processes that supervisors used varied widely.

Gadlin suggested consideration of a process for any employment-related dispute that would begin with mediation, after informal attempts through the ombuds. If no settlement was reached, an internal peer-panel using adjudication would follow. To use the new system, the employees did not have to charge discrimination if that was not the basis of their concern. The mediation process would be confidential, with the aim of discussing real issues and reducing or preventing the tensions caused by formal discrimination accusations when not justified. The peer panel's decision in the absence of settlement would not preclude a complaint with the EEOC when discrimination was alleged. For the non-EEO complaints, the peer jury's decision would be final. (Complaints that fit within the union grievance process would be excluded from the pilot.) Gadlin worked with stakeholders within the NIH for about two years and ultimately found support to pilot the process within some NIH divisions. He and his colleagues trained more than a hundred potential peer panelists.

After three years, all of the divisions piloting the new series of processes decided to continue using them, but Gadlin began to notice a change in results. With the prospect of a fair internal adjudication process, more employees opted to file with the new internal system. All of them reached settlement at the mediation phase during the first 18 months of the pilot.

In the subsequent 18 months, though, about half of those filing did not settle at the mediation stage. Gadlin discovered that those using the peer panel adjudication increasingly brought lawyers; the adjudication portion lengthened and became more complex. When that occurred, the peers who had volunteered to serve on panels found the experience unpleasant. On balance, executive officers preferred the new system, but Gadlin began a new effort to improve the system before recommending expansion.

Narrow litigation accompanied by broad mediation: A cross-racial police shooting in Cincinnati in 2001 ignited racial tensions and three days of rioting. Prior to the shooting, plaintiffs had filed a federal class action against the police department, charging a pattern of racial discrimination in previous incidents. The judge appointed a special master mediator. Once rioting began, the federal judge in the discrimination suit directed the mediator to facilitate a citywide collaborative effort to improve police-community relations, which had been a cause of racial tensions. Ultimately, 3,500 people participated in the collaborative process, including major stakeholders like the Fraternal Order of Police who were not parties to the litigation. The results of that collaborative effort—agreements on the use of force policy, police community collaboration, police training, identification of crime patterns, and more—became the basis for settling the litigation. The judge appointed monitors to assess compliance over a five-year period.

In both the NIH and Cincinnati matters, the order and timing of the mediation within the litigation process mattered. In Cincinnati, the mediation might not have occurred absent the pending litigation. At NIH, the hearing process that would immediately follow mediation in the event of no settlement seemed, over time, to formalize the mediation phase and make it less productive of settlement.

The proximity of the NIH hearing process to the mediation may have caused some to use mediation in adversarial ways. How does the prospect of future adjudication change negotiations? Robert Mnookin and Lewis Kornhauser suggest that negotiating parties' views of what they can secure through further adjudication affects the fairness of the settlement discussions in a positive way. Rather than two separate processes, the "shadow of the law," they note, permeates negotiations that are interspersed with litigation (Mnookin and Kornhauser, 1979:968-969). Other commentators attach negative connotations to litigation's shadow, noting that settlement discussions held in the litigation context more narrowly focus on legal issues to the exclusion of the parties' other issues (pp. 150-151).

The processes within a system do not have to operate in progression. One of the innovations of Canada's Indian Residential Schools Settlement Agreement was to separate processes that had been combined in other nations dealing with wide-scale child abuse in government institutions and allow them to operate simultaneously.

Truth and
Reconciliation
Commission of Canada

Canadian process in the aftermath of the Indian Residential Schools: In 2007, the following processes were created or allowed to continue:

- A government entity dealt solely with monetary claims by survivors. That process worked expeditiously, at least as to those claimants who were literate and could prove what school they attended (Jung, 2009a:11, 14). Those who opted out of the government's claims process could sue.
- The Prime Minister apologized in 2008 (p. 36, n. 12) and polling indicated that 83 percent of Canadians heard about the apology and that most approved of it (Jung, 2009:18).
- No immunity from prosecution was granted by the settlement; criminal prosecutions of perpetrators proceeded through prosecutors, adding yet other entities that could operate simultaneously.
- The government provided funding until 2012 (when the government withdrew funding) that a private and independent entity (the Aboriginal Healing Foundation) could immediately re-grant for research and programs on healing those harmed while the other processes proceeded.

- A new government-funded entity, the Truth and Reconciliation Commission of Canada, would operate for five years (issuing a final report in 2015). The Truth and Reconciliation Commission would disburse funds allocated by the settlement for commemorative activities to honor "the resiliency and courage of former students, their families, and communities," promote storytelling and hearing, document what occurred and the harm it caused, and make recommendations to the government and others (Truth and Reconciliation Commission of Canada , 2012:1-2). To avoid mixing processes, the Commission did not hold perpetrators individually accountable—that was left to prosecutors—and therefore the Commission could use an expedited and supportive process, and when requested a confidential one. The Commission issued interim findings and recommendations in 2012 and held national hearings.

The simultaneous processes fit the desire for swift progress on some fronts while allowing the Truth and Reconciliation Process to operate over a period of years.

Other sequencing considerations: Chapter 7 discusses another sequencing issue—the flow of information from one process to the next. This was a design feature of the collaborative law process—the same attorney could not use the information from negotiations in litigation, or even litigation strategy. Chapter 6 addresses the related problems of using the same intervenor in multiple processes. As discussed there, the parties may clam up or act strategically in ways that undermine negotiations while also undermining the fairness of the adjudicative process if the same intervenor will facilitate negotiations and make decisions, or if the information can flow from a facilitative intervenor to a judge or arbitrator.

6. Exercising creativity in process and system design

The system designs and processes that you read about can spur your thinking about processes or systems, but they should not limit your thinking. The designers profiled in this book sometimes created new processes, adapted or renamed old ones, and ordered processes in novel ways.

Processes are fluid and must often be adapted to new situations. They can be modified, as Jennifer Llewellyn, the Aboriginal leaders, and church and Canadian government representatives did with the Truth and Reconciliation Commission (pp. 33-36).[3] Designers also rename processes. For example,

---

3. An exception would be when one needs to keep the processes within legal definitions for legal benefits, as for the mediation privilege or the summary enforcement for arbitration (*see* Chapters 7, 12, and 13).

This book mentions a variety of processes and a partial list of these might get you thinking about yet others: violence interruption (pp. 117); claims facilities (pp. 80-81); healing circles (p. 202-203); deliberative democracy, including online deliberations; deliberative polling; citizen juries, citizen congresses, and e-democracy (pp. 164, 167, 251); arbitration (Appendix B); truth and reconciliation commissions (pp. 197-198); conflict mapping (pp. 76-77); community courts (pp. 114-115); problem-solving courts (pp. 123-124); online, world-wide small claims court (pp. 119-120); transformative, facilitative, or evaluative mediation (Appendix C); storytelling (pp. 201-203, 205); negotiated rulemaking (pp. 248, 280); Navajo peacemaking (p. 269); collaborative law (pp. 114-115); structured negotiations (pp. 115-116); police-community dialogue (p. 297); victim-offender dialogues (pp. 204-205); dispute resolution advisors (pp. 284-286); good offices and shuttle diplomacy (pp. 226, 238-239); partnering agreements (pp. 30-31); intensive camps (pp. 229-230); town hall meetings (pp. 187-188); peer review panels (pp. 125-126); national issue forums (p. 167); facilitation (Chapter 15); and public policy consensus (p. 149).

this book refers to Michael Young as a mediator in the South African negotiations, but Young did not use that term. Young described his work instead as individual meetings, phone conversations, lunches, dinners, bilateral meetings, bilateral talks, and bilateral conferences. Prospective participants may have found it easier to agree to participate in these discrete events than in something that sounded more formal, like mediation (*see also* Carpenter, 1999:68). Conversely, a process may be given a formal name to make it sound inviting and even novel, such as "visioning," "search for common ground," "the listening project" (Dukes, 1996:67, 71, 73), and "family group conferencing" (Burford, 2000).

You may want to develop your own file of process and systems employed by others, but consider the file contents as a resource to stimulate your thinking and imagination rather than a constraint on the possibilities you consider.

C. A COLLABORATIVE APPROACH TO CREATING PROCESSES AND SYSTEMS

Costantino and Merchant argue for collaborative designing, based on their extensive experience in designing within government agencies and private organizations, noting, "Just as disputants are more likely to comply with a resolution reached through mediation because they were integral to the process, so too are stakeholders more likely to use and be satisfied with a conflict management system that they have helped to design" (Costantino and Merchant, 1996:66). In their view, designers are the expert fellow travelers who listen, teach, nudge, and persuade from the side as the stakeholders develop a design (*see* designer skills and client relations discussions in Chapters 3 and 15).

Other theorists seem to lend support to involving stakeholders in the design process. For example, Roger Fisher and Dan Shapiro underscore the importance of "core concerns" that can stimulate either positive or negative emotions in negotiation (2005:72-93). One of these core concerns is *autonomy*. Individuals want to have a sense that they have some independent ability to make decisions about their lives and their choices. When they lack a sense of autonomy, they may experience emotions that are negative and this may result in dissatisfaction with a dispute resolution forum and unproductive behavior in any kind of collaborative process. Applying this negotiation advice to secure party or stakeholder acceptance of a new dispute system, designers might make certain that the process or system has features that protect individual stakeholders' psychological sense of autonomy.

Maryland Chief Judge Robert M. Bell took a collaborative approach, beginning his dispute resolution initiative by listening and facilitating, as chair of a commission and through his staff director and her colleagues. Staff director Rachel Wohl and deputy director Lou Gieszl coordinated sessions to educate and get feedback from 700 people who joined to plan the new systems for Maryland. The schema below reflects that two-year collaborative planning process that culminated in a report and a decision by the Maryland legislature to fund the initiative.

Wohl could convene stakeholders as she began the planning; that is not always feasible. At times, designers gauge stakeholder reaction while the process operates. For example, Cure Violence administrators could ask police, neighbors, the faith community, and public officials to provide input into the plans for using violence interrupters, but the interrupters themselves had to predict the reactions of potential retaliators as the mediations began, and then adjust (pp. 27-28).

In most situations, though, creative designers can find ways to reach and involve many stakeholders. In that way, they can accommodate more interests and engage a group that will assist in implementation. For example, during the mortgage foreclosure crisis that began in 2008, some government and private groups, aware that foreclosure litigation served neither the banks nor the

consumers, sought to design their own interest-based dispute resolution system (*see, e.g.*, Schneider and Fleury, 2011:368-371). In some cases, those charged with designing these processes could have decided that it would be difficult to identify and include in the design process individuals whose homes were to be foreclosed. After all, how could you identify at-risk homeowners and invite them into the process? Moreover, what purpose would it serve? Was it not obvious that the interest of most homeowners would be to simply stay in their homes?

In the foreclosure mediation initiative, the design team thought it wise to find a way to include mortgage holders. They contacted various agencies set up to assist homeowners in jeopardy of losing their houses. The designers created a brochure about their work and asked these agencies to hand it out when they met with clients. The brochure invited homeowners to phone the design team and then asked them to be a part of an interview and collaborative design process. This approach proved largely effective, resulting in a creative system design, one that accounted for the fact that at least some homeowners in fact preferred to vacate their homes rather than continue to pay for underwater mortgages.[4] Even more importantly, it identified a major issue that otherwise would have been missed—namely that letters from banks inviting homeowners into a mediation foreclosure program would be unlikely to work because homeowners often so feared a letter from a bank that they either did not open it or would not trust any promises or offers it contained.

4. An underwater mortgage is one for a property that is worth less than the debtor owes on the mortgage.

Like the mortgage foreclosure designers, Deborah Katz encountered resistance when she began a collaborative planning process to set up a system to deal with employee disputes or grievances for the U.S. Transportation Security Administration's employees at airports across the country. Congress created the agency following the September 11, 2001 terrorist attacks, and administrators needed to act quickly to deal with future terrorist threats. Katz recalls, "There was a lot of pressure on us to, as one executive urged us, 'buy something off the shelf'—just implement it nationwide rather than engage in a collaborative design process. I believe, however, that the [conflict management system] would have been short-lived had we just mapped it all out at headquarters and dictated. . . . Moreover, the iterative collaborative process has produced a startling amount of innovation, understanding, and a level of involvement by employees that we would not otherwise have been able to generate" (Cohen, 2009:89).

These collaborative design stories share common themes:

- Whenever possible, include all stakeholders in the design process.
- Avoid being presumptuous about what the interests of a particular stakeholder group might be.
- Practice humility in your work with clients and stakeholders alike.

THOUGHTS GOING FORWARD

Process and system creation lies at the heart of what you will do as a designer. Such work depends for its success not only on a thoughtful and thorough assessment but also on an appreciation of the ways in which the processes and systems fit into the lives of people and the structures within which they operate. The design goals may be as mundane as saving money and as profound as improving justice more broadly. So you will be listening for people's interests, reading theoretical writings, and sorting out your own role as these interests conflict. Remember that you can create entirely new processes or sequence them in new ways. In all of this, watch out for ways in which sequencing the processes can change their character. You can achieve breakthroughs if you work collaboratively with stakeholders, focus on tailoring to interests and broader concerns, and open your mind to new processes and combinations.

QUESTIONS

5.1   A local merchant asked you to design an online (asynchronous emails) negotiation process for disgruntled customers. The merchant explains, "It's cheaper that way. Also, emotions sometimes dissipate when we slow down the negotiations. Besides, we'll have a record of what we said." In what ways do you agree with what the merchant says? In what ways might there be shortcomings to the merchant's approach (*see also* Chapter 10)?

5.2 The Old Hat County Court has had a mediation program for 25 years, used in about 10 percent of general civil cases and 15 percent of the domestic relations cases. No other statistics are available. The chief judge recalls no complaints from the bar about the mediation program but nonetheless asks you, as an outside consultant, to revisit some of the decisions that were made previously and to point out the advantages and disadvantages of continuing it. The chief judge found this checklist for designing a court-connected dispute resolution program and has filled it in with notes on current practices:

a. *Goals:* Provides services that litigants and their attorneys value; has no negative impact on the court budget.

b. *Process:* Offers only mediation (see Appendix C if you are not familiar with mediation)—no other dispute resolution processes.

c. *Screening for appropriateness and timing:* Judges may do that in first pre-trial conference. Mediation is not suggested for domestic relations cases in which a party has alleged physical violence. All other cases are appropriate for mediation.

d. *Conduct of the mediation:* Does not regulate whether the mediator can evaluate for the parties what is likely to occur absent a settlement, and does not regulate whether the mediator ever holds a joint session attended by all parties.

e. *Who pays/access to justice:* Requires the parties to pay the mediator and, if no settlement results, permits mediator's fees to be taxed as "court costs" to be paid by the losing party at judgment. Has a list of mediators who will volunteer services for those who cannot afford the fee.

f. *Mandatory or voluntary:* Encourages judges to suggest mediation but does not authorize judges to mandate parties to participate in mediation (and therefore also does not require that the parties participate in good faith or come with bargaining authority).

g. *Staffing:* Uses only private mediators who do not work for the court. Has no court mediation manager. No program to recruit diverse mediators.

h. *Mediator qualifications/ethics:* Sets no qualifications or ongoing requirements for mediators except that they are lawyers, have had 25 hours of mediation training, and will abide by the Standards of Conduct for Mediators.

i. *Technology:* Has no online or virtual qualities.

j. *Mediator immunity:* Does not provide mediators with immunity from liability.

k. *Mediation privilege:* States that mediation communications are privileged from disclosure during legal proceedings, under a state statute modeled on the Uniform Mediation Act (Appendix E).

l. *Settlement enforcement:* Requires mediated agreements to be recorded to secure court enforcement.

m. *Self-represented parties:* These persons have choice about whether to mediate, and they can refer to court's self-help center to do research on law. No provision of counsel for mediation parties though legal aid often represents low-income parties.

n. *Mediation-related laws:* Has court rules governing items h, j, and l.

o. *Support from bar, court and others:* This seems to be okay.

p. *Evaluation:* Has never been evaluated.

Imagine that you have a 30-minute meeting scheduled with the chief judge. What potential changes in this program strike you as important enough to discuss at least preliminarily at this initial meeting? How would you begin the conversation with the chief judge?

5.3   How might lawyers be trained and incentivized to think more systematically about helping their clients manage and resolve disputes? What barriers might there be to implementing your ideas?

5.4   Not all efforts to re-structure negotiations have proved as successful as collaborative law, eBay's online negotiation, and the National Institutes of Health's structured collaboration agreements. For example, some courts have tried to overcome the law practice organization barrier that results in delayed negotiations by requiring lawyers to sign statements that they have met and conferred. Lawyers submit the statements, but there is little evidence of earlier or more settlements (Wissler and Dauber, 2005:266; McAdoo, 2002:425). What might explain this apparent failure to overcome barriers by re-structuring negotiations?

5.5   One practitioner suggests that collaborative law could be effective in overcoming barriers to earlier settlement in medical malpractice cases (Clark, 2007:21). Compare medical malpractice disputes and family law disputes in terms of the parties' goals and the barriers to a settlement that meets those goals. Do you predict success for collaborative law in medical malpractice disputes? Why or why not?

5.6   A group of Wisconsin family lawyers uses a process much like collaborative law but without requiring agreement that the divorcing parties will secure new counsel if the parties fail to reach agreement. Analyze the likely advantages and disadvantages of the Wisconsin process, called cooperative law, compared to (a) collaborative law and (b) traditional practice (*see* Lande, 2008).

5.7   What are (i) the stakeholders' interests regarding the process and (ii) the barriers to achieving them though a negotiated agreement, and what should be (iii) the designer's actions in reaction to (i) and (ii) in one of the examples listed below?

a. A chemical fire in a commercial refuse dump has spewed noxious fumes for two months, and the owner cannot figure out how to extinguish it. In the meantime, adjoining landowners' crops and animals have been harmed and people as far as a half mile away have had exposure to the fumes, though they do not yet know the health implications.

b. Robots will soon replace 400 non-union assembly line employees of the Widget Factory. Management has contacted you before telling the employees. Most of the employees have the skills to work in a new customer service initiative, but management fears that selecting some but not all of the current employees would result in discrimination suits, as those with poor communications skills probably would not be selected, and those without strong English language skills might more often fall into that category. Management could also find positions for all of these assembly line workers if all agreed to take a 15 percent cut in pay. Management would like you to try building a consensus on an approach that would not cause as much human suffering as laying off all of the assembly line workers. But if doing something short of laying off all of these workers will generate significant litigation, management leans in favor of laying off all workers.

c. Read parts of the report and watch portions of the videos on the deliberative polling used by Professor James Fishkin as an intervenor in order to allow informed and representative Michigan citizens to reach consensus, or at least to achieve a policy perspective with significant support, on the way that Michigan government officials should manage budget problems, http://cdd.stanford.edu/polls/btp/ (click on video under "Hard Times, Hard Choices: Michigan Citizens Deliberate").

5.8 Some U.S. prosecutors refer a portion of criminal matters to mediation between alleged perpetrator and victim. If the mediation parties reach agreement and abide by it, the prosecutors have a practice of not prosecuting. Mediation referral criteria might include: all school truancy cases, first offense bad check cases, and others in which the alleged offense does not implicate public safety and the alleged victim and defender have a continuing relationship. What are the pros and cons of this approach?

5.9 eBay's Community Court (pp. 114-115) provides an inexpensive and quick way to protect against the possibility that a single arbitrator is biased, inattentive, or irrational on a given day or in a given matter. When it is important to simplify an adjudication process in order to meet the time and cost needs, what is the essence that should be preserved in the arbitration process in each of the following contexts and how would you suggest accomplishing that without adding significant costs or delays? For each, what is the Francis McGovern (pp. 80-81) "rough justice" explanation, and would the users and other stakeholders agree with the tradeoffs if they heard the explanation?

a. Disputes among contractors in ongoing construction.
b. Post-judgment child custody disputes between parents.
c. Disputes between collaborating scientists at the National Institutes of Health (pp. 30-32).
d. Conflict between developed and developing countries over intellectual property protection or environmental regulation.

5.10   Colin Rule selected India to pilot his new idea in part because its courts employ a common law adversary process similar to the eBay Community Court's process. Tradition also influenced the Rwandan government when it selected a customary Rwandan process, a lay adjudication tribunal called Gacaca, to handle criminal trials for more than 100,000 persons still in custody in 2001 in connection with the 1994 genocide.

Suppose you work for an oil company that would like you to design a simplified claims process to be available in case of an oil spill. What would be the advantages and disadvantages of using a claims process that fits local traditions? How might the claims process differ (if at all) if the spill occurred off the East Coast of the United States as opposed to somewhere in the Persian Gulf?

5.11   The collective bargaining agreements for both the National Hockey League and Major League Baseball contain salary arbitration clauses. In one, the arbitrator sets the salary after considering the salary proposals of owners and players; in the other, the arbitrator selects one or the other of the salary proposals submitted by the parties but not anything in between ("final offer arbitration"). Under both systems, player salaries have increased dramatically above inflation rates over the last 15 years (Yoost, 2006:494-495, 504-506). Which system is likely to promote more pre-arbitration settlement and why? If you were invited to design a system or process to help players and teams prevent or resolve contract disputes, in what ways might it resemble one of the two arbitration regimes currently in place and in what ways might it differ?

5.12   You have been asked to create a claims process to distribute a $50 million class action settlement fund to employees in several nations who experienced gender discrimination by the Acme Company. In some of these nations, the courts use a civil law, inquisitorial approach, while the courts in other nations, like the United States, use a common law, adversarial approach. What procedural safeguards should be a part of the adjudicative process used to distribute the settlement fund to victims? Before you answer, consider Mark Freeman's list (pp. 81-82) of the procedural values weighed in the creation of truth commissions.

5.13   How do you explain Roselle Wissler's results in the court context (p. 125)? What does the research suggest in terms of the timing of the National Institutes of Health mediation? What might make you hesitant to apply Wissler's research in the NIH context?

5.14   California was one of the first states to introduce mandatory mediation for contested custody issues within divorce proceedings. In some California counties, the mediators made a report and recommendation to the judge in those cases that did not settle in mediation. Gadlin's NIH design took a different approach—mediators could not comment to the peer panels; what was said in mediation remained there. How would you expect the dynamics of mediation to differ in these two contexts? What differences would you expect in settlement rates? Apart from settlement rates, under what circumstances would the California approach seem to be an appropriate design feature and under what circumstances might the NIH seem an appropriate design feature (*see* Chapter 7)?

5.15 In light of research and commentary about the "shadow" that litigation casts on settlement discussions, what are the pros and cons of the decision by the judge in Cincinnati (pp. 126-127) to encourage the mediator to promote discussion of more than just the legal issues of the pending case? How might other judges broaden the issues discussed in mediation sessions (Riskin and Welsh, 2008:863)?

5.16 Individuals who experience harassment in some situations may care more about stopping the harassment and prefer to avoid processes that expose them to publicity even if those processes might punish the offender. In designing a dispute resolution system to deal with these issues, how would you weigh (1) the preferences of the complainants and (2) community interests related to establishing justice and tracking repeat offenders? What if the corporate client prefers to avoid any confidential processes because of fear that this will be perceived as trying to hide—rather than address—a problem?

Exercise 5.1 *Tallahoya University processes:* University counsel left the following voicemail for you: "Hey, I know I promised not to ask you to make formal proposals until you had finished your class and had an opportunity to do research. But, I just learned that the University budget for the next couple of years will be tentatively set soon. After that, it will be much harder to get new projects funded. So—with hopes you will forgive me—what is your best guess as to what processes you will ultimately recommend for each of the first five issues I described to you (pp. 42-44), and why do you recommend these processes? With your analysis in hand, I can make my pitch. Don't worry—I know that you will want to change your recommendations after you learn more. At this stage, I just need to give the rough outlines of our proposal and be persuasive. Thanks!"

BIBLIOGRAPHY AND REFERENCES

AMERICAN BAR ASSOCIATION SECTION ON DISPUTE RESOLUTION (2008) *Task Force on Improving Mediation Quality Final Report.* Chicago: ABA.

AMSLER, Lisa Blomgren (2017) "The Dispute Resolver's Role Within a Dispute System Design: Justice, Accountability, and Impact," 13 *U. St. Thomas L.J.* 168.

ARROW, Kenneth et al. eds. (1995) *Barriers to Conflict Resolution.* New York: W.W. Norton.

AUERBACH, Jerold (1983) *Justice Without Law?* New York: Oxford University Press.

BASS, Jack (1993) *Taming the Storm: The Life and Times of Judge Frank M. Johnson, Jr. and the South's Fight over Civil Rights.* New York: Doubleday.

BAZERMAN, Max H., and Katie SHONK (2005) "The Decision Perspective to Negotiation," in Michael L. Moffitt and Robert C. Bordone eds., *The Handbook of Dispute Resolution* 52. San Francisco: Jossey-Bass.

BENNETT, L. Michelle, Howard GADLIN, and Samantha LEVINE-FINLEY (2010) *Collaboration and Team Science: A Field Guide.* Washington, DC: National Institutes of Health.

BERMAN, Greg, and John FEINBLATT (2005) *Good Courts: The Case for Problem-Solving Justice.* New York: New Press.

BRAND, Ronald A. (2012) "Party Autonomy and Access to Justice in the UNCITRAL Online Dispute Resolution Project," 10 *Loy. U. Chi. Int'l L. Rev.* 11. (2012)

BROWN, Jennifer Gerarda, and Ian AYRES (1994) "Economic Rationales for Mediation," 80 *Va. L. Rev.* 323.

BURFORD, Gale, and Joe HUDSON eds. (2000) *Family Group Conferencing: New Directions in Community-Centered Child and Family Practice.* Piscataway, NJ: Transaction Publishers.

BURGER, Warren (1977) "Our Vicious Legal Spiral," 16 *Judges J.*, Fall 22.

BUSCH, Dominic, Claude-Helene MAYER, and Christian BONESS eds. (2010) *International and Regional Perspectives on Cross-Cultural Mediation.* Frankfurt: Peter Lang.

BUSH, Robert A. Baruch, and Joseph P. FOLGER (2012) "Mediation and Social Justice: Risks and Opportunities," 27 *Ohio St. J. on Disp. Resol.* 1.

CARPENTER, Susan (1999) "Choosing Appropriate Consensus Building Techniques and Strategies," in Lawrence Susskind, Sarah McKearnan, and Jennifer Thomas-Larmer eds., *The Consensus Building Handbook: A Comprehensive Guide to Reaching Agreement* 61. Thousand Oaks, CA: Sage Publications, Inc.

CARPENTER, Susan L., and W.J.D. KENNEDY (2001) *Managing Public Disputes: A Practical Guide for Government, Business, and Citizens' Groups.* San Francisco: Jossey-Bass.

CLARK, Kathleen (2007) "The Use of Collaborative Law in Medical Error Situations," 19 *Health L.* 19.

COHEN, Amy J. (2009) "Dispute Systems Design, Neoliberalism, and the Problem of Scale," 14 *Harv. Negot. L. Rev.* 51.

COHEN, Judith (2009a) "Why Programs Are No Longer Enough: An Interview on Collaborating at the U.S. TSA," 27 *Alternatives* 81.

COHEN, Judith (2009b) "What Corporations Need to Know About How to Install an Integrated Conflict Management System," 27 *Alternatives* 99.

COLE, Sarah R., Nancy H. ROGERS, Craig A. McEWEN, James R. COBEN, and Peter N. THOMPSON (2017-2018) *Mediation: Law, Policy, Practice* (3rd ed.). Minneapolis: West.

COSTANTINO, Cathy, and Christina Sickles MERCHANT (1996) *Designing Conflict Management Systems: A Guide to Creating Productive and Healthy Organizations.* San Francisco: Jossey-Bass.

DELGADO, Richard (1988) "ADR and the Dispossessed: Recent Books About the Deformalization Movement," 13 *Law & Soc. Inquiry* 145.

DUKES, E. Franklin (1996) *Resolving Public Conflict: Transforming Community and Governance.* Manchester, UK: Manchester University Press.

FADER, Hallie (2008) "Designing the Forum to Fit the Fuss: Dispute System Design for the State Trial Courts," 13 *Harv. Negot. L. Rev.* 481.

FASLER, Karen (2007) "Show Me the Money!! The Potential for Cost Savings Associated with a Parallel Program and Collaborative Law," 20 No. 2 *Health L.* 15.

FEINBERG, Kenneth R. (2005) *What Is Life Worth?* New York: Public Affairs.

FELSTINER, William L.F. (1974) "Influences of Social Organization on Dispute Processing," 9 *Law & Soc'y Rev.* 63.

FISHER, Roger, and Daniel SHAPIRO (2005) *Beyond Reason: Using Emotions as You Negotiate.* New York: Viking.

FISHER, Roger, William URY, and Bruce PATTON (2011) *Getting to Yes: Negotiating Agreement Without Giving In* (3rd ed.). New York: Penguin Group.

FISS, Owen M. (1984) "Against Settlement," 93 *Yale L.J.* 1073.

FISS, Owen M. (2009) "The History of an Idea," 78 *Fordham L. Rev.* 1273.

FREEMAN, Mark (2006) *Truth Commissions and Procedural Fairness.* Cambridge: Cambridge University Press.

GADLIN, Howard et al. (2010) *Collaboration and Team Science: A Field Guide.* Bethesda, MD: National Institutes of Health.

GASTIL, John, and Peter LEVINE eds. (2005) *The Deliberative Democracy Handbook.* San Francisco: John Wiley & Sons.

GOLANN, Dwight (1996) *Mediating Legal Disputes: Effective Strategies for Lawyers and Mediators.* New York: Aspen Publishers.

GOLANN, Dwight, and Jay FOLBERG (2011) *Mediation: The Roles of Advocate and Neutral* (2d ed.). New York: Wolters Kluwer.

GOLDBERG, Stephen, Jeanne BRETT, and William URY (2012) "Designing an Effective Dispute Resolution System," in Stephen Goldberg, Frank Sander, Nancy Rogers, and Sarah Cole, *Dispute Resolution: Negotiation, Mediation, Arbitration, and Other Processes* (6th ed.) 483. New York: Wolters Kluwer.

GOLDBERG, Stephen B., Frank E.A. SANDER, Nancy H. ROGERS, and Sarah R. COLE (2012) *Dispute Resolution: Negotiation, Mediation, Arbitration, and Other Processes* (6th ed.). New York: Wolters Kluwer.

GOLDSTONE, Richard (2000) *For Humanity: Reflections of a War Crimes Investigator.* New Haven, CT: Yale University Press.

GREENBERG, Elayne E. (2009) "We Can Work It Out: Entertaining a Dispute Resolution System for Bankruptcy Court," 17 *Am. Bankr. Inst. L. Rev.* 545.

HEUMANN, Milton, and Jonathan M. HYMAN (1997) "Negotiation Method and Litigation Settlement Methods in New Jersey: You Can't Always Get What You Want," 12 *Ohio St. J. on Disp. Resol.* 253.

HOLLANDER-BLUMOFF, Rebecca, and Tom R. TYLER (2008) "Procedural Justice in Negotiation: Procedural Fairness, Outcome Acceptance, and Integrative Potential," 33 *Law & Soc. Inquiry* 473.

JUNG, Courtney (2009) "Canada and the Legacy of the Indian Residential Schools: Transitional Justice for Indigenous People in a Non-Transitional Society," http://ssrn.com/abstract+1374950.

KOROBKIN, Russell (2006) "Psychological Impediments to Mediation Success: Theory and Practice," 21 *Ohio St. J. on Disp. Resol.* 281.

KOROBKIN, Russell, and Chris GUTHRIE (1997) "Psychology, Economics and Settlement: A New Look at the Role of the Lawyer," 76 *Tex. L. Rev.* 77.

KOROBKIN, Russell, and Chris GUTHRIE (1994) "Psychological Barriers to Litigation Settlement: An Experimental Approach," 93 *Mich. L. Rev.* 107.

LANDE, John (2008) "Practical Insights from an Empirical Study of Cooperative Lawyers in Wisconsin," 2008 *J. Disp. Resol.* 203.

LANDE, John (2008) "The Movement Toward Early Case Handling in Courts and Private Dispute Resolution," 24 *Ohio St. J. on Disp. Resol.* 83.

LLEWELLYN, Jennifer J. (2002) "Dealing with the Legacy of Native Residential School Abuse in Canada: Litigation, ADR, and Restorative Justice," 52 *U. Toronto L.J.* 253.

LOVE, Lela (1997) "The Top Ten Reasons Why Mediators Should Not Evaluate," 24 *Fla. St. U. L. Rev.* 937.

MACFARLANE, Julie (2008) *The New Lawyer: How Settlement Is Transforming the Practice of Law.* Vancouver: UBC Press.

MAYER, Bernard S. (2004) *Beyond Neutrality: Confronting the Crisis in Conflict Resolution.* San Francisco: Jossey-Bass.

McADOO, Bobbi (2002) "A Report to the Minnesota Supreme Court: The Impact of Rule 114 on Civil Litigation Practice in Minnesota," 25 *Hamline L. Rev.* 401.

McEWEN, Craig A. et al. (1994) "Lawyers, Mediation, and the Management of Divorce," 28 *Law & Soc'y Rev.* 149.

MNOOKIN, Robert, and Lewis KORNHAUSER (1979) "Bargaining in the Shadow of the Law: The Case of Divorce," 88 *Yale L.J.* 950.

MNOOKIN, Robert H. (1993) "Why Negotiations Fail: An Exploration of Barriers to the Resolution of Conflict," 8 *Ohio St. J. on Disp. Resol.* 235.

MNOOKIN, Robert H., and Ronald GILSON (1994) "Disputing Through Agents: Cooperation Between Lawyers in Litigation," 94 *Colum. L. Rev.* 509.

MNOOKIN, Robert H., and Lee ROSS (1995) "Introduction," in Kenneth Arrow et al. eds., *Barriers to Conflict Resolution* 20. New York: W.W. Norton & Co.

MNOOKIN, Robert H., Scott R. PEPPET, and Andrew S. TULUMELLO (2004) *Beyond Winning: Negotiating to Create Value in Deals and Disputes* (2d ed.). Cambridge, MA: Belknap Press of Harvard University Press.

MOFFITT, Michael L. (2005) "Disputes as Opportunities to Create Value," in Michael L. Moffitt and Robert C. Bordone eds., *The Handbook of Dispute Resolution* 173. San Francisco: Jossey Bass.

MOSTEN, Forrest S. (2009) *Collaborative Divorce: Helping Families Without Going to Court.* San Francisco: Jossey-Bass.

NADER, Laura (1993) "Controlling Processes in the Practice of Law: Hierarchy and Pacification in the Movement to Re-Form Dispute Ideology," 9 *Ohio St. J. on Disp. Resol.* 1.

NOLAN, James L., Jr. (2001) *Reinventing Justice: The American Drug Court Movement.* Princeton, NJ: Princeton University Press.

PATTON, Bruce (2005) "Negotiation," in Michael L. Moffitt and Robert C. Bordone eds., *The Handbook of Dispute Resolution* 279. San Francisco: Jossey-Bass.

PEPPET, Scott (2008) "The Ethics of Collaborative Law," 2008 *J. Disp. Resol.* 131.

RAIFFA, Howard, with John RICHARDSON and David METCALFE (2002) *Negotiation Analysis: The Science and Art of Collaborative Decision-Making.* San Francisco: Jossey-Bass.

REGAN, Paulette (2010) *Unsettling the Settler Within: Indian Residential Schools, Truth Telling, and Reconciliation in Canada.* Vancouver, BC: The University of British Columbia Press.

REILLY, Peter (2009) "Was Machiavelli Right? Lying in Negotiation and the Art of Defensive Self-Help," 25 *Ohio St. J. on Disp. Resol.* 481.

RELIS, Tamara (2009) *Perceptions in Litigation and Mediation: Lawyers, Defendants, Plaintiffs, and Gendered Parties.* Cambridge, UK: Cambridge University Press.

REUBEN, Richard C. (2005) "Democracy and Dispute Resolution: Systems Design and the New Workplace," 10 *Harv. Negot. L. Rev.* 11.

RISKIN, Leonard L., and Nancy A. WELSH (2008) "Is That All There Is? 'The Problem' in Court-Connected Mediation," 15 *Geo. Mason L. Rev.* 863.

RISKIN, Leonard L. (1996) "Understanding Mediators' Orientations, Strategies, and Techniques: A Grid for the Perplexed," 1 *Harv. Negot. L. Rev.* 7.

ROSS, Lee (1999) "Reactive Devaluation in Negotiation and Conflict Resolution," in K.J. ARROW et al. eds., *Barriers to Conflict Resolution* 26. Cambridge, MA: PON Books.

ROTHMAN, Jay, and Randi LAND (2003-2004) "The Cincinnati Police-Community Collaborative," 18 *Crim. Just.* 35.

RULE, Colin, Vikki ROGERS, and Louis DEL DUCA (2010) "Designing a Global Consumer Online Dispute Resolution (ODR) System for Cross-Border Small Value-High Volume Claims—OAS Developments," 42 *UCC L.J.* 221.

SANDER, Frank E.A., and Stephen B. GOLDBERG (1994) "Fitting the Forum to the Fuss: A User-Friendly Guide to Selecting an ADR Procedure," 10 *Negot. J.* 49 (1994).

SANDER, Frank E.A., and Lukasz ROZDEICZER (2006) "Matching Cases and Dispute Resolution Procedures: Detailed Analysis Leading to a Mediation-Centered Approach," 11 *Harv. Negot. L. Rev.* 1.

SCHEPARD, Andrew ed. (2010) "Special Issue on Collaborative Law," 38 *Hofstra L. Rev.* 411.

SCHMITZ, Amy J. (2010) "Legislating in the Light: Considering Empirical Data in Crafting Arbitration Reforms," 15 *Harv. Negot. L. Rev.* 115.

SCHNEIDER, Andrea Kupfer, and Natalie C. FLEURY (2011) "There's No Place Like Home: Applying Dispute Systems Design Theory to Create a Foreclosure Mediation System," 11 *Nev. L.J.* 368.

SHAPIRO, Daniel L. (2005) "Enemies, Allies, and Emotions: The Power of Positive Emotions in Negotiation," in Michael L. Moffitt and Robert C. Bordone eds., *The Handbook of Dispute Resolution* 66. San Francisco: Jossey-Bass.

SCHOENY, Mara, and Wallace WARFIELD (2000) "Reconnecting Systems Maintenance with Social Justice: A Critical Role for Conflict Resolution," 16 *Negot. J.* 253.

SCHWAB, William H. (2004) "Collaborative Lawyering: A Closer Look at an Emerging Practice," 4 *Pepp. Disp. Resol. L.J.* 351.

SIMON, William (1985) "Legal Informality and Redistributive Politics," 19 *Clearinghouse Rev.* 385.

STIPANOWICH, Thomas J., Curtis E. von KANN, and Deborah ROTHMAN eds. (2010) *Protocols for Expeditious, Cost-Effective Commercial Arbitration: Key Action Steps for Business Users, Counsel, Arbitrators and Arbitration Provider Institutions.* Austin, TX: College of Commercial Arbitrators.

STULBERG, Joseph (1997) "Facilitative Versus Evaluative Mediator Orientations: Piercing the 'Gridlock,'" 24 *Fla. St. L. Rev.* 985.

STURM, Susan, and Howard GADLIN (2007) "Conflict Resolution and Systemic Change," 2007 *J. Disp. Resol.* 1.

SUSSKIND, Lawrence, Sarah McKEARNAN, and Jennifer THOMAS-LARMER eds. (1999) *The Consensus Building Handbook: A Comprehensive Guide to Reaching Agreement.* Thousand Oaks, CA: Sage Publications.

TESLER, Pauline H. (2007) *Collaborative Law: Achieving Effective Resolution Without Litigation* (2d ed.). Chicago: ABA.

TRUTH AND RECONCILIATION COMMISSION OF CANADA (2012) *Interim Report.* Winnipeg, Manitoba: TRC of Canada.

TRUTH AND RECONCILIATION COMMISSION OF CANADA (2015) *Honouring the Truth, Reconciling for the Future: Summary of the Final Report of the Truth and Reconciliation Commission of Canada.* Winnipeg, Manitoba: TRC of Canada.

UMBREIT, Mark, Betty VOS, Robert B. COATES, and Elizabeth LIGHTFOOT (2005) "Symposium: Restorative Justice in Action: Restorative Justice in the Twenty-First Century: A Social Movement Full of Opportunities and Pitfalls" 89 *Marq. L. Rev.* 251.

URY, William L., Jeanne M. BRETT, and Stephen B. GOLDBERG (1988) *Getting Disputes Resolved: Designing Systems to Cut the Costs of Conflict.* San Francisco: Jossey-Bass.

WARFIELD, Wallace (1996) "Building Consensus for Racial Harmony in American Cities: Case Model Approach," 1996 *J. Disp. Resol.* 151.

WEBB, Stuart G., and Ronald D. OUSKY (2006) *The Collaborative Way to Divorce: The Revolutionary Method That Results in Less Stress, Lower Costs and Happier Kids—Without Going to Court.* London: Penguin Books.

WEINSTEIN, Jack B. (2009) "Comments on Owen M. Fiss, Against Settlement (1984)," 78 *Fordham L. Rev.* 1265.

WISSLER, Roselle L. (2002) "Court-Connected Mediation in General Civil Cases: What We Know from Empirical Research," 17 *Ohio St. J. on Disp. Resol.* 641.

WISSLER, Roselle L. (2004) "The Effectiveness of Court-Connected Dispute Resolution in Civil Cases," 22 *Conflict Resol. Q.* 55.

WISSLER, Roselle L., and Bob DAUBER (2005) "Leading Horses to Water: The Impact of an ADR 'Confer and Report' Rule," 26 *Just. Sys. J.* 253.

WETLAUFER, Gerald B. (1990) "The Ethics of Lying in Negotiations," 75 *Iowa L. Rev.* 1219.

YOOST, Stephen M. (2006) "The National Hockey League and Salary Arbitration: Time for a Line Change," 21 *Ohio St. J. on Disp. Resol.* 485.

ZEHR, Howard (2002) *The Little Book of Restorative Justice.* Intercourse, PA: Good Books.

KEY PLANNING ISSUES IN MORE DETAIL

The chapters in Part Three focus on the newly designed process or system, as distinct from the design process. For example, Chapter 6 examines the process or system itself—not the stakeholders in the process of designing. The Part Three chapters will enable you to answer the following questions:

- Who should be the intervenors and participants in the process or system you are designing and how will that process or system attract their participation and prepare them to participate effectively (Chapter 6)?
- How open and how confidential should this new process or system be, and how can that be accomplished (Chapter 7)?
- How can the process or system satisfy desires for justice, deterrence, safety, reconciliation, punishment, truth, public acknowledgment, and understanding that arise especially in contexts where inequality exists or where parties have experienced intentional wrongdoing or terrible violations and harm, and where the risk of recurrence may be high and the consequences grave? (Chapter 8)?
- How can the process or system be designed in ways that help enhance relationships over time (Chapter 9)?
- How can technology help with the effectiveness of the new process or system, and how can a designer manage the problems introduced by the use of technology (Chapter 10)?

CHAPTER 6

Selecting, Engaging, and Preparing the Participants in the New Process

The success of your design depends on involving the right *people* at the right *time* who are prepared to deploy the right *skill* set in the right *roles*. We focus in this chapter on those who do the conflict management work in the newly designed process. In other words, the topic is the parties to the disputes themselves, their representatives, and the intervenors, not the stakeholders engaged in collaborative planning—though many of the lessons apply to both groups. This chapter covers how to engage participants in a single process as well as how to engage them in a broader dispute management system (as in eBay). After reading this chapter, you will have a list of issues related to selecting, involving, and educating participants in the process and ideas for strategies to handle the issues.

Designers sometimes compromise the success of a design as a result of choices they make regarding participants. For example, designers may exclude either the lawyers or the parties from attending the sessions, often changing the fairness or dynamic of the process considerably. Or they may fail to identify the intervenors whose skill set is best suited for the particular dispute. For example, an organization may over-emphasize the value of a mediator's reputation for success without assessing whether the mediator has the talents, values, or style required for the particular dispute at hand. The designers may fail to recognize the difficulty of getting people caught in bitter conflicts to agree on

---

DESIGNING STEPS

1. Design initiative
2. Basic planning steps
   - Assessing stakeholders, their goals and interests, and contexts
   - Creating processes and systems
3. Key planning issues (that may arise throughout the planning)
   - **Planning how to select, engage, and prepare intervenors and parties**
   - Determining the extent of confidentiality and openness in the process
   - Dealing with desires for change, justice, accountability, understanding, safety, reconciliation
   - Enhancing relationships
   - Incorporating technology
4. Implementing and institutionalizing the system or process
   - Implementing
   - Using contracts
   - Using law
   - Evaluating, revising

---

using a particular approach, and subsequently fail to demonstrate enough "case volume" to persuade funders to provide resources. They may also forget to consider that the fairness or effectiveness of a process or system depends on how prepared the parties are. At times, a design might look good on paper but the designer might not have taken into account that some of the most important participants will lack the resources, time, skills, or knowledge to access the system.

Each section of the chapter responds to a design decision that might precipitate failure if made poorly, even if the process or system is otherwise well designed:

- Who should participate in the new process or system (Section A)?
- Who should be the intervenors (Section B)?
- How should the process or system encourage participants to become and stay involved and when should that encouragement occur (Section C)?
- How should the process or system prepare the participants (Section D)?

A. IDENTIFYING PARTICIPANTS

Buyers and sellers are the obvious parties in most eBay disputes. In other situations, by contrast, careful thought about who participates may be a prerequisite to ensuring that the new system or process achieves its goals. To get a sense of just how much the "who should participate" issues differ by context, ask yourself:

- Who should participate in truancy mediations?
- Should injured first responders (police, fire, ambulance) who provided aid after a terrorist attack be able to participate in a claims facility for attack victims? What about those individuals who suffered psychological harm because they lost a loved one? What about those who suffered psychological harm because they watched the attack unfold on TV from afar?
- Should a court-sponsored mediation in a discrimination suit against police include non-party community leaders (pp. 126-127)?
- Should an organization's employment manual preclude all parties from bringing attorneys to the dispute resolution sessions (p. 427, section 10)?

Your answers to these questions might suggest different criteria for selecting participants in each setting. In addition, your answers will probably also underscore for you the importance of identifying participants thoughtfully. The story segment below illustrates this latter point.

Negotiations about South Africa: Mediator Michael Young decided to initiate the process (that included elements of both a collaborative planning process and a mediation) with participants who could predict what would be acceptable to the decision-makers and who had ties to and influence with decision-makers, but who were not decision-makers themselves. If official negotiations on ending apartheid were held, the South African President and the African National Congress (ANC) would be two key participants. The ANC was the most powerful of the insurgent groups, but it was by no means the only insurgent group. Young surmised based on the preparatory work he had done, however, that if the government and

Reuters photo

ANC agreed on how official talks would be held, their agreement would carry the day with other stakeholders who might not otherwise be at the table.

Thabo Mbeki clearly fit Young's criterion as someone who had influence with the ANC but was not the immediate decision-maker himself. He agreed to join by the second meeting and soon emerged as the leading voice in the ANC delegation to the mediation. Mbeki had grown up around the ANC; his father was active in the organization and the younger Mbeki knew the original leaders. At the time of the talks, Thabo Mbeki was a member of the ANC executive committee and considered by many to be the second in command. The ANC had yet other reasons, tragic ones, to trust Mbeki's devotion to the cause—Mbeki's brother was killed because of his involvement with the ANC, and Mbeki's son was killed as he tried to leave South Africa to join his father's work with the ANC. In addition, Young assessed that Mbeki would be thoughtful about alternative choices for South Africa's future. Mbeki had taken advantage of his 28 years outside South Africa to earn bachelor's and master's degrees in economics at the University of Sussex and receive military training in the Soviet Union, and he had worked throughout Africa.

Who could predict the government's stance and be an effective negotiator with the ANC? It could not be a member of the government that considered the ANC an illegal organization and publicly refused to negotiate with the ANC until it stopped its violence. Young selected Willie Esterhuyse, a prominent Afrikaner professor who grew up as an insider in the Afrikaner community that dominated the government but was a staunch opponent of apartheid. Esterhuyse would want the negotiations to succeed and would be realistic about what it would take.

As negotiations progressed, Michael Young and the original participants decided to add others. Once bilateral talks started, these choices were group choices, not Young's alone. Young reflected, "We discussed [how the South African economy would function post-apartheid] at length during the second stage of our activities and I exposed the players to those who run and have experience of running sophisticated and complex economies in the developed and developing world. This was not to condition the players to any particular model but to show what might be possible if [gross domestic product] growth is important for sustained economic activity. Equally the geo-political and economic environment in which our discussions were being conducted was important so that all remained current and were fully briefed on what the world was doing and thinking."[1]

Esterhuyse's anti-apartheid activities meant that the government did not have the confidence in him that the ANC had in Mbeki. In fact, once Esterhuyse became involved with the mediation, South African government agents began trailing him. Soon President P.W. Botha's head of security met privately with Esterhuyse and issued an ultimatum—Esterhuyse had to inform him regularly about the "secret" discussions. Esterhuyse decided to confide in Mbeki that he was having secret discussions with government security. In this way, the government had become a participant in the negotiations, but only in the "one-way" sense that the government heard what was going on while not disclosing its positions. Making matters more complicated, the Minister of Justice also was negotiating with the imprisoned Nelson Mandela, who had been cut off from confidential communications with others in the ANC. At some risk, the ANC smuggled word to Mandela about the Michael Young talks to thwart the possibility that government negotiators would play Mandela and the ANC against each other.

After five years of talks, the negotiating teams were getting close to agreement and Esterhuyse's inability to speak for the incoming President loomed as the next obstacle. F.W. de Klerk would probably soon become President and he seemed not to take the head of security into his confidence. Young knew that he needed to expand participants—to reach someone who had de Klerk's ear. He made an unusual choice, inviting the next President's brother to join the talks. It worked. De Klerk's brother communicated periodically with de Klerk, and that removed the obstacle to continuing talks to reach the agreement discussed above (pp. 58-60) to hold official talks on the end of apartheid, release Nelson Mandela, and end the banning of the ANC (Harvey, 2001:163, 169).

---

1. Email to authors, April 25, 2011.

Choosing in order to achieve enduring resolution: Young's initial thoughtfulness in selecting participants and then in modifying the selections averted impasse at several points in the negotiations. Given the importance of participant selection in this example, you may want to consult commentary by designers who work in a similar context to yours in order to spur thought about whether you have the right participants. Michael Young, for example, might have decided that his mediation had dynamics similar to public policy mediation. In that setting, Susan Carpenter suggests asking who is:

- "knowledgeable about the issues at hand;
- "able to work productively with others;
- "supported by their constituency;
- "interested in participating; and
- "available for periodic meetings . . ."? (Carpenter, 1999:93).

Similar commentary might help you, as a new designer in a given context, ask some of the questions that Young knew to ask, given his experience. The importance and complexity of selecting the right participants also counsels for spending time to understand the context for those choices, as the South African process demonstrates.

Special considerations when systemic change is a goal: One of the critical questions in selecting participants is whether systemic change ought to be considered in addition to, or even, at times, instead of the presenting dispute among parties (Sturm and Gadlin, 2007:3). If systemic change is to be considered at the beginning or later in the process, designers may want to include as parties those organizational actors with authority to act and others who might assist in doing the "root cause analysis" that will help move discussion from the individual case to underlying system problems (Sturm and Gadlin, 2007:42). Alternately, designers may bifurcate the process choices—focusing some on resolving the immediate disputes and organize others aimed at systems change. This point guided the Truth and Reconciliation Commission of Canada, particularly in its role to bring about reconciliation:

Truth and
Reconciliation
Commission of Canada

The aftermath of Canada's Indian Residential Schools: The class action settlement group specified that the Truth and Reconciliation Commission include participation from the broader Aboriginal communities who sought changes. The Commission should reach well beyond compensation of the survivors, should hear from more than the survivors of the schools, and should hold events that would include and educate the general public. In its interim report, the Truth and Reconciliation Commission of Canada points out the importance of involving the government and opinion leaders within the nation in any initiatives for change. As for the government, the report notes that the Indian Residential Schools were only one aspect of a general assimilationist policy. "Reconciliation . . . will require changes in the relationships between Aboriginal people and the government of Canada." As for the people in general, the report notes that reconciliation is not possible with all Canadians until they respect the

Aboriginal people. "Canadians generally have been led to believe—by what has been taught and not taught in schools—that Aboriginal people were and are uncivilized, primitive, and inferior, and continue to need to be civilized…. It will take time to re-establish respect. Effective reconciliation will see Aboriginal people regaining their sense of self-respect, and the development of relations of mutual respect between Aboriginal and non-Aboriginal people" (Truth and Reconciliation Commission of Canada, 2012:26-27; *see also* the final report, Truth and Reconciliation Commission of Canada, 2015).

Involving lawyers, represented clients, and other representatives: Sometimes lawyers overcome barriers by promoting more informed agreements and bringing their experience on how to organize negotiations and on workable outcomes from similar cases. In both consensual and litigation contexts, lawyer representatives may contribute to the fairness of the result, reduce overconfidence, and help in handling strong emotions of parties. Depending on their training and experience, however, these same representatives may impede the process and escalate conflict, introducing new barriers to success in negotiations. Research about barriers to agreement and satisfaction with dispute resolution processes suggests caution when any representatives are negotiating on behalf of others.

RESEARCH ON BARRIERS SOMETIMES INTRODUCED WHEN PEOPLE ARE REPRESENTED BY COUNSEL

Legalizing the dispute: When civil litigation is underway, negotiation frequently revolves narrowly around the monetized outcomes typical in courts and thus does not "expand the pie" to include the wide range of party interests (Relis, 2009:232; Riskin and Welsh, 2008:868) or the involvement of others who would not be parties to litigation. This approach tends to "fix the pie," limiting value creation and making it more difficult for the parties to achieve a wide range of interests—for example, in telling their stories, enhancing relationships, hearing an explanation. All of this can leave the parties feeling that they have not been heard and understood during the process (Macfarlane, 2008:71).

Principal/agent tension: "The interests of lawyers … in a negotiation may differ from those of [their clients,] creating the potential for greater than necessary transaction costs and for outcomes that do not fully address the interests of the parties. The financial interests of lawyers may be in tension with the interests of their clients. Contingent fee lawyers, for example, tend to give priority to monetized settlement outcomes and perhaps to quick settlement" (Mnookin et al., 2004:228), and hourly fee lawyers have few incentives to settle quickly, especially when there are good professional reasons to seek more information (Kritzer, 1991:45). Further, attorneys have their reputations and relationships to consider, especially when negotiating with repeat players—insurance claims agents or other lawyers, for example (Mnookin and Gilson, 1994:552-553).

"Tolerance for ambiguity and risk—alternatively the desire for complete information—may vary between lawyer and client, especially when the client bears the marginal costs of seeking more information. . . . Former general counsel of Motorola, Richard Weise, observed that '[l]awyers, as a class, are not up for much risk. They like to get all the facts before making a decision'" (Mnookin et al., 2004:230).

"Attorneys, as well as other agents, also bring to the resolution of disputes their own perspectives, experiences and preferences, and these may differ from those of the principals" (Cole et al., 2017-2018:§3:9).

Strategic protection of litigation information: Disclosure of information in negotiation can lead to its use by the opposing counsel to shape the discovery of evidence that will not be privileged if settlement is not achieved. As a consequence, lawyers often advise clients to hold back disclosing information that might provide the basis for enlarging the pie and widening settlement options out of fear of its strategic use in subsequent litigation.

Law practice organization: Hectic law practices with many open cases and multiple court deadlines makes it likely that lawyers will not be able to respond quickly to communications from clients or opposing counsel to help move negotiation forward efficiently. Moreover, negotiation among attorneys does not directly include clients whose only experience of case resolution may be the receipt of copies of correspondence between lawyers and reviews of proposed settlements. The limited contact with the settlement process and with either the other party or legal authorities limits the sense of "procedural justice" experienced by clients in negotiation. These perceptions of procedural justice—of the role that parties have and of how others treat them—count as much or more heavily as the outcomes or costs when people assess their experience with a dispute resolution process (Lind et al., 1990; Lind and Tyler, 1988:1-2).

Negotiation approach: "The empirical evidence supports the widespread perception that competitive rather than cooperative negotiation dominates in the context of litigation, even though lawyers commonly prefer a cooperative approach" (Cole et al., 2017-2018:§3:10).

Designers who identify these representation-related issues may seek ways to use the design to overcome them. They may involve the clients as well as their representatives in the process as a means to overcome principal-agent dissonance, for example.

Delegating the choice: In designing systems, as distinct from the single-conflict mediation like the South African example, the designer and the intervenor may be different persons. In the system context, should the designer then identify participants or leave the choice to the intervenor? For example, should a teacher always be asked to participate in truancy mediation or should the mediator decide in each case? Shifting to an adjudication example, should an investigatory commission be given subpoena power and the decision-making capacity to select the participants and subpoena them to hearings? You may elect to delegate the selection of participants to the intervenor as a means of tailoring participation in each dispute.

B. CHOOSING INTERVENORS

Both perception and reality count in choosing effective intervenors.[2] The intervenors should be good at what they do, of course. But the participants' confidence in an intervenor also matters as it affects their willingness to participate, to be candid, and to feel confident about the result. In fact, researchers report that in mediation between represented parties, "the mediator's inability to gain the confidence of the parties was the major reason for his or her lack of success" (Goldberg et al., 2009:277. *See also* Poitras, 2009:307). So, too, perceptions of an intervenor can influence whether funders commit resources for the initiative and whether the public has confidence in the outcomes. Being good and being assumed to be good thus overlap for intervenors.

Still, intervenors assumed by attorneys or participants to be good at the start may not be effective, and intervenors not assumed to be good at the start may gain participants' and others' confidence during the process. For example, attorneys tend to believe that experts in the substantive area of the mediation will perform best but will afterward give as high marks to non-expert mediators, as discussed below. Designers can expand the potential pool of mediators by considering:

- what it takes to be an effective intervenor and then how to develop confidence in that effective intervenor, even if others do not assume the intervenor to be good at the start; and
- how to help intervenors who already have the confidence of potential participants become more effective.

1. What it takes to be selected and accepted as an intervenor

Whether the intervenor will be selected by participants or earn their trust depends on the context. Consider these contexts and the effects on the parties' or public's willingness to participate in or trust in either the mediator or the adjudicator:

- A former U.S. federal judge and congressional leader, George Mitchell, was the successful mediator of the Belfast Peace Agreement (also called the "Good Friday Accords"), though he had no track record mediating sectarian violence.
- Justice Murray Sinclair, the first Aboriginal judge in the Manitoba courts, a

---

2. An "intervenor" becomes involved to help resolve a dispute, either by assisting in negotiations or by making a decision. Mediators, arbitrators, and facilitators, for example, are intervenors.

respected figure with awards from the Aboriginal community for his work in Aboriginal law and honorary degrees from several universities, serves as Chair of the Truth and Reconciliation Commission of Canada.

- Two Jewish students with no experience with Catholicism successfully facilitated learning dialogues among Catholic clergy and lay people while many of the same Catholics balked at suggestions that a neutral priest or nun serve as facilitators.

In each instance, and in the example below, perceptions of the intervenor mattered, but not always for the same reasons.

Cure Violence Chicago: Fundamental to Cure Violence's approach is the recognition that shootings often arise from disputes, and many are solvable conflicts if workable options to violence can be found. The potential shooter might be trying to respond to the problem of someone stealing a girlfriend, to retaliate for another shooting, or to react to perceived disrespect. But, even the most experienced mediators in the nation would not be able to help negotiate peaceful solutions if the parties were reluctant to talk to the mediator. Cure Violence would have to find mediators whom the potential shooters would trust, and who could be counted upon not to be police informers. To solve this problem, as we have seen, Cure Violence employed individuals—many of whom had criminal records—who had considerable "street credentials."

How would other stakeholders view the hiring of persons from the neighborhood, often with serious criminal records? Executive Director Gary Slutkin and Chicago Director Hardiman explored this with funders, police, and neighbors. "We cannot do this with angels," Hardiman would say; Slutkin explained, "We are not doing this to be nice, but because it is needed. To change behavior, you need access, credibility, and trust." Some people understood. Some did not. Later, the Cure Violence national and international training unit developed training and support for violence interrupters and reinforced their resolve not to re-offend. The interrupters were taught to detect, interrupt, mediate, and follow through. Research in several cities indicates that Cure Violence has reduced gun violence in program neighborhoods (*see* pp. 336-338). The risks that Cure Violence took in employing ex-offenders to do this work appear to have paid off, although it risked undermining the confidence in the program of some stakeholders—particularly police, but also government funders. Program leaders dealt with that issue by explaining the choice persistently, and the evidence of effectiveness has buttressed their explanations.

Like the Cure Violence designers, you may encounter the need to explain your intervenor selection. For example, attorneys may ask for intervenors who are former judges or experts in the pertinent area of law, but the client might be able to afford only intervenors with a general knowledge of the law and not at the salary level that would attract a former judge. Moreover, in many cases, former judges are seasoned lawyers and less likely to have the skills and process-design creativity needed to be as effective as those with less legal knowledge but more experience helping parties resolve complex problems.

This mismatch between desires and resources may not be fatal to the design, however. Research documents a disconnect between the characteristics attorneys value *when they select* mediators for their cases and the characteristics that lead to settlement and positive reactions from attorneys and parties *after mediation*. When asked who would be the best mediators before mediation, attorneys tend to give considerable weight to judicial experience and expertise in the field of law at issue in the case (McAdoo, 2002:434-435). Afterwards, attorneys give as high, if not higher, evaluation to mediators who have never served as judges and who do not have special expertise in the legal issues of the case (Wissler, 2011a:320). Also, the parties seem to settle as often whether or not their mediator had expertise in the field of law at issue and have no different perceptions of the fairness or benefit of the process depending on this expertise by the mediator (Pearson and Thoennes, 1988:434-436, 450). In such situations someone who *is* good is not always assumed to be good. Because both matter, part of the design challenge may be to help participants appreciate the quality of the intervenor, much as Hardiman and Slutkin did for the Cure Violence interrupters.

2. What it takes to be an effective intervenor, once accepted

In the movie version of the early South African negotiations, the participants concluded their final session by watching on television the President's announcement that the government ended its ban of the African National Congress and was ready to begin official negotiations on a new constitution. Then they viewed live shots of Nelson Mandela leaving prison after 27 years. That represented an emotion-tinged culmination of years of negotiations—and one negotiator stopped to say to mediator Michael Young, "It takes a big man to make himself invisible" (PBS, "Endgame," 2009). This scripted suggestion of character and dedication to role as related to mediator success brings to mind the characteristics often sought in neutrals—temperament, dedication, and ability (ABA, 2010 (regarding judges)).

Most people would subscribe to these general traits for an intervenor, but they differ in the details of training, background, and approach. Some differences stem from context; others are more philosophical. In Maryland, the collaborative planning group convened by Chief Judge Bell (pp. 38-40) reached agreement within two years on how to expand the use of mediation but was less successful in agreeing on how to assure the quality of mediators in the system. What happened next in Maryland demonstrates the principal arguments in the debate about what constitutes a good mediation. Related to "seeming good," the story also demonstrates how a designer can bring about consensus in the midst of a debate about defining what constitutes "being good."

Maryland's collaborative process on mediator quality: The commentary and legal research provided to the Maryland commission showed disagreement nationally on assuring mediator quality. On the one hand, many states used entry-level qualifications that required educational degrees and specified the hours of mediation training for court mediators. Some included special mediation training for particular kinds of disputes or expertise in the substantive law at issue in the mediation. In addition, a number of mediator groups considered "certification" of mediators, who then could use that credential to gain certain appointments, and again debated criteria for the certification (ACR, 2004; ACR, 2010; ABA, 2008). Had a national consensus been reached on what level of qualifications were necessary to protect consumers? Some said yes. Mediators bolstered a consumer protection justification for the entry-level requirements with an argument that mediators would not gain regard as a profession unless entry-level requirements were high.

On the other hand, researchers could not substantiate that mediators with higher education, more mediation training, or expertise in the subject matter of the dispute mediated more effectively than those without. In fact, the only criterion tested that research could relate to a measure of higher quality was experience mediating, creating a chicken and egg problem of gaining experience before meeting entry-level requirements or a multi-stage qualification process (ACR, 2004).

Photo by Jonathan Franz

A national mediator organization opposed licensure for mediators and noted the positive effects of party-chosen mediators. The group urged caution before institutionalizing entry-level criteria that applied broadly and would reduce the size and diversity of the pool of mediators before being shown to improve quality. This national group noted a lack of agreement over what was quality mediation. It also urged research to develop performance-based testing methods for mediators (SPIDR, 1989; SPIDR, 1995; ACR, 2004). Adding another level of complexity to the debate, mediators disagreed on what should be the goal of mediation—settlement, reconciliation, respect, or something else (*see* pp. 264-265).

The Maryland commission's division mirrored the national debate. Ultimately, Chief Judge Bell and Director Wohl suggested that they issue their plan for increasing dispute resolution choices for the state, including the only statement regarding mediator quality on which they agreed—that Maryland should use high-quality mediators and that Wohl and her staff should continue consensus building on the details.

The staff of the Maryland program then hired a consultant to work with a group of stakeholders on providing these details. That process took another three years.

At the beginning of the three-year process, the consultant noted that the multiple positions on mediator quality might be synthesized as choices between high and low initial hurdles to become a mediator and high and low maintenance requirements to remain a mediator, thus reframing the discussions to an examination of pros and cons of each cell in the chart below:

High initial hurdle/Low maintenance	High initial hurdle/High maintenance
Low initial hurdle/Low maintenance	Low initial hurdle/High maintenance

The stakeholder group held hearings throughout the state and listened to hundreds of mediators. Group members asked the mediators what contributed to making them good. Few mentioned educational qualifications and other aspects of the "high initial hurdle" requirements, and many mentioned ongoing mentoring, experience, education, and ethics. The stakeholder group began to realize that the professional image they sought for mediators could emerge from a membership organization that required this ongoing improvement. Eventually, most of the group favored a low initial hurdle/high maintenance approach to quality—what the consultant framed as "quality assistance" rather than the illusive "quality assurance."

After another series of public hearings and new stakeholder group meetings, those involved reached consensus on assisting mediators to achieve quality without requiring that they meet entry-level requirements beyond 40 class hours of mediation training. They also expressed agreement that the training could be for a variety of mediation approaches. Those mediators who joined the new Maryland quality initiative had to agree to abide by Maryland's mediator ethics, cooperate in the event that consumers complained, take ethics classes, and engage in skills improvement every year. For these members, the newly created entity provided free training, updates, and networking, and publicized the mediators in an online directory. Performance testing was available for improvement, not as an entry-level requirement. Maryland's online directory for consumers gave information about member mediators' substantive law expertise and mediation experience, but let the consumer decide the importance of each criterion.

The stakeholder group made another decision that facilitated consensus. They would not seek to require courts, government programs, or community programs to use only members to mediate, though they hoped that would occur. Though not compelled to do so, many courts and some other providers have followed their approach voluntarily. More than 1,000 Maryland mediators have joined the initiative. Few consumers have complained to the ombuds.

In 2010, MACRO's Deputy Director Lou Gieszl became president of the Association for Conflict Resolution, a professional organization for ADR practitioners in and beyond the United States. In 2011, the Association for Conflict

Resolution adopted mediation program standards that reflected much of what was learned through collaborative discourse in Maryland. https://cdn.ymaws .com/acrnet.org/resource/resmgr/docs/ModelStandardsCertification.pdf. In 2012, a performance-based certification program for community mediators in Maryland became the first to meet ACR's new standards. In other words, though at first stymied by debates about mediator quality, Maryland's commission eventually helped change the national approaches to this difficult issue.

The viewpoint among Maryland stakeholders shifted and coalesced regarding criteria to determine a good mediator. That new consensus on mediator quality removed a logjam. It also produced an implicit commitment to what Donald Schön called "reflective practice"—that a central part of quality is to engage practitioners in active self-examination about and collective discussion of issues, techniques, ethical questions, successes and failures (Schön, 1983:128-167). In this view, quality is emergent and always in the process of creation and refinement. Does the Maryland program in fact produce better mediators? It is too early to tell, but an April 2014 report offers some answers, https://www.courts.state.md.us/ sites/default/files/import/courtoperations/pdfs/adrlandscape.pdf (pp.35-46).

Law professor Susan Sturm and former NIH Ombuds Howard Gadlin suggest another important criterion for selecting intervenors. They note that when the system designer anticipates both dealing with individual disputes and promoting or enabling systemic changes to prevent future problems and strengthen the organization, this might affect who should serve as intervenor. They describe the "boundary-spanning, institutional intermediary" as a person or office "located at the intersection of multiple, interrelated systems" but in some sense independent of them (Sturm and Gadlin, 2007:39). NIH's Center for Cooperative Resolution is just such an office. Reporting only to the NIH Director, the office nonetheless is relatively autonomous but works collaboratively with the many centers and institutes at NIH. By position and reputation, its staff can convene relevant parties at various stages of conflict resolution efforts so that, when appropriate, systemic problems can be identified and addressed.

Because most traits for intervenors would add value, stakeholders may want them all. But resources and circumstances may force prioritization among these traits. For example, budgetary constraints may lead designers to use intervenors from within an organization, whether or not they have the talent, training, or disposition to be effective. At other times, the client may have selected an "implementation team" to launch the new dispute resolution system. Members of a design and implementation team who have spent many hours collaboratively creating a system may reasonably expect to be among the set of those who will be used as mediators, facilitators, or other intervenors. If some members of the implementation team clearly lack the talent to be effective intervenors, designers must devise strategies to train those individuals or find ways to keep them out of roles that would be destructive to the overall success of the system.

In one organizational context, the client had already designated a team to implement the system recommended by the design team. As the designers started to work with the new implementation team it became clear that at least one member of the team lacked the interpersonal demeanor and disposition to be effective in the effort. Simply cutting this person out was risky, however, because she held sway with an important constituency in the organization. To deal with this, the designers brainstormed a productive role for this person in the execution of the overall system—one that was better aligned with her talents and less likely to threaten the overall success of the new system. Thus, the pre-designation of the intervenors led the designers to prioritize among the desired traits for the intervenors.

Another approach to the practical limitations on securing intervenors with all desired traits is to expand the pool of effective intervenors. In the next example, a designer seized on the fact that a large number of people can serve effectively as adjudicators if they are part of a jury or group. He also realized he could leverage the inherent trust that some people have for traditional tribunals as part of his system design. He used these observations to create a more accessible adjudicative process.

---

eBay and Afghan traditions: The United States Agency for International Development (USAID) sought ideas from eBay resolutions executives on ways to improve the Afghan justice system so that Afghan citizens would have more confidence in the rule of law. USAID had focused on helping to improve the quality and independence of the nation's official court system. Geography and travel conditions impeded USAID's initiative to train judges and to educate people about their rights, however. One judge, who walked for eight days to reach the training, detailed the challenges:

> "'As you can see, I am an old man,' [said] the judge, who walked 14 hours per day, sleeping in mosques and in homes of distant relatives and strangers. 'Along the way, there were many problems. It was raining, there were no roads, and we had to cross mountains'" (USAID, 2008).

These same conditions made it difficult for some parties to appear in Afghan courts if they did not live nearby. Experts also noted that people often expressed more confidence in traditional village justice than the justice delivered by the courts. When USAID officials heard about eBay's community court in India, they invited Rule to offer ideas for a supplementary type of intervenor for Afghanistan.

The judges in the traditional Afghan system are village elders. The process, as well as the identity of the judges, contributes to public confidence in their tribunal. If the parties are from different villages or ethnic groups, the elders asked by one party to convene a tribunal will invite equal numbers of elders from the other party's village or group. The panel gathers beneath a tree, in a mosque, or elsewhere. It operates based on traditions rather than laws. The elders deliberate until reaching a decision, but junior members defer by tradition to the opinions of the most respected senior members, who in turn listen first to the more junior members. Although enjoying the confidence of many Afghans, the traditional system faces geographic challenges as disputes develop between people from different parts of the nation.

The eBay resolutions executives assumed the accuracy of the assumptions about the village elder system just stated (though see Chapter 5 for process questions one might pose) and suggested allowing disputants to access the tribunal of elders on cell phones. The traditional intervenors had been good decision-makers in the eyes of the people for centuries. They were plentiful in number and worked without pay. To preserve trusted intervenors but overcome cost and travel obstacles, the parties could record statements back and forth on cell phones and send the accumulated recording to the tribunal, which could deliberate in person or by phone (Rule and Nagarajan, 2010:9-12).

Having a "good" intervenor may often include, as it did in the Afghan proposal, a trusted and accessible intervenor. To facilitate use of these trusted individuals, the designer may suggest eliminating high entry-level required credentials for intervenors, at least on a trial basis.

The Maryland experience, over time, may demonstrate the importance of enhancing intervenors' learning from experience through reflective practice. It may also underscore the importance of developing shared values among the intervenors. Both the Afghan and Maryland stories emphasize that "being good" and "being assumed to be good" overlap, and that a designer can play a role in improving both perception and quality.

C.   ENGAGING PARTICIPANTS: HOW AND WHEN

Former Indian Residential Schools students took advantage of the revised Canadian claims facility (replacing the process put in place by the government a few years earlier) with relatively few exercising their rights to opt out (pp. 33-34). Unfortunately, it is not always, or perhaps even typically, the case that the targeted parties are willing to become involved in the processes created by dispute design teams and their stakeholder partners. At times, people in conflict will flock to a process; other times they will demur or even resist. In six of the seven examples introduced in Chapter 2, designers had to devise strategies to persuade those in conflict to use the processes they had created or made available. Figuring out when and how to engage participants is a critical part of designers' work.

There are challenges in engaging participants in all types of processes. For example, this book discusses proposals for cell phone participation in proceedings before elders in Afghanistan (pp. 158-159), the pressures to comply with online arbitration awards through eBay (pp. 118-119), the proposal for a United Nations protocol for online consumer disputes (pp. 119-120), and arbitration clauses (Appendix B).

Of course, there is always the possibility that the processes do not meet stakeholders' needs. But that may not be the reason that stakeholders may balk at participating. The research discussed below regarding mandatory mediation indicates that those reluctant to participate often find that mediation meets their needs. People and organizations resist mediating for a variety of reasons including that they distrust the other parties to the dispute (*see* Chapter 9 on relationships), desire to appear confident about success in litigation or another process, lack understanding of the process or even of the availability of the forum, receive counsel from an attorney not to join the process, had a past bad experience with a process, or simply tend to avoid or procrastinate (*see* Matz, 1987:4-5). In the face of such barriers, even publicized and high-quality processes might not attract voluntary participation.

Persuading participants to become engaged: The designers found ways to get the parties engaged, despite their initial reluctance, in each of the examples below.

 Sanford, Florida: Bringing in the U.S. Community Relations Service to help engage key parties: Sanford city official Andrew Thomas suggested that fellow city officials call the U.S. Department of Justice's Community Relations Service, understanding that community-wide mediations often fail because at least one stakeholder refuses to come to the table. Aware of this problem, the Community Relations Service sends mediators to intervene in civil rights conflicts without an agreement by some stakeholders to mediate. The mediators often angle for an invitation and sponsorship by city officials or others, but, failing that, they sometimes begin their work without invitation. The mediators shuttle among groups that resist a joint mediation, such as police, hate groups, civil rights advocates, and fearful neighbors. The Justice Department affiliation may make some persons wary of refusing to talk with these mediators or perhaps more trusting of their intentions. The mediators use the involvement of some stakeholders to bring aboard reluctant ones. "If the mayor and city council are going to make a decision, wouldn't you like them to have your input?" (Levine, 2005:25-29.) Whatever the reason, the Community Relations Service has achieved impressive success in helping stakeholders agree to parade routes that avoid violence, plan for police-community dialogue, change discriminatory policies, and avert violence in many other contexts. The CRS mediators have succeeded, when other mediation efforts have failed, because of their ability to convene discussions, even if not face to face, about the controversy (id.). In Sanford, they reached many stakeholders by organizing local clergy into a new organization, Sanford Pastors Connecting, and through that group reached a number of additional stakeholders.

The community mediation experience of offering mediation, but few coming: During the late 1970s, the U.S. Justice Department invested in community mediation programs that could serve as alternatives to court for ordinary people. Mediation was free for the parties, and evaluations showed that those using them settled in high percentages and found the programs satisfying, fair, and inexpensive. Nonetheless, the centers failed to attract many users, even in large cities. The community mediation programs kept costs low by using volunteer mediators. The volume was so low, though, that one program's cost per case exceeded $1,000 in today's dollars, an expense that seemed high in relation to the stakes of the disputes.

Some community mediation programs survived because they revised the ways that they convened the parties, thereby increasing volume. They encouraged police and prosecutor referrals to mediation, for example, often with both parties uncertain whether a prosecution would occur if the parties did not participate in the mediation. In some cities, the courts began requiring parties to use mediators from the local community mediation program. The increased volume lowered per case costs, making it possible to justify the benefits to funders. Surprisingly, the settlement and party satisfaction rates persisted despite pressures to participate (Cole et al., 2017-2018:§4:2).

Inside a legal department reticent to change: Corporate in-house counsel estimate that they spend over $10,000 for every month that a business-to-business case is in litigation. A number of large corporations support the International Institute for Conflict Prevention and Resolution (CPR) in an effort to reduce the costs of conflict, though also with the expectation of other benefits such as reducing disruption of business relationships. A team of researchers sampled the business disputing in six large corporations. In four of the corporations, general counsel had signed the CPR pledge to explore the use of dispute resolution (such as mediation) before resorting to litigation. The research showed, nonetheless, no greater use of mediation by two of these four corporations than by the corporations in which the general counsel did not encourage the use of mediation.

At the first of the companies making greater use of mediation, the lawyers usually did not suggest mediation until late in the dispute, after formal discovery. Overall, that company's use of mediation did not shorten litigation.

At the second of the companies making greater use of mediation, the lawyers instead suggested mediation before formal discovery in most disputes. We will call this company that made frequent early use of mediation the Acme Company. Disputes involving Acme were resolved with about ten fewer months of litigation than disputes involving any of the other five companies.

The researchers interviewed lawyers in each of the six corporations. They discovered that lawyers for all corporations making little use of mediation were reluctant to bring their clients to mediation. These in-house counsel thought client involvement caused problems and so found ways to avoid using mediation even if their superiors were urging greater use. In fact, in all but the corporation using mediation early, the lawyers thought that it was irresponsible to discuss settlement seriously in big cases until they had completed discovery. By that time, as one lawyer said, the case was usually ready for trial and would likely settle anyway, even without mediation.

But, at Acme, the lawyers viewed client participation as a positive and saw no problems with settling early, as the mediator could facilitate an informal exchange of the information needed to assess the value of the case. Acme's in-house counsel usually tried to schedule mediation before litigating.

Acme's general counsel confided in researchers that his lawyers had once embraced the same views researchers found at the other five corporations. At first, the general counsel sent the lawyers to educational programs about mediation and told them to make greater use of mediation. Nothing changed. Ultimately, general counsel required the lawyers to fill out a detailed, multipage form any time that they did not suggest mediation before beginning formal discovery. The form asked them to explain to general counsel in excruciating detail what each aspect of discovery would cost the client and why it would be better, taking into account these costs, to complete that aspect of discovery before mediation. They also explicitly tracked time to resolution and adopted a clear goal of continuing to reduce that time interval, knowing that earlier settlement generally entailed lower costs. Immediately, the lawyers on his staff began routinely suggesting mediation before filing litigation.

The Acme lawyers' next challenge was to persuade opposing counsel to agree to mediation. They developed a number of strategies. Concerned that their counterparts were distrustful of their suggestion (*see* reactive devaluation, p. 417), they allowed opposing counsel to propose the mediator, saying that Acme would insist only that the mediator had substantial experience mediating. These lawyers reasoned that they lost no strategic advantage, relying on mediation qualifications research that could identify no factor other than experience mediating as related to improved settlement.

They also engaged opposing counsel in conversations about which corporate representatives should attend the mediation, assuring them that it would be best to have comparable parties attend. Acme lawyers suggested to opposing counsel that all parties should select persons who were not so involved as to be emotionally attached while close enough to the dispute to be knowledgeable and helpful.

Acme's lawyers enthusiastically endorsed the frequent and early use of mediation by the time researchers interviewed them. They did not mention the organizational incentives and disincentives that helped them come to this view (Rogers and McEwen, 1998:841-845).

Each of the situations just discussed involved an intervention after a dispute arose. Each required ingenuity to engage the participants at the right time to meet stakeholders' goals for the process, even though participation was not mandatory in the sense of a court order, statutory requirement, or contract clause. Different strategies were used each time—police referral, invoking the Justice Department name, and creating a "speed bump" to the expensive formal discovery phase of litigation by requiring attorneys fill out a form—to secure participation by reluctant participants.

Providing multiple entry points: Research suggests that if one goal of a dispute processing system is to surface and address conflict within an organization or system, it can be helpful to provide multiple points of entry into the system (Sturm and Gadlin, 2007:14). The reason is simple. Persons in conflict may have different sensitivities and varying degrees of trust in particular individuals and offices within an organization. As discussed regarding the National Institutes of Health system (pp. 125-127), if the only entry way into a dispute resolution system is through a supervisor and the aggrieved party does not trust or feel comfortable with the supervisor, then the participant is unlikely to use the system. If, on the other hand, aggrieved individuals know they can turn to an ombuds, a union steward, an EEOC office, or a supervisor in another division for advice on how to proceed, it is more likely that the conflict will surface and be addressed. Of course, the more entry points into a system, the more important it is that each potential entry point person be well trained in how to handle complaints and how to advise a disputant.

Considering whether to make certain processes mandatory: Is it counterproductive to engage parties using organizational handbooks, court or administrative agency orders, statutory requirements, or pre-dispute contract clauses that require participation? Will the parties merely "go through the motions" if they attend unwillingly? Psychologist Roselle Wissler found little difference in party or lawyer satisfaction with mediation or settlement rates between the group that was ordered to mediation and the group that participated voluntarily (looking at state and federal courts in Ohio). In one study, settlement rates increased slightly when one party had suggested the mediation, though the court may have required the other party to participate (Wissler, 2004:(2):69). Wissler's findings in this respect resemble those in a variety of court programs throughout the nation (Cole et al., 2017-2018:§14:21).

Research on parties mediating pursuant to pre-dispute mediation clauses also found settlement rates similar to those who decided to mediate after the dispute arose (Brett et al., 1996:262). Thus, mandatory programs, if structured well, seem well-received even by participants who were reluctant to participate at first unless the process will result in a decision. Participants often resist complying in the case of arbitration clauses (*see* discussion in Chapter 12; Appendix B).

Lawyers may be reluctant to ask for mediation until formal discovery is complete (pp. 127-128), so courts often direct the parties to mediation in order to shorten disposition time and therefore reduce the parties' costs. As discussed in the last chapter, research on court-annexed mediation shows that settlement rates are roughly the same for mediation set early in the dispute as for mediation nearer to trial. Generally, the early mediation referral will be less costly to the parties than referral nearer to trial. One sweet spot, in terms of settlement rates and cost reduction, seems to be after the start of formal discovery but before it ends (Cole et al., 2017-2018:§§14:22-23).

In sum, people in conflict may not act like typical consumers. They may reject, at least initially, a process that seems to be the right fit and to have the right price for reaching the kind of outcomes they want. Persuasion, listening, and empathy may overcome reluctance in some situations. At other times, ease of entry makes participant involvement more likely. Sometimes designers need to develop sophisticated strategies or even apply some leverage to convene participants. As you design processes and systems, you will want to consider the challenges you may face in getting participants to use the system and you will want to ensure that the design has features to address the barriers that might exist in your particular context.

D. PROVIDING RESOURCES FOR THE PARTICIPANTS

Research indicates that preparation of the participants increases their chances to reach a settlement (ABA, 2008), and it seems likely that similar results would occur if the goals are reaching consensus or improving understanding. In addition, as discussed above, when parties understand the processes in which they are participating, they report a higher degree of satisfaction with them (pp. 74-75). Certainly respect for the equity of the process increases if all parties are prepared. The comment below suggests yet another benefit in the public policy context— greater respect for the outcome.

> *Law professor Peter Shane on online deliberations:* "When people engage with difficult issues in a deliberate and informed way, the quality of their input improves, and it becomes more likely that government policy makers will take [their expression of] public opinion into account. Because there is likely to be a significant gap between the knowledge of government officials and the ability of most public participants to address public policy issues, the quality of information provided to participants is central to the success of online deliberation" (Shane, 2008:4).

Because preparation improves the success of, satisfaction within, fairness of, and respect for the process and result, you will want to consider ways to design a process or system so that participants have the preparation, information, and resources they need. Approaches to preparation for design initiatives, some already mentioned in this book, including:

- participation by child-development, financial, and other experts in collaborative law negotiations in the divorce context (pp. 114-115);
- eBay's negotiation preparation and techniques (pp. 25-26);
- inclusion of economics experts in the South African negotiations (p. 148);
- encouragement of lawyers' participation with their clients in mediation sessions (pp. 150-151);
- provision of information and question-and-answer sessions about how the process works, as Ken Feinberg did after designing the 9/11 compensation system (p. 79);
- design of a training program to give participants the skills they need to engage successfully in a difficult conversation, as designers working in the Catholic Church did when creating a safe space dialogue; and
- distribution of a list of questions for participants to consider in advance of a process so that they are less caught off guard or emotionally aroused in a negative way when a sensitive issue is raised.

Unfortunately, a design client does not always share the designer's desire for prepared participants. For example, an employer might ask the designer to put a waiver of counsel during dispute resolution sessions into the employment agreement. This request creates a dilemma for the designer, as this waiver might create an uneven playing field between the novice employee and the legally sophisticated corporate representative. Or, a developer in a residential neighborhood anxious to get the zoning variance he needs to build a mall might argue that widely advertising community meetings about the proposed plan are unnecessary and that simply providing notice through a small advertisement in the community paper will suffice. In another example, a paying institutional client may demur when a designer suggests that sharing some financial and strategy planning with union membership in advance of negotiations might improve relations and allow for more amicable and successful negotiations.

These examples underscore the importance of educating the client, along with other stakeholders, in a collaborative planning process (Chapters 3 and 5.C; Appendix D). The prepared client may understand some of the benefits of participant preparation and seek strategies to achieve that. As discussed in the eBay example, one of the chief advantages of online dispute resolution has been the ease of educating parties so that a more balanced and therefore satisfying and just negotiation occurs (*see* Chapter 10). The eBay example underscores the importance of considering the resources and capabilities of the parties who would likely use the system as part of the design. It also suggests the importance of continuous evaluation and modification. What might look sensible on paper may not work out as planned in practice—for preparation of the parties as well as for others aspects of design. Whatever the context, preparation of participants should be on the list of pivotal design decisions.

THOUGHTS GOING FORWARD

The process or system that you design will work only if the people respond to it as you anticipate. If you leave out key participants, the design may lose effectiveness, fairness, or legitimacy. Identifying the participants will not be enough; in the midst of a dispute, at least one crucial prospective participant may be reticent to participate at all or to join in at the best time. Your design should take that into account. The choice of participants and intervenors may facilitate a broader focus for the process—even structural change—if you consider that aspect in the choice. You may decide to educate clients or stakeholders about the research concerning effective intervenors and the role of broader interests in the selection of participants, as much of this will be counterintuitive to them. Their understanding of the broader public needs and fairness concerns reduces the need for you as the designer to face tough policy issues about your role in a process that might not be fair or include public interests. Finally, your designed process or system should prepare those who will participate in the process or make certain, through representation or other means, that they will be prepared. Otherwise, parties will be less likely to reach agreement and may not respect its fairness, and those who learn about the process or system may question its legitimacy.

QUESTIONS

6.1   State officials of both major political parties have been vocal about their desires to change the redistricting process used to re-draw district boundaries for state legislators after the census every decade. Several nonprofit groups want to see this happen—they say that they exaggerate only slightly when they characterize the current redistricting system as allowing representatives to choose their voters rather than vice versa. In this state, redistricting change could be accomplished only by a voter-approved amendment to the state constitution that provides how members of the redistricting board are selected and/or the criteria the board applies. These groups have asked you to design and facilitate a process to build the consensus necessary for a state constitutional amendment to succeed.

They advise that few voters understand redistricting law and why it matters. As a result, their political experts counsel that a constitutional amendment would fail if a major political party opposes it or even if any group with the resources to buy television advertisements opposes it, unless those favoring it are willing and able to invest at least $5 million in publicity. Your clients think it unlikely anyone with resources would choose this issue for that level of investment. Who would you plan to involve initially in a process to build consensus on a constitutional change? Why?

6.2   In the South Africa mediation, each team was headed by someone of prominence. What are the pros and cons of seeking prominence in each of the redistricting negotiators discussed in question 6.1? What might be the possible effect if some negotiators are the heads of their organizations and others are junior staff members?

6.3 Question 6.2 pre-supposes that the designer will use an influential stakeholder approach to achieve public policy consensus. Suppose the designer decides instead to involve the general public as participants in shaping consensus on a revision of redistricting laws. What are the advantages and disadvantages of structuring the public's involvement in each of the ways below? Some scholars call this "deliberative democracy." ("Even in a representative democracy, direct, participatory democracy plays an important role in emphasizing and furthering public discussion, dialogue, or deliberation and thereby addressing public problems in ways that respect diverse interests and values" (Gastil and Keith, 2005:3).) If one of these "deliberative democracy" approaches is followed, will it also be necessary to use a process to build consensus among the political party leaders, business leaders, and other representatives of influential stakeholders?

    a. "*Citizen juries*": Organizers begin with a public opinion poll on the target topic and then select paid jurors who hold opinions in the same proportions as the survey respondents. The citizen jurors meet, often for several days, hear from experts, deliberate, and vote (Crosby and Nethercut, 2005:112-115).

    b. "*Deliberative polling*": The deliberative poll organizers select about 100 to 500 citizens by lot to represent the broader community and pay them to become educated and deliberate on a topic (Fishkin and Farrar, 2005:72-75). The deliberations and the votes that are taken are public, in one case televised by Public Broadcasting Service (watch at http://cdd.stanford.edu/polls/btp/).

    c. "*National issue forums*": Community groups frame issues of public importance and invite citizen participants, who receive a book with background on the issues and several prominent options for resolving the issue. A moderator guides discussion and leads the group to identify common ground (Melville et al., 2005:41-45).

6.4 One of Pauline Tesler's additions to the collaborative law process for family law negotiations was to involve jointly selected experts—financial, child-development, or others—as negotiation participants (pp. 114-115). In a similar vein, Michael Young added experts to discuss the South African economy post-apartheid (p. 148). What is another context in which it would help to invite experts to attend and participate in negotiations? For the context you suggest, what would be the advantages and disadvantages of including jointly selected rather than individual party-selected experts?

6.5 The Irish government paid for attorneys to represent the claimants before the Residential Institutions Redress Board, a government-created facility for claims arising from child abuse and neglect in government-funded, church-run institutions (http://www.rirb.ie). Most claims were resolved in negotiations with the government representative at the pre-hearing stage. As discussed above (pp. 150-151), research indicates that negotiations change with the involvement of attorneys as participants. How could a designer set up Redress Board settlement conferences to maximize the positive contributions attorneys made to these negotiations and minimize the negative contributions?

6.6 As a designer for a new court mediation program, what would you do to gain attorney confidence and trust in the court staff mediators if the court cannot afford to hire former judges or experts in each pertinent area of law?

6.7 What are a few of the pros and cons of selecting a well-known human rights advocate and Anglican archbishop, Desmond Tutu, to chair South Africa's Truth and Reconciliation Commission rather than a former judge or other law-trained person?

6.8 A survey of lawyers with cases in a federal district court indicates that they prefer a court staff mediator to all of the following: mediators who are federal judges, individuals in private mediation practice, and volunteer mediators (Wissler, 2011a:298). In light of the last question, how would you explain this result?

6.9 Select a situation—perhaps a dispute you have read about in the national news or learned about through this class—and imagine yourself as the designer of a system or process for that situation. List the questions you would ask yourself as you select the best intervenor for your forum.

6.10 As noted above, other high-volume, court-connected mediation programs that use non-staff mediators require the mediators to have educational qualifications, a certain number of hours of mediation training, and, occasionally, experience. However, research can confirm only that experienced mediators are sometimes better than inexperienced mediators in achieving settlements. Moreover, the body of research in high volume settings suggests that pre-mediation preparation of the parties, timing, and choice of participants matter more than mediator experience. In light of this research, how would you suggest that a university select mediators for its student-to-student mediation program?

6.11 Bar associations who rate judicial candidates rely on reputation—sometimes determined through attorney polls—supplemented by interviews of the candidate, opposing counsel, and others, and reviews of experience. They tend not to quantify their criteria. What are the pros and cons of using a similar approach to select mediators in a large-volume system? How should the judicial rating approach be adapted for mediator selection?

6.12 Major multinational companies now have units dedicated to corporate social responsibility (CSR). CSR efforts in China often focus on creating dispute processing systems for the many thousands of employees who might live and work in a factory. These employees are often short term, uneducated, and unaware of any rights that the law may or may not provide them. They frequently balk at raising issues to the management for fear of being fired or subjected to other reprisals. As a designer, what steps could you take to increase the likelihood of their participation, ensure that it is effective, and protect them from reprisal? What challenges might you face?

6.13 What factors would you consider in deciding how to advise the National Institutes of Health ombuds on whether to mandate participation in its mediation program through a clause in the employment contract?

6.14 Research indicates that parties tend to follow their attorney's counsel about whether and when to use mediation (Pearson et al., 1982:29; Wissler, 2004(1):478-479). In one study, attorneys indicated that their cases most often went to mediation because of judicial referral (Wissler, 2004(1):489). Outside of litigation, how might a designer influence the bar to recommend participation in other dispute resolution processes and do so at an early point in the dispute? What resistance might a designer face and how might she address it?

6.15 Designers develop their own lists of ideas for persuading reluctant parties to participate. For example, public policy mediator Susan Carpenter sometimes calls the initial gathering a "dialogue" or "workshop" because those terms do not seem to imply reaching agreement and therefore are less threatening (Carpenter, 1999:68). Name a few ideas that would be on your list.

Exercise 6.1 *Convening questions from Tallahoya University (see basic facts on pp. 42-44)*: You received this email from University counsel:

Hi!

I am forwarding a note that the Provost sent as he considers my budget requests to implement new disputing processes and systems. This is a good sign—senior administrators are taking my proposal seriously. Give me some of your thoughts—I need to send a response quickly.
Best wishes,
Sally

Sally,

I got your request to set aside funds for new processes. Life would be better if we could resolve these issues, so I am interested. But, I admit to being dubious about what you propose to deal with the mascot mess. Who would have to participate in this process? Wouldn't we just end up upsetting more people who don't know enough to understand the options? And why would we have to pay for intervenors for the proposed new harassment procedures and campus expansion issues process—can't we just use your lawyers as intervenors? One other thing—we're just renewing the agreement for landlords who want their apartments listed by our off-campus housing office—is that the point at which we should insert a clause requiring them to use the new off-campus housing processes? Can you get me some new language on the timing, etc. now? Sorry but I need this soon.
Cheers,
Rattan

BIBLIOGRAPHY AND REFERENCES

AMERICAN BAR ASSOCIATION SECTION OF DISPUTE RESOLUTION TASK FORCE ON IMPROVING MEDIATION QUALITY (2008) *Final Report*. Washington, DC: American Bar Association Section on Dispute Resolution.

AMERICAN BAR ASSOCIATION STANDING COMMITTEE ON THE FEDERAL JUDICIARY (2010) "What It Is and How It Works."

ASSOCIATION FOR CONFLICT RESOLUTION (2010) *2010 Model Standards for Mediation Certification*. Washington, DC: ACR.

ASSOCIATION FOR CONFLICT RESOLUTION TASK FORCE ON MEDIATOR CERTIFICATION (2004) *Report and Recommendations to the Board of Directors*. Washington, DC: ACR.

BOWN, Chad P., and Bernard M. HOEKMAN (2005) "WTO Dispute Settlement and the Missing Developing Country Cases: Engaging the Private Sector" 8 No. 4 *J. Int'l Econ. L.* 261.

BRANDON, Barbara H., and Robert D. CARLITZ (2002) "Online Rulemaking and Other Tools for Strengthening Our Civil Infrastructure," 54 *Admin. L. Rev.* 1421.

BRETT, Jeanne, Zoe I. BARSNESS, and Stephen B. GOLDBERG (1996) "The Effectiveness of Mediation: An Independent Analysis of Cases Handled by Four Major Service Providers," 12 *Negot. J.* 259.

CARPENTER, Susan (1999) "Choosing Appropriate Consensus Building Techniques and Strategies," in Lawrence Susskind, Sarah McKearnan, and Jennifer Thomas-Larmer eds., *The Consensus Building Handbook: A Comprehensive Guide to Reaching Agreement* 62. Thousand Oaks, CA: Sage Publications, Inc.

COLE, Sarah R. (2005) "Mediator Certification: Has the Time Come?," 11 (3) *Disp. Resol. Mag.* 7.

COLE, Sarah R., Nancy H. ROGERS, Craig A. McEWEN, James R. COBEN, and Peter N. THOMPSON (2017-2018) *Mediation: Law, Policy, Practice* (3rd ed.). Minneapolis: West.

CROSBY, Ned, and Doug NETHERCUT (2005) "Citizens Juries: Creating a Trustworthy Voice of the People," in John Gastil and Peter Levine eds., *The Deliberative Democracy Handbook: Strategies for Effective Civic Engagement in the Twenty-First Century* 111. San Francisco: Jossey-Bass.

FISHKIN, James, and Cynthia FARRAR (2005) "Deliberative Polling: From Experiment to Community Resource," in John Gastil and Peter Levine eds., *The Deliberative Democracy Handbook: Strategies for Effective Civic Engagement in the Twenty-First Century* 68. San Francisco: Jossey-Bass.

GALANTER, Marc (1974) "Why the 'Haves' Come Out Ahead: Speculations on the Limits of Legal Change," 9 *Law & Soc'y Rev.* 95.

GASTIL, John, and William M. KEITH (2005) "A Nation That (Sometimes) Likes to Talk: A Brief History of Public Deliberation in the United States," in John Gastil and Peter Levine eds., *The Deliberative Democracy Handbook: Strategies for Effective Civic Engagement in the Twenty-First Century* 3. San Francisco: Jossey-Bass.

GOLDBERG, Stephen B., Margaret L. SHAW, and Jeanne M. BRETT (2009) "What Difference Does a Robe Make? Comparing Mediators with and without Prior Judicial Experience," 25(3) *Negot. J.* 277 (July).

HARVEY, Robert (2001) *The Fall of Apartheid: The Inside Story from Smuts to Mbeki*. New York: Palgrave Macmillan.

HYMAN, Jonathan (2010) "Four Ways of Looking at a Lawsuit: How Lawyers Can Use the Cognitive Frameworks of Mediation," 34 *Wash. U. J.L. & Pol'y* 11.

KRITZER, Herbert (1991) *Let's Make a Deal: Understanding the Negotiating Process*. Madison, WI: University of Wisconsin Press.

LEVINE, BERTRAM J. (2005) *Resolving Racial Conflict: The Community Relations Service and Civil Rights, 1964-1989*. Columbia: University of Missouri Press.

LIND, E. Allen, and Tom R. TYLER (1988) *The Social Psychology of Procedural Justice*. New York: Plenum Press.

LIND, E. Allen, Robert J. MACCOUN, Patricia A. EBENER, William L.F. FELSTINER, Deborah R. HENSLER, Judith RESNIK, and Tom R. TYLER (1990) "In the Eye of the Beholder: Tort Litigants' Evaluation of Their Experiences in the Civil Justice System," 24 *Law & Soc'y Rev.* 953.

MACFARLANE, Julie (2008) *The New Lawyer: How Settlement Is Transforming the Practice of Law.* Vancouver: UBC Press.

MATZ, David E. (1987) "Why Disputes Don't Go to Mediation," *Conflict Resol. Q.* 3 (Fall).

McADOO, Bobbi (2002) "A Report to the Minnesota Supreme Court: The Impact of Rule 114 on Civil Litigation Practice in Minnesota," 25 *Hamline L. Rev.* 401.

McEWEN, Craig A., and Thomas MILBURN (1993) "Examining a Paradox of Mediation," 9 *Negot. J.* 23.

McGINN, Kathleen L., and Eric WILSON (2004) "How to Negotiate Successfully Online," *Negot.* (No. 3) 7.

McGOVERN, Francis (1986) "Toward a Functional Approach for Managing Complex Litigation," 53 *U. Chi. L. Rev.* 440.

MELVILLE, Keith, Taylor L. WILLINGHAM, and John R. DEDRICK (2005) "National Issues Forums: A Network of Communities Promoting Public Deliberation," in John Gastil and Peter Levine eds., *The Deliberative Democracy Handbook: Strategies for Effective Civic Engagement in the Twenty-First Century* 37. San Francisco: Jossey-Bass.

MNOOKIN, Robert H., and Ronald GILSON (1994) "Disputing Through Agents: Cooperation Between Lawyers in Litigation," 94 *Colum. L. Rev.* 509.

MNOOKIN, Robert H., Scott R. PEPPET, and Andrew S. TULUMELLO (2004) *Beyond Winning: Negotiating to Create Value in Deals and Dispute* (2d ed.). Cambridge, MA: Belnap Press of Harvard University Press.

MOFFITT, Michael L. (2009) "The Four Ways to Assure Mediator Quality (and Why None of Them Work)," 24 *Ohio St. J. on Disp. Resol.* 191.

PBS, Interview with Michael Young, *available at* http://mpt-legacy.wgbhdigital.org/wgbh/masterpiece/endgame/young.html (last visited June 19, 2018).

PEARSON, Jessica, Nancy THOENNES, and Lois VANDERKOOI (1982) "The Decision to Mediate: Profiles of Individuals Who Accept and Reject the Opportunity to Mediate Contested Child Custody and Visitation Issues," 6 *J. Divorce*, Fall/Winter 17.

PEARSON, Jessica, and Nancy THOENNES (1988) "Divorce Mediation Research Results," in Jay Folberg and Ann L. Milne eds., *Divorce Mediation: Theory and Practice* 429. New York: Guilford Press.

POITRAS, Jean (2009) "What Makes Parties Trust Mediators?," 25(3) *Negot. J.* 307 (July).

POU, Charles, Jr. (2004) "Assuring Excellence, or Merely Reassuring? Policy and Practice in Promoting Mediator Quality," 2004 *J. Disp. Resol.* 303.

PUTNAM, Robert D. (2000) *Bowling Alone: The Collapse and Revival of American Community.* New York: Simon & Schuster.

RELIS, Tamara (2009) *Perceptions in Litigation and Mediation: Lawyers, Defendants, Plaintiffs, and Gendered Parties.* Cambridge, UK: Cambridge University Press.

RISKIN, Leonard L., and Nancy A. WELSH (2008) "Is That All There Is? 'The Problem' in Court-Connected Mediation," 15 *Geo. Mason L. Rev.* 863.

ROGERS, Nancy H., and Craig A. McEWEN (1998) "Employing the Law to Increase the Use of Mediation and to Encourage Direct and Early Negotiations," 13 *Ohio St. J. on Disp. Resol.* 831.

RULE, Colin, and Chittu NAGARAJAN (2010) *Crowdsourcing Dispute Resolution over Mobile Devices* (eBay self-published).

SCHMITZ, Amy J. (2010) "Legislating in the Light: Considering Empirical Data in Crafting Arbitration Reforms," 15 *Harv. Negot. L. Rev.* 115.

SCHÖN, Donald A. (1983) *The Reflective Practitioner: How Professionals Think in Action.* New York: Basic Books.

SHANE, Peter M. ed. (2008) *Building Democracy Through Online Citizen Deliberation: A Framework for Action*. Columbus, OH: Ohio State University.

SOCIETY OF PROFESSIONALS IN DISPUTE RESOLUTION (SPIDR) (1989) *Report of the SPIDR Commission on Qualifications*. Washington, DC: SPIDR.

SOCIETY OF PROFESSIONALS IN DISPUTE RESOLUTION (SPIDR) (1995) *Ensuring Competence and Quality in Dispute Resolution Practice, Report #2 of the SPIDR Commission on Qualifications*. Washington, DC: SPIDR.

STERNLIGHT, Jean R. (2010) "Lawyerless Dispute Resolution: Rethinking a Paradigm," 37 *Fordham Urb. L.J.* 381.

STURM, Susan, and Howard GADLIN (2007) "Conflict Resolution and Systemic Change," 2007 *J. Disp. Resol.* 1.

SUSSKIND, Lawrence, Sarah McKEARNAN, and Jennifer THOMAS-LARMER eds. (1999) "Introduction," in *The Consensus Building Handbook* xvii. Thousand Oaks, CA: Sage Publications.

TRUTH AND RECONCILIATION COMMISSION OF CANADA (2012) *Interim Report*. Winnipeg, Manitoba: TRC of Canada.

TRUTH AND RECONCILIATION COMMISSION OF CANADA (2015) *Honouring the Truth, Reconciling for the Future: Summary of the Final Report of the Truth and Reconciliation Commission of Canada*. Winnipeg, Manitoba: TRC of Canada.

U.S. AID (2008) "Judge Walks Eight Days for Rule of Law Training" (U.S. AID, archived).

VINING, Richard L. Jr., Amy STEIGERWALT, and Susan Navarro SMELCER (2009) *Bias and the Bar: Evaluating the ABA Ratings of Federal Judicial Nominees*. Atlanta: Emory University SSRN.

WISSLER, Roselle L. (2002) "Court-Connected Mediation in General Civil Cases: What We Know from Empirical Research," 17 *Ohio St. J. on Disp. Resol.* 641.

WISSLER, Roselle L. (2004) "Barriers to Attorneys' Discussion and Use of ADR," 19 *Ohio St. J. on Disp. Resol.* 459.

WISSLER, Roselle L. (2004) "The Effectiveness of Court-Connected Dispute Resolution in Civil Cases," 22 *Conflict Resol. Q.* 55.

WISSLER, Roselle L. (2011a) "Court-Connected Settlement Procedures: Mediation and Judicial Settlement Conferences," 26 *Ohio St. J. on Disp. Resol.* 271.

WISSLER, Roselle L. (2011b) "Judicial Settlement Conferences and Staff Mediation," 17 (4) *Disp. Resol. Mag.* 18.

Determining the Extent of Confidentiality and Openness in the Processes

In this chapter, we examine some of the considerations designers weigh in determining where to place a particular process (or parts of the process) on the continuum between, at one end, absolute confidentiality or secrecy and, at the other end, complete openness (including active publicity, transparency, warnings issued to affected people). When you complete the chapter, you will have a sense of the competing interests to consider, ideas on how designers have resolved these competing concerns, and a better idea of when you need to do legal research to be certain that your approach will be feasible under the law.

Confidentiality and openness decisions are complicated. For one thing, stakeholders' interests may differ with respect to confidentiality and openness, but that is just part of the challenge. In addition, the interests of the public or others not represented at the table may diverge from the preferences of those who would be participating in the process (discussed further in Section A). And U.S. law (and sometimes that of other nations) may constrain choices (Section C).

The challenge, discussed in Section B, is to find creative ways to accommodate competing interests within the law and among stakeholders. Gary Slutkin

DESIGNING STEPS

1. Design initiative
2. Basic planning steps
- Assessing stakeholders, their goals and interests, and contexts
- Creating processes and systems
3. Key planning issues (that may arise throughout the planning)
- Planning how to select, engage, and prepare intervenors and parties
- **Determining the extent of confidentiality and openness in the process**
- Dealing with desires for change, justice, accountability, understanding, safety, reconciliation
- Enhancing relationships
- Incorporating technology
4. Implementing and institutionalizing the system or process
- Implementing
- Using contracts
- Using law
- Evaluating, revising

and Tio Hardiman, for example, worked with Chicago law enforcement officials so that they would understand the significance of compelling Cure Violence's interrupters to divulge their conversations. The goal? So that law enforcement officials would rarely seek to compel them to do so. Slutkin and Hardiman could explain the important results Cure Violence achieved and help law enforcement understand that the violence interrupters would not be able to get people talking without assurances of confidentiality.

Other stories in this book also illustrate the variety in confidentiality/openness issues—Michael Young's concerns for the safety of the South African negotiators if word of negotiations leaked out, Canada's Indian Residential Schools survivors' desires to tell the story broadly and yet allow some to give confidential accounts, and more. Despite the variety, common threads emerge both in the interests and legal issues. This chapter discusses these threads briefly, with references to sources that provide more depth of analysis.

A. COMPETING CONSIDERATIONS

A designer might begin by identifying the often-competing confidentiality-openness interests, the topic of this section, before considering how these might be accommodated in a design, the topic of Section B.

1. Legitimacy

A designer works in the midst of traditions, past practice, cultural expectations, and/or legal constraints regarding what is open and what is confidential —all of which affect the perceived legitimacy of a process. For example, in the U.S. context, most private individuals expect to be able to conduct private negotiations, especially when such negotiations will promote candid discussion. At the same time, the U.S. legal approach is rooted in free speech guarantees, jury trial rights, transparent representative democracy, and a history of reliance on public scrutiny of court and administrative proceedings. And the law recognizes the need for limits on what can remain confidential—for example, the need to require individuals who hear about imminent or past serious harm to report it to the appropriate authorities under some circumstances. When a design varies from these traditions, the designer may want to consider whether people will view it as legitimate.

Other nations do not embrace all U.S. traditions, have similar laws, or react in the same ways to openness and confidentiality. Communal customs in other nations, as well as within portions of the U.S. population, increase the likelihood that a conflict between two people may be treated as the "business" of many more, thus indicating an approach to confidentiality distinct from the typical U.S. approach. Thus, the legitimacy concerns may differ substantially, especially outside the United States.

So, too, the political situation may affect whether the public views as legitimate an attempt to resolve difference outside the public view. For example, after a long stalemate over basic government budget issues, the public may welcome a confidential conclave among members of both parties in an effort to hammer out agreement, though the public might otherwise resent exclusion of the media from such work. Major shifts in power structures or societal values can cause rapid and seismic shifts in the public's expectation of what should remain confidential and what should be available to the public. In the latter part of 2017, for example, the #MeToo movement responding to sexual harassment in the workplace may have led public expectations to a shift away from confidentiality in settlement procedures and more toward transparency and public exposure.

2. Strategic considerations

Designers have more than laws and traditions to consider. They also must take into account strategic considerations. Whether participants will avail themselves of a particular process—the focus of Chapter 6.C—depends, at least in part, on the openness or confidentiality of the procedure.

Quite apart from whether people will use the procedure at all, the success of a system also hinges on matching the openness or confidentiality of a process to the characteristics of a particular dispute and the disputants. For example, people sometimes react differently in discussions when they think that what they say will be used elsewhere. It is not simply a question of whether adversaries will use their statement in legal proceedings. In some contexts, a few participants will posture to gain approval of an outside constituency, while others will respond to possible outside knowledge of what was said by clamming up or choosing each word carefully. If any participants represent constituents who will later hear about what they say, they may decline not only to commit to a position but also even to predict their constituents' interests. The South African talks provide an extreme illustration of this, as the negotiators represented groups with "hard-line" factions. The negotiators would have been in physical danger from some of the extremists if word of their willingness to compromise leaked out early in the talks, and all would have suffered political consequences.

3. Fairness

Confidentiality and openness concerns may also affect fairness. For example, beyond participation and candor concerns just discussed, confidentiality contributes an additional positive effect in mediation: the mediator cannot threaten to report to the public or a key decision-maker (judge or prosecutor, for example) as a way to pressure a reluctant party to settle. The dynamics of the mediation may change considerably depending on this latter point—whether the mediator can make a recommendation to the judge or other influential individual if the parties do not settle. Suppose parents cannot resolve a child custody matter and the mediator responded as below:

> "When Linda protested that, because of Jerry's work schedule, Kenny would have frequent and continuing contact with neither parent when he was staying with Jerry, the mediator made it clear that if Linda did not agree to sharing custody on the terms she suggested, she would recommend to the court that Jerry get sole custody" (Grillo, 1991:1595).

One can imagine that Linda in this example believed that a judge would follow the court mediator's recommendation; Linda felt left with little choice but to go along. The Uniform Mediation Act prohibits mediator recommendations in such a situation. One reason given by the drafters was their desire to avoid arming the mediator with the ability to pressure settlement (Uniform Mediation Act §7 cmt., Appendix E; *see also* "SPIDR" report quoted in Goldberg et al., 2012:522-523).

The other side of the fairness coin is that people may misbehave in secret sessions because no one will learn about it (Delgado, 1988:153). Thus, a public that does not trust the honesty of its government may question the fairness of a private arbitration between its government and private interests over a matter of public utilities. The public may worry that elected officials will not zealously pursue public interests against private entities that have contributed to their campaigns or corrupted them (*see* example on p. 179).

4. Desires or requirements to warn

Occasionally, people too quickly promise confidentiality and then realize that they want to violate the agreement because they feel morally obligated to report something they have learned—a consumer product that malfunctions may spark a fire, for example. In other instances, they may have professional or legal obligations to warn, as in the case of some professionals who hear that a child is being neglected or abused. Thus, you may want to consider the likely exceptions and build these exceptions into any promise to maintain confidentiality in the processes and systems you design.

5. Questions to ask as a designer

You will notice that some considerations just discussed relate to:

- the *type of process*—mediation versus adjudication, for example (confidentiality may not improve the dynamics of adjudication but may play a role in making mediation more successful);

- the *subject matter* of the dispute—like a product that may spark a fire or a nuclear plant defect—that triggers a desire for openness;
- *trust or distrust of the fairness of the tribunal,* such as decision-making bodies with powerful repeat players on one side and consumers on the other;
- *what occurs or is said* during a process—a lawyer acting unethically or a person admitting ongoing child abuse—that triggers a call for permitting later use of the information;
- the *importance of reaching settlement,* as in the congressional debt ceiling discussions, may play a role in moving the balance toward confidentiality;
- the *importance of being heard* broadly and of public education, as in the Canadian Truth and Reconciliation Commission (pp. 200-201);
- the *desire for consistency of results*, as in the 9/11 claims tribunal (p. 79);
- the *nature of the parties,* such as officeholders holding public policy discussions; and
- *whether the public needs to know*, as in the product liability settlement or arbitration regarding a dangerous product.

You can analyze these considerations as a starting point, perhaps even using the interest mapping discussed in Chapter 4 for this purpose. If you map these considerations and others that you may observe, which may weigh in different directions for different purposes, you may be able to create a design that takes many of them into account—the topic of the next section.

B. DESIGNING IN THE MIDST OF CONFLICTING STRATEGIC GOALS

As a designer, you can sometimes accommodate competing interests regarding openness and confidentiality. Suppose, for example, that a legislature engages you to design a process for building bipartisan consensus on key policy issues, such as the state funding formula for nursing homes. You may fear "grandstanding" to the media by some participants, both during the session and outside it, because that behavior dampens other participants' candor and escalates anger and mistrust. Referring to the list of issues just discussed, you might note that the type of process (consensus-building) and its dynamics as well as the importance to the public of reaching agreement both weigh in favor of confidentiality. But other considerations weigh in favor of openness—the involvement of public officials and the public nature of the substance (perhaps leading the public to worry about the legitimacy of a "secret" or "back-room" process). One option might be to announce the process, seek input, provide public updates, and give a public report, but hold the meeting in private. Of course, you would seek the participants' agreement that those giving public updates avoid "grandstanding" mentioned above.

Demonstrating design creativity in this context, James Kunde suggests: "If a group decides that *all* participants should speak to the press . . . , they might include a ground rule that they should talk only about their own interests and perspectives and not try to characterize the views of others" (Kunde, 1999:448). In a variation on this approach, participants agree that they may use information from their discussions but will not disclose a speaker's identity or affiliation, an approach called the Chatham House Rule after a British nonprofit that employs the rule (www.chathamhouse.org).

The success of the Kunde and Chatham House approaches depends on the participants' willingness to keep their word rather than on legal enforceability. So, these ideas might not work in polarized contexts.

In polarized contexts, designers look for options with more certainty. They may design a process that involves shuttling among parties. Public policy mediations may be designed to augment public meetings with private conversations among individual members of a deliberative body. People then cannot disclose statements made by others; they have not heard them. In the court context, the accommodation of private interests might be achieved by offering the option of keeping settlement terms out of the court's judgment. For arbitration, the parties might arrange to hold proceedings in a private office.

Designers may be able to accommodate competing interests by refining the confidentiality-openness rules for different parts of the process, as the story below illustrates.

Truth and
Reconciliation
Commission of Canada

Planning the Truth and Reconciliation Commission of Canada: The planners of the Truth and Reconciliation Commission wanted to capture the best balance between desires for openness and confidentiality. On the one hand, they recognized the importance of the larger public hearing the voices of the Indian Residential Schools survivors. Public education could be the bridge to political change necessary to establishing the right relationship between Aboriginal citizens and other citizens of Canada. It would also help in the healing process to publicly acknowledge the harm, as in the past survivors had been called liars when they spoke of their ordeals. In addition, public disclosure might be a way to hold perpetrators of abuse publicly accountable. On the other hand, some survivors had never been able to tell even their own families about the abuse they had suffered, variously because of trauma or a desire to keep it private. Those survivors would not speak in a public setting. At the same time, it would seem unfair to base a report that attributed fault to particular people or institutions on secret accounts.

The planners concluded at last that the Commission should let the survivors decide whether they told their stories confidentially or publicly but should forgo the naming of perpetrators in the Commission report. A series of factors were weighed in that decision. The Commission did not offer criminal immunity, so perpetrators could still be prosecuted to secure accountability.[1] And, nothing precluded those who testified from giving their story to the media independent of the process. The Commission wanted to facilitate the process that gave the greatest voice to survivors and permitted the Commission to base its report (absent naming names of perpetrators) and recommendations on the broadest survivor input.

Ultimately, the planners discovered that survivors who spoke confidentially often gained the courage to speak later in a public setting. As the result, they satisfied more of the competing interests regarding confidentiality and openness than they previously thought feasible.

Like processes to build a consensus or combined processes such as the Truth and Reconciliation Commission of Canada, an arbitration system might also be designed to allow some openness and some confidentiality. In one illustration of this, city residents demanded access to a confidential arbitration between their government (Bolivia) and a private foreign company. They believed that the arbitration result would affect the cost of their water and wanted both to be heard during the arbitration and to observe and listen to the proceedings to be assured that the government advocated strongly for their concerns and that the tribunal took them into account. The controversy attracted international attention. Eventually, the arbitration administrator, the World Bank's International Centre for the Settlement of Investment Disputes, modified its arbitration rules to open its arbitrations in two ways: requiring prompt release of the arbitrators' legal reasoning and allowing non-disputants to submit input (Norris and Metzidakis, 2010:31-33, 74; *see also* Boyarsky, 2015:36).

In many contexts, people differ on what is the "right balance." For example, people may also worry about or be pleased with the long-term effects of openness or confidentiality, as the excerpt below illustrates.

Former South African Justice Richard J. Goldstone on openness in South Africa's Truth and Reconciliation Commission: "Many of [the Truth and Reconciliation Commission's] hearings were televised and broadcast live to the nation on radio and television, and its activities were covered in almost all news bulletins. In my view, its most signal success is that the evidence it amassed of gross abuses during the apartheid era has made it literally impossible for those abuses to be credibly denied. The refrain I have heard from a substantial number of white people during the last year or so of the TRC's work was that there had been 'more than enough of re-opening wounds.' 'Whose wounds are they?' I would inquire. 'Surely not yours. And what makes you think that those wounds have ever healed?'" (Goldstone, 2000:70).

---

1. Only a few prosecutions have resulted in convictions, however, because of lost evidence. And many alleged perpetrators had died before prosecutions began.

Designers may help stakeholders resolve some differences by helping them examine what has happened in other similar contexts.

C. THE U.S. LAW REGARDING CONFIDENTIALITY AND OPENNESS

When creating new processes, the law may constrain the choices regarding openness and confidentiality. Thus, there is a practical, legal research aspect of planning for confidentiality and openness. Reading this section should help you spot legal issues, at least in the domestic U.S. context. Unfortunately, a lack of common themes in legal approaches to mediation confidentiality in other nations precludes any quick international guidance (Hopt and Steffek eds., 2013:51).

Failing to spot and research the legal issues might lead to undesirable results. For example, if a proposed process or system includes a practice of asking parties to contract for confidentiality, the designer may want to research:

- when the courts override privacy agreements by the parties if their testimony is subpoenaed;
- whether the planned process fits within the definition of mediation in the applicable privilege law;
- whether public meeting and records laws make the agreement unenforceable; and
- whether participants in the process are likely to say things that ought to be reported for the protection of others.

Parties who relied on the confidentiality agreement would be justifiably upset if they are surprised that their candid statements could be used in ways that harmed them.

Dispute resolution and evidence textbooks and treatises more thoroughly analyze the law (*see, e.g.,* Cole et al., 2017-2018:Ch.8). This section instead provides a problem that may serve to remind you of some issues that occur frequently, even though the law varies by jurisdiction, and sometimes by process within a jurisdiction. The problem deals only with mediation and arbitration, though some of the law in those contexts applies as well for different processes. Also, it deals with U.S. law; increasingly, similar legal issues and doctrines are emerging for cross-border disputes[2] and within other nations.[3]

---

2. *See, e.g.,* the UNCITRAL provisions for confidentiality of international commercial conciliation at http://www.uniformlaws.org/shared/docs/mediation/uma_final_03.pdf, Section 11 and Appendix A of the Act.

3. *See, e.g.,* Directive 2008/52/EC (23) of the European Parliament and of the Council (2008).

Legal Practice Notes: Law Regarding Confidentiality and Openness

1. Mediation

If the information is not legally protected, achieving confidentiality in mediation may be more difficult than achieving openness. Consider, for example, a confidentiality agreement, often suggested by designers of mediation programs in order to increase candor and encourage participation. Despite its purpose, a confidentiality agreement has limited effectiveness. The courts may enforce the agreement in a dispute over confidentiality between signatories to the confidentiality agreement. Still, when a public body subpoenas evidence, the courts will rarely allow people to decline to provide the information merely because they had promised each other privacy. And confidentiality agreements are unavailing if public meetings or records law provide otherwise or if the law places on a mediation participant a legal duty to report certain facts or the court finds a contract defense or public policy exception to enforcement.

In the United States, the legal provisions that most often affect the confidentiality and openness in mediation are tucked into a variety of types of law, including:

- evidence rules, especially for compromise discussions;
- privilege laws;
- public meetings and open records laws;
- common law doctrines regarding open courts;
- common law doctrines dealing with protective orders;
- ethics requirements for preserving confidences;
- court and agency rules and orders prohibiting disclosure;
- statutory or ethical duties to report;
- rules regarding formal discovery; and
- contract law regarding explicit or implied confidentiality agreements.

To get a flavor of what designers must research in the mediation context, consider a few of these provisions in the context of a problem that unfolds and is litigated solely within the United States. Keep in mind the hypothetical situation below as we examine the provisions.

Confidentiality hypothetical: During an eight-hour summer electricity outage in a major city, stores closed in the central business district, and people began milling in the streets. By evening, small groups of people began breaking windows and looting stores. When police arrived, some in the crowd threw rocks at them. Rescue squads removed two injured officers, and the conflict between the crowds and police intensified. By morning, 14 people had been hospitalized for injuries, and 50 arrested. For weeks afterward, bitterness grew over whether the police profiled by race and religion that evening. Some of those arrested filed a class action against the police, charging racial profiling over the course of years.

The federal judge who was assigned the discrimination case asks you what processes might be created if parties sought to settle the litigation and if the parties sought to work to bring about consensus on what should happen in the future in police practices dealing with unruly crowds. It seems likely that if part of the design is a mediation about future police practices, you might want to include in that mediation community representatives who were not parties to the discrimination suit. You might have the mediator ask all participants to sign an agreement to keep what was said during mediation sessions confidential and request them all to acknowledge that discussions fall under the state's mediation privilege statute. If the parties were to reach agreement, they might ask the judge to enter the agreement as a consent order.

a. Evidentiary exclusions for compromise discussions

Evidentiary exclusions for compromise discussions typically protect those discussions in narrow circumstances. Suppose that some of those injured during the hypothetical conflict described above file a separate civil rights action against a police officer in federal court and seek to depose the mediator. Suppose further that counsel for these plaintiffs will ask what the defendant said about the source of the plaintiffs' injuries during the mediation conducted in the class action litigation.[4] The defendant then moves the court to exclude the mediator's testimony.

Federal Rule of Evidence 408, on compromise discussions, provides:

> (a) Prohibited uses. Evidence of the following is not admissible on behalf of any party, when offered to prove liability for, invalidity of, or amount of a claim that was disputed as to validity or amount, or to impeach through a prior inconsistent statement or contradiction:
>
> (1) furnishing or offering or promising to furnish—or accepting or offering or promising to accept—a valuable consideration in compromising or attempting to compromise *the claim*; and
>
> (2) conduct or statements made in compromise negotiations regarding the claim, except when offered in a criminal case and the negotiations related to a claim by a public office or agency in the exercise of regulatory, investigative, or enforcement authority.
>
> (b) Permitted uses. This rule does not require exclusion if the evidence is offered for purposes not prohibited by subdivision (a). Examples of permissible purposes include proving a witness's bias or prejudice; negating a contention of undue delay; and proving an effort to obstruct a criminal investigation or prosecution.

Returning to the hypothetical, the defendant may argue that the mediator's testimony cannot be used to show the source of the injury under this compromise discussion exclusion and therefore that the plaintiff should be precluded from asking about it during a deposition. But plaintiff will counter with alternative arguments: (1) that the mediation discussions did not pertain to a disputed legal "claim," but rather had a broader scope regarding future plans for the police and community; (2) that the testimony might be offered to demonstrate the bias of a particular witness—a "permitted use"; and (3) that formal discovery is not limited to admissible evidence as long as it appears reasonably likely to lead to admissible evidence.

Notice what a slender reed the compromise discussions rule provides as a basis for the defendant to defend against the discovery requests. If the defendant has no other legal basis for protecting the mediation communications (e.g., a mediation privilege), the court will probably allow the mediator to be deposed about conversations that occurred during the mediation. The protection provided by evidentiary rules for compromise discussions might be narrower yet if the hypothetical problem changes so that the action is filed in some state courts, though most states follow the federal approach (Cole, 2017-2018:§8:7).

b. Mediation privilege

Mediation privileges often provide broad confidentiality protection but do not apply to all mediations. Assume that the pertinent state where the electrical outage occurred was one of the twelve jurisdictions that have enacted the Uniform Mediation Act (Appendix E). The privilege statute provides in pertinent part:

> §4(b)(1) A mediation party may refuse to disclose, and may prevent any other person from disclosing, a mediation communication.
>
> (2) A mediator may refuse to disclose a mediation communication, and may prevent any other person from disclosing a mediation communication of the mediator.

---

4. The mediator's statement as to what the defendant said during mediation would not be hearsay if offered by the plaintiff. FRE 801(d)(2*).

(3) A nonparty participant may refuse to disclose, and may prevent any other person from disclosing, a mediation communication of the mediator.

§5(a) There is no privilege under Section 4 for a mediation communication that is:

(1) in an agreement evidenced by a record signed by all parties to the agreement;

(2) available to the public under the open records act or made during a session of a mediation which is open, or is required by law to be open, to the public;

(3) a threat or statement of a plan to inflict bodily injury or commit a crime of violence [followed by other exceptions not at issue here] [*see* full Act in Appendix E].

Assuming the same hypothetical facts, the defendant's arguments become stronger under the privilege statute than they were if based solely on the evidentiary exclusion for compromise discussions: (1) that the scope of formal discovery does not extend to privileged communications and that the mediator (probably joined by one of the parties) asserts the mediator privilege to preclude disclosing mediation communications; and (2) that all trial testimony by the mediator is also precluded by the mediation privilege. Defendant would assure the court that the key requirements are met because:

- The mediation fits the statutory *definition* to be covered by the privilege (*see* Uniform Mediation Act §3).
- The mediator is a *"holder"* of the privilege (one of those authorized to assert or waive it) and asserts the privilege.

- The privilege is *absolute*; that is, it does not yield to a great need for the evidence (as does a *qualified* privilege) unless a party has a constitutional right to it.
- The testimony is sought as to mediation *communications* and therefore within the coverage of this communications privilege.

The problem is that this civil rights action is pending in federal court. Will the federal court apply the state privilege statute? Yes, if it were a diversity action, as Federal Rule of Evidence 501 applies state law whenever state law covers the substantive claim:

Except as otherwise required by the Constitution of the United States or provided by Act of Congress or in rules prescribed by the Supreme Court pursuant to statutory authority, the privilege of a witness, person, government, State, or political subdivision thereof shall be governed by the principles of the common law as they may be interpreted by the courts of the United States in the light of reason and experience. However, in civil actions and proceedings, *with respect to an element of a claim or defense as to which State law supplies the rule of decision*, the privilege of a witness, person, government, State, or political subdivision thereof *shall be determined in accordance with State law.*

But the answer would be "no" in this federal civil rights law action. Rule 501 requires the court to apply federal privilege law.

The federal courts have split on the question of whether a federal statute authorizes a privilege[5] and whether there is a common

---

5. The federal Alternative Dispute Resolution Act of 1998, 28 U.S.C. §652(d), authorizes local court rules on the confidentiality of dispute resolution processes adopted by the court until a broader federal law is adopted, but there remains uncertainty about whether these local rules create privileges. *Compare Fed. Deposit Ins. Corp. v. White*, No. 3-96-CV-0560-BD, 199 WL 1201793, at *1 (N.D. Tex. 1999) (no privilege) *and Yelder v. U.S. Dept. of Defense*, 577 F. Supp. 2d 342, 346 (D.D.C. 2008) (recognizing ADR Act as basis for protecting mediation communication).

law federal mediation privilege (Cole et al., 2017-2018:§§8:15, 8:16; Deason, 2002). Some, but not all, federal courts have given weight to the pertinent state common law privilege in determining federal common law (*see, e.g., Teligent v. K & L Gates*, 640 F.3d 53, 57-61 (2d Cir. 2011); *see generally* Deason, 2002).

So, the federal court might allow the deposition of the mediator if it related to a federal claim. But a state court or federal court considering a state claim probably would not allow the deposition. In other words, the confidentiality of the mediation discussion may depend not only on the scope of the privilege law but also on what sort of litigation occurs subsequently.

In sum, mediation privileges protect mediation discussions against future use more broadly than compromise discussions exclusions, but only when the mediation fits within the definition of the applicable privilege.

c. Public access laws

Suppose a local news reporter asks to attend the class action mediation related to the electrical outage incident and, when refused entry, seeks a court order that would permit attendance. Public access laws may open the mediation (or other consensus building activity) to the public in spite of that jurisdiction's mediation privilege; the result depends on whether the privilege law pre-empts public access laws or vice versa. The reporter might argue: (1) this is a court proceeding and open to the public under common law doctrines based on the First Amendment to the U.S. Constitution, and (2) this is a public meeting involving public officials making public decisions and state public meeting laws therefore require it to be open.

Regarding the right of access to court proceedings, the U.S. Court of Appeals for the Sixth Circuit explained the U.S. Supreme Court's analysis as involving "complementary considerations": "First, the proceeding must be one for which there has been a 'tradition of accessibility.' . . . Second, public access must play a 'significant positive role in the functioning of the particular process in question.'" (*Cincinnati Gas & Electric Gas Co. v. General Electric Co.*, 854 F.2d 900, 903 (6th Cir. 1988) (*citing Press-Enterprise Co. v. Superior Court*, 478 U.S. 1, 6-13 (1986))). The Sixth Circuit reasoned that settlement processes do not fall within these criteria and therefore do not come within the right of access.

Having failed on the court proceedings access argument, the reporter may next argue a right of access under the state's public meeting statute. Suppose the statute provides:

> Except as otherwise specifically provided by law, all meetings, formal or informal, special or regular, of the governing bodies of all municipalities, counties, townships, and school districts and all boards, bureaus, commissions, or organizations of the State, except grand juries, supported wholly or in part by public funds or expending public funds, shall be public meetings.

The reporter will probably fail to gain access if the mediator chooses participants who do not fall within these definitions. Sometimes, public policy mediators meet separately with just one or two members of a larger public body, for example, to get their views confidentially as to how to structure a more public meeting so that it can be successful.

d. Laws regarding confidentiality agreements

Returning to the electrical outage, suppose a community leader who participated in the class action mediation and signed an agreement to keep it confidential, tells a reporter about what a police officer said during mediation. The courts generally enforce agreements to keep discussions confidential under contract law against other signatories to the confidentiality agreement who voluntarily disclose (in contrast to the courts' stance on the effectiveness of agreements against a subpoena for evidence). Of course, contract defenses such as unconscionability or violation of public policy or law can be asserted against a confidentiality agreement. Also, research suggests that many parties ignore such contracts and even the confidentially laws discussed above (Coben and Thompson, 2006:66-69). In the police and public unrest hypothetical, for example, what would be the police officer's damages if a community mediation participant voluntarily disclosed what the police officer said during mediation? Perhaps little.

But the situation might be different if the court had ordered mediation confidentiality or required it by rule. Courts have been willing to award sanctions, ranging from dismissal of an action to disqualification of an expert, when a mediation participant violates a court order or rule (*Hand v. Walnut Valley Sailing Club*, 2012 WL 1111137, at *2 (10th Cir. 2012); *Paranzino v. Barnett Bank*, 690 So. 2d 725 (Fla. Dist. Ct. App. 1997); *Irwin Seating Co. v. International Business Machines Corp.*, No. 1:04-CV-568, 2006 WL 3446584 (W.D. Mich. Nov. 29, 2006), *aff'd*, 2007 WL 518866 (W.D. Mich. Feb. 15, 2007); Cole et al., 2011:§8:47).

Because of the differential treatment of court orders, some mediation parties ask the court to enter their confidentiality agreement as a court ruling—sometimes called a consent protective order. They may do this to increase the chances that signatories will comply. In addition, they also thereby place the burden to secure a change in the order on non-signatories that want to set aside the protective order.

e. Putting it together

As a designer, you might want to research the pertinent law and make a chart to help you navigate these laws. For the mediation following the electrical outage, the chart might look like the one on the next page, with an X indicating that the law probably provides protection against the desired use of the information (but you should research to be certain).

You may have to devote extra research time to confidentiality related to mediation because the legal situation is complex. Legal constraints may also affect the design

process in unanticipated ways. For example, the mediation communications privilege might not apply if the designer modified the traditional format, such as using a non-neutral facilitator.

2. Arbitration

Arbitration confidentiality largely rests on contract law, often broadly construed by courts supportive of encouraging private resolution of disputes (Drahozal, 2015). Privately bargained-for confidential arbitration might be considered a tradition—one that lies between open adjudication and private settlement discussions. Not only is arbitration confidentiality justified as an inducement to arbitrate, but also as a means to attract witnesses absent subpoena power, to resolve differences without affecting investments and markets, and to encourage settlement within arbitration proceedings (Norris and Metzidakis, 2010:56-58).

When setting up the arbitration clause, the drafter has a number of choices:

- the parties agree specifically to maintain confidentiality;
- the parties agree to use a tribunal, knowing that the tribunal imposes confidentiality as a part of its rules; or
- the parties could agree that the arbitrator will decide about confidentiality.

Whatever the choice, the contract provisions regarding confidentiality do not provide unshakeable protection. The courts may nonetheless decline to enforce these arbitration confidentiality agreements. Privilege laws do not usually cover arbitration. As a consequence, the court may require disclosure—even when the parties agreed to confidentiality—when required by contract defense, discovery rules, the need for evidence, and public policy. In addition, litigation to enforce the arbitration agreement or award often results in disclosure of arbitration evidence (*see* Bennett, 2013; Farkas, 2018:14).

Scholars increasingly criticize broad enforcement of confidentiality agreements for arbitration. They reference the "bipolar" view of adjudication, depending on the court or arbitration setting (Dore, 2006:513). Further, they recount stories that demonstrate the increasingly broad impact of some arbitration decisions (Norris and Metzidakis, 2010:31-32, 71-72; Lo, 2012:154-155). That raises the question of whether the courts will become more reluctant to enforce confidentiality as arbitration reaches more frequently into public policy, affects parties with differing resources, and involves (through treaties) entire nations as parties. (Already the U.S. Court of Appeals for the Third Circuit has ruled that the Delaware Chancery Court Arbitration cannot be closed. *Del. Coalition for Open Government, Inc. v. Strine*, 733 F.3d 510 (3rd Cir. 2013), *cert. denied*, 134 S. Ct. 155 (2014).)

Law ⟶ Desired Use of Evidence ↓	Federal Rule of Evidence 408 or comparable state rule (compromise discussions exclusion)	Mediation privilege	Contract law	Public meetings and public records laws
Formal discovery to secure mediation discussions		X, but only if this federal court recognizes a mediation privilege		
Admission of mediation discussions into evidence	X, but only if mediation concerned a claim and offered to prove liability or amount	X		
Voluntary disclosure to the media			X	
Whether a reporter can attend the mediation				X

Returning to the strategic considerations discussed in Sections A and B, it may be possible to design around the U.S. legal provisions discussed briefly in this section, as well as any legal provisions in other nations. To illustrate: The drafters of the United Nations protocol for a world-wide, online small claims "court" might designate which law will apply to the confidentiality and openness of that process. In addition, they might allow the parties to vary that "default" provision by agreement. These drafters then might ask signatory nations to adopt laws giving effect to the protocol or the parties' agreement.

That ability to work around existing laws then places drafters into the processes of considering what provisions for openness/transparency and confidentiality/secrecy would make the new online court legitimate in the eyes of a world-wide public and especially in the view of those who might use it; what would make the facilitated negotiations and arbitration processes most effective; what would serve fairness; and what exceptions would be necessary to permit participants to warn others concerning threats to inflict serious harm. The answer might vary for the facilitated negotiations phase and the arbitration phase; for certain types of claims; for certain disclosures; and for certain parties, as discussed above (pp. 180-186). Drafters would also consider how a blended approach to these issues would be received in a world with varying traditions regarding confidentiality and openness. Also, too much fine-tuning might make the provisions for confidentiality and openness too complex for the users to understand (*see* Chapter 13).

Even within the United States, designers might be able to change the laws regarding openness and confidentiality when necessary to make a process or systems effective (*see* Chapter 13). For this reason, you may want to begin with strategic considerations and only then move to legal research about existing constraints.

THOUGHTS GOING FORWARD

You can improve the design by working with stakeholders to think carefully at the start about what should be open and what should be confidential and, with respect to each, to what extent. You often can combine elements of openness and confidentiality within a single design. As a designer, the long-term legitimacy of the process and its outcomes matters; it is not just a question of protecting the narrow interests of the parties. Even if a process is traditionally confidential or open, people may lose confidence in the process when it covers particular subject matters or when it involves suspect tribunals, particular types of parties, and circumstances. Planning regarding confidentiality is constrained by law; you may need to research what will be possible under the law in a variety of jurisdictions where the issue might arise, or what change in the law might be feasible.

QUESTIONS

7.1 Early in 1993, President William Clinton appointed his wife, Hillary Clinton, as chair of the Health Care Task Force to generate a proposal for universal health care. She maintained the confidentiality of the task force members and its meetings, despite criticism and even litigation challenging the confidentiality. Presumably, she hoped to forge agreement on the best package, with stakeholders being more candid and feeling free to try out ideas without the risk of having to defend each statement or position publicly. By fall of 1993, President Clinton made his 1,000-plus-page health care reform proposal public, but Congress did not pass it, at least in part because of anger related to the closed-door nature of the proceedings.

President Barack Obama promised a more open approach during his 2008 presidential campaign and encouraged public health care reform discussions. Members of Congress hosted "town hall meetings." America Speaks describes town hall meetings as designed to "restore the public voice in decision making by creating an opportunity for the general public to give those in leadership positions direct, substantive feedback on key issues" (http://usabudgetdiscussion. org/what-is-a-national-town-meeting-2/). But CNN reported (August 10, 2009) a different result for the health care meetings—yelling exchanges, insulting signs, and little ability to hear those speaking about health care.[6]

For his part, President Obama, a Democrat, organized a day-long, CSPAN-televised health care reform meeting with Republicans. A Washington Post reporter noted there was "little sign that the two parties are any closer together than they were before, or that there's any more likelihood of a bipartisan deal today than there was yesterday." One blogger asked rhetorically whether anyone listened "with an open mind" or learned anything new.[7] Nor did President Obama escape criticism for secrecy—news media criticized him for holding closed-door strategy meetings with Democrats. In the end, Congress passed the health care reform legislation with Republican opposition.

Suppose that a new U.S. President seeks to build national consensus on a wide-ranging new approach to providing affordable health care to all Americans. What are the confidentiality-related lessons from the Clinton and Obama federal health care forums on building public consensus for this initiative?

7.2   A dance event that packed a university residence hall cafeteria devolved into a fistfight. Injured students tested positive for alcohol and drugs. In addition to instituting disciplinary proceedings against the students, the university began searches for drugs and alcohol at the doors to on-campus parties. To protest the new search policy, students organized a "strike," with two-thirds stopping their dorm fee payments. They called a press conference to demand that the university president "immediately" hold an "open town hall meeting" to discuss the situation. What would you tell the university president about the advantages and disadvantages of trying to resolve the issues through an "open town hall meeting"? What other processes would you suggest? What should be done about openness and confidentiality in these processes, taking into account the students' demands and all of the stakeholders' needs?

---

6. http://articles.cnn.com/2009-08-10/politics/health.care.questions_1_health-care-president-s-plan-clinton-s-plan?_s=PM:POLITICS.

7. http://voices.washingtonpost.com/44/2010/02/health-care-summit-live-analys.html.

7.3   Acme Corporation owns five dumps. Six months ago, one of the dumps began spewing fumes that sickened many who lived or worked nearby. Acme immediately notified state and federal environmental authorities. Federal, state, and company experts believe that a unique combination of chemicals set off the reaction, but there is no proven method to stop it. The company is earnestly trying to solve the problem, spending millions of dollars—all of its profits for the year to date—on experts and attempts to fix the problem. So far, nothing has worked, though Acme is currently applying yet another chemical to the dump in an attempt to extinguish the fire. Already, four nearby farms have closed operations. Traffic must be diverted from one stretch of a nearby state highway on some days. Fortunately, there has not been a storm with high winds during the last six months.

Acme now proposes to create a claims forum but will only do so with the blessing of federal and state environmental authorities. The company would sell two "healthy" dumps in order to create the fund to pay claims. The company proposes that those who elect to use the claims forum would agree to use mediation and, if the parties do not settle there, participate in arbitration and abide by the decision of the arbitrator. Acme has offered federal and state authorities a veto on mediators and arbitrators, and these authorities have approved the mediation and arbitration process in principle.

After talking with attorneys for claimants, Acme's counsel believes that people will likely elect to use the claims forum, if created, because they fear that Acme will go out of business within a year if Acme cannot find a cure by then. Counsel explains that, for claimants, it is a matter of recovering either all of what the arbitrator awards in a matter of months or a small portion of what a court awards several years from now.

Acme will announce the claims facility as soon as the company resolves one remaining detail—what will be open and what will remain confidential in the claims process. Acme has hired you to advise the company on this. Acme's lawyer reminds you that Acme wants approval of the design by federal and state environmental authorities, so your design regarding openness and confidentiality needs to meet their interests as well as Acme's. Acme would prefer to keep all of the processes as confidential as possible but especially wants settlement amounts to remain confidential to preserve Acme's abilities to negotiate in the future. Acme and the government parties would like a high settlement rate because the claims fund will be limited, and they prefer that Acme pay the claimants rather than deplete their funds paying litigation expenses. What should the agreement to mediate and arbitrate claims provide with respect to confidentiality? What practices related to openness and confidentiality should be adopted? Be prepared to explain your recommendations to Acme's lawyer.

7.4   The director of a nonprofit community mediation program seeks your counsel on whether and how the program should change its confidentiality practices in light of a new development. Currently, mediation communications are privileged under that state's version of the Uniform Mediation Act (Appendix

E). The center asks all mediators to abide by the Model Standards of Conduct for Mediators, which require mediators to maintain the "confidentiality of all information obtained by the mediator in mediation, unless otherwise agreed to by the parties or required by applicable law" (Standard V.A.). All agreements to mediate include promises by the parties and mediator not to disclose what is discussed in mediation.

The director now questions this approach because of a series of mediations involving a local air purifier manufacturer. In each case, the complainants charged that the air purifier overheated, burning a hole in a carpet or table. When the manufacturer offered a monetary settlement contingent upon a release of claims and an agreement to be silent about the complaint, the parties accepted the offer in all eight mediations. Some mediators want to warn others who may have the purifiers. The director asks you to re-design their system as it relates to confidentiality so that mediators can warn other consumers about potential safety hazards. What changes in practice and/or law would be required to meet the director's goal? On balance, is this a good idea?

7.5   Imagine that you have been approached by the President and a bipartisan group of U.S. Senators and Representatives. Exhausted by what seems to be constant infighting and stalemates in dealing with the country's most pressing issues—health care, taxes, the budget deficit, the environment, education—the group has asked you to design an approach to break the impasse and help Congress and the President govern more effectively. What advice would you give them with respect to how they should deal with considerations of transparency and privacy in the design of the system?

Exercise 7.1   *Tallahoya University—confidentiality:* You just had a conversation with University counsel about a proposed sexual harassment policy and the processes in place for dealing with complaints. The University counsel wants you to advise on how confidentiality should be handled at various stages in the system design. Stakeholders have differing interests in this respect:

a. *Students:* Some student complainants are unlikely to come forward unless they are assured of confidentiality. Others do not care. Some complainants seek to begin a process that will lead to punishment of the respondent and publicity that will warn others to steer clear of this person. Other complainants take the opposite approach—they have no interest in punishment but want to secure assurance that their individual difficulties will end, without any disclosure that the harassment occurred.

b. *Counsel:* The University's attorneys note that the federal Crime Awareness and Campus Security Act, 20 U.S.C. §1092(f), requires the University to collect and disclose reports of criminal offenses. This state has adopted the Uniform Mediation Act (Appendix E).

c. *Attorneys for the accused:* Attorneys for the accused typically ask whether their clients' statements during the university process can be used against them in civil or criminal litigation. They also seek a confidentiality clause in any settlement agreement or disciplinary report.

d. *University student affairs administration:* The University's vice president for student affairs wants to send a clear message that the University will not tolerate sexual harassment. That office will adjudicate through its disciplinary process any complaints that are filed there rather than or in addition to having been filed with the proposed new procedures.

Give University counsel your assessment of what is best and why. Are there some accommodations of these interests that you think unprincipled and, if adopted, would cause you to quit your job on the University's design team?

BIBLIOGRAPHY AND REFERENCES

BENNETT, Steven C. (2013) "Confidentiality Issues in Arbitration," 68 *Disp. Resol. J.* 1.

BOYARSKY, Stuart (2015) "Transparency in Investor-State Arbitration," 21 (4) *Disp. Resol. Mag.* 34.

COBEN, James R., and Peter N. THOMPSON (2006) "Disputing Irony: A Systematic Look at Litigation About Mediation," 17 *Harv. Negot. L. Rev.* 43.

COLE, Sarah R., Nancy H. ROGERS, Craig A. McEWEN, James R. COBEN, and Peter N. THOMPSON (2017-2018) *Mediation: Law, Policy, and Practice* (3rd ed.). Minneapolis: West.

DEASON, Ellen E. (2001) "Enforcing Mediated Settlement Agreements: Contract Law Collides with Confidentiality," 35 *U. Davis L. Rev.* 33.

DEASON, Ellen E. (2002) "Predictable Mediation Confidentiality in the U.S. Federal System," 17 *Ohio St. J. on Disp. Resol.* 239.

DEASON, Ellen E. (2006) "The Need for Trust as a Justification for Confidentiality in Mediation: A Cross-Disciplinary Approach," 54 *U. Kan. L. Rev.* 1387.

DELGADO, Richard (1988) "ADR and the Dispossessed: Recent Books About the Deformalization Movement," 13 *Law & Soc. Inquiry* 145.

DORE, Laurie Kratky (2006) "Public Courts Versus Private Justice: It's Time to Let Some Sun Shine in on Alternative Dispute Resolution," 81 *Chi.-Kent L. Rev.* 463.

DRAHOZAL, Christopher R. (2015) "Confidentiality in Consumer and Employment Arbitration," 7 *Y.B. Arb. & Mediation* 28.

FARKAS, Brian (2018) "Donald Trump and Stormy Daniels: An Arbitration Case Study," 24 (3) *Disp. Resol. Mag.* 12.

FISHKIN, James S. (2009) *When the People Speak: Deliberative Democracy and Public Consultation.* Oxford, UK: Oxford University Press.

FUNG, Archon, Mary GRAHAM, and David WEIL (2007) *Full Disclosure: The Perils and Promise of Transparency.* Cambridge, UK: Cambridge University Press.

GOLDBERG, Stephen B., Frank E.A. SANDER, Nancy H. ROGERS, and Sarah R. COLE (2012) *Dispute Resolution: Negotiation, Mediation, Arbitration, and Other Processes* (6th ed.). New York: Wolters Kluwer.

GOLDSTONE, Richard J. (2000) *For Humanity: Reflections of a War Crimes Investigator.* New Haven, CT: Yale University Press.

GRILLO, Trina (1991) "The Mediation Alternative: Process Dangers for Women," 100 *Yale L.J.* 1545.

HAGER, L. Michael (2010) "Congress Needs a Mediation Tool to Dissolve Gridlock," *The Washington Post,* June 18, p. A27.

HOPT, Klaus J., and Felix STEFFEK eds. (2013) *Mediation: Principles and Regulation in a Comparative Perspective.* Oxford, UK: Oxford University Press.

KUNDE, James E. (1999) "Dealing with the Press," in Lawrence Susskind, Sarah McKearnan, and Jennifer Thomas-Larmer eds., *The Consensus Building Handbook: A Comprehensive Guide to Reaching Agreement* 435. Thousand Oaks, CA: Sage Publications.

LO, Alex (2012) "Too Much Privacy for Repeat Players? The Problem of Confidentiality Clauses and a Possible Solution," 5 *Contemp. Asian Arb. J.* 149.

MENKEL-MEADOW, Carrie (2009) "Are There Systemic Ethics Issues in Dispute System Design? And What We Should [Not] Do About It: Lessons from International and Domestic Fronts," 14 *Harv. Negot. L. Rev.* 195.

MOFFITT, Michael (2005) "Pleading in an Age of Settlement," 80 *Ind. L.J.* 727.

NORRIS, Amanda L., and Katina E. METZIDAKIS (2010) "Public Protests, Private Contracts: Confidentiality in ICSID Arbitration and the Cochabamba Water War," 15 *Harv. Negot. L. Rev.* 31.

REUBEN, Richard C. (2004) "Democracy and Dispute Resolution: The Problem of Arbitration," 67 *Law & Contemp. Probs.* 279.

RITZ, Philipp (2010) "Privacy and Confidentiality Obligation on Parties in Arbitration Under Swiss Law," 27 *J. Int'l Arb.* 221.

ROGERS, Nancy H. (2017) "Mediation and the Law," in Stephen B. Goldberg et al., *How Mediation Works: Theory, Research, and Practice* Ch.5. Bingley, UK: Emerald Press.

SUN, Jeffrey C. (1999) "University Officials as Administrator and Mediators: The Dual Role Conflict and Confidentiality Problems," 1 *BYU Educ. & L.J.* 19.

SUSSKIND, Lawrence, and Patrick FIELD (1996) *Dealing with an Angry Public: The Mutual Gains Approach to Resolving Disputes.* New York: The Free Press.

Seeking Justice, Safety, Reconciliation, Change, Public and Personal Understanding, and Other Goals

People interested in design work have developed a self-critique—that designers have been too quick to assume that stakeholder goals and interests can be satisfied by the sequencing of settlement or civil adjudication processes. These commentators variously raise practical, philosophical, and political issues regarding the failure to consider the broader implications of designing conflict management systems, as noted in Chapter 5.A.[1] When you have read this chapter, you will have in mind many of the questions to ask to avoid such a narrow approach. In addition, you will have ideas on how processes can be adapted, combined, and set within particular contexts to respond to those who seek more than resolution of

---

1. *See also* Mayer, 2004:16-17; Cohen, 2009:55-57; Schoeny and Warfield, 2000:259-260; Bingham, 2008.2-3, Schneider, 2009.290-293; Sturm and Gadlin, 2007:3; Menkel-Meadow, 2009:198-199; Menkel-Meadow, 2006:553; Mitchell, 2002:2; Llewellyn, 2002:253; Regan, 2010:117-120; Bush and Folger, 2005.

DESIGNING STEPS

1. Design initiative
2. Basic planning steps
- Assessing stakeholders, their goals and interests, and contexts
- Creating processes and systems
3. Key planning issues (that may arise throughout the planning)
- Planning how to select, engage, and prepare intervenors and parties
- Determining the extent of confidentiality and openness in the process
- **Dealing with desires for change, justice, accountability, understanding, safety, reconciliation**
- Enhancing relationships
- Incorporating technology
4. Implementing and institutionalizing the system or process
- Implementing
- Using contracts
- Using law
- Evaluating, revising

the immediate dispute, including those who want justice (Section A), safety (Section B), change (Section C), public understanding (Section D), personal understanding (Section E), personal accountability (Section F), and reconciliation (Section G). You will also have a sense of how the designing process might unfold with these when the aim is not solely resolution (Section H). The chapter that follows this one explores yet another non-settlement goal—enhancing relationships (Chapter 9), and other goals.

While you might find these non-resolution interests in any conflict, they occur especially in situations when some sense deep inequality, terrible wrongdoing, or harms that might recur.

In 2014, Bruno Augusto Santos Oliveira, a Brazilian federal judge with an LL .M. in dispute resolution and 12 years of judicial and dispute resolution experience, noticed that a significant portion of the 10,000 legal matters pending before him related to the creation of a national park. Judge Oliveira sensed that the parties involved longed for more than settlement or a court ruling.

Judge Oliveira's account of the Canastra National Park process: In 1972, the military regime ruling Brazil announced the creation of Serra da Canastra National Park, which would encompass two major river basins—the Rio Grande Basin and the São Francisco River Basin—and cover 494,210 acres, an area ten times the size of the District of Columbia. To acquire the land, the government sometimes paid prices below market value. In other instances, it seized the land without paying. In fact, the police used violence to take land that had been inhabited by indigenous populations for more than 150 years.

By 2002, the government had acquired only a little over a third of the area originally intended to comprise the park. During that 30-year period, owners of the remaining areas of the designated park developed agricultural, cattle-raising, and mining industries. In 2002, the government announced that it would acquire the remaining areas identified for the park and initiated a new wave of inspections, controls, fines, and restrictions. The government interrupted mining but did not pay the owners. The government placed restrictions on agriculture, including the farming by Canastreiros, the traditional residents of Serra da Canastra. A climate of distrust, revolt, and conflict emerged. Protestors set fires, many of which raged out of control. Environmental advocates accused residents of being responsible for environmental degradation when these residents used their own methods to fight the fires. Villagers accused government agents of arbitrariness and complained that they had confiscated the lands. The mines, paralyzed without warning, sacked thousands of employees. The government scheduled entire villages for removal.

Some judges might have simply tried to settle or set for trial the park-related cases, some of which had been pending since 1972. As Bernard Mayer has said of designers, "We often seem too eager for resolution, and, as a result, it sometimes seems that we are seeking solutions that do not match the level of depth at which participants experience a conflict" (Mayer, 2004:16-17). But Judge Oliveira had a different reaction. He recalls, "I recognized the ineffectiveness of judicial mechanisms to resolve a complex set of disputes and realized that varied parties were interested in:

- Gaining a voice,
- Establishing justice,
- Creating a safe, fire-free environment,
- Changing the status quo, and
- (Perhaps) promoting reconciliation.

I began to study ways of dealing with underlying conflicts."

You will read in Part H about Judge Oliveira's design steps and the processes that Judge Oliveira ultimately put in place—none of which would have occurred without his sensitivity to the parties' non-resolution interests.

In addition to the challenging task of figuring out the optimal combination of processes for situations such as the Serra da Canastra disputes, designers face practical and moral dilemmas in prioritizing a wide range of interests beyond settlement. In reading Chapters 4 and 5, you encountered commentators' views on how to handle these tough choices (*see* pp. 80-83 and 106-113), and in this chapter you will read about how designers have dealt with them creatively. The designer's primary roles may include involving stakeholders who represent this wider array of interests, helping other stakeholders to recognize unarticulated interests, and putting process options before them that might help them achieve these varied interests—and then encouraging the stakeholders to be the decision-makers about process options. Dilemmas for the designer will persist in this situation as well, but this collaborative approach may reduce the designer's potential to miscalculate the ways that stakeholders weigh and prioritize interests.

While the risks of designing processes and systems in situations like the Brazilian national park are high, so too are the potential rewards. When carefully conceived, these processes and systems facilitate peaceful co-existence, save lives, and bring about change. Your expertise as a designer will make you a valuable contributor when you help people achieve these goals.

A. SEEKING JUSTICE

If an act violates criminal laws, then successful prosecution could convey legal accountability and might also deter future unlawful conduct, thus contributing to safety. In situations where the conflict is caused by a crime, conviction and punishment might also change the perpetrator; at any rate that individual might be imprisoned and not able to commit a crime again, or might be discharged and not in a position to commit similar offenses. A conviction may occasionally establish precedent that particular behavior constitutes a crime (*see* Koh, 2002:312-313). But resort to a criminal process does not always produce a conviction or meet all of the varied interests discussed just above in the Brazilian park example and in other situations.

A group of designers and stakeholders often do not have to choose between prosecution and another process such as a truth and reconciliation commission; they can pursue both or choose from other options entirely. This contrasts with the unusual situation faced by a nation transitioning to a new government after civil war; there, amnesty—not prosecution—may be required to achieve peace, and with much controversy about that choice. In situations that do not involve transitions to a new government, the issue is often what, if any, processes could be deployed in addition to prosecution (assuming prosecution is warranted).

In the aftermath of Canada's Indian Residential Schools, designers faced just this question. A handful of people had been convicted of abusing children. Many more suspected perpetrators had already died, or children could not identify them, or memories had faded. The survivors and Aboriginal communities sought something more than occasional and non-systematic prosecution.

Thousands of residential school survivors filed civil suits as well. When courts certified several suits as class actions, this contributed pressure for the government to do something more, as did some of the cases in which motions by the government and churches to dismiss claims were unavailing.

While ultimately contributing to the pressure for a broader settlement, the civil suits did not themselves meet the stakeholders' needs. Sometimes the courts would award damages only for physical and sexual abuses, which were often difficult to prove years later. The courts often did not recognize a remedy for the students' forcible removal from families, their loss of language and culture, the cold and unfeeling reception at the schools, the denigration and disruption of their communities. And the adversarial process felt neither natural in the cultures of survivors nor responsive to the matters most important to them.

Truth and
Reconciliation
Commission of Canada

The first dispute resolution process created in the aftermath of the Indian Residential Schools: Aware of the civil suits and the desires for something additional, the Canadian government established a simplified claims process option called the "ADR process," though geared to the recoveries the courts would award. The statement below by an 88-year-old survivor indicates one reaction to the insufficiency of civil recovery through the government's ADR process:

"'I cannot forget one painful memory. It occurred in 1932 when I was 15 years old. My father came to the Portage la Prairie resident school to tell my sister and I that our mother had died and to take us to the funeral. The principal of the school would not let us go with our father to the funeral. My sister and I cried so much, we were locked in a dark room for about two weeks. After I was released from the dark room and allowed to be with other residents, I tried to run away to my father and family. I was caught in the bush by teachers and taken back to the school and strapped so severely that my arms were black and blue for several weeks. . . . I told this story during my ADR hearing. . . . I was told that my experience did not fit into the rigid categories for being compensated under the ADR. However, the adjudicator, Mr. Chin, after hearing my story at my hearing, awarded me $1,500. The federal government appealed to take even that small award from me.'" (Regan, 2010:128).

Stories like this one helped the broader public understand the desire for much more than the prosecutions, the civil litigation, and the government's "ADR" claims tribunal. The Canadian Bar Association was among those supporting the convening of a Truth and Reconciliation Commission and experience-based, rather than law-based, compensation. The Association said, "'[T]here are legal arguments and there is justice. It is time for justice'" (Regan, 2010:125-126).

Another situation in which both prosecution and civil recovery occurred, but many people sought more, occurred in the United States. In contrast to the Canadian situation, Greensboro, North Carolina waited 26 years before it created a process to augment traditional ones to deal with the aftermath of violent community conflict.

Bitterness within a U.S. community 26 years after killings: In 1979, the Communist Workers Party organized a demonstration against the Ku Klux Klan in a Greensboro, North Carolina, public housing project in which most residents were African American. As they prepared and as local residents of this southern U.S. city stood nearby, members of the Klan and a neo-Nazi party drove past the demonstrators. Demonstrators carried signs that read, "Death to the Klan." When a demonstrator slapped some of the caravan cars, several of those in the cars jumped out, grabbed guns from a car trunk, and fired at the demonstrators, killing five people and wounding ten others. During the gunfire, one of the demonstrators shot his gun as well and then was killed.

When prosecuted, those who shot at the demonstrators claimed self-defense. All-white juries acquitted the shooters of state murder charges and federal charges of violating the victims' civil rights.

In 1985, a court found the police department, which did not station officers at the gathering point, and some Klan and Nazi members liable in one of the shootings. Subsequently, the city paid $400,000 in settlement to resolve the civil litigation.

In 2005, the shootings remained a divisive community issue. A news reporter's videotape of the shootings depicted unarmed demonstrators being shot at close range. With the 1979 videotape now posted on the web, residents continued to speculate about how a fair trial could have resulted in acquittals. Residents asked the city council to investigate and make public statements about what occurred years before. The city council declined, 6 to 3, with all white members voting no and all African-American members voting yes.

Hundreds of local citizens, though, offered to donate the needed funding for a process to deal with the shootings and their aftermath. After studying truth and reconciliation commissions around the world, the citizens group ultimately implemented such a commission. The commission publicized its work, investigated, and heard testimony. Though the private commission lacked subpoena power, many testified, including former members of the Ku Klux Klan, former Nazi Party members, former Communist Party members, demonstrators, and police. Some apologized for their roles. A year later, in 2006, the commission issued findings and recommendations to governments, schools, and community groups. The commission recommended finding ways to remember, advocacy for investigations of police corruption, changes to diversify jury pools, and efforts to reconcile. In 2009, the city council expressed regret on behalf of the City of Greensboro regarding the 1979 shootings (*see* http://www.greensborotrc.org/; Williams, 2009).

In Greensboro and in Canada, people sought justice through traditional court processes, but what happened in the courts did not satisfy their desire for justice. In Canada, they returned to ask more of the government, and the Canadian government responded. In Greensboro, when the city said no, the citizens were so intent on supplementing the justice system processes that they donated the funds themselves to create a process to meet stakeholder interests. Each of the succeeding sections in this chapter discusses common stakeholder interests and process responses in situations like these—ones with a backdrop of inequality or involving terrible wrongdoing, particularly if that wrongdoing might recur.

B. SEEKING SAFETY

Sociologist Louis Kriesberg points out that after violence people want sufficient deterrence and/or a plan for the future that assures them that they are safe (Kriesberg, 1998:188). Under this viewpoint, if a police officer who used excessive violence committed a crime and did so acting alone, his imprisonment might assure others in the community that their children were not at risk. But if his actions were part of a broader pattern of abuse, these persons might fear for their children until the pattern changed.

The analogy may extend to non-criminal acts like a chemical spill caused by negligent company officials and to reckless acts like drag racers who kill a pedestrian. In some instances, people may feel safer presuming a deterrent effect of the punishment or civil recovery, although evidence is thin that punishment consistently produces a deterrent effect (*see, e.g.,* Pratt et al., 2006; Paternoster, 2010). In other instances, they feel safe only after new regulations for the companies or more severe penalties for drag racing.

Enhanced perceptions of safety may also require a degree of reconciliation (*see* Section F), as it is not always possible, desirable, or healthy for people to have nothing to do with each other after violence (Lederach, 1998:26). In Rwanda, for example, tens of thousands of prisoners, mostly Hutus, were released from incarceration to return to their neighborhoods where they would live among Tutsis whose families they had been convicted of brutalizing and killing in 1994. Members of neither ethnic group could feel safe without some level of mutual understanding that one would not now attack the other.

In other words, a designer may use or create a variety of processes to deal with stakeholder interests in a future with less likelihood of harm. People may worry about their safety or others' safety even years after an incident. Traditional dispute management processes and systems do not always satisfy that need.

C. SEEKING CHANGE

People sometimes seek change—change that is more fundamental than resolving the presenting dispute. They may seek changes in organizational practices and structures, in public perceptions and attitudes, in distribution of power and resources, and in law. A designer who identifies a desire to achieve change in any of these respects can sometimes find or create processes that will help achieve it. A designer's assessment may point to a need to seek fundamental change even though the stakeholders seem interested in merely resolving a dispute. As discussed below (p. 208), a designer in that situation may want to add stakeholders or devise another strategy to help existing stakeholders understand this assessment. Of course, as noted by the commentators quoted in Chapter 5.A, litigation might lead to reform in some situations. Other commentators suggest that designers might also let the disputes fester, hoping that doing so will create the political will to bring about political or economic changes, but that route may also lead to unrest and suffering. The unrest and suffering in turn may interfere with planning for change. These are not easy choices.

The stories you have already read in this book demonstrate a variety of processes aimed at leading to change:

- former ombuds Howard Gadlin's advice to the National Institutes of Health to change certain practices based on the accumulated knowledge from individual disputes showing that the practices are problematic for many individuals (pp. 30-31; *see also* Rowe, 2009:284);
- the class action settlement of the Canadian Indian Residential Schools issues, which included a truth and reconciliation commission tasked with making findings and educating the general public (pp. 33-36);

- the South African mediation to set up direct conversations for a transition of a new constitution and universal suffrage (pp. 17-19); and
- the U.S. Justice Department's Community Relations Service that broadens the conversations to include those who can improve racial and ethnic justice, such as with Sanford, Florida's committee to recommend changes to its police department and then its committee to monitor implementation of the recommendations (pp. 160-162).

The processes were more complex in the sense that they were created in the midst of other attempts to achieve change. In the last three of these stories, other actions set the framework for the final process to change: class action litigation in the Canadian example, violence and economic sanctions in South Africa, and probably demonstrations after the delay in prosecuting the neighborhood watch shooting in Sanford, Florida.

As you work with stakeholders to design a process that will result in change, they may disagree about the optimal change process. For example, Mark Freeman, a lawyer working in the field of transitional justice, points out that a truth and reconciliation commission can "analyze the social causes of a conflict" (Freeman, 2006:71-72), but in some contexts people may feel that they know the cause and the solution, and want to use a political organization or even a violent approach to achieve that change. In another example of disagreement about the optimal approach, some in Canada praised the truth and reconciliation commission process for its potential to change public opinion—a "bridge" to societal change—while others saw it as a "wall"—putting the conflict firmly in the past and leaving unchanged the power and resource distribution that helped produce the harms addressed by the Commission (Jung, 2009:13). Former civil rights mediators have extolled mediation about "root causes" as a path to change, while others have blamed the process for reducing pressures to change (Warfield, 1996:153-154; Schoeny and Warfield, 2000:266 (mediators can mediate root causes); Nader, 1993:3; Auerbach, 1983:144 (both: dispute resolution may make change less likely)).

Change work is tempered by what is feasible, but designers who do not strive to incorporate the desire or need for change into the systems or processes they assist in creating may miss opportunities to contribute or, if they are not careful, may treat symptoms without addressing some of the root causes of conflict. Chapter 5.A suggests some of the effects of failing to address a need for change.

D. SEEKING PUBLIC UNDERSTANDING

The Truth and Reconciliation Commission of Canada listed as its vision:

> "We will reveal the truth about residential schools, and establish a renewed sense of Canada that is inclusive and respectful, and enables reconciliation" (Truth and Reconciliation Commission of Canada, 2012:2).

Thus the Commission saw its role in revealing the truth as also producing fundamental changes in perceptions and relationships in Canada. Some proponents hoped that these in turn would lead to structural changes in the power and resources available to Aboriginal peoples. Indeed, people are animated to seek public understanding of what occurred by different interests—achieving change, validating their suffering, promoting reconciliation, or a combination of these.

To produce public understanding of past injustice and cruelty, a designer may need to create a new process. Truth and reconciliation commissions represent one such process innovation. The Greensboro Truth and Reconciliation Commission decided that transmitting its findings to the public had value even though criminal prosecutions, civil litigation, and media sources had already focused on what had occurred. The Commission explained:

> "The [Greensboro Truth and Reconciliation Commission] recognizes that for many in our society and in our community, the justice system and media are usually reliable and sufficient guarantees of respect for rights and avenues for discovering the truth about events and the people involved. This is not necessarily true for all. . . . [E]ven a free and vigorous media reflects the opinions and biases of its time and, to a large extent, the interests of its owners. A look back years later by a truth commission may reveal a story different from the one media outlets originally told. We also believe that one of the strengths of the truth commission is that we have been able to engage many members of the community in the process of seeking and dealing with the truth in a way that is very different from the casual or momentary attention one may give to even the best reporting. . . . We hope that our modest examination of a difficult chapter of Greensboro's history and how those events shape the community today may serve as a profound and timely reminder of the importance of facing shameful events honestly and acknowledging the brutal consequences of political spin, calculated blindness and passive ignorance. While the [Commission] recognizes the differences between Greensboro's history and the abuses addressed by other truth commissions, we share a common aspiration: that the truth about the past will help us build a better, more just and more inclusive future" (Greensboro Truth and Reconciliation Commission, 2006:14-15).

For individuals, public understanding of what they went through may help with healing (Sternlight and Robbennolt, 2012). Former South African justice Richard Goldstone noted the importance of allowing people to be heard in a dignified public setting, as exemplified by what occurred when he hosted hearings designed to ascertain the causes of political violence and intimidation during the transition period from apartheid to democracy.

Justice Goldstone: "Four South African victims of apartheid were invited to talk about their experiences. One of them was Albie Sachs, who spoke of the trauma of having an arm and an eye blown away by a bomb that South African agents had placed under his car in Maputo, the capital of Mozambique. Then came the turn of Mrs. Gcina, the widow of a small town lawyer whose only political activity was representing community leaders who were brought to court under draconian apartheid security laws. She spoke of how the security police had terrorized her and their young children with midnight raids and repeated detentions of her husband. One day after the police had taken away her husband for the final time, she heard on the radio that his bullet-riddled body had been found in a field some distance from their home. When Mrs. Gcina described how her twelve-year-old son came to her and asked when his father would be home, her composure dissolved and she began to weep. No one who was present will forget the scene of Albie Sachs attempting to console Mrs. Gcina with the stump of his right arm.

"[T]he following morning at breakfast . . . I complimented her on her courage in coming to speak of her experiences. She responded by expressing her gratitude for having been able to do so: 'You know, Judge, last night was the first night since I lost my husband that I have slept through and not been awakened by nightmares.' When I asked her how she explained that, she responded without a moment's hesitation: 'There were so many important people here who were interested in hearing my story'" (Goldstone, 2000:64-65).

When people who have been harmed want to be heard publicly, as did Mrs. Gcina, it may help for designers to build an opportunity for expression into existing processes. U.S. District Judge Jack Weinstein, for example, held meetings around the country so that veterans could talk about their suffering from the wartime use of Agent Orange even though the litigation was headed to settlement (Weinstein, 2009:1268-1269). Restorative justice advocate Howard Zehr describes the healing aspect as follows:

> "[I]t is often important for a victim to be able to retell [the story of what happened] many times. There are good therapeutic reasons for this. Part of the trauma of crime is the way it upsets our views of ourselves and our world, our life-stories. Transcendence of these experiences means 're-storying' our lives by telling the stories in significant settings, often where they can receive public acknowledgment. Often, too, it is important for victims to tell their stories to the ones who caused the harm and to have them understand the impact of their actions" (Zehr, 2002:14-15).

Processes to enhance public understanding are not only instruments for change or individual healing, but also a way to help a broader public move to a common view of the complexities of a matter. Law professor Janine Geske was looking for a process that would help "the Catholic Church, as a community of people . . . to look from different perspectives at the deep-seated and far-ranging effect of the sex abuse scandal" (Geske, 2009). She adopted a circle process, often designed for the individual members' healing, and had it recorded for the use of parishes throughout the country. The circle process, based on Native American traditions, operates like this:

> "In a circle process, participants arrange themselves in a circle. They pass a 'talking piece' around the circle to assure that each person speaks, one at a time,

in the order in which each is seated in the circle. . . . One or two 'circle keepers' serve as facilitators of the circle. . . . Circles consciously enlarge the circle of participants. Victims, offenders, family members, sometimes justice officials, are included, but community members are essential participants as well" (Zehr, 2002:51).

In her videotaped version of the circle process, Geske included "clergy-abuse survivors and a variety of other kinds of people: then-Archbishop of Milwaukee . . . , parish staff, an offending priest, two parish priests, a woman who left the church over the scandal, and another parishioner whose children are no longer Catholic" (Geske, 2009). She notes that all knew that they were being videotaped. The videotape, in her view, became "a powerful springboard for meaningful discussion that can extend the healing process in all of us" (id.).

In a similar vein, an intervention by the White House in 2009, described below, was a means to de-escalate national tensions resulting from disagreement about the arrest of an innocent man by using a dispute management process and publicity about it.

The beer summit: In 2009, a white police officer arrested an African-American Harvard professor at home in Cambridge, Massachusetts after a call from a passerby that two men—who turned out to be the professor and his cab driver—forcibly opened the door to what turned out to be the professor's residence. The professor was tired and had just arrived home after a flight from China to find the lock on his door jammed. Was this a story about the understandable response by a police officer or an example of racial profiling by a white police officer of an African-American man? Public reaction split. President Barack Obama made a remark in response to a news conference question that implied his belief that the police officer used racial profiling. Subsequently, a new controversy emerged about whether the President should have commented before an administrative inquiry was completed. The President and Vice President then invited the arresting officer and professor to the White House for beers and discussion. The "beer summit" was held in private. Afterward the police officer and professor

White House photo

made public statements that they disagreed about what occurred in the past but agreed on their goals for the future. The President issued this statement:

> I am thankful to Professor Gates and Sergeant Crowley for joining me at the White House this evening for a friendly, thoughtful conversation. Even before we sat

down for the beer, I learned that the two gentlemen spent some time together listening to one another, which is a testament to them. I have always believed that what brings us together is stronger than what pulls us apart. I am confident that has happened here tonight, and I am hopeful that all of us are able to draw this positive lesson from this episode.[2]

White House photo

The White House also released the photos in this box, emphasizing the conciliatory nature of the event.

Processes like Geske's and the White House's can promote public understanding of and respect for diverse views and experiences even in the midst of disagreement (*see* Bush and Folger, 1996:2, 20).

E. SEEKING PERSONAL UNDERSTANDING

People often want to understand what occurred; knowing that may help them to achieve peace of mind. For example, the parties in a medical malpractice case may need money to pay for their child's continuing medical difficulties but also seek to understand what caused their child's condition (Riskin and Welsh, 2008:879). A process that provides for discussion with doctors and hospital staff as well as insurers would be more likely than one with insurers only to address parental interests in communicating about what went medically wrong as well as financial settlement.

In a criminal context, Howard Zehr reports a similar dynamic:

"Victims need answers to questions they have about the offense—why it happened and what has happened since. They need real information, not speculation or the legally constrained information that comes from a trial or plea bargain. . . ." (Zehr, 2002:14).

Designers can create these conversations in a number of contexts: in a protected setting like mediation, assuming the mediator will broaden the discussions beyond what is legally relevant (Riskin and Welsh, 2008:879); after litigation is over when people might speak more freely, as in post-conviction

---

2. https://www.npr.org/sections/thetwo-way/2009/07/obama_beer_photo_op_now_part_o .html (last visited Aug. 15, 2018).

victim-offender dialogues; or as entirely new processes, such as in Greensboro's truth and reconciliation hearings.

The storytelling after traumatic experience may serve the goals of public and personal understanding as well as lay the groundwork for change. Conflict scholar Al Fuertes reported these multiple effects of storytelling by Philippine war victims:

> "[Victims] found the experience of telling cathartic. As they told their stories individually and in groups, they acquired new knowledge and understanding about the nature and dynamics of the impact of war and displacement and also gained new skills in dealing with its effects. Many were confirmed in the strengths they possessed and were validated in their stories and coping mechanisms. Problems they shared were discussed, and aspirations, including dreams of a future reality, were defined further. Healing is an ongoing process, and the storytelling workshop made these people become more cohesive as a displaced community" (Fuertes, 2012:346-347).

F. STRENGTHENING PERSONAL ACCOUNTABILITY

Legal accountability—being found civilly liable or settling a lawsuit or pleading or being found guilty in a criminal proceeding—does not always result in establishing personal accountability for wrongdoing. Lawyers may sometimes gloss over this distinction as they represent clients. After research on lawyer representation, Tamara Relis noted:

> "[P]laintiffs' objectives of obtaining admissions of fault, acknowledgments of harm, retribution for defendant conduct, prevention of reoccurrences, answers, and apologies remain invisible to most lawyers throughout the duration of litigation and mediation" (Relis, 2009:34).

In contrast to the lawyers Relis observed, people who are hurt or injured know the difference. For example, one of the plaintiffs in litigation against W.R. Grace for polluting groundwater in Woburn, Massachusetts resisted a confidential settlement that nullified the verdict against Grace and failed to include an acknowledgment of responsibility by the company:

> "'A settlement is one thing,' he said, 'but I'm not willing to throw out the verdict in order to settle. They're guilty of polluting. My child died from their stupidity. I didn't get into this for the money. I got into this because I want to find them guilty for what they did. I want the world to know that'" (Harr, 1995:442).
>
> "Most seemed to agree with this. Pasquale Zona said, 'A settlement without disclosure is no settlement at all.' . . ."
>
> "'Saying they're not guilty of any illness or death,' Ron Zona said with disgust. 'That's why we're in this to begin with'" (id.:443).

While these comments related to settlement, a similar point might be made about the lack of personal accountability when a corporation enters a guilty plea in court. It does not necessarily result in shame for those doing the act, recognize their personal responsibility for the harm, or express community disapproval of those responsible (Poveda, 1994:150, 951). But, the process could be designed to change that, as the following example demonstrates:

"Charged with spilling 75,000 gallons of cancer-causing chemicals into Washington's Puget Sound, Pennwalt had agreed to plead guilty to a felony and pay $1.1 million in fines. . . . When Pennwalt's lawyers appeared before him with the plea agreement, [federal district] Judge [Jack E.] Tanner turned them away, ordering them not to return unless they brought Pennwalt's 'top man' with them. 'Who is the corporation? I think the public is entitled to know who's responsible,' barked Tanner. When the lawyers returned with three top-level local Pennwalt executives, Tanner again refused the plea. Only when CEO Edwin E. Tuttle appeared in court, flying in from across the country, did Tanner accept the company's guilty plea. He did so, however, only after questioning Tuttle carefully on how the chemical spill could have happened and how (in light of Pennwalt's imminent sale to an overseas acquirer) the people of the state of Washington could be assured that nothing so destructive could ever happen again. Tuttle, composed and courteous, responded to all of Judge Tanner's questions. Later, Tanner recalled, 'The only way to get their attention [was] to make the top guy responsible'" (Barnard, 1999:959, 961).

Even in criminal cases involving individuals, the impersonality of the justice process and the minimal participation of crime victims limit the extent to which a guilty plea or a conviction produce in the offender a sense of personal accountability for harm done.

"Accountability in most juvenile justice systems is interpreted as punishment or adherence to a set of rules laid down by the system. However, neither being punished nor following a set of rules involves taking full responsibility for behavior or making repairs for the harm caused. Punishment and adherence to rules do not facilitate moral development at a level that is achieved by taking full responsibility for behavior" (Guide, 1998:9).

To increase personal accountability, some schools asked student offenders to meet with the people their actions have harmed:

"For many students, full participation in a restorative justice process is much more difficult and burdensome than conventional forms of punishment. It is easier simply to be suspended, or to serve time in detention, than to confront the consequences of your conduct and the people your actions have harmed, and then to help construct a remedy or response for which you will be responsible. . . . [quotes student who resisted RJ] 'I don't want to face my teacher and in detention all I have to do is sit there for an hour and I'm done'" (Abregu, 2012:13).

The restorative justice approach taken by these schools and Judge Tanner's insistence on personalizing the corporate errors represent just two options in a broad array of approaches in which designers might accommodate the desire to strengthen personal accountability on the part of wrongdoers.

G. SEEKING RECONCILIATION

Even after violence, people sometimes must live or work together, and they want to feel secure in these relationships. For these and other reasons, they sometimes aim for a level of reconciliation that will make that feasible. When he accepted the Prime Minister's apology for the decades of abuse at the Indian Residential Schools, Assembly of First Nations National Chief Phil Fontaine, a survivor of the residential schools, immediately put the focus on reconciliation: "Together we can achieve the greatness our country deserves" (Truth and Reconciliation Commission of Canada, 2012:27). This was not a naïve statement; he also said:

> "We heard the Government of Canada take full responsibility for this dreadful chapter in our shared history. We heard the Prime Minister declare that this will never happen again. Finally, we heard Canada say it is sorry. Brave survivors, through the telling of their painful stories, have stripped white supremacy of its authority and legitimacy. The irresistibility of speaking truth to power is real. Today is not the result of a political game. Instead, it is something that shows the righteousness and importance of our struggle" (Jung, 2009:18).

As law professor Jennifer Llewellyn put it, "[Reconciliation] is not the stuff of greeting cards and intimate reunions. . . ." (Llewellyn, 2008:190). It is the stuff of moving forward.

Some have said that reconciliation, change, and truth are linked. After decades of discrimination and suffering under South Africa's apartheid policies, all parties opted to seek reconciliation but with constitutional changes that ensured universal suffrage along with other rights and with months of public hearings that made known the experiences of victims, the personal confessions of perpetrators, and detailed findings regarding what had occurred. Bishop Desmond Tutu, former Chair of South Africa's Truth and Reconciliation Commission, explained the necessary combination:

> "For us, truth was at the heart of reconciliation: the need to find out the truth about the horrors of the past, the better to ensure that they never happen again. And that is the central significance of reconciliation. Without it people have no sense of safety, no trust, no confidence in the future. The aim must be . . . 'to build a shared future from a divided past'" (Tutu, in Bloomfield et al., 2003:3).

Because of the link between reconciliation and truth, those who write about truth and reconciliation commissions emphasize the value of making findings about what occurred in the past as part of the reconciliation process (*see, e.g.*, Kriesberg, 1998:188; Freeman, 2006:71-72).

H. DESIGNING PROCESSES TO SERVE NON-RESOLUTION INTERESTS

Designers work through the same steps discussed in earlier chapters to this book, but with somewhat different considerations, when encountering interests other than resolving the dispute. Once Judge Oliveira identified these additional interests in the Brazilian park cases referenced in the introduction to this chapter, he conferred with a dispute system design expert at Sao Paulo law school, Diego Faleck (see pp. 194-195), who recommended that he read an earlier edition of this book. Judge Oliveira describes below what he did to take design initiative, assess the situation, create processes, and implement the process (Chapters 2-5, 11-13).

Judge Oliveira's account of the Canastra National Park process: Taking design *initiative and clarifying roles:* "As the only federal judge for the region, with almost ten thousand lawsuits under my responsibility, I knew the personal time investment that taking initiative for dispute system design would demand. I would not only need to deal with the conflict itself but also to introduce and work toward the acceptance in our judicial culture of a new way of dealing with conflicts. I first sought support from our Appellate Court for this undertaking and found another judge to collaborate with me—Judge Marco Antonio. I also sought support from the Association of Federal Judges of Brazil. Before Judge Antonio and I started, we gathered our families and, during the school holidays, did an 'undercover tourist trip' to the National Park. We came back convinced, that, despite the sacrifice of family time to deal with the problem, it would be worthwhile."

Diagnosing or assessing stakeholders, goals, and contexts: "A careful analysis of the cases was a good start to identifying the stakeholders. The complexity of the dispute and the number of stakeholders was difficult to communicate. To deal with that issue, I constructed a website with visual appeal, which would condense all information for quick reading. Further, I named the project *Canastra: Justice and Reconciliation* and created a logo for it.

"Through direct personal contact we reached out to stakeholders: the Federal Justice Department, Federal Public Defender's Office (which agreed to represent the interests of the Canastreiros who would not otherwise have had legal representation), Canastreiros Association, Brazilian Bar Association, Federal Public Prosecutor's Office, Miners' Association, municipal leaders in the region, National Association of Federal Judges, Brazilian House of Representatives, Catholic Church, Federal University of Minas Gerais, Workers' Party in the State of Minas Gerais, and ICMBio—the Brazilian Ministry of the Environment's administrative arm.

"As I listened to these persons, I realized again that designing processes for this conflict would be a question of following the lessons of the book—escaping from legal nomenclature and going straight to the interests."

Creating dispute management processes and systems: "The first breakthrough resulted from difficult meetings between the Canastreiros and ICMBio about fire containment. ICMBio agents had been punishing Canastreiros for their efforts at fire prevention which did not accord with the environmental agency's guidelines. Considerable anger and mutual suspicion shadowed the meetings. At the same time, both parties wanted to reduce distrust and the temperature of the conflict, as it was severely damaging both day-to-day peace and the environment itself. Widespread and uncontrolled fires had been burning on both government and Canastreiros' lands.

"An idea to establish a form of collaborative fire fighting led to the breakthrough. The central idea was to create 'aceiros'—small fire breaks where vegetation is removed to keep fires from spreading.

"It was a beautiful experience. Free from the ballast of conflict and distrust, they worked together in great harmony, and it was possible to perceive the reciprocal admiration when technicians could see the wisdom of the elders to fight the fire, and also when the Canastreiros perceived the value of new techniques brought by the agents of the government. This 2014 agreement has proved itself highly effective. Widespread and uncontrolled fires are now almost nonexistent. And, underlying these concrete results, the agreement launched seeds of trust that have made other agreements possible.

"Building on this success, multiple parties engaged in planning a First Joint Public Hearing to address the outcry about a government order to remove the São Francisco statue, located at the source of the São Francisco River. It is a sacred place for the traditional populations, who celebrate their religious festivals there, as well as a national symbol related to the preservation of the

Photo of Canastra National Park by Judge Oliveira

environment, because for many Saint Francis was one of the first environmentalists. An agreement was reached to preserve the statue and altar and to set aside the land on which it stands.

"The agreement regarding the statue was a milestone, as it gave impulse to a virtuous cycle that had already begun with the aceiros' partnership. Since then, the engagement of the parties has become denser, and very important measures have been taken by public agents, even without formal agreements. One example is that the 'Land Consolidation' letters that the Government sends to the inhabitants, telling them about compulsory purchase of their lands, will not apply to traditional populations, thus for the first time recognizing the Canastra people's claim to the land and opening up the possibility of their staying in the territory.

"The second milestone was the adoption by ICMBio of the Integrated Fire Management technique. In June 2017, ICMBio communicated the adoption of this technique, which consists in the use of traditional knowledge of the use of fire, involving the local community in actions of participatory management of fire.

"Another dimension of our design was the creation of the Truth and Reconciliation Commission of Serra da Canastra with the purpose of recording and dealing with the facts related to the violence in the region during the period of the military regime, opening ways for the the viability of a consensual solution. The Bar Association assists the Truth and Reconciliation Commission. Its work is underway."

Reaching an Agreement: In October of 2018 the parties reached a broad agreement on a new dispute resolution system. Entitled Agreement of Coexistence, it builds on previous successes, such as a collaborative fire prevention agreement, the preservation of the Statue of St. Francis, and respect for the rights of traditional communities. In the new system, the government provides to traditional residents three essential rights that had been denied for more than forty years: 1) perpetual ownership in the lands, with right of sale and hereditary transmission; 2) annulment of all environmental fines proven to have arisen from activities related to the maintenance of the Canastreiros' traditional way of life; 3) rectification of the areas of traditional properties. In areas considered as the National Park under Government ownership, the management plan will be done in a participatory manner going forward. A Commission for Follow-up of the Agreement will be created, formed by the Canastreiros themselves, the Public Defender, the Public Ministry, and the Environmental Agency, with right of withdrawal in case of noncompliance. Canastreiros may invoke a confidentiality clause when they participate in the new system. In addition, the new Agreement of Coexistence does not force parties to waive any judicial rights that may be already available to them from the state. Those who want to continue with their individual legal action will be able to do so while those who want to participate in the new system can choose that route instead.

Reflections on his role: "When my fellow judge, Judge Marco Antonio Guimaraes, and I arrived at a small village by the mountains, we were approached by some startled old men. One asked, 'Judges here? I never knew there were judges with legs.' We were, and we are, judges-with-legs. And the number of judges-with-legs has been increasing each day, throughout the Brazilian federal justice system. This story, to me, sums up what it takes to be a designer: you have to get up and leave. Leave the courtroom; leave your office; leave the comfort zone, get out of yourself, your position of authority; get out of the pre-shaped solutions, in search of new types, of dialogue. One must walk toward a new way of doing things."

Judge Oliveira recognized from the start that the multiplicity of interests both warranted a novel design and increased the complexity of the design work. Still he took the same series of steps as designers follow when settlement or adjudication is the stakeholders' only goal. In weighing these broader stakeholder interests as he followed typical designer steps, Judge Oliveira found himself acting in nontraditional ways for a judge—ultimately blazing a new path for other judges.

THOUGHTS GOING FORWARD

Your challenge as a designer is to find "the right level of depth at which to engage" stakeholder interests and goals (Mayer, 2004:184). This is particularly true against a backdrop of inequality and when there has been wrongdoing and suffering that might recur. In this context, be prepared to ask more questions and think more broadly about the goals a design should achieve. For those situations involving more than resolution in particular, the processes and systems should be tailored to the circumstances. In addition to or instead of creating processes or systems simply for resolving disputes, can you develop ones that permit those involved to achieve their deeper yearnings to make an organization or society more just or to make fundamental changes in organizational practices, in public perceptions and attitudes, in distribution of power and resources, or in law? How can you be sensitive to the desires, and at times, unspoken but critical needs for validation, healing, accountability, and reconciliation as you design? What will it take to create a process that will make it possible for people to feel safe from repetition of harm? There may be concerns that these "softer" processes leave perpetrators unaccountable, but that need not always be the case. Further, as part of an integrated system, several processes can often proceed at once, preserving or even enhancing accountability. There will often be conflicts among stakeholders or the larger public's interests in these situations, leaving you as the designer with moral and strategic quandaries to address and handle.

QUESTIONS

8.1 For the Brazilian park disputes described at the start of this chapter, (i) what stakeholders should be a part of a collaborative design process? (ii) what are they likely to seek from the process? (iii) what processes would likely be feasible and responsive to these needs?

8.2 Suppose the government refuses to be involved in the process that other stakeholders in question 8.1 have chosen. What are the pros and cons of proceeding without explicit federal government involvement? In this regard, you might consider what Michael Young did in the South African negotiations (pp. 147-148).

8.3 In Canada, people are still debating whether the Truth and Reconciliation processes achieved their aims. What would you ask to satisfy your own concerns about the success of the processes?

8.4 In 2011, Governor Paul LePage of Maine and the Wabanaki Tribal Governments agreed to create a truth and reconciliation process on child welfare issues. The truth and reconciliation organizers issued this list of reasons:

- "The United States government has tried many different ways to solve what they called 'the Indian problem'—stealing land, killing off entire tribes by war and disease and by taking Indian children away from their families and communities.

- "In the 1800's, different church groups with the support of the government took Indian children and sent them to boarding schools far away from their communities where they couldn't speak their own language, wear their own clothes or practice their own religion. They also treated Indian children badly, abusing them physically, emotionally and sexually. Many of these children died. The ones who made it home after years in these schools were not the same as when they left.

- "In the 1950's, the Bureau of Indian Affairs and the Child Welfare League of America did an experiment where they took hundreds of Indian children from their families to raise them in white homes, thinking it was better for them.

- "In Maine, Indian children were taken from their families and placed in white foster homes at a higher rate than most other states.

- "In 1978, the federal government passed a law called the Indian Child Welfare Act that gave Indian children more protection and recognized a child's tribal citizenship is as important as their family relationship. Maine child welfare has been working with Wabanaki tribes to have an improved relationship and to work better with Wabanaki people. A lot of progress has been made, but there are still some problems. This TRC will identify the problems and make suggestions to help fix these problems" (https://ptla.org/wabanaki/truth-and-reconciliation).

You have joined the truth and reconciliation's advisory committee of stakeholders as the design expert. You will listen, of course, to what stakeholders seek from the process but want to do research first on other situations in which stakeholders sought something similar and in which the context resembles this one. What do you think are the likely interests of stakeholders? What comparable processes come to mind as you think about meeting these interests through process design?

Maine was the first U.S. state to organize a truth and reconciliation commission. Should the United States convene a truth and reconciliation commission to deal with past injustices against Native Americans or other groups of persons who experienced or endured the legacy of, for example, slavery, government-sanctioned discrimination and violence, or internments during war (*see* Goldstone, 2006)?

8.5 The South African truth and reconciliation commission had the authority to subpoena witnesses. In contrast, the Canadian commission did not, although the settlement agreement required all of the involved churches and the government to supply the information the commission requested and left the settlement agreement under the supervision of the court. What might be the arguments for and against subpoena power in each of these situations?

8.6 The South African truth and reconciliation commission named perpetrators, though it also accorded many of these individuals amnesty from criminal prosecution. What is likely to be lost or gained if another truth and reconciliation commission does not name perpetrators of crime in a situation in which there will be no amnesty, that is, where the perpetrators remain subject to criminal prosecution?

8.7 A local chemical company sent trucks under cover of darkness to dump, illegally of course, chemical waste into a stream. Later several individuals filed a class action against the company on behalf of over 500 persons who claimed to have become ill, many with permanent health damage, as the result of the dumped chemicals leaking into their food or water. As the law clerk to the judge assigned the class action, what counsel might you offer the judge about the process(es) that could and should be used, in addition to that required by the rules of civil procedure, before the judge approves a settlement reached by the company and class representatives?

Exercise 8.1 A student kills 20 people on the Tallahoya University campus and then kills himself. In their grief, people begin blaming the university administration for not providing enough counseling or admissions vigilance, the police and campus security for not responding sooner, professors who noticed aberrant behavior for doing nothing further, residence hall administrators for not evacuating students quickly enough, and builders of the residence halls for not creating automatic hallway barriers that could be lowered in a crisis. Students are grief-stricken and no longer feel safe. Some blame those students who ran and hid from the shooter rather than trying to stop him, and one such student has already withdrawn from school. University counsel calls you. "Is there a design that might help in this tragic situation," counsel asks, "and, if so, are we the office to create it?"

BIBLIOGRAPHY AND REFERENCES

ABREGU, Lisa (2012) "Restorative Justice in Schools: Restoring Relationships and Building Community," 18 (4) *Disp. Resol. Mag.* 10.

ALLRED, Keith G. (2005) "Relationship Dynamics in Disputes: Replacing Contention with Cooperation," in Michael L. Moffitt and Robert C. Bordone eds., *The Handbook of Dispute Resolution* 83. San Francisco: Jossey-Bass.

AMSTUTZ, Mark R. (2005) *The Healing of Nations: The Promise and Limits of Political Forgiveness.* New York: Lanham.

ASMAL, Kader (2000) "International Law and Practice: Dealing with the Past in the South African Experience," 15 *Am. U. Int'l L. Rev.* 1211.

AUERBACH, Jerome (1983) *Justice Without Law?* New York: Oxford University Press.

BARNARD, Jayne W. (1999) "Reintegrative Shaming in Corporate Sentencing," 72 *S. Cal. L. Rev.* 959.

BINGHAM, Lisa B. (2008) "Designing Justice: Legal Institutions and Other Systems for Managing Conflict," 14 *Ohio St. J. on Disp. Resol.* 1.

BLOOMFIELD, David, Teresa BARNES, and Luc HUYSE eds. (2003) *Reconciliation After Violent Conflict: A Handbook.* Stockholm: International Institute for Democracy and Electoral Assistance.

BOUTROS-GHALI, Boutros (1995) *An Agenda for Peace* (2d ed.). New York: United Nations.

BUSH, Robert A. Baruch, and Joseph FOLGER (2005) *The Promise of Mediation* (2d ed.). San Francisco: Jossey Bass.

BUSH, Robert A. Baruch, and Joseph FOLGER (1996) *The Promise of Mediation.* San Francisco: Jossey-Bass.

CHAYES, Antonia, and Martha MINOW eds. (2003*) Imagine Coexistence: Restoring Humanity After Violent Ethnic Conflict.* San Francisco: Jossey-Bass.

CHIGAS, Diana, and Brian GANSON (2003) "Grand Visions and Small Projects," in Antonia Chayes and Martha Minow eds., *Imagine Coexistence* 59. San Francisco: Jossey-Bass.

COHEN, Amy J. (2009) "Dispute Systems Design, Neoliberalism, and the Problem of Scale," 14 *Harv. Negot. L. Rev.* 51.

CROCKER, David A. (2002) "Punishment, Reconciliation, and Democratic Deliberation," 5 *Buff. Crim. L. Rev.* 509.

DEUTSCH, Morton (1998) "Constructive Conflict Resolution: Principles, Training, and Research" in Eugene Weiner ed., *The Handbook of Interethnic Coexistence* 199. New York: Continuum.

DUBINSKY, Paul R. (2005) "Human Rights Law Meets Private Law Harmonization: The Coming Conflict," 30 *Yale J. Int'l L.* 211.

FISS, Owen M. (2009) "The History of an Idea," 78 *Fordham L. Rev.* 1273.

FREEMAN, Mark (2006) *Truth Commissions and Procedural Fairness.* Cambridge: Cambridge University Press.

FUERTES, Al (2012) "Storytelling and Its Transformative Impact in the Philippines," 29 *Conflict Resol. Q.* 333.

GESKE, Janine (2009) "Repairing the Harm from Clergy Sex Abuse," *available at* http://law.marquette.edu/facultyblog/2009/05/25/repairing-the-harm-from-clergy-sex-abuse/.

GOLDSTONE, Richard (2000) *For Humanity: Reflections of a War Crimes Investigator.* New Haven, CT: Yale University Press.

GOLDSTONE, Richard J. (2006) "The South African Truth and Reconciliation Commission: Is It Relevant to the United States," 12 (3) *Disp. Resol. Mag.* 19.

GREENSBORO TRUTH AND RECONCILIATION COMMISSION (2006) *Greensboro Truth and Reconciliation Commission Report, available at* http://www.greensborotrc.org/.

NATIONAL CRIMINAL JUSTICE REFERENCE SERVICE (1998) *Guide for Implementing the Balanced and Restorative Justice Model* (1998) https://www.ncjrs.gov/pdffiles/167887.pdf.

HAMBURG, David A. (1998) "Preventing Contemporary Intergroup Violence," in Eugene Weiner ed., *The Handbook of Interethnic Coexistence* 27. New York: Continuum.

HARR, Jonathan (1995) *A Civil Action.* New York: Random House.

HARVEY, Robert (2001) *The Fall of Apartheid: The Inside Story from Smuts to Mbeki.* New York: Palgrave Macmillan.

HUFF, C. Ronald, Nancy H. ROGERS, and Richard A. SALEM (1987) "Mediation of Cohabitant Violence Cases," in Nancy H. Rogers and Richard A. Salem eds., *A Student's Guide to Mediation and the Law.* New York: Matthew Bender.

INTERNATIONAL CIVIL RIGHTS CLINIC AT HARVARD LAW SCHOOL, ed. (2009) *Prosecuting Apartheid-Era Crimes?: A South African Dialogue on Justice*. Cambridge, MA: International Civil Rights Clinic at Harvard Law School.

JUNG, Courtney (2009) "Canada and the Legacy of the Indian Residential Schools: Transitional Justice for Indigenous People in a Non-Transitional Society," https://papers.ssrn.com/sol3/Papers.cfm?abstract_id=1374950.

KNOBLOCK-WESTERWICK, Silvia, and Jingbo MENG (2009) "Looking the Other Way," 36 *Communication Research* 426.

KOH, Harold (2002) "A United States Human Rights Policy for the 21st Century," 46 *St. Louis U. L.J.* 293.

KRIESBERG, Louis (1998) "Coexistence and the Reconciliation of Communal Conflicts," in Eugene Weiner ed., *The Handbook of Interethnic Coexistence* 182. New York: Continuum.

LEDERACH, John Paul (1998) "Beyond Violence: Building Sustainable Peace," in Eugene Weiner ed., *The Handbook of Interethnic Coexistence* 236. New York: Continuum.

LLEWELLYN, Jennifer J. (2002) "Dealing with the Legacy of Native Residential School Abuse in Canada: Litigation, ADR, and Restorative Justice," 52 *U. Toronto L.J.* 253.

MAYER, Bernard S. (2004) *Beyond Neutrality: Confronting the Crisis in Conflict Resolution*. San Francisco: Jossey-Bass.

MENKEL-MEADOW, Carrie (2005) "Roots and Inspirations: A Brief History of the Foundations of Dispute Resolution," in Michael L. Moffitt and Robert C. Bordone eds., *The Handbook of Dispute Resolution* 13. San Francisco: Jossey-Bass.

MENKEL-MEADOW, Carrie (2006) "Peace and Justice: Notes on the Evolution and Purposes of Legal Processes," 94 *Geo. L.J.* 553 (2006).

MENKEL-MEADOW, Carrie (2009) "Are There Systemic Ethics Issues in Dispute System Design? And What We Should [Not] Do About It: Lessons from International and Domestic Fronts," 14 *Harv. Negot. L. Rev.* 195.

MENKEL-MEADOW, Carrie (2014) "Unsettling the Lawyers: Other Forms of Justice in Indigenous Claims of Expropriation, Abuse, and Injustice," 64 *U. Toronto L.J.* 620.

MINOW, Martha (1998) *Between Vengeance and Forgiveness*. Boston, MA: Beacon Press.

MINOW, Martha (2002) "Memory and Hate," in Martha Minow and Nancy L. Rosenblum eds. (2002) *Breaking the Cycles of Hatred: Memory, Law, and Repair* 14. Princeton: Princeton University Press.

MITCHELL, Christopher (2002) "Beyond Resolution: What Does Conflict Transformation Actually Transform?" 9 *Peace and Conflict Studies* 1.

MNOOKIN, Robert (2010) *Bargaining with the Devil: When to Negotiate, When to Fight*. New York: Simon & Schuster.

NADER, Laura (1993) "Controlling Processes in the Practice of Law: Hierarchy and Pacification in the Movement to Re-Form Dispute Ideology," 9 *Ohio St. J. on Disp. Resol.* 1.

NOLAN-HALEY, Jacqueline (2017) "Dispute System Design: Justice, Accountability, and Impact," 13 *U. St. Thomas L.J.* 315.

O'CONNOR, Sandra Day (2000) "Foreword," in Richard J. Goldstone, *For Humanity: Reflections of a War Crimes Investigator*. New Haven, CT: Yale University Press.

PAOLINI, Stefania, Miles HEWSTONE, Ed CAIRNS, and Alberto VOCI (2004) "Effects of Direct and Indirect Cross-Group Friendships on Judgments of Catholics and Protestants in Northern Ireland: The Mediating Role of an Anxiety-Reduction Mechanism," 30 *Personality and Social Psychology Bulletin* 770.

PATERNOSTER, Raymond (2010) "How Much Do We Really Know About Criminal Deterrence?," 100 (3) *J. Crim. L. & Criminology* 765.

PHELPS, Teresa Godwin (2004) *Shattered Voices: Language, Violence, and the Work of the Truth Commissions*. Philadelphia: University of Pennsylvania Press.

POVEDA, Tony G. (1994) *Re-Thinking White Collar Crime*. Westport, CT: Praeger Publishers.

PRATT, Travis C., Frances T. CULLEN, Kristie R. BLEVINS, Leah E. DAIGLE, and Tamara D. MADENSEN (2006) "The Empirical Status of Deterrence Theory: A Meta-Analysis," in Frances T. Cullen, John Paul Wright, and Kristie R. Blevins eds., *Taking Stock: The Status of Criminological Theory* 367. New Brunswick, NJ: Transaction Publishers.

PUTNAM, Robert D. (2000) *Bowling Alone: The Collapse and Revival of American Community*. New York: Simon & Schuster.

QUIGLEY, John B. (2006) *The Genocide Convention: An International Law Analysis*. London: Ashgate Publishing Ltd.

REGAN, Paulette (2010) *Unsettling the Settler Within: Indian Residential Schools, Truth Telling, and Reconciliation in Canada*. Vancouver, BC: The University of British Columbia Press.

RELIS, Tamara (2009) *Perceptions in Litigation and Mediation: Lawyers, Defendants, Plaintiffs, and Gendered Parties*. Cambridge, UK: Cambridge University Press.

RISKIN, Leonard L., and Nancy A. WELSH (2008) "Is That All There Is? 'The Problem' in Court-Connected Mediation," 15 *Geo. Mason L. Rev.* 863.

ROBINSON, Paul H. (2011) "The Ongoing Revolution in Punishment Theory: Doing Justice as Controlling Crime." 42 *Ariz. St. L.J.* 1089.

ROSS, Marc Howard (1993) *The Culture of Conflict*. New Haven, CT: Yale University Press.

ROTBERG, Robert I., and Dennis THOMPSON (2000) *Truth v. Justice: The Morality of Truth Commissions*. Princeton, NJ: Princeton University Press.

ROWE, Mary (2009) "An Organizational Ombuds Office in a System for Dealing with Conflict and Learning from Conflict, or 'Conflict Management System,'" 14 *Harv. Negot. L. Rev.* 279.

RULE, Colin (2008) "Making Peace on eBay: Resolving Disputes in the World's Largest Marketplace," *ACResolution* (Fall).

SCHNEIDER, Andrea Kupfer (2009) "The Intersection of Dispute Systems Design and Transitional Justice," 14 *Harv. Negot. L. Rev.* 289.

SCHOENY, Mara, and Wallace WARFIELD (2000) "Reconnecting Systems Maintenance with Social Justice: A Critical Role for Conflict Resolution," 16 *Negot. J.* 253.

SISK, Timothy (2001) "Peacemaking Processes: Forestalling Return to Ethnic Violence," in I. William Zartman ed., *Preventive Negotiation: Avoiding Conflict Escalation* 67. Lanham, MD: Rowman & Littlefield Publishers, Inc.

SKOGAN, Wesley G., Susan M. HARTNETT, Natalie BUMP, and Jill DUBOIS (2008) *Executive Summary, Evaluation of CeaseFire-Chicago, available at* https://www.ipr.northwestern.edu/publications/papers/urban-policy-and-community-development/docs/ceasefire-pdfs/executivesummary.pdf.

SLUZKI, Carlos E. (2003) "The Process Toward Reconciliation," in Antonia Chayes and Martha Minow eds., *Imagine Coexistence* 21. San Francisco: Jossey-Bass.

SOSNOV, Maya (2008) "The Adjudication of Genocide: Gacaca and the Road to Reconciliation in Rwanda," 36 *Denv. J. Int'l L. & Pol'y* 125.

STERNLIGHT, Jean, and Jennifer ROBBENNOLT (2012) *Psychology for Lawyers: Understanding the Human Factors in Negotiation, Litigation and Decisionmaking*. Chicago: ABA.

STURM, Susan, and Howard GADLIN (2007) "Conflict Resolution and Systemic Change," 2007 *J. Disp. Resol.* 1.

"Symposium: Dialogues of Transitional Justice" (2014) 32 *Quinnipiac L. Rev. 579.*

TEITEL, Ruti (2000) *Transitional Justice*. New York: Oxford University Press.

TITTLE, Charles, Ekaterina BOTCHKOVAR, and Olena ANTONACCIO (2011) "Criminal Contemplation, National Context, and Deterrence," 27(2) *J. Quantitative Criminology* 225-249.

TRUTH AND RECONCILIATION COMMISSION OF CANADA (2012) *Interim Report*. Winnipeg, Manitoba: TRC of Canada.

TRUTH AND RECONCILIATION COMMISSION OF CANADA (2015) *Honouring the Truth, Reconciling for the Future: Summary of the Final Report of the Truth and Reconciliation Commission of Canada.* Winnipeg, Manitoba: TRC of Canada.

TYLER, Tom (2009) "Governing Pluralistic Societies," 72 *Law & Contemp. Probs.* 187 (Spring).

VAN NESS, Daniel W., and Karen Heetderks STRONG (2002) *Restoring Justice* (2d ed.). Cincinnati, OH: Anderson Publishing Co.

VOLPE, Maria R (1998) "Using Town Meetings to Foster Peaceful Coexistence," in Eugene Weiner ed., *The Handbook of Interethnic Coexistence* 382. New York: Continuum.

WARFIELD, Wallace (1996) "Building Consensus for Racial Harmony in American Cities: Case Model Approach," 1996 *J. Disp. Resol.* 151.

WEINSTEIN, Jack B. (2009) "Comments on Owen M. Fiss, Against Settlement (1984)," 78 *Fordham L. Rev.* 1265.

WILLIAMS, Jill E. (2009) "Legitimacy and Effectiveness of a Grassroots Truth and Reconciliation Commission," 72 *Law & Contemp. Probs.* 143 (Spring).

ZARTMAN, I. William (2000) "Introduction," in I. William Zartman ed., *Traditional Cures for Modern Conflicts: African Conflict "Medicine."* Boulder, CO: Lynne Rienner Publishers.

ZARTMAN, I. William ed. (2001) *Preventive Negotiation: Avoiding Conflict Escalation.* Lanham, MD: Rowman & Littlefield Publishers, Inc.

ZEHR, Howard (2002) *The Little Book of Restorative Justice.* Intercourse, PA: Good Books.

Enhancing Relationships

A designer will be unable to achieve design goals in some situations unless the design creates ways for the stakeholders to build and improve relationships over time. When you have completed this chapter, you will have sampled the pertinent research and theory and have a number of ideas to enhance relationships as you create and modify processes and systems.

A note on language: In this chapter we refer to "constructive relationships." By this, we mean relationships among the participants that help achieve the goals for the system or process. In some instances, a more constructive relationship is a more trusting one. It may also be one that does not involve as much hate or prejudice. After a period of violence, the most constructive relationship that can be achieved between members of warring factions may simply be a relationship in which one person does not choose to inflict violence on the other; it may not be possible for people to trust each other or set aside their hatred (Minow, 1998).

The violence-related example is extreme, of course. In other situations, a designer may find that the participants are on relatively good terms and simply need specialized help to create a more dynamic and effective dispute resolution system. Designers take their parties where they find them. Whether the relationship between them is good or bad, intimate or nearly non-existent, designers

---

DESIGNING STEPS

1. Design initiative
2. Basic planning steps
   - Assessing stakeholders, their goals and interests, and contexts
   - Creating processes and systems
3. Key planning issues (that may arise throughout the planning)
   - Planning how to select, engage, and prepare intervenors and parties
   - Determining the extent of confidentiality and openness in the process
   - Dealing with desires for change, justice, accountability, understanding, safety, reconciliation
   - **Enhancing relationships**
   - Incorporating technology
4. Implementing and institutionalizing the system or process
   - Implementing
   - Using contracts
   - Using law
   - Evaluating, revising

---

can establish new processes to increase the likelihood that the future relationship will have a positive or constructive trajectory.

The process-relationship interaction occurs in multiple ways: First, the more constructive the relationships, the *less likely that a conflict will escalate*. To get a sense of this dynamic, consider your own reaction to the following incident in a U.S. city:

> Bullets fly into the house the night after one of the children declined to join a gang. The mother calls the police, while the father puts a gun under his belt and steps out in front of the house to watch for the shooters. Police officers arrive and order the father to hit the ground. The father does not immediately comply and moves his arm. The police officers see the gun in the belt and kill the father.

A tragedy certainly. A demand from community members to review police use of force policies and to investigate the officers who fired on the homeowner may follow. Perhaps litigation or criminal charges will come next. What would you want to know in order to predict whether the conflict will escalate beyond this to divide the community or even trigger civil unrest and violence? No doubt some of the information you would seek would relate to the details of the incident and the racial, ethnic, or religious identities of those involved in it. You would also want to know the history and quality of the relationships between police and citizens within that community—their mutual perceptions and levels of trust and communication. Answers to such questions will help provide insight into whether people will view the father's killing as a tragic, but isolated incident; a product of poor or inadequate training or lack of experience; or part of a pattern or practice, perhaps based on race, ethnicity, or religion. (Be aware that the answers to these questions may also affect you as a designer; how might the circumstances of the tragedy affect your capacity to work effectively as a designer?)

Second, the relationships affect *how well processes to build consensus will work*. People who are angry or fearful may refuse to meet. If they meet, their distrust may undermine the use of interest-based techniques and cause individuals to eschew any overture to seek resolution (*see* p. 417). If people still remain distrustful, they may reject any agreement that depends on future actions by the other players. "There is no use speaking with them. They will never follow through on an agreement."

Third, the relationships among disputing parties affect more than just whether disputing parties will reach consensual resolutions. As former ombuds at the National Institutes of Health Howard Gadlin points out, clients often want you to design the *system in order to retain and encourage collaborative relationships*. Building, preserving, or restoring relationships, not simply resolving a dispute, may be the primary goal. An adjudication process that resolves the dispute but does not deal with relationships may result in highly valued scientists leaving for a different institution, as in the case of NIH. In the case of eBay, distrust of other traders may mean that customers feel so much at risk that they avoid using eBay at all. Former eBay Resolution Center director Colin Rule explained that this may sound like a vague loss, but businesses know it is real: "While the concept may be difficult to quantify, . . . businesses have come to understand that trust has a very positive effect on the bottom line, and that is why they are willing to spend money to foster it" (Rule, 2008).

Despite the importance of constructive relationships to your design, designers rarely have at their disposal all the levers that affect those relationships. You will probably have to operate without the ability to change the segregated housing, the bad office layout, or the divisive history, to note a few influences on relationships. Still, designers have found ways to use the levers that they can control in ways that enhance relationships among those involved or affected by the process or system of processes.

This chapter focuses first on the theory designers need to understand in order to enhance relationships (Section A) and then on the common tools to do so (Section B).

A. RESEARCH AND THEORY

As you work to improve relationships, three areas of research and theory may be especially helpful. Scholars describe these areas with labels like "social capital," "constructive contacts," and "trust and mistrust within negotiations." As you read about their work, ask what lessons they provide a designer about (1) how relationships affect disputing, and (2) how a design might improve those critical relationships. You will want to explore additional research and theory as you work as a designer.

1. Social capital

Political scientist Robert D. Putnam and colleagues refer to "social capital" as the positive social networks that affect not only the people within them but also others.[1] They view positive social networks as having high degrees of "reciprocity, mutual assistance, and trustworthiness" (Putnam and Feldman,

---

1. Other disciplines and authors have given the term "social capital" different meanings than Putnam and his colleagues.

2003:2). People within these positive social networks will be more likely to trust each other, thus increasing the chances that designers can create processes in which interest-based negotiations will occur. They also more often trust the acquaintances of those within their social networks. Further, in positive social networks, reputations spread quickly, acting as a deterrent to dishonest actions within negotiations.

Social capital within a broader community helps make processes to build consensus more effective. It is especially unfortunate, then, that social capital has decreased in the United States in recent years, according to their research. Putnam and Lewis Feldstein suggest, for example, that Americans have become less active in parent-teacher organizations, other civic activity, or even family discussions over the last few decades. "Beginning, roughly speaking, in the late 1960s, Americans in massive numbers began to join less, trust less, give less, vote less, and schmooze less" (Putnam and Feldstein, 2003:4; *updated in* Putnam and Sander, 2010:12-15). Some of the causes they cite seem beyond the control of dispute system designers, including that Americans increasingly spend time watching television and engaged with other digital media, commuting (usually alone) longer distances, and managing two career marriages (Putnam, 2000:283-284). Other causes may be within the designer's control, especially in the context of a single organization; we will examine these in Section B.

A second unfortunate effect of the decline in social capital relates to the inter-group conflicts discussed often throughout this book. Social scientists refer to relationships across group boundaries as "bridging social capital" and also see a decline in it. They note the potential effects on disputing:

> ***Robert D. Putnam and Lewis M. Feldstein:*** "[A]nalysts find it helpful to distinguish between "bonding social capital" (ties that link individuals or groups with much in common) and "bridging social capital" (ties that link individuals or groups across a greater social distance). Both kinds of connections are valuable to us as individuals, but bridging is especially important for reconciling democracy and diversity. A society that has only bonding social capital risks looking like Bosnia or Belfast" (2003:279).

Commentators refer to the reduction in bridging social capital as "polarization," and note its corrosive effects on reaching political agreement among groups within the United States. Given the effects on conflict management systems across groups, designers may work to re-build bridging social capital. Section B offers examples of this work. The research and commentary on "constructive contacts" in the next section provide another source for ideas to do so.

2. Constructive contacts

"Constructive contact" research relates to a common design challenge: many people mistrust or dislike people belonging to a particular group. To draw from just one of hundreds of inter-group conflicts around the world, a Protestant individual in Northern Ireland may have learned to distrust all Catholics. Such inter-group distrust and dislike can lead to bitter divides within communities and, pertinent to the designer, can undermine a design for conflict resolution. Differences between members of groups that distrust and dislike one another can lead individuals to attribute ulterior motives for innocent actions, insult each other, and even be more willing to be dishonest with one another. Conflict prevention and resolution designs must take these barriers into account.

Social scientists have studied what sorts of contacts among people in different groups increase respect and a sense of joint purpose and which types of contacts increase divisions, hatred, and prejudice. They have identified the following characteristics of situations that tend to promote constructive contacts:

a. *positive,* sometimes fun, shared *activities* (Amir, 1998:178; Kriesberg, 1998:192);

b. participation of people who are *personable* and have *common values* (Amir, 1998;176-178);

c. *extensive interaction,* not just greetings as people pass (Amir, 1998:172-174);

d. activities in which members from both groups work together toward a *common goal* (Amir, 1998:170-172, citing especially Sherif, 1966:146-147); and

e. situations in which members from both groups have *equal status* (Amir, 1998:166-168; Kriesberg, 1998:191-192).

In the absence of these situational characteristics, bringing together people who distrust and misunderstand one another runs the risk of reinforcing divisions, hatred, and prejudice (Amir, 1998:178).

Through their research, social scientists continue to look for strategies that hold promise in building trust across groups, but the characteristics noted above provide important clues for designers. In the process of creating a system, designers might consider building in activities that promote or even force constructive contacts (*see* Section B for more ideas).

Some of the research occurs in the most difficult situations, like the one that follows, where violence has diminished trust.

Northern Ireland: "The Troubles" between Catholic and Protestant partisans in Northern Ireland have produced a largely segregated society. More than 90 percent of the children attended segregated schools in 2005 although about half lived in integrated neighborhoods. Even nonpartisan members of these religious groups, particularly among those directly affected by violence, often do not trust members of the other religious group. In research among students at an integrated university, roughly 10 percent had moved from a house because of sectarian intimidation, 12 percent had homes damaged by bombs, and 13 percent had been affected by a sectarian-incident-related injury. In all, 22 percent had had one of these experiences and nearly half had close friends who had suffered in one of these ways. These students were more prejudiced and wary of students in the other religious group than were other students.

This research makes clear the challenges designers face operating effective conflict management systems involving Catholics and Protestants in Northern Ireland. But other research provides hope that efforts to reverse the mistrust across groups will succeed. Students who had friends across groups—even if those students were harmed directly by sectarian actions—had lower fears and prejudices. Even students whose friends had friends in the other group showed less fear and prejudice (Paolini et al., 2004:779-784).

In other words, those who bridge groups create more constructive relationships for themselves and also for their friends who do not bridge. The ripple effect of constructive contacts holds promise for reversing a downward trust cycle, even if not all persons have cross-group friendships.

As discussed in Section B, designers in all contexts can experiment with contacts like these to enhance relationships between persons.

3. Trust and mistrust within negotiations

Social scientists who study negotiations note that constructive relationships affect negotiations positively. Negotiators with higher levels of trust for each other are more likely to use cooperative negotiation techniques, disclose information, and understand the other's perspective, for example (Lewicki, 2006:197-199). Conversely, if people distrust each other, agreements will be less stable (Hall and Heckscher, 2003:296). Trust between the parties to a single dispute therefore increases the chances of reaching both agreement and lasting agreement. Because parties negotiate ways to simplify process even when they adjudicate their disputes, trust can reduce the cost of litigation or arbitration. As a result, designers have plenty of reasons to consider aspects of process design that encourage trust among parties. We move now to consider some tools that a designer might use.

B. PRACTICE IMPLICATIONS

As you work to enhance relationships, the research on social capital, constructive contacts, and trust provides a basis for thinking through how to do it. It may help as well to consider approaches taken by other designers. This section offers a few.

1. Intervene early

In their anger, people tend to do things that sour relations. Designers have a potent strategy to avoid this—get involved early and begin structuring relations between people in ways that preserve relationships.

One way to do this is to suggest non-accusatory language within the system even before a dispute occurs, as eBay does for trading disputes.

eBay on intervening early to preserve trust: eBay begins its intervention even before a complaint is raised, when feasible. Buyers can report problems (such as item non-receipt) and have the issue resolved immediately (for example, with a tracking number) before the seller even realizes the buyer is concerned. eBay also seeks to avoid development of mistrust between users, suggesting the use of less inflammatory language and process, as discussed above (pp. 115-116). Former eBay Director of Online Dispute Resolution Colin Rule explains, "Some members acknowledge that their actions resulted in the transaction problem initially, but once the problem escalates (perhaps to name calling, insults, recriminations, fraud filings, etc.), the original agent of the action that caused the problem no longer feels like the perpetrator, and both sides can quickly take on the mantle of the victim" (Rule, 2008).

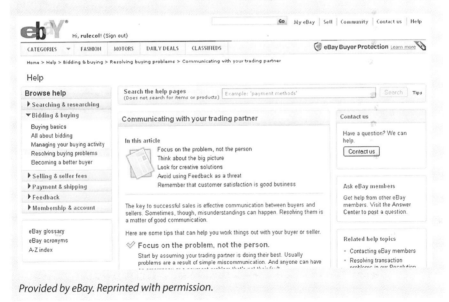

Provided by eBay. Reprinted with permission.

Another early intervention strategy is to involve staff members who watch for conflict escalation, sending an intermediary quickly when they observe the trouble, even before an invitation. The United Nations has learned the importance of this approach:

> *Internationalists on intervening early to preserve trust:* Because successes in negotiating about future relationships rarely succeed after violence, designers consider how to intervene before conflict escalates. Boutros Boutros-Ghali, then United Nations Secretary General, wrote about the lack of success in intervening post-violence and noted that "the most doable and efficient employment of diplomacy is to ease tensions before they result in conflict" (1995:46). The United Nations developed its "good offices" approach and provides envoys in an effort to intervene when crisis seems imminent (Sisk, 2001).

Early intervention can also be used to assure people that others take them seriously and that they will have an opportunity to have their views considered, as well as to set up clear paths of communication about a problem. Consider the theory below by two prominent public policy mediators.

> *Public policy mediators Susan Carpenter and W.J.D. Kennedy on intervening early to preserve relationships:* "Many conflicts start with a resolvable problem and grow beyond hope of resolution because they are not dealt with early. . . . Unmanaged conflicts seldom stay constant for long. . . . One or more parties choose not to acknowledge that a problem exists. Other groups are forced to escalate their activities to gain recognition for their concerns. Eventually everyone engages in an adversarial battle. . . . Unmanaged conflicts tend to become more serious because the people involved in them are anxious, fearful, and suspicious of the other side. . . . They do not notice that their perceptions of their adversaries and themselves are changing and that they are progressively incurring risks and costs that would have seemed intolerable earlier in the struggle. . . . [The rumor mill operates absent credible information, conspiracy theories abound, and an] unfortunate consequence of insufficient information is that when the complete story is finally told, no one believes it" (Carpenter and Kennedy, 2001:207, 11, 16-17).

The theme of beginning early might be accompanied by the next series of ideas—ways to improve the interactions among disputants.

2. Encourage constructive interaction among disputants

Applying the theory and research about constructive contacts summarized above, a number of designers found ways to improve relationships.

a. Creating positive activities

A designer may encourage social conversation or discussion of easier issues before turning to more difficult and substantive ones. Michael Young's approach provides an example within a single process, though a designer could also build such an approach into a system. Young's first face-to-face meeting of the Afrikaner and African National Congress delegations occurred after Young had worked with the negotiators separately for two years. Still, when Michael Young began the first mediation session, the participants had little trust for one another. It understates to say that they were just members of rival groups—the South African regime had imprisoned ANC negotiator Thabo Mbeki's father, killed his son, and banned the ANC, and the ANC had planted bombs in Afrikaner neighborhoods. In the account below, Robert Harvey describes Young's deliberate use of a pleasant environment and an easier agenda for the first meeting.

"That the others were human after all": "The Compleat Angler at Marlow, in England, is the kind of delightful, quaint, olde-English rustic retreat . . . ideally suited for [mediator Michael] Young's purposes in organizing the first-ever meeting between senior Afrikaners with government connections and exiled [African National Congress (ANC)] leaders: it was the most improbable place conceivable for such a venue—and the talks had 'above all to be secret' to protect both sides. There, on a pleasant October morning in 1987, . . . the three white South Africans . . . met [with] the ANC delegation. . . .

Reuters photo

"Young says that there were 'enormous tensions' as they met for the first time. 'It was like the Pope shaking hands with the devil.' They sat down at the small table. Conversation was tense and disjointed, and Young had to be 'forceful' in controlling the discussion. More than mere politics and race divided them. The whites were well-heeled, well-fed, at ease with their surroundings. Pahad, living in North London, was the most urbane of the ANC members. They were poorly dressed and fed after years of living life on a shoe-string as political exiles. . . .

"Within a day, both concur, the two sides had noticeably relaxed. They found there was much more to talk about than they had expected. Neither was unreasonable; instead they proceeded to find common ground.

"Young ensured that the discussions were deliberately vague, and ranged over major issues without touching on specifics. . . . Their only conclusion was that they must meet again at a senior level, and with a more specific agenda. . . .

"That had been a first encounter between ANC leaders and senior Afrikaners. After the initial tension, these men, who up to then had regarded each other as murderer and oppressor respectively, and whose followers had been geared up to fight to the death back home, had been pleasantly surprised by the basic reasonableness of the other side. But what had actually been achieved? Handshakes and the discovery that the others were human after all in the comforting glow of a small English hotel in mid-winter, so different from their homeland in midsummer. A significant measure of common ground between strikingly opposed political positions. Young could point to nothing specific. But that, to him, had not been the intention" (Harvey, 2001:127-129).

b. Coaching participants on effective interaction and helping them recognize their common values

In addition to establishing the best environment and agenda, as Young did, teaching and coaching can also be design options that enhance constructive relationships. The collaborative law process between divorcing couples takes that approach.

Collaborative law, re-building trust as a marriage ends: Collaborative law negotiations consciously re-build trust (pp. 114-115). The model requires all negotiators to take trainings in interest-based negotiation and to agree to be candid and open to discussing interests. The lawyers and other professionals seek to model this trusting approach to the conversations. They talk with their clients before the negotiation, letting the client know that it is natural to have difficulty being open, trusting, and trustworthy in the midst of dissolution and asking the client to give them a signal when they feel they are at risk of losing their ability to do so. When the client acts in a manner likely to produce mis-trust, the lawyer or mental health professional coach who assists that party can remind the client of the previous conversation. When this does not work, the parties and professionals sometimes stop the negotiations for a conference on how to interact in ways more likely to lead to trust and agreement (Tesler, 2010).

The teaching and coaching approach might also be assisted by the processes that are used when disputes occur. The U.S. Post Office, for example, chose transformative mediation as its primary process for disputes among employees (pp. 321-322). Transformative mediation focuses on transforming the interaction between parties by empowering them and restoring their capacity to be open and responsive to one another (*see* Appendix C).

In a related strategy, some designers believe that they can foster more constructive relationships if intervenors or another visible group of persons model this approach. Thus, the designer might train intervenors to seek input from the parties on the meeting place, agenda, and other items primarily as a way to model that level of respect for each person. Using more dramatic modeling, a group called "Cornerstone Community" of Protestants and Catholics live in a house on the border of Protestant and Catholic segregated communities in Belfast, Northern Ireland, where they openly collaborate on joint community projects (Nelson et al., 2003:6).

c. Establishing extensive interaction

The research demonstrates the value of extensive interaction, but it may be difficult to achieve that. The Seeds of Peace story below illustrates a creative way to build constructive relationships by bringing people together for the sorts of interactions shown by research to improve interactions. The Seeds of Peace approach is designed to increase trust over time between members of groups with histories of violence, tensions, and distrust.

Seeds of Peace—creating friendships to achieve broader bridging: Founded in 1993, Seeds of Peace brings together teenagers from conflict zones such as Israel-Palestine or India-Pakistan for a three-week intensive summer camp in Maine. During the course of the camp, young people on opposite sides of the conflict engage in daily structured dialogue sessions. They also participate in various activities designed to build relationships and trust between the parties. While the teenagers participate in dialogue sessions, their chaperones, often teachers from their home countries, participate in parallel trainings and learning conversations. The dialogue sessions for teens and adults can often be intense and emotionally exhausting.

Those who designed the camp were committed to an intentional process of evaluation and modification through the years. Through this iterative learning, Seeds of Peace was able to design a series of activities and dialogues that maximize the likelihood of honest, sometimes heart-wrenching, exchange in a relatively low-risk environment.

As the tension, violence, and conflict escalated in the years following the start of the Second Intifada in 2000, Seeds of Peace leaders realized that simply inviting teenagers to a three-week camp in Maine was inadequate. As part of its continuing commitment to review and improve processes and structures, Seeds started to create and implement programs "on the ground" in the conflict zones for alumni of the three-week camp to find new ways to renew and continue their engagement with others. Beginning in January 2012, for example, student-designers from Harvard's Negotiation and Mediation Clinic teamed up with Seeds of Peace to deliver a program for older graduates of the Seeds of Peace camp designed to build mediation and conflict intervention skills among Israeli and Palestinian young adults at the same time it renewed and expanded bonds made years earlier in the United States.

d. Fostering common goals

As noted above, social scientists suggest that people working toward a common mission are more likely to form constructive relationships. That research suggests strategies like the one described next.

Steve Goldberg on creating a shared task: "One designer (though that term was unused at the time) was asked to intervene at a coal mine at which the relationship between union and management was quite poor, resulting in frequent strikes and low productivity. He formed a joint union-management group to consider means by which to improve the situation. Shortly after the group was formed, he told them that as bad as the union-management relationship was at their mine it was considerably worse at another mine a few hundred miles away at which he had also been engaged. He proposed that the group go to that mine so that they could give him advice on how to improve relationships there. After a long ride on a chartered bus, followed by drinks and dinner, as well as a day talking in union-management pairs to people at the second mine, then a long bus ride home and a meeting devoted to advice on improving the situation at the visited mine, guess what? The joint committee members, having joined together to forge a solution to problems at the other mine, realized that they could do the same at their mine, which had been the designer's intention all along" (2012, email to authors).

Designers may encounter even larger-scale situations that call for trying to set the stage for relationship building, such as the South African transition that has often been the focus of this book.

The South African experience in articulating common aspirations: In the late 1990s, South Africa was "emerging from brutal government-imposed white supremacy and violent insurgency by the oppressed racial majorities. To move toward universal suffrage, the nation needed people to work together on a new constitution. President Nelson Mandela spoke often about a unique, common, and deeply-ingrained trait of South Africans—*Ubuntu*. President Mandela, joined by other leaders such as Truth and Reconciliation Commission Chairman Bishop Desmond Tutu, called upon history and current examples to justify *Ubuntu*, which they explained as appreciating the humanity of each individual—not demonizing other groups of people—and conducting their affairs so that others benefitted in addition to themselves. This proposed South African spirit seemed to resonate, and it pointed toward forgiveness and collaboration about the future—traits that the internal violence had placed at grave risk. South Africans ultimately adopted a new constitution and enshrined the human dignity and healing aspects of *Ubuntu* in the opening paragraph of their new constitution" (Rogers, 2018:30-31).

---

e. Trying to achieve equal status

Sometimes the design can easily provide the equal status that helps enhance relationships. Between businesses, for example, the design might encourage parties to send the same level of representative from within their organizations. In another context, a well-run, multi-stakeholder consensus-building process might provide for the hiring of technical experts who would then make their reports available to all stakeholders, thereby leveling the difference in playing field that might otherwise exist because of asymmetries in information and in access to the resources needed to secure expert information.

The task becomes more difficult when those who will participate have different levels of power within society. The Truth and Reconciliation Commission of Canada noted this issue within the process designed to lead to reconciliation.

Truth and
Reconciliation
Commission of Canada

Interim report by the Truth and Reconciliation Commission of Canada: "Reconciliation implies relationship. The residential schools badly damaged relationships within Aboriginal families and communities, between Aboriginal peoples and churches, between Aboriginal peoples and the government, and between Aboriginal and non-Aboriginal peoples within Canadian Society. The Commissioners believe these relationships can and must be repaired....

"Reconciliation . . . will require changes in the relationship between the Aboriginal people and the government of Canada. The federal government, along with the provincial governments, historically has taken a social welfare approach to its dealings with Aboriginal people. This approach fails to recognize the unique legal status of Aboriginal peoples as the original peoples of this country" (2012a:26-27).

Those from the Aboriginal communities hoped that the processes created through the class action settlement in the residential schools case would readjust their status so that reconciliation would be possible. It is too soon to know whether the strategy will be successful. While it has detractors, there are some signs that the people of Canada are beginning to change their understanding of Aboriginal communities (cf. James, 2012:202). A survey of the Canadian public indicated that 83 percent had heard about the Prime Minister's apology to the Aboriginal peoples in 2008, and 71 percent approved (Jung, 2009:18). The Commission publicized many victims' accounts and recommended that they become a part of the Canadian history taught in schools (Truth and Reconciliation Commission of Canada, 2012b).

The Canadian story provides reminders about the importance of attending to the status of participants, particularly in a process aimed at reconciling relationships.

3. Improve communications

Insufficient, excessive, bad, or hurtful communication among parties is both a cause of conflict and an impediment to achieving design goals. Fortunately, designers can deploy a range of strategies to optimize the frequency and improve the quality of communication among them. At times, disputes arise because parties simply do not have the means or the skills to communicate directly. In such situations, the lack of communication leads persons on all sides of the disputes to form negative impressions of the other.

There are many ways designers can help improve communications. For example, they may recommend intensive communication training for all the parties. A stakeholder assessment may find that the presenting problem is really a symptom of unskilled communication rituals or dynamics. A process that merely resolves the presenting conflict will not stabilize the organization. Instead, designers may provide negotiation training and consulting in an effort to alter more fundamentally the unhelpful dynamic faced by the parties (see negotiation training suggestions in Appendix D).

Designers may try to enhance, or at least preserve, a relationship by taking charge of communications, making certain that they are clear. Quakers have chosen this shuttle diplomacy approach to remove miscalculation as a reason for violence. As you read the story that follows, which occurred during the armed conflict in Sri Lanka, think about how mere communication assistance helped to preserve and even build trust in the midst of sectarian violence.

Professor Thomas Princen on Quaker Joseph Elder's shuttling in Sri Lanka: "Sri Lanka is an island nation of sixteen million people just off the southeastern coast of India. It has been long troubled by tension between the majority and largely Buddhist Sinhalese (about 74 percent of the population), and the minority and largely Hindu Tamils (about 18 percent). Since it gained independence in 1948, Sri Lanka (formerly Ceylon) has been a democratically ruled country with a fast-growing economy."

In the 1980s, the government, largely Sinhalese, instituted policies that discriminated against Tamils, who largely withdrew from the government. Various groups of Tamil guerrillas formed, and violence escalated. It took nearly 20 years before a peace agreement was signed.

For at least a decade of the civil war, American Quaker Joseph Elder and colleagues shuttled between the rival groups. They simply arrived and began networking their way to the leaders.

Over ten years, the Quakers encouraged messages that would dispel misimpressions. For example, Sinhalese hardliners who were close to the government gave Elder permission to tell the Tamil that, despite the government's public stance that there "were only four or five hundred militants" who could be "driven off the island" in a few months, they recognized that the war would go on for many years unless they settled their disagreements. Among the messages Elder took to hardliners from the Tamil rebels was that at "various times the militants have reduced operations to promote a peace process, but the signal was not adequately conveyed, and the reduction in operations was too often interpreted as a sign of weakness" (Princen, 1994:430-431, 437, 441).

Communication assistance may not always be as direct as in the Quaker example. In the United States, the media have historically played a communications role in giving people roughly similar accounts on current issues. However, the highly varied media sources in the digital era can provide quite different accounts of events and issues. The proliferation of false accounts, especially through social media, sows confusion (Pew, 2016b). Further, with heightened political polarization, norms favoring learning about different viewpoints appear to have broken down in the United States. Research indicates that people prefer watching news on TV to reading it (Pew, 2016a) and that they tend to watch the news programs that reflect their own views (Knobloch-Westerwick and Meng, 2009; Pew, 2014). Almost 40 percent of Americans get their news primarily online. Newspapers were the preferred news source for only 20 percent of Americans in 2016 (Pew, 2016a). Spending more time listening to only one of several diverse viewpoints has the effect of increasing in-group feelings of being right and that the out-group is wrong (Allred, 2005). In response to the increasing political polarization in the United States, individual and citizen groups have formed to create in-person and online opportunities for dialogue and conversation across political difference. These movements include Better Angels (www.better-angels.org) and the Listen First Project (www.listenfirstproject.org).

Designers may have few options to change this new reality in the larger society. However, an effective and balanced communication strategy within an organization or particular groups within a community might increase intergroup understanding (see p. 235 on study circle process). The Cure Violence Chicago approach (below) of maintaining strong communications even among rival gangs illustrates this approach.

4. Increase positive interactions within the larger community

As a designer, you may decide to take a long-term approach to building constructive relationships. Former National Institutes of Health ombuds Howard Gadlin used this approach. He encouraged collaborative leadership as he consulted with supervisors. He also encouraged collaborating scientists to use techniques that are consistent with building more constructive relationships, such as giving individual credit when a project succeeds and agreeing in advance who will handle the media if they jointly make an important advance in health research.

Cure Violence Chicago also worked to encourage positive interactions between gangs well in advance of any conflicts.

Preventive work by Cure Violence Chicago: Rival Chicago gangs, factions, and cliques can recount reasons why they should not trust each other. Nonetheless, some level of trust might increase willingness to check with the other group or at least engage with Cure Violence's violence interrupters (pp. 27-28). For this reason, Cure Violence Chicago held regular workshops with individual groups, beginning with discussions in their vernacular and then helping them to understand the destructive force of violence. After a year of the separate workshops for each group, Cure Violence hosted peace summits involving multiple groups—often 300 young people. After discussions, the groups often signed "peace treaties" in which the groups agreed that they would not use violence and that they would call Cure Violence at the first sign of trouble. Cure Violence continued, even after the peace treaties were signed, to invite the groups to common social events. Cure Violence credited this trust-building activity as contributing to the reduction in violence in Cure Violence neighborhoods (pp. 336-338).

Designers with a long-term view may also encourage people to be joiners. People who join organizations have more empathy and more often help to solve common problems (Putnam, 2000). This civic engagement thus enhances constructive relationships that serve to make dispute resolution systems work more effectively when needed. This engagement has the potential to enhance constructive relationships even if like-minded people join. And it will help even more if activities join people from different groups, creating the "bridging social capital" discussed above (pp. 221-222). To achieve the latter, designers might encourage involvement with a common goal that all groups share. Because the designers encourage involvement in order to enhance constructive relationships in this hypothetical situation, they may avoid focusing on the points of disagreement (Cleven et al., 2018:62). To encourage engagement, designers endeavor to create organizations that meet members' needs. They may train leaders or provide facilitators to structure positive interactions among members. In the story below, the designers used all of these strategies in bringing together disparate groups on the topic of a new direction for a public school system.

Building relationships on the way to forge agreement on improving education: The Montgomery County, Maryland school system is the nation's sixteenth largest, with 156,000 students. Bordering on the District of Columbia, the school system's students were predominantly white and from affluent families in the mid-1980s. By 2008, the demographics had changed; the district had a mix of economic levels and races and students spoke 134 first languages. The student performance levels fell, with much lower performance in the schools serving students from poorer families. The Montgomery County superintendent could approach the problem by moving resources from high-performing schools to low-performing schools, but such a decision would likely divide the community (Childress et al., 2009:18-20).

Instead, in 1999 the superintendent worked with planning consultants to create a process for joint decision-making among the stakeholders—"parents, the general public, county and state government officials, colleges and universities, advocacy groups [including unions] and civil organizations, and the business community"—on a strategy that would bring better education for every student (id.:23).

Parents in particular were encouraged to join groups, beginning in 2000. The superintendent and his staff held forums for parents throughout the county, facilitating participation by including interpreting services in five languages. They used the forums to encourage parents to join small working groups. The working groups focused not just on the reform that had been initially contemplated but on other reforms as well. (For example, all parents wanted more access to their children's records so that they could monitor progress on a daily basis—something included in the final plan.) Later, the district created a district-wide parents' council. The superintendent made certain that suggestions from all of these groups were addressed in the final report, which made broad recommendations for change across the district. Still later, in 2006-2007, the superintendent formed 15-member "study circles" of parents, teachers, and students to talk about racial and ethnic barriers to success (id.:65-66, 124).

The District has documented improved student performance overall and within each of the demographic groups of students since 2001. The planning consultants attributed part of the success to the groups built during the period discussed above. They noted about the general approach: the superintendent "created the conditions under which multiple stakeholder groups felt as if they owned the results" (id.:137).

Of significance to this chapter on relationships, the groups also contributed to more constructive relationships among parents, another factor in achieving support for the plan: "Nearly 90 percent of participants—both parents and staff—reported an increase in their understanding of each others' attitudes and beliefs" (id.:124).

Just as social media and technology such as Facebook, Twitter, and even Netflix might reduce traditional "land-based" social engagement because people spend more time online than with others in their communities, designers can consider using the same technologies to build new forms of social capital in the online environment. The Divided Community Project at the Ohio State

University Moritz College of Law suggests, for example, that local leaders consider the following potentially positive uses of social media:

1. "Use social media, websites, and apps to create widely-used and _trusted online information sources_ for residents that will help maintain and enhance residents' confidence and become an antidote to inaccurate news and unsubstantiated rumors.

2. "Use social media, websites, and apps to _increase input from residents_ in ongoing decisions respond to residents' concerns.

3. "Use social media, websites, and apps to promote offline, face-to-face events and to _support online dialogue_ among residents in order to build community resiliency.

4. "Work to reduce and _combat online hate speech/discriminatory conduct_ through social media so as to reduce the effects.

5. "_Mine_ social media and other online data as part of an overall ongoing initiative to better understand community concerns [with discussion of privacy limitations on this strategy]" (Divided Community Project, 2017).

In each of these initiatives, enhancing relationships was not the only purpose served by engaging people broadly, but that aspect of the engagement played or might in the future play a key role in the overall success of the design.

5. Set boundaries on the need to trust

Sometimes the process can be structured to reduce the need for trust in every aspect of the interactions. Otherwise, the failure of one participant to act as expected might escalate mistrust by the others. For example, divorcing parents might be encouraged to agree to exchange income tax returns instead of relying on mutual trust on the financial aspect of bargaining. Bounded interactions like this might at least preserve existing levels of trust. Similarly, divorcing parents reduce noncompliance risks by incorporating their settlement into a consent decree that the judge approves and enforces as a court judgment. Providing another example of bounded trust, Cure Violence interrupters shuttle among hostile parties, so that one set of parties does not have to trust that the other set of parties would not hurt them if they met. So, too, prosecutors may say to the complainant in the presence of the alleged perpetrator, "Let me know if he does not comply with this agreement to make restitution. I can still review your original complaint and decide whether to prosecute."

In some situations, setting boundaries on trust may be the only feasible goal. Imagine developing a systems design for property disputes between existing Rwandan residents and the Rwandans who return to their neighborhoods and find others living in their houses, after they served prison sentences for killing neighbors during the 1994 ethnic massacres. The neighbors can continue to "co-exist" (Chayes and Minow, 2003:xix) if they trust each other enough to talk, even if through intermediaries, and set out an agreement that each is likely to respect.

If one person will not likely act as promised, and nothing can assure compliance, of course, negotiations may not be worth the risk (*see* Zwier, 2013:7 on talking to the "wicked" but not to the "truly evil"; *see also* Mnookin, 2010).

While structuring interactions may reduce the need for the parties to trust each other, eliminating all need for trust among disputants may not be constructive if a goal of the system is to develop that very trust. Research suggests that people may not develop trusting and trustworthy patterns without some aspect of the process that requires their reliance on trusting and being trustworthy (Bohnet and Baytelman, 2007:114-115). Thus, mediation programs among divorcing parents may want to establish some low-risk areas where it is necessary for one parent to trust the other, as a way of establishing enough trust for the divorced parents to handle parenting matters going forward.

6. Deal with structures that enhance fairness

Some designers are able to intervene more deeply to avert division. One set of strategies is beyond the control of most designers—changes in governmental and social structures that reduce inequality and protect people's rights. This structural approach avoids creating disparately entitled groups, who might then lose trust in members of dominant groups (Ross, 1993:ix). But in a smaller setting, for example an organization like the National Institutes for Health, the ombuds can sometimes provide an effective voice for workplace equality and rights protection. Designer contributions to creating fair structures also help to prevent conflict and to resolve it more effectively.

7. Develop new approaches

You can develop new ideas by following the research and experience regarding relationships. For example, sociologist Louis Kriesberg notes that, in addition to the constructive contacts discussed above, a number of other trust re-building activities seem to hold promise in some post-violence settings, though there is little research to substantiate their effectiveness: leaders who present themselves as representing all of the people, education preparing people for constructive interactions and dealing with conflict, public events that are shared across groups, and treatment of individuals traumatized by threats or violence (1998:192-196).

THOUGHTS GOING FORWARD

Your designs will succeed more often if you understand how to enhance relationships among those interacting as part of the processes you create. By studying research and theory related to constructive relationships, you increase your sensitivity to this aspect of designing. In addition, you will begin to note how others factor this pivotal consideration into their designs. The research points to the need for nuanced design; simply throwing people of different groups into a room together is unlikely to work and can be risky. But, as the research indicates, designers who are attentive to creating common goals, keeping people on equal footing, making the interactions enjoyable, and increasing the depth of interaction may succeed in improving interactions more broadly.

Designers who work within a particular context may also find ways to work preventively, in advance of conflicts, to build relationships among individuals and the groups that are important to their identities. A community in which people feel that they are treated fairly and that has constructive relationships will deal with conflicts more effectively. Further, individuals will succeed more frequently in resolving disputes if they already respect and trust each other and wish each other well.

As designers, you may find that the ideas in the chapter spur others for you and that the spirit of the designers who worked to enhance relationships may inspire you to look for even more possibilities.

QUESTIONS

9.1   Drawing on what Young did to help the South African participants realize that the "others were human after all," suggest what might be done to build trust while developing a dispute management design for conflicts about the location of residences for groups of developmentally disabled adults.

9.2   What strategies might a court employ to intervene before loss of trust between civil litigants?

9.3   Former U.S. Attorney General Eric Holder created controversy by commenting that Americans avoid significant contacts and discussions with those of different races:

> "As a nation we have done a pretty good job in melding the races in the workplace. We work with one another, lunch together and, when the event is at the workplace during work hours or shortly thereafter, we socialize with one another fairly well, irrespective of race. And yet even this interaction operates within certain limitations. We know, by "American instinct" and by learned behavior, that certain subjects are off limits and that to explore them risks, at best, embarrassment, and, at worst, the questioning of one's character. And outside the workplace the situation is even more bleak in that there is almost no significant interaction between us. On Saturdays and Sundays America in the year 2009 does not, in some ways, differ significantly from the country that existed some fifty years ago" (2009).

Holder suggests as one way to ameliorate the situation that "if we are to make progress in this area we must feel comfortable enough with one another, and tolerant enough of each other, to have frank conversations about the racial matters that continue to divide us" (2009). Suggest an approach, based on the constructive contacts scholarship, to achieve Holder's goal.

Exercise 9.1 *Taking the initiative at Tallahoya University:* University counsel still has not asked you to make suggestions to enhance positive cross-group contacts among students. But you attended Tallahoya as an undergraduate and feel strongly that as the social class, racial, and religious diversity increases in the student population, students nonetheless end up confining their relationships to others who share their own social and cultural backgrounds. This diminishes the educational value of "diversity" and helps spawn group or individual actions that produce overt tensions. You worry that if the University does not do something more proactively to address these divisions and latent tensions, there will inevitably be an event that will spark deep bitterness and division on campus and result in worsened relations and bad publicity for the University. And you are concerned that student learning experiences are diminished by the divisions. You decide to take the initiative. What ideas seem most fruitful to discuss with University counsel?

BIBLIOGRAPHY AND REFERENCES

ALLRED, Keith G. (2005) "Relationship Dynamics in Disputes: Replacing Contention with Cooperation," in Michael L. Moffitt and Robert C. Bordone eds., *The Handbook of Dispute Resolution* 83. San Francisco: Jossey-Bass.

AMIR, Yehuda (1998) "Contact Hypothesis in Ethnic Relations," in Eugene Weiner ed., *The Handbook of Interethnic Coexistence* 162. New York: Continuum.

BOHNET, Iris, and Yael BAYTELMAN (2007) "Institutions and Trust: Implications for Preferences, Beliefs and Behavior," 19 *Rationality and Society* 99.

BORDONE, Robert C. (2018) "Building Conflict Resilience: It's Not Just About Problem-Solving," 2018 *J. Disp. Resol.* 65.

BOUTROS-GHALI, Boutros (1995) *An Agenda for Peace 1995* (2d ed.). New York: United Nations.

BRAZIL, Wayne D. (2007) "Hosting Mediations as a Representative of the System of Civil Justice," 22 *Ohio St. J. on Disp. Resol.* 208.

CARPENTER, Susan L., and W.J.D. KENNEDY (2001) *Managing Public Disputes: A Practical Guide for Government, Business, and Citizens' Groups*. San Francisco: Jossey-Bass.

CHAYES, Antonia, and Martha MINOW eds. (2003) *Imagine Coexistence: Restoring Humanity After Violent Ethnic Conflict*. San Francisco: Jossey-Bass.

CHILDRESS, Stacy M., Denis P. DOYLE, and David A. THOMAS (2009) *Leading for Equity: The Pursuit of Excellence in Montgomery County Public Schools*. Cambridge, MA: Harvard Education Press.

CLEVEN, Erik, Robert A. Baruch BUSH, and Judith A. SAUL (2018) "Living with No: Political Polarization and Transformative Dialogue," 2018 *J. Disp. Resol.* 53.

COLEMAN, Peter T., and Morton DEUTSCH (1998) "The Mediation of Interethnic Conflict in Schools," in Eugene Weiner ed., *The Handbook of Interethnic Coexistence*. New York: Continuum.

DEUTSCH, Morton (1998) "Constructive Conflict Resolution: Principles, Training, and Research" in Eugene Weiner ed., *The Handbook of Interethnic Coexistence* 199. New York: Continuum.

FOLGER, Joseph P., and Robert A. Baruch BUSH (2010) "Conclusion: The Development of Transformative Mediation: Challenges and Future Prospects," in Joseph P. Folger et al. eds., *Transformative Mediation: A Sourcebook* 453. New York: Institute for the Study of Conflict Transformation.

FRANKEL, Tamar (2010) "Trust and the Internet," in James R. Silkenat, Jeffrey M. Aresty, and Jacqueline Klosek eds., *The ABA Guide to International Business Negotiations: A Comparison of Cross-Cultural Issues and Successful Approaches* (3rd ed.). Chicago: ABA.

HALL, Lavina, and Charles HECKSCHER (2003) "Negotiating Identity," in Thomas A. Kochan and David B. Lipsky eds., *Negotiations and Change: From Workplace to Society* 279. Ithaca, NY: Cornell University Press.

HARVEY, Robert (2001) *The Fall of Apartheid: The Inside Story from Smuts to Mbeki.* New York: Palgrave Macmillan.

HERZIG, Maggie, and Laura CHASIN (2006) *Fostering Dialogue Across Divides.* Watertown, MA: Public Conversations Project.

HOLDER, Eric (2009) Speech: Attorney General Eric Holder at the Department of Justice African American History Month Program (February 18). https://www.justice.gov/opa/speech/attorney-general-eric-holder-department-justice-african-american-history-month-program.

JAMES, Matt (2012) "A Carnival of Truth? Knowledge, Ignorance and the Canadian Truth and Reconciliation Commission," 6 *Int'l J. Transitional Just.* 182.

JUNG, Courtney (2009a) "Transitional Justice for Indigenous People in a Non-Transitional Society," *ICTJ Research Brief,* www.ictj.org.

JUNG, Courtney (2009b) "Canada and the Legacy of the Indian Residential Schools: Transitional Justice for Indigenous People in a Non-Transitional Society," https://papers.ssrn.com/sol3/papers.cfm?abstract_id=1374950.

KNOBLOCK-WESTERWICK, Silvia, and Jingbo MENG (2009) "Looking the Other Way," 36 *Communication Research* 426.

KRIESBERG, Louis (1998) "Coexistence and the Reconciliation of Communal Conflicts," in Eugene Weiner ed., *The Handbook of Interethnic Coexistence* 182. New York: Continuum.

LEDERACH, John Paul (1998) "Beyond Violence: Building Sustainable Peace," in Eugene Weiner ed., *The Handbook of Interethnic Coexistence* 236. New York: Continuum.

LEWICKI, Roy J. (2006) "Trust and Distrust," in Andrea Kupfer Schneider and Christopher Honeyman eds., *The Negotiator's Fieldbook.* Washington, D.C.: ABA Section of Dispute Resolution.

LEWICKI, Roy J., and Edward C. TOMLINSON (2003) "Distrust," Beyond Intractability, *available at* https://www.beyondintractability.org/essay/distrust.

MENKEL-MEADOW, Carrie (2018) "Why We Can't 'Just All Get Along': Dysfunction in the Polity and Conflict Resolution and What We Might Do About It," 2018 *J. Disp. Resol.* 5.

MINOW, Martha (1998) *Between Vengeance and Forgiveness.* Boston, MA: Beacon Press.

MINOW, Martha (2002) "Memory and Hate," in Martha Minow and Nancy L. Rosenblum eds., *Breaking the Cycles of Hatred: Memory, Law, and Repair* 14. Princeton: Princeton University Press.

MNOOKIN, Robert (2010) *Bargaining with the Devil: When to Negotiate, When to Fight.* New York: Simon & Schuster.

NELSON, Barbara J., Linda KABOOLIAN, and Kathryn A. CARVER (2003) *How to Build Social Capital Across Communities.* Los Angeles: UCLA.

PAOLINI, Stefania, Miles HEWSTONE, Ed CAIRNS, and Alberto VOCI (2004) "Effects of Direct and Indirect Cross-Group Friendships on Judgments of Catholics and Protestants in Northern Ireland: The Mediating Role of an Anxiety-Reduction Mechanism," 30 *Personality and Social Psychology Bulletin* 770.

PEW RESEARCH CENTER (2014) "Political Polarization and Media Habits," *available at* http://www.journalism.org/2014/10/21/political-polarization-media-habits/.

PEW RESEARCH CENTER (2016a) "Pathways to News," *available at* http://www.journalism.org/2016/07/07/pathways-to-news/.

PEW RESEARCH CENTER (2016b) "Many Americans Believe Fake News Is Sowing Confusion," *available at* http://www.journalism.org/2016/12/15/many-americans-believe-fake-news-is-sowing-confusion/.

PRINCEN, Thomas (1994) "Joseph Elder: Quiet Peacemaking in a Civil War," in Deborah M. Kolb and associates eds., *When Talk Works: Profiles of Mediators.* San Francisco: Jossey-Bass.

PUTNAM, Robert D. (2000) *Bowling Alone: The Collapse and Revival of American Community.* New York: Simon & Schuster.

PUTNAM, Robert D., and Lewis M. FELDSTEIN (2003) *Better Together: Restoring the American Community.* New York: Simon & Shuster.

PUTNAM, Robert D., and Thomas H. SANDER (2010) "Still Bowling Alone: The Post 9-11 Split," 21 *J. Democracy* 9.

ROGERS, Nancy H. (2018) "One Idea for Ameliorating Polarization: Reviving Conversations About an American Spirit," 2018 *J. Disp. Resol.* 27.

ROSS, Marc Howard (1993) *The Culture of Conflict.* New Haven, CT: Yale University Press.

RULE, Colin (2008) "Making Peace on eBay: Resolving Disputes in the World's Largest Marketplace," *ACResolution* (Fall).

SHARIFF, Khalil Z. (2003) "Designing Institutions to Manage Conflict: Principles for the Problem Solving Organization," 8 *Harv. Negot. J.* 133.

SHERIF, Muzafer (1966) *Group Conflict and Cooperation.* London: Routledge & Kegan Paul.

SISK, Timothy (2001) "Peacemaking Processes: Forestalling Return to Ethnic Violence," in William I. Zartman ed., *Preventive Negotiation: Avoiding Conflict Escalation* 67. Lanham, MD: Rowman & Littlefield Publishers, Inc.

TESLER, Pauline H. (2007) *Collaborative Law: Achieving Effective Resolution Without Litigation* (2d ed.). Chicago: ABA.

TESLER, Pauline (2008) "Collaborative Family Law, the New Lawyer, and Deep Resolution of Divorce-Related Conflicts," 2008 *J. Disp. Resol.* 83.

TESLER, Pauline (2010) Interview at the Ohio State University Moritz College of Law.

TRUTH AND RECONCILIATION COMMISSION OF CANADA (2012a) *Interim Report.* Winnipeg, Manitoba: TRC of Canada.

TRUTH AND RECONCILIATION COMMISSION OF CANADA (2012b) *Canada, Aboriginal Peoples, and Residential Schools: They Came for the Children.* Winnipeg, Manitoba: TRC of Canada.

TRUTH AND RECONCILIATION COMMISSION OF CANADA (2015) *Honouring the Truth, Reconciling for the Future: Summary of the Final Report of the Truth and Reconciliation Commission of Canada.* Winnipeg, Manitoba: TRC of Canada.

ZARTMAN, I. William ed. (2001) *Preventive Negotiation: Avoiding Conflict Escalation.* Lanham, MD: Rowman & Littlefield Publishers, Inc.

ZWIER, Paul J. (2013) *Talking with Evil: Principled Negotiation and Mediation in the International Arena.* Cambridge, UK: Cambridge University Press.

Using Technology

DESIGNING STEPS

1. Design initiative
2. Basic planning steps
- Assessing stakeholders, their goals and interests, and contexts
- Creating processes and systems
3. Key planning issues (that may arise throughout the planning)
- Planning how to select, engage, and prepare intervenors and parties
- Determining the extent of confidentiality and openness in the process
- Dealing with desires for change, justice, accountability, understanding, safety, reconciliation
- Enhancing relationships
4. **Incorporating technology**
5. Implementing and institutionalizing the system or process
- Implementing
- Using contracts
- Using law
- Evaluating, revising

The use of technology can enhance the ways that you and your design colleagues work together and conduct research. It also has the potential to make the process or system you design more suited to the stakeholders' goals and the context. In this chapter, we use the term "technology" broadly to include use of teleconferencing or videoconferencing, texting, web-based tools, artificial intelligence for analysis or translation, social media, robots that hold "conversations" with parties and answer their questions, audience participation devices ("clickers"), mind maps, and more. With the breakneck pace of digital innovation, the technologies we describe as "ground-breaking" here might be common or even outdated as these descriptions reach our readers. For these reasons, we raise broader questions related to technological innovation and its role in systems design instead of focusing on particular technologies. This chapter should give you a start on the research related to technology's effects and help you appreciate why you might always ask the three questions that serve to organize this chapter:

- What benefits might technology offer in the design process (Section A) and as part of the design (Section B)?
- What problems might technology introduce (Section C)?
- How might these problems be overcome or reduced enough to make the use of technology a net benefit (Section D)?

A. POTENTIAL BENEFITS OF TECHNOLOGY IN THE WORK OF PROCESS OR SYSTEM DESIGN

Technology could improve the designing process, in addition to being used within the processes and systems that the design creates and implements (discussed in Section B). It is not simply a question of easing communications among designers and stakeholders or even of online polling as a tool to learn from stakeholders (*see* Chapter 4.E). For example, designers for an online retailer could mine the wealth of data generated in online purchasing and dispute resolution, thus improving the assessment of strengths and weaknesses of existing processes and the ways they are used. With about 60 million disputes annually, eBay monitored these data and used them to create new processes and systems, as discussed preliminarily below by two online dispute resolution experts and in more detail in Chapter 14.

 eBay's data mining for process and system design: "eBay discovered that disputes [between buyer and seller] primarily arise due to miscommunication and that the transfer of key information can clarify the nature of the problem and assist in assigning responsibility and devising a solution. Under this [new] system, parties are asked to answer questions and supply documents that have been found to shed light on the type of conflict in question" (Rabinovich-Einy and Katsh, 2012:174).

After instituting this new system, Colin Rule and his colleagues again used data generated by online transactions to find that that those participating in eBay's dispute process actually increased their use of eBay after disputes rather than being deterred from use by the dispute they had experienced (pp. 317-319).

Other technologies such as mind maps can help designers create sophisticated conflict assessment visuals that map stakeholders, identify deference patterns among them, and help designers to get a better sense of possible avenues for identifying joint gains.[1] As a result, mind maps can support creation of a consensus-based process for system design and implementation.

B. POTENTIAL BENEFITS OF TECHNOLOGY IN IMPLEMENTING SYSTEMS AND PROCESSES

It seems worthwhile to consider employing technology in any new process or system, because its use could facilitate communication in myriad ways, bridging some of the challenges of dispute management related to time, space, scale, and cost; open new ways to analyze information; and more. Online dispute resolution, often shortened to ODR, augments other dispute resolution processes not only in private settings such as eBay but also in the justice systems in the United States and abroad. Web portals, or even robots that can observe facial expressions and voice tone and respond appropriately, can equip self-represented parties with tailored legal information, assist them to prepare legal documents, coach them in effective negotiation of their type of matter, and help them understand dispute resolution processes (Larson, 2010:140). Case referral technology can closely tailor recommendations for the process to the particular dispute. Negotiation software allows the parties to try out negotiating positions, with the software disclosing to the other party only whether there is common ground for a resolution. But designers will likely uncover uses of technology beyond these more established ways.

In the first story that follows, consider how the designers used imaging technology to overcome confusion and analyze problems that arose in a public consultation process. In later sections, we will explore what new problems technology introduced (Section C), and what strategies were developed to manage the technology-introduced problems (Section D).

Using digital resources to gain public input and acceptance of renewable energy plans: "Germany seeks a substantial transformation of its energy system," explains Arne Spieker, an expert in technology and citizen participation procedures. "By 2025 renewables should generate up to 45 percent of the country's energy production and up to 60 percent in 2035. [All parties in parliament support the outlines of the renewable energy plan and it has been] widely accepted among the general public. . . . In . . . 2017, 95 percent of Germans thought the [renewable energy plans were] an important or very important political project; . . . [but] only 57 percent stated they would approve the construction of wind turbines [or energy grids] in their neighborhood."

---

1. Both freeware and commercially available software support the creation of mind maps. *See, e.g.,* www.thebrain.com or www.mindmeister.com or www.mindjet.com.

Given this "not in my neighborhood" reaction to renewable energy plans, German authorities decided to encourage public hearings. They were eager to avoid what happened in 2010 when community resistance to proposed infrastructure changes generated weeks of demonstrations involving tens of thousands of people and "violent clashes between police and demonstrators." Unfortunately, the public hearings on renewable energy attracted large crowds and degenerated into hostile confrontations—not public input or acceptance.

German planners encountered better success with a series of structured small group discussions facilitated by experienced environmental moderators. They discovered a barrier to productive discussions though even in this setting. Neighbors could not visualize the proposed developments based on technical descriptions or even drawings, and so the planners and public participants could not achieve a "common understanding of the issues at stake." Further, planners could not reach their audience in the midst of the meeting to help them understand how alternatives might work or how a speaker's proposed modification would change the impact of the project on the neighborhood.

In response to these barriers to promoting public input and acceptance, Spieker and his group suggested introducing virtual reality versions of each proposed project. In pilot projects using virtual reality, they discovered that people understood this highly technical information more clearly than when they had only technical descriptions or drawings. Also, the moderator could modify the virtual model in just a few seconds, helping participants to compare alternatives and visualize their proposed variants (Spieker, 2018:75-86).[2]

The German planners were partially successful using strong facilitation skills (*see* Chapter 15), but they strengthened the process significantly by employing technology. The story demonstrates the importance of involving technology experts who understand dispute system design principles and so can identify potential benefits of introducing digital approaches. In a second example, just below, city officials asked for help in overcoming collaborative process problems created by use of social media.

---

2. While overcoming a major barrier to gaining public input and acceptance, the introduction of visual technology introduced a new problem. Stereoscopy helped people visualize but made 10 percent of them dizzy. Thus, the operators may have to offer two versions of the virtual reality technologies so that all participants can benefit.

Sanford, Florida: In the aftermath of the Trayvon Martin shooting (pp. 20-22), city officials discovered that demonstrations involving tens of thousands of people could be prompted by notices on social media and materialize in only a few hours. To give one example, the demonstrators were often angry because of inaccurate information transmitted through social media calls for action (such as a bogus announcement about the city hiring for summer jobs at a time and location that the city had set for a listening session by city officials with residents). Traditional news outlets were not reaching many potential demonstrators to correct the information in a timely way. In fact, nationally, almost two-thirds of American adults get some or most of their news from social media sites (Pew Research Center, 2018).

Student designers as well as members of the Divided Community Project at the Ohio State University Moritz College of Law convened experts in social media and community-wide conflict for counsel on how to deal with situations such as Sanford's. Based on input from those with experience, the designers outlined for local leaders a series of combined social media and in-person responses, discussed in Chapter 9.D.4. Through searching online, the Divided Community Project could include examples of cities across the nation that had already implemented these strategies (Divided Community Project, 2017).

These illustrations highlight the importance of considering whether and how technology might be productively employed whenever you are creating new processes and systems. They also suggest the issue addressed in the next section—that thoughtful use of technology by designers can help overcome challenges that themselves are created by uses of technologies.

C. TECHNOLOGY-INTRODUCED DESIGN PROBLEMS

Now the other side of the coin: technology can also create problems that a designer must be attentive to, address, or manage for a process or system to succeed. Existing research may help you to identify the problems. More likely, though, logic and your research and experience will be the primary means of identifying the technology-introduced problems. To look for these issues, you might ask at least how the digital approaches will affect:

- the honesty and accuracy of communications;
- trust among community members and understanding across community divides;
- susceptibility to bullying, identity theft, discriminatory and hate speech, and other victimization;
- equal access;
- fairness of any dispute resolution mechanism;

- privacy interests; and
- public access to information.

1. Research

Though we take a broad approach to the use of technology, the research on the use of digital solutions in dispute resolution processes is sparse and narrow, focusing typically on the differences among asynchronous online message platforms, social media, telephone, and in-person communications. Research on online communication shows that it can be used effectively between people who know each other and work within an organization—such as a group of designers sharing a wiki to gather and process information or a group of colleagues using a service such as Slack to communicate and update each other on progress in their day-to-day work. Online polling holds promise for planners who seek quick input from a broad group of persons as part of a planning process (*see* Chapter 4.B on polling issues).

Several studies document, though, that compared to face-to-face negotiation, unstructured, asynchronous online exchanges between strangers not within a common group will:

- *reduce "trust* in the process" (Nadler, 2001:333; Nadler and Shestowsky, 2006:155);
- "*escalate negative* emotion and negative attributions about other participants" (Nadler, 2001:333; Friedman and Currall, 2004:9-19);
- *be less likely to build "stable relationships"* (Nadler and Shestowsky, 2005:157; McGinn and Wilson, 2004:7; Putnam, 2000:174-179);
- *spread inaccurate news more quickly* than accurate news (Vosoughi, 2018, dealing with Twitter); and
- *produce less forthright* discussions (McGinn and Wilson, 2004:8).

In an e-democracy application, law professor Jeffrey Lubbers surveyed federal agency rulemakers on the usefulness of online comments on proposed regulations, learning that these rulemakers had received more comments since allowing online participation. At the same time, rulemakers reported a greater tendency for those posting online comments to give generalized opinions without facts or reasoning to support them. They also saw an increase in form responses, likely generated by special interest campaigns. In general, they believed that they had learned little that was new as the result of moving from hard copy to online comments on proposed regulations (Lubbers, 2012:240-245, 248-249).

Those who frequent private comment networks such as Twitter report consistent, and additional, effects—the comments seem unorganized, sometimes uncivil, and include people who seem to have no stake in the outcome or desire for resolution. Making matters worse, people increasingly seem drawn to networks that do not challenge their opinions, creating private "echo chambers" and deepening divisions (*see* Sunstein, 2017).

2. Fairness and practical considerations

The commentary, as well as the research, provides guidance on additional potential problems, particularly fairness and practical concerns. Here are a few examples:

The digital divide: Use of technology may not affect everyone in the same way. Income level and geography also may determine access to and skill in using technology (Shane, 2012:6). Younger persons may be more adept in using certain new technologies than their elders; businesses more adept than consumers.[3] Some segments of the population, sometimes splitting by generation, may prefer Instagram or Snapchat, for example, while others still primarily use Facebook. Still, the evidence indicates that differences are narrowing in some ways. For example, in one program 36 percent of those opting into online negotiation and mediation of their small claims cases had household incomes below the statewide average.[4]

The invisible software: Novel fairness issues emerge when software mediates or resolves disputes. Participants using a private online negotiation service to resolve buyer-seller disputes cannot tell whether the software operates neutrally. That ignorance may lead buyers to suspect that the provider designs the software to favor sellers who typically pay the provider for the service and to certify them as compliant with dispute resolution results. Transparency might help, but private providers protect the trade secrets in their software.

Even if the invisible software rarely contributes to unfairness, people may refuse to put themselves in a situation of having to use the software if they do not trust it. In a changing situation, it may be difficult to design a reliable regulatory or even certification system for the fairness of the software. The European Union now offers its own platform and permits parties to "opt out"—in other words, to use an in-person court procedure rather than online dispute resolution.[5]

The staffing requirements: The e-deliberations in particular generate high comment volumes, with the contributors expecting that their viewpoints will be considered. The staffing required for such listening rarely seems to be present, however. Law professor Peter Shane reports that after various forms of government-connected online forums have operated for 15 years, "few are tied in any ascertainable, accountable way to actual governmental policy making" (Shane, 2012:3).

---

3. For example, in 2010 a survey revealed that those 18 to 25 years of age were more likely to use the internet than those who were older. But the internet gap by age is narrowing. *See* http://www.pewinternet.org/2010/12/16/generations-2010/. Regarding businesses and consumers, *see* Schmitz, 2018.

4. Franklin County [Ohio] Municipal Court, 2018 statistics (Alex Sanchez, speech at Ohio Supreme Court Dispute Resolution Conference, March 13, 2018).

5. https://ec.europa.eu/consumers/odr/main/?event=main.home.show.

3. Privacy, security, and public access

Privacy and security: With identity theft on the rise and increasing concerns about cyber hacking and infiltration and cyber-terrorism, designers must consider carefully the limits of technology both as a tool in the design process and in the actual systems themselves. For example, the transmission of metadata via email may increase the likelihood of identity theft and, in a growing number of contexts and jurisdictions, is required by law to be transmitted through secure servers. In addition, depending on the context in which a designer is working, there may be concerns about the transmission of other information traditionally considered personal or private. For example, designers working in a health care context will likely be subject to constraints regarding the use of private medical information, and designers working in a labor context may have to follow special procedures with respect to the use of human resource information.

People may be unnerved and concerned about discrimination and unfairness when sophisticated digital experts collect data about them from multiple sources and analyze those data and then apply the results of the analytics to the detriment of the persons targeted. For example, data experts may help to pitch political candidates in ways that take advantage of individual vulnerabilities or deny insurance or employment based on a psychological assessment. In addition to the risk of exploitation, this use of data analytics raises issues of mistakes, discrimination, and privacy loss (Hirsch, 2018). The norms defining what information is private and what is public are constantly in flux (Maxwell et al., 2012) and may vary across age groups. As new technologies emerge, new debates about the use of technology in process design will surely emerge, forcing designers to balance the advantages of such tools with limits that might be cultural, generational, and, at times, legal.

Public access to the system: Public entities such as courts may contract with private online providers, thus raising questions about the public's ability to gain access to the issues giving rise to complaints, to assess whether the system delivers equal justice, and to learn from patterns among complaints (Schmitz, 2018; Resnik, 2018:112-114). At the same time, online dispute resolution might provide even greater public understanding of process fairness and trends in complaints than the traditional systems if the vast data trails could be accessed and analyzed (Katch and Rule, 2016; Schmidt, 2018).

In sum, these and other potential technology-triggered problems affect relationships of the participants in the design process and in the system resulting from it, as well as the fairness, feasibility, and attractiveness of the process and of the design. Thus, even this short list of problems illustrates the advantages of anticipating problems early and developing strategies to manage them.

D. MANAGING TECHNOLOGY'S PROBLEMS

We have already discussed a number of management strategies for problems caused by technology:

- To counteract fast-spreading inaccurate information in places such as Sanford, Florida (p. 247), public officials can try to become the trusted information source for the community in conflict and stand ready to increase staff during a crisis to maintain that trust.
- Because people may be more likely to lie and act uncivilly online than in person, eBay has constructed and scored reputations for buyers and sellers that are compiled from their postings and ratings of one another. This reputation scoring encourages greater civility and honesty (p. 248).
- To avoid escalation of emotions, Colin Rule's evolving design of online dispute resolution for eBay users with no ties but that of buyer and seller imposes considerable structure on the exchanges and offers advice about the appropriate language to deescalate conflict. For example, eBay decided after reading some angry opening complaints to avoid providing the complainant a text box that would allow the complainant to describe the concern in prose that could sometimes be inflammatory. Instead, eBay offered a series of politely phrased statements and the complainant could check the pertinent ones. After that change, settlements increased.
- To deal with those without the skills or capacity to communicate online, the Franklin County Municipal Court gives each small claims party a choice of in-person, phone, or online mediation.

In the example that follows, a government website incorporates suggestions from online deliberation experts to counteract tendencies for website communications to be disorganized and uncivil.

U.S. Office of Science and Technology Blog: Government sites that invite citizen views on proposed regulations and other initiatives often require them to register real names and email addresses (though other bloggers see only the pseudonyms they submit). As they register, participants agree to the site's "terms of participation," a list that has grown over time as the administrators observe new forms of counterproductive participation. Some agencies post comments only after a moderator screens them for compliance with these terms, but a U.S. Office of Science and Technology Blog tried a less costly approach. If several participants flagged a comment as violating the site's terms, the site would automatically remove that comment until an administrator could review it and decide whether to re-post it. Participants also could vote for comments that seemed especially pertinent and vote against off-point comments. Postings with negative scores over time would "collapse," requiring the user to click a line to see them, though they could be rescued from "collapse" by enough positive votes. Periodically, administrators synthesized the pertinent comments and then posed new questions that built on previous submissions (*see* more on these and other suggestions in Shane, 2008).

Though organization and civility are primary goals addressed through these blog rules, the U.S. Office of Science and Technology Blog's registration may also increase honesty in the process.

Another strategy for overcoming disorganization and extreme comments on such websites is to allow participation by invitation only and to open the website for scheduled times, thus resembling in-person discussions. In two such initiatives, a university-based group invited randomly selected individuals to take part in scheduled online public policy discussions over a year's period and reported coherent discussions and positive reactions (Price, 2012:141).

Strategies for dealing with technology-introduced problems may sometimes only reduce—not fully overcome—them. Still, reducing the problem may allow the digital approach to be worth it, on balance. The management and consent-based strategies discussed thus far may be insufficient ways to manage technology's problems. Commentators are more frequently calling for regulatory approaches, including legislation and aggressive intervention by the Federal Trade Commission and other agencies (e.g., Hirsch, 2018; Sunstein, 2017; Miller, 2013). As designers, you may want to consider law-based approaches to overcoming problems introduced by technology (*see* Chapter 13). The point of these examples is not for you to learn these management strategies, but to prepare you to search for approaches that respond effectively to the problems you perceive, or to develop your own strategies.

THOUGHTS GOING FORWARD

Can technology be part of the answer as you design a dispute management system or process? The question seems always worth asking. If so, try to anticipate the problems technology will introduce and develop a plan to overcome them. With limited existing research to guide you, you may need to introduce a pilot version and evaluate its success yourself (Chapter 14).

QUESTIONS

10.1   In this chapter, we discussed the use of technology not only in the design itself, but also during the design process. As a designer, what mode of communication (online text, phone voice communication, in-person, hard-copy memorandum, etc.) would you use for each of the following:

a. Explaining to a client the reasons for considering the opposition of employees before instituting a binding arbitration system for employee complaints?

b. Asking neighbors, clergy, and police officers in a neighborhood whether they would support a Cure Violence–type approach of mediation plus caseworkers to reducing violence?

c. Finding out what students think of the university's ombuds?

10.2   Designers assess whether the less wealthy or educated will fare worse in a new process, as well as whether a new design might reduce existing inequities between the "haves" and "have nots" (Galanter, 1974:103, regarding litigation and the quoted language; Nadler and Shestowsky, 2006:148; Schmitz, 2010b:139-143 regarding negotiation; Mann, 2009:110-112 regarding arbitration). Research now provides conflicting evidence on whether placing the processes online affects outcomes for the "have nots." Suppose that the wealthy fare better than others in online arbitration because they more often can hire experts to advocate and have greater capacities to take risks, wait, and secure information (Mann, 2009:83, 110-112). What avenues could a designer pursue to help even the playing field for online arbitration? What would you say to a wealthy dispute systems client who prefers to have an advantage?

10.3   Some federal appellate mediators hold most of their sessions by conference calls with attorneys for the parties. The results of telephone mediation resemble those for in-person mediation in terms of settlement and attorney satisfaction (*see* Eaglin, 1990:Ch.3). How would you explain the lack of difference in results between their telephone and in-person mediation sessions? Explain whether the introduction of Skype or similar video communication might improve settlement or satisfaction rates.

Exercise 10.1   *Using technology to deal with Tallahoya University's campus expansion issues:* The University's counsel sent you the following note: "As you might remember from our early conversations, from our standpoint, there is good and bad news about the plans to expand the campus to the west, which as you know is a residential district with single-family homes. The good news is that the University plans to use the expansion for low-rise buildings. These will be used primarily for auxiliary administrative functions, like fundraising and public relations, which will be minimally disruptive. Also, the University is willing to modify plans for exteriors, egress, and landscaping to improve the fit with what neighbors want.

"But remember that there is also bad news. The bad news is that the homeowners have just learned that the property purchasers who acquired these properties have done so on behalf of the University. They are steamed about the deception and fearing the worst: noisy athletic fields with massive night lighting and 20-story buildings with our mascot—if we ever settle on one—out in front.

"So that also affects the good news. With trust of the University diminished, the neighbors may not believe us when we tell them that our plans are tamer than they fear. They may suspect that the University will shift uses of the property once we secure neighborhood acquiescence to a University presence.

"About 300 neighbors may be affected, and these people will change as moves in and out of the neighborhood occur. Some will attend meetings called by the University; some will not.

"In addition to what you suggested as the primary process in response to my questions several weeks ago, I wonder if the University should supplement that with an ongoing internet-based process for educating neighbors about the situation and gaining their input." What do you think are the pros and cons of that idea? If there will be an internet-based approach, what do you suggest that it should be? What are the downsides of your suggested approach and how would you deal with them?

BIBLIOGRAPHY REFERENCES

AMERICAN BAR ASSOCIATION TASK FORCE ON ᴇCOMMERCE AND ADR (2002) *Recommended Best Practices for Online Dispute Resolution Service Providers, available at* http://www.abanet.org/dispute/documents/BestPracticesFinal102802.pdf.

BORDONE, Robert C. (1998) "Electronic Online Dispute Resolution: Approach, Potential, Problems and a Proposal," 3 *Harv. Negot. L. Rev.* 175.

BRANDON, Barbara H., and Robert D. CARLITZ (2002) "Online Rulemaking and Other Tools for Strengthening Our Civil Infrastructure," 54 *Admin. L. Rev.* 1421.

BRENNAN, Becca (2015) "Match or Mismatch.com? Online Dispute Resolution and Divorce," 21 (2) *Disp. Resol. Mag.* 15.

COLE, Sarah R., and Kristen M. BLANKLEY (2006) "Online Mediation: Where We Have Been, Where We Are Now, and Where We Should Be," 38 *U. Tol. L. Rev.* 193.

COLE, Sarah R., Nancy H. ROGERS, Craig A. McEWEN, James R. COBEN, and Peter N. THOMPSON (2017-2018) *Mediation: Law, Policy, and Practice* (3rd ed.). Minneapolis: West.

CORTES, Pablo (2008) "Can I Afford Not to Mediate? Mandatory Online Mediation for European Consumers: Legal Constraints and Policy Issues," 35 *Rutgers Computer & Tech. L.J.* 1.

CORTES, Pablo (2016) "The Brave New World of Consumer Redress in the European Union and the United Kingdom," 22 (3) *Disp. Resol. Mag.* 41.

CRAVER, Charles B. (2015) "How to Conduct Effective Telephone and E-Mail Negotiations, 17 *Cardozo J. Conflict Resol.* 1.

DAVIS, Benjamin G., and Keefe SNYDER (2010) "Online Influence Space(s) and Digital Influence Waves: In Honor of Charly," 25 *Ohio St. J. on Disp. Resol.* 201.

DIVIDED COMMUNITY PROJECT (2017) *Divided Communities and Social Media: Strategies for Community Leaders.* Columbus, OH: The Ohio State University Moritz College of Law, http://moritzlaw.osu.edu/dividedcommunityproject/.

EAGLIN, James B. (1990) *The Pre-Argument Conference Program in the Sixth Circuit Court of Appeals: An Evaluation.* Washington, DC: Federal Judicial Center.

EUROSTAT (2009) *Statistical Books: Consumers in Europe.* Luxembourg: Office for Official Publications of the European Communities.

EXON, Susan Nauss (2017) "Ethics and Online Dispute Resolution: From Evolution to Revolution," 32 *Ohio St. J. on Disp. Resol.* 609.

FISHKIN, James, and Cynthia FARRAR (2005) "Deliberative Polling: From Experiment to Community Resource," in John Gastil and Peter Levine eds., *The Deliberative Democracy Handbook: Strategies for Effective Civic Engagement in the Twenty-First Century* 68. San Francisco: Jossey-Bass.

FRIEDMAN, Ray, and Steven C. CURRALL (2004) "Conflict Escalation: Dispute Exacerbating Elements of E-Mail Communication," *available at* http://papers.ssrn.com/sol3/Delivery. cfm/ SSRN_ID459429_code031108500.pdf?abstrac tid=459429&mirid=5.

GALANTER, Marc (1974) "Why the 'Haves' Come Out Ahead: Speculations on the Limits of Legal Change," 9 *Law & Soc'y Rev.* 95.

GALVES, Fred (2009) "Virtual Justice as Reality: Making the Resolution of e-Commerce Disputes More Convenient, Legitimate, Efficient, and Secure," 2009 *U. Ill. J.L. Tech. & Pol'y* 1.

GASTIL, John, and William M. KEITH (2005) "A Nation That (Sometimes) Likes to Talk: A Brief History of Public Deliberation in the United States," in John Gastil and Peter Levine eds., *The Deliberative Democracy Handbook: Strategies for Effective Civic Engagement in the Twenty-First Century* 3. San Francisco: Jossey-Bass.

GLADWELL, Malcolm (2010) "Small Change: Why the Revolution Will Not Be Tweeted," *New Yorker* 42 (Oct. 4).

GOLDBERG, Jordan (2014) "Online Alternative Dispute Resolution and Why Law Schools Should Prepare Future Lawyers for the Online Forum," 14 *Pepp. Disp. Resol. L.J.* 1.

GRAMATIKOV, Martin, and Laura KLAMING (2012) "Getting Divorced Online: Procedural and Outcome Justice in Online Divorce Mediation," 14 *J.L. & Fam. Studies* 97.

HALOUSH, Haitham A., and Bashar H. MALKAWI (2007) "The Liberty of Participation in Online Alternative Dispute Resolution Schemes," 1 *SMU Sci. & Tech. L. Rev.* 119.

HARTER, Philip J. (2000) "Assessing the Assessors: The Actual Performance of Negotiated Rulemaking," 9 *N.Y.U. Envtl. L.J.* 32.

HIRSCH, Dennis (2018) "To Solve the Facebook Problem Think Big (Data)," *The Hill,* April 24, 2018.

HIRSCH, Dennis (2018) "Predictive Analytics Law and Policy: A New Field Emerges," 14 *I/S: J.L. & Pol'y for the Info. Soc'y* 1.

JENSEN, Astrid (2009) "Discourse Strategies in Professional E-mail Negotiation: A Case Study," 28 *Eng. for Specific Purposes* 4.

JOHNSON, Norman A., and Randolph B. COOPER (2009) "Power and Concession in Computer-Mediated Negotiations: An Examination of First Offers," 33(1) *Mgmt. Info. Systems Q.* 147-170.

KATSH, Ethan, and Janet RIFKIN (2001) *Online Dispute Resolution: Resolving Conflicts in Cyberspace.* San Francisco: Jossey-Bass.

KATSH, Ethan (2006) "Online Dispute Resolution: Some Implications for the Emergence of Law in Cyberspace," 10 *Lex Electronica, available at* http://cedires.be/index_bestanden/Katsh_ODR.pdf.

KATSH, Ethan (2009) "Online Dispute Resolution: Moving Beyond Convenience and Communication," in James R. Silkenat, Jeffrey M. Aresty, and Jacqueline Klosek eds., *The ABA Guide to International Business Negotiations: A Comparison of Cross-Cultural Issues and Successful Approaches* (3rd ed.) 235. Chicago: ABA.

KATSH, Ethan, and Orna RABINOVICH-EINY (2017) *Digital Justice: Technology and the Internet of Disputes.* Oxford, UK: Oxford University Press.

KATSH, Ethan, and Colin RULE (2016) "What We Know and Need to Know About Online Dispute Resolution," 67 *S.C. L. Rev.* 329.

KUMAR, Shekhar (2009) "Virtual Venues: Improving Online Dispute Resolution as an Alternative to Cost Intensive Litigation," 27 *J. Marshall J. Computer & Info. L.* 81.

LARSON, David Allen (2006) "Technology Mediated Dispute Resolution (TMDR): A New Paradigm for ADR," 21 *Ohio St. J. on Disp. Resol.* 629.

LARSON, David Allen (2010) "Artificial Intelligence: Robots, Avatars, and the Demise of the Human Mediator," 25 *Ohio St. J. on Disp. Resol.* 105.

LARSON, David Allen (2011) "'Brother, Can You Spare a Dime?' Technology Can Reduce Dispute Resolution Costs When Times Are Tough and Improve Outcomes," 11 *Nev. L.J.* 523.

LUBBERS, Jeffrey (2012) "A Survey of Federal Agency Rulemakers' Attitudes About E-Rulemaking," in Stephen Coleman and Peter M. Shane eds., *Connecting Democracy: Online Consultation and the Flow of Political Communication* 229. Cambridge, MA: The MIT Press.

MANN, Bruce L. (2009) "Smoothing Some Wrinkles in Online Dispute Resolution," 17 *Int'l J.L. & Info. Tech.* 83.

MAXWELL, Jeremy C., Annie I. ANTON, Peter SWIRE, Maria RIAZ, and Christopher M. McCRAW (2012) "A Legal Cross-References Taxonomy for Reasoning About Compliance Requirements," 17 *J. Requirements Engineering* 99.

McGINN, Kathleen L., and Eric WILSON (2004) "How to Negotiate Successfully Online," *Negot.* (No. 3) 7.

MELVILLE, Keith, Taylor L. WILLINGHAM, and John R. DEDRICK (2005) "National Issues Forums: A Network of Communities Promoting Public Deliberation," in John Gastil and Peter Levine eds., *The Deliberative Democracy Handbook: Strategies for Effective Civic Engagement in the Twenty-First Century* 37. San Francisco: Jossey-Bass.

MILLER, David (2013) "Legislating Our Reasonable Expectations: Making the Case for a Statutory Framework to Protect Workplace Privacy in the Age of Social Media," 22 *U. Miami Bus. L. Rev.* 49.

NADLER, Janice (2001) "Electronically-Mediated Dispute Resolution and E-Commerce," 17 *Negot. J.* 333.

NADLER, Janice, and Donna SHESTOWSKY (2006) "Negotiation, Information Technology, and the Problem of the Faceless Other," in L. Thompson ed., *Negotiation Theory and Research* 145. London: Taylor & Francis.

PEW RESEARCH CENTER (2018) "News Use Across Social Media Platforms 2017," *available at* http://www.journalism.org/2017/09/07/news-use-across-social-media-platforms-2017/.

PRICE, Vincent (2012) "Playing Politics: The Experience of E-Participation," in Stephen Coleman and Peter M. Shane eds., *Connecting Democracy: Online Consultation and the Flow of Political Communication* 125. Cambridge, MA: The MIT Press.

PUTNAM, Robert D. (2000) *Bowling Alone: The Collapse and Revival of American Community.* New York: Simon & Schuster.

RABINOVICH-EINY, Orna, and Ethan KATSH (2012) "Technology and the Future of Dispute Systems Design," 17 *Harv. Negot. L. Rev.* 141.

RAINEY, Daniel (2015) "Glimmers on the Horizon: Unique Ethical Issues Created by ODR," 21 (2) *Disp. Resol. Mag.* 20.

RESNIK, Judith (2018) "2J/A2K: Access to Justice, Access to Knowledge, and Economic Inequalities in Open Courts and Arbitrations," 96 *N.C. L. Rev.* 101.

RULE, Colin, and Chittu NAGARAJAN (2010) *Crowdsourcing Dispute Resolution over Mobile Devices* (eBay self-published).

SCHMITZ, Amy J. (2010a) "'Drive-Thru' Arbitration in the Digital Age: Empowering Consumers Through Binding ODR," 62 *Baylor L. Rev.* 178.

SCHMITZ, Amy J. (2010b) "Legislating in the Light: Considering Empirical Data in Crafting Arbitration Reforms," 15 *Harv. Negot. L. Rev.* 115.

SCHMITZ, Amy J. (2014) "Secret Consumer Scores and Segmentations: Separating Consumer 'Haves' from the 'Have-Nots,'" 2014 *Mich. St. L. Rev.* 1411.

SCHMITZ, Amy J. (2016) "Building Trust in E-commerce Through Online Dispute Resolution," in John A. Rothchild ed., *Research Handbook on Electronic Commerce Law.* Northampton, MA: Edward Elgar Publishing.

SCHMITZ, Amy J., and Colin RULE (2017) *The New Handshake: Online Dispute Resolution and the Future of Consumer Protection.* Chicago: ABA.

SCHMITZ, Amy J. (2018) "A Blueprint for Online Dispute Resolution System Design," 21 *J. Internet L.* 3.

SELA, Ayelet (2017) "The Effect of Online Technologies on Dispute Resolution System Design: Antecedents, Current Trends, and Future Directions," 21 *Lewis & Clark L. Rev.* 635.

SHACKELFORD, Scott J., and Anjanette H. RAYMOND (2014) "Building the Virtual Courthouse: Ethical Considerations for Design, Implementation, and Regulation in the World of ODR," 2014 *Wis. L. Rev.* 615.

SHANE, Peter M. ed. (2008) *Building Democracy Through Online Citizen Deliberation: A Framework for Action.* Columbus, OH: Ohio State University.

SHANE, Peter M. (2012) "Online Consultation and Political Communication in the Era of Obama: An Introduction," in Stephen Coleman and Peter M. Shane eds., *Connecting Democracy: Online Consultation and the Flow of Political Communication* 1. Cambridge, MA: The MIT Press.

SPIEKER, Arne (2018) "Stakeholder Dialogues and Virtual Reality for the German Energiewende," 2018 *J. Disp. Resol.* 75.

SUNSTEIN, Cass (2017) *#Republic: Divided Democracy in the Age of Social Media.* Princeton, NJ: Princeton University Press.

VERDONSCHOT, Jin Ho (2015) "In the Netherlands, Online Application Helps Divorcing Couples in Their Own Words, on Their Own Time," 21 (2) *Disp. Resol. Mag.* 19.

VOSOUGHI, Soroush, Deb ROY, and Sinan ARAL (2018) "The Spread of True and False News Online," 2018 *Science* 359.

WAHAB, Mohamed S. Abdel, Ethan KATSH, and Daniel RAINEY eds. (2012) *Online Dispute Resolution: Theory and Practice.* The Hague, The Netherlands: Eleven International Publishing.

IMPLEMENTING

The fourth phase of designing is implementation. Part Four is organized into three narrowly focused chapters and one broader chapter. The narrowly focused chapters cover the use of contracts (Chapter 12), law (Chapter 13), and systematic collection of evidence to determine and document the success and the need for any modifications of the design (Chapter 14). We begin with the broader chapter on implementing (Chapter 11).

Implementing

Implementation may be the fourth phase of designing in this book, but it has to be considered from the start. If a new process or system cannot be implemented successfully, it is nothing more than an idea. You already have learned about implementation through the stories in the book. Anticipating implementation, designers:

- changed processes to make them easier to implement;
- involved certain stakeholders who might support or block implementation; and
- modified the design as a result of evaluation done early in the implementation phase.

By reading this chapter, you will organize what you already know about implementation into a mental checklist to use throughout your work as a designer.

This chapter focuses on seven items for your checklist:

- anticipating from the start who must support or might derail a new approach and *incorporating these stakeholders into the planning,* or at least considering their interests in the plans (Section A);
- *encouraging a receptive climate* for the new system, through training, communications, and other approaches (Section B);
- when appropriate, *fitting the design within existing patterns* of disputing or mechanisms for resolution within the organization or culture in order to decrease resistance (Section C);

- *developing resources* for the initiative while assuring that fairness and accessibility will be achieved (Section D);
- considering carefully *who should lead* (Section E);
- when possible, beginning on a small scale—often with a *pilot program* (Section F); and
- *preparing for the long-term operation*, considering the potential to drift away from original goals, often by placing the system or process within the appropriate institution (Section G).

The book covers three other aspects of implementation—using contracts (Chapter 12), law (Chapter 13), and evaluation (Chapter 14)—in the chapters following this one.

A. ANTICIPATING THE NEED FOR SUPPORT AND THE POSSIBLE RESISTANCE

As part of this first theme, we return to the initial identification of stakeholders (Chapter 4.A). Did it include questions like: Whose support will later be needed? Who might seek to block or impede implementation? If you understand these individuals' or organizations' needs, you can often find creative ways to meet them in the design. Also, people will often support what they helped to create. Anticipating the need for support and the power of resistance is a preventive strategy—the low-hanging fruit of implementation—that depends on early identification and involvement of these key people.

Of course, those who might later resist change may not be obvious. For example, imagine that a general counsel seeks your help because the company wants to reduce employment litigation and improve relations with employees. You ask the general counsel whether you should involve the executives, the direct supervisors, or the lawyers working for the general counsel in the early discussions in order to ease implementation later. The general counsel responds that it is unnecessary: "They are the ones who most want something better. They have to testify and deal with the bitterness and expense that follow a formal claim."

Those who have designed in the workplace, though, will counsel you to persist. One reason to do so is that people who would seem to benefit may not perceive the new program as a net benefit, as the research below explains.

> *Improving workplace disputing systems—a surprise:* Employment experts David Lipsky, Ronald Seeber, and Richard Fincher point out the unexpected news that resisters to a new workplace mediation program are often those who will benefit from it. They warn to expect opposition from "first-line supervisors who feel that the system's values and flexibility interfere with traditional paths of communication and give too many rights to those with meritless claims. Sometimes the strongest resistance comes from human resource personnel who feel that the new system changes the power structure, diminishes their role in conflict resolution, and decreases the emphasis on rights-based determination of employee disputes" (2003:165). They note that even in-house lawyers often oppose such systems and that sometimes senior management fear a "flood of complaints" (id.).

All of these concerns might have been resolved if those mentioned had participated in the design process.

In order to anticipate the less obvious reasons to resist or decline support—those that eluded the general counsel above—you can develop a list of questions to use in a variety of contexts. Then, you can augment these questions by interviews with others who have designed programs in similar milieus—the equivalents of Lipsky, Seeber, and Fincher in other settings. For example, your list might include:

- Whose job status will be affected (including in informal ways as in the workplace example above)?
- Who will have to do extra work?
- Who feels disaffected from the leaders and therefore will support a new program only if someone they trust supports it (e.g., were health care insurers included in plans to design a process to reform the state's approach to medical insurance)?
- Does the design challenge the conventional wisdom of a particular group?
- Whose budget or staff resources will be cut to operate the new initiative?
- Who feels entitled to be consulted about changes in this context?

Involving all of the stakeholders early on does not necessarily make it harder to reach agreement or finalize the system. If all of the stakeholders are involved, it may be possible to implement the parts of a system on which there is broad agreement while continuing to discuss those issues that are unresolved. This can be more problematic if the design team purposefully left out those who disagreed with their views at an early stage in the process, assuming that it would be easier to implement without the opposition. The likelihood that those left out will expend energy to ensure the failure of the new approach is much higher when they are "outsiders" than when they are simply dissenting voices from within (Fader, 2008:497-498).

Consider this example in Maryland where planners, unable to agree on how to measure "quality assurance" for mediators, were nonetheless able to find creative ways to spread mediation, improve quality, and manage their differences.

Implementing Maryland's "quality assistance" approach to mediator quality: Maryland's designers (MACRO) helped stakeholders reach consensus on a plan to assure mediator quality—that mediators would be judged by an ongoing commitment to improving their effectiveness rather than by high entry-level qualifications (pp. 155-157). The stakeholders also had reached consensus that the implementation would be accomplished without forcing a court or organization to use only mediators who had joined the statewide organization. Also, they agreed that mediators would not be required to join. So, implementation success depended upon widespread acceptance of the ongoing quality improvement approach.

MACRO hired Cheryl Jamison, a lawyer with a mental health counseling background, to implement the mediator assistance initiative. Jamison worked over three years to develop mediators' trust in the process, to help mediators understand why they should invest their time in ongoing improvement, and to show mediators the worth of the online searchable

Photo by Jonathan Franz

database. Membership grew and some courts began referring only to members, but one thorny issue kept arising—what approach to mediation (e.g., facilitative? evaluative?) would be the focus of the training and ongoing skills assessment?

MACRO established a 22-person council for the mediator quality initiative, drawn from sectors that used each of the primary mediation approaches. Council members could not agree on the best mediation goal or procedures. Some thought that mediators should not evaluate the merits of the underlying legal claim. Some thought that transformation of the conflict interaction should be the goal, not settlement.

After several years, it was apparent that the initiative was taking hold even while this disagreement remained. About 800 mediators had joined and reacted positively to the free ongoing skills and ethics courses and activities. Courts were beginning to select mediators from the membership.

Although Council members still could not agree on the optimal goal and therefore the optimal mediation training approach, they now had strong reasons to maintain the momentum. They did so by putting the disagreement about the mediation approach behind them.

The council members, still in disagreement about the best approach, jointly acknowledged that mediators in Maryland were legitimately using four major mediation frameworks: facilitative mediation, transformative mediation, analytical mediation (which might include some evaluation), and inclusive mediation (which included community mediation approaches).[1] Training could focus on any or all, as could mediator assessment. They had found a way to surmount this obstacle. After all, the initiative proved valuable once implemented—so much so that they did not want it threatened by this disagreement.

By including those in disagreement while delaying a decision on the standoff regarding mediation approaches, Maryland planners used the time to help stakeholders understand their shared interest in expanding the use of mediation and developing self-improvement in whatever approach they were using. Though delay was a successful strategy in terms of choosing a preferred mediation approach, Maryland planners resolved other concerns, when they could, early in their planning (pp. 70-71). Early planning also helps with climate issues, the topic of the next section.

B. IMPROVING THE CLIMATE FOR IMPLEMENTATION

Changing dispute management processes and systems means changing behaviors. As you read about Cure Violence, think about the counterfactual situation: what would have happened had Cure Violence started using interrupters without persuading those in the community to let it know about brewing trouble?

Cure Violence's efforts to get reports: The Cure Violence Chicago staff noticed three frequent sources of violence: retaliation, gang rivalries, and interpersonal disputes. They had mediators but needed a strategy to secure tips that violence might occur.

To prevent retaliation, Cure Violence needed to learn quickly about a violent crime and notify mediators to work with the victim's family and friends. The police would have to call Cure Violence immediately after learning of the violence. So, Cure Violence stayed in constant contact with police, asking about violent incidents. Once the program had operated for a while, Cure Violence made certain police officers knew that retaliatory violence was down, due in part to police referrals to Cure Violence. As trust and confidence developed over time, the police began routinely calling Cure Violence about violence likely to lead to retaliation.

---

1. In facilitative mediation, the mediator does not evaluate. In a transformative mediation, the mediator defers more (than in facilitative and evaluative mediation) to the parties to set the agenda and seeks mutual understanding and respect but not necessarily a resolution of the dispute. Community mediation often occurs between unrepresented parties and flexibly deals with more than the presenting dispute if that seems to serve the parties' interests. For more on mediation approaches, see Appendix C.

To get word of possible gang-related violence, Cure Violence's Tio Hardiman and colleagues negotiated peace treaties among gangs; gang members agreed to call Cure Violence if they anticipated violence. Cure Violence also provided transportation for gang members to attend its workshops and social events, thus staying in regular contact with gang members, just as they did with police.

To learn about potentially violent interpersonal disputes, Cure Violence had to change the practices of scattered individuals—relatives, friends, and neighbors of the disputing individuals. Cure Violence used a community and media outreach strategy to let them know the benefits of contacting Cure Violence when they feared that a relative or friend might resort to violence.

Cure Violence's strategies to get tips are common ones for designers who seek to change practices:

- communicating beforehand about the program and how it might help individuals, groups, agencies, communities;
- communicating after implementation about its successes; and
- securing commitments from key collaborators and resources to help.

Additional strategies in other contexts may include:

- changing economic or other incentives and
- building the capacity of various stakeholders by teaching effective dispute resolution techniques.

Communications: A well-conceived communication strategy can help secure necessary resources and participation in a program. As the next segment on the National Institutes of Health ombuds demonstrates, "word of mouth" is rarely sufficient. Indeed, worth of mouth alone can easily lead to misconceptions and bad rumors about how a program runs.

National Institutes of Health ombuds: Who knew? After ten years as NIH's ombuds, Howard Gadlin asked the Harvard Law School Negotiation and Mediation Clinical Program to examine how users perceived the service. The Harvard clinic students interviewed 46 ombuds staff, administrators, and users; emailed others; conducted six focus groups; and surveyed over 34,000 NIH staff members. They found positive results among users: users trusted the ombuds staff, felt treated with respect, and most often found them helpful. The problem the design students uncovered was that one in four NIH staff members had never heard of the ombuds office. Even more thought that consulting the ombuds would escalate a conflict. In a typical response, one staff member said, "I would worry that taking an issue to this level would inflate its seriousness; I would also worry about possible repercussions, such as being seen as a troublemaker, someone hard to please, or setting something in motion I couldn't control." How should the ombuds communicate with the 34,000 staff members who already complained of the "information overload" age? The design students recommended periodic email/electronic newsletter transmittal of "stories" that conveyed the essence of the service. The stories could be written to deal with the fears about conflict escalation. They suggested website revision and other targeted means as well.

Public relations can be expensive, so groups like Cure Violence Chicago engage the media as part of the strategy to build support and resources for the initiative while also relying on word of mouth and supportive local community organizations such as churches or neighborhood groups to spread the word. Cure Violence must communicate with young people and other community residents who are directly affected by violence and can assist the organization in responding to it. In addition, Cure Violence builds broader public support for city and state leaders' decisions to fund its work and seeks ways to reach potential private donors.

Cure Violence's media strategy: Cure Violence Chicago regularly celebrated related news, such as a Cure Violence community that had gone a year without a shooting, and issued media releases. In addition, Cure Violence Chicago staff were available to the media as experts on a variety of crime-related topics. As a result, the local or national media carried Cure Violence stories several times a month. In addition, members of Cure Violence worked with award winning filmmakers Steve James and Alex Kotlowitz to produce a feature-length documentary about their program called "The Interrupters" (*see* http://interrupters.kartemquin.com/).

Filming Cure Violence interrupter Ameena Matthews for the documentary "The Interrupters." Photo courtesy of Kartemquin Films.

Education: Educational programs that are designed to change behavior range from informative sessions about how a new system might work to more intensive programs aimed at equipping stakeholders to participate more fully and effectively in the various roles (mediator, facilitator, party) that comprise the dispute resolution system. Those leading the collaborative lawyering initiative, for example, require lawyers to take classes in interest-based negotiation as a prerequisite to practicing collaborative law (pp. 114-115). Sometimes the educational strategy is expansive, as when designers teach all key court employees how to mediate as a means to help them understand when it would be valuable to refer cases to mediation and how they should explain the process (*but see* Costantino and Merchant, 1996:136). Designers also teach by modeling, during the planning process, the collaborative approach they know will make the workplace or community receptive to a consensus-based dispute resolution system.

Financial or other incentives: What incentives do people have to change their behavior as contemplated by the design? At times, aligning financial incentives may change behavior. In a role-played experiment, settlements occurred more quickly if attorneys financed litigation expenses (Inglis and McCabe, 2010:149). Suppose a university charges the pertinent department's budget for all payments the university must make to resolve claims arising in that department, but the university administration pays litigation costs, including attorney's fees. If fiscal incentives influence behavior, one can imagine that the department head may want to drag out litigation longer than the central university.

But not all people respond to incentives in the same ways. For some, the crucial incentive may be recognition ("If you implement this successfully, you will be the first company to have done so. We will then nominate you for a national problem-solving award!"). Alternatively, people may find it fascinating to learn new skills or be part of an innovative program. They may gain personal satisfaction in being a key part of a change that improves the quality of life for disputants. In order for these incentives to help secure cooperation, the designer may have to train, involve, and communicate with key people with these incentives in mind.

C. USING EXISTING PATTERNS

If focused solely on what should be changed, designers might fail to appreciate the value of other aspects of what the organizations or individuals have been doing in the past. Sometimes currently existing patterns, processes, and behaviors can be leveraged in the new system. In fact, this might be the only avenue; it is not always possible or efficient to change people's values or the ways that they go about their daily activities. With creativity and sensitivity to those with whom you are working, you may be able to fit the design within these existing practices and values and the incentives, resources, and structures that help sustain them. This strategy resembles shifting a sail to take advantage of prevailing winds; it can often facilitate a quicker start for a new program and one that will be received with greater warmth and enthusiasm.

The strategy for fitting within existing patterns might be as simple as scheduling the new process at the time of an already established event. For example, designers schedule a truancy mediation at about the time that teachers would have previously met with parents to discuss unexcused absences. Teachers need to adjust only to new participants—the mediator, the student, and perhaps counselors—who can help to formulate a plan that will increase attendance going forward. If the teachers do not view the mediation as more burdensome than the status quo, the designers avoid dealing with a major hurdle—persuading teachers to take on another time-consuming task—and the new program can be implemented more quickly and with less resistance.

Employing a similar strategy, a designer might fit the process to current disputing values, hoping that the parties will embrace it from the start. In the story below, the judges did just that.

Navajo peacemakers: In the 1980s, several Navajo Nation judges decided that the adversarial court process did not provide what many local Navajo people wanted in a process—"healing, respect, consensus, harmony, individual autonomy [of the Navajo peoples] and the wisdom of elders" (Nielson, 1998:11, 16-18). Mediation might increase consensus, but mediators tend to encourage settlement between disputants; the family and community elders play no role. Using a different approach, the traditional Navajo peace leaders, called "Naat'aanii," had used an informal, story-based process that combined consensus building and arbitration. The Naat'aanii brought the parties' families and sometimes others into the discussions, thus responding to the desire for community harmony.

The judges secured resources for a few Navajo Peacemakers. They observed that this traditional process resonated with many of the Navajo people. In fact, people began voluntarily submitting their disputes to the Peacemakers, even when not court-referred. By 1998, there were 250 Navajo Peacemakers resolving disputes such as minor criminal matters and family conflicts (id.:8, 12-14, 17).

Of course, some existing patterns, structures, incentives, and values conflict with the aims of the new system or process, necessitating a return to the task described in Section B. Suppose, for example, that the claims process for clergy child abuse could be organized to preserve a culture of secrecy and extreme deferral to hierarchal authority within particular religious organizations. The designer might conclude that to reinforce these tendencies in a new design would perpetuate the very problems that had occurred, undetected, for decades. At the same time, ignoring these tendencies might ensure the ultimate failure of the system as well. The task for the designer is to leverage those aspects that might prove fruitful (the focus of Section C) while designing the system in a way that curbs the unhealthy or destructive patterns of the past (Section B).

D. MARSHALING RESOURCES

Mediator Michael Young listed private company sponsorship of the South Africa talks as a key component of success (pp. 17-19)—the company made considerable resources available for these high-stakes negotiations. But designers seldom begin with such resources. Instead they must often negotiate for the human and financial resources they need to ensure the success of a system. Many times, they must cajole, improvise, and be creative. In some instances, when they simply cannot persuade decision-makers of the need for support, they may exercise their discretion to withdraw from the work.

Designers may be familiar with the up and down state and city budget allocations and various fundraising efforts of nonprofit organizations like Cure Violence. Novice designers may be surprised though when a private for-profit organization balks at allocating resources to hire an ombuds person, to train staff, or to publicize and educate about new procedures. Consider the viewpoint of institutional decision-makers who must make hard financial choices: from their perspective, they are spending organizational time and effort on the design process itself. After all, they may be paying your fee as a designer, as well as the fee for additional facilitators. In addition, if you have created a collaborative design process, you have also diverted a substantial amount of staff time away from existing work and toward design meetings, interviews, surveys, and the like. When you now suggest hiring additional permanent staff or instituting a firm-wide training program, you may encounter resistance or even anger. You may be wondering why an organization would spend so much time and energy on a design process only to balk at proper implementation, but the viewpoint of the institutional decision-maker in charge of allocating resources may be different.

Given the challenges of securing resources, a design might be geared from the start to save them. Two strategies already discussed demonstrate prominent cost-cutting options—leveraging technology (Chapter 10) and the creative use of volunteer mediators and adjudicators (Chapter 6.B). Such approaches may make the new initiative feasible, and therefore might be worth the potential downsides.

While creativity helps to deal with resource constraints, imaginative funding strategies may also have pitfalls. For example, the idea of making the mediator's fee contingent on the outcome came from a desire to overcome reluctance to provide resources when a mediation might not result in agreement. But that idea met with resistance because of concern that the economic incentives might compromise mediator neutrality. With this concern in mind, the dominant aspirational ethics standards for U.S. mediators discourage mediator fees contingent on the outcome (Model Standards of Conduct for Mediators, 2005:Standard VIII.B.1).

In the excerpt below, Wayne Brazil, a U.S. magistrate judge for more than 20 years, reflects on the problems implicit in another resource-creating strategy—requiring litigation parties to participate in mediation and also pay the mediator's fee, even if an exception is made for indigent parties.

> **Wayne Brazil:** "With privatization being so fashionable, . . . policymakers will surely be asked why court provision of free or low-cost ADR services should not be confined to litigants with limited resources or to cases of limited monetary value. . . . [T]he percentage of civil cases that could be deemed to 'need' free or low-cost ADR services might be quite substantial. . . . Trying to restrict court provision of ADR services to small cases or poor litigants also would increase the risk of creating, or of being perceived as having created, a two-tiered system of 'ADR justice.' . . . The suggestion that courts limit the provision of ADR services to certain classes of cases also raises some larger policy concerns. Is it appropriate for courts to provide all classes of cases the full complement of adjudicatory and case management services for free, but to make the parties in some classes of cases pay for ADR services? . . . And why should public courts endorse—by providing for free—only one kind of procedure, adjudication, for addressing disputes, especially when that procedure arguably sanctions—or at least is assumed to offer safe harbor to—aggressive and self-serving conduct, tolerates considerable inter-party friction, imposes massive transaction costs, and is very slow to yield results? These questions become more difficult to answer satisfactorily in courts that compel parties to participate in an ADR process. Why should mediation, for example, be the only mandatory component of a court process for which parties are required to pay a substantial fee? And why should the parties be forced to pay such a fee to some private provider . . . ?" (Brazil, 2006:258-261).

E. BUILDING LEADERSHIP

Two schools have students with similar backgrounds, but a dispute system design dies at one school and thrives in the other. A designer suggests the reason—at the second school, the principal has a warmer, more outgoing personality, and, perhaps partly as a result, the teachers and students enjoy a culture of innovation and mutual support. Leadership matters.

Sometimes it seems that leadership alone makes the difference—not just leadership combined with environment—because a successful program at times fails shortly after its first leader retires and a new leader takes over. So a designer may try to guide selection and development of the leader in order to implement successfully.

Leader attributes—an interview with Rachel Wohl of the Maryland Court of Appeals dispute resolution program: Rachel Wohl pointed out that she did not have to spend much time managing because she trusted every member of her staff—staff members participated in determining the direction of the office and they held common values. She said that she made certain that they had rewarding tasks and sufficient resources. She commented that her friendship with and respect for these talented people pulled her to remain as director for 15 years.

Wohl's comments suggest that she exemplified one of the criteria of an effective manager. Management researchers note that effective managers of people typically care about their employees, including whether their office colleagues find satisfaction in their jobs, and they provide praise, clarity of task, and resources (Wagner and Harter, 2006:202-203).

But leaders of innovation may need more than good management skills. To find out what leadership strengths are specific to implementing new designs, we asked Wohl what criteria she recommends to another state's chief justice who was hiring someone to direct the court's dispute resolution program. She responded: has energy, cares about people, is able to connect with them, and is dogged in efforts to achieve the mission. In part, these characteristics come to the forefront because Wohl prefers a collaborative design approach, but they are consistent with leadership theory in the innovation context. Collaborative leadership of innovation may require strengths in "taking initiative when there is inertia, living with uncertainty, learning from mistakes, learning to accept the inevitable failures of innovation, experimenting, learning to live with the stress that accompanies innovation . . . , and helping others deal with inevitable consequences of risk-taking and of change" (Kuttner, 2011:120).

In designing dispute management systems, designers will want to identify and cultivate inspiring leaders with qualities similar to the ones articulated by Wohl, as well as strategies for improving succession to other exceptional leaders when the first leaves. They may also seek to instill organizational practices that might create receptive climates for the design in the absence of outstanding leaders (*see* question 11.4). Despite efforts to reduce reliance on exceptional leadership, however, some designs may depend for their success on having the right kind of leader and may founder when they do not. Steve Goldberg notes this phenomenon in union-management relations where new designs tend to include interest-based negotiation or mediation. He adds:

> "Interest-based negotiation with management can always be seen from the union perspective as collaboration. The cooperative union leader is 'in bed with management,' or 'sold out the rank-and-file.' There is often a hawkish element in the membership that produces a leader who says, 'I could do better than those wimps,' and there is no way to prove that he/she could not. As a result, many efforts at installing better, more interest-based systems in the union-management context have a limited life span, no matter how careful the designer."[2]

---

2. Note to authors, September 23, 2011.

F. USING A PILOT PROGRAM

Administrators know that they can bring some doubters on board with a new initiative by suggesting a carefully monitored pilot of the program. A pilot version of the overall design also serves to test the concept while preserving the flexibility to improve it (or abandon it) before applying it broadly. In addition, by piloting a program on a small scale, designers can strategically begin in a division or part of the organization that might be more open to trying something new. Successful results in one domain may well be contagious, persuading others across the organization to be more open. Piloting may also allow adjustment for surprise results, such as learning in a given situation that litigation may produce larger settlement offers than a private claims facility with lower transaction costs because the class action assures the defendant of finality regarding all potential claimants (*see* Issacharoff and Rave, 2013). Whenever possible, then, introducing a dispute management system on a small scale in a pilot program merits consideration.

A pilot program that fails, however, may end the initiative. So, designers plan pilot programs carefully. Keeping in mind the multiple purposes for beginning with a pilot program, Costantino and Merchant suggest the following criteria for choosing where to institute the pilot for a new intra-organization process:

- "Are there sufficient numbers of disputes to test success?
- "Are there sufficient resources (time, staff, money) to allocate to the pilot?
- "Are the results of the pilot measurable and easily evaluated?
- "Is the area of the pilot important to the rest of the organization?" (Costantino and Merchant, 1996:156).

G. TAKING SUCCESSFUL INNOVATION TO SCALE; INSTITUTIONALIZING IT

Ask a designer what initiatives are underway, and you will typically learn that the designer is working on new initiatives to improve an existing process or is seeking a way to make it more permanent—to "institutionalize" it. In the institutionalization process, the questions of how to deal with "drift" from the original goals and the choice of institution loom large.

1. Taking successful innovation to scale: anticipating drift from original goals

The results achieved in the pilot or initial operations of a new dispute management system may change as the system operates over time or expands. Employees settled nearly all disputes they submitted to the National Institutes of Health mediation process during the first 18 months of the program, but a large portion were handled instead through the peer panel adjudication process in the next year, and that process became more complicated over time (pp. 125-126).

Designers seeking to get a program back on track may return to the original design considerations and ask whether important design questions may have been overlooked or not explored fully. For example:

- Did the designers identify all relevant stakeholders and do a thorough and adequate stakeholder assessment?
- Did the designers take into account possible resistance by some individuals or constituencies?
- Was there something about the local culture, organizational structure, or incentives that was missed or inadequately understood?
- What has been the role of organizational leaders?
- Was the proper funding in place?
- Were potential participants effectively incentivized through a rewards program or other organizational structure to avail themselves of the new system?
- Have the needs of the organization changed in some way that simply could not have been detected or designed for at an earlier stage?

In the example that follows, the designers anticipated drift and prepared to deal with it.

Collaborative law, drift as the initiative expanded: Collaborative lawyering in the family law field began with groups of lawyers in Minneapolis and San Francisco (pp. 114-115) but now has spread to virtually all U.S. cities, and to cities in other nations as well. The innovative initiative dealt with the potential for drift in several ways.

The first approach was to organize collaborative lawyers into a community for mutual encouragement and reinforcement of values. The organizers created a national, now international, organization of collaborative lawyers that provided an avenue to discuss issues as the field grew.

Pauline Tesler recalls that the organizers examined what had occurred as mediation programs were implemented and decided to try to avoid the credentialing debates that they viewed as slowing implementation. They made the lack of credentialing a key aspect of collaborative lawyering that could be suggested as a part of the policies of each local program. Through this informal approach, they built anticipation of resistance to credentialing into the design.

A way to deal with a second kind of drift appeared by chance. With family law practitioners accustomed by practice, and perhaps by personality, to engage in cagey, adversarial bargaining, there was concern that collaborative law negotiations would move in that direction over time. Reports of a similar drift in mediation provided an added reason for concern. Early in the development of collaborative law, the organizers expanded the model to include mental health and other experts in the negotiations. These professionals did not come from the adversarial tradition and expressed concern when negotiations turned in that direction. Then organizers had the idea to institutionalize the reports by the interdisciplinary experts—a post-negotiation interdisciplinary debriefing became a part of the model.

The organizers also noticed that most collaborative lawyers were willing to take some risks to be part of the process. Another group of more risk-averse family lawyers held back, concerned that there had not been a definitive ruling on the ethics of the agreement to withdraw as counsel in the event that the parties did not reach agreement in the collaborative lawyering negotiations. Also, there were concerns about whether the courts would enforce the confidentiality agreements in the event of a subpoena for communications. These doubts could limit the growth of collaborative lawyering and might even undermine its success. Collaborative lawyers successfully lobbied for enactment of individual statutes in some states and court rules in others to clarify the law. A national movement led in 2009 to a Uniform Collaborative Law Act, in an attempt to add certainty. Since then, the membership of local practice groups has expanded.[3]

2. Institutionalizing

Dispute systems designs often begin as a cooperative initiative of spirited organizers. Designers worry about what will happen as these people leave or lose enthusiasm. Once leadership changes and the novelty wears off, will the initiative:

- decline in quality?
- lack a steady stream of resources?
- veer away from the initial focus?
- fail to achieve enough visibility to attract users?

Designers may seek to assure continuance and oversight by placing the initiative within an institution. Consider the example below involving the leaders of the Montgomery County, Maryland public school district and their efforts to improve and institutionalize collaborative and consensus-based processes developed over a ten-year period.

Montgomery County Public Schools (MCPS): In 1999, the Montgomery County, Maryland public school district adopted a comprehensive ten-year plan entitled Our Call to Action: Pursuit of Excellence. Part of that plan involved an unprecedented commitment to collaborative, problem-solving processes at every level of school administration—from dealing with unions, to working with parents, addressing diversity issues, and dealing with conflict between students,

---

3. Interview with Pauline Tesler, Sept. 29, 2010.

teachers, and administrators. In order to institutionalize collaborative processes within the school district, MCPS established a leadership group, called the "ADC," that included leaders of the school district's various unions as well as the deputy superintendent of schools and the chief operating officer of the district. The idea was that regular communications and continuous meetings would help identify problem areas early on and would ensure the continuity, growth, and adaptability of the system.

In the fall of 2009, ten years after *Our Call to Action*, the ADC invited students from the Harvard Negotiation and Mediation Clinical Program to evaluate and assess the collaborative and dispute resolution processes that existed across the organization. Part of the purpose was to ensure the dynamism of the processes in place and identify areas for growth, modification, and change. But the ADC had a second reason for enlisting the help of the Harvard clinic: after a decade serving as district and union leaders, many in the leadership group realized that they needed to think about transition. They wanted to ensure the collaborative values and vision that they had forged more than a decade earlier were passed on to a new generation of leadership. The ADC leadership sought to do so by commissioning a comprehensive study, one that would both help them improve the collaborative processes in place and serve as an educational tool for a new generation of leadership and thereby prevent program drift and inertia. In June 2010, the Montgomery County public school district released a new five-year strategic plan drawing upon the Harvard clinic study as well as other outside and self-assessments.

The choice of institution will affect the initiative's tone, scope, and future, as the stories below illustrate.

Institutionalizing Canada's Truth and Reconciliation Commission: As law professor Jennifer Llewellyn recalls the conversations of the design group, the Commission was to play a creative role, "discovering the truth of past wrongdoing, its implications for relationships, and what will be required to address the related and resulting harm and equip parties to live together differently in the future." The Commission might, for example, "bring the involved parties together in a process that reflects and models the values of reconciled relationships" (Llewellyn, 2008:190). But the Commission would determine optimal activities over time.

The class action Indian Residential Schools Settlement Agreement authorized the Truth and Reconciliation Commission and provided continuing oversight by the court, but did not designate an institutional home for the Commission. Ultimately, the government made the Commission a government agency, reporting its progress regularly to a group of lawyers overseeing it, under the auspices of the court. Llewellyn notes that the Commission then began to view its mission in terms of discrete tasks and timelines, and she worries that these might eclipse the broader mandate, that the Commission members might have lost sight of the forest for the trees.

The Commission story counsels for giving the institutional home more thought at the start. To practice doing that, suppose that a commission comprised of volunteer designers seeks to institutionalize its efforts through a paid staff—a state dispute resolution office that will design new programs, help them grow, and improve their quality over time (*see* Drake, 1989:259). One could imagine the comments regarding the optimal institutional home:

- Placing the new office within the governor's office enhances its visibility, but will a new governor treat it as a pet project of the predecessor and remove its funding?
- Locating the office instead within the state supreme court might promote more permanence, but over time will chief justices insist that the court office limit its resources to court-connected programs? Will the court naturally encourage a narrow, legal-focused form of mediation?
- If the state office answers to a commission appointed by all three branches, will any branch deem it a high enough priority to find funding for it over time? If different political parties control these branches of government, will commission members engage in partisan bickering?

Because these are fair questions, one might expect that the designers will begin to canvass existing offices in other states, looking for information on similar or analogous efforts to institutionalize a dispute resolution initiative.

In the next example, organizers could not canvass the experience institutionalizing a similar initiative elsewhere, as the program was novel. But their ultimate choice of the U.S. Justice Department as the home for the new program seems to have contributed to its long-term success.

Determining the institutional auspices for federal civil rights mediators: Racial unrest occurred broadly and frequently in the United States during the 1960s. Mediators helped citizen avert violence on a number of occasions. Foundations provided funding for some mediations. In one instance, an Assistant U.S. Attorney General helped negotiate an agreement that resolved bitter differences.

These *ad hoc* mediation successes fueled interest in institutionalizing federal civil rights mediation. Individuals differed in what institution should house the federal mediators, proposing variously the Civil Rights Commission, the Federal Mediation and Conciliation Service (which mediates collective bargaining conflicts), and the Commerce Department (Levine, 2005:6-12). Just hours before the U.S. House passed the Civil Rights Act of 1964, an amendment added a "Community Relations Service" with a staff who could mediate (id.:13). First, Congress placed the mediators in the Commerce Department. Soon after, the President with the consent of Congress chose yet another institutional home—the Department of Justice. The Senate added a key provision—a criminal penalty for Community Relations Service employees who disclosed

confidential information, even to those in other divisions of its federal depart-
mental home (id.:14).

For about a half-century, the Community Relations Service has provided
mediators for hundreds of civil rights disputes each year (p. 160). The mediators' ability to identify with the Justice Department may make people hesitant
to turn them away and the assurance of confidentiality may increase candor as
they shuttle between factions.

That institutional choice allowed the Community Relations Service to take
advantage over the years of the Justice Department's credibility to secure cooperation, and the statute guaranteeing confidentiality overcame the major disad-
vantage of placing it there.

As these stories illustrate, designers' attention to institutionalization can
positively influence success over time and can be among the most creative and
significant parts of design work.

THOUGHTS GOING FORWARD

You can ease successful implementation by planning for it from the beginning.
Who must support the new initiative for it to succeed? Who could block its success? Can these stakeholders be engaged in the planning? Taken into account?
Taught? Led? Given incentives? How will you help create a receptive climate?
Avoid unnecessarily disrupting existing work and values? Find the necessary
resources? How will you try out the new process or system? Assure its success
over time? Remember that much can be achieved informally—through leadership, incentives, communications, teaching, placement within an organizational structure, and even modeling. By maximizing use of these informal
approaches, you may be able to reduce the need for the formal, and often less
flexible, approaches of contract and law discussed in the next two chapters.

QUESTIONS

11.1   "Your emergency is not my problem." One can buy a sign that says this.
More confrontational signs also are in shops: "Poor planning on YOUR part does
not constitute an emergency on MY part," to name one. The signs sell because
of a strong impulse not to feel responsible for something invented elsewhere,
particularly when a person asked to implement believes it will not be beneficial
or when implementation feels burdensome or risky. If a court has hired you to
design and implement a court mediation program, who might block its effectiveness because of this sort of reaction? What would you suggest to avoid this
impediment to successful implementation?

11.2   With an eye to marshaling resources, a designer might invite the
pertinent program officer from a large foundation to participate in the design

process. Suppose the goal of the initiative is to plan a process for creating consensus on how to make the Sanford, Florida community one in which people work across their divisions to solve community problems (pp. 20-22). What are the pros and cons of inviting the foundation's program officer to participate in the deliberations that will define the new process?

11.3 A military high school administrator asks you to design a process and/or system to reduce hazing of new students by older, upper class students. As you begin your assessment, you discover that administrators foster a culture of not complaining. In fact, they belittle students who are "whiners." It's a century-old practice at the school. What should you do?

11.4 Suppose a problem-solving climate will be crucial to implementation of a new dispute management process or system. In such a situation, designers trying to create these qualities of the organizational environment might try to "hard-wire" that process or system for problem-solving even in the absence of effective leadership. Khalil Shariff suggests a few qualities in this chart (the "institution" refers to the planned process or system) (language below taken from Shariff, 2003:156). Do any of these ideas seem promising?

Variable	Principle
Membership	*Principle 1:* Institutions should strive for *inclusiveness* by incorporating into their structure all stakeholders likely to be affected by the institution's work.
Scope	*Principle 2:* Institutions should seek *broad coverage* of many related issues of interest to the institutional membership rather than being limited to a specific narrow issue area. *Principle 3:* Institutions should seek *depth of jurisdiction* on individual issue areas such that they are empowered to take many kinds of action on issues within their mandate.
Centralization	*Principle 4:* Institutions should seek to build *central sources of information gathering and dissemination*. *Principle 5:* Institutions should *decentralize and proliferate discussions and conversations among institutional members* in multiple forums and forms.
Control	*Principle 6:* Institutions should vest control over decisions in those *most interested and affected by them*.
Flexibility	*Principle 7:* Institutions should embed opportunities for regular review of principal design decisions in order to integrate learning from experience.

Exercise 11.1   *Tallahoya University's budget issues:*   If the proposed design to deal with harassment complaints requires no new budget allocation, it can be started in the coming year. Otherwise, the University will implement the design at some uncertain future time. What would you explore to determine whether a new design could be implemented without a new budget allocation? If you will propose charging a user fee, what are the implications of doing so?

Exercise 11.2   *Implementing the intellectual property dispute resolution system at Tallahoya University:*   A voicemail from University counsel: "Hey. Time to celebrate. The Provost has just approved your plan to use a collaborative approach, modeled on regulatory negotiations used by the federal government,[4] as the first step in the effort to resolve disputes that pit the desire to protect intellectual property against the needs of developing nations in such matters as research to improve seeds and drugs. The Provost also liked your backup plan to make the Board of Trustees' Development Committee the final arbitrator of whether the University will allow the research to go forward when an agreed approach is submitted after the 'regulatory negotiations' or when agreement cannot be resolved through the regulatory negotiations approach. And, get this—the Provost has approved an annual operating budget of $250,000! What's next? Please give me a plan to implement, including rough job descriptions for the person we hire to lead the initiative."

Exercise 11.3   *Dealing over time with divisive student issues at Tallahoya University:* As you prepare for your first days of work as one of the University's designers, a thought occurs to you. University administrators seem to deal with issues related to diversity as unique events, but predictably these issues recur. Perhaps University administrators would be open to institutionalizing an approach like that developed in response to Exercise 9.1 (p. 239). Create a chart that lists the pros and cons of two or three possible institutional homes for such a program.

REFERENCES

BORDONE, Robert C. (1998) "Electronic Online Dispute Resolution: Approach, Potential, Problems and a Proposal," 3 *Harv. Negot. L. Rev.* 175.

BRAZIL, Wayne D. (2006) "Should Court-Sponsored ADR Survive?," 21 *Ohio St. J. on Disp. Resol.* 241.

COSTANTINO, Cathy A., and Christina Sickles MERCHANT (1996) *Designing Conflict Management Systems.* San Francisco: Jossey-Bass.

COSTANTINO, Cathy A., and Melinda R. Lewis (2015) "What Dispute Systems Design Can Learn from Project Management," *Negot. J.* (July) 175.

---

4. Congress authorized regulatory negotiation, sometimes called "reg-neg," in 1990. An agency may decide to use the reg-neg process for particular rules, allowing parties with important stakes to engage in facilitated discussions on the language of the rule. The process encourages collaboration in seeking technical assistance, for example. If agreement is reached, the negotiated rule is published for comment in the traditional process.

DRAKE, William R. (1989) "Practice Dispute Systems Design: A Special Section—Statewide Offices of Mediation," 5 *Negot. J.* 359.

FADER, Hallie (2008) "Designing the Forum to Fit the Fuss: Dispute System Design for the State Trial Courts," 13 *Harv. Negot. L. Rev.* 481.

GLADWELL, Malcolm (2000) *The Tipping Point: How Little Things Can Make a Difference.* Boston: Little Brown.

GOLDBERG, Stephen B., Frank E.A. SANDER, Nancy H. ROGERS, and Sarah R. COLE (2012) *Dispute Resolution: Negotiation, Mediation, Arbitration, and Other Processes* (6th ed.). New York: Wolters Kluwer.

INGLIS, Laura, and Kevin MCCABE (2010) "The Effects of Litigation Financing Rules on Settlement Rates," 18 *Sup. Ct. Econ. Rev.* 135.

ISSACHAROFF, Samuel, and D. Theodore RAVE (2014) "The BP Oil Spill Settlement and the Paradox of Public Litigation," 74 *La. L. Rev.* 397.

KUTTNER, Ran (2011) "Conflict Specialists as Leaders: Revisiting the Role of the Conflict Specialist from a Leadership Perspective," 29(2) *Conflict Resol. Q.* 103.

LEVINE, Bertram J. (2005) *Resolving Racial Conflict: The Community Relations Service and Civil Rights, 1964-1989.* Columbia: University of Missouri Press.

LIPSKY, David B., Ronald L. SEEBER, and Richard D. FINCHER (2003) *Emerging Systems for Managing Workplace Conflict: Lessons from American Corporations for Managers and Dispute Resolution Professionals.* San Francisco: Jossey-Bass.

LIU, Leigh Anne, Lin INLOW, and Jing Betty FENG (2015) "Institutionalizing Sustainable Conflict Management in Organizations: Leaders, Networks, and Sensemaking," 32 *Conflict Resol. Q.* 155.

LLEWELLYN, Jennifer (2008) "Bridging the Gap Between Truth and Reconciliation: Restorative Justice and the Indian Residential School Truth and Reconciliation Commission," in M. Brant-Castellano, L. Archibald, and M. DeGagne eds., *From Truth to Reconciliation: Transforming the Legacy of Residential Schools* 183. Ottawa: Aboriginal Healing Foundation.

McHALE, M. Jerry, et al. (2009) "Building a Child Protection Mediation Program in British Columbia," 47 *Fam. Ct. Rev.* 86.

Model Standards of Conduct for Mediators (2005). Washington, DC and New York: American Bar Association, Association for Conflict Resolution, American Arbitration Association.

MOON, Yuseok, and Lisa B. BINGHAM (2007) "Transformative Mediation at Work: Employee and Supervisor Perceptions on USPS REDRESS Program," 11 *Int'l Rev. Pub. Admin.* 43.

MOSTEN, Forrest S., and John LANDE (2009) "The Uniform Collaborative Law Act's Contribution to Informed Client Decision Making in Choosing a Dispute Resolution Process," 38 *Hofstra L. Rev.* 611.

NIELSEN, Marianne O. (1998) "A Comparison of Canadian Native Youth Justice Committees and Navajo Peacemakers: A Summary of Research Results," 14 *J. Contemp. Crim. Just.* 6.

PUTNAM, Robert D. (2000) *Bowling Alone: The Collapse and Revival of American Community.* New York: Simon & Schuster.

RAPHELSON, Samantha (2018) "Trump Budget Would Eliminate Justice Department's Peacemaking Office," NPR, https://www.npr.org/2018/03/27/597304508/trump-budget-would-eliminate-justice-departments-peacemaking-office, March 18, 2018.

ROGERS, Nancy H. (2015) "When Conflicts Polarize Communities: Designing Localized Offices That Intervene Collaboratively," 30 *Ohio St. J. on Disp. Resol.* 173.

SHARIFF, Khalil Z. (2003) "Designing Institutions to Manage Conflict: Principles for the Problem Solving Organization," 8 *Harv. Negot. L. Rev.* 133 (2003).

SMITH, Stephanie, and Janet MARTINEZ (2009) "An Analytical Framework for Dispute Systems Design," 14 *Harv. Negot. L. Rev.* 123.

TESLER, Pauline H. (2007) *Collaborative Law: Achieving Effective Resolution Without Litigation* (2d ed.). Chicago: ABA.

TESLER, Pauline (2008) "Collaborative Family Law, the New Lawyer, and Deep Resolution of Divorce-Related Conflicts," 2008 *J. Disp. Resol.* 83.

WAGNER, Rodd, and James K. HARTER (2006) *12: The Elements of Great Managing.* New York: Gallup Press.

WISSLER, Roselle L. (2004) "The Effectiveness of Court-Connected Dispute Resolution in Civil Cases," 22 *Conflict Resol. Q.* 55.

WISSLER, Roselle L. (2002) "Court-Connected Mediation in General Civil Cases: What We Know from Empirical Research," 17 *Ohio St. J. on Disp. Resol.* 641.

Using Contracts

DESIGNING STEPS

1. Design initiative
2. Basic planning steps
- Assessing stakeholders, their goals and interests, and contexts
- Creating processes and systems
3. Key planning issues (that may arise throughout the planning)
- Planning how to select, engage, and prepare intervenors and parties
- Determining the extent of confidentiality and openness in the process
- Dealing with desires for change, justice, accountability, understanding, safety, reconciliation
- Enhancing relationships
- Incorporating technology
4. Implementing and institutionalizing the system or process
- Implementing
- **Using contracts**
- Using law
- Evaluating, revising

A contractual approach to implementing a dispute management system takes advantage of friendly relations to establish procedures that parties commit to using if they become antagonists. The process you design could arrange for people to contract about a variety of process matters: what processes they will use, the level of confidentiality, what documents they will provide to other participants, when they will give notice of a dispute, and more. If you have not studied arbitration law, you can read Sarah Cole's and Kristen Blankley's overview of arbitration law in Appendix B. When you have read this chapter, you will have ideas about the practical significance, aside from legal enforceability, of eliciting contractual promises for processes other than arbitration. You will also understand the courts' general approach to contract clause enforcement for collaborative processes (though see Appendix B for arbitration clauses) and a few of the numerous drafting issues to consider.

The contract approach may work best in combination with adjustments of organizational practices, such as those discussed in Chapter 11. The sections within this chapter recognize that legal enforcement is but one of the strategic considerations in using contracts:

- the interplay between contract and organizational innovations and practices (Section A);

- court enforcement of dispute resolution clauses (Section B); and
- drafting strategies for a designer (Section C).

A. THE "PEOPLE" PART OF CONTRACTING FOR PROCESS

1. Usefulness aside from enforceability

A contract can be useful even if not legally enforceable. We have already discussed an example of this—the "peace treaties" Cure Violence Chicago elicits among gangs. Gang members who agree to notify Cure Violence at the first sign of trouble seem more often to do so, though courts are unlikely to enforce that agreement. Even when contracts are enforceable, research supports the notion that people who contract for particular actions commonly work things out without reference to court enforcement of their contract in the context of ongoing relationships and informal norms of industries and occupations (Macaulay, 1963:61; Macaulay, 1985:467-468).

Contracts setting out the process for disputes may have informal value beyond the benefit of exchanging promises—in getting the parties to talk about issues they might encounter as they work together and the processes they want to employ post-dispute.

National Institutes of Health—talking out issues in advance: Former ombuds Howard Gadlin's checklist for collaborating scientists included such matters as who would take the media inquiries if the collaboration led to findings of public interest and how disputes about that would be resolved. The goal was to fix those matters likely to result in disruption while the scientists were still getting along well. In addition, the dispute resolution clause reminded them about a situation they would like to and could avoid, by being attentive to positive relations with their colleagues at all points in the process.

In the story below, designers exploited the potential of organizational adaptations, rules, and practices. Designers suggested that the parties agree to jointly employ someone who would work on the preventive and informal side. They supplemented this informal process with a default clause setting forth formal dispute resolution processes.

Thomas Stipanowich on an informal and contract-based approach in a construction setting: "The contract for the renovation of Queen Mary Hospital, a venerable 56-year-old edifice, required intricate demolition and construction services to be performed while keeping the hospital and operating theatres operational—a complex and challenging scheme likely to prove a hotbed of conflict. The project owner, the Hong Kong Government's Architectural Services Department, desirous of strict budget control, required a system which would identify and resolve disputes in the shortest possible time and prior to completion of the project. [That government department] retained the services of an international team of consultants to develop an appropriate dispute resolution system for the project.

"The consultants first spoke confidentially with project participants (including pre-qualified contractors) regarding the nature of the project, their objectives and concerns and potential areas of dispute. The result was a report setting forth specific recommendations for project organization and administration aimed at avoiding or minimizing areas of dispute. These included tight time frames for jobsite decision-making and handling of claims, and the establishment of a flexible, dynamic dispute resolution system centered upon the figure of a Dispute Resolution Adviser (DRA).

"The resulting agreement called for joint appointment of a neutral, a construction expert possessing dispute resolution skills as the DRA at the time the construction contract commenced. A default mechanism was established for independent appointment of a DRA should the parties fail to agree on an appointee. The DRA's fees were to be shared equally between the owner and general contractor.

"The DRA's first function was to meet with job participants to explain and build support for a cooperative approach to problem solving on the project. Among other things, the DRA was to discuss basic rules of communication and attitudinal changes necessary to avoid adversarial positions. Thereafter, the DRA was to make monthly visits to the site for the purpose of consulting with project participants on the status of the job and facilitating discussions respecting any conflicts which arose since the last visit. . . .

"In the event of a formal challenge to a project decision, certificate or evaluation, the parties were given four weeks to negotiate pertinent issues (with or without the assistance of the DRA). In the event the problem remained unresolved, a party's written notice of dispute would trigger a more formal stage of dispute resolution in which the DRA had freedom to employ any of several methods of third-party-assisted dispute resolution including mediation, mini-trial and expert fact-finding. The proceeding would involve site level representatives and would be conducted with the assistance of the DRA or a qualified third party.

"If assisted site level negotiations failed, the DRA was to prepare a report identifying the key issues in dispute, the positions of the parties, and the perceived barriers to settlement and making either a recommendation for settlement or a nonbinding evaluation of the dispute. The report would be used by senior off-site representatives of the parties in further negotiations, perhaps assisted by the DRA.

"Should matters not be resolved within fourteen days of the issuance of the DRA's report, the DRA would set into motion a short-form arbitration procedure or other mutually acceptable means recommended by the DRA. The arbitrator would be appointed by the parties; failing their agreement, the DRA would make the selection.

"The DRA procedure worked well. Despite the usual problems and several hundred owner-ordered changes, no disputes reached the stage of nonbinding evaluation. In other words, the informal process resolved all disputes. The DRA system has since been applied on at least one other hospital project for the same owner" (Stipanowich, 1998:387-389).

While the Dispute Resolution Advisor assisted parties in resolving disputes before invoking the more expensive hearing-based processes, it may also have helped that the parties recognized the enforceability of the tiered dispute resolution clause. That clause constrained their future actions in the event of non-settlement (see Groton et al., 2017).

2. Resentment of pre-dispute clauses?

Will people rail against a process when they participate because they are bound by a contract entered before the dispute arises? The counterintuitive answer for mediation: "probably not." The intuitive answer for arbitration: "probably so," particularly if they could not bargain about inclusion of the clause. Examining the differing reactions to mediation and arbitration may help you anticipate the likely reaction to pre-dispute clauses regarding other processes that you might create.

Mediation: Apparently, people typically do not resent being compelled to talk with each other with an intervenor's help, particularly pursuant to a contract clause. In a study of 449 mediated cases, those persons who participated in mediation pursuant to a pre-dispute mediation clause in a contract were as likely to settle as those who agreed to mediation after the dispute arose (Brett et al., 1996:253).

Arbitration: Unlike the cooperative reaction to mediation clauses, people tend to resent pre-dispute arbitration clauses if they feel that they had no real choice but to accept the arbitration clause. They worry that a contracted-for adjudication designed by the more powerful party will hurt them. For this reason, arbitration clauses in consumer or employment agreements generate controversy. Empirical evidence may not substantiate their fears that they will fare worse in arbitration than litigation (see, e.g., Drahozal and Zyontz, 2011:102-104), but consumers and employees harbor these fears nonetheless.

Because of these differing reactions to pre-dispute clauses for mediation and arbitration, those whose strongest interests lie in the disputing parties' sense of fairness may suggest dispute management designs with clauses for consensual processes but not clauses for adjudication outside the courts.

B. COURT ENFORCEMENT AND CONTRACTUAL PROCESSES

These differing reactions to mediation as compared to arbitration clauses carry over into the amount of litigation generated by them. In contrast to an entire field of jurisprudence that has developed as people resist enforcement of arbitration clauses, relatively few reported court decisions deal with mediation clause enforcement (largely handled through existing contract law doctrines) or other non-binding dispute management clauses (regarding mediation clauses, see Cole et al., 2017-2018:§6.1; regarding arbitration clauses, see Appendix B).

When a dispute resolution clause creates a new process—like the advisory hearing clause in the Hong Kong construction contract—it seems likely that the courts will treat enforcement as a contract law question just as they have largely done for mediation. As with other contracts, courts will recognize contract defenses such as unconscionability. Overall, though, attorneys for the parties are likely to advise them that the courts will enforce these innovative process clauses. The fact that the courts allow, and enforce, a great deal of what Professor Jaime Dodge terms "procedural private ordering," which might work to the detriment of one of the parties, presents dilemmas for designers—do they assist in designing a one-sided process through a contract clause (regarding the dilemmas, see Chapter 4.B; regarding private ordering, see Dodge, 2011:727-278.

C. MORE VERSUS LESS DETAIL ABOUT PROCEDURES

Though arbitration is discussed in Appendix B rather than in this chapter, it offers lessons on the pros and cons of providing contractually for the details of other dispute management processes. In Chapter 5.D, we discussed a counterintuitive lesson—that those contracting for arbitration often provide for a more complex process than they ultimately want to pay for or take the time to participate in (Stipanowich et al., 2010:1). In fact, 70 percent of business attorneys responding to a survey said that arbitration failed to meet expectations concerning "speed, efficiency and economy" more than half of the time (Stipanowich et al., 2010:3). Attorneys afterward resent the cost and time of discovery and motion practice particularly (Stipanowich et al., 2010:6-9).

Why is there not an instant cure to this bias toward complexity—drafting arbitration clauses to reduce the procedures that introduce expense and delay? Thomas Stipanowich points to several possible answers:

- transactional lawyers who insert arbitration clauses may lack expertise in process;
- lawyers may be exhausted at the "eleventh hour" of the talks leading to a deal when clauses are inserted;

- lawyers may not want to "kill the deal" by talking about potential conflict between partners;
- lawyers may be compulsively protective of client's interests; and
- lawyers may not be able to predict what kinds of disputes will arise (Stipanowich, 2009; Stipanowich, 2010).

Having read about the tendency to agree to more complexity than you will later value, a designer like you might improve the form of dispute resolution clauses, even providing stepped processes corresponding to what is at stake in the dispute. Still, Stipanowich's last point—the inability to predict the dynamics of future disputes—remains a challenge for clauses regarding all sorts of dispute resolution processes. That does not mean, however, that designers should not try their best to forecast future issues and provide for their resolution, as the following "cautionary tale" demonstrates:

Truth and
Reconciliation
Commission of Canada

The Truth and Reconciliation Commission of Canada—providing for document exchanges: The government, survivor and Aboriginal representatives, and churches set up the Truth and Reconciliation Commission in the settlement agreement for a class action, leaving the court with continuing supervisory authority. Instead of agreeing that the Commission had subpoena power, the drafters provided that all parties would supply the documents needed by the Commission. As time went on, the churches began refusing to provide documents unless the Commission paid their expenses in doing so, and the Commission could not always afford to do so. By the time this issue arose, the parties' lawyers were unable to agree to modify the settlement agreement to provide explicitly for expenses (see Llewellyn interviews, Appendix F).

In light of the fact that it is rarely possible to predict every single kind of dispute that might arise under a contract, what might you do as a designer? The experiences discussed in this section suggest several possibilities:

- Wait until after the dispute arises and then agree on a process (Delaying the decision would cut down on unwise choices, though the parties might be too angry or distrustful to agree at that point (see Blankley, 2016:757).);
- Agree prior to any disputes only on mediation-like processes or provision for a dispute resolution expert (see Groton and Dettman, 2011:183), commitments that permit considerable flexibility as circumstances dictate;
- Include a dispute resolution contract clause but devote energy to maintaining or building productive interpersonal and inter-organizational relations so that resort to the clause is unlikely (see Macaulay, 1985:467-468); or
- Design into the organization of relationships structures or roles (such as the Dispute Resolution Advisor referenced in the Hong Kong hospital example earlier in this chapter) that will facilitate identification and informal resolution of disputes.

THOUGHTS GOING FORWARD

When you implement a design, you have several tools to use to get key people "on board" with the roles that they will play under the new design—organizational rules and structures, contract, and law. Contracting prior to a dispute can produce substantial acquiescence but also may produce unintended consequences. You will want to gauge before using contract clauses: the likely level of later resentment; the ability to predict what kinds of process will be warranted; the likelihood that the clause will produce litigation about process; and whether the cost and time are worth it on balance. Even informal or unenforceable promises may sometimes help because the mere promise may increase the likelihood of compliance in the heat of a dispute or the press of a busy day. Ultimately, combining formal, informal, and organizational methods may prove the best approach.

QUESTIONS

12.1 After a plane crashed into an urban center, leaving 200 dead and many injured, the likely defendants in any tort actions have asked you to draft an agreement that prospective claimants could sign to use an alternative process rather than suing. What would you suggest be included in the agreement? What concerns would you have about agreeing to such an engagement?

12.2 If you were corporate in-house counsel, what are the pros and cons of drafting the dispute resolution clauses in business contracts yourself rather than leaving that to the outside counsel drafting the overall contracts?

12.3 A bipartisan commission to revise your state's constitution has just begun work. The executive director wants to keep members from criticizing each other in the media, concerned that such actions would polarize the commission (see Chapter 7). The executive director seeks your help. Specifically, she asks you to analyze what would be gained or lost in asking each commission member to promise that, when speaking to the media, the member would endeavor not to characterize the position of another member. The executive director acknowledges that such a promise would probably not be legally enforceable.

12.4 Analyze the pros and cons of the following statute on settlement agreements reached by divorcing parents, as it relates to using contracts to implement a design system:

> (2) . . . The permanent parenting plan shall contain provisions for resolution of future disputes between the parents. . . .
>
> (4) . . . A process for resolving disputes, other than court action, shall be provided. . . . A dispute resolution process may include counseling, mediation, or arbitration by a specified individual or agency, or court action. In the dispute resolution process:
>
> > (a) Preference shall be given to carrying out the parenting plan;

(b) The parents shall use the designated process to resolve disputes relating to implementation of the plan, except those related to financial support, unless an emergency exists;

(c) A written record shall be prepared of any agreement reached in counseling or mediation and of each arbitration award and shall be provided to each party;

(d) If the court finds that a parent has used or frustrated the dispute resolution process without good reason, the court shall award attorneys' fees and financial sanctions to the prevailing parent;

(e) The parties have the right of review from the dispute resolution process to the superior court; and

(f) The provisions of (a) through (e) of this subsection shall be set forth in the decree (Wash. Rev. Code §26.09.184).

Exercise 12.1   *Tallahoya University counsel left you this voicemail:* "I just had an idea. What if we put this clause in the form that students sign when they accept admission to Tallahoya? 'I agree that I will submit any dispute I have with another student, a teacher, or an administrator to the University ombuds for informal dispute resolution before I file a court or administrative complaint.' The only exceptions would be for emergencies or criminal matters. The contract clause I have in mind would acknowledge: 'In exchange for my promise, the University agrees to provide an ombuds services for students without charge.'"

How might you respond to the University counsel's "proposal"?

REFERENCES

AMERICAN ARBITRATION ASSOCIATION (2007) Drafting Dispute Resolution Clauses: A Practical Guide. New York: AAA.

BLANKLEY, Kristen M. (2016) "The Ethics and Practice of Drafting Pre-Dispute Resolution Clauses," 49 Creighton L. Rev. 743.

BRETT, Jeanne, Zoe I. BARSNESS, and Stephen B. GOLDBERG (1996) "The Effectiveness of Mediation: An Independent Analysis of Cases Handled by Four Major Service Providers," 12 Negot. J. 259.

COLE, Sarah R., and Kristen M. BLANKLEY (2005) "Arbitration," in Michael L. Moffitt and Robert C. Bordone eds., The Handbook of Dispute Resolution 52. San Francisco: Jossey-Bass.

COLE, Sarah R., Nancy H. ROGERS, Craig A. McEWEN, James R. COBEN, and Peter N. THOMPSON (2017-2018) Mediation: Law, Policy, and Practice (3rd ed.). Minneapolis: West.

COOPER, Corinne, and Bruce E. MEYERSON eds. (1991) A Drafter's Guide to Alternative Dispute Resolution. Chicago: ABA.

DODGE, Jaime (2011) "The Limits of Procedural Private Ordering," 97 Va. L. Rev. 723.

DOMKE, Martin, Larry EDMONSON, and Gabriel M. WILNER (2017) *Domke on Commercial Arbitration* (3rd ed.) Thomson Reuters/West Group.

DRAHOZAL, Christopher R., and Stephen J. WARE (2010) "Why Do Businesses Use (or Not Use) Arbitration Clauses?," 25 Ohio St. J. on Disp. Resol. 433.

DRAHOZAL, Christopher R., and Samantha ZYONTZ (2011) "Creditor Claims in Arbitration and in Court," 7 Hastings Bus. L.J. 77.

GROTON, James P., and Kurt L. DETTMAN (2011) "How and Why the Standing Neutral Dispute Prevention and Resolution Technique Can Be Applied," 29 Alternatives 177.

GROTON, James P., Chris HONEYMAN, and Andrea Kupfer SCHNEIDER (2017) "Thinking Ahead," in Chris Honeyman and Andrea Kupfer Schneider eds., 1 The Negotiator's Desk Reference 265. St. Paul, MN: Hamline University DRI Press.

MACAULAY, Stewart (1985) "An Empirical View of Contract," 1985 Wis. L. Rev. 465.

MACAULAY, Stewart (1963) "Non-Contractual Relations in Business," 20 Am. Soc. Rev. 85.

MAZADOORIAN, Harry N. (1999) "Building an ADR Program: What Works, What Doesn't," 8 Business Law Today 37.

NIELSEN, Marianne O. (1998) "A Comparison of Canadian Native Youth Justice Committees and Navajo Peacemakers: A Summary of Research Results," 14 J. Contemp. Crim. Just. 6.

NIELSON, Marianne O., and James W. ZION (2005) Navajo Nation Peacemaking: Living Traditional Justice. Tucson: University of Arizona Press.

SCANLON, Kathleen M. (2006) Drafting Dispute Resolution Clauses. New York: CPR (see also 2008 supplement by Helena Tavares Erickson).

STIPANOWICH, Thomas J. (2010) "Arbitration: The 'New Litigation,'" 2010 U. Ill. L. Rev. 1.

STIPANOWICH, Thomas J., Curtis E. VON KANN, and Deborah ROTHMAN eds. (2010) *Protocols for Expeditious, Cost-Effective Commercial Arbitration: Key Action Steps for Business Users, Counsel, Abitrators and Arbitration Provider Institutions*. Austin, TX: The College of Commercial Arbitrators.

STIPANOWICH, Thomas J. (2009) "Arbitration and Choice: Taking Charge of the 'New Litigation,'" 7 DePaul Bus. & Com. L.J. 383.

STIPANOWICH, Thomas J. (1998) "The Multi-Door Contract and Other Possibilities," 13 Ohio St. J. on Disp. Resol. 303.

WESTON, Maureen A., Kristen M. BLANKLEY, Jill I. GROSS, and Stephen HUBER (2018) Arbitration: Law, Policy, and Practice. Durham, NC: Carolina Academic Press.

Using Law

The designers in the seven stories discussed throughout the book implemented their designs largely without a change in law.[1] In fact, research supports the notion that social relationships, practices, and norms exert a powerful influence on behavior, perhaps making changes in law unnecessary for most designs. Law professor Cass Sunstein points out:

> "It has long been understood that people are more likely to engage in healthy behavior if they live or work with others who engage in such behavior. And if people are in a social network with other people who are obese, they are more likely to become obese themselves. The behavior of relevant others can provide valuable information about sensible or appropriate courses of action" (Sunstein, 2011:1408).

Still, occasionally you may want to secure a change in law to implement a design effectively. Because of this opportunity, the chapter focuses on laws that are especially pertinent for the designer (for more comprehensive coverage, *see* Macneil et al., 1994; Cole et al., 2017-2018; on confidentiality, *see* Chapter 7). The chapter samples an extensive literature that examines in more depth the role of law in achieving change. When you have read this chapter, you will identify a few of the most promising opportunities to use law and have in mind warnings that a change in law can do more harm than good.

Those planning government sponsored dispute resolution programs seem to believe that changes in law will help in implementation. Indeed, the breadth of this chapter may seem narrower than that of other chapters because designers

---

1. The exception might arguably be the Canadian tribunals regarding the Indian Residential Schools that were created by the court order approving a class action settlement.

DESIGNING STEPS

1. Design initiative
2. Basic planning steps
- Assessing stakeholders, their goals and interests, and contexts
- Creating processes and systems
3. Key planning issues (that may arise throughout the planning)
- Planning how to select, engage, and prepare intervenors and parties
- Determining the extent of confidentiality and openness in the process
- Dealing with desires for change, justice, accountability, understanding, safety, reconciliation
- Enhancing relationships
- Incorporating technology
4. Implementing and institutionalizing the system or process
- Implementing
- Using contracts
- **Using law**
- Evaluating, revising

use laws more often when the design occurs within a court or administrative agency (*but see* Section B). Laws in the United States related to dispute resolution in courts and administrative agencies have been changed in thousands of ways during the last few decades. For mediation alone, the volume of statutory language increased about fivefold between 1998 and 2016 (Cole, et al., 2017-2018:§16.1). A similar phenomenon occurred elsewhere in the world. The European Union, for example, has issued mediation directives both for online dispute resolution and cases within the courts, and member states have followed with their own detailed laws to implement the directives.[2]

These changes provide grist for discussing key design issues. One can examine existing laws with questions like the following concerning the law's effectiveness:

- Can a change in law alter behavior by changing people's incentives or disincentives (Section A)?
- What are ways to change law in order to encourage the constructive relationships discussed in Chapter 9 (Section B)?
- Does a change in law assist in institutionalizing a new system within the public sector (Section C; on institutionalization, *see* Chapter 11)?
- Can the law make culture or customary practice more receptive to the new system or process (Section D; *see also* discussion of receptive atmospheres in Chapter 11)?
- What negative fallout should a designer anticipate from a change in law (Section E)?

The preceding questions relate to a single design, but laws reach more broadly. These broader implications present yet another dilemma for you as a designer — what is your role if a change in law might assist in achieving success in your design but have negative consequences for others? For example, what if the proposed new law increases the complexity of the law related to dispute resolution? Will people be deterred from taking advantage of more regulated processes? Will variance by jurisdiction interfere with the effectiveness of the laws?

---

2. Directive 2008/52, of the European Parliament and of the Council of 24 May 2008 on certain aspects of mediation in civil and commercial matters, 2008 O.J. (L 136) 003(EC); Directive 2000/31, of the European Parliament and of the Council of 8 June 2000 on certain legal aspects of information society services in particular electronic commerce, 2000 O.J. (L 178)12 (EC); for implementation, *see, e.g.,* Amendment to the Civil Procedure Rules for United Kingdom's Senior Courts, England and Wales and County Courts, England and Wales, 2011 No. 88 (L. 1).

A.   CHANGING LAW TO CHANGE INCENTIVES

Law can be a powerful force in changing human behavior when it creates incentives to act in pertinent ways or removes incentives to do the opposite. People act in particular ways for many reasons, of course — because they think it right, because they want to please others, because of habits, because they promised to do so, and more. The most powerful tools for those implementing a design may be those already discussed in the last two chapters. But, if a designer is seeking a change in law, it may be because none of these approaches has worked and examining incentives may be in order.

Consider a situation in which designers fear that mediators might pressure the parties to settle. They might try a number of law-based options, which vary in terms of whether they create incentives:

1. Mediators shall not pressure parties to settle.[3]
2. Mediators shall not charge a fee "contingent upon the result of the mediation or the amount of the settlement."[4]
3. Mediators shall disclose financial and personal interests and past relationships that a "reasonable person would consider likely to affect the impartiality of the mediator. . . ."[5]

Would Option 1 dissuade mediators from leaning on the weaker party to secure settlement? There is reason to doubt that result. Social scientists note that people comply less frequently with requirements that they do not consider moral imperatives, especially if following the practice favored by the law is not an established custom or professional norm, and they do not fear detection and therefore negative consequences for violating the law (*see* Kagan, 2000:375; Hawkins, 2003:256-265; Black, 1997:28-29). So, an analysis of Option 1 might include the following notes: "Some mediators think it appropriate to pressure settlement and have market-based incentives to do so. The law is new, so professional norms do not support compliance. Mediation communications are typically privileged, so evidence to show noncompliance may not be available to show that a mediator violated the law. On the other hand, the law expresses a public view as to appropriate behavior and that expression may change mediators' perspectives over time, as discussed in Section D. On balance, though, the research would make one pessimistic that Option 1 would result in fewer mediators pressuring the parties to settle, particularly in the short term."

Options 2 and 3 deal directly with mediators' incentives. Option 2 removes a possible powerful economic incentive to pressure settlement. Option 3 might prevent mediators who have an incentive to pressure one of the parties to settle

---

3. *See* Rules of Practice, Civ. Dist. Ct. for the Parish of Orleans (LA), 8(b).

4. Model Standards of Conduct for Mediators, Standard VII.B.1 (2005) (the wording is drawn from the Standards, though the text suggests its use instead in a statute).

5. Uniform Mediation Act, Section 9(a)-(b) (though the Standards use "should" rather than "shall") (Appendix E of this book).

from mediating particular cases (assuming that the conflict disclosures will not be secret). Targeting incentives and disincentives, as Options 2 and 3 do, may offer more promise for achieving results. A key issue regarding the effectiveness of Options 2 and 3 might be whether other more powerful incentives cut in a different direction (*see* Lathan, 1996:410-413). For example, will mediators try to increase settlement rates through pressures to settle in order to enhance their reputations and referral sources in a competitive market (Kolb, 1994:483)?

A federal law, discussed in the next story, illustrates thoughtful use of law to encourage participation and to reduce mediator settlement pressures. The law removes an impediment to participation. It also blocks mediators who might have an incentive to coerce settlement from using their strongest ammunition — a threat to tell their Justice Department colleagues about illegal activities.

The law creating the Justice Department's Community Relations Service: Congress enacted the Civil Rights Act of 1964 to strengthen the nation's civil rights laws. The 1960s were years of heightened unrest and violence over civil rights. To expand civil rights progress while reducing violence, a little noticed section of the Civil Rights Act of 1964 established the Community Relations Service (CRS). From its initial placement in the U.S. Commerce Department, CRS was moved in 1966 to the Justice Department. Congress charged it with assisting in "resolving disputes, disagreements, or difficulties relating to discriminatory practices based on race, color, or national origin...."[6] In essence, the Act created a staff of system designers for these conflicts. Assistant Attorney General Burke Marshall, who had some experience intervening in civil rights cases, reportedly drafted the section (Levine, 2005:8).

President Lyndon Johnson signing the Civil Rights Act of 1965 that created the Community Relations Service. Standing are civil rights and congressional leaders.

---

6. 42 U.S.C. §2000g-1.

In the only substantive provision regarding the CRS, the Act required CRS employees to preserve confidentiality. In other words, mediators had to maintain the expectations of those with whom they worked regarding confidentiality and to avoid allowing the information from mediations to be used in the Justice Department's investigative and prosecuting functions. The Act created criminal penalties for CRS employees who breached confidentiality.[7] As a result, the CRS mediators could not threaten to pass on information that might lead to prosecution and could promote candor by promising confidentiality.

Over the next 40+ years, CRS facilitators designed forums and facilitated peaceful resolutions that included agreements to diversify police department staffing, create community dialogue, arrange security and timing of protest marches to avert arrests and violence, integrate schools, change police practices, and more. Those who worked with the CRS reported that they used a facilitative rather than high-pressure approach when they mediated. Former CRS employee Bertram Levine described a facilitative mediation style, as he noted that they "worked with antagonists to find solutions and to avoid or lessen violence" and that they tried "to find, motivate, assist, and help target the resources of potential allies" (Levine, 2005:xi).

One can easily imagine that using the law to make the process confidential, even with regard to the mediator's Justice Department law enforcement colleagues who might decide to prosecute one of the mediation participants, had a greater effect than would have a statute encouraging participation and prohibiting mediator coercion. The Uniform Mediation Act adopted an analogous approach in a provision designed to keep mediators from pressuring parties to settle in court-connected, prosecutor-connected, or administrative agency–connected mediation. That provision prohibits mediators from telling those who might make rulings on the dispute what was said in mediation.[8] Because telling judges or others who might rule on the case would be illegal, mediators are unlikely to threaten to "tell on" parties who are reluctant to settle or to suggest that non-settlement might result in an influential mediator recommendation to the decision-maker.

B. CHANGING LAW TO ENCOURAGE CONSTRUCTIVE CONTACTS

Can changes in law help to promote constructive contacts that may prevent disputes from arising or escalating? If so, law might be a positive design tool even outside the court and public agency context that is the focus of most of this chapter. As discussed above, some kinds of contacts (working on equal levels,

---

7. 42 U.S.C. §2000g-2(b).
8. Uniform Mediation Act §7, Appendix E of this book.

toward a common goal, relatively pleasant circumstances, with personable individuals, etc.) are constructive of the kinds of relationships that de-escalate conflict (Chapter 9). Especially those designers working in ethnic, racial, religious, and other identity-based conflicts endeavor to build constructive contacts across these groups. Designers can seek a change in law to encourage particular kinds of constructive contact or, at least, to limit "destructive" contact.

Examples of the use of law to structure inter-group contacts so that they will increase understanding come from South Africa. When it transitioned from apartheid, South Africa established landlord-tenant mediation and regular meetings between police and residents. Both were arenas often producing clashes across racial lines.

Laws may also interfere with constructive contacts and changing these laws to remove that interference may help reduce the escalation of conflict and disputing. For example, one party to litigation often succeeds in getting the other party's out-of-court apology admitted into evidence, as a "party admission." So, lawyers and insurance companies discourage apologies. The medical treatment context provides an illustration of the other consequences. If "patients and loosen family members perceive they are being told the whole truth, they are much less likely to initiate litigation" (Geckeler, 2007:192-193) and patient-physician relations might improve, even resulting in prevention of future errors (Alberstein and Davidovitch, 2011:175). Several states recently changed their laws to exclude from evidence a range of statements — from expressions of sympathy to apologies — but usually in one limited context — statements by medical providers in civil actions against them.[9] Such laws thus seek to remove the disincentive to make constructive contacts in this narrow setting.

C. CHANGING LAW TO ESTABLISH NEW PROCESSES

In hundreds of instances over the last several decades, those who design new dispute resolution programs in courts and administrative agencies have secured changes in statutes, rules of procedure, court rules, executive orders, or administrative regulations just to establish the new initiative and determine how the new program interacts with the existing justice system. Often the statutes modify confidentiality, deal with statutes of limitations, set out qualifications for the mediator or judge, provide immunities from liability, and sometimes authorize mandatory participation by the parties. The laws that establish a program may encourage risk-averse public officials to start such programs (*see* Section D, below). Many of these statutes seem unnecessary, however. Similar programs are established in other jurisdictions and flourish without the authorizing authority.

---

9. *See, e.g.,* Cal. Evid. Code §1160 (sympathy expressions); Mont. Code Ann. §26-1-814 (apologies); S.C. Code Ann. §19-1-190 (apologies, beyond medical); Wash. Rev. Code Ann. §5.64.010 (apologies); 12 Vt. Code §1912 (apologies).

For example, the Maryland initiative in courts, schools, and public agencies, discussed above (p. 38), proceeded without statutory authorization, whereas Nebraska enacted a statute establishing its agency (comparable to MACRO in Maryland) as well as mediator qualifications and provisions for confidentiality, mediator immunity, enforcement of agreements, and tolling of statute of limitations (Neb. Rev. Stat. §§25-2901 et seq.).

The program-specific provisions on such matters as confidentiality, enforcement of agreements, and tolling statutes of limitations may also contribute to complexity. New York law illustrates the complexity regarding whether conversations in a particular mediation program will be admissible in evidence. Eight New York statutes govern mediation confidentiality in various contexts (N.Y. Civ. Serv. Law §205(4)(b); N.Y. Educ. Law §§313(5)(c), 4404-a(5); N.Y. Exec. Law §§297(3)(a), 465.7(c); N.Y. Fam. Ct. §915, N.Y. Jud. Law §849-b; N.Y. Lab. Law §804). For a mediation conducted by telephone between New York and North Carolina, the parties would also need to consult 21 North Carolina statutory provisions on mediation confidentiality (N.C. Gen. Stat. §§1-5657.81, 7A-38.1(1), 7A-38.2, 7A-38.3B, 7A-38.3D(i), (j), (k), 7A-38.4A, 7B-202, 8-110, 20-301.1(b)(9), 41A-7(d), (g), 50-13.1(e), (f), 50-77, 58-44-100(h), 95-36, 95-242(d), 115C-109.4, 115C-431, 116-3.3, 143-215.22L(h), 143.318.11, 150B-23.1(j), as listed in Cole et al., 2017-2018:App.A). In addition, the parties may want to research what the pertinent federal courts would do about applying their own or state laws on mediation confidentiality. If a party in France is brought into the conference, that individual probably will want to insist on conducting the mediation under French or other laws, though then all parties will have to research those laws and also whether the pertinent courts would give effect to such a provision.

As discussed below, participants may avoid processes when participation seems complex. Increasingly, uniform laws that apply across programs provide an alternative to program specific laws on such matters as confidentiality, tolling statutes of limitations, and so forth. The Uniform Mediation Act provides an example of such a law (Appendix E), as does the United Nations Commission on International Trade Law model rules for international conciliation of commercial disputes, which some U.S. states have adopted (http://www.uncitral.org/uncitral/en/uncitral_texts/arbitration/2002Model_conciliation.html). The program-specific laws might not contribute unnecessarily to the complexity of the law if the laws incorporate more generic laws regarding how the process will unfold.

D. CHANGING LAW TO CHANGE CULTURE AND CUSTOMARY PRACTICES

The longstanding debate about whether "law ways" can change "folkways"[10] seems to have the answer, "Sometimes." Social scientists note that robust change

---

10. *See, e.g.,* Helle Porsdam, *Folkways and Law Ways: Law in American Studies* (2001).

has at its base a change in culture and organizational structures, not just law, but that such changes can be difficult to achieve and take time. One can sometimes change law and institutions quickly, carefully targeting the laws to modify culture and organizational incentives over time. The change in law may be one of many changes that might be combined, as the late Professor Frank Sander pointed out in his "mediation receptivity index," to reach a point of changing patterns of behavior (Sander, 2007:599).

A common target for designers has been the legal culture. Former judge Wayne Brazil noted that a positive effect of the federal Alternative Dispute Resolution Act of 1998 was that it shifted federal judges' attitudes toward the view that courts ought to serve the needs of parties, not simply adjudicate disputes (Brazil, 2002:112). In the first example below, the designers began with the problem of how to shift lawyers' culture and then analyzed the role that a change in law might play.

A process for assessing how to use law to change the culture among lawyers: In the 1990s, Ohio Chief Justice Thomas Moyer charged that court's advisory group on dispute resolution to determine how to encourage lawyers to advise their clients to mediate before suing. One by one, members of the committee argued that the court could best change the culture of Ohio lawyers regarding earlier referral to mediation if it:

- required lawyers to attend continuing education sessions on mediation;
- offered to train lawyers to mediate, free;
- required bar applicants to have taken a dispute resolution course in law school or before the bar examination and/or include dispute resolution as a bar examination topic;
- initiated a mediation program in every county;
- steered new mandatory mediation programs into that part of the docket in which parties were usually represented by counsel; or
- expanded court mediation programs that used large numbers of volunteer lawyers to serve as mediators.

Recognizing that the court would not be able to implement all six strategies, the committee members began discussing which would have the greatest effect. A social scientist who attended the meeting suggested that they get more information before deciding. Heeding that counsel, the committee asked Chief Justice Moyer to send a survey, designed with the help of the social scientist, to all Ohio attorneys. Half responded and the survey results identified those attorneys who were referring clients to mediation or inserting mediation clauses into contracts. Were these lawyers more likely than non-referring attorneys to have attended a continuing education session on mediation, been trained as a mediator, served as a volunteer mediator, taken a law school dispute resolution course, worked in a county with a mediation program operating, or

---

participated as an attorney in a court mediation? After hearing the analysis of results, the committee decided that the strongest influence on attorney culture and practice was the attorney's attendance at court mediation sessions with clients, though most of the committee's other ideas had some small positive effect (Wissler, 1996). As a result, the committee recommended to Chief Justice Moyer two changes requiring legislative action:

- an amendment to the filing fee statute, making it clear that courts could use the income from a raised filing fee to fund court mediation programs; and
- a budget allocation that would permit two-year grants to courts seeking to establish mediation programs.

The committee also suggested that the court give preference in making grants to those courts that would use mediation in cases typically involving represented parties and to those courts that intended to use the filing fee increase to fund the continuation of the program after the initial grant expired.

The court secured the recommended legislative changes and administered the program over a decade to implement a court mediation program in nearly every county. When possible, the grants were given for mediation initiatives that focused on the cases involving lawyers. During that period more and more private mediators, depending on lawyer referrals, could sustain a mediation practice, one indication of a shift in culture and practice among lawyers.

This example shows how careful study on what could bring about positive cultural change can send the designer in a completely different, and more successful, direction in changing the law. In the next example, the culture change may not have been the goal of the change in law, but it was the effect.

A study of difference in laws, differences in legal culture: In 1992, when researchers studied lawyers' culture in the two states, Maine (by statute) required mediation in all divorce cases with disputed child custody, but New Hampshire did not. In Maine, lawyers typically attended mediation sessions with their clients, and most domestic relations lawyers had attended many such sessions. In New Hampshire, domestic relations lawyers rarely attended a mediation session. When asked what they most sought in representing their domestic relations clients, New Hampshire lawyers were most likely to respond that they would "get as much as possible" for their client while Maine lawyers were most likely to say that they sought to reach "a settlement fair to both parties" (McEwen et al., 1994:178).

Now that research has shown that lawyers involved with mediation may change their ways of practicing, others may decide to adopt mandatory mediation with the explicit goal of changing attorneys' customary practices.

These explicit goals for enacting legislation may also be frustrated by the failure to adopt effective practices for implementation. Sunstein points out, for example, that "smoking and seat belt regulations appear to have worked hand in hand with emerging social norms, helping to reduce deaths and injuries" (Sunstein, 2011:1408). To look at another implementation issue, a study showed that consumers in Vermont were more likely to achieve the remedies listed in the law than were consumers in California though both states enacted similar "Lemon Laws" regarding consumer complaints about defective automobiles. So, too, Russian courts that applied identical mediation laws, adopted in 2010, had higher or lower rates of voluntary mediation usage depending on the judges' support for and explanations of mediation (Hendley, 2013:754). Thus, laws may change conduct, but their success also depends upon work to implement and create a receptive climate.

E. ANTICIPATING THE UNINTENDED CONSEQUENCES OF CHANGING THE LAW

The "law of unintended consequences" is not a law, despite its name. But, the phrase describes a phenomenon particularly pertinent to changes in law. The study of domestic lawyers in Maine and New Hampshire discussed above demonstrates unintended *positive* consequences. In that study, a law aimed at improving results for divorcing parties who participated in mediation may also have affected how their lawyers negotiated outside of mediation.

Often the law has an unintended *negative* effect, however. People may react more formally and rigidly in a heavily regulated context, for example. Or, they may hesitate to use the regulated process if they find it to be complicated to do so (Sunstein, 2011:1411) or if they must exercise extreme care to avoid negative consequences. In an instance of the latter, one might speculate that prospective mediation parties might react hesitantly if the law imposed criminal penalties on *parties* (as opposed to on *mediators* in the Community Relations Service example above) for disclosing mediation communications. In another context that does not involve law but an analogous situation, a complex regulatory regime created following a string of hazing incidents at a university was so complicated and out of keeping with the institutional structure that students and administrators regularly ignored the newly instituted processes and simply moved the prevailing approaches to conflict management underground and out of view of senior administrators, creating an even more problematic situation for all.

For designers who work across national borders, yet other unintended consequences follow the regulation of various dispute management processes — these designers may have to hire local attorneys to find out what laws apply. One can imagine that such a requirement would pose an insurmountable financial barrier for some and would cause others to make a business decision not to use a process like mediation that will likely be governed by local laws.

Illustrating other new problems presented by law, a senior federal district judge noted the unanticipated consequences of laws permitting mandatory mediation. The problems occurred when courts began ordering parties both to mediate and to pay for the mediation. Notice that the judge suggests the problem could be ameliorated in the same way that it was for appointed counsel, through rules requiring the court to jointly vet attorneys and clear them for possible appointments. But she also suggests a more practical solution — staff mediators.

Judge Sandra Beckwith's comments on a proposed federal court guide: "The topic I wish to address is the practice, which I understand may be growing, of sending litigants out to private mediators for pay before allowing them to proceed to disposition by the court.

"I see no major objections in principle to so called mandatory mediation when the courts provide it at no cost to litigants, either by a magistrate judge, a staff mediator, or volunteers. . . . What concerns me is:

"1. Adding litigation costs in the form of mediation fees to litigants who come to us seeking judicial resolutions. After all, they already pay for our services as taxpayers.

"2. Creating business relationships between courts/judges and a growing private mediation sector. . . .

"I suggest that the responsibility should lie with the court to determine if the circumstances of a specific case or situation justify forcing litigants to hire and pay outside mediators. Further, I suggest that the criteria for making that determination be similar to those for appointing special masters. Judges should determine that the stakes in a particular case are high enough, and the parties have sufficient means, that requiring parties to pay for private mediation is both warranted and not unduly burdensome.

"My second concern, about creating business relationships with private mediators, is based principally on the need for judicial independence and public perceptions of independence. When courts provide lists of available mediators, even if they are not paid, we enhance their business stature in at least two ways: We imply or actually represent to the public that those on the list have skills and professional standing that warrant a court's imprimatur; and we provide them with the opportunity to gain mediation experience that helps them build their private practices. . . .

"Obviously, in programs that provide for payment of the mediators, the value of referrals is much greater and can create an economic sector heavily and directly dependent on judges and program administrators for its livelihood. I realize the risks posed by this situation are greater in state courts where judges run for election and depend on campaign contributions, but the perceptions that can be created by these circumstances could undermine the public's confidence in our independence and neutrality. I see little difference between

---

referring litigants to mediators for hire and referring criminal defendants to private [appointed] attorneys, a practice [recently addressed by appointing a court committee charged with establishing the panel of private attorneys, limiting judges to appointment of panel members except in unusual circumstances, and other best practices.][11] ...

[After proposing a transparent selection process, Judge Beckwith notes that it is also difficult to remove mediators from the list.] "[T]he issues raised here can be largely solved by employing an in-house court mediator who can provide high quality mediation at no cost to litigants. This model is not without its challenges, but it avoids entirely the problems addressed here" (letter, later modified into an article, Beckwith, 2011:357-361).

Because of possible unintended consequences like those noted by Judge Beckwith, you may want to exploit informal practices or contract-based approaches to implementation issues before seeking a change in law. In the mediation area, for example, commentators suggest asking a series of questions before deciding that new law is the best approach:

- "Will the law achieve its goals if mediation is confidential?" Duties for mediators and mediation parties may run afoul of this problem, for example, because the mediation privilege may prevent those who might enforce the legal duties from learning whether the participants violated the law.
- "Will mediation participants know about the law?" If not, behavior is unlikely to change.
- "Does the law conflict with deeply engrained practices?" If so, does it provide sufficient incentives for changing those practices, as discussed in Section A?
- "Are the lines between adjudication and mediation [or other types of processes] clear?
- "What are other 'unintended consequences' of the law?
- "Can the goals be achieved without changing the law?" (Cole et al., 2017-2018:§§16:1-16:8).

THOUGHTS GOING FORWARD

Changing the law can sometimes help you implement a design. A law stating that people should do something does not make it necessarily so, but a thoughtful approach can sometimes achieve real change, particularly if accompanied by changes in practices. Even if the law is likely to change behavior in a way that assists successful implementation, you will want to ask about the unintended consequences, not only for your program but also for others affected by the law's reach.

---

11. 18 U.S.C. §3006A. The Guide to Judiciary Policy, Vol. 7A, Appx. 2B sets for the best practices (*available at* http://www.uscourts.gov/rules-policies/judiciary-policies/cja-guidelines/chapter-2-ss-210-representation-under-cja (last visited August 20, 2018)).

These unintended consequences may render the change in law not worth it on balance.

QUESTIONS

13.1 Lawyers sometimes offer clients a "collaborative law" option, especially in the area of marital law (pp. 114-115). If both parties and their lawyers agree to negotiate with a collaborative law approach, the lawyers will help their clients resolve all issues through candid, interest-based negotiations. Some jurisdictions have court rules or statutes setting forth the parameters of collaborative law. The National Conference of Commissioners on Uniform State Laws approved a draft law, though the American Bar Association House of Delegates declined in 2011 to endorse the proposed uniform law. A hotly disputed drafting issue was whether the laws should require clients and lawyers to agree that the clients engage new counsel if they do not settle with the assistance of a collaborative lawyer (also called a disqualification provision) (*see generally* Peppet, 2008; Lande, 2009; Lande, 2011). Switching lawyers in the event of impasse, of course, may be expensive for the clients and possibly diminish income for the collaborative lawyers. But proponents for requiring the change in lawyers argue that collaborative lawyers will not be candid about interests, despite the provisions requiring that approach, unless they have no incentives to use the negotiations for trial preparation — in other words, no reason to conduct informal discovery and to avoid disclosures that could be damaging in litigation. Based on what social scientists say (pp. 150-151) and your own views of attorney conduct, will the collaborative negotiations be achieved without requiring a change in lawyers if there is impasse? Would it be sufficient to require those who agree to the collaborative approach to negotiate candidly and use an interest-based approach? Is there any reason to place the provisions requiring disqualification of counsel in the rules of professional conduct rather than in a statute?

13.2 Courts and clients generally gain when they reach the same settlement earlier. More than a century ago, Abraham Lincoln noted this effect when he wrote, "Point out to [your neighbors] how the nominal winner is often a real loser — in fees, expenses, and waste of time." Citing this quote, the Pennsylvania Supreme Court noted that legal malpractice case law provided a disincentive for lawyers to recommend early settlement, even when early settlement would serve the client's interests, because a lawyer risked malpractice liability for recommending settlement before engaging in a thorough investigation of the law and facts. The court in 1991 created almost the equivalent of a safe harbor that removed this disincentive, ruling that lawyers should be liable only for malpractice when they recommended settlement before completing a thorough investigation of law and fact.[12] But the ruling attracted no followers.

---

12. *Muhammad v. Strassburger, McKenna, Messer, Shilobod and Gutnick*, 526 Pa. 541, 587 A.2d 1346, 1351, cert. denied, 112 S. Ct. 196 (1991).

Other state supreme courts acknowledged that malpractice liability does provide a disincentive to recommending early settlement, but declined to create a safe harbor out of concern that the change in law could have a negative consequence — that lawyers who were engaged in negligent conduct might recommend settlement to absolve themselves of responsibility for their errors.[13] Ultimately, noting this unanticipated possible consequence, the Pennsylvania Supreme Court backed off its safe harbor approach in 1996, limiting its 1991 ruling to its facts.[14] How might you tailor the malpractice law so as to remove the disincentive to recommending early settlement without excusing lawyers who had already engaged in negligent practice at the time they recommended settlement? (*See McKay v. Owens*, 130 Idaho 148, 937 P.2d 1222 (1997); Cole et al., 2017-2018:§12:3.)

13.3   Law professors Leonard Riskin and Nancy Welsh advocate court rules that require mediators to ask mediation parties some specific questions. Their goal is to broaden the problems addressed in mediation, to overcome a narrow legalistic approach becoming more prevalent in court-connected mediation (*see* Relis, 2009:9-17). To achieve this, they suggest questions such as "If the mediation focuses on the legal strengths and weaknesses of your case and the likely cost of continuing in litigation, will this be sufficient to help you reach a complete resolution of your dispute with the other party? If not, what other non-litigation issues need to be addressed? . . ." (Riskin and Welsh, 2009:20). What is the likelihood that such a rule would succeed in achieving Riskin's and Welsh's goal? What, if any, are the possible unintended consequences, both positive and negative?

13.4   What are the advantages and disadvantages of extending the evidentiary exclusion for medical professional apologies to apologies by all people?

13.5   Law professor Maria Volpe observes that town meetings help develop "a mindset regarding dialogues among members of the community." She notes that the town meetings "can play a role in helping to set the tone for culturally diverse parties to communicate with greater ease, a key ingredient for constructive ethnic coexistence" (Volpe, 1998:386, 396). Would you recommend a legal requirement for town hall meetings in small communities? How would you analyze the advantages and disadvantages? If you had full authority to change the law to require some kind of forum within a small community (town hall meeting, small group dialogues, etc.), would you? What features would it have? Is there a version of this idea that would be constructive in urban areas?

13.6   In a number of jurisdictions, court rules or statutes require lawyers to confer with opposing counsel and sometimes with clients about dispute resolution practices or settlement possibilities. The goal of these laws is to encourage

---

13 *Grayson v. Wofsey, Rosen, Kweskin*, 231 Conn. 168, 174-175, 646 A.2d 195, 199-200 (1994); *Ziegelheim v. Apollo*, 128 N.J. 250, 267, 607 A.2d 1298, 1306 (1992); *McMahon v. Shea*, 547 Pa. 124, 132, 688 A.2d 1179, 1183 (1996).

14 *McMahon v. Sheu*, 688 A.2d 1179, 1182 (Pa. 1996).

early settlement. But, studies in Arizona and Minnesota showed no increases in early settlement, in early negotiations, or in lawyer referrals to dispute resolution processes after the "confer and report" requirements were put in place (Wissler and Dauber, 2005:266; McAdoo, 2002:425). Of course, like the Ohio advisory committee example above, these are not definitive results. What might explain this outcome? How might you re-design the regulatory regime to increase the likelihood of a better result? Explain why the increased mediation participation by lawyers might have a more profound effect on lawyer's culture than the "confer and report" requirements.

13.7   The United States is party to a number of transnational trade agreements that require use of arbitration. Argue why the United States should urge inclusion of a mediation clause, as a prerequisite to arbitration, in future trade agreement negotiations in order to change the culture of lawyers representing the trade entities (*see* Peters, 2008:1304).

13.8   How does Judge Beckwith's proposal deal with the possibility of private mediators' pressuring the parties to settle so as to achieve a settlement rate that will lead the courts to select them again?

13.9   Divorce cases with contested custody issues may be sent to mediation in both Ohio and Maine. A study in both states concluded that there were similar settlement rates in Maine and Ohio, though in Maine more issues were resolved through settlement. Parties were highly satisfied with mediation and similarly so in both states.

At the time of the study, the pertinent laws differed as follows: Maine had no mediator qualifications. In Ohio, mediators had to have a bachelor's degree or equivalent and to have completed court-approved mediation training. Ohio mediators could address only parenting issues, not money matters, whereas Maine mediators addressed all contested issues. Probably as a result, lawyers almost always accompanied clients to mediation in Maine and rarely did so in Ohio.

Predict the unintended as well as the intended consequences of these laws. Which legal regime is best and why?

13.10   Some European and Asian nations adopted laws that apply nationwide regarding mediation and arbitration (*see* Alexander, 2009:103-03). By contrast, in the United States, the key laws (judging by court rulings) regarding arbitration are federal while state law provides the most important legal provisions for mediation affecting state courts (which handle the bulk of U.S. litigation). What are the pros and cons of the U.S. federal-state approach?

Exercise 13.1   *Using law to incentivize participation:* Tallahoya University's counsel sent you the following email: "Do you remember the problem about the university-area landlords and student tenants — the problem that we think contributes to lower four-year graduation rates (p. 43)? I have just had an idea on how to overcome the problem we had of getting landlords — and sometimes student tenants — to participate in mediation before they sue. Suppose you draft a statute that makes some of the benefits in state landlord-tenant law dependent on willingness to participate in mediation if the rental property at issue lies within a specified number of feet of a university campus. I could ask our government affairs department to look for a sponsor in the legislature.

Here's how I see the new statute: Landlords will not get interest on money owed or court costs if they sue tenants before mediating (unless the tenants decline to participate in mediation). Tenants will not be entitled to the statutory penalty of double their security deposits if they prevail in the event that they sue for a return of the security deposits before mediating (unless the landlord declines to participate in mediation).

What are the pros and cons of my idea? If we go this direction, what else would you put into the statute?"

REFERENCES

ALBERSTEIN, Michal, and Nadav DAVIDOVITCH (2011) "Apologies in the Healthcare System: From Clinical Medicine to Public Health," 74 *Law & Contemp. Probs.* 151.

ALEXANDER, Nadia (2009) *International and Comparative Mediation: Legal Perspectives.* The Netherlands: Wolters Kluwer Law and Business.

BARRETT, Jerome T., and Joseph P. BARRETT (2004) *A History of Alternative Dispute Resolution.* San Francisco: Jossey-Bass.

BARTELS, William K. (2000-2001) "The Stormy Seas of Apologies: California Evidence Code Section 1160 Provides a Safe Harbor for Apologies Made After Accidents," 28 *W. St. U. L. Rev.* 141.

BECKWITH, Sandra (2011) "District Court Mediation Programs: A View from the Bench," 26 *Ohio St. J. on Disp. Resol.* 357.

BLACK, Julia (1997) *Rules and Regulators.* Oxford, UK: Oxford University Press.

BORN, Gary (2010) *International Arbitration: Cases and Materials.* New York: Wolters Kluwer.

BRAZIL, Wayne D. (2002) "Court ADR 25 Years After *Pound*: Have We Found a Better Way?," 18 *Ohio St. J. on Disp. Resol.* 93.

COBEN, James, and Peter THOMPSON, The Mediation Case Law Project, a website at https://digitalcommons.hamline.edu/dri_mclsummaries/

COLE, Sarah R., Nancy H. ROGERS, Craig A. McEWEN, James R. COBEN, and Peter N. THOMPSON (2017-2018) *Mediation: Law, Policy, and Practice* (3rd ed.). Minneapolis: West.

COLE, Sarah R., Craig A. McEWEN, Nancy H. ROGERS, James COBEN, and Peter THOMPSON (2014) "Where Mediation Is Concerned, Sometimes 'There Ought Not to Be a Law!,'" 20 *Disp. Resol. Mag.* 34 (Winter).

FOLBERG, Jay, Dwight GOLANN, Thomas J. STIPANOWICH, and Lisa A. KLOPPENBERG (2016) *Resolving Disputes: Theory, Practice, and Law* (3rd ed.). New York: Wolters Kluwer.

GECKELER, Grant Wood (2007) "The Clinton-Obama Approach to Medical Malpractice Reform: Reviving the Most Meaningful Features of Alternative Dispute Resolution," 8 *Pepp. Disp. Resol. L.J.* 171.

HAMILTON, Michael, and Dominic BRYAN (2006-2007) "Deepening Democracy? Dispute System Design and the Mediation of Contested Parades in Northern Ireland," 22 *Ohio St. J. on Disp. Resol.* 133.

HAWKINS, Keith (2003) *Law as Last Resort: Prosecution Decision-Making in a Regulatory Agency.* Oxford, UK: Oxford Socio-Legal Studies.

HENDLEY, Kathryn (2013) "What If You Build It and No One Comes? The Introduction of Mediation to Russia," 14 *Cardozo J. Conflict Resol.* 727.

KAGAN, Robert A. (2000) "The Consequences of Adversarial Legalism," in Robert A. Kagan and Lee Axelrad eds., *Regulatory Encounters: Multinational Corporations and American Adversarial Legalism* 372.

KOLB, Deborah, and Associates (1994) *When Talk Works: Profiles of Mediators*. San Francisco: Jossey-Bass.

KRIESBERG, Louis (1998) "Coexistence and the Reconciliation of Communal Conflicts," in Eugene Weiner ed., *The Handbook of Interethnic Coexistence* 182. NY: Continuum.

LANDE, John (2011) "An Empirical Analysis of Collaborative Practice," 49 *Fam. Ct. Rev.* 257.

LANDE, John (2009) "'Cooperative' Negotiators in Wisconsin," 15 (2) *Disp. Resol. Mag.* 20.

LATHAM, Stephen R. (1996) "Regulation of Managed Care Incentive Payments to Physicians," 22 *Am. J.L. & Med.* 399.

LEVINE, Bertram J. (2005) *Resolving Racial Conflict: The Community Relations Service and Civil Rights, 1964-1989*. Columbia: University of Missouri Press.

MacNEIL, Ian R., Richard E. SPEIDEL, and Thomas J. STIPANOWICH (1994) *Federal Arbitration Law: Agreements, Awards, and Remedies Under the Federal Arbitration Act*. Boston: Little Brown.

McADOO, Bobbi (2002) "A Report to the Minnesota Supreme Court: The Impact of Rule 114 on Civil Litigation Practice in Minnesota," 25 *Hamline L. Rev.* 401.

McEWEN, Craig A. (2007) "Note on Mediation Research," in Stephen Goldberg et al., *Dispute Resolution: Negotiation, Mediation and Other Processes* (5th ed.) 156. New York: Aspen.

McEWEN, Craig A., Richard MAIMAN, and Lynn MATHER (1994) "Lawyers, Mediation, and the Management of Divorce Practice," 28 *Law & Soc'y Rev.* 149.

MENKEL-MEADOW, Carrie J. (1991) "Pursuing Settlement in an Adversary Culture: A Tale of Innovation Co-Opted or 'The Law of ADR,'" 19 *Fla. St. U. L. Rev.* 1.

MENKEL-MEADOW, Carrie J., Lela Porter LOVE, Andrea Kupfer SCHNEIDER, and Jean R. STERNLIGHT (2010) *Dispute Resolution: Beyond the Adversarial Model* (2d ed.). New York: Aspen.

PEPPET, Scott (2008) "The Ethics of Collaborative Law," 2008 *J. Disp. Resol.* 131.

PETERS, Don (2008) "Can We Talk? Overcoming Barriers to Mediating Private Transborder Commercial Disputes in the Americas," 41 *Vand. J. Transnat'l L.* 1251.

RELIS, Tamara (2009) *Perceptions in Litigation and Mediation: Lawyers, Defendants, Plaintiffs, and Gendered Parties*. Cambridge, UK: Cambridge Univ. Press.

RISKIN, Leonard L., and Nancy A. WELSH (2009) "What's It All About? Finding the Appropriate Problem Definition in Mediation," 15 *Disp. Resol. Mag.* 19 (Summer).

SANDER, Frank E.A. (2007) "Developing the MRI (Mediation Receptivity Index)," 22 *Ohio St. J. on Disp. Resol.* 599.

SANDER, Frank E.A. (2002) "Some Concluding Thoughts," 17 *Ohio St. J. on Disp. Resol.* 705.

SUNSTEIN, Cass R. (2011) "Empirically Informed Regulation," 78 *U. Chi. L. Rev.* 1349.

TALESH, Shauhin A. (2012) "How Dispute Resolution System Design Matters: An Organizational Analysis of Dispute Resolution Structures and Consumer Lemon Laws," 46 *Law & Soc'y Rev.* 463.

VOLPE, Maria R. (1998) "Using Town Meetings to Foster Peaceful Coexistence," in Eugene Weinger ed., *The Handbook of Interethnic Coexistence* 382. New York: Continuum.

WARFIELD, Wallace (1996) "Building Consensus for Racial Harmony in American Cities: Case Model Approach," 1996 *J. Disp. Resol.* 151.

WISSLER, Roselle L. (1996) *Ohio Attorneys' Experience with and Views of Alternative Dispute Resolution Procedures*. Columbus: Supreme Court of Ohio Committee on Dispute Resolution.

WISSLER, Roselle (2002) "Court-Connected Mediation in General Civil Cases: What We Know from Empirical Research," 17 *Ohio St. J. on Disp. Resol.* 641.

WISSLER, Roselle L., and Bob DAUBER (2005) "Leading Horses to Water: The Impact of an ADR 'Confer and Report' Rule," 26 *Just. Sys. J.* 253.

WISSLER, Roselle L., and Art HINSHAW (2005) "How Do We Know That Mediation Training Works?," 12 *Disp. Resol. Mag.* 21 (Fall).

CHAPTER 14

Evaluating and Revising

This chapter provides an overview of evaluation for designers and suggests how a designer might use the resulting information. We employ the term "evaluation" to mean the use of systematic data collection techniques to help understand the operation and effects of a dispute system design (Rossi et al., 1999:4), whether the data are gathered by independent professionals or program designers and managers. After reading this chapter, you should understand how and when to use outside professional evaluators, how to undertake systematic data collection on your own if hiring a professional evaluator is not feasible, and some of the challenges in and techniques for interpreting the data gathered. You should also have been challenged to broaden your thinking about the kinds of intended and unintended impacts that dispute processing systems might have.

DESIGNING STEPS

1. Design initiative
2. Basic planning steps
- Assessing stakeholders, their goals and interests, and contexts
- Creating processes and systems
3. Key planning issues (that may arise throughout the planning)
- Planning how to select, engage, and prepare intervenors and parties
- Determining the extent of confidentiality and openness in the process
- Dealing with desires for change, justice, accountability, understanding, safety, reconciliation
- Enhancing relationships
- Incorporating technology
4. Implementing and institutionalizing the system or process
- Implementing
- Using contracts
- Using law
- **Evaluating, revising**

Evaluation moves the design beyond translating an interesting idea into practice and toward a commitment to examining evidence to determine whether the design achieves the stakeholders' aims. In some rare instances, the proof is arguably in the result—the peace process in South Africa was one of a kind, and its outcome provided the test of the effectiveness of the process that generated it. The nature of such outcomes and how they are read varies significantly, however—the fall of apartheid generally won acclaim but many other peace accords have been widely criticized. In most other instances, the proof is not in the perceived quality of a single "pudding." Designers develop dispute *systems* to deal with recurring instances of conflict—for example, between managers and those managed or among scientists at the National Institutes of Health (NIH), among customers of eBay, between residents of Chicago neighborhoods, or between litigants who have filed cases in court. In these circumstances, there are many outcomes for varied people, groups, or communities in conflict. This chapter covers designs that deal with repeated instances of conflict and focuses on the challenges of gathering information and making sense of it in ways that can assist designers and decision-makers.

This chapter is not written for professional researchers but rather is primarily aimed at the many program designers who are unlikely to have outside evaluators working for them and who can and should undertake some systematic data collection on their own. This is not a text on formal evaluation such as the professionals might use (*see, e.g.,* Fitzpatrick et al., 2010; Rossi et al., 2003; Weiss, 1999; or Wholey et al., 2010) or on social research (*see, e.g.,* Babbie, 2010), although it is informed by these works. Nor is it a guide to critical reading of formal evaluation research about dispute systems. Rather, it is meant to be an accessible overview of approaches to systematic and disciplined data (information) collection in order to encourage you as a designer to build data collection into your designs from the start and to make use of that information in the implementation process and beyond. We hope this proves especially useful to law students whose clinical project involves evaluating a dispute management system.

We view evaluation here essentially as an approach to collecting data that will inform decision-making about a program. Most of these judgments will be based on much more than narrowly defined and empirically examined criteria of success. Evaluation—judgments about what works or what needs changing, the extent to which a program has achieved its varied goals, how it achieves its objectives and can be replicated elsewhere, whether it is worth the cost and bother—is really a management (and sometimes political) process that uses the information coming from evaluation along with other evidence and perspectives reflecting values and interests. If you are the designer, you will need to make those judgments based on the best evidence available.

Program evaluation should always be undertaken with a commitment to the principles of "scientific rigor" (*see, e.g.,* Hoover, 1984:3-15). That means, in essence, being systematic in gathering data; careful in creating measures (for example, survey questions); disciplined and critical in evaluating alternative explanations for results; and resistant to the tendency to see only what you may want to see. Committing to rigor thus means that you adopt a disciplined and critical approach to gathering and evaluating information. It does not dictate particular techniques or research design, which you will always select in the context of your goals, time frame, and resources.

A quest for the best should not get in the way of collecting useful information with the limited resources available, even though some techniques of data collection and analysis are more systematic than others (Kaplan, 1964:28-29). Of course, the less systematic and planned your evidence collecting (e.g., informal conversations with several available disputants served by the dispute processing system versus formal interviews with a random sample), the more careful and critical you should be in interpreting and employing the results. But in the absence of other information (or along with it), those informal conversations may provide you with insights and ideas that improve system design and implementation. Thus, limited resources may constrain the kinds, extent, and quality of information you collect but should not prevent you from gathering evidence that can inform decision-making. As physicist Percy Bridgman observed, the scientific method is nothing more than "doing your damnedest" to answer particular questions (Kaplan, 1964:27).

A. WHY DO EVALUATION AND FOR WHOM?

Designers need to gather evidence thoughtfully and systematically about their work during the diagnosis and early implementation stages and again after the system appears to be complete and operational. Two general sorts of questions will help you as a designer to understand how well the design has been implemented and what its impact has been: (1) what are you actually doing "on the ground" compared to what you hoped to be doing in "theory," and (2) how are you doing at managing the problems or disputes the system was designed to address? If system change plays a part in your design, you will also want to ask a third question: what evidence is there that fewer problems or disputes are emerging after systemic changes?

The first of these questions rests on the well-supported assumption that practice is much messier than theory; recruiting or training personnel falls short of goals; unanticipated resistance to aspects of the implementation crop up; and changes in a community or organization affect the way a system operates. A primary goal of evaluation work is to monitor program implementation and to provide guidance in adjusting it to meet changed, unanticipated, or problematic circumstances.

The second question asks not only whether the design appears to be accomplishing some or all of the goals set for it but inquires as well about the unanticipated effects of the design (for example, on the organization, on resources). Answering these "outcome" questions typically requires designers to respond to the question: "compared to what?" That is, if 60 percent of workplace conflicts are now resolved within 40 days and 55 percent of employees feel good about their workplace, is that better, the same, or worse than it was before? Assessing impact usually requires that we know something about a baseline—what sorts of disputes take place, how they are handled, what their consequences are—at the start of the design process when designers are assessing the problem. As Carol Weiss notes, the key outcomes are "net outcomes"—ones that can be attributed to the dispute system (1999:9). Indeed, the assessment stage of system design (*see* Chapter 4) is a good time to build in data gathering components that lay the groundwork for later evaluation by describing the sets of issues and problems that a design must address.

Answering the third question requires attention to the same issues highlighted for the second question. What are current rates of problems now—compared to the rates before implementing the new system? But it also reminds you to examine whether the organization or community has changed systemically—for example, as in NIH, instituting new procedures that anticipate possible conflicts and prevent them. What else is going on—for example, are people now simply more reluctant to complain (a problematic side effect) or is there evidence of apparent increase in disputes—perhaps because the new system has opened up access to their hearing and resolution?

If you are working in an organizational setting, you will also want to know how the dispute management system affects the organization overall, and how it is perceived and utilized. And, to what degree is the design achieving client goals such as maintaining customers, improving work morale, reducing violence, and saving money? Here too, having baseline data about what work morale was like before the design as well as pre-design organizational perceptions of disputing and other matters will provide a crucial reference point for subsequent evaluation. All of this underscores just how important the assessment phase of any design process is for evaluation: even from the start of a design initiative, you will be gathering data that will assist in later evaluation. Remember that many organizations already gather information—often using technology to do so—that could be of use both in assessment and in later evaluation (Rabinovich-Einy and Katsh, 2012:176-177).

Along the way in the process/system creation and implementation stages, you might want to test alternative models for intervention to decide which works better along a variety of dimensions. This approach will require comparative evidence on such issues as how disputes are handled, organizational costs, and effects. As we will see later, such tests open up possibilities for *field experiments* using random assignment to different mechanisms for intervention. Such a design for implementation and evaluation would provide the greatest confidence in drawing conclusions about which model works best.

Designers and their clients are major consumers of evaluative data, which enable them to discover problems with their system design and correct them as well as to develop confidence that the system design accomplishes much of what was hoped for it. However, others too often have an interest in evaluative information. Grant funders typically require reports based on an evaluation plan. State legislatures may mandate such reports too. For example, the Joint Chairmen of Maryland's Senate Budget and Taxation Committee and House Committee on Appropriations requested a report on "the impact of the Mediation and Conflict Resolution Office's Alternative Dispute Resolution Program [MACRO] on the courts' overall caseload" (MACRO, 2009:1). Clearly, for Chief Judge Robert M. Bell and Rachel Wohl this report provided an opportunity to explain and justify their program more broadly.

At times, dispute system designers report evaluations that they do themselves for purposes of documenting—and promoting—their work. To make such reports effective requires gathering credible data thoughtfully, both quantitative evidence and qualitative evidence; indeed, success stories are often particularly effective tools for communicating about the work of a program (Krueger, 2010). MACRO made use of these approaches in its report to the Maryland General Assembly and took a much broader approach than the one the legislature requested—a report on impact on court caseload.

MACRO: Rachel Wohl and Chief Judge Robert Bell were fully aware of the danger of permitting program evaluations to be narrowly focused on a single outcome indicator such as court caseload. The MACRO report to the General Assembly might be used to determine MACRO's future funding. As a result, MACRO's report included evidence of process—of program implementation and growth. Their document does the following:

- describes how MACRO has assisted courts in improving the quality of mediators on their rosters and strengthened mediator training;
- summarizes evidence from university research about earlier and more frequent settlement and fewer discovery motions in workers' compensation cases randomly assigned to mediation as compared to those on the regular track;
- reports results of district court ADR users' surveys indicating 90 percent would recommend using ADR to others (this measure parallels the Net

> Promoter Score used as a crucial indicator of client loyalty by PayPal, as we will see later in this chapter) and 86 percent were satisfied with the overall experience;
>
> - reports 35,000 hours of time donated by community mediators to conduct mediations and nearly 28,000 hours donated for community education and training;
> - and finally, in direct response to the request of the legislative committees, reports over 16,000 cases were referred to mediation in circuit and district courts and community mediation centers and over 8,000 cases were actually mediated, with more than 5,000 settling and 4,700 cases "removed from the Courts' dockets."
>
> Throughout the report to the legislative committees, MACRO uses testimonials from judges, prosecutors, police officers, and mediation participants that give voice to those affected by dispute resolution in an effort to tell a complex story about program implementation and impact to the legislative committees that provide their funding.
>
> For a broader audience, MACRO's tenth anniversary report recounts the progress of the Maryland Mediation and Conflict Resolution Office. Many of the Maryland ADR Commission's goals for MACRO focus on implementation and program delivery—for example, "advancing the appropriate use of ADR statewide" and "launching a comprehensive, web-based court ADR program assessment, improvement, and evaluation system." The report thus presents evidence of implementation efforts and successes. A centerpiece of the report is evidence about the significant increase in ADR programs available—illustrated by maps showing program locations in 1998 and 2008 (*see* Chapter 2.C), and descriptions of kind and numbers of programs available.
>
> The report also describes the new ADR evaluation support system that provides refined *exit survey* tools for program users, a scanning system for data entry from these surveys, and tools that connect these data with other data from the state's judicial information system. With regard to the goal of increasing mediator excellence, the report describes the development of the Maryland Program for Mediator Excellence and an extensive series of professional development events and resources for mediators. Without direct evidence of "increased public awareness of ADR and its benefits," the MACRO report describes in detail its outreach efforts, including a multi-lingual public awareness campaign employing posters, a consumers' guide, a newsletter, and two short videos.

Even if grant funders, legislators, or others do not require an evaluation, designers can improve future management by systematic data collection. These data can guide changes in implementation and later might help with management by providing information about "what is happening on the ground" and what the outcomes of the dispute system appear to be.

B. WHAT KINDS OF EVALUATION APPROACHES ARE THERE?

Those in the program evaluation business distinguish *formative* from *summative* evaluation (*see, e.g.*, Weiss, 1999:31). *Formative* evaluations are intended to help program designers and administrators learn how their program implementation is going and to discover ways to refine and improve it. Formative evaluations also permit comparisons among different modes or models of implementation to figure out which one(s) seems to work best. *Summative* evaluation, by contrast, looks at the "bottom line"—what impact does the "finished" program have on the people, conflicts, organizations that it is designed to serve and at what costs were those results achieved? Formative evaluation assumes a dispute system design in progress; summative evaluation presumes it is done. In reality, of course, all dispute system designs need to continue to evolve, and even early in the implementation phase some outcome evidence can assist in system re-design. The strongest evaluation research thus has elements of both formative and summative approaches.

At one extreme, pure summative evaluation often places inordinate emphasis on one or two quantitative measures of program impact. The legislative request that prompted the MACRO report illustrates the dangers of isolated "bottom line" evaluations—that request focused exclusively on reducing court caseload, perhaps under the (naïve) assumption that it would save money. Most dispute management system designs will have multiple effects, however—some unanticipated. And focusing only on a particular "bottom line" tells designers, program managers, and funders virtually nothing about what the program actually does, how it does it, and the varied ways in which it might improve—or harm—an organization and people's relationships and lives. That is why blending evidence about varied outcomes and implementation makes the most sense. It underscores MACRO's wisdom in adopting a broad approach in reporting back to the legislature.

As a business, eBay and PayPal (hereafter eBay) had a bottom-line orientation in looking at outcomes for its dispute processing system—measures of customer reactivation—but it also attended to a wide range of other evidence to inform designers about user perceptions of the system in relation to varying cultural contexts for its use.

---

eBay: As eBay developed, it was clear to Colin Rule and others that they needed data to monitor the ways that customers reacted to problems encountered in using PayPal and eBay and to assess quickly user responses to an evolving system for responding to 60 million or more disputes annually (Schmitz and Rule, 2018). eBay wants to keep its customers and have them return for more sales or purchases, even if they perceive problems with buyers or sellers. It also wants them to think positively about their experiences and to recommend eBay to others. These criteria—as well as cost—have turned out to be central for judging the efficacy of the dispute resolution systems that evolved at eBay and to modifying them over time. As an online business, eBay has unusual capacity to collect and track data about users—every keyboard or mouse click, in fact, for millions of users across the globe. And much of this data collection was in place already; it did not have to be created by Colin Rule. The challenge was not the collection of data but rather selecting the data that could meaningfully guide improvements in the dispute system design.

eBay's goals led to the identification of two key variables for outcome evaluation—reactivation rates and Net Promoter Scores:

- Reactivation measures gauge the likelihood that customers experiencing disputes will re-use eBay. To solve the "compared to what" question, the company asked whether the volume of eBay use for each customer in a dispute was lower, higher, or the same in the six months after the dispute as in the six months prior to it. The finding that both "winners" and "losers" in disputes had higher use rates after their disputes than before they were resolved affirmed that the system was working. In fact, people who used online dispute resolution actually increased their use of the eBay site compared to those who did not use online dispute resolution. Only those who took a long time (three to four weeks or more) to resolve disputes showed a decline in reactivation; by their actions users showed that they would rather lose a low value case quickly than win but have it take a long time.

- eBay wants its customers to promote use among others. To measure user support for its product, the company makes use of a common survey tool, the Net Promoter Score.[1] eBay regularly samples its customers and surveys them, asking simply, "How likely is it that you would recommend this site to a friend or family member?" on a scale of 0 (not at all likely) to 10 (extremely likely). Net Promoter Scores offer eBay a sense of the response of its customers generally and also allows it to compare the responses of customers who employ online dispute resolution with those who do not.

eBay uses another tool to assess in greater depth the responses of customers to varying dispute resolution options. A sample of clients using these options receives an online version of the Subjective Values Inventory[2]—a social psychological tool for gauging feelings about the instrumental outcome of a negotiation (e.g., win or lose), about oneself in the process (e.g., loss of face), about the process (e.g., fairness), and about the relationship with the other party (e.g., trust). Data from these surveys provide eBay a perspective on the overall satisfaction of users and help to identify any areas of the process requiring improvement.

---

1. *See* https://www.netpromoter.com/know/.

2. *See* http://subjectivevalue.com/.

To refine the dispute resolution process and its presentation to users in different cultural and linguistic contexts, eBay has also employed focus groups with users reacting to their online experience. eBay recognized early on that the explanation for dispute resolution processes had to vary across sites to account for differences in cultural perceptions. This has meant employing staff native to various language communities to assist in shaping online instructions that are localized in ways that recognize cultural nuances. eBay can also gauge usability of its website to some extent by the length of pauses on each of its pages and at each stage of a branching process. The dispute resolution process itself can also be continuously assessed for usability, for example by monitoring "drop off rates," that is the rate and point at which users who have entered the online dispute resolution site leave it. Comments in the online user community also provide information about perceptions and problems that help refine process and delivery systems as do comments left on each page in response to a comment icon.

Clearly, eBay did not simply look at the bottom line—did users return to similar or higher rates of use after online dispute resolution than they showed before a dispute experience? It also looked more broadly at perceptions of fairness and worked hard to understand how people in very different settings interacted with its online system. Examining a wide range of outcomes and experiences contributes significantly to improved system designs. For MACRO, the numbers of cases heard and resolved by mediators mattered but so did the expansion of available alternatives for people and businesses using courts and the testimonials of citizens and court officials about the impacts of innovation. MACRO understood and believed in the value of these expanded alternatives but used a variety of evidence to convince decision-makers with a narrower view of outcomes of its perspective.

The MACRO approach challenges us to think about the points of convergence and divergence between public relations and disciplined or rigorous evaluation. MACRO's report was crafted to promote the program to legislators and to present the most favorable portrait of the program that the available evidence supported. Self-evaluations by programs or designers for external decision-makers make this approach virtually inevitable. One can suppose that at the same time, MACRO leaders looked at the evidence critically and in disciplined ways so that they were not deceiving themselves about the program's strengths and weaknesses.

The most useful evaluation research pays attention to key criteria set by decision-makers but also provides a much wider and richer look at what the program does and how it does it. At the same time, designers themselves are the most critical consumers of that information—using it not (only or mainly) to defend or promote, but also to help make programmatic and management choices that can improve the system that they have designed. Evaluation is a state of mind after all—a disposition to assess in a disciplined way the worth of practices in the light of evidence and to make changes in response to that evaluation. From this perspective, it makes sense to use as broad a range of quantitative and qualitative data from varied sources as it is feasible to collect and interpret in order to provide information about outcomes and process that can be used for system improvement.

C.   HOW DO YOU IDENTIFY THE OUTCOME CRITERIA FOR EVALUATION?

Not surprisingly, Maryland's legislative committees responsible for the state budget selected a criterion for evaluation that in their view related to the costs of running the state courts—caseload. As we saw, however, MACRO took a broader view of its mission and "assessed" accordingly, reporting on mediation program implementation, mediation quality initiatives, and public education, for example. MACRO's self-evaluation implicitly underlined evidence that activities seen to have intrinsic value (such as implementation of mediation programs and professional development activities for mediators) were now taking place. The criteria for assessing Cure Violence Chicago could also be viewed narrowly or more broadly, focusing only on the level of community violence or more expansively on the results of work helping individuals most exposed to violent retaliation to gain access to education and work.

Cure Violence: How would you know if—and how—the Cure Violence Chicago program was working to reduce urban violence? A summative evaluation might ask a single question—do shootings and lethal violence decline in Cure Violence neighborhoods? However, a central goal of Cure Violence is to change community norms about violence. Because community norms are difficult to measure, Northwestern University evaluators focused instead on whether there was evidence that shootings and homicides declined in Cure Violence neighborhoods in Chicago (Skogan et al. 7-37). It turns out evidence existed, but as discussed later, that fact alone does not demonstrate that Cure Violence caused the declines. Later evaluations of Cure Violence neighborhoods in New York City also found declines in shooting victimizations and injuries in treatment neighborhoods over time and compared to control neighborhoods (https://johnjayrec.nyc/2017/10/02/cvinsobronxeastny/).

The New York evaluators of Cure Violence took on the challenge of assessing normative change. They employed indicators of willingness to use violence in response to 17 hypothetical scenarios for a sample of over 2,200 youths. The results show steeper declines over time in propensity for violence among young men in Cure Violence neighborhoods than in comparison areas (https://johnjayrec.nyc/2017/10/02/cvinsobronxeastny/).

The Chicago evaluators did not rely exclusively on bottom-line evidence about the violence reduction goal. They also examined the impact of the other services Cure Violence workers provided for clients as part of the original system design, which grew in part from a "root cause analysis" that located problems of violence partly in the economic marginalization of many young people. Interviews with almost 300 of those clients revealed that of the many who needed a job, over 80 percent received help preparing a resume and for job interviews, and 86 percent "reported that Cure Violence helped them find a job opening" (Skogan et al., 2008:ES-11). Both outreach workers and their clients also described considerable time and effort devoted to supporting additional schooling as well as to aiding practical efforts to obtain driver's licenses and social security cards and to be advocates with attorneys or probation officers. What impact did such services have? Those who received services were nearly twice as likely to be employed and four times more likely to have completed high school or further education and training.

Cure Violence interrupters Ameena Matthews and Cobe Williams. Photo courtesy of Kartemquin Films.

Also broadening evaluation criteria, the researchers who evaluated the United States Postal Service's REDRESS (Resolve Employment Disputes, Reach Equitable Solutions Swiftly) system for responding to EEO complaints looked not only at the ways that complainants and respondents perceived the fairness of the mediation process and outcomes, but also at the aggregate impact of the system on the workplace (Bingham et al., 2009:1-50). Through exit surveys of participants in workplace mediation they learned that well over 90 percent of complainants and supervisors viewed the mediators as respectful, impartial, and fair, and 91 percent expressed satisfaction with the process and 64 percent to 70 percent with the outcome.

Interviews carried out before and after implementation of REDRESS indicated a substantial decline in reports that supervisors dealt with conflict by "yelling, arguing, disciplining, or intimidating" their opponents (Bingham et al., 2009:44) and a large increase in the percentage describing an "open door" for communication. Comparisons across options for dealing with workplace problems (EEO complaint, REDRESS, and formal grievance process) indicated REDRESS was far more likely than either of the other processes to improve communication and relationships between the parties. A review of Postal Service records showed steady increases in use of REDRESS since its inception and a decline in filings of EEO complaints.

Providing another illustration of expanding evaluation criteria, the University of Michigan Hospital attended to costs as it redesigned its procedures for handling unexpected medical events and outcomes, but costs were not all that mattered (Boothman et al., 2009). At the hospital, for example, innovations in patient care were just as important a result of the dispute management system and could not be summarized in terms of dollars saved.

University of Michigan Hospital: The University of Michigan Hospital designed and implemented a system for managing "unanticipated patient outcomes" so that the costs in time, money, and reputation to the hospital would be reduced and the quality of patient care improved. The system was based on three principles that differed radically from the "deny and defend" approach common in medical malpractice:

1. "Compensate quickly and fairly when unreasonable medical care causes injury.
2. "Defend medically reasonable care vigorously.
3. "Reduce patient injuries (and therefore claims) by learning from patients' experiences" (Boothman et al., 2009:139).

University of Michigan Hospital photo. Used with permission.

The system put in place relies on quick and thorough review by experienced caregivers of claims by patients or their families or of reports by physicians and nurses of unanticipated patient outcomes. A medical specialty committee (that also includes members outside the specialty to provide added perspectives and independence) then reviews each report. The goal of this review process is to find out what happened and why, to determine whether the care in question was reasonable or not by professional standards, and to share the results of the review with all parties concerned. Where care was inappropriate, apologies are made, open discussion with patient and attorney (if there is one) is initiated, and appropriate compensation offered (Boothman et al., 2009:140-143).

The University of Michigan risk managers undertook their own ongoing evaluation of this system using financial data, surveys, and accounts of organizational changes over time. First, it was essential to measure the impact of the new system on malpractice litigation and costs to the hospital. They could answer that question in part by a time series analysis of new claims (declining from 136 in 1999 to 61 by 2006), of open claims (dropping from 262 in 2001 to 83 in 2007), of claim processing time (falling from 20.3 months in 2001 to 8 months in 2007), and by the drop in insurance reserves by two-thirds and of litigation costs by 50 percent. They had to acknowledge, however, because they had no comparison group, that not all of this decline could be attributed to the new program since there was simultaneously a national decline in tort claims filings (Boothman et al., 2009:143-144).

Boothman and colleagues (2009:145) also attributed a series of clinical improvements to initiation of the new claims review process and to the real-location of resources that would have gone to pay lawyers and settle claims. These include, for example, development of an online incident reporting system, establishment of rapid response teams, creation of a hospitalist service, use of patient safety coordinators, changes in the organization of clinical and supervisory staffing, and adoption of new technologies to better monitor patient care.

In addition to measuring the financial and clinical impacts of the new system, the University of Michigan Hospital employed survey tools to judge the satisfaction of both medical faculty and of the plaintiffs' bar with the hospital's malpractice approach. These surveys showed that virtually all medical staff members perceived a change in the hospital's approach to malpractice claims and approved of those changes and that a majority indicated that the approach contributed importantly to their decision to stay at the hospital. Meanwhile, all of the 26 members of the plaintiffs' bar specializing in medical malpractice viewed the University of Michigan Hospital as either "the best" or "among the best" health systems for its transparency, and four-fifths indicated that the information the system provided enabled them to make better decisions about which claims to pursue through the courts and that the system lowered the costs for their clients (Boothman et al., 2009:145-146).

Clearly, no formula identifies the appropriate criteria for evaluating the outcomes of a dispute management system. External or internal audiences may demand a focus on a narrow set of goals, but wise system designers and managers typically understand a broad variety of potential program impacts and want to examine those through quantitative data and through descriptions and stories. Dispute processing systems can affect not just those directly involved in conflicts but the communities and organizations of which they are a part. Basic human values matter to policy makers and managers, not just money and efficiency, so examining how people experience a dispute system, their sense of justice and fairness, their morale as employees, and their success as community members should be part of evaluation efforts.

Developing evaluation criteria and methods requires, you will find, the same collaborative processes that shape dispute system designs. Consultation with stakeholders about what it would mean for the design to be successful and what evidence their constituencies might expect will help you develop your evaluation approach. This consultation requires more than accumulating a laundry list of things that stakeholders might like to know. Data collection and analysis have significant costs so you will have to be tough-minded in deciding where to devote scarce resources. In doing so you will be wise to focus on how information would actually be useful to improve design and operation and would answer the concerns of critics and funders. "Gee, it would be interesting to know . . ." is not an adequate criterion for gathering data.

D. WHY SHOULD YOU LOOK AT PROGRAM IMPLEMENTATION AS WELL AS PROGRAM OUTCOMES?

Without documentation of what the program actually does, how it is organized, how people are trained, and who is served, it is hard to know what you are evaluating (Rossi et al., 1999:191-232; Love, 2004). Apparent program failures are often failures of implementation. Inadequate funding, training, or supervision may undermine a good design. So knowing what actually happens on the ground is a crucial part of both program management and evaluation.

System or program administrators do not always know the answers to all of these questions, although they may think they do. Ideally, through some form of program monitoring—regular reporting and record-keeping—an organization should be collecting much of this information. Evolving technologies for gathering data in organizations have the potential to assist system designers both in the assessment stage and in evaluation (Rabinovich-Einy and Katsh, 2012). But additional data collection through observation, surveys, and interviews can substantially enrich and perhaps alter the picture of what actually goes on. For example, how many mediations take place, how long do they take, how quickly are they held after an initial referral, how often do participants not show up, how many lead to additional mediations, how often do parties to mediation bring supporters or advocates with them? All of this could be learned from systematic record-keeping as was undertaken by the Postal Service's REDRESS program, for example, through mediator tracking forms. What approach do mediators take—do they recommend settlement terms to parties, pressure them to settle, or caucus with parties? Surveys of mediation participants (and of mediators) might help answer that question as they did for REDRESS.

The United States Postal Service's REDRESS program was designed to provide "transformative mediation"—a version of mediation that focuses on helping disputing parties to recognize and understand one another's viewpoints. Mediators who follow this approach encourage communication among parties about understanding and changing "their interactions with others." As a result, according to the Postal Service website, "[t]he mediation is considered successful when the parties participate in interactive communication that results in a clearer understanding of their situation and each other's perspective. Often, this leads to resolution of the dispute."[3] One of the central implementation questions then for the REDRESS program was whether or not mediators were consistently using this approach. To discover whether they were or not, the program used an exit survey that asked several questions of disputants about mediator conduct (for example, did the mediator help them understand the other party's point of view?).

Implementation was also a key challenge for Cure Violence and particularly tricky because program success depended on hiring workers who were connected to the world of gangs and street violence that was the target of change and relied upon the capacity of widely variant and unevenly funded community organizations to implement the program in local neighborhoods.

Cure Violence Chicago: Prior to completion of a formal and extended program evaluation in 2008, the administrator of locally hosted Cure Violence programs collected standardized reporting data from outreach workers and violence interrupters on their work hours and on client contacts and characteristics. These data permitted monitoring of program implementation and administrative adjustments to ensure that each of the local programs was reaching the target audience of high-risk community members and that staff were available at key hours when escalating conflict might occur. Cure Violence also tracked the operation and context of the 25 differing organizations that served as local host organizations and gathered qualitative data about the advantages and disadvantages of differing kinds of sponsorship and the consequences of unstable funding for the program.

A major part of the Northwestern University evaluation of Cure Violence focused on implementation. With support of a large grant from the National Institute of Justice, the researchers looked at implementation, reviewing program records and undertaking site visits, observations, surveys of program staff, interviews with possible collaborating organizations (e.g., local police, churches, schools) and with almost 300 clients.

This work enabled the research team to develop a profile of the clients served (confirming that they were indeed "high risk"—e.g., involved in gangs, with substantial arrest records); of the problems they faced (joblessness and lack of educational preparation, anger management, low self-esteem); and of the

---

3. United States Postal Service, Transformative Mediation, https://about.usps.com/what-we-are-doing/redress/transformative-mediation.htm (last visited June 27, 2018).

challenges in "managing" their cases. They were able to document the nature of the violence that interrupters intervened in, the neighborhood contexts for this work, and the risks and challenges of intervening. They described in some detail the collaborative relationships that Cure Violence Chicago had established with churches, schools, police, and others and the role of political leaders in the key funding decisions that contributed to the instability of resources and staffing for Cure Violence programs. The evaluation also examined in detail the issues of selecting and managing staff—background checks, drug testing, credentials, training, supervision of work, and turnover. In doing so, it also documented an important side effect of Cure Violence's work—providing meaningful work and job experience for many ex-offenders as program staff.

You cannot take for granted the implementation of a dispute system design. Thoughtful data collection will assist you in understanding what is actually happening "on the ground." Clearly, early collection of information relating to process can help you do formative or process evaluation that will assist you in adjusting implementation practices to align with design goals. That data collection can be done in many different ways, including—especially when resources are scarce—informal observations of implementation work and conversations with those who deliver the services. More formal data collection and evaluation raise a series of issues that we examine below.

E. WHAT QUESTIONS SHOULD GUIDE EVALUATION RESEARCH?

Helpful evaluation research requires clarity about the questions that it will help you answer. As suggested earlier in Section A, the sorts of key questions that you will want to answer with the best information you can afford to collect include:

- What is the system design delivering "on the ground"? And if the design delivery is falling short of what was planned, what is keeping the system from operating in the ways you hoped it would?
- What kinds of claims and disputes are being processed, through what processes, how fast, with what results?
- How do parties experience the processes/system?
- What effects if any has the system design had on the organizations or institutions or communities that surround it?
- How, if at all, does all of this differ from what happened before the new design?

The sections that follow address some of the strategies for answering these questions as systematically as possible and several of the central challenges in doing so.

In addressing these core questions with whatever evidence you can gather, you and your client will focus particularly on the set of interventions and outcomes you planned and hoped for. But there can be unintended consequences of innovations—both positive and negative. Some unintended and unwanted consequences can be anticipated; others not. In collecting evidence, you need to leave open the possibility of discovering that the implementation did not go quite as you planned or that at least some of the people and organizations with disputes reacted differently than you hoped. Qualitative research (talking with even a few people in semi-structured ways and observing what is happening on the ground) can provide the flexibility and open-endedness that help expose unintended consequences.

Those studying the implementation of one aspect of the Indian Residential Schools Settlement Agreement in Canada—the payment of standardized amounts to former students based on the number of years of residence—used such interviews to identify some responses that were hoped for and some that were not. For example, on the negative side, they found significant instances of emotional trauma prompted by the application process and patterns of self-destructive behavior and community disruption in the wake of payments. Although these were not the most common responses, the severity of the negative effects for a few may have outweighed some of the important benefits of these payments. Data collection helps identify such effects—and if detected early enough—could prompt enhancing or altering design elements that might minimize or compensate for them. In fact, some of these effects appear to have been anticipated in Canada, and the resources provided by the Aboriginal Healing Foundation may have helped buffer them in limited ways.

Truth and
Reconciliation
Commission of Canada

The Truth and Reconciliation Commission of Canada: How would you begin to think about evaluating the impact of the 2006 Indian Residential Schools Settlement Agreement or even part of its implementation? Over 100,000 people from many communities across Canada ultimately applied for Common Experience Payments (CEP) that were directed to past residents of a list of government-supported schools and paid at a standard rate of $10,000 for the first year of residence and $3,000 per year for each additional year Ultimately, nearly 78,000 people received compensation (Reimer et al., 2010:5-6). But how was the compensation process experienced by these individuals, and what impact did it have on them and on their communities?

To answer these questions, researchers from a social science consulting firm completed semi-structured interviews of 281 Inuit, First Nations, and Metis persons who were either CEP recipients or unsuccessful applicants (one-quarter of interviewees) from 17 communities (Reimer et al., 2010:9).

- "Participants generally agreed that the compensation process seemed inconsistent, leaving them at the mercy of an outside agency in control of yet another aspect of their lives" (id.:xiii).

- "Forty per cent of participants found the CEP application process difficult or challenging [logistically or emotionally]" (id.:xiii).
- "More Survivors described positive types of impacts of payments than did those who described negative impacts; however, this frequency should not be confused with magnitude. The negative impacts described by participants were profoundly destructive [self-destructive behavior, conflicts among relatives] for many survivors and their families and in some communities outweighed any positive, material benefits of the payments" (id.:xiv).
- For half of the study group, compensation was both positive (allowing relief of financial stress) and negative "because these benefits did not outweigh the sense of injustice . . . nor did they alleviate the pain of triggered emotions and memories of trauma . . ." (id.:xiv).
- "The majority of Survivors in the study group required or wanted some kind of support during the CEP process, whether it was assistance with form-filling or counseling related to the triggered emotions and traumatic memories" (id.:xiv).
- "Almost half of the participants in the study said compensation made no difference in their well-being. . . . [They saw] no connection between money and healing . . ." (id.:xv).

F. WHAT DATA SHOULD YOU COLLECT?

1. Selecting from the repertoire of data collection techniques

The same data collection techniques available for the assessment phase discussed in Chapter 4 are the ones that you might use in an evaluation. In that phase, ideally, you will have collected evidence that serves as a basis of comparison for later evaluation of both process and outcomes. Chapter 4.E provided a detailed discussion of data collection techniques that you should review. This section summarizes those techniques in the context of evaluation.

Many people think first of *surveys* as the way to collect data about a program and its impacts. Indeed, surveys can play an important role but typically provide incomplete information, limited by the structure of the questions, the partial perspectives of those who respond to them, and constraints of time and space (*see generally* Newcomer and Triplett, 2010). However, eBay and other organizations learn much of central importance to them from their use of a single survey question generating the Net Promoter Score; this question can be quickly administered and scored online for millions of users. Surveys can and do provide important—but limited—information. For eBay the most important evidence came not from those surveys but from routinely collected *organizational records* of the behavior of users, the rates at which they used eBay before and after disputes.

If you use surveys, online surveys are far and away the least costly to administer. Links to an online survey through Qualtrics or SurveyMonkey, for example, could be sent to an email list of individuals or distributed in some fashion through other networks (an online newsletter, for example). Such surveys have huge advantages over paper and pencil surveys, which must be coded and entered into a data analysis program—thus, the costs of these rise directly with the number administered. These steps—which often mean that paper and pencil surveys are never analyzed—are done automatically in online surveys. When using online surveys recognize, of course, that good lists of email addresses may not be available, that respondents are self-selected, and the greater the burden of getting to the survey, the heavier the self-selection will be.

Court mediation programs have often employed *exit surveys*—surveys given to parties who just experienced mediation and collected before they leave. As paper and pen surveys, they typically require some labor to tabulate and summarize. Those summaries provide some helpful information, typically documenting that almost everyone trusts the mediators and finds their experience fair. These affirmations can provide useful support in reports to supervising agencies and applications for funds but may offer limited insight to program managers. Surveys are only one of many data collection tools that designers might consider as they try to extract multiple and rich perspectives on how the system design works in practice (*see generally* Weiss, 1998:152-175; Wholey et al., 2010:247-422).

Structured or partly structured interviews let respondents tell stories and provide accounts of experiences and responses to them in their own words. They thus can add much more nuanced perspectives to the evidence than might come from checks or circles on surveys. Stories themselves humanize what a dispute processing system actually does and may provide compelling parts of an evaluation of the system design.

Focus groups may be among the most widely used tools for efficiently collecting qualitative data that could bear on system design implementation and impact (Krueger and Casey, 2010). As noted in Chapter 4.E, focus groups also can be particularly useful in the assessment stage of design because they permit guided conversations with stakeholders.

Organizational or public records also provide extremely important sources of data that can help establish a baseline (e.g., number of complaints filed with EEOC) and allow managers to monitor program operation—for example, through regular reports of activity by mediators (Hatry, 2010). Refining and improving internal organizational data collection and analysis tools early on will smooth and enrich later evaluation. For example, intake data gathering may be routinized but not include all of the information that might prove useful later in an evaluation; if necessary, negotiate to modify the form. Make sure as well that the intake data are actually tabulated rather than left in folders to accumulate.

Observations can add much to the answers to survey or interview questions and to data routinely collected by an organization. They can provide the basis for a picture and account of processes—what does a Maryland court mediation session look like, or a violence interrupter's meeting with a victim of an earlier assault? What is a day in the life of an NIH ombuds? Such observations may be informal but still systematic in recording what one sees, or more highly formalized like eBay's recording of how long web users linger on a page and whether or not they move further into the site as a consequence.

Clearly, data collection needs to be thought of broadly and in relation to the objectives of evaluation and the resources available to undertake it. In all data collection, however, remember a basic rule. Do not collect data unless there are tools in place to analyze and make use of the information. We know of both court and community programs, for example, that regularly collect exit survey or self-evaluation forms from program participants and carefully file them but never analyze them. The year's worth of paper files may be of some use to later researchers but have little or no operational value to the organization. Interviews can provide rich insights but transcribing them takes enormous time and care; good notes taken during the interviews and enriched immediately after should suffice. Routine organizational data may also go unanalyzed. Thus, designing data collection means also figuring out a realistic plan for making use of the information that results.

2. Measurement and description

Measuring key concepts poses one of the central challenges of evaluation research (Weiss, 1998:114-151). How do you gauge fairness of process, workplace morale, or customer satisfaction, for example? Happily, for these and many other variables, social scientists have developed metrics that can be adapted or used directly. eBay, for example, adopted the Net Promoter Score as well as the Subjective Values Inventory (Curhan et al., 2006) to measure customer responses. Such measures are published and, when not copyrighted, can be replicated freely. For example, you could readily find measures of procedural justice perceptions in the extensive research literature. By examining published evaluations of other dispute systems—such as the extensive research on the United States Postal Services' REDRESS program—one can often discern the key indicators of system effects and of effectiveness used by other evaluators. Feel free to ask evaluators to share their research instruments if they are not published. Generally, it is far better to rely on and replicate measures that others have validated than to invent your own.

Measurement is rarely straightforward, even when measuring costs where the dollar (or other currency) is the standard unit of measure. When it comes to costs or cost savings, figuring out which costs to count and which not to count turns out to be a central challenge. Cost savings are even harder to measure in many cases, but not all. The University of Michigan Hospital could with relative ease measure the dollars leaving the organization for outside counsel and lawsuit settlements or awards. It did not report, however, the costs to the hospital of organizing its internal investigation and review processes. Those may or may not be marginal costs of operation; they could represent simple reallocation of tasks among existing personnel. Should those costs have been considered in weighing the success of the system design? If so, how?

Evaluation work should not turn exclusively on measurement that typically produces quantitative measures. Stories and voices matter as well—for policy makers sometimes much more than quantitative evidence. Thus, accounts of both process (what people do and how programs operate) and more or less detailed case studies of or stories about cases, events, or community life can communicate powerfully about how a dispute system works and how it affects people, relationships, and organizational practices. Such stories humanize abstract systems and allow the voices of those people delivering a service or impacted by it to be heard. These voices can illustrate the values reflected by the system (for example, empowerment of parties) and describe systemic changes that cannot be captured quantitatively. Thus, the University of Michigan Hospital evaluation not only reports on dollars apparently saved but also describes specific improvements in care resulting from changed medical practices.

Although all designers will have stories to tell about the implementation and impacts of a new system, it takes planning to collect them systematically, to record quotations and comments, and to obtain appropriate consent for sharing them (with names attached or without them). You will be well served by developing a system for recording stories over time, ideally beginning at an early stage in the implementation. Qualitative interviewing can be a valuable data collection tool to help you gather systematically the accounts and perceptions of those implementing a dispute processing system or employing it. Your data collection may well begin in the assessment phase of your work when the "before" story and evidence can be gathered in ways that will later permit comparisons to the data about "during" and "after" implementation of a new design.

3. Confidentiality and the ethics (and effects) of data collection

Although your data collection may not always accord with the most rigorous methods of social science, it should always live up to high ethical standards and appropriately make and honor promises of confidentiality (*see generally* Weiss, 1998:175-178; Babbie, 2010:62-75). The fundamental principle of "do no harm" applies to data collection. Avoid deceiving or misleading those from whom data are collected, honor organizational or professional commitments to confidentiality, and be careful of intruding on the privacy of individuals and groups. Be sure to obtain consent from parties about using any stories that might identify them and be sure to disguise in published reports individuals or organizations that have not consented to be identified. Professional social science organizations have codes of ethics that include useful reminders about protections for confidentiality and informed consent (*see, e.g.*, American Sociological Association

Code of Ethics at http://www.asanet.org/membership/code-ethics). When you are doing design work as part of a clinical program in a law school, make certain you know and comply with university rules on the use of human subjects and follow the procedures of your institutional review board.

Anonymity and confidentiality are not synonymous. Anonymity means that the person who gathers the data does not know the identities of those providing responses (e.g., a web survey with no identifiers); confidentiality means that identities are or may be known but not revealed and in fact are actively protected. If you solicit comments, for example, the respondent may say something that an enterprising reader could link to a specific person or case. Thus, it is vitally important to be clear with yourself and with those providing information what level of protection you are prepared and able to provide.

This challenge becomes particularly vexing when there would be considerable value in linking pieces of information to the individuals to whom they apply. So if there are case records and survey responses, can they be linked together? Not if the surveys are filled out anonymously. Will attaching an identification number that permits linkage inhibit responses? If not (or not much), then make those links, but do not promise that the responses will be *anonymous*. Presuming that the data can be linked but their confidentiality protected, promises of confidentiality can be honored while linking pieces of data.

The law in pertinent jurisdictions may, however, block a designer from protecting the confidentiality of identifiable data (*see generally* Chapter 7). If the client or designer is a public entity, can the data be protected from public records disclosure? If the data become pertinent to litigation, can they be protected from discovery? If the pertinent jurisdiction recognizes a scholarly research privilege, would the privilege apply to research designed to improve a particular design rather than for general scholarly purposes?[4] Is the client willing to expend resources for attorney's fees to protect the privacy of the data? Because of the potential risks and costs of collecting data with the uncertain ability to protect promised confidentiality, when working in the public sphere, designers will want to consider collecting at least some data anonymously instead.

In addition to care with regard to confidentiality, you should be thoughtful about the potential unanticipated effects of gathering the information. For example, social scientists guard against the "Hawthorne effect"[5]—the possibility that a group singled out for study will perform differently not because of

---

4. *Compare In re Bextra and Celebrex Mktg. Sales Practices and Prod. Liab. Litig.*, 249 F.R.D. 10 (D. Mass. 2008) (recognizes scholarly research privilege) *with In re Grand Jury Proceedings*, 5 F.3d 397 (9th Cir. 1993) (no scholarly research privilege).

5. The "Hawthorne effect" references studies of worker productivity at Hawthorne Works in the 1920s and 1930s in which worker productivity improved with many of the changes in their work environment (e.g., lighting), even changes that returned them to the original work environment. Researchers speculate that the workers may have worked harder because they knew that their productivity was being monitored, rather than because of the changes in working conditions (Adair, 1984:334).

the intervention being studied but rather because *they* are being studied. There may be other possible consequences as well. For example, a well-meaning group of law students might survey bar association membership to explore new options for dispute resolution service delivery, but in doing so provoke organizational turmoil by broaching possibilities that threaten the self-interest of some members.

Perhaps even more significant, designers must address up front the question of who will see the evaluation data and any written evaluation reports and how possible it is, in fact, to protect the confidentiality of informants in those reports and data. For example, a joint working committee between school unions and a school board might agree to commission an evaluation and review of existing dispute management practices in the district. Some teachers may want access to the final report as a condition of their participation while others may not participate unless they have assurances that only members of the joint working committee will have a final copy of the report. How might you handle this situation? There may be many solutions or none, depending on the underlying interests and concerns of those involved. At times, offering to share an abstract of the final report or offering to hold a public session with a broad overview of the results might satisfy the teachers insisting on transparency while meeting the privacy interests of the teachers who only want the joint working committee to see the work product.

Consider another challenge: In the same evaluation, one of the stakeholders is the school superintendent. How can you as a designer capture the views of the school superintendent but also protect her confidentiality in a final report or assessment? One possibility might be to have a somewhat broader stakeholder category such as "District Administrative Leadership" that might encompass assistant superintendents and senior administrators within the school district as well as the human resources director or general counsel.

G. FROM WHOM DO YOU COLLECT DATA? SAMPLING AND REPRESENTATIVENESS

Random or probability sampling[6] of people or case files provides greater confidence that the evidence collected will be representative of a larger population of individuals or cases (Babbie, 2010:196). Sampling enables a data gatherer

---

6. Random or probability sampling means ensuring that each case or person has an equal (or at least a known) chance of being chosen for the sample in order to represent the same variability in the sample as in the population from which it is drawn (Babbie, 2010:196). One way to do random sampling is to use a table of random numbers (available on the web) and use it to select a sample from a list of cases, each of which has a unique number attached. Often close approximations to random samples can be done by systematic sampling—taking every fifth or eighth case or person in a list.

to focus more energy on a smaller group than the population as a whole, perhaps sending follow-up surveys and reminders to try to get a higher response rate, using interviews (often with higher response rates) rather than surveys, or doing more detailed analysis of fewer case files. Random sampling does not, of course, always produce a good "cross-section" of the population, especially when people can refuse to participate or simply are unavailable.

There is no "correct" sample size, and statisticians' recommendations about "the best" sample size do not relate to the size of the population sampled; instead, statistical choices about sample size relate to the absolute size of the sample—the larger the sample, the greater the power of statistical inference (Babbie, 2010:207). Of course, in the world of practice, resources often dictate sample size. So also does the method of data collection. Personal interviews, especially if recorded and transcribed, demand far more time than surveys and inevitably mean smaller samples. If the data come from mailed surveys that require someone to enter the data by hand, each survey raises the cost. But if you can use an online tool such as SurveyMonkey or Qualtrics to ask questions of members of a population with an existing email list, there are few advantages of sampling or marginal costs in seeking more rather than less data (unless it is in creating a longer or shorter email list to send to). If you are sampling from a population without online tools, it sometimes makes sense to use a smaller sample but to follow up with participants more intensively to encourage higher response rates.

In gathering information from program participants or about conflict situations, an important consideration is how representative the actual respondents are of the "total population" of participants or conflicts. Thus, in seeking to understand the impact of a new dispute system on employee morale, a survey could be an important tool. But how confident are you that those who respond to the survey tell the same story as those who do not? Response rates to surveys become one gauge of representativeness, but in fact response rates more frequently hover closer to 20 percent or lower than to 90 percent, leaving significant doubts about whether those responding represent accurately the whole population.

In that likely eventuality, you could do what the students at Harvard Law School did in their evaluation of NIH staff views of the ombuds office. They had a response rate to their staff survey of only 3.3 percent, but because they surveyed the whole population of NIH staff, they had over 1,100 respondents. They compared the demographic characteristics of respondents (job type, age, and so on) with known demographic data about the NIH employee/contractor population and found that the profiles of the respondents largely mirrored the population. With appropriate cautions, the students made use of the survey data, recognizing that it provided more information than the students would have had without the survey at all. It is always important to be aware of the limits of representativeness and generalizability of data collected and thus to resist making overly strong claims or drawing inappropriate conclusions from the data. But in the real world, practitioners will make decisions based on the information available rather than waiting for the perfect study. Evaluation research in practice often means using what you have and trying to make sense of it, while recognizing (but not being paralyzed by) the imperfections of the data.

H. HOW DO YOU MAKE SENSE OF YOUR DATA?

1. Compared to what?

Comparisons, we have seen, are vital to making sense of much of the data collected to evaluate a dispute management system. Before versus after is one important kind of comparison. Measuring "reactivation" of PayPal users with disputes has value because it permits comparisons of individuals' PayPal use rates six months before utilizing online dispute resolution with those rates six months after. Maryland's description of mediation impact implicitly compares court caseload without mediation and with it, and its maps of ADR programs in 1998 and 2008 (*see* Chapter 2.C) tell a powerful story of change. Postal Service interviews before and after implementing REDRESS allowed evaluators to conclude that workplace interactions appeared much better along several dimensions after implementation than before. In each of these instances, a central point of comparison is organizational characteristics or individual behavior before and after the intervention. Such comparisons permit judgments about change and of relative effectiveness, and they can help test assumptions about cause and effect relationships. The challenge of making the right comparisons lies at the center of the design of data collection and the interpretation of the evidence collected (Weiss, 1998:199-212; Rossi et al., 1999:281-285).

Comparisons, of course, can be tricky. Two interrelated and key questions must be answered. Are the groups or time periods being compared really comparable? Are there other changes besides the system design change that may explain differences between the time periods or groups? Experimental designs (discussed in the next section) give the researcher the greatest confidence that *control* and *experimental* groups are comparable, but such designs are often difficult or inappropriate to implement. As discussed below, the Cure Violence evaluators compared changes in rates of shooting and homicide in Cure Violence neighborhoods with changes in rates in "comparable" neighborhoods without the program. These comparisons required great care and some statistical sophistication. Comparisons of the same organization or neighborhood over time can be problematic when many things are changing together. If there is a difference in key variables such as workplace climate or dollars expended for malpractice litigation between time one (before dispute system) and time two (after dispute system), it does not necessarily follow that the difference results from the new system. Historical events, long-term trends (as in Chicago's violence levels or declines in malpractice filings), and other interventions may explain equally well the observed changes in indicators of program success. This leads us to the challenge of causal inference.

2. Causal inference

How do we know that we can attribute any changes in key indicators of impact such as cost, workplace morale, customer satisfaction, conflict or complaint/dispute levels, or violence to implementation of a new dispute management system design? Logic provides part of the answer (*see* Hoover, 1984:91; Babbie, 2010:94-95). To infer causation you need to establish:

- time priority (that is, the causal variable precedes the effect variable);
- consistency of relationship between cause and effect variables (for example, the same system design is followed by higher worker morale in all or most locations it is put into effect); and
- absence of causation by a "third" variable that can explain impact (for example, self-selection of participants most disposed to resolving conflict explains high rate of resolution and satisfaction or new organizational leadership that prompts the system design also brings other changes that may have produced the observed results).

Of these, the third will likely be most problematic. If baseline data are collected on key indicators before the design is implemented, they can be compared to similar measures collected after implementation; in this case it should be clear that design implementation precedes whatever "effects" are measured. The design is often implemented only once so consistency of relationships cannot be examined (but it is important if multiple implementations occur—as happened with Cure Violence—to make sure that the results are relatively consistent across sites). The remaining issue and the one that you will find most challenging is the question of whether some other variable or phenomena could be causing whatever impacts appear to come from the new dispute system design.

Cure Violence Chicago: During the years of the first Cure Violence implementations, Chicago continued to experience a long-term decline in homicides that began in 1992 (for example, from 824 in 1995 to 628 in 2000 to 528 in 2008). So it was not surprising that shootings and murders declined in Cure Violence areas. Two fundamental and related challenges for evaluation thus appeared—the "compared to what" problem and the "did our program cause it" problem (because the Cure Violence program was not the only change occurring in Chicago). To address the first, researchers used two approaches to comparison: a time series analysis with 16 years of data—in essence comparing Cure Violence neighborhoods with themselves prior to Cure Violence—and matching—that is, identifying similar neighborhoods that had no Cure Violence programs and comparing them over time with the Cure Violence areas. "The analysis of crime hot spots contrasted shooting patterns before and after the introduction of Cure Violence, with parallel maps detailing changes in shooting patterns in the matched comparison areas" (Skogan et al., 815). These comparisons helped address the second question—did Cure Violence cause the observed reductions. Researchers also needed complex statistical techniques to figure out whether declines in shootings in the Cure Violence neighborhoods occurred more quickly and more steeply than did declines in comparison neighborhoods. In fact, they did in six of seven neighborhoods studied (consistency of result); evidence of a decline in the seventh could not be linked to Cure Violence. This sort of data analysis could only be done credibly by those with substantial statistical expertise. Overall, the evaluators concluded, the program areas grew noticeably safer in six of the seven sites (Skogan et al., ES-17).

Two basic strategies test or control for the effects of confounding, or "third" variables (that is, variables other than system design change): experimental design and statistical controls in the analysis of any quantitative data that the research may generate:

- *Experimental design* provides the most straightforward method (*see* Rossi et al., 1999:279-306; Torgerson et al., 2010). It requires the random assignment of eligible (either by mandate or volunteer) cases to be handled by the dispute system or by an alternative or no process. Random or chance assignment presumably makes essentially equal the experimental group receiving service and the control group that does not, thus making unlikely the possibility that confounding variables explain any differences in outcomes between the two groups. Of course, the suggestion of random assignment may seem politically unwise for the administrator who wants to defend use of resources for the "most appropriate" cases.[7] However, absent random assignment, skeptics can attribute differences in result to such factors as self-selection (those most likely to settle are picked for or themselves choose the designed process). Researchers will typically be satisfied with a lower number of cases in the groups studied if an experimental design has been used, because they are less pressed to account for other reasons for the results they see. The lower case numbers could reduce research expenses and leave fewer evaluators underfoot.
- *Statistical controls* provide some help with causal inference when, as in most instances, experimental design has not been employed (Babbie, 2010:449-465). To use those statistical controls requires, however, both the collection of additional data (for example, on individual characteristics of program users or of organizations deploying the dispute system design) and some level of statistical sophistication in multivariate analysis. Such analysis

---

7. Experimentation also may face legal hurdles. *See generally* Walker, 1988:77-81.

techniques (multiple regression, for example) permit the analyst to test the relationship of some variables (voluntary versus mandated participation) with others (perceived fairness of process) while holding all other measured variables constant (for example, age, gender, employment status). These statistical methods aid interpretation of outcome data and can help with causal inference, especially when the data include comparable cases that were not part of the dispute system design. These might be similar cases or disputes that occurred prior to the new design or ones occurring in roughly comparable settings not covered by the design. Cure Violence evaluators used multivariate techniques to help contrast program neighborhoods with others not using the program in a non-experimental setting. Using statistical controls makes it advantageous to study larger numbers of people or groups because it increases the likelihood of finding differences not statistically attributable to chance between those affected by the new system design and those not experiencing it (*see* Babbie, 2010:207).

As noted earlier, causal inference was a big issue for the Cure Violence evaluation. Although shootings and homicides appeared to have declined in Cure Violence areas, they were declining all over Chicago over a period of two decades. Clearly, there were forces at work other than Cure Violence. How could you tell whether the program "added value"—that is, accelerated a decline already occurring? This "added value" question is a central one for all designers to consider, using whatever data they are able to collect, even if neither experimental design nor statistical controls are feasible.

3. Using statistics to analyze and present data

Statistics can help summarize and communicate some of the information that you have collected (*see generally* Newcomer and Conger, 2010). Some statistics are descriptive and others are inferential. Descriptive statistics include percentages, means and medians, cross-tabulations and correlations (measures of relationships between variables); they provide summary "descriptions" of the data collected and of relationships within those data (Babbie, 2010:467-476). More complex multivariate techniques such as regression analyses can help "control" for the effects of several variables at once, thus helping to eliminate (or confirm) alternative plausible explanations for findings, as discussed in the section above on causal inference. Such techniques can also help designers test the possibility that the design affects individuals or groups differently. Thus, eBay could assess whether its online dispute resolution system was used differently in Japan and the United States by statistically controlling for country when looking at evidence on reactivation rates.

Inferential statistics help the data analyst project from the data collected to the larger population from which a sample was taken (Babbie, 2010:476-488). These statistics thus provide guidance about levels of confidence in the generalizability of the data from the sample to the whole population. Typically, these statistics assume random sampling, an assumption that often cannot be met. If data are collected about an entire population, of course, inferential statistics are not necessary.

For many purposes, the careful use of *descriptive statistics* will be most important in summarizing quantitative data. Visual representations of those data are likely to communicate information more effectively to a wider audience. Such representations might include the usual line and bar graphs and pie charts but also the use of maps (as MACRO used to show with dots both the growth in and wide distribution of dispute resolution programs in Maryland at two different points in time—*see* pp. 39-40), timelines, and other visual representations.

Both web resources and introductory statistics texts (for social scientists) can help you with selecting and interpreting appropriate statistical tools (*see, e.g.,* Levin, Fox, and Forde, 2016). Some statistical consultation with graduate students or faculty at your university may help you out as well.

I. WHAT RESOURCES DO YOU NEED TO DO EVALUATION RESEARCH AND WHO SHOULD DO IT?

Outside evaluators—independent or university-based academics, consulting organizations, graduate or professional students engaged in clinical work or community-based research—have the virtue of independence and the credibility that goes with it. They can also bring time, energy, and skills that are not available to those managing a new and evolving dispute management system. Although students and volunteers may provide no- or low-cost assistance, large-scale, professionally done evaluation often carries a large price tag. For example, the evaluation of Cure Violence Chicago was funded by part of a $999,662 grant from the National Institute of Justice and took three years to complete. Academic researchers often work on their own timetables and measure completion time in years rather than weeks. Private consulting firms probably provide the major resource for outside evaluation and deliver their products according to an agreed-upon schedule. How much and what they do will obviously be shaped by resources and time, but helpful small-scale evaluation efforts are common. In any event, outside evaluators need clear guidance and direction about the shape any evaluation takes—the research design, like the system design, should result from collaboration. And they need the system designers who hire them to understand the value of collecting evidence systematically as a way of improving design.

Do-it-yourself data collection may need to be adopted by many designers. Alternatively, an intermediate level can be achieved by the happy coincidence of a designer's need for research and the interest and availability of faculty and/ or students in local law schools, universities, or colleges. These academics might help carry out a low-cost evaluation or provide advice throughout the course of a do-it-yourself evaluation.

But without those resources—or in anticipation of them—you as a designer will want to build the need for data collection into your program design early on and do as much as you can to collect and record information in the context of limited resources. For some organizations with considerable resources, like eBay/PayPal, collection of data is relatively easy and low cost as they monitor the use of their websites and use patterns and regularly send out online surveys to users. For others like Cure Violence, evaluation was much more difficult, in part because each of the sites was separately administered, often by organizations with very limited resources and no professional staff.

Sometimes, as in the case of highly public claims processes like that administered by Ken Feinberg for the families of 9/11 victims, evaluation is ongoing, not systematic, and is carried out quite publicly by outside groups. On the one hand, Feinberg himself measured "success by the percentage of claimants who sign on—a stunning 97 percent in the 9/11 fund, surpassing his initial hope for as much as 90 percent" (Carter, 2011:37). On the other hand, he responded to public evaluations and criticism, for example, about his comment to grief-stricken families that they should file with the 9/11 fund because "it was the only game in town" (Carter, 2011:36). The critical response led him to engage personally with the claims process, to conduct over 900 hearings himself, and to let those hearings become opportunities for emotional release of traumatized families rather than simply evidentiary tests of the dollar amounts of claims (Carter, 2011:36).

MACRO also operates in a political environment, as the request for a report from the legislative committees makes clear. And, anticipating that, MACRO took the initiative to broaden the criteria for evaluation and to provide its own report of evidence about the organization's successes in building a state-wide system of high-quality dispute resolution. Such reports permit the designers to shape their self-presentation but could leave a skeptical outsider wondering about the objectivity of the evaluation. Thus, MACRO has also sought to encourage independent researchers to examine their programs both so that designers can learn from that widened base of evidence and to help satisfy any remaining skeptics about the impact of MACRO's programs.

J. WHEN SHOULD YOU GATHER EVALUATION DATA?

From the beginning. Evaluation of one sort or another—that is, collecting evidence to gauge how the program is doing—can achieve more if it is ongoing, although its formality and focus will shift over time as the dispute system design takes shape and is implemented. Although it is crucial to build in data collection tools from the beginning, it is never too late to get started.

As noted earlier, Howard Gadlin decided that the NIH ombuds program could use outside evaluation once again 12 years after an initial evaluation of a pilot ombuds program had been completed. The ombuds program was well established at NIH and had developed a well-earned reputation as one of the model ombuds programs in the United States. Its ombuds were busy with cases, and word-of-mouth accounts suggested clients were well served. What then could be learned from an evaluation, especially one where there was no budget to support it? Howard Gadlin was not sure, but he was game to learn new things.

National Institutes of Health: Two students in a Harvard Law School clinical course took on the evaluation task on a shoestring budget. Their focus was on the perception and understanding of the work of the ombuds among NIH administrative leaders; perceptions of the ombuds office's reputation and effectiveness and identification of unmet needs among a cross-section of NIH staff; and perceptions of experience among users of ombuds services (Krol and Tomezsko, 2010). Working from a distance, the students relied on telephone interviews with administrative leaders, an online survey of all NIH employees and contractors (34,505 people), and several in-person focus groups with small groups of ombuds office users and non-users who volunteered to participate in response to the earlier online survey.

The results of the data collection generally showed that most users trusted the ombuds, respected their skill, and perceived the ombuds to have treated them with respect and understood their viewpoint. Pie charts in their report show the quantitative findings, and these are supplemented by quotations from interviews and focus groups about the experience of users. These results were reassuring but not unexpected. Less anticipated were a series of other findings from survey and interview data. One finding reflected a central challenge of organizational systems for dispute resolution among employees—the confidentiality of the process and results provided little guidance and information to the vast majority of employees who never use the system. This reflected a more general sense that the ombuds office and its work were relatively unknown. The data also revealed that some potential users feared use of the ombuds because of concerns about "escalation, stigma and retaliation" (Krol and Tomezsko, 2010:19). The student researchers also uncovered perceptions of the organizational structure and culture that they believed exacerbated employee-supervisor conflicts, leading perhaps to insight about organizational change that might prevent conflict.

Managing evaluation in the context of limited resources: Formal data gathering and analysis take time, cost money, and require some level of expertise. Many organizations implementing system change lack one or more of these resources. Data gathering can also impose burdens on overstretched staff or volunteers or require skills they do not have. These burdens are hidden costs of poorly crafted evaluation efforts. They are a major reason why data routinely collected lie unanalyzed in program files. Engaging office or service delivery staff in the research design process can help to avoid these hidden costs and make it more likely that evaluation efforts produce useful information.

It is never easy to find the resources to analyze data regularly gathered, to collect new data (for example, by follow-up interviews with participants or organizational representatives), and to keep records of stories of the work. But some such resources may be more within reach than might be assumed. On occasion, skilled volunteers can do some of this work. Partnerships with colleges or universities can involve talented undergraduate and graduate and law students along with expert faculty as advisors and contributors, adding value both to education and to the dispute system design effort.

In the context of scarce resources, you will likely focus first on collecting the information required by funders or sponsors to document program implementation and success. Data collection is much less difficult and costly to do if planned from the beginning rather than in a catch-up effort after implementation. As you respond to external audiences, remember that funders or decision-makers may define overly narrow criteria of success, as did the Maryland legislature for MACRO. It is in your interest as a designer to widen the evidence collected and provided to document the program for selected external audiences.

This approach may or may not also serve you in monitoring and improving the design, however. Strategic and low-cost evaluation will require that you bootstrap the collection of as much evidence as you can about how the process is going and what effects it is having. The more limited the resources, of course, the more limited the approach to collecting information. Talking with at least a few people (partly structured interviews or even a few focus groups) from stakeholder groups or constituencies in the new system can give you a sense of what is going on and expose you to the unexpected (or unwanted). These are unlikely to be formal, transcribed interviews. However, be self-aware about this data collection and record notes as systematically as you can about what you see and hear. That documentation imposes a degree of discipline on the data collection that provides a modest check on selective memory and inevitable bias.

If you are in a position to do so, design administrative data collection in an automated format that permits easy analysis and a more systematic look at how the system is working. As noted earlier, electronic surveys could efficiently broaden your access to participants. Use follow-up emails to remind people to participate. Interviewing informally or holding one or more focus groups before finalizing the survey will improve your selection of which questions to ask. Walking around to observe can tell a thoughtful designer much about how the design is working. Remember also to find ways to record some of the compelling stories about individuals or organizations affected by the design—perhaps ask staff to tell those stories to volunteers who can record and document them (*see generally* Krueger, 2010).

Ultimately, effective evaluation means doing everything you can given the constraints on resources to answer key questions like those in Section E.1 above.

K. PROGRAM REVIEW AS AN ADDED APPROACH TO EVALUATION

The scores of capable professionals who have been involved in designing and implementing dispute processing systems in different contexts constitute an untapped resource for designers interested in examining the operation and performance of their programs and in gathering ideas for improvement (*see* Averch, 2004). The program or expert review model appears to be untried in conflict management but has a long history in higher education where re-accreditation and program reviews require self-studies, bring in visiting committees of academics from other institutions, and produce extensive, evaluative reports by the outside reviewers. This model could offer low-cost, expert, peer consultation and could help build shared knowledge and understanding in the world of dispute management system design.

Program reviews bring the perspectives of "outsiders" and thus widen significantly the understanding of what is being done and what might be possible and done differently in a dispute management system. They also permit program organizers to see things that they may take for granted—the ways that the particular community or organizational context in which they operate shape and limit the operation of the program and its effectiveness, for example. It is for just these reasons—to break away from insular perspectives—that academic institutions regularly use outside reviewers to evaluate departments and programs.

How might a program review be organized for a pioneering program such as Cure Violence Chicago? It would require the Cure Violence staff to put together a self-study describing program goals, history, budgets, and program operation and to include summaries of whatever data they had collected about their work. In that self-study, the staff might note pressing problems like inconsistent funding streams and attrition of staff. They would identify professionals in other cities engaged with violence prevention work with gangs and in communities along with several social scientists who study such work and invite them to work as a team to review the self-study, observe the program in Chicago or another location, and talk selectively to staff and perhaps to "clients." The review team would then use its collective experience and perspective to evaluate the Cure Violence program, to respond to the questions raised by the self-study, and to make suggestions for program improvement.

Although outside program reviews make use of data collected through evaluations or monitoring, they do not rely exclusively on those data. Rather, they depend heavily on professional community standards and on the experiential knowledge of those doing similar (but not identical) work in other locales. In the world of dispute processing system design, designers are often local pioneers in their community or organization. They can learn much, however, from pioneers in other, parallel contexts and can share their learning with others. Program reviews thus could promise both relatively low-cost consulting and an opportunity to build the knowledge base for dispute processing system design.

THOUGHTS GOING FORWARD

An important part of implementing a design is determining whether or not it runs as planned and has the desired effects—and perhaps some unanticipated effects as well. Systematic and thoughtful collection and analysis of data with the resources you have available will assist you in strengthening the design and help your client or sponsor know whether or not they are achieving their goals. Of course, partnering with a social scientist or law school clinic is preferable for this evaluation process, but often not feasible. That should not stop you from doing the best data gathering and analysis that you can do. Give careful thought to what you will want to learn about and to measure and be ready to collect stories about implementation and how it plays out for those it serves. Rarely will learning about just one or two things be sufficient. The approaches to evaluation described in this chapter may not be easily replicable, but they should remind you of the range of possible outcomes you might look for and some of the varied ways to gather useful information. Remember to start early, before implementation of the new design, so that you have a basis for analysis of the later data. Also, consider a variety of evaluation approaches, including peer reviews.

QUESTIONS

14.1   Your client, the general counsel of a large corporation, asks you to replicate the employee mediation program used by the U.S. Postal Service. "The Postal Service program has been so well evaluated," she says, "can't we just make sure ours has a mediation delivery system just like theirs? Clearly if we did so, we should achieve similar results and thus avoid the need for costly evaluation research. Anyway, we don't have time or money to do that research on our own." How would you respond to the general counsel?

14.2   What should former National Institutes of Health ombuds Howard Gadlin have done with the evaluation evidence collected by the Harvard Law School design students? What might he have gained by having the evaluation done five years earlier? When should the evaluation be done again, and how might it be improved in the next round?

Exercise 14.1   *Evaluating one of Tallahoya University's new designs:* You are now a full-time member of the University's design staff. University counsel sent you this email: "Good news—the Provost has decided to implement a part of your proposal for dealing with off-campus housing disputes. From now on, any landlord who wants to be listed by the University housing office must agree to include a mediation clause in all leases with Tallahoya students. The landlords will agree to mediation by the local small claims court before instituting litigation. (Thanks for letting me know that the pre-filing mediation at the court is free—that was a key piece in making this work.) The Provost says, however, that the landlords will be hopping mad. He's going to ask the Board of Trustees to give him a year to make your approach work, despite the political pressures the landlords will bring to bear to terminate the program. At the end of the year, he would like evidence that the mediation clauses have made a difference somehow."

Think of all the things the University cares about related to off-campus housing. What sorts of data might be collected to gauge the impact of these leases? How would you know whether things are "better" or "worse" with the mediation clauses in place—that is, what is your comparison? What might be the challenges in data collection?

BIBLIOGRAPHY AND REFERENCES

ADAIR, John G. (1984) "The Hawthorne Effect: A Reconsideration of the Methodological Artifact," 69(2) *J. Applied Psychology* 334.

AMERICAN SOCIOLOGICAL ASSOCIATION (2018) *Code of Ethics* (*see especially* Ethical Standards 10 and 11 on Confidentiality and Informed Consent), www.asanet.org/sites/default/files/asa_code_of_ethics-june2018.pdf.

AVERCH, Harry A. (2004) "Using Expert Judgment," in Joseph S. Wholey, Harry P. Hatry, and Kathryn E. Newcomer eds., *Handbook of Practical Program Evaluation* (2d ed.) 292. San Francisco: Jossey-Bass.

BABBIE, Earl (2010) *The Practice of Social Research* (12th ed.). Belmont, CA: Wadsworth.

BELL, Robert M., and Rachel WOHL (2008) *The Impact of the Mediation and Conflict Resolution Office's Work to Advance the Appropriate Use of Alternative Dispute Resolution in the Courts.* Annapolis, MD: Maryland Mediation and Conflict Resolution Office.

BINGHAM, Lisa Blomgren, Cynthia J. HALLBERLIN, Denise A. WALKER, and Won-Tae CHUNG (2009) "Dispute System Design and Justice in Employment Dispute Resolution: Mediation at the Workplace," 14 *Harv. Negot. L. Rev.* 1.

BOOTHMAN, Richard C., Amy C. BLACKWELL, Darrell A. CAMPBELL, Jr., Elaine COMMISKEY, and Susan ANDERSON (2009) "A Better Approach to Medical Malpractice Claims? The University of Michigan Experience," 2 *J. Health & Life Sciences L.* 125.

CARTER, Terry (2011) "The Master of Disaster," 97 *ABA J.* 32 (January).

CURHAN, Jared R., Hillary Anger ELFENBEIN, and Heng XU (2006) "What Do People Value When They Negotiate? Mapping the Domain of Subjective Value in Negotiation," 91 *J. Personality & Soc. Psychol.* 493.

FITZPATRICK, Jody L., James R. SANDERS, and Blaine R. WORTHEN (2010) *Program Evaluation: Alternative Approaches and Practical Guidelines* (4th ed.). Englewood Cliffs, NJ: Prentice-Hall.

HATRY, Harry P. (2004) "Using Agency Records," in Joseph S. Wholey, Harry P. Hatry, and Kathryn E. Newcomer eds., *Handbook of Practical Program Evaluation* (2d ed.) 243. San Francisco: Jossey-Bass.

HOOVER, Kenneth R. (1984) *The Elements of Social Scientific Thinking* (3rd ed.). New York: St. Martin's Press.

KAPLAN, Abraham (1964) *The Conduct of Inquiry: Methodology for Behavioral Science.* San Francisco: Chandler.

KROL, Rachel, and Diana TOMEZSKO (2010) *2010 Evaluation of the Office of the Ombudsman, Center for Cooperative Resolution at the National Institutes of Health.* Cambridge, MA: Harvard Negotiation and Mediation Clinical Program.

KRUEGER, Richard A. (2010) "Using Stories in Program Evaluation," in Joseph S. Wholey, Harry P. Hatry, and Kathryn E. Newcomer eds., *Handbook of Practical Program Evaluation* (3rd ed.) 404. San Francisco: Jossey-Bass.

KRUEGER, Richard A., and Mary Anne CASEY (2010) "Focus Group Interviewing," in Joseph S. Wholey, Harry P. Hatry, and Kathryn E. Newcomer eds., *Handbook of Practical Program Evaluation* (3rd ed.) 378. San Francisco: Jossey-Bass.

LEVIN, Jack, James Alan FOX, and David Forde (2016) *Elementary Statistics in Social Research* (12th ed.). London: Pearson.

LOVE, Arthur (2004) "Implementation Evaluation," in Joseph S. Wholey, Harry P. Hatry, and Kathryn E. Newcomer eds., *Handbook of Practical Program Evaluation* (2d ed.) 69. San Francisco: Jossey-Bass.

MARYLAND MEDIATION AND CONFLICT RESOLUTION OFFICE (2009) *MACRO Progress Report: 10 Years of Achievement, available at* http://www.courts.state.md.us/macro/pdfs/reports/macroprogressreport2009.pdf.

NET PROMOTER, http://www.netpromoter.com/netpromoter_community/index.jspa.

NEWCOMER, Kathryn E., and Dylan CONGER (2010) "Using Statistics in Program Evaluation," in Joseph S. Wholey, Harry P. Hatry, and Kathryn E. Newcomer eds., *Handbook of Practical Program Evaluation* (3rd ed.) 454. San Francisco: Jossey-Bass.

NEWCOMER, Kathryn E., and Timothy TRIPLETT (2010) "Using Surveys," in Joseph S. Wholey, Harry P. Hatry, and Kathryn E. Newcomer eds., *Handbook of Practical Program Evaluation* (3rd ed.) 262. San Francisco: Jossey-Bass.

RABINOVICH-EINY, Orna, and Ethan KATSH (2012) "Technology and the Future of Dispute Systems Design," 17 *Harv. Negot. L. Rev.* 141.

REIMER, Gwen, Amy BOMBAY, Lena ELLSWORTH, Sara FRYER, and Tricia LOGARS (2010) *The Indian Residential Schools Settlement Agreement's Common Experience Payment and Healing: A Qualitative Study Exploring Impacts on Recipients.* Ottawa: Aboriginal Healing Foundation.

ROSSI, Peter H., Mark W. LIPSEY, and Howard E. FREEMAN (2003) *Evaluation: A Systematic Approach* (7th ed.). Thousands Oaks, CA: Sage Publications.

SCHMITZ, Amy J., and Colin RULE (2017) "Lessons Learned from eBay," in Amy Schmitz and Colin Rule, *The New Handshake: Online Dispute Resolution and the Future of Consumer Protection,* Washington, DC: ABA Book Publishing.

SKOGAN, Wesley, Susan M. HARTNETT, Natalie BUMP, and Jill DUBOIS (with the assistance of Ryan Hollon and Danielle Morris) (2008) *Evaluation of CeaseFire-Chicago* (2008). Evanston, IL: Northwestern University, *available at* https://www.ncjrs.gov/pdffiles1/nij/grants/227181.pdf.

TORGERSON, Carole J., David J. TORGERSON, and Celia A. TAYLOR (2010) "Randomized Controlled Trials and Nonrandomized Designs," in Joseph S. Wholey, Harry P. Hatry, and Kathryn E. Newcomer eds., *Handbook of Practical Program Evaluation* (3rd ed.) 144. San Francisco: Jossey-Bass.

WALKER, Laurens (1988) "Perfecting Federal Civil Rules: A Proposal for Restricted Field Experiments," 51 *Law & Contemp. Probs.* 67.

WEISS, Carol H. (1999) *Evaluation* (2d ed.). Englewood Cliffs, NJ: Prentice-Hall.

WEISS, Robert S. (1995) *Learning from Strangers: The Art and Method of Qualitative Interview Studies.* New York: Simon and Schuster.

WHOLEY, Joseph S., Harry P. HATRY, and Kathryn E. NEWCOMER eds. (2010) *Handbook of Practical Program Evaluation* (3rd ed.). San Francisco: Jossey-Bass.

PART FIVE

SKILLS FOR DESIGNERS

CHAPTER 15

Facilitation and Related Skills for Designers

Designers deploy a full range of dispute resolution skills in their work. They negotiate, mediate, and often build systems that include arbitration as one process in the broader system. Appendices B, C, and D of this book offer broad guidance on negotiation, mediation, and arbitration. This chapter focuses on facilitation. Mediation, negotiation, and facilitation skills overlap substantially, although success with each of these processes requires some unique capabilities, and the ways in which the skills are deployed vary based on the person facilitating, process, context, timing, and purpose. Among the component skills required for these processes are active listening; effective interviewing; preparation; creativity; and managing time, resources, and behaviors. Mastering these skills will not make a designer successful, but succeeding without them is unlikely. As Bernard Mayer put it, "What makes a successful peacemaker or conflict resolver is not a set of processes, methodologies or tactics; it is a way of thinking, a set of values, an array of analytical and interpersonal skills, and a clear focus" (Mayer, 2000:ix).

We focus on the steps and skills required for effective facilitation both because they are so essential and because fewer classes build facilitation skills. The text below augments the discussion of focus group facilitation in Chapter 4, though those new to it may want to take advantage of the chapter-end references.

When you have read this chapter, you will have a basic understanding of the steps, skills, and challenges of facilitation. In addition, you will appreciate that being a facilitator encompasses a broad array of component skills that are necessary to being an effective designer. Finally, you will have an awareness of some of the special challenges of facilitation and some tips for addressing those challenges.

A. WHAT AND WHY

A facilitator's primary role is to *assist* or *promote* conversation and exchange among people and groups. Facilitators use their knowledge of group process and their skills for managing groups to design meetings and structures that enable groups to interact effectively and with purpose. At the most general and abstract level, facilitation is the art of enabling conversations to unfold productively by creating conditions that maximize the likelihood that participants can engage fully and authentically with each other. Designers facilitate in countless contexts. These include running focus groups (*see* Chapter 4), dialogue sessions, negotiations, consensus-building processes, or informational meetings, to name just a few examples of designer-as-facilitator.

How designers facilitate depends on their style, the parties' needs, the prevailing climate and customs, the time frame, and the purpose of meeting or interaction that they are planning. For example, a dialogue session comprised of Irish Catholic religious leaders and victims of clergy abuse will require different norms and skills than will an informational session at the National Institutes of Health describing a new resource available to those experiencing workplace conflict. But both examples involve facilitation.

To encourage open exchange, facilitators deploy a variety of tools to build rapport and trust. Active listening and process design are two of those tools. In addition, facilitators often "hold" the space for a group. This entails monitoring participation in a group—encouraging those who tend to be quiet to participate more actively and managing those who may over-participate to self-monitor and make room for other voices and perspectives.

Whether facilitators are planning to moderate a challenging conversation, a negotiation, or an informational session, they should keep in mind a number of considerations before, during, and after a session. We discuss these below.

B. STEPS OF EFFECTIVE FACILITATION

As you work with the multitude of stakeholders in the design process, you will find yourself called upon to facilitate in multiple contexts. It will help you to be aware of key steps in the facilitation process, whatever the setting. But as with system design itself, facilitation is neither formulaic nor linear. The steps we outline below represent a rough sequence, but designers often loop back and re-consider decisions and approaches as they gather new information in their work.

1. Preparation and set-up

Successfully planning and set-up for facilitation requires a myriad of activities for which most people have almost no formal training.

Purpose: In planning to facilitate, the designer must first consider carefully the purpose of any meeting or session. Possible purposes might include:

- To facilitate learning and discussion among individuals with differing but strongly held views. Such meetings are sometimes called dialogues or learning conversations;
- To brainstorm possible solutions to a particular problem or situation;
- To attain a better understanding of a particular context or conflict situation;
- To promote healing and reconciliation among individuals or groups who may feel aggrieved. One type of meeting that is designed to promote healing and reconciliation is called a restorative circle. But there are many other variations and names for these meetings;
- To discuss interests of parties who are considering entering into a transaction;
- To negotiate the terms of a resolution to an ongoing dispute; and
- To decide on a strategy for an upcoming enterprise.

At times, of course, facilitators may not be certain of the purpose of particular meetings until they have spent time interviewing key stakeholders and getting a better assessment of the situation; at other times, the designer will have a good sense of the purpose of a meeting before reaching out to stakeholders. In the former case, designers may need to adjust or modify the purpose of a session as they learn more.

A common pitfall for designers is to say, "Oh, we'll just get some people together in a room and hash things out." This strategy may work at times, but, more often than not, it complicates matters. For example, those who are not centrally involved in decision-making may become frustrated because they were summoned to a meeting with no sense of why they were called or what their roles might be; similarly, stakeholders essential to the implementation of a given procedure may be miffed to learn that three planning meetings had been organized before they were involved. Identifying the purpose for any given session helps ensure that the right people will be invited to the meeting, avoiding the problem of over- or under-inclusion.

Another common pitfall in facilitating is to have too many or conflicting purposes in a single meeting. This might happen when a design team feels rushed to reach decisions or finds it difficult to get all essential players into a room at one time. The temptation to have an ambitious array of purposes in such cases is strong, but experience suggests that inefficient or unsustainable long-term outcomes may result. Even if you accomplish short-term goals, you will find that people resent it if they sense that too many decisions were made without ample input and consideration. Moreover, rushed decision-making often leads to bad decisions that fail to consider the downstream implications of early decisions on the system, organization, or stakeholders.

With a clearly articulated and appropriately defined purpose, however, a designer is in a better place to provide answers to other critically important questions for preparation and planning:

1. Who should be invited?
2. What questions (if any) should be asked of invitees before a session and what information might be provided to them or needed from them?
3. What should the agenda be?
4. What roles should invitees be given, and which roles should be present at the meeting?
5. What is the best forum for the purpose or task I have articulated?
6. If decisions are to be made at this meeting, what should be the decision rule? If the decision rule is already established, how should that affect your agenda and approach?
7. What is required/needed for implementation after the session? What deadlines should be set for various decisions, tasks, and meetings that will follow?

Below we provide some guidance on issues that a designer should consider in responding to these questions as part of a meeting design. A number of books provide additional ideas (*see* Hoffman, 2018; Adams et al., 2007; Parker and Hoffman, 2006; Harvard Business School Press, 2006; Wilkinson, 2004; Lencioni, 2004; Kelsey et al., 2004; Doyle and Straus, 1993; Straus, 1999; Kayser, 1995).

Deciding whom to invite: If you are like most of us, you have had the experience of sitting in a meeting to which you have been invited and wondering to yourself, "Why on earth am I here? Did the organizers think about whether this would be a good use of my time or whether my presence here really mattered?"

Creating an invitation list for a meeting, consensus-building session, or focus group is more an art than a science, as with many design decisions. But there are some general considerations to keep in mind:

First, you should distinguish the question of whom to involve in the overall design process from the question of whom to invite to a particular meeting or brainstorming session. As we indicated earlier, in most cases, designers should seek to engage a broad and representative array of stakeholders in a design process.

With respect to each meeting, however, a designer should be more judicious in thinking about whom to include. For example, if the purpose of a given meeting is to brainstorm possible ways of addressing stakeholder concerns, it may not be wise to invite the senior decision-makers to a meeting. Why? Because of their decision-making authority, senior decision-makers may be reluctant to engage openly in a brainstorming session, as Michael Young's facilitated planning for South Africa illustrated (*see* pp. 147-149). A thoughtful facilitator would do much better by inviting mid-level managers or career diplomats to a brainstorming meeting. No one thinks they have plenary decision-making power so they are more able to engage freely in brainstorming. Because these individuals nonetheless have access to senior decision-makers, they can bring the brainstormed list of ideas back to the key decision-makers for discussion and consideration later, a process so powerfully demonstrated in South Africa.

Similarly, if the purpose of a meeting is to identify standards by which to make a policy decision, it may help to include substantive experts at a meeting. For example, if government and industrial leaders convene to determine a safe level of emissions for a particular substance, the conversation will be more fruitful if the needed epidemiologists and chemists are at the table to provide the relevant information, analyze data, and answer questions.

It may be tempting to include people in a session just so they will hear the discussion, but such a strategy can be risky. Unengaged people tend to dampen the enthusiasm of others or take the conversations off track.

Consulting with stakeholders: Once you have decided on and invited an initial group of participants to a session or meeting, you may consider consulting with them, and other stakeholders, in advance of the session, either through interviews or surveys. Pre-facilitation consultation with stakeholders can help manage participant expectations about your role in the session, the purpose of a particular meeting or process, and what they might reasonably expect as an output or result. It also helps you as facilitator to gather critical information that can assist you with designing the agenda for the meeting or meetings and identifying possible challenges that may arise in the course of those meeting(s).

Some questions you may consider asking stakeholders as part of a pre-session consultation (and depending on the purpose of the facilitation) include:

- What should I know?
- Who is involved?
- What issues are you hoping to address?
- What are the consequences of the current situation?
- Whom do these consequences impact?
- What barriers do you anticipate?
- What have you tried so far?

- How has it worked?
- How do you imagine a facilitator might help?
- What information would you like to have in advance in order to be prepared to participate effectively at the meeting? "Research shows that participant input improves [in facilitated public policy deliberations] when people are given high-quality information that provides context and history, is neutral and objective, and includes all perspectives" (Amsler and Nabatchi, 2016).
- What would be a good outcome of the session in your view?
- What worries/concerns do you have about the session?
- What else would you like to share with me?
- What have I not asked that I should?

In Section C.1 of this chapter, we offer some strategies for how to interview stakeholders as part of a preparation process.

Choosing the forum and setting up the space: Once you have established the purpose of the meeting and identified and invited participants, choose carefully the right kind of meeting type to accomplish this purpose. All too often, designers simply set up the same kind of meeting they have been holding all along. Effective planning requires matching the type of meeting with its purpose. Some common types of meetings include:

- formal plenary meetings,
- formal small groups or breakouts,
- informal consultations/caucuses,
- task-specific working groups,
- unstructured gatherings,
- dialogue sessions,
- focus groups, and
- healing/restorative circles.

Choosing the forum that best fits goals and context will help drive who should be invited and what the ground rules and process norms will be. If a goal is to understand the interests and concerns of stakeholders, there may be an advantage to small group meetings over a large plenary session. Why? Because people may be more reluctant to be candid about their concerns and interests in a large group. On the other hand, if a meeting goal is to build trust among parties, there may be an advantage in gathering all stakeholders at the same meeting and then engaging in activities designed to facilitate trust-building.

Once you have a sense of purpose, size of group, and forum, consider how best to set up the physical space. This includes details such as the arrangement of any chairs and tables, as well as visuals such as flipcharts, possible PowerPoint projection, and any other required materials or technology. Facilitators cannot always choose the space they use or the room architecture that is best suited to their purposes, but advance planning and consultation with stakeholders can increase the likelihood that appropriate space can be identified and booked.

Experience suggests that the room set-up has a big impact on how participants experience a given session. For example, a restorative circle might benefit from a set-up with chairs in a circle without a table whereas small working groups would benefit from pods of chairs arranged in a room with enough distance between each pod so that the groups do not distract each other. Arranging for food and drink can also increase the likelihood that participants will engage constructively during a session, but the how, when, and what will also depend on context.

The diagram below identifies room set-ups that tend to encourage group participation. Contrast these set-ups with a more traditional lecture hall or theater arrangements that tend to inhibit or discourage maximum participation.

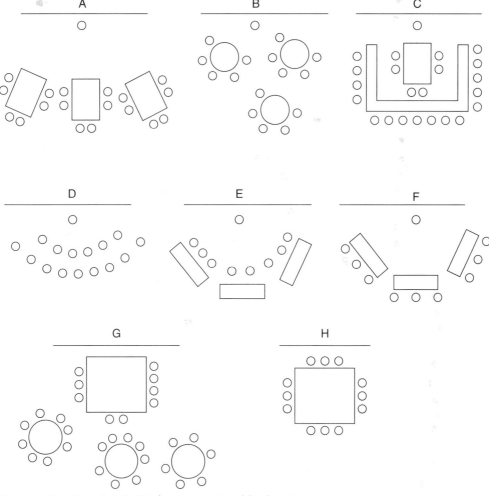

Examples of configurations designed to encourage participation.

Agenda setting: As with so much of dispute systems design, there is no formulaic way to set agendas for meetings. However, effective agenda-setting entails attention to typical component parts of many meetings, to assess whether to include them, and to estimate how long each agenda item might take. A common though non-exhaustive list of agenda items might include:

- welcome and introductions;
- agenda overview and agreement/modification;
- agreement on ground rules or group expectations, including any expectations about confidentiality. Confidentiality norms vary with the purpose of the meeting. For example, opinions collected in a focus group designed to understand community views related to the construction of a new high school need to be shared with decision-makers. In this case, an appropriate confidentiality norm may be that no comment gets attached to any particular participant but that all of the ideas generated will be shared with decision-makers. In a restorative justice session, however, you may set a norm that everything said will be held confidential. Remember that confidentiality norms should be consistent with public meetings or other disclosure requirements set by law (*see* Chapter 7). For example, even in a restorative justice setting, a facilitator might be under obligation to disclose a threat of physical harm to another person.
- identification of issues;
- exploration of issues;
- brainstorming and option development;
- option evaluation;
- generation of norms, criteria, decision-making principles;
- framework agreement; and
- drafting.

You will think of other agenda items. What matters most is that you think through the activities and items you would like to see covered in the meeting and map them out clearly in advance of the meeting.

Circulating a draft agenda of a meeting to participants in advance of a session allows attendees to offer suggestions and modifications when appropriate as well as to prepare adequately for what will be discussed. At times, this preparation might be substantive, such as obtaining the information needed to be useful and informed in a session, and/or talking with internal constituents, supervisors, and colleagues. By distributing an agenda to attendees well in advance of the event and asking attendees to come prepared, a designer contributes both to the efficiency of the facilitated session and the entire design process.

The checklist below represents one approach to systematic preparation that a facilitator might use in preparing for a facilitation.

Facilitation Preparation Checklist

At the end of the meeting, I hope:

- The group will reach agreement.
- Most people will support a particular approach, and others will agree not to oppose.
- The decision-maker will have heard what is needed to make a sound decision.
- People will have become interested in this project and willing to continue involvement.
- I will have a sense of where each person stands.
- The people attending will have a better appreciation of each other.
- Other:

1. This is why a meeting is better than other means to achieve this goal:
2. Persons who should come:
   - Because they are key stakeholders:
   - Because they will be part of implementation:
   - Because they might block the outcome otherwise:
   - Because they have ideas or expertise:
   - Because others will respect the outcome if they support it:
   - For other reasons:
3. Of this group, these persons should be excluded because they are not interested and/or will distract others:
   - Reasonable substitutes for these persons:
5. Will the meeting be open to the media (*see generally* Chapter 7)?
6. How I will deal with the likely group interactions because of:
   - Size:

     (Professor Robert Kelly (quoted in Kayser, 1995:59): "Everyone wants some air time—if only to show how persuasive they can be—and meetings with 10 or more participants tend to digress from their formal agendas and run hours longer than they should.")

   - Power differentials (discussed in Section D.3 below):
   - Desire not to be quoted:
   - Cultural differences:
   - Other group chemistry issues:
   - Inexperienced negotiators who might threaten, etc.:
7. How I will engage each participant and keep that person engaged throughout the meetings:
   - Calls ahead to each person:
   - Meet as they enter the room:
   - Ask each to speak on something related to the topic of the meeting during the first 20 minutes either in the large group or subgroup:

     An Essential Partners manual suggests, "Can you tell us something about your life experience or current situation that will help us understand your views and concerns about _____ [topic of day]" (*available at* https://whatisessential.org/fdad).

   - Note progress:
   - Other strategy:
8. The agenda:
   - What to include in the opening and introductions:
   - When participants should have information before they discuss:
   - When should a common illustration be provided for discussions?

- "Easy" issues to be resolved early to create optimism and deepen engagement:
- How options can be expanded before commitments are encouraged:
- Is the timing realistic?
- What must be done as the meeting ends in terms of next steps:

9. How people should be seated:
   - Will they face each other or a shared board, flipchart, or computer screen?
   - Does the seating strategy enhance informal exchange when facilitating such exchange would be helpful?
   - Have seats been arranged to make it easy to break into subgroups when needed?
   - How will team members, observers, or other representatives be seated?

10. Questions to help bring about closure:
    - How should issues be framed?
    - What are likely barriers to successful result?
    - How might these barriers be overcome?

11. How people should be asked to respond:
    - Will voting cause bitterness among losers?
    - Should people respond anonymously (technology)?
    - Other techniques:

12. What should be confidential and what open?

13. What is the desired tone for the meeting and how should it be achieved?
    - Meal before meeting?
    - Celebrity speaking on importance of meeting task?
    - Expert panel presentation before meeting and dialogue?
    - Other:

14. Ways in which technology may help:
    - Videoconferencing:
    - "Clicker" voting:
    - "Wikis" for single-text drafting:
    - Computer modeling (*see* Chapter 10):
    - Other technology ideas:

15. What could go wrong?

16. Will ground rules or revisions in plans help deal with what could go wrong?

17. What participants should be told in advance of this meeting for:
    - Clarity:
    - Preparation in the substance:
    - Preparation in meeting techniques:
    - Other preparation:

2. Openings and shared norms

As you can see, successful facilitation involves an enormous amount of preparation and planning before the actual meeting, planning session, mediation, or consensus-building event.

Ground rules: Meetings or other events run more smoothly when everyone present shares an understanding of why they are there, what the behavioral norms are, and what your role is as a facilitator.

Facilitators tailor ground rules to the preferences, skills, and values of the group as well as to the topic and purpose of the discussion. They differ as to whether they should develop a list of ground rules in advance of a session and present them to a group for questions and approval or whether the group should develop its own ground rules (Vick, 2015:139). If a group is going to be working over many meetings and has some experience with group process, there could be advantages to having it develop its own ground rules. Doing so will honor the group members' interest in autonomy and increase the likelihood that participants will follow the rules because they created them together.

On the other hand, if the interaction is one-shot or relatively short-term and/or if the participants have less experience with group process, there are advantages to a facilitator suggesting ground rules and then seeking consent of the group. These advantages include promoting efficiency, avoiding the adoption of conflicting or unhelpful group norms, and preventing the possibility that a facilitator might overrule an inappropriate group norm and thus undercut the appearance of neutrality with the group. In at least one ill-fated facilitated dialogue between parties on opposite sides of an emotional and strife-filled conflict, the group-generated list of ground rules included one that said, "No touchy-feely listening" and another norm urged, "Listen with compassion and curiosity." Wanting to avoid favoring one participant over the other, the facilitators awkwardly adopted both ground rules, confusing all engaged in the conversation and undermining the legitimacy of the group norms that had been generated.

When facilitating a challenging dialogue, a list of sample ground rules might include:

- Honor the right of everyone to speak, question, disagree, change their view, be heard, and be treated with respect.
- Speak personally, for yourself as an individual, not as a representative of an organization, identity, or position.
- Avoid assigning intentions, beliefs, or motives to others. (Ask others questions instead of stating untested assumptions about them.)
- Honor each person's right to "pass" if he or she is not ready or willing to speak.
- Allow others to finish before you speak.
- Share "air time."
- Avoid criticism of identifiable individuals.
- Respect all confidentiality or anonymity requests that the group has agreed to honor.
- Stay on the topic.

Discussion of purpose, product, and process: Facilitators should make clear the purpose of a session at its beginning. If there is a product to be delivered or agreed upon at the end, facilitators can make certain that participants realize that at the start of a session. The table on the next page lists some possible products that facilitated groups might create.

POSSIBLE PRODUCTS FROM A FACILITATED SESSION

- Brainstormed list of potential approaches
- A product or program outline
- A binding agreement or resolution
- A list of next steps for the group
- Assigned tasks for individuals in the group
- A timeline for creation or implementation
- A list of agreed-upon principles to govern future decision-making

---

Introductions: Facilitators can decide whether individual introductions of participants would be helpful given the purpose and time constraints of the meeting and the size and composition of the group. In some cases, participants may already know each other, but it may be worthwhile to design an introductory exercise to help the group members build comradery, focus on a shared task, or see each other in a new perspective. In other cases, participants may not know each other at all, but individual introductions would be unproductive or not feasible, as, for example, at a large town hall session.

If you decide that introductions or ice-breakers make sense, consider carefully what you might ask individuals to share. For example, asking each participant to mention titles, roles, or past experience might help provide insight on the perspective individuals bring to the meeting. In some contexts, however, this can be counterproductive, leading people to use titles and roles to claim expertise, power, or leverage in a way that reinforces stereotypes or is counterproductive later. Instead, a facilitator might ask, "What is one hope you have for the group today?" or "What made you decide to participate in today's conversation?" As you consider what prompt you might use, keep in mind the size of the group and the duration of the meeting to ensure that your question is appropriately calibrated. In some cases, you may consider modeling the answer yourself. Doing this helps set appropriate time expectations but also serves as a model for the level of depth and detail you hope others might share.

Explaining role: Finally, clarify your role as a facilitator in a given session. As a designer, your role in many contexts will be to help the group achieve its purpose by managing the process, ensuring progress, attending to deadlines, and keeping the group productive and on task. To this end, in many cases you will remain impartial or neutral with respect to the outcome, but active and involved with regard to the process used in the session.

At other times, however, you may have more of a hybrid role. For example, you may be assisting the group in designing one feature of its dispute management system by offering your professional expertise while also working with the group to help it arrive at the outcome that works best for the group and its needs and values. Imagine, for example, a management team considering the pros and cons of an interest-based approach to decision-making versus a more top-down, command-control approach. You may have views about the best way to move forward, views worth sharing based on what you know about systems design and human psychology.

In some contexts, those involved may ask for your professional advice and/or you may think it appropriate to share even if not asked. In such moments, you will need to balance the challenge of advocating a particular approach with your role as facilitator in creating space for all parties to air their views and for the group to decide on its own. One way of handling such a scenario is to be transparent about taking off your "facilitator hat" and putting on your "expertise hat." You might then offer the group your best advice, linking that counsel to what you understand to be the broader interests of the group. Then you would verbally put your "facilitator hat" back on and give the group space to make its own decision.

Whether you take an entirely neutral approach or a hybrid approach as part-expert/advocate and part-impartial facilitator, be clear up front about the role you expect to play and get approval and buy-in from the group.

Considering decision rules: Not every meeting you facilitate will be organized to make decisions, so whether this step matters will depend on the nature of your session. Sometimes, the rule or process for making a substantive decision (i.e., a decision about the issues being discussed) will differ from the rule of decision for a process choice (i.e., how a meeting will be conducted and how long it might last, for example).

Some common "decision rules" include:

- unanimity,
- broad consensus,
- majority vote,
- giving a "rough sense" of the group's view while vesting authority in a single chairperson or an established decision-making process, and
- compound vote/hybrid.

For meetings where decisions are likely to be made, a facilitator should be clear about the decision rules that will prevail. In some cases, a facilitator may suggest these rules; in other cases, a facilitator may actively involve the stakeholders in jointly determining the decision rule; and in still other situations, the decision rules will already have been made, for example, in organizational by-laws. In all instances, clarifying the decision rule helps you as a facilitator to design the rest of the process and assists group members in understanding what to expect from a meeting.

Decision rules drive substantive outcomes in design contexts. For example, if you are working with officials in a Roman Catholic diocese to establish a system for deciding which parishes to consolidate because of declining church attendance, the local bishop will likely be the sole decision-maker—even though many stakeholders may care about the outcome and many may have formal or informal ways of influencing the decision. On the other hand, if you are assisting physicians in a mid-size medical practice in Santa Fe in their decision about whether and how to negotiate the acquisition of their practice by a larger hospital-owned practice, each individual physician may have an equal vote and the final decision may be made based on majority rule. Even in such a situation, however, stakeholders may decide at the beginning of their meeting that they would prefer to make decisions by consensus, unanimity, or a super-majority. Choices made about the decision rule will affect how you organize and structure your meeting or meetings to ensure that voices get heard as thoroughly and frankly as possible.

Depending on the nature of the meeting, the broader purposes of the design, and the values of those involved in the design process, one can articulate strong arguments on behalf of virtually any decision rule. What matters is that a facilitator should be aware of the pros and the cons of various decision rules and, when asked to suggest or recommend one, can tailor the recommendation carefully to meet the needs and purpose of the group.

3. Managing the process, agenda, and relationships

The bulk of your work as facilitator involves managing the process, agenda, and relationships of the meeting, dialogue, focus-group, or brainstorming session that you are facilitating. The kind and form of questions you will ask and the manner of your engagement will vary depending on the particular kind of session. Accordingly, this section simply offers some considerations that may guide your thinking as you approach the facilitation.

When *managing the process*, your goal will frequently be to empower participants to both speak and to listen. This means you will endeavor to:

- Create space for a wide range of views, approaches, and opinions;
- Check assumptions and work to avoid situations where real differences between the parties do not get adequately raised or discussed in the group. This kind of opinion convergence is sometimes called "groupthink" and, while it can make a facilitated session easier and more harmonious in the moment, the failure to dig deeply and get at underlying assumptions and different reasoning can lead to bad decisions and false consensus that will haunt the parties at a later stage in reaching or implementing an agreement;
- Consider "provoking" participants when variable voices are not expressed;
- Ensure that all views are adequately heard and recognized.

When *managing the agenda*, your goal might be to:

- Help the group accomplish its substantive goals;
- Continue to clarify purpose for each task and connect to overall purpose;
- Ensure everyone has information, materials, and directions needed to complete the task;
- Provide problem-solving approaches to challenges or barriers the group faces;
- Capture critical information for the group;
- Manage time effectively and keep the group on task.

When *managing relationships*, your objectives might be to:

- Help group members maintain good working relationships;
- Uncover and describe underlying interests;
- Address group members' psychological or emotional concerns;
- Reframe issues in mutually agreeable terms;
- Prevent personal attacks.

Developing questions: Facilitators consider carefully the kinds of questions they will ask participants and tailor the type of question to the intended purpose. Broadly speaking, questions from a facilitator will either be *open-ended* or *closed*. Both types are useful at particular moments.

Open-ended questions are questions that do not have "yes" or "no" as an answer. They invite broad and deep inquiry. They can be particularly helpful at the start of a session or to get participants thinking across contexts and in general ways. Questions such as, "How would you . . . ", "Say more about that . . ." or "Why is that?" all invite open and expansive answers (Tippett, 2017:29-30).

Closed questions, on the other hand, typically yield a "yes" or "no" answer or force participants to respond to an "either/or" prompt. As a general rule, they are less useful to facilitators when trying to promote discussion, dig more deeply into an issue, or understand more fully the basis for stakeholders' viewpoints, emotions, or perspectives. However, when a facilitator wants to close a conversation or move on to a new topic, a closed question can signal to the group that you want to move on and give people who feel a strong need to be heard a final chance to add their voice to the discussion. For example, in an effort to ensure all agenda items get covered after a fulsome discussion on a particular topic, you might ask, "Before we move on, are there any last points worth mentioning?" as a way to signal a transition to the group.

Image-building questions represent a third form of question that can be particularly helpful when a facilitator wants to encourage creativity or invite participants to imagine a situation from a perspective different from their own. They are particularly useful to open certain kinds of dialogue sessions or consensus-building facilitations. For example, if you are facilitating a public meeting of citizens expressing views about how to handle conflicts that have arisen over competing uses of a public park in an urban center, you might ask: "Imagine that it is two years from now and that you are a visitor to your cherished park from another state. What would you notice during your visit that would be a sign that the community had succeeded in creating an ideal space for park users?" A question like this transports the focus group outside of its current situation to imagine what a "good outcome" looks like. A follow-up, open-ended question might ask, "What barriers currently exist to achieving this outcome?"

In addition to asking good questions, facilitators manage the relationships between the parties. They accomplish this by *active listening* to participants, a skill we discuss in more detail in Section C.2 of this chapter, and by enforcing the agreed-upon shared norms or ground rules. When helping a group manage its relational space, a designer works to:

- ensure everyone *is* heard;
- ensure everyone *feels* heard;
- clarify what is actually being said (or not said);
- hear behind what may be said (or not said) and push for what may help unexpressed statements, demands, or positions to surface;
- model and encourage productive behavior among participants.

At times, a facilitator may need to reckon with particularly challenging behaviors from participants who are angry, feel unheard, violate ground rules, or seem unreasonable in some way. We address these issues in more detail in Section D.2 of this chapter.

Deadlines: Agenda setting in facilitation involves more than establishing a start and an end time. In many cases, it also involves setting internal deadlines for discussing certain topics and making particular decisions. Experienced facilitators work to establish deadlines as part of the design of their meetings. In setting deadlines, a meeting planner should have a few basic principles in mind:

First, groups work best when they have a tangible short-term goal and deadline, a mid-point goal that seems within reach yet is challenging, and a long-term goal that inspires. Within the course of a particular meeting, then, it can be helpful to set deadlines for ending discussion on certain issues and making decisions when appropriate. But within the course of the broader planning process as well, a designer might consider how to build in short-term objectives, mid-term milestones, and an inspiring longer-term goal (Fisher and Sharp, 1998:53-54).

Second, setting unrealistic deadlines can backfire even though setting deadlines can help and establishing ambitious deadlines can demonstrate an aggressive, hard-working, and can-do spirit. When a designer builds in process deadlines that are nearly impossible to achieve, the likelihood of a bad outcome grows: participants make reckless decisions, constituent stakeholders burn out, or the group persistently misses deadlines. When many deadlines start to fall by the wayside, participants may question the viability of an entire project. Parties may become dispirited and jaded, and the project becomes uncomfortable and could collapse.

The role of the United States in brokering the Northern Ireland peace accords in 1998 demonstrates appropriate attention to timing. The U.S. Special Envoy to the negotiations, former U.S. Senator George Mitchell, had spent enormous amounts of time working with all involved parties, facilitating many conversations, formal and informal. However, at some point in late 1997, it became apparent to Mitchell that both parties were simply dragging the negotiation forward indefinitely in an attempt to extract additional concessions before they agreed to a deal they both knew they would ultimately sign. Aware that imposing a firm but reasonable deadline could actually facilitate agreement, Senator

Mitchell convinced then-U.S. President Bill Clinton to announce publicly a deadline of Good Friday 1998 as the date by which the parties would either reach agreement or have Senator Mitchell and the assistance of a U.S. mediator withdrawn. Because the use of a deadline was carefully considered and appropriately timed, the parties successfully reached agreement on Good Friday 1998 (Curran et al., 2004). The careful facilitator, then, builds realistic deadlines into the process design to assure that decisions get made with both care and efficiency.

4. Providing closure

An important role of facilitators is to bring appropriate closure to whatever kind of meeting or session they run. The ideal form of closure varies depending on the kind of meeting, the context, and the purpose. Closure activities might include:

- *Reviewing decisions that were made:* In some cases, this might include drafting a written agreement to be signed by parties; in others, it might be agreeing to the wording that would appear in meeting minutes; in still others less formality may be appropriate. Reviewing decisions ensures that all present leave the room with a shared understanding of what may have been decided.

- *Reviewing next steps:* Depending on the context, you may want to confirm an action plan; assign specific tasks to particular individuals or groups; and set deadlines, benchmarks, or check-ins for the parties. As you work with a group around next steps, remember that facilitators think critically and in detail about what is needed for implementation. You may also want to build in feedback loops for the parties if a plan is complicated, will take place over time, and involves many stakeholders.

  In some facilitations, stakeholders who are not present may expect an update on what occurred in the session. In such cases, the next steps might entail the drafting of a press release either by a subcommittee of participants with help from the facilitator or by the facilitator and with the approval of the participants. If the drafting is to occur after the session, a facilitator might consider working with the parties to coordinate on joint messaging to constituencies or the public in the interim period between the release of the press release and the end of the meeting. In still other cases, there may be a required public disclosure of outcomes or minutes from a session or a requirement that such information be made available upon formal request. In such cases, of course, the requirement of public disclosure should have been made known to the parties at the beginning of the session, during the discussion on ground rules and confidentiality expectations.

- *Sharing learnings or reflections:* In cases where you have been facilitating a dialogue on a challenging issue, closure might entail inviting participants to share a key lesson, takeaway, insight, or reflection about their experience. You may choose to do this *popcorn style,* allowing participants to speak whenever they choose or, at times, you may think it appropriate to use a *go-around* as a way to bring closure, allowing people to speak in turn, around the room. In either case, you may choose to allow people to "pass" or "opt out" if they prefer not to share.

- *Inviting feedback:* At times, it may be appropriate to bring closure by inviting participants to provide feedback about the session itself. Doing so can benefit you as the facilitator, and it might also benefit others who participated. For example, inviting feedback can be useful in situations where a designer holds a series of focus groups or informational meetings and has the chance to modify and integrate the feedback for future sessions. But even in a situation where you will not be conducting a second session, allowing participants to provide feedback can serve important psychological and emotional needs for participants to be heard and to register their experience of the session.

In short, the kind of closure you bring as a facilitator to a particular experience will vary enormously depending on context, purpose, audience, and timing but makes a meaningful difference in the way stakeholders experience the entire design process.

C. SKILLS FOR EFFECTIVE FACILITATION

The skills required for effective facilitation are too numerous to be addressed in detail in this book. The references in this chapter offer resources to designers who want an in-depth and detailed accounting of these skills. Here we address a few of the most critical skills for effective facilitation. Many of these skills are important not just for facilitation, but for virtually every aspect of design work.

1. Active listening

The most effective facilitators and designers have sharpened their active listening skills. Listening skills help enable you to build trust with stakeholders, elicit tangible and intangible interests, and provide a sense of security to stakeholders that allows them to participate more fully in a design process.

Many imagine themselves to be excellent listeners but experience suggests that most people listen less effectively than is optimal. Active listening is one of the most exhausting and valuable tools in the designer's tool kit.

There are three component parts of active listening:

1. paraphrasing,
2. inquiry, and
3. acknowledging emotion.

Photo courtesy of Divided Community Project, The Ohio State University Moritz College of Law.

Paraphrasing involves reflecting what you heard a speaker say back to the speaker as accurately as you can. It is a critical skill for three reasons: (1) it ensures that you have an accurate and full understanding of another's perspective; (2) it invites the other to expand upon, correct, and supplement your understanding when it is incorrect or incomplete; and (3) it makes the speaker feel heard and understood.

Paraphrasing is best deployed when the speaker talks in long paragraphs and chapters and becomes repetitive. Skillful active listeners sometimes interrupt the speaker to reflect back what they have heard and to provide the speaker with a sense of feeling heard. Paraphrasing is less useful and can be perceived as condescending when it simply repeats verbatim what a speaker utters.

For example, if a speaker remarks, "I am planning on filing a lawsuit," it would not be helpful to follow by saying, "So, you are planning on filing a lawsuit."

But suppose the speaker said, "I am planning on filing a lawsuit. In addition, I want him to know how angry I am, how unfairly he treated me, and how horrible the impact on me has been. His behavior has been simply outrageous. If I would have known what an unethical person he was, I would never have entered into this partnership!" This might be a good opportunity to paraphrase by saying, "So, it sounds as if you are prepared to file a lawsuit. From your perspective it is important for him to know about your anger, the negative impact his behavior has had, and how unfairly treated you feel. Part of what upsets you relates to your experience of him as unethical and the sense that, had you known he would act this way, you would never have entered into the partnership."

It may be tempting to agree with the speaker, perhaps in order to establish rapport. "Wow. That really is awful!" comes quickly to mind as a friendly response. But, a judgmental reaction, even a positive one, may distort future responses and undermine your role as an independent designer or neutral facilitator. A more neutral response might sound like, "For you, this was just a really awful experience."

Inquiry in active listening involves asking non-judgmental, open-ended questions of another, at least at the beginning:

- Help me understand why . . .
- Say a bit more about . . .
- What matters most to you in this situation?
- What would be a good outcome in this matter from your perspective?

In designing a new disputing system for Levi Strauss, for example, interviewers asked employees to give their thoughts about the current disputing system and "what they thought a new system should look like" (Mares-Dixon et al., 1999:1069). When an interviewee is upset about something that happened, public policy mediators Lawrence Susskind and Jennifer Thomas-Larmer suggest "What is the history of the conflict?" as a starting question even though they may know most of the history by the third or fourth interview (1999:112).

Based on the psychological literature, Jennifer Robbennolt and Jean Sternlight point out a number of advantages of beginning with open-ended questions:

> "When conducting the interview, it is useful to begin with open-ended questions rather than questions that can be answered yes or no or that provide only a limited number of options. Open-ended questions allow the interviewee lots of flexibility in providing an answer, giving clients and witnesses the freedom to tell their story in a manner that makes sense to them and encouraging them to tell a more complete story. . . . Another advantage of open-ended questions is that they allow interviewees, and particularly clients to explain their interests and nonlegal concerns. . . . Allowing clients to speak fully in response to open-ended questions may also address clients' desire for procedural justice. . . . Allowing interviewees to tell the story in their own ways, and asking broad questions before narrowing in, will also aid memory" (Robbennolt and Sternlight, 2012:199).

Inquiry in active listening can be deployed whenever someone makes a statement that you find surprising, disconcerting, too general to comprehend, or in some way inconsistent with your understanding. Imagine an NIH scientist commenting to someone on a design team, "The place is hopelessly bureaucratic. It's really hard to work here!" A skillful active listener might respond by saying, "When you talk about the bureaucracy, what are the specific things you have in mind? And tell me more about the ways that you find it hard to work here."

In inquiry mode, a facilitator must be careful not to use questions that suggest a shortcoming of the speaker. For example, a question such as, "Why has your process moved so slowly?" will likely draw a defensive response. More helpful questions invite explanations from the speaker. For example, "Tell me a bit about the process, how you designed it, and how you've experienced the pace so far."

In addition, facilitators must pay careful attention to the tone they use when asking a question. If the tone is argumentative, short, or combative, it is likely to draw a short and argumentative response. Genuine, open questions with a curious and inquisitive tone will yield more expansive and information-filled responses.

Acknowledging emotion is an aspect of active listening that seeks to bring to the surface the underlying feeling(s) hidden in the speaker's words and reflect them back to the speaker as accurately as possible. The purpose of acknowledging emotion is not to agree or disagree with the reasonableness of the speaker's feelings but rather to help the speaker feel heard. By capturing the emotion accurately, an effective active listener often learns more about the interests and concerns of the speaker. More importantly, however, acknowledging emotion often helps the speaker move beyond an emotionally charged moment in a way that builds trust and frees up cognitive space to be a more constructive participant in the design process.

Acknowledging emotion is different from agreement. Suppose a colleague with whom you work greets you one morning by saying, "I just can't figure out why Sandy is unable to finish the project in a timely way again and again! Sandy is maddening!" A good active listener might demonstrate acknowledgment by saying:

- "I can see that this is frustrating to you."
- "It must be disappointing and irritating for you to feel that a colleague in this situation is late on projects frequently."

Acknowledging emotion can be hard, especially when the active listener is the target of the content. Often people resist acknowledging another's feelings because they may disagree or do not believe that the speaker has sufficient justification for feeling a certain way. Suppose the speaker targets you rather than Sandy as the one who is late. In situations like this, an unhelpful response would be to defend yourself: "The only reason why I am late with the project is because I didn't have the support or time I needed to get it done correctly."

Other times people avoid acknowledging emotion because they assume that it is inappropriate or intrusive to bring up feelings in a professional context, and they want to avoid a responsive outburst. In cases like this, it might be tempting for you to move first to problem solving: "Next time I'll get started on the project earlier." While this response is more likely to avoid confrontation, it may be dissatisfying to both listener and speaker. Yet another reason for resisting acknowledging feelings is the concern that doing so looks weak or will be perceived in some way as "touchy-feely." It is important to remember that in acknowledging feelings, the purpose is not to defend, agree, fix, or persuade. It is simply to draw out the emotion in a way that helps other persons express themselves and move to a place where problem solving and an effective discussion about the issues causing the negative emotions might be more possible.

Doug Stone, Bruce Patton, and Sheila Heen (2010:Ch.9) provide additional practical insights on these three component skills of active listening—paraphrasing, inquiry, and acknowledging emotions—that are central skills of effective facilitators.

2. Creativity

The most effective designers are those who can harness the power of creative thinking. The same is true for facilitators—both in their role in designing processes and agendas and in encouraging participants to call upon their own creative skills. Creativity allows a designer to think about a problem in a way that ventures outside the customary approach and thereby generates new or potentially unconventional ways of solving or addressing a problem.

Creativity often involves thinking more expansively about a problem. For example, it might mean reframing the problem, expanding issues, or changing the time frame for decision-making in order to re-orient the way parties are addressing the situation. In many cases, it will mean working with the parties to move beyond positions to underlying interests and then encouraging them to be relentless in coming up with ideas for addressing the interests while putting aside positions.

For example, during the 2017 football season in the United States, some NFL players began to kneel during the singing of the national anthem at the start of games to protest racial discrimination and profiling in police activity and other sectors. Some people, including U.S. President Donald Trump, some team owners, and many fans, saw this protest activity as disrespectful of the flag and/or unpatriotic. Trying to find a "middle ground" between kneeling and standing leaves little room for creativity. But thinking expansively about the dispute—imagining the interests of some players as being to draw attention to historic and ongoing inequalities in the United States based on race, and the interests of another constituency as being to honor the sacrifice that Americans have made to protect and preserve freedoms, imperfect as those freedoms may still be—can open up space for more generative and creative thinking about how to achieve both goals.

Creativity may be spurred by reframing the problem and the way it is analyzed. Reframing enables people to generate solutions that are less conventional and that transform a situation from one of seeming impasse to one with value-creating potential. Earlier in this chapter, we suggested that by using questions that invite participants to conjure up images or imagine themselves in different contexts—perhaps in the past or in the future or in a different role—facilitators could stir creativity in a group of stakeholders.

Of all the skills in this chapter, creativity is the hardest to teach. While it is true that there may be differential natural propensity for creativity, it is nonetheless a skill that individuals can improve. Moreover, choices made by designers in their work can help facilitate or impede creativity in a group setting. Designers can initiate activities and processes to promote conditions that support creative thinking, both their own and others.

The classic creativity exercise is called brainstorming. If it is well executed, brainstorming can involve people with varying intellectual and experiential strengths in the creative process (*see* Menkel-Meadow, 2001:117). Brainstorming is a word used so frequently, however, that the mere suggestion of brainstorming can conjure up thoughts of painful, bureaucratic, and perhaps pointless meetings. Brainstorming often produces far less of value than it might because, in most instances, what individuals describe as brainstorming is not well executed.

Groups engaged in an activity loosely called "brainstorming" make predictable mistakes that set the exercise up for failure or frustration. Chief among these is that someone will suggest brainstorming without articulating clearly the rules to be followed, how long the brainstorming will last, or what will happen next. As a result, it does not take long for ideas to be criticized, evaluated, or picked apart. In short order, the brainstorming ends as parties begin to wrangle over one or two options.

To increase the likelihood that brainstorming will be productive, designers should announce clearly an explicit period for it. They should do this after they have asked individuals to work alone, jotting down their own ideas, as research suggests brainstorming in a group before allowing individuals to come up with ideas on their own can stunt creativity (Markman, 2017). They can also articulate the ground rules for brainstorming instead of assuming that everyone generally knows them. The following rules will help create an environment for productive brainstorming:

1. *Avoid evaluating ideas as they are presented:* It is tempting while brainstorming to evaluate ideas: "Here is why this won't work . . ." or "One problem with that idea is . . . ." Even if the criticisms have merit, this kind of evaluation dampens participation from the group and makes it less likely that someone will share an idea for fear of being judged.

   In some cases, a group avoids negative evaluation, but errs by evaluating positively. If three ideas receive lukewarm acknowledgment or no comment and the fourth gets a "Fantastic idea!," the implicit message is that the first three ideas are in some way inferior to the fourth. In order to keep the ideas coming, it is important to avoid evaluation of *all* ideas, appreciate the value of every idea, and ensure that the ideas are captured in some way—either on flipchart, white board, or projected via a computer and projector.

   An important note: At some point, it is appropriate to assess the viability and quality of ideas created as part of a brainstorming session. But this should be done *after* the brainstorming is over and with reference to the criteria and interests the group has agreed upon for assessment, not at the moment of the ideas' generation.

2. *Avoid attributing ideas to individuals:* When capturing ideas, do not attribute ideas to individual persons by name. Research on the psychological heuristic called *reactive devaluation* suggests that individuals tend to be more critical of ideas that come from people they perceive as opposed to them and more in favor of ideas that come from their side, entirely apart from the merits of the ideas themselves. For example, researchers in the

1980s presented to Stanford University students a plan for the university to divest from South Africa in response to that nation's policy of apartheid. In one version, they told the students that the plan was generated by the Stanford student government. In the second version, the experimenters told students that it had been generated by the Stanford University Board of Trustees. Students who believed that their own student government had generated the plan rated it more favorably than those who believed it had come from the board of trustees. It is helpful in brainstorming, then, to capture all the ideas without attaching specific names or identities to them.

3. *Encourage "crazy" ideas:* In design processes, it is generally valuable to remain pragmatic and realistic about what might be done given institutional constraints, resource limitations, past history, and the like. But when it comes to brainstorming, maximum creativity, regardless of feasibility, should reign. Even if some of the ideas suggested ultimately prove implausible, often these crazy ideas lead to more plausible ones that would not have emerged absent the space to think freely.

4. *Remind participants that there is no commitment expected simply because they suggest an idea:* At times during a brainstorming session, people may generate ideas that they or their constituency might not support. When fearful that simply suggesting an idea implies support, the person says nothing. Failure to capture that idea means failure to capture the derivative ideas that would flow from it. One way to avoid this unhelpful self-censoring is to state this principle up front.

The four brainstorming ground rules listed above seem simple enough. But facilitators find it difficult to implement them. Even seasoned professionals can find themselves stuck in a cycle of evaluation or self-censoring of their own ideas. Constant reminders about the ground rules as well as setting clear time limits on brainstorming can increase the likelihood that participants follow the rules. And when participants do follow the rules, brainstorming can often prove amazingly productive and satisfying.

Brainstorming is just one of many ways to stimulate creative thinking. Jennifer Gerarda Brown offers a host of other techniques to promote creativity (2006). For example, once a person articulates a problem, the facilitator can play with the words expressing the problem in ways that may yield new solutions. This can be done by shifting the emphasis of the words or changing, deleting, or adding a word.

Perspective-taking or role reversal can be a powerful way to spur creativity. At times, people find themselves limited by the "rightness" of their own perspectives. But if they can imagine the world in the shoes of either the other side or simply of others who may not be similarly situated (whether or not they are at the dispute resolution table), they can often start to imagine a host of solutions that address the problem and break the impasse.

Yet another way to stimulate creative thinking is what Fisher and colleagues call the "atlas of approaches" method (Fisher et al., 1996:67). Similar to perspective-taking, this "atlas of approaches" method invites participants to view a

372

problem from the vantage point of professionals in a variety of fields. Using this approach, a facilitator might ask, "What would a doctor do?" or "What would a city planner do?" or "What would the mayor do?" or "What would a psychologist do?" The very act of taking on these different personas forces creative thinking in ways that can yield out-of-the-box proposals (*see also* Menkel-Meadow, 2001:97-98).

Though some groups might resist, using drawing, art, games, improv acting, or sketching can be powerful ways to access creativity and get participants to see problems from new perspectives. Structured activities that draw on these activities can work because they invite participants to leave their world with the ordinary rules of life and enter a different space, with the rules of the activity governing, for a discrete period of bounded time. Replacing one set of "ordinary rules" with a set of "new rules" within the context of the game or activity can provide both the freedom and the structure for creative results (Gray et al., 2006:2).

One of the most powerful ways to encourage creativity is to identify analogous situations, often across different contexts, and then to look to them for patterns and solutions that can be applied to the current problem in the current context. For example, some years ago a major national conservatory was faced with the challenge of persuading some of its top recruits to choose its school over other top-tier music schools. In addition to looking to industry best practices, team members also looked outside their industry: How did sports teams attract top talent? What about investment banks? What strategies might be available that would seem simply out of the box in the tradition-steeped world of classical music?

The literature on creativity suggests how to develop one's own creativity and encourage a group to be creative collectively as well. A starting point for more on creativity is *The Handbook of Creativity* (Robert J. Sternberg ed., 1999).

3. Self-reflection

Like creativity, self-reflection is an important, yet hard-to-teach skill for effective facilitators. Virtually every text on facilitation contains a section on the role of understanding and managing yourself, your triggers, and your strengths, weaknesses, and values as a key component of successful facilitation. It is no surprise that self-awareness and self-reflection matter in facilitation; it is exhausting work, requiring you to manage personalities, substantive issues, and your own emotions and triggers simultaneously.

Below are what two facilitation experts write about this topic:

Wayne J. Vick: "An effective facilitator is someone who:
- "Knows and understands their natural style.
- "Is intimately familiar with their hot buttons.
- "Adapts their behavior to the needs of others and the environment.
- "Has a plan for development and improvement." (Vick, 2015:64).

> *Suzanne Ghais:* "You cannot enhance your strengths if you don't know what they are; you cannot rein in your weaknesses if you do not realize you have them; you aren't going to develop your personal 'brand' if you are unaware of what people already think of you. Knowing yourself is a lifelong endeavor..." (Ghais, 2005:18; *see also* Schuman, 2005:543 on knowing personal values).

A number of practices will help you improve skills of self-reflection. First, when possible, seek feedback from others with an openness and curiosity. Second, you may consider taking one of many personality inventories such as the Thomas-Kilmann Management of Differences Exercise or the Kantor Baseline Instrument, to name a few. Third, you may consider keeping a personal journal where you write about your experience of facilitation shortly after completing a meeting. In this journal you might record what you did that worked well, where you got stuck, what you could have done differently, and why it might be hard or challenging in the moment to enact the advice you provide yourself. Though journal writing requires a personal time commitment, it can be a great and relatively low-cost investment in enhancing your own ability to self-reflect and improve over time.

Finally, while it may not be realistic or possible in many contexts, seeking out opportunities to observe yourself in action can be a valuable way to self-reflect and improve over time. This can perhaps be achieved by scheduling a mock facilitation with colleagues or friends and arranging to be video-recorded. Despite the temptation to be forward-looking, taking the time to cultivate self-reflection as a disciplined part of your practice and professional growth will increase your effectiveness and your confidence as a facilitator over time.

D. SPECIAL CHALLENGES

Successful facilitators plan for surprises as best they can. Like designers, they have a sense of the terrain and their destination while cultivating a nimble adaptability to adjust when they encounter detours in the road. While it would be impossible to cover every challenge a facilitator might face, six common challenges are discussed in the subsections below.

1. Difficult participant behaviors

One of the most challenging aspects of facilitation is handling participants who—whether intentionally or because of lack of skill or both—disrupt the group. Participants exhibiting difficult or challenging behaviors come in many forms. Some may repeatedly break the ground rules by interrupting; others may attack or blame; still others may insist on discussing their desired topic regardless of whether it is relevant. You should recognize that in some cases, difficult or intransigent behavior results from a feeling of not having been heard or listened to.

There are many strategies for dealing with individuals exhibiting these behaviors. Chief among them is excellent and patient active listening. The chart below provides some quick tips for specific situations:

Problem Behavior	Possible Intervention
• Negative comment or accusation: "All of those who think it's OK for kindergarteners to read books about families with two mommies are undermining the notions of family that make this country great."	• Remind the participant of the group norms and ask him to avoid making personal opinions sound as if they are statements of fact, especially when they will seem negative to other participants.
• Someone who is quiet or non-participatory	• Consider checking in with such persons during a break or at a time when others are not around and asking them how they think the process is going. • Depending on their responses, you may consider inviting them to participate more actively.
• Someone who interrupts	• Remind the person who interrupted of the ground rule to let others finish. Then return to the original speaker. After the original speaker is done (or later if there is queue), you may return to the person who interrupted and invite her to make a statement.
• Someone who is making sweeping generalizations: "The managers here never trust us with anything that matters. All they ever do is sweet-talk us."	• Try to focus the discussion on a particular time that this may have happened by saying, "Perhaps you can tell us about a time you experienced being sweet-talked to instead of trusted, so we can understand more fully what you mean."
• Someone who challenges your credibility: "I'm sorry, can you tell us again what experience you have with this topic? You've been working on this issue for three months; we've been here for 20 years."	• Paraphrase his concern, ask him to elaborate or say more about it with specificity, and consider reminding the participants of your role.
• Someone who pontificates or goes off on tangents: "As the only person in the room who has done serious work on child welfare issues, let me tell you how this plays out in the real world . . ."	• Reframe her comment as "her perspective" and open up the room for others' views.

2. The problem of "neutrality"

As discussed earlier in this chapter, there are times when parties will ask you for your expert advice as a designer. The very act of sharing that advice will be perceived by those who disagree with your approach as "taking sides" or "being biased" or as not being "neutral." But even in situations where you are not asked to render an "expert" opinion, the question of what neutrality means as a facilitator and whether it is ever possible is a vexing one.

If you are like most of us, you will have opinions about the substantive issues that are part of your design work; you will also have opinions about the people involved. You will like some stakeholders more than others; feel more sympathetic to some constituent groups than others; and believe that some with whom you work are more reasonable, generous, conscientious, kind, or charismatic than others. Facilitators work hard to be aware of these biases and feelings. Pretending they do not exist is not an effective strategy. Keen self-awareness empowers a facilitator to enact behaviors to avoid the appearance of favoritism of person, constituency, or point of view.

Because complete neutrality may not be possible, one way of reframing your role as a facilitator is to think of yourself as the individual charged with helping create a space where *all* participants feel empowered and enabled to speak and be heard by others. At the same time, you are helping them listen to others whose views may be different from their own. If you conceive of your role as *enabling voice* and *enabling listening*, the "problem of neutrality" may seem less fraught. Indeed, at times—and depending on your style—it might even suggest facilitator transparency as a strategy to encourage more people to speak. For example, in a challenging facilitation about race and voting, your admission that your views reflect your own race and position and might have influenced some decisions about how to design the session could *encourage* people to speak frankly.

In addition to transparency, facilitators practice other strategies in their efforts to retain their credibility and legitimacy as fair process-brokers for the group. For example, when asked for their opinion on a substantive issue, they could turn it back to the group or the individual by saying, "While I appreciate your interest in how I see it, ultimately, the wisdom and views of you and the other stakeholders are what will bring about any resolution, so let me open up your question more broadly to others."

At times, it may be appropriate to address the question of neutrality as part of your opening. In situations where a facilitator is being paid by a single stakeholder, addressing concerns around neutrality up front will be important to your success. Similarly, you might address neutrality questions up front in situations that raise identity questions. For example, the choice of the mayor to facilitate a dialogue between youth of color and police officials may be a red flag for some participants who believe that the mayor is necessarily biased toward the police. Addressing this question explicitly and openly may be a skillful move that allays concerns and creates openness for others to model the behavior you have demonstrated. Alternately, and perhaps preferably, co-facilitating a session such as this with someone who may have legitimacy with the youth of color might address concerns of neutrality.

Finally, as a facilitator, do your best to monitor participation levels and check in with participants at breaks so that any possible concerns about your neutrality can be expressed and addressed as early as possible.

3. Dealing with inherent power differences

In certain situations, facilitators may find themselves facing a hard choice about the appropriateness of facilitating between individuals and groups where there are significant power differentials for fear of replicating those inequalities in the facilitated session. Effective designers are always sensitive to the role that power plays in their work, of course: when employees, supervisors and managers, and union stewards work on designing a grievance mechanism, power is in play. The same is true in any corporate, governmental, academic, or political structure. Good facilitators and designers understand this, but it does not stop them in their work (*see generally* Chapter 2.A).

In some cases, however, the inherent structural power differentials—perhaps because of history, war, economic circumstances, racial discrimination, and more—may be so lopsided that a facilitator needs to consider whether it is wise to bring groups together across these divides for a dialogue. The risk could be great of replicating the same problems within the session as exist in the broader culture or system. However, if a facilitator decides to bring these individuals together, she will often take measures to ensure that the power differential is minimized even while striving to maintain the neutrality discussed above.

A facilitator should think carefully about power imbalances before convening a session. For example, in some conversations on race between white and black Americans, a facilitator might exercise extra vigilance regarding the historical, political, and structural inequities that could affect the way a conversation gets framed and the voices that are heard and validated. In the international context, facilitators who work with Israelis and Palestinians may face similar challenges.

Designers and facilitators are likely to have differing views about whether and how to engage groups and individuals when serious power differentials are in play. As a facilitator, you should be conscious of power dynamics and seek to educate yourself about various ways to address them in the room. For example, you might consider inviting a co-facilitator who identifies with the less powerful constituency to join you in a particular session; or you might design activities that encourage role reversal or that allow for more voices to be heard. One example of this is to use a "pair-and-share" approach to facilitation, in which the facilitator offers a discussion question or prompt to the group and then invites participants to discuss it one on one with representatives from different constituencies with whom they are paired. This increases the likelihood that less powerful voices will get expressed. A facilitator then can invite "report backs" from the pair-and-share where the "reporter" is tasked with sharing all the views expressed in the small dyadic conversation. Finally, as you educate yourself on power dynamics in the room, you will also want to reflect on how decisions you make regarding facilitation in situations of inherent power differentials meshes with your broader personal and professional values.

4. Co-facilitation

As indicated in Section D.3 above, there may be benefits to facilitating a session, group, or meeting in collaboration with another facilitator. Co-facilitation can be advantageous for the group and for the facilitators, but it comes with risks and costs.

Some common advantages of co-facilitation are that it:

- aids in handling difficult situations or behaviors, especially in situations where one facilitator may be triggered or may feel overwhelmed and stuck;
- increases the likelihood that participants will "connect" with or "affiliate" with at least one of the facilitators;
- assists with processing complex information in the room, recording information, and managing an agenda;
- models the kind of open, transparent communication that the facilitators promote within the group itself.

Photo courtesy of Divided Community Project, The Ohio State University Moritz College of Law.

Of course, there are downsides to co-facilitation as well. They include:

- increasing preparation time for facilitators who need to coordinate on approach, style, and roles;
- inviting the possibility of clashes between facilitators, whether related to style, content, or simply competition between them;
- potentially increasing the client's expenses.

As you consider whether to work with a co-facilitator, you will want to ask about the needs of the group as well as what resources and potential facilitators are available.

If you have decided to work with a co-facilitator, whenever possible you should strive to engage someone who will complement your strengths and weaknesses, who will support you in your role, and with whom you can have an open and transparent relationship. At times, however, designers do not have the ability to choose their co-facilitator. For example, if you were working with villagers in Canastra National Park, the stakeholders might insist that a particular village elder or respected member of the community co-facilitate with you. Similarly, if you were working in a major corporation to design a grievance mechanism for workers, the vice president of human resources might designate a senior human resources officer to co-facilitate sessions with you.

Whether you can select your co-facilitator or are charged with working with a designated person, in addition to doing all of the work of facilitation outlined in Section B of this chapter, you should also discuss with your co-facilitator questions such as the following:

- What is your preferred style of facilitation?
- What roles should each of us play? Some ways of dividing roles can include primary/secondary; intervenor/recorder; online/offline; task/relation-ship; intervenor/reaction; or no explicit division of labor (Schwarz, 2007:306-313).
- What is your preferred style of feedback?
- How will we handle any differences that may come up between us in the room?
- How will we handle challenging participant behaviors?

While it is impossible to think through every eventuality, spending time with a co-facilitator in advance of a session discussing these questions will increase the likelihood that your work together will be enjoyable and as seamless as possible.

5. Facilitating conference calls

Conference calls seem likely to continue as a common facilitation method despite rapid changes in technology (*see* Chapter 10). Most of the steps and skills we discussed earlier in this chapter apply with equal force when facilitators moderate a conference call among stakeholders. But the lack of shared physical space simplifies in some ways and complicates in others. Issues such as room set-up and refreshments disappear, while issues such as managing participation, keeping participants engaged and on track, and perceiving and handling tension in the meeting can be more challenging.

When facilitating a conference call, establishing a protocol for who will speak promotes orderly discussion. At the time of this writing, technology such as Zoom, BlueJeans, and Google Hangouts represent just three of several services that assist facilitators in organizing conference meetings. Each of these tools allow participants to "raise their hands" electronically or otherwise signal that they would like to speak. They also allow participants to make comments or ask questions online while a conversation is happening. Finally, these services typically allow multiple participants to appear on screen at the same time, capturing some of the benefits of in-person conversations where facial gestures and eye contact can assist a facilitator in managing group dynamics and energy.

Facilitators will need to develop other ways to manage participation when these tools are not available because of bad or limited internet connectivity. For example, you may ask individuals always to state their name when they begin to speak and you may make more extensive use of "go arounds" that give each participant a chance to comment.

In addition, facilitators of a conference call might ask participants to allow three to five seconds of silence between each comment. Many participants on a conference call will be on "mute" during the call and typically will need a few seconds to unmute their phone before speaking. Setting an expectation of a slower pace of question-and-response can reduce the awkwardness of silence in between comments by setting it as an expectation.

When a facilitator coordinates a "hybrid" meeting where some participants are physically present while others are participating by conference call, those physically present tend to dominate the conversation while those participating by conference become silent listeners. To encourage participation by the absent participants, facilitators running a hybrid meeting can check in repeatedly with them.

Finally, when there is no videoconferencing capability, facilitators lose the benefits of facial gestures, body movements, posture, and eye contact that can provide important information to them as they work. In light of this, facilitators pay extra attention to tone, participation dynamics such as interrupting or speaking over each other, and frequency of participation by stakeholders on a call.

6. Managing internal voices

Facilitating effectively taxes the facilitator emotionally as well as physically. Facilitators manage substance, process, and relationships in real time, often with participants who are distrustful, angry, impatient, and not at their best. Developing a capacity to facilitate effectively requires working on all of the skills we have discussed in this chapter and through other parts of the book. But it also requires managing your own internal voices—the stories you tell about the parties or about yourself to yourself while you are facilitating in the room. If not handled well, these voices can trip you up and make you less effective than you might be. When the progress of a particular meeting, mediation, or consensus-building session stalls, the volume of a facilitator's internal voice tends to rise, making skillful intervention even harder.

Stories about "them": For some moments, contexts, and personalities, facilitators can find themselves telling negative or unhelpful stories about the participants in a meeting. These stories are typically hypotheses about others, but at times the voices become loud enough to make it challenging for the facilitator to be present, in the moment and in the room. Stories about others sound like this:

- "These people are idiots."
- "They are acting so confident of their viewpoint. Why can't they listen?"
- "They are trying to trip me up."
- "They deserve the bad situation in which they find themselves."
- "They think I'm completely awful."
- "They are making no sense at all!"

Stories about self: At other times, a facilitator's internal voice focuses on the self in a way that harms the work at hand. These stories sound like this:

- "I am a fraud."
- "I am incompetent."
- "I am unqualified, too young, too inexperienced, etc."

These stories can, at times, overwhelm, thwart, limit, and distract facilitators from concentrating on the task at hand. Effective facilitators develop strategies to handle these voices when they find them distracting. Some of the prescriptions outlined in Section C.3 on self-reflection can be helpful. In addition, developing a mindfulness practice can also assist in cultivating a sophisticated self-concept that acknowledges one's strengths, weaknesses, and imperfections. In a moment when things are going badly, it may well be because of an error you made, but the error does not make you incompetent; it makes you human. In the moment when you start to see a particular unskillful move as representing or encapsulating your whole identity as a facilitator, being able to take a step back and place it within the broader context of your work and experience can help you regain your balance and focus on being present again.

At moments when internal stories about self or others crop up, consider asking yourself:

- What is triggering these stories?
- What is holding me back from being open and curious about the participants?
- What is holding me back from being compassionate with myself and with others in the room?

- What do I need now to re-center myself and be present with the participants right now and how can I ask for that? (Davidson, 2005:282)

These and other questions for reflection and self-diagnosis can help you get back on track by adding nuance to the relatively simple stories of judgment and attri-bution that cloud your perception. As you develop skills of reflection in your facil-itation practice, you will come upon your own strategies for handling the internal judgments about yourself and others that can keep you from being your best self.

THOUGHTS GOING FORWARD

All designers facilitate. If you are highly skilled, thoughtful, and prepared in facilitation and related skills, you will contribute more to trust, candor, devel-opment of relationships, sense of engagement, surfacing of ideas, and move-ment toward consensus—all central components of taking design initiative, assessing or diagnosing, creating processes, implementing, and evaluating. Like so much of what a designer does, you will become more skilled in facilita-tion over time, especially if you study, observe, practice, reflect, and solicit peer feedback. These skills will also make you a better leader and professional, which in turn will provide more opportunities for you to take design initiative. As you develop professionally as a designer, consider how you may deepen your knowl-edge of facilitation by practicing some of the skills outlined in this chapter and by exploring the topic in more depth through materials in the References that address facilitation from a wide range of perspectives and contexts.

QUESTIONS

15.1   Imagine that a meeting has been called to discuss ways the Catholic Church in Ireland might be able to establish a better system in the future for handling allegations of sexual misconduct. Whom might you want to invite to this meeting? If the Archbishop of Dublin asked to come, what would you do? What would be the advantages or disadvantages of his presence? Fill out the checklist at the end of Section B.1 for this meeting.

15.2   Early in 2010 during the height of the debate over health care reform in the United States, then-U.S.-President Barack Obama organized a one-day "health care summit" and invited congressional leaders from both parties to participate in a dialogue on health care issues that would be broadcast live on C-SPAN (and any other news outlet interested in covering the event). The pur-ported purpose of the summit was to have an honest and open conversation about the proposed health care legislation. Given this purpose, what do you think about the choice of an open, public forum for the President and congres-sional leaders? What other forums might have been more conducive to this purpose? For what purpose might a large, nationally televised town hall con-versation be well suited?

15.3 Imagine that you have been enlisted by the Chaplaincy of Tallahoya University to facilitate a meeting between campus ministers of various religious groups on campus. You expect a broad array of religious groups to be represented, including Jews, Christians of various denominations, Muslims, Buddhists, Hindus, and representatives from the campus humanist society. The topic of the session is "Promoting Tolerance and Respect." You are worried that at least one or two of the campus ministers will be disruptive. One minister, a fundamentalist Christian, has argued in the past that putting other faiths on an equal footing with Christianity promotes relativism and undermines the truth of the Gospel; another minister has argued that the humanist chaplain ought not have a seat at the table since secular humanism is not a religion at all. As a facilitator, what ground rules might you want to establish in advance of this session as a condition for participation? Imagine that all parties agree to them but that during the session one of the chaplains continually interrupts others and insists that they are living in a Judeo-Christian country and that people of other faiths should conform to Judeo-Christian precepts. How might you intervene to ensure a safe and productive conversation?

15.4 Encouraging genuine creativity is challenging for designers even when relationships between parties are strong. When conflict is rampant, however, and conditions tense, creating an environment conducive to creativity is even more challenging. Imagine a conflict situation—perhaps a strike situation or hostage taking—where emotions run high, tempers flare, and time is short. What are the special barriers you would face as a designer trying to encourage creativity in such a situation? What might you do to transform the situation from one that seems zero-sum and ready to boil over into a more productive opportunity for creativity?

15.5 Imagine you have been hired by the CEO of a fast-growing tech company to design a curriculum to help bridge the communication gap between millennials and other older workers who are employed at the company. The CEO has insisted that she co-facilitate with you a brainstorming session with her direct reports, the senior management team. What concerns might you have about this? What might you say to her in preparation? What measures could you take to increase the likelihood that all who are participating will feel empowered to speak and be heard?

15.6 In October 2017, NFL owners, players, and league executives met to discuss the fallout from the decision of some NFL players to kneel during the national anthem. Despite NFL Commissioner Roger Goodell's request to "make sure we keep this confidential," The New York Times obtained an audio recording of the three-hour meeting and published a report found at https://www.nytimes.com/2018/04/25/sports/nfl-owners-kaepernick.html. Read the article and imagine that you had been hired to facilitate this meeting. Based on the information in this chapter, what predictable problems occurred in this meeting that a facilitator might have anticipated? What design features, ground rules, or interventions might you have made to reduce the occurrence of these problems or to address them as they arose?

REFERENCES

ADAMS, Tammy, Janet A. MEANS, and Michael SPIVEY (2007) *The Project Meeting Facilitator: Facilitation Skills to Make the Most of Project Meetings*. San Francisco: Jossey-Bass.

AMSLER, Lisa Blomgren, and Tina NABATCHI (2016) "Public Engagements and Decision-Making: Moving Minnesota Forward to Dialogue and Deliberation," 42 *Mitchell Hamline L. Rev.* 1629.

BALZ, Dan (2010) "In Health-Care Debate, a Great Divide over Style and Substance," *Washington Post*, February 28, p. A02.

BELSON, Ken, and Mark LEIBOVICH (2018) "Inside the Confidential N.F.L. Meeting to Discuss National Anthem Protests," *New York Times*, April 25, p. A1.

BENS, Ingrid (2017) *Facilitating with Ease!: Core Skills for Facilitators, Team Leaders and Members, Managers, Consultants, and Trainers*. Hoboken, NJ: John Wiley & Sons.

BINDER, David A., Paul BERGMAN, Susan C. PRICE, and Paul R. TREMBLAY (2004) *Lawyers as Counselors: A Client-Centered Approach*. St Paul, MN: Thomson West.

BORDONE, Robert C. (2018) "Building Conflict Resilience: It's Not Just About Problem-Solving," 2018 *J. Disp. Resol.* 65.

BROOKS, David (2010) "Not as Dull as Expected!," *The New York Times*, February 26, p. 27.

BROWN, Jennifer Gerarda (2006) "Creativity and Problem-Solving," in Andrea Kupfer Schneider and Christopher Honeyman eds., *The Negotiator's Field Book: The Desk Reference for the Experienced Negotiator* 407. Washington, DC: ABA, Section of Dispute Resolution.

BURNS, Robert (2010) "Mideast Peace Talks Round Ends with No Deal; Palestinians Launch Mortars, Israelis Drop Bombs," *Associated Press Newswires*, Sept. 15.

CARPENTER, Susan L, and W.J.D. KENNEDY (2001) *Managing Public Disputes: A Practical Guide for Government, Business, and Citizens' Groups*. San Francisco: Jossey-Bass.

COSTANTINO, Cathy, and Christina Sickles MERCHANT (1996) *Designing Conflict Management Systems*. San Francisco: Jossey-Bass.

CURRAN, Daniel, James K. SEBENIUS, and Michael WATKINS (2004) "Two Paths to Peace: Contrasting George Mitchell in Northern Ireland with Richard Holbrooke in Bosnia-Herzegovina," 20 *Negot. J.* 513.

DAVIDSON, Anne (2005) "Finding Your Voice," in Roger Schwarz, Anne Davidson, Peg Carlson, and Sue McKinney eds., *The Skilled Facilitator Fieldbook: Tips, Tools, and Tested Methods for Consultants, Facilitators, Managers, Trainers, and Coaches*, 279. San Francisco: Jossey-Bass

DOYLE, Michael, and David STRAUS (1993) *How to Make Meetings Work!* New York: Berkley Books.

FISHER, Roger, and Alan SHARP (1998) *Getting It Done: How to Lead When You're Not in Charge*. New York: Harper Business.

FISHER, Roger, Elizabeth KOPELMAN, and Andrea Kupfer SCHNEIDER (1996) *Beyond Machiavelli: Tools for Coping with Conflict*. New York: Penguin Books.

FISHER, Roger, and Daniel SHAPIRO (2005) *Beyond Reason: Using Emotions as You Negotiate*. New York: Penguin Books.

FRENKEL, Douglas N., and James H. STARK (2009) *The Practice of Mediation*. New York: Wolters Kluwer.

GEARAN, Anne (2010) "Analysis: Obama Seeking Elusive Diplomatic Prize—Deal to End Decades of Mideast Conflict," *Associated Press Newswires*, August 21.

GHAIS, Suzanne (2005) *Extreme Facilitation: Guiding Groups Through Controversy and Complexity*. San Francisco: Jossey-Bass.

GRAY, Dave, Sunni BROWN, and James MACANUFO (2010) *Gamestorming: A Playbook for Innovators*. Sebastopol, CA: O'Reilly Media, Inc.

HARVARD BUSINESS SCHOOL PRESS (2006) *Running Meetings: Expert Solutions to Everyday Challenges*. Cambridge, MA: Harvard Business School Publications.

HERZIG, Maggie, and Laura CHASIN (2006) *Fostering Dialogue Across Divides: A Nuts and Bolts Guide from the Public Conversations Project*. Watertown, MA: Public Conversations Project.

HOFFMAN, Kevin M. (2018) *Meeting Design: For Managers, Makers, and Everyone*. Brooklyn, NY: Two Waves Books.

HOLLINS, Caprice, and Ilsa GOWAN (2015) *Diversity, Equity, and Inclusion: Strategies for Facilitating Conversations on Race*. London: Rowman & Littlefield.

KANTOR, David (2012) *Reading the Room: Group Dynamics for Coaches and Leaders*. San Francisco: John Wiley & Sons.

KAYSER, Thomas A. (1995) *Mining Group Gold: How to Cash in on the Collaborative Brain Power of a Group* (2d ed.). New York: McGraw-Hill.

KELSEY, Dee, Pam PLUMB, and Beth BRAGANCA (2004) *Great Meetings! Great Results*. Portland, ME: Great Meetings.

KESSLER, Glenn (2010) "Obama: Mideast Talks May Focus First on Border," *Washington Post*, Sept. 11, p. A09.

KILLERMAN, Sam, and Meg BOLGER (2016) *Unlocking the Magic of Facilitation: 11 Key Concepts You Didn't Know You Didn't Know*. Austin, TX: Impetus Books.

LANDLER, Mark, and Ethan BRONNER (2010) "U.S. Believes Arab States Won't Scuttle Mideast Talks," *New York Times*, Oct. 8, p. 4.

LENCIONI, Patrick (2004) *Death by Meeting: A Leadership Fable—About Solving the Most Painful Problem in Business*. San Francisco: Jossey-Bass.

LISNEK, Paul Michael (1992) *Effective Client Communication: A Lawyer's Handbook for Interviewing and Counseling*. St. Paul, MN: West.

MARES-DIXON, Judy, Julie A. McKAY, and Scott PEPPET (1999) "Building Consensus for Change Within a Major Corporation: The Case of Levi Strauss & Co.," in Lawrence Susskind, Sarah McKearnan, and Jennifer Thomas-Larmer eds., *The Consensus Building Handbook* 1065. Thousand Oaks, CA: Sage Publications.

MARKMAN, Art (2017) "Your Team Is Brainstorming All Wrong," *Harv. Bus. Rev.*, https://hbr.org/2017/05/your-team-is-brainstorming-all-wrong.

MAYER, Bernard (2000) *The Dynamics of Conflict Resolution: A Practitioner's Guide*. San Francisco: Jossey-Bass.

MENKEL-MEADOW, Carrie (2001) "Aha? Is Creativity Possible in Legal Problem Solving and Teachable in Legal Education?," 6 *Harv. Negot. L. Rev.* 97.

NELSON, Jo (2003) "Facilitation: A Tool for Evoking and Creating Wisdom," 19 *Interspectives* 12.

PARKER, Glenn M., and Robert HOFFMAN (2006) *Meeting Excellence: 33 Tools to Lead Meetings That Get Results*. San Francisco: Jossey-Bass.

ROBBENNOLT, Jennifer K., and Jean R. STERNLIGHT (2012) *Psychology for Lawyers: Understanding the Human Factors in Negotiation, Litigation, and Decision Making*. Chicago: ABA Publishing.

RUETE, Edward S. (2000) "Facilitation 101," in *Proceedings of the 6th Annual IAF Conference: Toronto 2000*. St. Paul, MN: International Association of Facilitators.

SCHIRCH, Lisa, and David CAMPT (2007) *The Little Book of Dialogue for Difficult Subjects: A Practical, Hands-On Guide*. New York, NY: Good Books.

SCHUMAN, Sandy ed. (2005) *The IAF Handbook of Group Facilitation: Best Practices from the Leading Organization in Facilitation*. San Francisco: Jossey-Bass.

SCHWARZ, Roger (2007) *The Skilled Facilitator: A Comprehensive Resource for Consultants, Facilitators, Coaches and Trainers* (3rd ed.). San Francisco: Jossey-Bass.

SCHWARZ, Roger, Anne DAVIDSON, Peg CARLSON, and Sue MCKINNEY (2005) *The Skilled Facilitator Fieldbook: Tips, Tools, and Tested Methods for Consultants, Facilitators, Managers, Trainers, and Coaches*. San Francisco: Jossey-Bass.

SEBENIUS, James K. (2001) "To Hell with the Future, Let's Get on with the Past: George Mitchell in Northern Ireland," *Harvard Business School Case 9-801-393*. Boston: Harvard Business School Publishing.

SHAFFER, Thomas L., and James R. ELKINS (2005) *Legal Interviewing and Counseling.* St. Paul, MN: Thomson West.

STERNBERG, Robert J. ed. (1999) *Handbook of Creativity.* New York: Cambridge University Press.

STONE, Doug, Bruce PATTON, and Sheila HEEN (2010) *Difficult Conversations: How to Discuss What Matters Most.* New York: Penguin Books.

STRAUS, David A. (1999) "Managing Meetings to Build Consensus," in Lawrence Susskind, Sarah McKearnan, and Jennifer Thomas-Larmer eds., *The Consensus Building Handbook* 287. Thousand Oaks, CA: Sage Publications.

SUSSKIND, Lawrence, and Jennifer THOMAS-LARMER (1999) "Conducting a Conflict Assessment," in Lawrence Susskind, Sarah McKearnan, and Jennifer Thomas-Larmer eds., *The Consensus Building Handbook* 99. Thousand Oaks, CA: Sage Publications.

TIPPETT, Krista (2017) *Becoming Wise: An Inquiry into the Mystery and Art of Living.* New York: Penguin Books.

TUECKE, Patricia (2005) "The Architecture of Participation," in Sandy Schulman ed., *The IAF Handbook of Group Facilitation: Best Practices from the Leading Organization in Facilitation.* San Francisco: Jossey-Bass.

VICK, Wayne J. (2015) *Process-Based Facilitation: Facilitating for Meeting Leaders, Constituents, and Group Facilitators.* Bloomington, IN: iUniverse.

WALL, Victor D., Jr., and Marcia L. DEWHIRST (1991) "Mediator Gender: Communication Differences in Resolved and Unresolved Mediations," 9 *Conflict Resol. Q.* 63.

WANGSNESS, Lisa, and Susan MILLIGAN (2010) "Health Care Summit Underscores Divisions; Democrats Lay Path to Pass Bill in Majority Vote," *Boston Globe,* Feb. 26, p. A1.

WILKINSON, Michael (2004) *The Secrets of Facilitation: The S.M.A.R.T. Guide to Getting Results with Groups.* San Francisco: Jossey-Bass.

WONG, Paul T.P. (2005) "Creating a Positive Participatory Climate: A Meaning-Centered Counseling Perspective," in Sandy Schuman ed., *The IAF Handbook of Group Facilitation: Best Practices from the Leading Organization in Facilitation* 186. San Francisco: Jossey-Bass.

APPENDIX A: DESIGNERS' STORIES

Recognizing that some of you wonder how to make use of your design expertise, we asked several people who have made a difference with their expertise to chronicle that for you.

Diego Faleck

"Late Justice is not Justice, but manifest injustice," wrote Ruy Barbosa de Oliveira (1849-1923), perhaps the most prominent jurist and statesman in the history of Brazil. I was struck by these words during my first year of law school in São Paulo. They haunted me during my years of litigation practice, and were ever-present in 2007, in the aftermath of the largest aircraft accident in the history of Latin America.

On July 17, 2007, TAM airlines Flight 3054 lost control and crashed into a building in the heart of São Paulo, killing 199 people. In an instant, hundreds of potential lawsuits were created.

In Brazil, the process of providing compensation and relief to the beneficiaries of victims of mass disasters typically resembles a long, painful crusade. Lawsuits for compensation of this kind last an average of 14 years. I knew there had to be a better way. And, in fact, I'd caught more than just a glimpse of it the year before, when I was a student at Harvard Law School.

Professor Robert Bordone and Professor Emeritus Frank E.A. Sander's Dispute Systems Design class helped me to see that a hard-headed, yet creative approach to lawyering could help transform seemingly intractable problems, giving people better, more just outcomes in a shorter period, with more stake-holder participation.

When the TAM plane crashed, I had been working as chief of staff at the Secretariat of Economic Law of the Ministry of Justice for three months. I was determined that DSD could be used to advance the interests of the families of those who lost their lives and to avoid the enormous costs that would have been borne by the already taxed Brazilian court system. I took it upon myself to propose an unprecedented compensation strategy for the beneficiaries of the victims. It took some persuading; the project involved many political risks. For one, the government would have to face the awkward discussion about the price we put on human life and the inadequacy of our compensation system. But the possible benefits outweighed the risks. I was given the go-ahead and began the next step, persuading stakeholders to design and participate in a sophisticated alternative dispute resolution system for the resolution of claims.

There, too, I was met with substantial skepticism and resistance. The airline and insurance companies were unwilling to try a new approach on an accident of such magnitude. Some attacked me for being overly academic. Companies that had supported the idea at first then rejected it completely. Many family members continued to distrust the airline. After nine months of negotiation over the design of the system, the beneficiaries of 80 victims decided to pursue their claims in court, rather than through ADR.

But I persisted, and the "Câmara de Indenização 3054"—the first-ever Brazilian claims resolution facility—was opened on April 24, 2008. It featured an assistance division, staffed by people hired and trained by me to assist the beneficiaries in filing their claims. Neutral representatives were present at every meeting the family members had with the companies. We also created an advisory arbitration committee, in which the public authorities would issue non-binding opinions to help the parties resolve their disputes. This reduced the distrust and unrealistic expectations among the beneficiaries, while protecting them from eventual opportunistic offers from the airline and insurance companies. One year after we opened the facility, 200 people—the beneficiaries of around 55 victims—were compensated. We also assisted the beneficiaries in litigation, leading 90 percent of them to settle.

The new system has received much attention and is widely viewed as a success. Legal counsel for both the airline and the insurance company said that they spent less on legal fees and more on compensating families than they would have under the old model, solving the problem as a whole with fewer costs. Family members reported that the system's transparency and impartiality helped them get through their ordeals with more tranquility.

It was then that a second airplane went down on May 31, 2009, Air France Flight 447, heading from Rio de Janeiro, Brazil, to Paris, France, leaving 228 victims from 32 different nationalities. This time, having had a strong precedent, full political support and higher education and motivation within stakeholders,

I was able to design and put to work a new system, the PI 447 (Programa de Indenização 447) by December 2009.

The system was very similar to the CI 3054, with few improvements and a track A and B for different types of cases. The case had different stakeholders and a smaller scope, since it was available only for the beneficiaries of the Brazilian victims. The system compensated over 80 beneficiaries of 20 Brazilian victims within two years of the accident. It is also viewed as a success in the country. Representatives from the insurers stated that Brazil was the country where disputes were by far handled with more tranquility and family members appreciated the support of a protected environment with neutral assistance to resolve their matters.

CI 3054 and PI 447 are milestones in the development of DSD, negotiation and ADR in Brazil. They offer real-life examples of how it is possible to fix complex problems by changing the way you think about and practice law. The case has drawn the attention of the Brazilian government and academics for research of possible applications of DSD in different scenarios and the inclusion of ADR in legislative bills.

In January 2011, I left my position in the government, then as Interim Secretary of Economic Law, and decided to open my own settlement counsel, mediation and disputes systems design practice, perhaps the one and only in the country at the time. This was, I thought, another leap of faith. Fortunately, it has quickly turned out to be an extremely exciting venture.

I always had the impression that the country—and the world—was thirsty for more efficient and humane ways to deal with their disputes. I always believed that dispute systems designers could find work, were they determined to get problems solved and to persuade stakeholders to keep talks alive and engage on resolution processes, while figuring out creative and thoughtful ways to organize ideas, procedures and resources to deal with their disputes. I always knew that, among the apparent old school hard-bargainers in the market, there are plenty of players with open minds and hearts for participating and being educated in innovative methods of dispute resolution. I was not wrong!

My first case there regarded a multi-party mediation and process design for a complex international dispute in the reinsurance market, involving a Brazilian steel-maker company, a local insurer and reinsurer, and over 30 foreign reinsurers, regarding a US $700 million claim. At a first glance, the case seemed insoluble. One could find there almost all kinds of textbook barriers a case could feature. It took some effort and time and the case was successfully settled, to everyone's surprise. It is considered by many in the market as one of the most complex cases in the history of Brazilian reinsurance.

From there on, year after year, the problem-solving practice has grown tremendously. I have been mediating a wide range of complex national and international commercial cases, on reinsurance, energy, construction, contractual and partnership disputes. I have also been working on interesting settlement counsel projects, mostly in the field of oil and gas and steel-making.

But most of the excitement still comes from the DSD cases. In the beginning of 2013, I was retained by the Colombian telecom Regulator for the design of a dispute resolution system for government-supported, interest-based channels to resolve claims between users and operators, with the use of mediation and online mechanisms. The project comprised consensus building among stakeholders—telecom operators, government offices, association of consumer protection—followed by a pilot project and external evaluation. The project was considered to be very successful and will be used as a basis for new regulation in the sector. I did it by the book . . . By this book!

And yet, my greatest DSD challenge was still to come, on early 2016. Mostly due to the success of the airline cases, I was retained for the design of a dispute resolution system for victim's compensation due to the largest environmental disaster in the history of Brazil—appointed by the Foundation created to implement remedial programs, with government supervision and support. The DNA of the system is pretty similar to the CI 3054 and PI 447, but the dimension and complexity of the case is of a much greater proportion. The program is designed for compensation of over 20,000 families for general damages (e.g. fishing, sand extraction, agriculture, tourism, damages to property and small business) and 450,000 beneficiaries for specific moral damages due to lack of water supply. After designing the system collaboratively with relevant stakeholders, I am serving as the chief mediator in the project and currently supervise a staff of 60 full time mediators. The work comprises mediations between communities and representatives of associations and the Foundation, to determine compensation criteria and also individual mediations for compensation.

It is very interesting to see the fast-paced evolution of DSD and ADR in the past 10 years in Brazil. One case led to another, adding on in complexity and size. After concluding my first DSD initiative, nearly 10 years ago, I craved that the effort would not end there. I hoped to inspire others and make sure that timely justice, true justice in the words of our statesman, was seen more often in the country.

Now, seeing how things have developed, I am overwhelmingly optimistic and enthusiastic about the future of DSD and ADR, not only in Brazil, but in many other places in the world. No matter how big, difficult, or daring the case I am working on is, I am now sure there will always be a new challenge ahead. I can only continue to envision plenty of opportunities and potential new cases for a problem-solving and DSD initiative to step up the cause of justice and improve the ways by which people and organizations resolve their disputes.

Since 2009, I have also been involved in academic work regarding negotiation, mediation and DSD. I have taught and trained students and coworkers and written a few seminal articles and a Ph.D. thesis introducing DSD in Brazil.

Indeed, there is no such thing yet as a clear map for becoming a dispute systems designer, and the footsteps left might be quite diverse. I believe, though, there are a few key lessons I have learned that have been helping me cut through this green field, that I usually like to share with my colleagues. They are: (i) it is possible to solve seemingly intractable problems with a thoughtful and creative approach; (ii) participation is key to success: share control; (iii) learn problem-solving negotiation and how to deal with difficult tactics; (iv) be committed to the cause, work relentlessly, and persist; and (v) negotiation and DSD classes really work!!

Cathy A. Costantino

My path to a career in systems design and alternative dispute resolution (ADR) has been non-linear and non-traditional. I have worked in multiple fields—social work, law, education—and in multiple arenas—public, private, and international. Each has contributed to my growth and evolution as an ADR professional.

I have always been fascinated by systems. As a kid, I spent a lot of time in the outdoors and quickly observed that everything in nature was connected—a system. During my undergraduate and graduate studies in Social Work at Catholic University in Washington, DC, I started to notice that there were overlaps and interconnections among different academic disciplines—systems. As a social worker and therapist, I studied and relied upon the principles of family systems theory in my practice with children and victims of domestic violence. After graduating law school from the University of California at Berkeley (Boalt Hall), I practiced at Steptoe and Johnson in Washington, DC where I litigated cases dealing with regulatory and administrative processes—systems. Simply put, systems were everywhere.

My first real thoughts about conflict management systems came in 1986 when I started working as a government attorney for the Federal Savings and Loan Insurance Corporation (FSLIC) during the S & L crisis. Although my primary responsibilities were in the litigation arena (we had more than 25,000 lawsuits), I quickly developed a love for and an expertise in negotiation and alternative dispute resolution (ADR). I helped design an ADR program which required entities controlled by the government that held parts of syndicated loans to mediate their disputes rather than sue each other. That program demonstrated that appropriate and early use of ADR in disputes involving distressed real estate loans could decrease carrying costs and reduce litigation expenses. Eventually, when FSLIC was transferred to the Federal Deposit Insurance Corporation (FDIC) in 1989, it occurred to me that we could expand the model to include all types of disputes. Knowing that the litigators might be resistant to using ADR and recognizing that we were working in a banking environment, I made a business case for the use of ADR, tracking litigation cost savings (eventually millions of dollars) as an initial metric. I was asked to create and lead an ADR Unit which facilitated, mediated, trained, evaluated, and designed processes to handle all types of disputes—both internal and external—in the FDIC's portfolio. After passage of the Administrative Dispute Resolution Act of 1990, I served on the Attorney General's ADR Working Group and Steering Committee, and chaired the ADR Design Committee, which helped federal agencies create and implement ADR programs. This gave me a unique opportunity to see and study different dispute resolution approaches throughout the entire federal government.

I still work at the FDIC as an attorney. Being in the public sector has allowed me to work with large organizations and handle complex, systemic issues. My mediation and negotiation work at the FDIC in labor and employment matters (both individual and class action cases) allows me to see individuals and systems in distress and to appreciate that both are capable of change. Serving as a facilitator for an organization-wide FDIC Culture Change Initiative helped me appreciate the ecological component that drives systems to adapt to changing environments, as well as the critical importance of involving all levels of stakeholders. Training FDIC bank closing personnel in negotiation strategies and tactics has enabled me to understand the issues that individuals in crisis situations must manage and resolve every day, particularly as a public servant.

In 1991, I had an "aha" moment at a conference when I was first introduced to the concept of Organization Development (OD)—how organizations seek and sustain change. Although I was well versed in ADR methods and principles, I still had questions: why would a system change how it handled its disputes, and what would increase the likelihood that the change would be sustained? OD was the missing link, and I soon started to play with the concept that if we had interest-based negotiation and interest-based mediation models, why not an interest-based conflict management systems design model which focused on involving the stakeholders in creating the systems they would use? And perhaps based in part on my background as a therapist, I came to understand that there were some conflicts that had only to be managed (not resolved), and some disputes that had to be resolved. I started to talk about these ideas at conferences and to dialogue with my ADR colleagues both within and outside the government. Because I kept getting so many inquiries about my conflict management systems design (CMSD) model and found myself having to explain the same ideas over and over again (and with the encouragement of Frank Sander who told me that if I wanted to teach in a law school I should write a book), I co-authored *Designing Conflict Management Systems Design: A Guide to Creating Productive and Healthy Organizations* (Jossey-Bass, 1996). The book was written every other Monday on my day off, with the initial CMSD concepts drawn with magic markers on storyboards and flipcharts in the basement of my townhouse.

Publication of the book opened up new worlds for me, and let me engage in spirited dialogue and learn from people all over the world. I served as the sole U.S. delegate to a United Nations International Labor Organization conference in Geneva on Structural Changes in the Banking Sector; helped the

Royal Canadian Mounted Police in Newfoundland and New Brunswick design a workplace disputes ADR system; trained the Singapore Arbitration Centre in CMSD principles; served as a consultant to the United Nations Development Program in Kampala, Uganda regarding conflict management capacity-building in Africa; did a podcast and spoke at the United Nations Conference on Trade and Development Joint Symposium on International Investment and ADR; and presented at a Systems Design Conference in The Netherlands. These experiences taught me that every culture has both implicit and explicit ways to manage conflict, and that CMSD around the world is as old as the sun and as fluid as the ocean.

I believe that CMSD practice must also be local, grounded in one's community. During my ten-plus years of facilitation, mediation, and design consultation with the Montgomery County Public School System, I coached teachers, para-professionals, service workers, principals, administrators, and union leadership to create workplace ADR programs and to promote a culture of inclusion and dialogue among stakeholders.

Thousands of students have entrusted me with the privilege of teaching and training them. I love to teach—it gives me the opportunity to test new ideas, to be exposed to new concepts and to learn from people of different backgrounds and disciplines. I have taught multiple courses (Negotiation, Mediation, Conflict Management Systems Design) at Georgetown University Law School since 1993, currently serve as an Adjunct Professor at Vermont Law School and Fordham Law School, occasionally guest lecture at Harvard Law School and teach Mediation Advocacy for the Department of Justice at its National Advocacy Center. I have also taught at Columbia University (Teacher's College), George Mason University (Institute for Conflict Analysis and Resolution), George Washington University School of Public Health, and the Federal Executive Institute.

The field of systems design has grown exponentially since my initial attempts to create a CMSD taxonomy. We now see CMSD used to manage conflict in the courts, workplaces, organizations, communities, governments, and in the global theater. We see it used to resolve complex disputes related to mass torts, mass disasters, national emergencies, class actions, and international transactions and treaties. Looking ahead, I believe that we are at the dawn of the "third generation" of CMSD. I have written about the many "second generation emerging issues" which challenge the Process, the Practitioner and the Profession. I honor those of you joining the field and invite you to be curious, creative, inquisitive and inventive—to find the work wherever it finds you and to approach each design and each client with respect, dignity, and a beginner's mind. Be assured that your path in this discipline can be non-traditional and non-linear, as mine has been. I am grateful for the opportunity to welcome and work with new colleagues in the field and I look forward with excitement and humility to the continued challenges that lie ahead and the many systems yet to be designed.

Oliver Quinn

My interest in, and appreciation for, ADR systems began during my undergraduate days in the late
1960s-early 1970s. I was part of the largest contingent of people of color to enter my University ("large"
being a relative term, since we represented a small
percentage of our entering class). Though small in
numbers, we were idealistic enough to believe that we
could materially change the culture at the University
toward more inclusion and equality, consistent with
the theme of that era in America.

What we discovered was that being admitted did
not mean being welcomed. Many faculty, students,
administrators and alumni felt that our presence at the University posed a threat
to its prestige—and they made their feelings known to us in many ways.

This circumstance taught me an important strategic lesson: There are
many ways to resolve disputes. We could not match the power behind the
status quo. So we had to convince people that our presence was an asset,
not a liability; that embracing diversity would strengthen the University, not
weaken it; and that while we shared many goals with our fellow students, we
also had some particular perspectives and goals that we intended to pursue.
These ranged from expanding the types of entertainment presented on
campus, to demands that the profile of the power structure at the University
(i.e., faculty and administrators) better resemble the emerging diverse profile
of the student body.

I was not aware of "ADR" at the time, but as I reflect on my experiences I
realize that we were engaging in the fundamental ADR paradigm of shifting the
discussions from "*positions*" to "*interests.*"

After graduating from law school I took a position as a civil rights enforcement attorney with the federal government. I did not approach my cases merely
to punish institutions that discriminated or otherwise violated federal laws; I
also looked for opportunities to help create remedial plans that would open
opportunities to populations who had historically been denied access, and to
ensure equality in the delivery of services. Again, ADR strategies proved useful
in the process of getting universities, hospitals, and other institutions not just to
pay fines for their prior discriminatory behavior, but to put in place programs
and processes to remediate past inequities.

My more experienced colleagues in the general counsel's office admonished
me to be more "adversarial." They told me that settling cases would not lead me
to better legal jobs down the line; that I needed to build a litigation track record
if I wanted to build my legal career.

But I was more interested in constructively addressing the factors that led to
the enforcement actions with which I was involved. Perhaps my life experiences

with discrimination, as well as the stories my parents and relatives shared with me of their own insulting, demeaning experiences, fueled my desire to get more out of these conflicts than just notches on my litigation gun. I wanted my work to produce systemic changes.

As my career moved on, I developed more interest in resolving disputes than participating in an adversarial process. I had a significant experience while serving as Assistant Dean at Rutgers Law School just after the Supreme Court's 1977 *Bakke* decision,[1] a watershed affirmative action case. My responsibilities at the law school included overseeing its Minority Student Program (MSP), a very high-profile affirmative action program designed to increase the representation of people of color and other disadvantaged people in the legal profession.

Bakke produced a very diverse set of opinions from the justices; there was something there for everyone. The law school faculty set out to examine the MSP to determine what impact the *Bakke* decision would have on its structure or operations. This review had the potential to become very adversarial, as the faculty held strong views on both sides. Through a series of intense discussions, the faculty recognized that there was almost universal support for the *goal* of increasing diversity in the student body; the points of difference related more to *how* to achieve that goal. Framing the discussions around methodology rather than goals helped to reduce the friction and resulted in a modified program that both passed constitutional muster and achieved the programmatic goal of diversifying the student body with qualified people.

Later, I became an administrative law judge. While this might appear as if I went to the "dark side" of litigation, it was in fact another opportunity to utilize ADR. Our dockets were overflowing, and I was sent to a judicial college to learn more about "settlement strategies and techniques." I was often able to work with parties to design resolutions to their disputes. I believed that leaving matters to me, the judge, to decide should be a last resort for the parties, who had to live with the outcomes. How could it not be better for them to build solutions rather than having my decisions imposed on them? Of course, I was fully prepared to issue decisions if the parties could not reach agreement on their own, or with my assistance. But I felt it was in the best interests of the parties to explore the possibilities of resolution as part of my management of cases.

This was my first experience in a formal dispute resolution *system*. Judges were trained how to settle matters before them. There was support and encouragement for resolution of disputes, not just disposition of cases. My prior experiences were ad hoc; working within a dispute resolution system made my efforts more effective.

Finally, later in my career I was able to use all of my relevant experiences, formal and informal, to construct and manage an employment dispute resolution system at a large corporation. The system allowed us to market, deliver

---

1. *Regents of the University of California v. Bakke*, 438 U.S. 265 (1978).

and assess the effectiveness of ADR in many types of workplace disputes. The challenges were to design and implement a system that was housed within the company, yet was perceived, and operated, as a "neutral" entity. The system had to respect the roles of Human Resources and the Law Department, as well as line and executive management. It had to be able to attract and retain skilled practitioners of ADR to work in the program. It had to be viewed by state and federal enforcement agencies as a legitimate internal effort to resolve disputes. And finally, the people working in the system constantly had to explain the value of third party neutrals to employees who were seeking either representation or adjudication from the program.

Providing an infrastructure for these dispute resolution activities was essential. The complexities would not allow ad hoc efforts to be effective. I realize now that my earlier activities would have been more effective if I had a system around me. Through my experiences in the public, private, academic, and non-profit sectors, I have concluded that ADR systems can strengthen any institution's capability to manage the inevitable conflicts that will occur in the course of business. The ability to design and implement such systems adds tremendous value to organizations in all sectors.

PD Villarreal

My long involvement with ADR began when, as a young lawyer in the late 1980s in Chicago, I started doing mediations with my rapidly becoming famous partner, Scott Turow. Scott and I were both with the Sonnenschein firm at the time (now SNR Denton) and we were working on a number of construction disputes for a family owned construction company. We were able to bring a number of difficult and important disputes to early resolution through mediation, still a relatively novel concept in corporate America. I realized then that, as much as I enjoy the thrill of trial combat, in most cases mediation represents a far superior way of resolving conflict than traditional litigation. This principle has served as one of the guiding stars of my career ever since.

After Sonnenschein, I accepted a position as litigation counsel for the General Electric Company in world headquarters in Fairfield, Connecticut. Upon my arrival in 1995 I was tasked, among other things, with "doing something" about ADR. GE had been an early corporate supporter of the concept of ADR, but in 1995, its use of ADR was still sporadic and ad hoc. Fortunately, my new assignment coincided nicely with the Company's commitment to Six Sigma, a quality methodology that emphasized the importance of process improvement, quantitative measurement, and customer focus. During my time at GE I was able to synthesize this new qualitative initiative (more like a crusade than an initiative) with my own rapidly evolving views of how a modern corporation should respond to the mounting litigation pressures of our time. We (I say we because many fine GE lawyers were involved) created an ADR program that attempted to take a systemic approach to conflict management. We called it EDR (Early Dispute Resolution) and I believe it was one of the first efforts in corporate America to fully integrate ADR into the way the company operated.

At GE, we treated litigation as a kind of "defect" analogous to the kinds of manufacturing defects Six Sigma had been developed to combat. We subjected each significant dispute to an Early Case Assessment (ECA) designed to quickly develop a view of the strengths and weaknesses of the case, potential settlement value, and appropriate litigation and settlement strategy. It was extremely well received and viewed as highly successful. It has served as a model for many similar programs throughout the country.

I left GE in 2005 to become head of litigation of Schering Plough, a major pharmaceutical manufacturer. At Schering, we created a very similar program, which was also a great success.

After Schering was acquired by Merck in 2009 I became head of litigation of Glaxo Smith Kline, one of the world's largest pharmaceutical manufacturing companies. Here too, we have instituted our own EDR program which we call MASTER. While we are still developing and refining the program, I believe it represents the state of the art in corporate conflict management systems design. We have used MASTER aggressively to reduce and control the overall costs of litigation to the Company.

Many years have passed since those first construction mediations in Chicago. Since then, the cases have gotten larger and more complex. My understanding of how disputes arise and how they are subdued has deepened. And the profession and Corporate America have made great strides in their acceptance and use of ADR. But my belief that ADR represents a better way of resolving conflict has never waivered.

APPENDIX B: ARBITRATION OVERVIEW

By Sarah R. Cole and Kristen M. Blankley[2]

Arbitration is a process by which a private (i.e., non-governmental) third-party neutral issues a binding determination of a matter in dispute. Like all dispute resolution processes, arbitration comes in many forms. In *contractual*

---

2. This is a revised version of a chapter by the authors in Michael L. Moffitt and Robert C. Bordone eds., *The Handbook of Dispute Resolution* 381 (2005). Sarah Cole is the John W. Bricker Professor of Law; Director, Program on Dispute Resolution, The Ohio State University Moritz College of Law. Kristen Blankley is Associate Professor of Law, University of Nebraska College of Law.

arbitrations, disputants agree by contract, either before or after a dispute arises, to resolve their dispute through a final and binding arbitration. In some jurisdictions, disputants may—and sometimes must—participate in *court-annexed* or *court-ordered arbitration*, raising unique opportunities and challenges. Court-annexed arbitration is a non-binding process that enables the parties to litigate in court if they are unsatisfied with the arbitration process. *Labor arbitrations*—those that take place specifically in the context of collective bargaining agreements—present a third type of arbitration, raising yet another set of procedures and issues.[3] *Treaty-imposed arbitrations* are international arbitrations that proceed to arbitration pursuant to international treaties. *Online arbitrations* occur entirely online, and these arbitrations stem largely (but not entirely) from contracts created over the internet. For reasons of clarity, and as a reflection of the prominence of this area of arbitration, this chapter focuses primarily on contractual arbitration.

Arbitration is a flexible process. Parties may negotiate virtually every aspect of the process, including the number of arbitrators who will hear the case; the location of the hearing; the applicable law; the availability, types, and amount of discovery; the timetable of events; the evidentiary standards; the appropriateness of expert witnesses; whether or not attorneys will represent the parties; and the use of pre- or post-hearing briefs. Arbitration's flexibility also enables parties to exercise considerable control over arbitrator selection. Thus, parties may select an arbitrator who is an expert in the field in which the dispute has arisen. Moreover, parties can and often do select arbitrators who are not lawyers. Thus, arbitration's flexibility enables parties to tailor the arbitral process for each particular dispute.

Although it seems unlikely that anything could be described as "typical" in a process that the participants design, most arbitrations follow a fairly predictable structure. Typically, arbitration hearings are non-public, if not confidential. The arbitrator usually opens an arbitration with a recitation of ground rules, followed by each party's opening statement.[4] Next, each party presents witnesses and other evidence. During the hearing, an arbitrator may ask questions of the witnesses and attorneys to clarify the evidence. Finally, the arbitrator hears closing statements. In most cases, the arbitrator allows the parties to submit post-hearing briefs that summarize each party's main arguments. The arbitrator then issues a written award, perhaps with an accompanying opinion, within the

---

3. This chapter will not address the topic of labor arbitration. Labor arbitration is typically governed by collective bargaining agreements between labor unions and management. Different principles and laws apply to labor arbitration than to contractual arbitration.

4. Arbitration ground rules focus on the arbitrator's personal preferences and the procedural rules that will govern the arbitration hearing. Among other issues, an arbitrator's ground rules might address introduction of documentary evidence, sequestration of witnesses, order of witness testimony, administration of witness oaths, time limitations on opening or closing statements, and length of hearing breaks. See J.W. Cooley, *The Arbitrator's Handbook* (South Bend, Ind.: National Institute for Trial Advocacy, 1998), p. 78.

time limit that the parties set. If the parties have not indicated when the award is due, arbitrators typically issue awards within a few weeks of the hearing.

I. Arbitration compared to other dispute resolution processes

Arbitration shares certain qualities with mediation. Like mediation, contractual arbitration is voluntary and non-public or confidential. Neither arbitral proceedings nor mediation proceedings may be used as evidence in a subsequent trial. Moreover, the arbitration hearing usually takes place in a private conference room rather than in a public courtroom. Both arbitration and mediation may save parties time and money as compared with litigation.[5] An arbitrator can be appointed and the hearing held in far less time than it would take for the same case to proceed through traditional litigation. In addition, limited discovery makes arbitration, like mediation, potentially a less expensive alternative to litigation.

Unlike mediation, arbitration is an adjudicative process. The arbitrator, like a judge, issues a decision based on the merits of the case. The parties do not create their own settlement. Instead, the arbitrator imposes a resolution on the parties, bounded only by the limitations articulated in the parties' agreement. Unlike traditional litigation, the arbitrator's decision generally cannot be appealed.

Arbitration is much more flexible than litigation. In civil litigation in federal courts, the Federal Rules of Civil Procedure and Evidence govern the process. Parties contracting for arbitration may or may not adopt formal rules of procedure or evidence to govern the arbitration. They may decide to use the rules already established by certain arbitration provider organizations, such as the American Arbitration Association. Parties may decide that a simple dispute requires only a few depositions and no pre- or post-hearing briefs, while a more complicated case may require more extensive procedures.

II. Historical treatment of arbitration agreements

Arbitration as we know it was developed by the merchant class in medieval Western Europe.[6] In the medieval period, merchants traveled to fairs where they

---

5. Because arbitration is a quicker and more streamlined process, it has the potential to save both parties money. Arbitration is especially cost-effective if processes such as discovery are kept to a minimum. However, as arbitration begins to adapt more characteristics of litigation, the length and cost of the process increases. See S.J. Ware, "Paying the Price of Process: Judicial Relegation of Consumer Arbitration Agreements," *Journal of Dispute Resolution*, 2001, pp. 89-100, for a discussion on how arbitration can be either cost-effective or costly.

6. See L.W. Craig, "Some Trends and Developments in the Laws and Practice of International Commercial Arbitration," *Texas International Law Journal*, 1995, 30, p. 5, stating that "[a]n important chapter in the development of private dispute resolution can be traced back to medieval Europe, when merchants and traders of different religions would assemble at markets and fairs to do business."

could meet and conduct business with other merchants. Because these fairs often occurred far from the merchants' homes, and because the merchants did not stay at any particular fair very long, it was important for the merchants to create a system to resolve the disputes that would inevitably arise from the business conducted at the fair. Unfortunately, the common law court system was not an appropriate venue for the resolution of these disputes because of its complex procedures. Moreover, the common law courts had little understanding of the customary norms the merchants followed. Merchants were interested in a system that would resolve disputes (1) quickly (so they could leave the fairs) and (2) in accordance with industry standards (to facilitate relationships among the parties).

Arbitration was developed to achieve these two goals. The arbitration system permitted parties to appoint a disinterested third party who was an industry expert to resolve the dispute quickly by applying understood customary norms. Arbitration successfully resolved mercantile disputes at least in part because informal marketplace sanctions (preserving parties' ongoing relationships and reputations within the industry) gave the parties strong incentives to abide by arbitration agreements and awards.

As the market grew wider and more impersonal, however, market sanctions became less effective and parties became more willing to simply ignore adverse arbitral decisions, undercutting arbitration's effectiveness as a binding, final dispute resolution mechanism. As arbitration's effectiveness declined in the nineteenth century, the commercial community, both in England and in America, turned toward the courts to assist them in strengthening the enforceability of arbitration agreements and awards. Until Congress passed the Federal Arbitration Act (FAA) in 1925, however, this effort proved largely fruitless. American courts refused to assist the merchants in strengthening arbitration, holding instead that arbitration agreements impermissibly divested the courts of jurisdiction. As a result, the courts refused to enforce agreements to arbitrate, and a party who did not want to go to arbitration could simply file a lawsuit in court instead of abiding by a contractual obligation to arbitrate a dispute.

Congress, in response to merchant lobbying, designed the FAA to overcome this judicial reluctance and to place agreements to arbitrate on equal footing with other types of contracts.[7] As a result of this legislation, American courts began to recognize the legitimacy of agreements to arbitrate, at least when those agreements involved parties who frequently participate in arbitration and claims arising out of contract or the common law. Arbitration agreements between commercial disputants, therefore, gained increasing acceptance for much of the twentieth century.

In the mid-1980s, arbitration agreements expanded beyond this traditional context. Contracts between a "repeat player" (usually a business) who arbitrates

---

7. See *Gilmer v. Interstate/Johnson Lane Corp.*, 500 U.S. 20 (1991), p. 24, stating that the purpose of the FAA is to "reverse the long-standing judicial hostility to arbitration agreements that had existed at English common law and had been adopted by American courts, and to place arbitration agreements upon the same footing as other contracts."

regularly and a "one-shot player" who may arbitrate once in a lifetime began to include broad arbitration clauses. Employers started including arbitration agreements in their employment contracts, and merchants started using arbitration agreements in sales to consumers. The scope of these agreements included not only contract and common law claims but also claims arising out of statutory violations. Although academics and others criticize predispute arbitration agreements, the Supreme Court routinely holds that these types of predispute arbitration agreements are valid, stating that there is a "federal policy favoring arbitration" when determining if arbitration is appropriate.[8]

III. Legal issues in arbitration

Even though arbitration is an alternative to litigation, it exists within a legal framework. For instance, the Federal Arbitration Act governs the enforcement of arbitration clauses in contract. Other legal issues that arise frequently in arbitration include the extent to which the states can regulate arbitration and what types of claims can be subject to arbitration.

A. Arbitration under the Federal Arbitration Act

The FAA governs all arbitration agreements that "involve commerce."[9] The Supreme Court has held that this language indicates that Congress intended the FAA to cover all arbitration agreements falling within the broad scope of Congress' power under the Constitution's commerce clause.[10] With few exceptions, Congress's ability to regulate interstate commerce extends to almost everything bought and sold within the United States, both products and services. This power also extends to most types of employment arrangements in the United States, with a statutory exception for certain interstate transportation workers.[11] Thus, the FAA regulates the vast majority of arbitration agreements.

Under the FAA, court involvement usually occurs, if at all, in two situations: prior to the start of arbitration and after the completion of arbitration. Prior to the start of an arbitration, a party with a valid arbitration agreement may obtain a stay of litigation from a court while the arbitration proceeds,[12] which has the effect of "freezing" the litigation until the arbitration is concluded. The FAA also allows a court to "compel" a party to arbitrate,[13] meaning that the court will

---

8. This quotation first appeared in *Moses H. Cone Memorial Hospital v. Mercury Construction Corp.*, 460 U.S. 1 (1983), p. 24, and it has been cited regularly ever since. See, for example, *Howsam v. Dean Witter Reynolds, Inc.*, 537 U.S. 79 (2002), p. 83; *EEOC v. Waffle House, Inc.*, 534 U.S. 279 (2002); p. 289; *Green Tree Fin. Corp.-Alabama v. Randolph*, 531 U.S. 79 (2000), p. 81; and *Gilmer v. Interstate/Johnson Lane Corp.*, 500 U.S. 20 (1991), p. 25.

9. See Federal Arbitration Act §2 (2003).

10. See *Circuit City Stores, Inc. v. Adams*, 352 U.S. 15 (2001), p. 112.

11. See Federal Arbitration Act §1 (2003); *Circuit City v. Adams*, 352 U.S. 105 (2001), p. 119.

12. See Federal Arbitration Act §3 (2003).

13. See Federal Arbitration Act §4 (2003).

enforce the agreement to arbitrate and put litigation on hold until the arbitration is resolved. The FAA also contains provisions for limited judicial review of arbitral awards, together with provisions articulating the process for vacating or modifying arbitration awards.[14]

B. Federal arbitration law

The two primary legal concerns raised in cases involving arbitration are preemption and arbitrability. The theory of preemption is that federal laws are supreme to state laws in all areas, including state efforts to regulate arbitration. Arbitrability refers to whether or not the parties intended that a particular claim be arbitrated or litigated.

Preemption. Under federal law, contracts to arbitrate under the FAA are to be treated like any other contract. In arbitration, the preemption doctrine applies to state law and state courts as well. In other words, states cannot pass laws treating contracts to arbitrate differently than other contracts. For example, a state cannot require that an arbitration clause appear in bold print for the contract to be enforceable.[15] Although a company can certainly put its arbitration clause in bold type, a state cannot require this action because doing so would have the effect of treating contracts to arbitrate differently from other contracts. The FAA, which does not permit special treatment of arbitration agreements, preempts state law that provides either preferential or adverse treatment of arbitration agreements.[16]

Arbitrability. "Arbitrability" relates to whether the parties agreed to arbitrate the merits of a particular dispute. The three main arbitrability questions include whether the parties have an agreement to arbitrate (i.e., the existence of an arbitration agreement), whether a particular dispute falls within the arbitration agreement (i.e., the scope of the arbitration agreement), and whether the contract is enforceable at all (i.e., whether the agreement is a valid contract).

One of the first questions a court asks with respect to each of these issues is "Who gets to decide?" That is, should a judge or an arbitrator decide whether a dispute is arbitrable? In *First Options of Chicago, Inc. v. Kaplan*,[17] the Supreme Court held that courts should determine whether the parties agreed to arbitrate a dispute and whether a dispute falls within the scope of the arbitration agreement.[18] Because arbitration is a creature of contract, parties who agreed to arbitrate should arbitrate, but the converse is also true. The *First Options* decision held that a party who may not have agreed to arbitrate should be allowed to have

---

14. See Federal Arbitration Act §§10-12 (2003).

15. See *Doctor's Assoc. Inc. v. Cassarotto*, 517 U.S. 681 (1996), p. 687.

16. See *Volt Information Sciences, Inc. v. Bd. of Trustees for the Leland Stanford Junior Univ.*, 489 U.S. 681 (1989), pp. 446-447; *see also AT&T Mobility v. Concepcion*, 131 S. Ct. 1740 (2011) (finding that the FAA preempted state law precedent invalidating class action waivers).

17. *First Options of Chicago, Inc. v. Kaplan*, 514 U.S. 938 (1995).

18. See also *Rent-a-Center, West, Inc. v. Jackson*, 130 S. Ct. 2772 (2010).

a court make the initial decision. One important exception exists, however, under *First Options*. If the parties "clearly and unmistakably" agreed that an arbitrator should resolve these initial questions, then the arbitrator should decide them.[19]

If the parties' *arbitration* agreement is enforceable and there is no dispute about whether the arbitration clause applies to the particular type of controversy at issue, the court will direct the case to arbitration. In arbitration, the arbitrator will decide the gateway procedural questions as well as the merits of the dispute. Gateway procedural questions include, among other things, allegations of waiver, delay, violation of limitations periods, and estoppel.[20]

Another doctrine, known as "separability," addresses the question of whether an arbitration agreement should be enforced when the contract containing the arbitration agreement is arguably unenforceable. For example, in *Prima Paint Corp. v. Flood & Conklin Mfg. Co.*, the plaintiff alleged that the defendant had fraudulently induced the plaintiff to sign a contract containing an arbitration clause. The Supreme Court held that an arbitrator, rather than a court, should decide the merits of the plaintiff's assertion that the entire contract was fraudulently induced.[21] The *Prima Paint* Court found that the parties' *arbitration agreement* was valid, even though it was contained in an arguably invalid contract.[22] As a result, the Court directed to the arbitrator the question of whether the defendant engaged in fraudulent inducement. The Court later refined the separability doctrine in *Buckeye Check Cashing, Inc. v. Cardegna*.[23] In that case, the Court held that a dispute over whether a void or voidable contract containing an arbitration provision is enforceable is a question for the arbitrator, not the court. In *Rent-a-Center v. Jackson*, the Supreme Court rejected an employee's challenge to the enforceability of an employer-promulgated arbitration clause because the clause delegated the power to decide enforceability questions to the arbitrator (referred to as the "delegation clause"). Unless the employee challenged the "delegation clause" as unconscionable, the Court held that the parties' desire to have the arbitrator decide enforceability questions, normally a question for the court, would remain undisturbed.[24] Commentators and some courts sharply criticize the separability doctrine.[25]

---

19. See *First Options of Chicago, Inc. v. Kaplan*, 514 U.S. 938 (1995), p. 946.

20. See *Howsam v. Dean Witter Reynolds, Inc.*, 537 U.S. 938 (2002), p. 86.

21. *Prima Paint Corp. v. Flood & Conklin Mfg. Co.*, 388 U.S. 395 (1967), p. 406.

22. The *Prima Paint* Court relied on Section 4 of the FAA, which states that "upon [a court's] being satisfied that the making of the agreement for arbitration," a court should direct "the parties to proceed to arbitration in accordance with the terms of the agreement." 9 U.S.C. §4.

23. 126 S. Ct. 1204 (2006).

24. *Rent-a-Center, West, Inc. v. Jackson*, 130 S. Ct. 2772 (2010).

25. *Shaffer v. Jeffery*, 915 P.2d 910 (Okla. 1996) (defense of fraudulent inducement of contract is for the court). See also R.C. Reuben, "First Options, Consent to Arbitration, and the Demise of Separability: Restoring Access to Justice for Contracts with Arbitration Provision," 56 *S.M.U. L. Rev.* 819, 838-855 (2003); S.J. Ware, "Employment Arbitration and Voluntary Consent," 25 *Hofstra L. Rev.* 83, 128-138 (1996).

C. Arbitration of statutory claims

Controversy surrounds the question of whether claims involving a violation of statutory rights can be resolved in arbitration. Congress enacted laws such as Title VII, the American with Disabilities act (ADA), and the age Discrimination in Employment Act (ADEA) to eliminate discrimination in the workforce. These statutes also give the aggrieved employees a federal forum in which to bring these "statutory claims." Not all statutory claims relate to discrimination, and courts regularly upheld arbitration agreements covering statutory claims as diverse as the Sherman Antitrust Act, the Securities and Exchange Act, and RICO.[26] In the mid-1980s, employers began to include arbitration agreements in employees' contracts. These agreements required employees to arbitrate all claims against the employer, including statutory claims. In the seminal *Gilmer v. Interstate/Johnson Lane Corp.* decision, the Supreme Court unequivocally held that an arbitrator was competent to hear cases involving the ADEA. The Court reasoned that arbitration under the New York Stock Exchange (NYSE) Rules adequately protected the plaintiff's interests and there was no reason to believe that a NYSE arbitrator was incapable of hearing and deciding a statutory claim.[27] Since *Gilmer*, the Supreme Court and lower courts have consistently upheld agreements to arbitrate statutory claims brought by employees against their employers.[28] Most recently, in 2018, the Supreme Court ruled in *Epic Systems v. Lewis* that courts should read together statutes to give them both effect.[29] In practice, that ruling means that cases involving statutory claims can be arbitrated unless Congress explicitly states otherwise.

IV. Arbitration clauses

When parties draft an agreement to resolve disputes, they should consider a variety of issues, including whether arbitration is appropriate. Parties who choose arbitration draft agreements covering a number of topics, the most common of which include type of dispute covered, arbitrator selection, number of arbitrators, applicable rules, type of award, available remedies, class actions, and arbitration fees and costs.

A. Appropriateness of arbitration

Arbitration may be used to resolve virtually any kind of dispute; however, some disputes may be better suited to arbitration than others. Because

---

26. See *Rodriquez de Quijas v. Shearson/American Express, Inc.*, 490 U.S. 477 (1989) (Securities Act claim); *Shearson/American Express, Inc. v. McMahon*, 482 U.S. 220 (1987) (RICO claim); and *Mitsubishi Motors Corp., Inc. v. Soler Chrysler-Plymouth Inc.*, 473 U.S. 614 (1985) (antitrust claim).

27. See *Gilmer v. Interstate/Johnson Lane Corp.*, 500 U.S. 20 (1001), pp. 30-35.

28. See *Rent-a-Center v. Jackson* (2010) (referring an employment discrimination claim to arbitration, and requiring the arbitrator to consider the legitimacy of an unconscionability defense).

29. *Epic Systems Corp. v. Lewis*, 138 S. Ct. 1612 (2018).

arbitration is less adversarial than litigation, the process may help preserve good will between the disputants. Moreover, arbitration is usually cheaper and more efficient than litigation, enabling parties to resolve their dispute more quickly and resume their relationship or business. In addition, arbitration decisions bring finality to the conflict because the decisions are very difficult to appeal.

B. Drafting arbitration clauses

Parties may draft an arbitration clause either before or after a dispute arises. Parties who draft post-dispute arbitration contracts can create a process to suit the specific needs of the parties depending on the complexity of the dispute and the needs of the parties. Parties can also draft agreements to arbitrate future disputes ("pre-dispute" arbitration agreements). Such agreements usually appear in the contract governing the parties' relationship, such as in an employment agreement, a consumer purchase agreement, or a joint venture agreement. When drafting a pre-dispute arbitration agreement, the parties try to anticipate the types of disputes that might arise out of the relationship and anticipate the procedure best able to resolve future disputes.

C. Arbitrator selection

Any arbitration agreement should either designate a particular person as the arbitrator or create a process for determining who the arbitrator will be. Parties most often choose specific arbitrators in post-dispute agreements to arbitrate or when the parties have a relationship with a certain arbitrator. More commonly, an arbitration agreement will specify an arbitrator selection *method*. The selection method usually indicates that an arbitration organization, such as the AAA, will provide a list of potential arbitrators, and the disputants will select an arbitrator from the list, either by eliminating arbitrators one-by-one or by listing the arbitrators in order of preference. Some arbitration agreements call for tripartite arbitration, in which each party appoints an arbitrator, and the two party-appointed arbitrators chose a third, neutral arbitrator.

D. Determining procedures

Parties have considerable flexibility in determining the arbitration procedures to govern the dispute. For example, the parties can designate how much discovery will take place and create a timetable for completing the discovery process. The parties can also dictate whether expert or lay witnesses may be called at the hearing, the order of party presentations, whether the arbitrator has subpoena powers, and whether rules of evidence or procedure will be strictly followed.

E. Form of the award

The arbitration agreement can also set forth how the award should look and a deadline for the arbitrator to issue the award. Parties who value time and cost-saving procedures may require that the arbitrator issue an award that indicates only who won and how much money that person will receive, if anything.

Parties can also require the arbitrator to write a reasoned opinion. Parties may request a written opinion for a variety of reasons, including understanding why the arbitrator ruled a specific way, requiring an arbitrator to think carefully about the case, and preserving a record for judicial review. Parties should be advised, however, that they will be required to pay the arbitrator for both writing the opinion and for study and research time associated with writing the opinions.

F. Available remedies

Courts have very limited powers in granting remedies to litigation parties. Arbitration, however, is not so limited. The parties can provide the arbitrator with discretion to award monetary damages, nonmonetary damages, or a combination of both. Thus, parties drafting an arbitration clause should consider whether they wish to authorize the arbitrator to award nonmonetary damages and, if so, consider limiting the potential scope of nonmonetary awards.

G. Consolidations and class actions

Consolidation and class action arbitration allow multiple claimants to proceed in arbitration against the same respondent. When arbitration cases are consolidated, each person with a claim against the same defendant joins his or her case to the others, so that there are multiple claimants but only one defendant. Class action arbitration occurs when one party brings an action against a defendant on behalf of him- or herself and all others similarly situated. As with a class action lawsuit in court, the class action arbitration can involve many people who are not named parties to the case.

Class action arbitrations are controversial. If an agreement to arbitrate is valid, the arbitrator, not the court, will decide whether a class action is appropriate for the particular case.[30] If the agreement is silent on the availability of classwide procedures, an arbitrator may not order class arbitration unless the arbitrator can point to a law authorizing such proceedings.[31] In contracts that specifically allow or ban class action arbitrations, the arbitrator is generally bound to respect his or her authority as defined in the contract. If the contract is silent, under a recent Supreme Court decision, the arbitrator cannot find that the contract permits class action arbitrations.[32] Nor can a state court declare an arbitration agreement unconscionable simply because the agreement includes a class action waiver.[33] State laws favorable to class action arbitration will likely be preempted under the Supreme Court's 2011 decision in *AT&T Mobility v. Concepcion*.[34] In 2018, the Supreme Court held the National Labor Relations

---

30. See *Green Tree Fin. Corp. v. Bazzle*, 539 U.S. 444 (2003).
31. *Stolt-Nielsen v. Animalfeeds Internat'l Corp.*, 130 S. Ct. 1758 (2010).
32. *Id.*
33. *AT&T Mobility v. Concepcion*, 131 S. Ct. 1740 (2011).
34. *Id.*

Act, which otherwise allows for concerted action such as unionizing and collective bargaining, does not provide employees with the right to proceed in a class action if the contract between the employee and employer prohibits class actions.[35]

H. Payment of fees

Arbitration agreements typically include provisions describing the allocation of arbitration costs. Arbitration costs typically include filing fees, administrator fees, and attorney's fees. In the absence of an agreement to the contrary, the filing party pays the filing fees. Arbitrator fees are usually split evenly between the parties for fairness reasons and to eliminate arbitrator bias. A number of courts, however, have held that it is unconscionable to require lower-paid workers or consumers to pay filing fees or pay for the arbitrator.[36] Parties usually pay their own attorney's fees, unless the parties give the arbitrator the power to require the loser to pay the winner's fees.

V. Enforceability of arbitration agreements

Challenges to arbitration often focus on contractual theories, particularly unconscionability. This section of the chapter explores some of the possible contractual challenges a party to an arbitration agreement might raise in court.

A. Conscionability

A court may declare an arbitration agreement void because it is unconscionable, or so one-sided that the courts refuse to enforce it. In most jurisdictions, a contract is void for reasons of unconscionability if it is both procedurally and substantively unconscionable. In some jurisdictions, however, substantive unconscionability alone may be enough to invalidate an agreement to arbitrate.

A contract is procedurally unconscionable if it is presented to the other party on a "take it or leave it" basis. Procedurally unconscionable contracts are most common in the employment and consumer contexts. A procedurally unconscionable contract almost always involves a disparity in bargaining power between the two parties, preventing the weaker party from successfully negotiating to change unfavorable terms. Often, courts examine the educational experience and sophistication of the party making the contract to determine if the contract is procedurally unconscionable.

To be unenforceable, a contract must also be substantively unconscionable. Substantively unconscionable contracts are those that contain terms that are harsh, oppressive, or unduly biased in favor of the party with greater bargaining

---

35. *Epic Systems Corp. v. Lewis*, 138 S. Ct. 1612 (2018).

36. See *Morrison v. Circuit City Stores, Inc.*, 317 F.3d 646 (6th Cir. 2003). The Supreme Court's opinion in *Green Tree Fin. Corp. v. Randolph*, 531 U.S. 79 (2000), puts a burden on the party complaining about the fees to show that the fees are burdensome.

power. When determining whether a contract is substantively unconscionable, a court will examine all of the terms contained in the arbitration agreement. Certain contract provisions are more troublesome than others. Exorbitant fees or costs for one-shot players trouble courts.[37] Inadequate discovery provisions may also be problematic. Courts also consider the availability of class procedures and the convenience of the location of the arbitration.[38] Finally, the courts will examine the arbitrator selection process to determine if the arbitrator will be unbiased.[39]

B. Contractual soundness

Because courts treat contracts to arbitrate just like any other contract, general contract defenses are available to challenge contracts to arbitrate. Thus, defenses such as duress, fraud, lack of consideration, illegality, and lack of capacity are available to a plaintiff when challenging an agreement in court or in front of the arbitrator. These types of defenses are generally used to challenge the validity of the contract or to prove that a contract was never formed. One must recall that the preemption doctrine prohibits states from passing laws that provide special defenses to those who are challenging the existence or validity of an agreement to arbitrate.[40] Whether the court or the arbitrator hears these defenses is a question of arbitrability.[41]

VI. Enforcement of arbitral awards

After a successful arbitration, one or more parties may petition the court to confirm the award.[42] The party seeking judicial confirmation of the award must physically take a copy of the award to the court and have it entered into the court's official record. After the award is confirmed, it can be enforced if one of the parties, usually the losing party, does not comply with its terms. A court

---

37. See, for example, *Morrison v. Circuit City Stores, Inc.*, 317 F.3d 646 (6th Cir. 2003), pp. 664-665, noting that a plaintiff in court would have a free judge and a lawyer on a contingency fee basis; and *Armendariz v. Foundation Health Psychare Services, Inc.*, 6 P.3d 669 (Cal. 2000), p. 687, stating that employees cannot pay for any "unreasonable costs or any arbitrator's fees or expenses as a condition of access to the arbitration forum."

38. See *Brower v. Gateway 2000*, 246 A.2d 246 (N.Y. App. Div. 1998), p. 256, holding an arbitration agreement unenforceable because it required arbitration in front of the International Chamber of Commerce in Paris, France.

39. For an example of a particularly egregious case, see *Hooters of America v. Phillips*, 173 F.3d 933 (4th Cir. 1999). In the *Hooters* case, the restaurant management compiled a list of potential arbitrators. Control of the list created the possibility that Hooters could "stack the deck" with favorable arbitrators.

40. See the earlier discussion on preemption in the Federal Arbitration Law section.

41. See the earlier discussion on arbitrability in the Federal Arbitration Law section.

42. See Federal Arbitration Act §9 (2003).

can enforce an arbitral award in the same manner as it enforces judicial awards, through judgment liens, garnishment, or other methods.

Under limited circumstances, a party may request a court to modify or correct an arbitration award. The FAA allows for modification or correction in three limited circumstances involving miscalculations or other errors.[43] The statute notes that the award may also be corrected or modified in order to "promote justice between the parties."[44] Under the FAA, courts can only review and vacate grounds under the following limited circumstances: (1) the award is procured by corruption or other undue means, (2) there is evident partiality on the part of the arbitrator, (3) the arbitrator has acted in a manner that constitutes misconduct, or (4) the arbitrator exceeded his or her powers as described in the agreement to arbitrate.[45] Some courts may review an award for a "manifest disregard of the law," but this review is also limited.[46] Parties, however, cannot contract for greater review than that provided in the FAA.[47] Limited review promotes the finality of arbitration, discouraging parties from engaging in protracted litigation following arbitration.

APPENDIX C: MEDIATION OVERVIEW[48]

Mediation takes somewhat different forms, but the core process focuses on assisted negotiation among two or more parties. The mediator's role is to help parties set the ground rules, to listen actively to them in order to understand the conflict and its context, and to facilitate discussion and exchange of ideas about how to resolve that dispute. Unlike some other ADR processes such as arbitration, mediation results are consensual—that is, the mediator has no authority to impose an outcome on the parties.

We over-simplify here as we focus first on the common ground in different mediation contexts and on the typical practices of mediators. Then we look briefly at significant variations in mediation approaches.

The prototypical mediation session (employing facilitative mediation—defined later in this appendix) occurs in a conference room in a neutral location.

---

43. See Federal Arbitration Act §11 (2003).

44. Federal Arbitration Act §11 (2003).

45. See Federal Arbitration Act §10 (2003).

46. Since 1953, parties in most jurisdictions could challenge an arbitration award for manifest disregard of the law. In *Hall Street Assoc, L.L.C. v. Mattel, Inc.*, 552 U.S. 576 (2008), the Court created some doubt as to whether the challenge was still possible. Then, in *Stolt-Nielsen S.A. v. Animalfeeds International Corp.*, 130 S. Ct. 1758 (2010), the Court implied in a footnote that a party may be able to challenge an arbitration award on the ground that the arbitrator manifestly disregarded the law.

47. *Hall Street Assoc, L.L.C. v. Mattel, Inc.*, 552 U.S. 576 (2008).

48. This appendix has been adapted, with permission, from Sarah Cole et al., *Mediation: Policy & Practice* ch. 3 (2017-2018), also available as a Westlaw database.

The mediator invites the participants in and seats them, usually so that the parties are closest to the mediator. If attorneys or other representatives are present, as we will assume them to be for purposes of this illustration, they sit further away. Frequently, these sessions are private. Often lasting several hours, a mediation session tends to be guided by the mediator firmly but informally, without formal rules of evidence or procedure.

The parties and their representatives may work with the mediator to shape some of the ground rules and the scheduling and function of future sessions. Mediation sessions frequently move between joint sessions with all parties present to separate caucuses (or private meetings) between each party (often with attorney or representative) and mediator. In introducing mediation, mediators usually caution parties about the confidentiality of their conversations in both joint meetings and caucuses. A mediation session typically concludes with an agreement to schedule another session with a particular agenda and often some "homework" (for example, consideration of new settlement alternatives or information gathering) or drafting of a tentative agreement. Of course, it may also conclude with the recognition that further mediation would be unproductive.

During this process, a mediator assists parties in discussing points of difference and agreement, in clarifying interests, in identifying alternative resolutions, and in accepting compromise, leaving to the parties the decision to accept or reject a settlement. Although some mediators are more aggressive than others in suggesting options and possible outcomes, their strongest control is over the process and in helping to shape the language framing both issues in dispute and potential outcomes.

The prototypical facilitative mediation involves several overlapping stages: introduction of the process by the mediator; presentation of viewpoints by each of the parties, including the range of their interests and goals and, often, expressions of feeling about the dispute and other party or parties; caucusing to discuss confidential information and views about settlement alternatives; joint exploration of alternative resolutions; and forging an agreement, when possible. The mediator's major challenge in moving through these stages is to assist parties, who often are initially distrustful and locked emotionally in conflicting positions, to reduce their antagonism and consider alternative possibilities for settlement.

In a facilitative mediation session, the mediator focuses attention on the parties and their perceptions, concerns, and interests. In the session's early stages, mediators want to establish their integrity, competence, and concern for the parties. Mediators convey their concern in large part by listening "actively" and sympathetically to the "stories" that each party has to tell (*see* Chapter 15.C.1, Active listening). Each party in turn sets out his or her concerns and understanding of the dispute without interruption, followed by questions from the mediator. These presentations may be followed by joint discussions of an agenda, needed information, and acceptable substantiation of that information.

These joint sessions promote the open exchange of information among parties and encourage candor about interests and goals as well as about the emotions and assumptions that may constrain the parties in moving forward toward resolution. Proponents of cooperative negotiation highlight the importance of this information sharing for building the best resolutions. The openness of these sessions, however, highlights the negotiator's dilemma—the decision to act cooperatively and share information or to act competitively and resist revealing information. A mediator's challenge is to build sufficient confidence in the process to encourage information sharing.

At some point in the process, many mediators will ask to meet separately (caucus) with each of the parties. Confidentiality is a concern in caucuses. At the close of the caucus, the mediator usually asks the parties whether there is anything they have said that they would be willing to have shared with the other party. The mediator will then share any information for which such permission has been granted at his or her discretion.

Early caucuses serve to alert the mediator to underlying interests, concerns, or facts not revealed in the joint session. In addition, the mediator may use the private sessions to challenge the interpretation or position of each party, to persuade a party to hear and understand the view of the other party, to separate one party from the threatening or disruptive conduct of the other, and to point out the consequences of intransigence and non-settlement. In later caucuses, the mediator may suggest alternative settlement ideas or test the parties' positions on proposals already on the table. Mediators expect parties to speak frankly in caucuses and may do so themselves in ways that would make that party hostile if done in a joint session.

One significant variation in mediation practice turns on the extent of use of caucuses. At the extremes, a mediation may occur only in joint sessions and never employ caucuses, while caucus-centered mediation may never or rarely bring the parties together in the same room to talk directly with one another. In this latter instance, the mediation consists largely of caucuses with the mediator shuttling back and forth between parties. Labor mediation, for example, relies heavily on separate caucuses with the parties in order to achieve agreements, whereas divorce and community mediation generally employ face-to-face sessions with some caucuses. Observers comment that "increasing numbers of mediators are abandoning or greatly minimizing the joint session," or that civil case mediation "in a significant number of court-annexed programs has begun to look more like the traditional pretrial settlement conference"[49] where lawyers argue their cases on the record to persuade a judge rather than engage in meaningful negotiation.

In the world of legal practice much commercial and civil mediation has either moved away from the prototypical facilitative mediation model or simply adopted a different one. An alternative prototype thus has emerged that

---

49. Senft and Savage, *ADR in the Courts: Progress, Problems, and Possibilities*, 108 PENN ST. L. REV. 327, 335 (2003).

minimizes the use of joint sessions, although these mediations often begin with all parties and lawyers present in order for the mediator to describe the process, time issues, ground rules, and confidentiality expectations. However, it may also begin in the caucus format that prevails thereafter. In general, this alternative version of mediation tends to be dominated by attorneys who often sit closest to the mediator and take the lead in presenting their arguments and in speaking for their clients. The discussions in caucus more likely focus on legal issues and claims, and less often on the underlying interests and preferences of parties who may participate little in the process. Mediators in this version of the process are much more likely to suggest possible outcomes to the parties—presumably based on what they hear in shuttling back and forth between parties. Some forms of this mediation may employ "bracketed bargaining" where mediators ask parties to make offers contingent on specific concessions by the other party.

The move to caucus-driven mediation reflects to some extent the preferences of attorneys who are not anxious to have their clients share information with the other party. The move also reflects mediator concerns about the problematic character of lawyer posturing in joint sessions. The absence of joint sessions for substantive discussions, however, eliminates opportunities for parties to hear one another directly and perhaps to better understand each other.

All mediation processes can accommodate advocacy and hard negotiation. Nonetheless, mediators encourage cooperative negotiation and tend to emphasize common views and values at the same time that they try to clarify points of disagreement. A central technique of mediators is to "reframe" or to translate parties' statements of positions into statements of interests. For example, a mediator may encourage environmentalists to look beyond their position that a power plant causing thermal pollution should be closed to consider their underlying interest in protecting fish populations that breed nearby. The goal of this technique is to help the parties to understand their own and the other party's interests, rather than to focus exclusively on defending positions or demands. In fact, many mediators discourage parties from stating their positions initially and ask instead for them to identify alternative ways of resolving the conflict.

Research makes clear that the actual practice and delivery of mediation vary significantly across courts, programs, locales, and mediators, creating notable departures from the prototypes described above. Research also suggests that even within particular programs, mediation processes vary substantially based on the aspirations, preparation, strategies, and skills of the parties and lawyers/ representatives who participate in them. All of these variations are likely to be consequential for the time and costs of mediation, the experiences of parties, and the kinds of outcomes achieved through it.

As suggested in the two prototypes above, over the last several decades, mediation practice in the United States has become more differentiated in philosophy, procedure, organization, and delivery. Distinctive styles of mediation have developed, along with extended debate about the merits of each. Mediation programs have developed and evolved, each organizing the delivery of mediation services in a somewhat different way (*see* question 5.2 in the text and think about how to implement a court mediation program).

Four major approaches to mediation have emerged in the United States: facilitative, evaluative, transformative, and "eclectic" mediation (using elements of two or more of the other approaches). Since the mid-1990s, mediators have engaged in an extended debate about the appropriateness and effectiveness of each of these approaches in varying contexts.

Facilitative mediation most closely resembles the first prototypical mediation described above. In it, the parties play a major role—encouraged by the mediators' questions—to find underlying interests, examine options, and shape outcomes. The mediator resists making recommendations to parties or providing opinions about the legal merits or likely legal outcomes in the case. Facilitative mediators rely heavily on joint sessions but also use caucuses where appropriate.

Evaluative mediation in a legal context more closely resembles judicial settlement conferences and centers on the critical examination of the strengths and weaknesses of each side's cases and the likely outcome of the case were it to reach trial. In whatever context evaluative mediation occurs, mediators are more assertive about their own judgments of best or likely outcomes and of the strengths and weaknesses of parties' cases and positions. They may also suggest settlement terms in the context of their case evaluation. In legal cases, evaluative mediations often are preceded by written submissions by attorneys for both sides, summarizing the facts as they know them and making best case arguments for their client. These sessions may begin in joint session with attorney opening statements (perhaps followed by party comments) for each side. These mediations are likely to rely more heavily on caucuses and to provide significantly less opportunity for direct party participation and for exploration of a wide range of underlying interests.

Transformative mediation will generally resemble the prototypical mediation in format but differs in philosophy and perhaps in process. Transformative mediation was proposed in 1994 by Bush and Folger in their book, *The Promise of Mediation*. Rather than focusing on settlement of a particular legal dispute, transformative mediators assist the parties in recognizing and understanding one another's points of view and the reasons for their actions. Mediators following this approach support parties (empower them) in communicating about changing "their interactions with others. . . . The mediation is considered successful when the parties participate in interactive communication that results in a clearer understanding of their situation and each other's perspective. Often, this leads to resolution of the dispute."[50] Transformed relationships and

---

50. United States Postal Service, Transformative Mediation, https://about.usps.com/what-we-are-doing/redress/transformative-mediation.htm (last visited June 28, 2018); see also Folger and Baruch Bush, Transformative Mediation and Third-Party Intervention: Ten Hallmarks of a Transformative Approach to Practice, 13 Mediation Q. 263, 275-276 (1996).

understandings of others are thus the central focus of mediation; resolution of the dispute is secondary. The United States Postal Service has adopted trans- formative mediation for its REDRESS (Resolve Employment Disputes Reach Equitable Solutions Swiftly) program as a matter of policy. This model connects closely to restorative justice practices and to truth and reconciliation processes such as those used in the aftermath of Indian Residential Schools in Canada (*see* Chapter 2.B).

The *eclectic or flexible model of mediation* involves some combination of these varied practices in the same mediation, depending on the preferences of the parties and/or the mediator's assessment of the demands of the particular situation. Many mediators resist being classified, for example, as evaluative or facilitative but combine elements of each as appropriate in a particular case.

The practices employed by mediators in the midst of community-wide civil rights protests—prominent recently in Ferguson, Baltimore, and other U.S. cities—differ from mediation practices for legal, family, business, or neighbor disputes described above. They more closely resemble those used by public policy mediators. This role involves organization and facilitation of discussion among multiple parties—often units of government and public and private organizations—in order to identify underlying interests and find viable solu- tions to complex problems. The facilitator role is broader and differs subtly from that of mediator; mediators may use their facilitation skills in convening and seeking consensus while also mediating specific disputes (*see* Chapter 15). The U.S. Justice Department's Community Relations Service (CRS) houses the most prominent of the community-wide civil rights mediators (called "conciliators" by statute), though other mediators do similar work through state or local gov- ernment or through contract with public entities.

APPENDIX D: INSTRUCTING STAKEHOLDERS ON OVERCOMING BARRIERS TO REACHING NEGOTIATION GOALS

Clients and stakeholders may doubt that a new consensual process will help the participants reach agreement. Perhaps they tried to get the parties to settle themselves, for example, and it did not work. Reading this appendix may help you teach clients and stakeholders to identify barriers to reaching agreement and then to be receptive to ideas for structuring the process to help participants overcome the barriers.

1. Beginning with common negotiating experiences

As a designer, you will sometimes structure a single process to build con- sensus, as Michael Young did with the South African negotiators (pp. 17-19), and sometimes create a system for a stream of ongoing disputes, as eBay did for online purchases or online comments (pp. 25-26). We begin in this section at the single dispute level, and then move to considerations in creating systems that incorporate consensus processes, sometimes linked to adjudication or other processes. The next few pages may help you prepare to teach stakeholders who will collaborate in the planning process.

To begin at the single dispute level, you can ask stakeholders to draw on their own experiences regarding typical barriers to reaching agreement, add other barriers identified through research, and then consider approaches that will help surmount those barriers. To learn how to do this, you can begin reflecting on your own experiences as you read the remainder of this section.

To give you practice at using an overcoming-barriers analysis, recall a conflict about a difficult situation that was important to you but did not go well. (Try not to pick one in which reaching agreement did not make sense to at least one negotiator, no matter how well negotiations proceeded.) First, what did you hope to achieve? Was complete agreement necessary or could your needs have been satisfied with something less, like a degree of understanding or an agreement on a way to resolve it? List your *outcome goals*. Did you care how the negotiation unfolded in terms of duration, timing, whether it was in person, openness or confidentiality, or how you and others dealt with each other? List your *process goals*.

Second, what stood in the way of success? Consider a series of questions to jog your memory:

- What challenges did you face in getting the others involved to meet with you?
- Was there trust between the parties?
- What role did events outside of your own negotiation play in facilitating or impeding progress in your discussions?
- Did you discuss issues in an order that led to generating and considering options?
- What information did you have about how others in similar situations (but perhaps in different contexts) resolved the issues?
- How did you and others express and handle emotions? In what ways did they facilitate or impede progress on your substantive goals?
- Did all negotiators prepare and communicate effectively regarding what you and others hoped for and your best alternatives to a negotiated agreement?
- What other barriers to effective negotiation can you identify?

Next to *your* outcome and process goals, list the *barriers* to reaching them.

Now, follow the same process for the other negotiators. Next begin to jot down ideas for process: if you could re-live this negotiation, how would you change the process to overcome the barriers you identified?

My unsuccessful negotiation:

My outcome goals: Other negotiators' outcome goals:
1.   1.
2.   2.
3.   3.

My process goals: Other negotiators' process goals:
1.   1.
2.   2.

Barriers to reaching these goals:
1.
2.
3.
4.
5.
6.
7.

Processes, or aspects of process, that might overcome these barriers:
1.
2.
3.
4.

As you read through this appendix and realize that you and other negotia-tors faced additional barriers, return to this chart and add to it, giving additional thought to processes to overcome the new barriers.

2. Cognitive barriers

When you identified barriers to agreement, did you consider cognitive bar-riers? Research indicates that people tend to react along certain patterns during negotiations. These decisional tendencies may interfere with reaching an agree-ment that meets the negotiators' interests. Skillful designers try to identify these barriers and design systems taking them into account.

The boxed discussion below synthesizes the research on a few of these pat-terns as potential barriers not only to agreement but also to agreement that resolves all of the issues the parties care about through a process that leaves the parties satisfied (*see*, regarding other cognitive barriers, Bazerman and Shonk, 2005:54-62). As you read this and recognize barriers that existed in your per-sonal conflict, add them to the list above.

THEORIES AND RESEARCH ABOUT COGNITIVE NEGOTIATION BARRIERS

Loss and risk aversion: "When parties must choose between a certain option (a settlement proposal) and a risky option (continue litigation), it matters a great deal whether the certain option is framed as a gain or as a loss (Korobkin, 2006:308). '[D]ecision makers tend to attach greater weight to prospective losses than to prospective gains of equivalent magnitude' and thus resist making even advantageous concessions when they are defined as 'losses' (Mnookin and Ross, 1995:20-21). As a result of this *loss aversion*, parties may prefer to risk the costs and uncertainties of further litigation and even trial rather than accept a favorable agreement. At the same time, people are typically averse to giving up certain gains in the face of risky alternatives; this *risk aversion* means that a settlement option which a party views as a gain is more likely to be adopted than a course of action that would result in litigation, even though litigation may produce greater gains" (Cole et al., 2017-2018:§3.67). Research indicates that frequently the same option or result can be framed either as a loss or a gain, but it also makes clear that "loss frames" are very hard to overcome (Korobkin and Guthrie, 1994:161-163).

Reactive devaluation: Parties in conflict tend to reject ideas for settlement from the other side simply because they originate from a party they distrust or are angry with. "If they want it, it must be bad for me" goes the "reasoning." For example, in the 1980s researchers at Stanford University presented a proposal for nuclear arms reductions to two groups of survey respondents who were asked to rate it in terms of how favorable it was to the United States. The first group was told that the proposal was originally made by then-U.S. President Ronald Reagan. The second group was told that the proposal was offered by the leader of the former Soviet Union, Mikhail Gorbachev. Respondents in the first group rated the proposal as more favorable to the United States than did those in the second condition even though the substance and content of both proposals were identical. Simply associating a proposal with someone perceived as an opponent caused people to rate it less favorably than when it came from their own side (Ross, 1995:29).

Overconfidence: "Parties to disputes share with most other people the cognitive bias toward *optimistic overconfidence*—a belief that 'the chances of good things happening to them are better than they are in reality' (Korobkin, 2006:284)" (Cole et al., 2017-2018:§3:13). Overconfidence makes parties reluctant to change their initial perceptions and assessments of the strength of their position, less likely that they will listen to and realistically assess the validity or strength of the other party's position, and more likely that they will overstate the likelihood of victory in any power contest that might be an option to agreement. Parties who lack objectivity about what they might gain through negotiation also "overlook the full range of possible outcomes" (Bazerman and Shonk, 2005:57).

Fixed pie bias: "Research . . . indicates that parties frequently enter negotiation with the view that their challenge is to divide up limited resources—a fixed-pie—in a win-lose fashion. To the degree that parties maintain that view, they will fail to capture value and achieve the best possible resolution" (Cole et al., 2017-2018:§3.13).

Once you identify cognitive barriers, you can design a process with an eye for overcoming them. For example, this discussion of "fixed pie bias" could lead you to introduce stakeholders to the idea of "value creation" in negotiation. As Bazerman and Shonk note, even what appears to be a simple negotiation between buyer and seller over price "could in fact expand to incorporate issues such as service, financing, delivery, long-term contracts, and so on" (2005:54). The "fixed pie bias" means that parties often need assistance in imagining alternative ways of thinking about their conflict, about the variables they might consider in negotiation, and possible options for resolution.

Value creation means identifying benefits to the parties beyond distribution of a "fixed pie." Value creation means that both (all) parties to a negotiation can "win" when the negotiation recognizes differences in time frames, priorities, capabilities, and risk preferences and includes variables such as shared interests, reduced transaction costs, and eased implementation (Ury et al.,1988; Moffitt, 2005:176-180). Thus, if a "fixed pie bias" barrier is identified, the designer might suggest structuring negotiations to create value or bring in an intervenor skilled in value creation, and one could use a similar analysis for other cognitive barriers.

3. Strategic, tactical, or unskillful approach to negotiation as a barrier

Negotiators may take a strategic approach to negotiation or deploy bargaining behaviors that become barriers to success. Inexperienced negotiators may be ineffective communicators or agenda-builders. Even experienced negotiators create barriers by selecting an approach that leads negotiating partners to lose trust, get angry, or miscalculate and miss opportunities to resolve matters (*see* p. 420). In addition, positional negotiators tend to play their cards "close to the vest" to avoid disclosures that might harm their negotiating positions. Alternately, to extract concessions they may exaggerate the strength of their alternatives, dig in their heels as an acting ploy, threaten, or escalate an already tense situation. Whether such behaviors are intentional or the byproduct of inadequate training or experience, hard bargaining and a positional approach to negotiation can exacerbate conflict and make it harder to discover joint gains. These behaviors inhibit the ability of designers to create processes that maximize value creation and efficiency, discussed in the previous paragraph. As you read this, consider whether the approaches used in your negotiation interfered with optimal agreement or even agreement at all.

Those with little training in negotiation may want to clarify what is meant by "optimal agreement" or negotiation efficiency. Patton, for example, identifies as key criteria for optimizing agreement in negotiation: (1) maximizing value creation (2) in the context of a solution the parties believe to be legitimate (3) that can be readily implemented and (4) a process that involves clear communication, (5) as few resources as possible and (6) strengthens relationships between the parties (Patton, 2005:285-287). An agreement is considered optimal when parties reach a deal in which no side can be made better off without another side being made worse off.

Returning to the byproducts of a hard and positional bargaining approach, such behaviors also may make it difficult to begin negotiations. In the prequel to the South African negotiations discussed above, positional negotiation tactics did just that.

Positional bargaining before the South African mediation: The South African government announced in the 1980s that it did not negotiate with illegal terrorist organizations and therefore would not speak with African National Congress (ANC) representatives until they stopped all violence. The ANC had decided that violence was a primary lever for persuading the apartheid gov- ernment to change. The ANC demanded an end to government attacks on the ANC and release of all ANC prisoners, including Nelson Mandela. As history played out, we learned that both sides ultimately preferred to reach agree- ment on a peaceful transition, but, until Michael Young's mediation, the positional nature of their negotiations may have played a role in blocking the way (Harvey, 2001:107, 115, 133, 166; *see* pp. 17-19).

Reuters photo

---

4. Attorneys and other representatives

Research, discussed in Chapter 6 (pp. 150-151), finds that representatives and particularly attorneys as representatives change the dynamics of negotia- tions. If representatives will participate, you can use that research to help clients and stakeholders identify the barriers their participation might create, and also the ways in which their participation might help overcome barriers.

5. Failing to deal effectively with emotions and self-image as barriers

Research on negotiations and self-image underscores that the parties' self-images may help or undermine successful negotiations (Fisher and Shapiro, 2005; Shapiro, 2005:66-82). Many dispute resolution processes fail to provide a means to acknowledge, address, and manage emotions. A too-oft-heard piece of advice is, "Don't get emotional." While this advice may work for computers and other non-human entities, it is unhelpful for humans engaged in conflict. Failure to create processes that handle emotions can serve as a serious barrier for a designer.

Likewise, issues of identity and self-image can also serve as a major impediment to successful consensual systems. For example, the physician, proud of the care taken at every moment, resists apologizing for a medical error, though an apology would clear the way for settlement of a malpractice dispute. Conversely, identity and self-image can increase the chances that the system will produce settlements. The designer can take advantage of a business person's pride in satisfying every customer, leading that person to strive for early settlement.

For these reasons, designers who recognize the role of emotions and self-image can take these powerful forces into account in the design. They might build processes that reduce the risks inherent in expressing emotion. They also identify levers for engaging self-identity positively. For example, a well-designed dispute resolution system for a hospital might lower the costs of an apology for a doctor. In addition, that system might provide a safe, moderated forum for doctor and patient to engage in a genuine and human conversation that reinforces the self-image of the doctor as a caregiver. Such a system might be more effective than traditional litigation—or even settlement discussions between lawyers in the midst of litigation—where defensiveness and denial tend to dominate.

Note on the list of barriers from your negotiation the circumstances when emotions and self-image interfered or assisted in reaching agreement.

6. Using mediation to overcome barriers to reaching agreement

Mediators have tools to surmount nearly all of the barriers listed above, though these tools vary by context and culture (Busch et al., 2010:9-13). The barrier-surmounting work often succeeds. For example, it is not unusual for mediation to result in settlement half of the time or more in high volume mediation programs. Mediators sometime list a hundred or more tools for overcoming barriers; mediators commonly:

- "encourage exchanges of information,
- "provide new information,
- "help the parties to understand each other's views,
- "let them know that their concerns are understood,
- "promote a productive level of emotional expression,

- "deal with differences in perceptions and interests between negotiators and constituents (including lawyer and client),
- "help negotiators realistically assess alternatives to settlement,
- "encourage flexibility,
- "shift the focus from the past to the future,
- "stimulate the parties to suggest creative settlements,
- "learn (often in separate sessions with each party) about those interests the parties are reluctant to disclose to each other, and
- "invent solutions that meet the fundamental interests of all parties" (Goldberg et al., 2012:121).

REFERENCES

BAZERMAN, Max H., and Katie SHONK (2005) "The Decision Perspective to Negotiation," in Michael L. Moffitt and Robert C. Bordone eds., *The Handbook of Dispute Resolution* 52. San Francisco: Jossey-Bass.

BUSCH, Dominic, Claude-Helene MAYER, and Christian BONESS eds. (2010) *International and Regional Perspectives on Cross-Cultural Mediation.* Frankfort: Peter Lang.

COLE, Sarah R., Nancy H. ROGERS, Craig A. McEWEN, James R. COBEN, and Peter N. THOMPSON (2017-2018) *Mediation: Law, Policy, and Practice* (3rd ed.). Minneapolis: West.

GOLDBERG, Stephen, Jeanne BRETT, and William URY (2012) "Designing an Effective Dispute Resolution System," in Stephen B. Goldberg, Frank E.A. Sander, Nancy H. Rogers, and Sarah R. Cole, *Dispute Resolution: Negotiation, Mediation, Arbitration, and Other Processes* (6th ed.) 483. New York: Wolters Kluwer.

GOLDBERG, Stephen B., Frank E.A. SANDER, Nancy H. ROGERS, and Sarah R. COLE (2012) *Dispute Resolution: Negotiation, Mediation, Arbitration, and Other Processes* (6th ed.). New York: Wolters Kluwer.

HARVEY, Robert (2001) *The Fall of Apartheid: The Inside Story from Smuts to Mbeki.* New York: Palgrave Macmillan.

KOROBKIN, Russell (2006) "Psychological Impediments to Mediation Success: Theory and Practice," 21 *Ohio St. J. on Disp. Resol.* 281.

KOROBKIN, Russell, and Chris GUTHRIE (1994) "Psychological Barriers to Litigation Settlement: An Experimental Approach," 93 *Mich. L. Rev.* 107.

MNOOKIN, Robert H., and Lee ROSS (1995) "Introduction," in Kenneth Arrow et al. eds., *Barriers to Conflict Resolution* 20. New York: W.W. Norton & Co.

MOFFITT, Michael L. (2005) "Disputes as Opportunities to Create Value," in Michael L. Moffitt and Robert C. Bordone eds., *The Handbook of Dispute Resolution* 173. San Francisco: Jossey-Bass.

PATTON, Bruce (2005) "Negotiation," in Michael L. Moffitt and Robert C. Bordone eds., *The Handbook of Dispute Resolution* 279. San Francisco: Jossey-Bass.

ROSS, Lee (1995) "Reactive Devaluation in Negotiation and Conflict Resolution," in Kenneth Arrow et al. eds., *Barriers to Conflict Resolution* 26. New York: W.W. Norton & Co.

SHAPIRO, Daniel L. (2005) "Enemies, Allies, and Emotions: The Power of Positive Emotions in Negotiation," in Michael L. Moffitt and Robert C. Bordone eds., *The Handbook of Dispute Resolution* 66. San Francisco: Jossey-Bass.

URY, William L., Jeanne M. BRETT, and Stephen B. GOLDBERG (1988) *Getting Disputes Resolved: Designing Systems to Cut the Costs of Conflict.* San Francisco: Jossey-Bass.

WEBB, Stuart G., and Ronald D. OUSKY (2006) *The Collaborative Way to Divorce: The Revolutionary Method That Results in Less Stress, Lower Costs and Happier Kids—Without Going to Court.* London: Penguin Books.

WEINSTEIN, Jack B. (2009) "Comments on Owen M. Fiss, Against Settlement (1984)," 78 *Fordham L. Rev.* 1265.

WETLAUFER, Gerald B. (1990) "The Ethics of Lying in Negotiations," 75 *Iowa L. Rev.* 1219.

WISSLER, Roselle L. (2002) "Court-Connected Mediation in General Civil Cases: What We Know from Empirical Research," 17 *Ohio St. J. on Disp. Resol.* 641.

WISSLER, Roselle L. (2004) "The Effectiveness of Court-Connected Dispute Resolution in Civil Cases," 22 *Conflict Resol. Q.* 55.

WISSLER, Roselle L., and Bob DAUBER (2005) "Leading Horses to Water: The Impact of an ADR 'Confer and Report' Rule," 26 *Just. Sys. J.* 253.

YOOST, Stephen M. (2006) "The National Hockey League and Salary Arbitration: Time for a Line Change," 21 *Ohio St. J. on Disp. Res.* 485.

APPENDIX E: UNIFORM MEDIATION ACT (2002)*

Section 1.

This [Act] may be cited as the Uniform Mediation Act.

Section 2. Definitions.

In this [Act]:

(1) "Mediation" means a process in which a mediator facilitates communication and negotiation between parties to assist them in reaching a voluntary agreement regarding their dispute.

(2) "Mediation communication" means a statement, whether oral or in a record or verbal or nonverbal, that occurs during a mediation or is made for purposes of considering, conducting, participating in, initiating, continuing, or reconvening a mediation or retaining a mediator.

(3) "Mediator" means an individual who conducts a mediation.

(4) "Nonparty participant" means a person, other than a party or mediator, that participates in a mediation.

(5) "Mediation party" means a person that participates in a mediation and whose agreement is necessary to resolve the dispute.

(6) "Person" means an individual, corporation, business trust, estate, trust, partnership, limited liability company, association, joint venture,

---

*Editors' Note: "The National Conference of Commissioners on Uniform State Law consists of lawyers appointed by the official designated by statute in each state, often the governor, to represent that state in the development, drafting, and adoption of uniform and model legislation. The Conference has approved many other uniform acts, including the Uniform Commercial Code and the Revised Uniform Arbitration Act. The Uniform Mediation Act was drafted in cooperation with a similar committee representing the American Bar Association Section on Dispute Resolution. Most citations in the comments have been omitted here. The full text including comments is posted at www.law.upenn.edu/bll/ulc/ulc_frame.htm." Stephen B. Goldberg et al., *Dispute Resolution: Negotiation, Mediation, Arbitration, and Other Processes* 617 (6th ed. 2012).

government; governmental subdivision, agency, or instrumentality; public corporation, or any other legal or commercial entity.

(7) "Proceeding" means:

(A) a judicial, administrative, arbitral, or other adjudicative process, including related pre-hearing and post-hearing motions, conferences, and discovery; or

(B) a legislative hearing or similar process.

(8) "Record" means information that is inscribed on a tangible medium or that is stored in an electronic or other medium and is retrievable in perceivable form.

(9) "Sign" means:

(A) to execute or adopt a tangible symbol with the present intent to authenticate a record; or

(B) to attach or logically associate an electronic symbol, sound, or process to or with a record with the present intent to authenticate a record.

to promote candor. . . .

Section 3. Scope.

(a) Except as otherwise provided in subsection (b) or (c), this [Act] applies to a mediation in which:

(1) the mediation parties are required to mediate by statute or court or administrative agency rule or referred to mediation by a court, administrative agency, or arbitrator;

(2) the mediation parties and the mediator agree to mediate in a record that demonstrates an expectation that mediation communications will be privileged against disclosure; or

(3) the mediation parties use as a mediator an individual who holds himself or herself out as a mediator or the mediation is provided by a person that holds itself out as providing mediation.

(b) The [Act] does not apply to a mediation:

(1) relating to the establishment, negotiation, administration, or termination of a collective bargaining relationship;

(2) relating to a dispute that is pending under or is part of the processes established by a collective bargaining agreement, except that the [Act] applies to a mediation arising out of a dispute that has been filed with an administrative agency or court;

(3) conducted by a judge who might make a ruling on the case; or

(4) conducted under the auspices of:

(A) a primary or secondary school if all the parties are students or

(B) a correctional institution for youths if all the parties are residents of that institution.

(c) If the parties agree in advance in a signed record, or a record of proceeding reflects agreement by the parties, that all or part of a mediation is not privileged, the privileges under Sections 4 through 6 do not apply to the mediation or part agreed upon. However, Sections 4 through 6 apply to a mediation communication made by a person that has not received actual notice of the agreement before the communication is made.

Section 4. Privilege Against Disclosure; Admissibility; Discovery.

(a) Except as otherwise provided in Section 6, a mediation communication is privileged as provided in subsection (b) and is not subject to discovery or admissible in evidence in a proceeding unless waived or precluded as provided by Section 5.

(b) In a proceeding, the following privileges apply:

(1) A mediation party may refuse to disclose, and may prevent any other person from disclosing, a mediation communication.

(2) A mediator may refuse to disclose a mediation communication, and may prevent any other person from disclosing a mediation communication of the mediator.

(3) A nonparty participant may refuse to disclose, and may prevent any other person from disclosing, a mediation communication of the nonparty participant.

(c) Evidence or information that is otherwise admissible or subject to discovery does not become inadmissible or protected from discovery solely by reason of its disclosure or use in a mediation.

Section 5. Waiver and Preclusion of Privilege.

(a) A privilege under Section 4 may be waived in a record or orally during a proceeding if it is expressly waived by all parties to the mediation and:

(1) in the case of the privilege of a mediator, it is expressly waived by the mediator; and

(2) in the case of the privilege of a nonparty participant, it is expressly waived by the nonparty participant.

(b) A person that discloses or makes a representation about a mediation communication which prejudices another person in a proceeding is precluded from asserting a privilege under Section 4, but only to the extent necessary for the person prejudiced to respond to the representation or disclosure.

(c) A person that intentionally uses a mediation to plan, attempt to commit or commit a crime, or to conceal an ongoing crime or ongoing criminal activity is precluded from asserting a privilege under Section 4.

Section 6. Exceptions to Privilege.

(a) There is no privilege under Section 4 for a mediation communication that is:

(1) in an agreement evidenced by a record signed by all parties to the agreement;

(2) available to the public under [insert statutory reference to open records act] or made during a session of a mediation which is open, or is required by law to be open, to the public;

(3) a threat or statement of a plan to inflict bodily injury or commit a crime of violence;

(4) intentionally used to plan a crime, attempt to commit or commit a crime, or to conceal an ongoing crime or ongoing criminal activity;

(5) sought or offered to prove or disprove a claim or complaint of professional misconduct or malpractice filed against a mediator;

(6) except as otherwise provided in subsection (c), sought or offered to prove or disprove a claim or complaint of professional misconduct or malpractice filed against a mediation party, nonparty participant, or representative of a party based on conduct occurring during a mediation; or

(7) sought or offered to prove or disprove abuse, neglect, abandonment, or exploitation in a proceeding in which a child or adult protective services agency is a party, unless the

[Alternative A: [State to insert, for example, child or adult protection] case is referred by a court to mediation and a public agency participates.]

[Alternative B: public agency participates in the [State to insert, for example, child or adult protection] mediation].

(b) There is no privilege under Section 4 if a court, administrative agency, or arbitrator finds, after a hearing in camera, that the party seeking discovery or the proponent of the evidence has shown that the evidence is not otherwise available, that there is a need for the evidence that substantially outweighs the interest in protecting confidentiality, and that the mediation communication is sought or offered in:

(1) a court proceeding involving a felony [or misdemeanor]; or

(2) except as otherwise provided in subsection (c), a proceeding to prove a claim to rescind or reform or a defense to avoid liability on a contract arising out of the mediation.

(c) A mediator may not be compelled to provide evidence of a mediation communication referred to in subsection (a)(6) or (b)(2).

(d) If a mediation communication is not privileged under subsection (a) or (b), only the portion of the communication necessary for the application of the exception from nondisclosure may be admitted. Admission of evidence under subsection (a) or (b) does not render the evidence, or any other mediation communication, discoverable or admissible for any other purpose.

Section 7. Prohibited Mediator Reports.

(a) Except as required in subsection (b), a mediator may not make a report, assessment, evaluation, recommendation, finding, or other communication regarding a mediation to a court, administrative agency, or other authority that may make a ruling on the dispute that is the subject of the mediation.

(b) A mediator may disclose:

(1) whether the mediation occurred or has terminated, whether a settlement was reached, and attendance;

(2) a mediation communication as permitted under Section 6; or

(3) a mediation communication evidencing abuse, neglect, abandonment, or exploitation of an individual to a public agency responsible for protecting individuals against such mistreatment.

(c) A communication made in violation of subsection (a) may not be considered by a court, administrative agency, or arbitrator.

Section 8. Confidentiality.

Unless subject to the [insert statutory references to open meetings act and open records act], mediation communications are confidential to the extent agreed by the parties or provided by other law or rule of this State.

Section 9. Mediator's Disclosure of Conflicts of Interest; Background.

(a) Before accepting a mediation, an individual who is requested to serve as a mediator shall:

(1) make an inquiry that is reasonable under the circumstances to determine whether there are any known facts that a reasonable individual would consider likely to affect the impartiality of the mediator, including a financial or personal interest in the outcome of the mediation and an existing or past relationship with a mediation party or foreseeable participant in the mediation; and

(2) disclose any such known fact to the mediation parties as soon as is practical before accepting a mediation.

(b) If a mediator learns any fact described in subsection (a)(1) after accepting a mediation, the mediator shall disclose it as soon as is practicable.

(c) At the request of a mediation party, an individual who is requested to serve as a mediator shall disclose the mediator's qualifications to mediate a dispute.

(d) A person that violates subsection [(a) or (b)] [(a), (b), or (g)] is precluded by the violation from asserting a privilege under Section 4.

(e) Subsections (a), (b), [and] (c), [and] [(g)] do not apply to an individual acting as a judge.

(f) This [Act] does not require that a mediator have a special qualification by background or profession.

(g) A mediator must be impartial, unless after disclosure of the facts required in subsections (a) and (b) to be disclosed, the parties agree otherwise.

Section 10. Participation in Mediation.

An attorney or other individual designated by a party may accompany the party to and participate in a mediation. A waiver of participation given before the mediation may be rescinded.[51]

APPENDIX F: CASE STUDY SOURCES AND ACKNOWLEDGMENTS

Throughout this book we have relied upon the stories of design work in South Africa, at NIH, in Maryland, in Sanford, Florida, at eBay, with Canada's Truth and Reconciliation Commission, and with Cure Violence Chicago. This material documents how we developed these stories and allows us to keep the accounts of the stories relatively uncluttered by footnotes.

Michael Young and the South African Talks

We thank Michael Young for visiting Harvard Law School on March 6, 2012 and Ohio State University Moritz College of Law on March 7, 2012. During those visits, he spoke with classes and at public colloquia, and Bob Bordone and Nancy Rogers had opportunities to interview him. You can watch and listen to one of Young's Ohio State lectures at http://moritzlaw.osu.edu/programs/adr/law-rence/young. You can also watch and download Young's address to the Harvard Law School community at http://www.law.harvard.edu/news/2012/03/30_michael-young-anti-apartheid-negotiations.html.

---

51. Editors' Note: "The National Conference of Commissioners on Uniform State Laws amended the Uniform Mediation Act in 2003. The purpose of the amendment was to encourage state adoption of the United Nations Commission on International Trade Law's Model Law on International Commercial Conciliation and to make the confidentiality provisions of that law consistent with the Uniform Mediation Act. The UN Commission urged member nations to vary the wording of the Commission's law as little as possible to facilitate international under-standing and thereby encourage the use of mediation for international commercial matters. To accommodate this desire, the UMA drafters incorporated the Model Law by reference in a new section 11. The original UMA sections 11-16 were renumbered as sections 12-17, and the Model Law was attached as an appendix to the UMA." Stephen B. Goldberg et al., *Dispute Resolution: Negotiation, Mediation, Arbitration, and Other Processes* 635-636 (6th ed. 2012).

Young also kindly reviewed our book draft and made comments on it through a September 3, 2012 email to the authors. At Young's suggestion, Nancy Rogers secured copies of Young's notes from the South African talks from the University of York Borthwick Institute for Archives. In addition, we reviewed the references that are cited in the stories. We are also grateful to Justice Richard Goldstone from South Africa, who, at Frank Sander's request, reviewed an earlier account of the South African experiences and gave us suggestions to increase the accuracy of our account.

Howard Gadlin and the NIH Ombuds Office

Howard Gadlin graciously allowed Nancy Rogers to interview him by phone on August 13, 2010 and permitted a video interview by Jonathan Franz on December 10, 2010. Excerpts from the video interview are available on the course web page. Gadlin also reviewed a draft of the summary and made suggestions by email to Nancy Rogers on December 7, 2010 and reviewed it again in 2012 (email to Nancy Rogers on September 27, 2012). We are also grateful to him for sending a copy of some of the work of his office, including the workbook developed for improving collaboration. In addition, we appreciate his giving permission to use a study of his work that was done by Harvard Law School's Dispute System Design Clinic, under Bob Bordone's supervision.

Rachel Wohl, Judge Robert Bell, Lou Gieszl, and Cheryl Jamison of the Maryland Program

Rachel Wohl and her staff were exceedingly helpful in the profile of their work. Nancy Rogers interviewed Wohl on August 25, 2010 and December 6, 2010; Lou Gieszl on October 6, 2010; and Cheryl Jamison on October 25, 2010. In addition, Jonathan Franz conducted video interviews of Judge Bell and Wohl on December 13, 2010; excerpts are posted on the course web page. Wohl, Gieszl and Cheryl Jamison reviewed the book draft and sent comments to Nancy Rogers on September 14, 2012; September 17, 2012; and September 17, 2012, respectively. In addition, they shared copies of reports and videos developed by the program.

Colin Rule and eBay

Colin Rule gave wonderful guidance to us when Rule headed both eBay's and PayPal's dispute resolution activities. Nancy Rogers interviewed Colin Rule by phone on August 24 and 25, 2010 and on October 22, 2010. He was also helpful in directing Rogers to various online and print resources, which are cited in the book, and sent screen shots on August 25, 2010 and October 22, 2010. Craig McEwen interviewed him on March 10, 2011 about evaluation approaches taken by eBay. Rule reviewed the draft of the book as it related to him and approved by email to Nancy Rogers on September 1, 2012. In addition, we are grateful that Colin allowed us to reference some of the findings of students working on behalf of eBay in Harvard Law School's Dispute Systems Design Clinic under Bob Bordone's direction.

Jennifer Llewellyn and the Truth and Reconciliation Commission of Canada

We thank Jennifer Llewellyn for providing an interview with Nancy Rogers by phone on August 8, 2012. Rogers then sent Llewellyn a copy of the book draft, and Llewellyn helped with suggestions by emails to Rogers on September 6, 2012 and September 26, 2012. In addition, we reviewed online and print resources that are cited in the book.

Gary Slutkin and Tio Hardiman of Cure Violence

The staff of Cure Violence helped us to understand this innovative program. Nancy Rogers interviewed Tio Hardiman in person on July 23, 2010 when he spoke in Columbus, Ohio, and then by phone on December 2, 2010 and February 2, 2010. Rogers interviewed Cure Violence's Candice M. Kane on August 4, 2010. In addition, Bob Bordone interviewed Gary Slutkin when Slutkin spoke at Harvard Law School class during spring semester, 2012. Tio Hardiman sent approval of a draft on December 29, 2010. Gary Slutkin sent Bob Bordone comments on the draft by email on August 9, 2012. In addition, Nancy Rogers heard speeches by several Cure Violence interrupters in connection with the screening of "The Interrupters" documentary in Columbus, Ohio on November 9, 2011. We reviewed additional sources that are cited in the book.

Andrew Thomas of Sanford, Florida

We are grateful to Andrew Thomas of the City of Sanford for his help in understanding the events unfolding there. Nancy Rogers interviewed Andrew Thomas and reviewed drafts with him by email, resulting in her article, *When Conflicts Polarize Communities: Designing Localized Offices That Intervene Collaboratively*, 30 Ohio St. J. on Disp. Resol. 173 (2015). Presentations by the Sanford city manager, former police chief, chair of a Sanford clergy group, and Andrew Thomas at the Ohio State University Moritz College of Law on April 9, 2015 supplemented this. In addition, Nancy Rogers emailed Andrew Thomas the portions of this book referencing Sanford on July 24, 2018, requesting any corrections for inaccuracies and modified the text in response to suggestions from Andrew Thomas' email on August 1, 2018.

Collected References

ABREGU, Lisa (2012) "Restorative Justice in Schools: Restoring Relationships and Building Community," 18(4) *Disp. Resol. Mag.* 10.

ADAIR, John G. (1984) "The Hawthorne Effect: A Reconsideration of the Methodological Artifact," 69(2) *J. Applied Psychol.* 334.

ADAMS, Tammy, Janet A. MEANS, and Michael SPIVEY (2007) *The Project Meeting Facilitator: Facilitation Skills to Make the Most of Project Meetings.* San Francisco: Jossey-Bass.

ALBERSTEIN, Michal, and Nadav DAVIDOVITCH (2011) "Apologies in the Healthcare System: From Clinical Medicine to Public Health," 74 *Law & Contemp. Probs.* 151.

ALEXANDER, Nadia (2009) *International and Comparative Mediation: Legal Perspectives.* The Netherlands: Wolters Kluwer Law and Business.

ALLRED, Keith G. (2005) "Relationship Dynamics in Disputes: Replacing Contention with Cooperation," in Michael L. Moffitt and Robert C. Bordone eds., *The Handbook of Dispute Resolution* 83. San Francisco: Jossey-Bass.

AMERICAN ARBITRATION ASSOCIATION (2007) *Drafting Dispute Resolution Clauses: A Practical Guide.* New York: AAA.

AMERICAN BAR ASSOCIATION SECTION OF DISPUTE RESOLUTION TASK FORCE ON IMPROVING MEDIATION QUALITY (2008) *Final Report.* Washington, DC: American Bar Association Section on Dispute Resolution.

AMERICAN BAR ASSOCIATION STANDING COMMITTEE ON THE FEDERAL JUDICIARY (2010) "What It Is and How It Works," http://www.abanet.org/scfedjud.

AMERICAN BAR ASSOCIATION TASK FORCE ON eCOMMERCE AND ADR (2002) *Recommended Best Practices for Online Dispute Resolution Service Providers, available at* http://www.abanet.org/dispute/documents/BestPracticesFinal102802.pdf.

AMERICAN SOCIOLOGICAL ASSOCIATION (1999) *Code of Ethics (see especially* Ethical Standards 10 and 11 on Confidentiality and Informed Consent), www.asanet.org/sites/default/files/asa_code_of_ethics-june2018.pdf.

AMIR, Yehuda (1998) "Contact Hypothesis in Ethnic Relations," in Eugene Weiner ed., *The Handbook of Interethnic Coexistence* 162. New York: Continuum.

AMSLER, Lisa Blomgren (2017) "The Dispute Resolver's Role Within a Dispute System Design: Justice, Accountability, and Impact," 13 *U. St. Thomas L.J.* 168.

AMSLER, Lisa Blomgren, and Tina NABATCHI (2016) "Public Engagements and Decision-Making: Moving Minnesota Forward to Dialogue and Deliberation," 42 *Mitchell Hamline L. Rev.* 1629.

AMSTUTZ, Mark R. (2005) *The Healing of Nations: The Promise and Limits of Political Forgiveness.* New York: Lanham.

ARROW, Kenneth, et al. eds. (1995) *Barriers to Conflict Resolution.* New York: W.W. Norton.

ASMAL, Kader (2000) "International Law and Practice: Dealing with the Past in the South African Experience," 15 *Am. U. Int'l L. Rev.* 1211.

ASSOCIATION FOR CONFLICT RESOLUTION (2010) *2010 Model Standards for Mediation Certification.* Washington, DC: ACR.

ASSOCIATION FOR CONFLICT RESOLUTION TASK FORCE ON MEDIATOR CERTIFICATION (2004) *Report and Recommendations to the Board of Directors.* Washington, D.C.: ACR.

AUERBACH, Jerold (1983) *Justice Without Law?* New York: Oxford University Press.

AVERCH, Harry A. (2004) "Using Expert Judgment" in Joseph S. Wholey, Harry P. Hatry, and Kathryn E. Newcomer eds., *Handbook of Practical Program Evaluation* (2d ed.) 292. San Francisco: Jossey-Bass.

AVRUCH, Kevin (1998) *Culture and Conflict Resolution.* Washington, DC: United States Institute of Peace Press.

――――――――――――――――― (2002) "What Do I Need to Know About Culture? A Researcher Says . . . ," in John Paul Lederach and Janice Moomaw Jenner eds., *A Handbook of International Peacebuilding: Into the Eye of the Storm* 75. San Francisco: Jossey-Bass.

BABBIE, Earl (2010) *The Practice of Social Research* (12th ed.). Belmont, CA: Wadsworth.

BALZ, Dan (2010). "In Health-Care Debate, a Great Divide over Style and Substance." *Washington Post,* February 28, p. A02.

BARNARD, Jayne W. (1999) "Reintegrative Shaming in Corporate Sentencing," 72 *S. Cal. L. Rev.* 959.

BARRETT, Jerome T., and Joseph P. BARRETT (2004) *A History of Alternative Dispute Resolution.* San Francisco: Jossey-Bass.

BARTELS, William K. (2000-2001) "The Stormy Seas of Apologies: California Evidence Code Section 1160 Provides a Safe Harbor for Apologies Made After Accidents," 28 *W. St. U. L. Rev.* 141.

BASS, Jack (1993) *Taming the Storm: The Life and Times of Judge Frank M. Johnson, Jr. and the South's Fight over Civil Rights.* New York: Doubleday.

BAZERMAN, Max H., and Katie SHONK (2005) "The Decision Perspective to Negotiation," in Michael L. Moffitt and Robert C. Bordone eds., *The Handbook of Dispute Resolution* 52. San Francisco: Jossey-Bass.

BECKWITH, Sandra (2011) "District Court Mediation Programs: A View from the Bench," 26 *Ohio St. J. on Disp. Resol.* 357.

BELL, Robert M., and Rachel WOHL (2008) *The Impact of the Mediation and Conflict Resolution Office's Work to Advance the Appropriate Use of Alternative Dispute Resolution in the Courts.* Annapolis, MD: Maryland Mediation and Conflict Resolution Office.

BELSON, Ken, and Mark LEIBOVICH (2018) "Inside the Confidential N.F.L. Meeting to Discuss National Anthem Protests," *New York Times,* April 25, p.A1.

BENNETT, L. Michelle, Howard GADLIN, and Samantha LEVINE-FINLEY (2010) *Collaboration and Team Science: A Field Guide.* Washington, DC: National Institutes of Health.

BENNETT, Steven C. (2013) "Confidentiality Issues in Arbitration," 68 *Disp. Resol. J.* 1.

BENS, Ingrid (2017) *Facilitating with Ease!: Core Skills for Facilitators, Team Leaders and Members, Managers, Consultants, and Trainers.* Hoboken, NJ: John Wiley & Sons.

BERMAN, Greg, and John FEINBLATT (2005) *Good Courts: The Case for Problem-Solving Justice.* New York: New Press.

BINDER, David A., Paul BERGMAN, Susan C. PRICE, and Paul R. TREMBLAY (2004) *Lawyers as Counselors: A Client-Centered Approach.* St. Paul, MN: Thomson West.

BINGHAM, Lisa B. (2003) *Mediation at Work: Transforming Workplace Conflict at the United States Postal Service.* Bloomington, IN: Human Capital Management Series, IBM Center for the Business of Government.

――――――――――――――――― (2004) "Employment Dispute Resolution: The Case for Mediation," 22 *Conflict Resol. Q.* 145.

――――――――――――――――― (2008) "Designing Justice: Legal Institutions and Other Systems for Managing Conflict," 24 *Ohio St. J. on Disp. Resol.* 1.

BINGHAM, Lisa B., Cynthia J. HALLBERLIN, Denise A. WALKER, and Won-Tae CHUNG (2009) "Dispute System Design and Justice in Employment Dispute Resolution: Mediation at the Workplace," 14 *Harv. Negot. L. Rev.* 1.

BIRKE, Richard (2010) "Neuroscience and Settlement: An Examination of Scientific Innovations and Practical Applications," 25 *Ohio St. J. on Disp. Resol.* 477.

BLACK, Julia (1997) *Rules and Regulators.* Oxford, UK: Oxford University Press.

BLANKLEY, Kristen M. (2016) "The Ethics and Practice of Drafting Pre-Dispute Resolution Clauses," 49 *Creighton L. Rev.* 743.

BLOOMFIELD, David, Teresa BARNES, and Luc HUYSE eds. (2003) *Reconciliation After Violent Conflict: A Handbook.* Stockholm: International Institute for Democracy and Electoral Assistance.

BOHNET, Iris, and Yael BAYTELMAN (2007) "Institutions and Trust: Implications for Preferences, Beliefs and Behavior," 19 *Rationality & Soc'y* 99.

BOOTHMAN, Richard C., Amy C. BLACKWELL, Darrell A. CAMPBELL, Jr., Elaine COMMISKEY, and Susan ANDERSON (2009) "A Better Approach to Medical Malpractice Claims? The University of Michigan Experience," 2 *J. Health & Life Sci. L.* 125.

BORDONE, Robert C. (1998) "Electronic Online Dispute Resolution: Approach, Potential, Problems and a Proposal," 3 *Harv. Negot. L. Rev.* 175.

_____ (2018) "Building Conflict Resilience: It's Not Just About Problem-Solving," 2018 *J. Disp. Resol.* 65.

BORN, Gary (2010) *International Arbitration: Cases and Materials.* New York: Wolters Kluwer.

BOUTROS-GHALI, Boutros (1995) *An Agenda for Peace* (2d ed.). New York: United Nations.

BOWN, Chad P., and Bernard M. HOEKMAN (2005) "WTO Dispute Settlement and the Missing Developing Country Cases: Engaging the Private Sector" 8(4) *J. Int'l Econ. L.* 261.

BOYARSKY, Stuart (2015) "Transparency in Investor-State Arbitration," 21(4) *Disp. Resol. Mag.* 34.

BRADY, Rory (undated, approximately 2002) *Report to the Government on the Review of the Laffoy Commission* (unpublished Irish government document).

BRAND, Ronald A. (2012) "Party Autonomy and Access to Justice in the UNCITRAL Online Dispute Resolution Project," 10 *Loy. U. Chi. Int'l L. Rev.* 11.

BRANDON, Barbara H., and Robert D. CARLITZ (2002) "Online Rulemaking and Other Tools for Strengthening Our Civil Infrastructure," 54 *Admin. L. Rev.* 1421.

BRAZIL, Wayne D. (2002) "Court ADR 25 Years After *Pound*: Have We Found a Better Way?," 18 *Ohio St. J. on Disp. Resol.* 93.

_____ (2006) "Should Court-Sponsored ADR Survive?," 21 *Ohio St. J. on Disp. Resol.* 241.

_____ (2007) "Hosting Mediations as a Representative of the System of Civil Justice," 22 *Ohio St. J. on Disp. Resol.* 208.

BRENNAN, Becca (2015) "Match or Mismatch.com? Online Dispute Resolution and Divorce," 21(2) *Disp. Resol. Mag.* 15.

BRETT, Jeanne M. (2007) *Negotiating Globally: How to Negotiate Deals, Resolve Disputes, and Make Decisions Across Cultural Boundaries* (2d ed.). San Francisco: John Wiley and Sons, Inc.

BRETT, Jeanne, Zoe I. BARSNESS, and Stephen B. GOLDBERG (1996) "The Effectiveness of Mediation: An Independent Analysis of Cases Handled by Four Major Service Providers," 12 *Negot. J.* 259.

BROOKS, David (2010). "Not as Dull as Expected!," *The New York Times*, February 26, p.27.

BROWN, Jennifer Gerarda (2006) "Creativity and Problem-Solving," in Andrea Kupfer Schneider and Christopher Honeyman eds., *The Negotiator's Field Book: The Desk Reference for the Experienced Negotiator* 407. Washington, DC: ABA, Section of Dispute Resolution.

BROWN, Jennifer Gerarda, and Ian AYRES (1994) "Economic Rationales for Mediation," 80 *Va. L. Rev.* 323.

BROWN, Louis M., and Edward A. DAUER (1978) *Planning by Lawyers: Materials on a Nonadversarial Legal Process.* New York: Foundation Press.

BRUNET, Edward, Charles B. CRAVER, and Ellen E. DEASON (2016) *Alternative Dispute Resolution: The Advocate's Perspective* (5th ed.). New York: LexisNexis.

BURFORD, Gale, and Joe HUDSON eds. (2000) *Family Group Conferencing: New Directions in Community-Centered Child and Family Practice.* Piscataway, NJ: Transaction Publishers.

BURGER, Warren (1977) "Our Vicious Legal Spiral," 16 *Judges J.* 22 (Fall).

BURGESS, Heidi, and Guy BURGESS (2002) "How Do I Get Good Information in a Short Time?," in John Paul Lederach and Janice Moomaw Jenner eds., *A Handbook of International Peacekeeping: Into the Eye of the Storm* 59. San Francisco: Jossey-Bass.

BURNS, Robert (2010). "Mideast Peace Talks Round Ends with No Deal; Palestinians Launch Mortars, Israelis Drop Bombs." *Associated Press Newswires*, Sept. 15.

BUSCH, Dominic, Claude-Helene MAYER, and Christian BONESS eds. (2010) *International and Regional Perspectives on Cross-Cultural Mediation.* Frankfort: Peter Lang.

BUSH, Robert A. Baruch, and Joseph FOLGER (1996) *The Promise of Mediation.* San Francisco: Jossey-Bass.

———————————————— (2005) *The Promise of Mediation* (2d ed.). San Francisco: Jossey-Bass.

———————————————— (2012) "Mediation and Social Justice: Risks and Opportunities," 27 *Ohio St. J. on Disp. Resol.* 1.

CAPITAINE, Brieg, and Karine VANTHUYNE eds. (2017) *Power Through Testimony: Reframing Residential Schools in the Age of Reconciliation.* Vancouver: UBC Press.

CARPENTER, Susan (1999) "Choosing Appropriate Consensus Building Techniques and Strategies," in Lawrence Susskind, Sarah McKearnan, and Jennifer Thomas-Larmer eds., *The Consensus Building Handbook: A Comprehensive Guide to Reaching Agreement* 62. Thousand Oaks, CA: Sage Publications, Inc.

CARPENTER, Susan L., and W.J.D. KENNEDY (2001) *Managing Public Disputes: A Practical Guide for Government, Business, and Citizens' Groups.* San Francisco: Jossey-Bass.

CARR, Alan, Barbara DOOLEY, Mark FITZPATRICK, Edel FLANAGAN, Roisin FLANAGAN-HOWARD, Kevin TIERNEY, Megan WHITE, Margaret DALY, and Jonathan EGAN (2010) "Adult Adjustment of Survivors of Institutional Child Abuse in Ireland," 34 *Child Abuse & Neglect* 477.

CARTER, Terry (2011) "The Master of Disaster," 97 *ABA J.* 32 (January).

CHAYES, Antonia, and Martha MINOW eds. (2003) *Imagine Coexistence: Restoring Humanity After Violent Ethnic Conflict.* San Francisco: Jossey-Bass.

CHEW, Pat K. (2001) *The Conflict and Culture Reader.* New York: New York University Press.

CHIGAS, Diana, and Brian GANSON (2003) "Grand Visions and Small Projects," in Antonia Chayes and Martha Minow eds., *Imagine Coexistence* 59. San Francisco: Jossey-Bass.

CHILDRESS, Stacy M., Denis P. DOYLE, and David A. THOMAS (2009) *Leading for Equity: The Pursuit of Excellence in Montgomery County Public Schools.* Cambridge, MA: Harvard Education Press.

CLARK, Kathleen (2007) "The Use of Collaborative Law in Medical Error Situations," 19 *Health L.* 19.

CLEVEN, Erik, Robert A. Baruch BUSH, and Judith A. SAUL (2018) "Living with No: Political Polarization and Transformative Dialogue," 2018 *J. Disp. Resol.* 53.

COBEN, James R., and Peter N. THOMPSON (2006), "Disputing Irony: A Systematic Look at Litigation About Mediation," 17 *Harv. Negot. L. Rev.* 43.

————————————————, The Mediation Case Law Project, a website at https://digitalcommons. hamline.edu/dri_mclsummaries/.

COHEN, Amy J. (2008) "Negotiation, Meet New Governance: Interests, Skills, and Selves," 32 *Law & Soc. Inquiry* 503.

———————————————— (2009) "Dispute Systems Design, Neoliberalism, and the Problem of Scale," 14 *Harv. Negot. L. Rev.* 51.

COHEN, Amy J., and Ellen E. DEASON (2006) "Comparative Considerations: Towards the Global Transfer of Ideas on Dispute System Design," 12(3) *Disp. Resol.* 23.

COHEN, Judith (2009a) "Why Programs Are No Longer Enough: An Interview on Collaborating at the U.S. TSA," 27 *Alternatives* 81.

———————————————— (2009b) "What Corporations Need to Know About How to Install an Integrated Conflict Management System," 27 *Alternatives* 99.

COLE, Sarah R. (2005) "Mediator Certification: Has the Time Come?," 11(3) *Disp. Resol. Mag.* 7.

COLE, Sarah R., and Kristen M. BLANKLEY (2005) "Arbitration," in Michael L. Moffitt and Robert C. Bordone eds., *The Handbook of Dispute Resolution* 52. San Francisco: Jossey-Bass.

_____ (2006) "Online Mediation: Where We Have Been, Where We Are Now, and Where We Should Be," 38 *U. Tol. L. Rev.* 193.

COLE, Sarah R., Craig A. McEWEN, Nancy H. ROGERS, James COBEN, and Peter THOMPSON (2014) "Where Mediation Is Concerned, Sometimes 'There Ought Not to Be a Law!,'" 20 *Disp. Resol. Mag.* 34 (Winter).

COLE, Sarah R., Nancy H. ROGERS, Craig A. McEWEN, James R. COBEN, and Peter N. THOMPSON (2017-2018) *Mediation: Law, Policy & Practice* (3rd ed.). Minneapolis: West.

COLEMAN, Peter T., and Morton DEUTSCH (1998) "The Mediation of Interethnic Conflict in Schools," in Eugene Weiner ed., *The Handbook of Interethnic Coexistence*. New York: Continuum.

COLL, Bryan (2009) "Why Ireland Is Running Out of Priests," *Time Mag.*, December 3, *available at* http://www.time.com/time/world/article/0,8599,1942665,00.html.

COOPER, Corinne, and Bruce E. MEYERSON eds. (1991) *A Drafter's Guide to Alternative Dispute Resolution*. Chicago: ABA.

CORTES, Pablo (2008) "Can I Afford Not to Mediate? Mandatory Online Mediation for European Consumers: Legal Constraints and Policy Issues," 35 *Rutgers Computer & Tech. L.J.* 1.

_____ (2016) "The Brave New World of Consumer Redress in the European Union and the United Kingdom," 22(3) *Disp. Resol. Mag.* 41.

COSTANTINO, Cathy A. (2009) "Second Generation Organizational Conflict Management Systems Design: A Practitioner's Perspective on Emerging Issues," 14 *Harv. Negot. L. Rev.* 81.

COSTANTINO, Cathy A., and Melinda R. LEWIS (2015) "What Dispute Systems Design Can Learn from Project Management," *Negot. J.* (July) 175.

COSTANTINO, Cathy A., and Christina Sickles MERCHANT (1995) *Designing Conflict Management Systems: A Guide to Creating Productive and Healthy Organizations*. San Francisco: Jossey-Bass.

CRAVER, Charles B. (2015) "How to Conduct Effective Telephone and E-Mail Negotiations, 17 *Cardozo J. Conflict Resol.* 1.

CROCKER, David A. (2002) "Punishment, Reconciliation, and Democratic Deliberation," 5 *Buff. Crim.* 509.

CROSBY, Ned, and Doug NETHERCUT (2005) "Citizens Juries: Creating a Trustworthy Voice of the People," in John Gastil and Peter Levine eds., *The Deliberative Democracy Handbook: Strategies for Effective Civic Engagement in the Twenty-First Century* 111. San Francisco: Jossey-Bass.

CURHAN, Jared R., Hillary Anger ELFENBEIN, and Heng XU (2006) "What Do People Value When They Negotiate? Mapping the Domain of Subjective Value in Negotiation," 91 *J. Personality & Soc. Psychol.* 493.

CURRAN, Daniel, James K. SEBENIUS, and Michael WATKINS (2004) "Two Paths to Peace: Contrasting George Mitchell in Northern Ireland with Richard Holbrooke in Bosnia-Herzegovina," 20 *Negot. J.* 513.

DAVIDSON, Anne (2005) "Finding Your Voice," in Roger Schwarz, Anne Davidson, Peg Carlson, and Sue McKinney eds., *The Skilled Facilitator Fieldbook: Tips, Tools, and Tested Methods for Consultants, Facilitators, Managers, Trainers, and Coaches* 279. San Francisco: Jossey-Bass.

DAVIS, Benjamin G., and Keefe SNYDER (2010) "Online Influence Space(s) and Digital Influence Waves: In Honor of Charly," 25 *Ohio St. J. on Disp. Resol.* 201.

DE COSTA, Ravi (2016) "Discursive Institutions in Non-Transitional Societies: The Truth and Reconciliation Commission of Canada," 38(2) *Int'l Pol. Sci. Rev.* 185.

DEASON, Ellen E. (2001) "Enforcing Mediated Settlement Agreements: Contract Law Collides with Confidentiality," 35 *U. Davis L. Rev.* 33.

_____ (2002) "Predictable Mediation Confidentiality in the U.S. Federal System," 17 *Ohio St. J. on Disp. Resol.* 239.

_____ (2006) "The Need for Trust as a Justification for Confidentiality in Mediation: A Cross-Disciplinary Approach," 54 *U. Kan. L. Rev.* 1387.

DELGADO, Richard (1988) "ADR and the Dispossessed: Recent Books About the Deformalization Movement," 13 *Law & Soc. Inquiry* 145.

DEUTSCH, Morton (1998) "Constructive Conflict Resolution: Principles, Training, and Research," in Eugene Weiner ed., *The Handbook of Interethnic Coexistence* 199. New York: Continuum.

DIAMOND, Louise (2002) "Who Else Is Working There?," in John Paul Lederach and Janice Moomaw Jenner eds., *A Handbook of International Peacebuilding: Into the Eye of the Storm* 25. San Francisco: Jossey-Bass.

DIVIDED COMMUNITY PROJECT (2017) *Divided Communities and Social Media: Strategies for Community Leaders.* Columbus, OH: The Ohio State University Moritz College of Law, http://moritzlaw.osu.edu/dividedcommunityproject/.

DODGE, Jaime (2011) "The Limits of Procedural Private Ordering," 97 *Va. L. Rev.* 723.

DOMKE, Martin, Larry EDMONSON, and Gabriel M. WILNER (2017) *Domke on Commercial Arbitration* (3rd ed.) Thomson Reuters/West Group.

DORE, Laurie Kratky (2006) "Public Courts Versus Private Justice: It's Time to Let Some Sun Shine in on Alternative Dispute Resolution," 81 *Chi.-Kent L. Rev.* 463.

DOYLE, Michael, and David STRAUS (1993) *How to Make Meetings Work!* New York: Berkley Books.

DRAHOZAL, Christopher R. (2015) "Confidentiality in Consumer and Employment Arbitration," 7 *Y.B. Arb. & Mediation* 28.

DRAHOZAL, Christopher R., and Stephen J. WARE (2010) "Why Do Businesses Use (or Not Use) Arbitration Clauses?," 25 *Ohio St. J. on Disp. Resol.* 433.

DRAHOZAL, Christopher R., and Samantha ZYONTZ (2011) "Creditor Claims in Arbitration and in Court," 7 *Hastings Bus. L.J.* 77.

DRAKE, William R. (1989) "Practice Dispute Systems Design: A Special Section—Statewide Offices of Mediation," 5 *Negot. J.* 359.

DUBINSKY, Paul R. (2005) "Human Rights Law Meets Private Law Harmonization: The Coming Conflict," 30 *Yale J. Int'l L.* 211.

DUKES, E. Franklin (1996) *Resolving Public Conflict: Transforming Community and Governance.* Manchester, UK: Manchester University Press.

DUNN, Seamus, and Jacqueline NOLAN-HALEY (1999) "Conflict in Northern Ireland After the Good Friday Agreement," 22 *Fordham Int'l L.J.* 1372.

EAGLIN, James B. (1990) *The Pre-Argument Conference Program in the Sixth Circuit Court of Appeals: An Evaluation.* Washington, DC: Federal Judicial Center.

ELLIOTT, Michael L. Poirier (1999) "The Role of Facilitators, Mediators, and Other Consensus Building Practitioners," in Lawrence Susskind, Sarah McKearnan, and Jennifer Thomas-Larmer eds., *The Consensus Building Handbook: A Comprehensive Guide to Reaching Agreement* 199. Thousand Oaks, CA: Sage Publications.

EUROSTAT (2009) *Statistical Books: Consumers in Europe.* Luxembourg: Office for Official Publications of the European Communities.

EXON, Susan Nauss (2017) "Ethics and Online Dispute Resolution: From Evolution to Revolution," 32 *Ohio St. J. on Disp. Resol.* 609.

FADER, Hallie (2008) "Designing the Forum to Fit the Fuss: Dispute System Design for the State Trial Courts," 13 *Harv. Negot. L. Rev.* 481.

FARKAS, Brian (2018) "Donald Trump and Stormy Daniels: An Arbitration Case Study," 24(3) *Disp. Resol. Mag.* 12.

FASLER, Karen (2007) "Show Me the Money!! The Potential for Cost Savings Associated with a Parallel Program and Collaborative Law," 20(2) *Health L.* 15.

FAURE, Guy Oliver (2011) "Practice Note: Informal Mediation in China," 29(1) *Conflict Resol. Q.* 85.

FEINBERG, Kenneth R. (2005) *What Is Life Worth?* New York: Public Affairs.

FELSTINER, William L.F. (1974) "Influences of Social Organization on Dispute Processing," 9 *Law & Soc'y Rev.* 63.

FISHER, Roger, and Daniel SHAPIRO (2005) *Beyond Reason: Using Emotions as You Negotiate.* New York: Viking.

FISHER, Roger, and Alan SHARP (1998) *Getting It Done: How to Lead When You're Not in Charge.* New York: Harper Business.

FISHER, Roger, Elizabeth KOPELMAN, and Andrea Kupfer SCHNEIDER (1996) *Beyond Machiavelli: Tools for Coping with Conflict*. New York: Penguin Books.

FISHER, Roger, William URY, and Bruce PATTON (1991) *Getting to Yes: Negotiating Agreement Without Giving In* (2d ed.). New York: Penguin Group.

————————————————————— (2011) *Getting to Yes: Negotiating Agreement Without Giving In* (3rd ed.). Boston: Houghton Mifflin.

FISHKIN, James S. (2009) *When the People Speak: Deliberative Democracy and Public Consultation*. Oxford, UK: Oxford University Press.

FISHKIN, James S., and Cynthia FARRAR (2005) "Deliberative Polling: From Experiment to Community Resource," in John Gastil and Peter Levine eds., *The Deliberative Democracy Handbook: Strategies for Effective Civic Engagement in the Twenty-First Century* 68. San Francisco: Jossey-Bass.

FISS, Owen M. (1984) "Against Settlement," 93 *Yale L.J.* 1073.

————————————————————— (2009) "The History of an Idea," 78 *Fordham L. Rev.* 1273.

FITZPATRICK, Jody L., James R. SANDERS, and Blaine R. WORTHEN (2010) *Program Evaluation: Alternative Approaches and Practical Guidelines* (4th ed.). Englewood Cliffs, NJ: Prentice-Hall.

FOLBERG, Jay, Dwight GOLANN, Thomas J. STIPANOWICH, and Lisa A. KLOPPENBERG (2016) *Resolving Disputes: Theory, Practice, and Law* (3rd ed.). New York: Wolters Kluwer.

FOLGER, Joseph P., and Robert A. Baruch BUSH (2010) "Conclusion: The Development of Transformative Mediation: Challenges and Future Prospects," in Joseph P. Folger et al. eds., *Transformative Mediation: A Sourcebook* 453. New York: Institute for the Study of Conflict Transformation.

FOLGER, Joseph P., Marshall Scott POOLE, and Randall K. STUTMAN (2012) *Working Through Conflict: Strategies for Relationships, Groups, and Organizations* (7th ed.). London: Pearson.

FORESTER, John (2009) *Dealing with Differences: Dramas of Mediating Public Disputes*. Oxford, UK: Oxford University Press.

FRANKEL, Tamar (2010) "Trust and the Internet," in James R. Silkenat, Jeffrey M. Aresty, and Jacqueline Klosek eds., *The ABA Guide to International Business Negotiations: A Comparison of Cross-Cultural Issues and Successful Approaches* (3rd ed.). Chicago: ABA.

FREEMAN, Mark (2006) *Truth Commissions and Procedural Fairness*. Cambridge: Cambridge University Press.

FRENKEL, Douglas N., and James H. STARK (2009) *The Practice of Mediation*. New York: Wolters Kluwer.

FRIEDMAN, Ray, and Steven C. CURRALL (2004) "Conflict Escalation: Dispute Exacerbating Elements of E-Mail Communication," *available at* http://papers.ssrn.com/sol3/Delivery.cfm/SSRN_ID459429_code031108500.pdf?abstractid=459429&mirid=5.

FUERTES, Al (2012) "Storytelling and Its Transformative Impact in the Philippines," 29 *Conflict Resol. Q.* 333.

FUNG, Archon, Mary GRAHAM and David WEIL (2007) *Full Disclosure: The Perils and Promise of Transparency*. Cambridge, UK: Cambridge University Press.

GADLIN, Howard et al. (2010) *Collaboration and Team Science: A Field Guide*. Bethesda, MD: National Institutes of Health.

GALANTER, Marc (1974) "Why the 'Haves' Come Out Ahead: Speculations on the Limits of Legal Change," 9 *Law & Soc'y Rev.* 95.

————————————————————— (1996) "Lawyers in the Mist: The Golden Age of Legal Nostalgia," 100 *Dick. L. Rev.* 549.

GALVES, Fred (2009) "Virtual Justice as Reality: Making the Resolution of e-Commerce Disputes More Convenient, Legitimate, Efficient, and Secure," 2009 *U. Ill. J.L. Tech. & Pol'y* 1.

GASTIL, John, and William M. KEITH (2005) "A Nation That (Sometimes) Likes to Talk: A Brief History of Public Deliberation in the United States," in John Gastil and Peter Levine eds., *The Deliberative Democracy Handbook: Strategies for Effective Civic Engagement in the Twenty-First Century* 3. San Francisco: Jossey-Bass.

GASTIL, John, and Peter LEVINE eds. (2005) *The Deliberative Democracy Handbook: Strategies for Effective Civic Engagement in the 21st Century*. San Francisco: Jossey-Bass.

GEARAN, Anne (2010) "Analysis: Obama Seeking Elusive Diplomatic Prize—Deal to End Decades of Mideast Conflict." *Associated Press Newswires*, August 21.

GECKELER, Grant Wood (2007) "The Clinton-Obama Approach to Medical Malpractice Reform: Reviving the Most Meaningful Features of Alternative Dispute Resolution," 8 *Pepp. Disp. Resol. L.J.* 171.

GELFAND, Michele J., and Jeanne M. BRETT (2004) *The Handbook of Negotiation and Culture*. Stanford: Stanford Business Books.

GESKE, Janine (2009) "Repairing the Harm from Clergy Sex Abuse," *available at* http://law.marquette.edu/facultyblog/2009/05/25/repairing-the-harm-from-clergy-sex-abuse/.

GHAIS, Suzanne (2005) *Extreme Facilitation: Guiding Groups Through Controversy and Complexity*. San Francisco: Jossey-Bass.

GLADWELL, Malcolm (2000) *The Tipping Point: How Little Things Can Make a Difference*. Boston: Little Brown.

_____ (2010) "Small Change: Why the Revolution Will Not Be Tweeted," *The New Yorker*, October 4, p.42

GLENDON, Mary Ann (1994) *A Nation Under Lawyers: How the Crisis in the Legal Profession Is Transforming American Society*. Cambridge, MA: Harvard University Press.

GOLANN, Dwight (1996) *Mediating Legal Disputes: Effective Strategies for Lawyers and Mediators*. New York: Aspen Publishers.

GOLANN, Dwight, and Jay FOLBERG (2011) *Mediation: The Roles of Advocate and Neutral* (2d ed.). New York: Wolters Kluwer.

GOLDBERG, Jordan (2014) "Online Alternative Dispute Resolution and Why Law Schools Should Prepare Future Lawyers for the Online Forum," 14 *Pepp. Disp. Resol. L.J.* 1.

GOLDBERG, Stephen B., Jeanne BRETT, and William URY (2012) "Designing an Effective Dispute Resolution System," in Stephen B. Goldberg, Frank E.A. Sander, Nancy H. Rogers, and Sarah R. Cole, *Dispute Resolution: Negotiation, Mediation, Arbitration, and Other Processes* (6th ed.) 483. New York: Wolters Kluwer.

GOLDBERG, Stephen B., Frank E.A. SANDER, Nancy H. ROGERS, and Sarah R. COLE (2012) *Dispute Resolution: Negotiation, Mediation, Arbitration, and Other Processes* (6th ed.). New York: Wolters Kluwer.

GOLDBERG, Stephen B., Margaret L. SHAW, and Jeanne M. BRETT (2009) "What Difference Does a Robe Make? Comparing Mediators with and without Prior Judicial Experience," 25(3) *Negot. J.* 277 (July).

GOLDBERG, Stephen B., et al. (2017) *How Mediation Works: Theory, Research, and Practice*. Bingley, UK: Emerald Press.

GOLDEN, Jim, H. Abigail MOY, and Adam LYONS (2008) "The Negotiation Counsel Model: An Empathic Model for Settling Catastrophic Personal Injury Cases," 13 *Harv. Negot. L. Rev.* 211.

GOLDSTONE, Richard J. (2000) *For Humanity: Reflections of a War Crimes Investigator*. New Haven, CT: Yale University Press.

_____ (2006) "The South African Truth and Reconciliation Commission: Is It Relevant to the United States," 12(3) *Disp. Resol. Mag.* 19.

GRAMATIKOV, Martin, and Laura KLAMING (2012) "Getting Divorced Online: Procedural and Outcome Justice in Online Divorce Mediation," 14 *J.L. & Fam. Studies* 97.

GRAY, Dave, Sunni BROWN, and James MACANUFO (2010) *Gamestorming: A Playbook for Innovators*. Sebastopol, CA: O'Reilly Media, Inc.

GREENBERG, Elayne E. (2009) "We Can Work It Out: Entertaining a Dispute Resolution System for Bankruptcy Court," 17 *Am. Bankr. Inst. L. Rev.* 545.

GREENSBORO TRUTH AND RECONCILIATION COMMISSION (2006) *Greensboro Truth and Reconciliation Commission Report*, *available at* http://www.greensborotrc.org/.

GRILLO, Trina (1991) "The Mediation Alternative: Process Dangers for Women," 100 *Yale L.J.* 1545.

GROSSMAN, Nienke (2009) "Legitimacy and International Adjudicative Bodies," 41 *Geo. Wash. Int'l L. Rev.* 107.

GROTON, James P., and Kurt L. DETTMAN (2011) "How and Why the Standing Neutral Dispute Prevention and Resolution Technique Can Be Applied," 29 *Alternatives* 177.

GROTON, James P., Chris HONEYMAN, and Andrea Kupfer SCHNEIDER (2017) "Thinking Ahead," in Chris Honeyman and Andrea Kupfer Schneider eds., 1 *The Negotiator's Desk Reference* 265. St. Paul, MN: Hamline University DRI Press.

Guide for Implementing the Balanced and Restorative Justice Model, https://www.ncjrs.gov/pdffiles/167887.pdf.

HAGER, L. Michael (2010) "Congress Needs a Mediation Tool to Dissolve Gridlock," *The Washington Post*, June 18, p. A27.

HALL, Lavina, and Charles HECKSCHER (2003) "Negotiating Identity," in Thomas A. Kochan and David B. Lipsky eds., *Negotiations and Change: From Workplace to Society* 279. Ithaca, NY: Cornell University Press.

HALOUSH, Haitham A., and Bashar H. MALKAWI (2007) "The Liberty of Participation in Online Alternative Dispute Resolution Schemes," 1 *SMU Sci. & Tech. L. Rev.* 119.

HAMBURG, David A. (1998) "Preventing Contemporary Intergroup Violence," in Eugene Weiner ed., *The Handbook of Interethnic Coexistence* 27. New York: Continuum.

HAMILTON, Michael, and Dominic BRYAN (2006-2007) "Deepening Democracy? Dispute System Design and the Mediation of Contested Parades in Northern Ireland," 22 *Ohio St. J. on Disp. Resol.* 133.

HARR, Jonathan (1995) *A Civil Action*. New York: Random House.

HARTER, Philip J. (2000) "Assessing the Assessors: The Actual Performance of Negotiated Rulemaking," 9 *N.Y.U. Envtl. L.J.* 32.

HARVARD BUSINESS SCHOOL PRESS (2006) *Running Meetings: Expert Solutions to Everyday Challenges*. Cambridge, MA: Harvard Business School Publications.

HARVEY, Robert (2001) *The Fall of Apartheid: The Inside Story from Smuts to Mbeki*. New York: Palgrave Macmillan.

HATRY, Harry P. (2004) "Using Agency Records," in Joseph S. Wholey, Harry P. Hatry, and Kathryn E. Newcomer eds., *Handbook of Practical Program Evaluation* (2d ed.) 243. San Francisco: Jossey-Bass.

HAWKINS, Keith (2003) *Law as Last Resort: Prosecution Decision-Making in a Regulatory Agency*. Oxford, UK: Oxford Socio-Legal Studies.

HENDLEY, Kathryn (2013) "What If You Build It and No One Comes? The Introduction of Mediation to Russia," 14 *Cardozo J. Conflict Resol.* 727.

HENRY, James F. (2001) "Lawyers as Agents of Change," in Russ Bleemer, Cynthia Blustein, Susan Scott, and Rosemarie Yu eds., *Into the 21st Century: Thought Pieces on Lawyering, Problem Solving and ADR* 49. New York: CPR Institute for Dispute Resolution.

HERZIG, Maggie, and Laura CHASIN (2006) *Fostering Dialogue Across Divides: A Nuts and Bolts Guide from the Public Conversations Project*. Watertown, MA: Public Conversations Project.

HEUMANN, Milton, and Jonathan M. HYMAN (1997) "Negotiation Method and Litigation Settlement Methods in New Jersey: You Can't Always Get What You Want," 12 *Ohio St. J. on Disp. Resol.* 253.

HIRSCH, Dennis (2018) "Predictive Analytics Law and Policy: A New Field Emerges," 14 *I/S: J.L. & Pol'y for the Info Soc'y* 1.

_____ (2018) "To Solve the Facebook Problem Think Big (Data)," *The Hill*, April 24.

HISCOCK, Mary E., "Cross-Border Online Consumer Dispute Resolution," 4(1) *Contemp. Asia Arb. J.* 1 (2011).

HOFFMAN, Kevin M. (2018) *Meeting Design: For Managers, Makers, and Everyone*. Brooklyn, NY: Two Waves Books.

HOLDER, Eric (2009) *Speech: Attorney General Eric Holder at the Department of Justice African American History Month Program* (February 18), https://www.justice.gov/opa/speech/attorney-general-eric-holder-department-justice-african-american-history-month-program.

HOLLANDER-BLUMOFF, Rebecca, and Tom R. TYLER (2008) "Procedural Justice in Negotiation: Procedural Fairness, Outcome Acceptance, and Integrative Potential," 33 *Law & Soc. Inquiry* 473.

HOLLINS, Caprice, and Ilsa GOWAN (2015) *Diversity, Equity, and Inclusion: Strategies for Facilitating Conversations on Race*. London: Rowman & Littlefield.

HOOVER, Kenneth R. (1984) *The Elements of Social Scientific Thinking* (3rd ed.) New York: St. Martin's Press.

HOPT, Klaus J., and Felix STEFFEK eds. (2013) *Mediation: Principles and Regulation in a Comparative Perspective*. Oxford, UK: Oxford University Press.

HUFF, C. Ronald, Nancy H. ROGERS, and Richard A. SALEM (1987) "Mediation of Cohabitant Violence Cases" in Nancy H. Rogers and Richard A. Salem eds., *A Student's Guide to Mediation and the Law.* New York: Matthew Bender.

HUFFINGTON POST (2009) *Interview with Michael Young,* http://www.huffingtonpost.com/michael-young/the-south-african-talks-a_b_327316.html.

HYMAN, Jonathan (2010) "Four Ways of Looking at a Lawsuit: How Lawyers Can Use the Cognitive Frameworks of Mediation," 34 *Wash. U. J.L. & Pol'y* 11.

INGLIS, Laura, and Kevin McCABE (2010) "The Effects of Litigation Financing Rules on Settlement Rates," 18 *Sup. Ct. Econ. Rev.* 135.

INTERNATIONAL CIVIL RIGHTS CLINIC AT HARVARD LAW SCHOOL ed. (2009) *Prosecuting Apartheid-Era Crimes?: A South African Dialogue on Justice.* Cambridge, MA: International Civil Rights Clinic at Harvard Law School.

ISSACHAROFF, Samuel, and D. Theodore RAVE (2014) "The BP Oil Spill Settlement and the Paradox of Public Litigation," 74 *La. L. Rev.* 397.

JAMES, Matt (2012) "A Carnival of Truth? Knowledge, Ignorance and the Canadian Truth and Reconciliation Commission," 6 *Int'l J. Transitional Just.* 182.

JENSEN, Astrid (2009) "Discourse Strategies in Professional E-mail Negotiation: A Case Study," 28 *Eng. for Specific Purposes* 4.

JOHNSON, Norman A., and Randolph B. COOPER (2009) "Power and Concession in Computer-Mediated Negotiations: An Examination of First Offers," 33(1) *Mgmt. Info. Systems Q.* 147-170.

JUNG, Courtney (2009a) "Transitional Justice for Indigenous People in a Non-Transitional Society," *ICTJ Research Brief,* www.ictj.org.

_____ (2009b) "Canada and the Legacy of the Indian Residential Schools: Transitional Justice for Indigenous People in a Non-Transitional Society," https://papers.ssrn.com/sol3/papers.cfm?abstract_id=1374950.

KAGAN, Robert A. (2000) "The Consequences of Adversarial Legalism," in Robert A. Kagan and Lee Axelrad eds., *Regulatory Encounters: Multinational Corporations and American Adversarial Legalism* 372.

KANTOR, David (2012) *Reading the Room: Group Dynamics for Coaches and Leaders.* San Francisco: John Wiley & Sons.

KAPLAN, Abraham (1964) *The Conduct of Inquiry: Methodology for Behavioral Science.* San Francisco: Chandler.

KATSH, Ethan (2006) "Online Dispute Resolution: Some Implications for the Emergence of Law in Cyberspace," 10 *Lex Electronica, available at* http://cedires.be/index_bestanden/Katsh_ODR.pdf.

_____ (2009) "Online Dispute Resolution: Moving Beyond Convenience and Communication," in James R. Silkenat, Jeffrey M. Aresty, and Jacqueline Klosek eds., *The ABA Guide to International Business Negotiations: A Comparison of Cross-Cultural Issues and Successful Approaches* (3rd ed.) 235. Chicago: ABA.

KATSH, Ethan, and Orna RABINOVICH-EINY (2017) *Digital Justice: Technology and the Internet of Disputes.* Oxford, UK: Oxford University Press.

KATSH, Ethan, and Janet RIFKIN (2001) *Online Dispute Resolution: Resolving Conflicts in Cyberspace.* San Francisco: Jossey-Bass.

KATSH, Ethan, and Colin RULE (2016) "What We Know and Need to Know About Online Dispute Resolution," 67 *S.C. L. Rev.* 329.

KAYSER, Thomas A. (1995) *Mining Group Gold: How to Cash in on the Collaborative Brain Power of a Group* (2d ed.). New York: McGraw-Hill.

KELSEY, Dee, Pam PLUMB, and Beth BRAGANCA (2004) *Great Meetings! Great Results.* Portland, ME: Great Meetings.

KESSLER, Glenn (2010). "Obama: Mideast Talks May Focus First on Border," *Washington Post,* Sept. 11, p. A09.

KILLERMAN, Sam, and Meg BOLGER (2016) *Unlocking the Magic of Facilitation: 11 Key Concepts You Didn't Know You Didn't Know.* Austin, TX: Impetus Books.

KNOBLOCK-WESTERWICK, Silvia, and Jingbo MENG (2009) "Looking the Other Way," 36 *Comm. Res.* 426.

KOH, Harold (2002) "A United States Human Rights Policy for the 21st Century," 46 *St. Louis U. L.J.* 293.

KOLB, Deborah, and Associates (1994) *When Talk Works: Profiles of Mediators.* San Francisco: Jossey-Bass.

KOROBKIN, Russell (2006) "Psychological Impediments to Mediation Success: Theory and Practice," 21 *Ohio St. J. on Disp. Resol.* 281.

KOROBKIN, Russell, and Chris GUTHRIE (1994) "Psychological Barriers to Litigation Settlement: An Experimental Approach," 93 *Mich. L. Rev.* 107.

_____ (1997) "Psychology, Economics and Settlement: A New Look at the Role of the Lawyer," 76 *Tex. L. Rev.* 77.

KRIESBERG, Louis (1998) "Coexistence and the Reconciliation of Communal Conflicts," in Eugene Weiner ed., *The Handbook of Interethnic Coexistence* 182. New York: Continuum.

KRITZER, Herbert (1991) *Let's Make a Deal: Understanding the Negotiating Process.* Madison, WI: University of Wisconsin Press.

KROL, Rachel, and Diana TOMEZSKO (2010) *2010 Evaluation of the Office of the Ombudsman, Center for Cooperative Resolution at the National Institutes of Health.* Cambridge, MA: Harvard Negotiation and Mediation Clinical Program.

KRONMAN, Anthony T. (1993) *The Lost Lawyer: Failing Ideals of the Legal Profession.* Cambridge, MA: The Belknap Press of Harvard University Press.

KRUEGER, Richard A. (2010) "Using Stories in Program Evaluation," in Joseph S. Wholey, Harry P. Hatry, and Kathryn E. Newcomer eds., *Handbook of Practical Program Evaluation* (3rd ed.) 404. San Francisco: Jossey-Bass.

KRUEGER, Richard A., and Mary Anne CASEY (2010) "Focus Group Interviewing," in Joseph S. Wholey, Harry P. Hatry, and Kathryn E. Newcomer eds., *Handbook of Practical Program Evaluation* (3rd ed.) 378. San Francisco: Jossey-Bass.

KUMAR, Shekhar (2009) "Virtual Venues: Improving Online Dispute Resolution as an Alternative to Cost Intensive Litigation," 27 *J. Marshall J. Computer & Info. L.* 81.

KUNDE, James E. (1999) "Dealing with the Press," in Lawrence Susskind, Sarah McKearnan, and Jennifer Thomas-Larmer eds., *The Consensus Building Handbook: A Comprehensive Guide to Reaching Agreement* 435. Thousand Oaks, CA: Sage Publications.

KUTTNER, Ran (2011) "Conflict Specialists as Leaders: Revisiting the Role of the Conflict Specialist from a Leadership Perspective," 29(2) *Conflict Resol. Q.* 103.

LANDE, John (2002) "Using Dispute Systems Design to Promote Good-Faith Participation in Court-Connected Mediation Programs," 50 *UCLA L. Rev.* 69.

_____ (2008) "The Movement Toward Early Case Handling in Courts and Private Dispute Resolution," 24 *Ohio St. J. on Disp. Resol.* 83.

_____ (2008) "Practical Insights from an Empirical Study of Cooperative Lawyers in Wisconsin," 2008 *J. Disp. Resol.* 203.

_____ (2009) "'Cooperative' Negotiators in Wisconsin," 15(2) *Dispute Resol. Mag.* 20.

_____ (2011) "An Empirical Analysis of Collaborative Practice," 49 *Fam. Ct. Rev.* 257.

LANDLER, Mark, and Ethan BRONNER (2010). "U.S. Believes Arab States Won't Scuttle Mideast Talks." *New York Times*, Oct. 8, p. 4.

LARSON, David Allen (2006) "Technology Mediated Dispute Resolution (TMDR): A New Paradigm for ADR," 21 *Ohio St. J. on Disp. Resol.* 629.

_____ (2010) "Artificial Intelligence: Robots, Avatars, and the Demise of the Human Mediator," 25 *Ohio St. J. on Disp. Resol.* 105.

_____ (2011) "'Brother, Can You Spare a Dime?' Technology Can Reduce Dispute Resolution Costs When Times Are Tough and Improve Outcomes," 11 *Nev. L.J.* 523.

LATHAM, Stephen R. (1996) "Regulation of Managed Care Incentive Payments to Physicians," 22 *Am. J.L. & Med.* 399.

LAUE, James H., Sharon BURDE, William POTAPCHUK, and Miranda SALKOFF (1988) "Getting to the Table in Policy Conflicts," 1988(20) *Conflict Resol. Q.* 6.

LEBARON, Michelle (2003) *Bridging Cultural Conflicts: A New Approach for a Changing World.* San Francisco: John Wiley and Sons, Inc.

LEDERACH, John Paul (1995) *Preparing for Peace: Conflict Transformation Across Cultures.* Syracuse: Syracuse University Press.

——————————————————— (1998) "Beyond Violence: Building Sustainable Peace," in Eugene Weiner ed., *The Handbook of Interethnic Coexistence* 236. New York: Continuum.

——————————————————— (2002) "Where Do I Fit In?" in John Paul Lederach and Janice Moomaw Jenner eds., *A Handbook of International Peacebuilding: Into the Eye of the Storm* 37. San Francisco: Jossey-Bass.

LEDERACH, John Paul, and Janice Moomaw JENNER (2001) *A Handbook of International Peacekeeping: Into the Eye of the Storm.* San Francisco: Jossey-Bass.

——————————————————— (2002) "So What Have We Learned?," in John Paul Lederach and Janice Moomaw Jenner eds., *A Handbook of International Peacebuilding: Into the Eye of the Storm* 315. San Francisco: Jossey-Bass.

LEIGHNINGER, Matt (2006) *The Next Form of Democracy: How Expert Rule Is Giving Way to Shared Governance . . . and Why Politics Will Never Be the Same.* Nashville: Vanderbilt University Press.

LENCIONI, Patrick (2004) *Death by Meeting: A Leadership Fable—About Solving the Most Painful Problem in Business.* San Francisco: Jossey-Bass.

LEVIN, Jack, James Alan FOX, and David FORDE (2016) *Elementary Statistics in Social Research* (12th ed.). London: Pearson.

LEVINE, BERTRAM J. (2005) *Resolving Racial Conflict: The Community Relations Service and Civil Rights, 1964-1989.* Columbia: University of Missouri Press.

LEWICKI, Roy J. (2006) "Trust and Distrust," in Andrea Kupfer Schneider and Christopher Honeyman eds., *The Negotiator's Fieldbook.* Washington, DC: ABA, Section of Dispute Resolution.

LEWICKI, Roy J., and Edward C. TOMLINSON (2003) "Distrust," *Beyond Intractability, available at* https://www.beyondintractability.org/essay/distrust/.

LIND, E. Allen, and Tom R. TYLER (1988) *The Social Psychology of Procedural Justice.* New York: Plenum Press.

LIND, E. Allen, Robert J. MACCOUN, Patricia A. EBENER, William L.F. FELSTINER, Deborah R. HENSLER, Judith RESNIK, and Tom R. TYLER (1990) "In the Eye of the Beholder: Tort Litigants' Evaluation of Their Experiences in the Civil Justice System," 24 *Law & Soc'y Rev.* 953.

LIPSKY, David B., Ronald L. SEEBER, and Richard D. FINCHER (2003) *Emerging Systems for Managing Workplace Conflict: Lessons from American Corporations for Managers and Dispute Resolution Professionals.* San Francisco: Jossey-Bass.

LISNEK, Paul Michael (1992) *Effective Client Communication: A Lawyer's Handbook for Interviewing and Counseling.* St. Paul, MN: West.

LIU, Leigh Anne, Lin INLOW, and Jing Betty FENG (2015) "Institutionalizing Sustainable Conflict Management in Organizations: Leaders, Networks, and Sensemaking," 32 *Conflict Resol. Q.* 155.

LLEWELLYN, Jennifer (2002) "Dealing with the Legacy of Native Residential School Abuse in Canada: Litigation, ADR, and Restorative Justice," 52 *U. Toronto L.J.* 253.

——————————————————— (2008) "Bridging the Gap Between Truth and Reconciliation: Restorative Justice and the Indian Residential School Truth and Reconciliation Commission" in M. Brant-Castellano, L. Archibald, and M. DeGagne eds., *From Truth to Reconciliation: Transforming the Legacy of Residential Schools* 183. Ottawa: Aboriginal Healing Foundation.

LO, Alex (2012) "Too Much Privacy for Repeat Players? The Problem of Confidentiality Clauses and a Possible Solution," 5 *Contemp. Asian Arb. J.* 149.

LOVE, Arthur (2004) "Implementation Evaluation," in Joseph S. Wholey, Harry P. Hatry, and Kathryn E. Newcomer eds., *Handbook of Practical Program Evaluation* (2d ed.) 69. San Francisco: Jossey-Bass.

LOVE, Lela (1997) "The Top Ten Reasons Why Mediators Should Not Evaluate," 24 *Fla. St. U. L. Rev.* 937.

LUBBERS, Jeffrey (2012) "A Survey of Federal Agency Rulemakers' Attitudes about E-Rulemaking," in Stephen Coleman and Peter M. Shane eds., *Connecting Democracy: Online Consultation and the Flow of Political Communication* 229. Cambridge, MA: The MIT Press.

MACAULAY, Stewart (1963) "Non-Contractual Relations in Business," 20 *Am. Soc. Rev.* 85.

_____ (1985) "An Empirical View of Contract," 1985 *Wis. L. Rev.* 465.

MACFARLANE, Julie (2008) *The New Lawyer: How Settlement Is Transforming the Practice of Law.* Vancouver: UBC Press.

MacNEIL, Ian R., Richard E. SPEIDEL, and Thomas J. STIPANOWICH (1994) *Federal Arbitration Law: Agreements, Awards, and Remedies Under the Federal Arbitration Act.* Boston: Little Brown.

MANN, Bruce L. (2009) "Smoothing Some Wrinkles in Online Dispute Resolution," 17 *Int'l J.L. & Info. Tech.* 83.

MARES-DIXON, Judy, Julie A. McKAY, and Scott PEPPET (1999) "Building Consensus for Change Within a Major Corporation: The Case of Levi Strauss & Co.," in Lawrence Susskind, Sarah McKearnan, and Jennifer Thomas-Larmer eds., *The Consensus Building Handbook: A Comprehensive Guide to Reaching Agreement* 1065. Thousand Oaks, CA: Sage Publications.

MARKMAN, Art (2017) "Your Team Is Brainstorming All Wrong," *Harv. Bus. Rev.*, https://hbr.org/2017/05/your-team-is-brainstorming-all-wrong.

MARYLAND MEDIATION AND CONFLICT RESOLUTION OFFICE (2009) *MACRO Progress Report: 10 Years of Achievement, available at* http://www.courts.state.md.us/macro/pdfs/reports/macro-progressreport2009.pdf.

MATZ, David E. (1987) "Why Disputes Don't Go to Mediation," *Conflict Resol. Q.* 3 (Fall).

MAXWELL, Jeremy C., Annie I. ANTON, Peter SWIRE, Maria RIAZ, and Christopher M. McCRAW (2012) "A Legal Cross-References Taxonomy for Reasoning About Compliance Requirements," 17 *J. Requirements Engineering* 99.

MAYER, Bernard (2000) *The Dynamics of Conflict Resolution: A Practitioner's Guide.* San Francisco: Jossey-Bass.

_____ _____ (2004) *Beyond Neutrality: Confronting the Crisis in Conflict Resolution.* San Francisco: Jossey-Bass.

MAZADOORIAN, Harry N. (1999) "Building an ADR Program: What Works, What Doesn't," 8 *Bus. L. Today* 37.

McADOO, Bobbi (2002) "A Report to the Minnesota Supreme Court: The Impact of Rule 114 on Civil Litigation Practice in Minnesota," 25 *Hamline L. Rev.* 401.

McEWEN, Craig A. (1998) "Managing Corporate Disputing: Overcoming Barriers to the Effective Use of Mediation for Reducing the Cost and Time of Litigation," 14 *Ohio St. J. on Disp. Resol.* 1.

_____ (2007) "Note on Mediation Research," in Stephen Goldberg et al., *Dispute Resolution: Negotiation, Mediation and Other Processes* (5th ed.) 156. New York: Aspen.

McEWEN, Craig A., and Thomas MILBURN (1993) "Examining a Paradox of Mediation," 9 *Negot. J.* 23.

McEWEN, Craig A., Richard MAIMAN, and Lynn MATHER (1994) "Lawyers, Mediation, and the Management of Divorce Practice," 28 *Law & Soc'y Rev.* 249.

McGINN, Kathleen L., and Eric WILSON (2004) "How to Negotiate Successfully Online," *Negot.* (No. 3) 7.

McGOVERN, Francis E. (1986) "Toward a Functional Approach for Managing Complex Litigation," 53 *U. Chi. L. Rev.* 440.

_____ (2009) "Dispute System Design: The United Nations Compensation Commission," 14 *Harv. Negot. L. Rev.* 171.

McHALE, M. Jerry, et al. (2009) "Building a Child Protection Mediation Program in British Columbia," 47 *Fam. Ct. Rev.* 86.

MELVILLE, Keith, Taylor L. WILLINGHAM, and John R. DEDRICK (2005) "National Issues Forums: A Network of Communities Promoting Public Deliberation," in John Gastil and Peter Levine eds., *The Deliberative Democracy Handbook: Strategies for Effective Civic Engagement in the Twenty-First Century* 37. San Francisco: Jossey-Bass.

MENKEL-MEADOW, Carrie (1991) "Pursuing Settlement in an Adversary Culture: A Tale of Innovation Co-opted or 'the Law of ADR,'" 19 *Fla. St. U. L. Rev.* 1.

——————————————— (2001) "Aha? Is Creativity Possible in Legal Problem Solving and Teachable in Legal Education?," 6 *Harv. Negot. L. Rev.* 97.

——————————————— (2001) "Lawyering, Dispute Resolution, Problem Solving and Creativity for the 21st Century," in Russ Bleemer, Cynthia Blustein, Susan Scott, and Rosemarie Yu eds., *Into the 21st Century: Thought Pieces on Lawyering, Problem Solving and ADR* 52. New York: CPR Institute for Dispute Resolution.

——————————————— (2002) "Practicing 'In the Interests of Justice' in the Twenty-First Century: Pursuing Peace and Justice," 70 *Fordham L. Rev.* 1761.

——————————————— (2005) "Roots and Inspirations: A Brief History of the Foundations of Dispute Resolution," in Michael L. Moffitt and Robert C. Bordone eds., *The Handbook of Dispute Resolution* 13. San Francisco: Jossey-Bass.

——————————————— (2006) "Peace and Justice: Notes on the Evolution and Purposes of Legal Processes," 94 *Geo. L.J.* 553 (2006).

——————————————— (2009) "Are There Systemic Ethics Issues in Dispute System Design? And What We Should [Not] Do About It: Lessons from International and Domestic Fronts," 14 *Harv. Negot. L. Rev.* 195.

——————————————— (2014) "Unsettling the Lawyers: Other Forms of Justice in Indigenous Claims of Expropriation, Abuse, and Injustice," 64 *U. Toronto L.J.* 620.

——————————————— (2018) "Why We Can't 'Just All Get Along': Dysfunction in the Polity and Conflict Resolution and What We Might Do About It," 2018 *J. Disp. Resol.* 5.

MENKEL-MEADOW, Carrie J., Lela P. LOVE, Andrea K. SCHNEIDER, and Jean R. STERNLIGHT (2010) *Dispute Resolution: Beyond the Adversarial Model* (2d ed.). New York: Aspen.

MILLER, David (2013) "Legislating Our Reasonable Expectations: Making the Case for a Statutory Framework to Protect Workplace Privacy in the Age of Social Media," 22 *U. Miami Bus. L. Rev.* 49.

MINOW, Martha (1998) *Between Vengeance and Forgiveness.* Boston: Beacon Press.

——————————————— (2002) "Memory and Hate," in Martha Minow and Nancy L. Rosenblum eds., *Breaking the Cycles of Hatred: Memory, Law, and Repair* 14. Princeton: Princeton University Press.

MITCHELL, Christopher (2002) "Beyond Resolution: What Does Conflict Transformation Actually Transform?" 9 *Peace & Conflict Stud.* 1.

——————————————— (2002) "How Much Do I Need to Know?," in John Paul Lederach and Janice Moomaw Jenner eds., *A Handbook of International Peacekeeping: Into the Eye of the Storm* 49. San Francisco: Jossey-Bass.

MNOOKIN, Robert (1993) "Why Negotiations Fail: An Exploration of Barriers to the Resolution of Conflict," 8 *Ohio St. J. on Disp. Resol.* 235.

——————————————— (2010) *Bargaining with the Devil: When to Negotiate, When to Fight.* New York: Simon & Schuster.

MNOOKIN, Robert H., and Ronald GILSON (1994) "Disputing Through Agents: Cooperation Between Lawyers in Litigation," 94 *Colum. L. Rev.* 509.

MNOOKIN, Robert, and Lewis KORNHAUSER (1979) "Bargaining in the Shadow of the Law: The Case of Divorce," 88 *Yale L.J.* 950.

MNOOKIN, Robert H., and Lee ROSS (1995) "Introduction," in Kenneth Arrow et al. eds., *Barriers to Conflict Resolution* 20. New York: W.W. Norton & Co.

MNOOKIN, Robert H., Scott R. PEPPET, and Andrew S. TULUMELLO (2004) *Beyond Winning: Negotiating to Create Value in Deals and Disputes* (2d ed.). Cambridge, MA: Belknap Press of Harvard University Press.

Model Standards of Conduct for Mediators (2005). Washington, DC and New York: American Bar Association, Association for Conflict Resolution, and American Arbitration Association.

MOFFITT, Michael L. (2005) "Disputes as Opportunities to Create Value," in Michael L. Moffitt and Robert C. Bordone eds., *The Handbook of Dispute Resolution* 173. San Francisco: Jossey-Bass.

_____ (2005) "Pleading in an Age of Settlement," 80 *Ind. L.J.* 727.

_____ (2009) "The Four Ways to Assure Mediator Quality (and Why None of Them Work)," 24 *Ohio St. J. on Disp. Resol.* 191.

MOFFITT, Michael, and Robert BORDONE eds. (2005) *Handbook of Dispute Resolution*. San Francisco: Jossey-Bass.

MOFFITT, Michael, and Andrea Kupfer SCHNEIDER (2014) *Examples and Explanations: Dispute Resolution* (3rd ed.). New York: Wolters Kluwer.

MOON, Yuseok, and Lisa B. BINGHAM (2007) "Transformative Mediation at Work: Employee and Supervisor Perceptions on USPS REDRESS Program," 11 *Int'l Rev. Pub. Admin.* 43.

MORGAN, David (1996) *Focus Groups as Qualitative Research* (2d ed.). Thousand Oaks, CA: Sage Publications.

MORRILL, Calvin (1995) *The Executive Way: Conflict Resolution in Corporations*. Chicago: University of Chicago Press.

MOSTEN, Forrest S. (2009) *Collaborative Divorce: Helping Families Without Going to Court*. San Francisco: Jossey-Bass.

MOSTEN, Forrest S., and John LANDE (2009) "The Uniform Collaborative Law Act's Contribution to Informed Client Decision Making in Choosing a Dispute Resolution Process," 38 *Hofstra L. Rev.* 611.

MURRAY, John S. (1984) "Third Party Intervention: Successful Entry for the Uninvited," 48 *Alb. L. Rev.* 573.

NADER, Laura (1993) "Controlling Processes in the Practice of Law: Hierarchy and Pacification in the Movement to Re-Form Dispute Ideology," 9 *Ohio St. J. on Disp. Resol.* 1.

NADLER, Janice (2001) "Electronically-Mediated Dispute Resolution and E-Commerce," 17 *Negot. J.* 333.

NADLER, Janice, and Donna SHESTOWSKY (2006) "Negotiation, Information Technology, and the Problem of the Faceless Other," in L. Thompson ed., *Negotiation Theory and Research* 145. London: Taylor & Francis.

NATIONAL CRIMINAL JUSTICE REFERENCE SERVICE (1998) *Guide for Implementing the Balanced and Restorative Justice Model*, https://www.ncjrs.gov/pdffiles/167887.pdf.

NELSON, Barbara J., Linda KABOOLIAN, and Kathryn A. CARVER (2003) *How to Build Social Capital Across Communities*. Los Angeles: UCLA.

NELSON, Dorothy (2001) "ADR in the New Era," in Russ Bleemer, Cynthia Blustein, Susan Scott, and Rosemarie Yu eds., *Into the 21st Century: Thought Pieces on Lawyering, Problem Solving and ADR* 65. New York: CPR Institute for Dispute Resolution.

NELSON, Jo (2003) "Facilitation: A Tool for Evoking and Creating Wisdom," 19 *Interspectives* 12.

NET PROMOTER, http://www.netpromoter.com/netpromoter_community/index.jspa.

NEWCOMER, Kathryn E., and Dylan CONGER (2010) "Using Statistics in Program Evaluation," in Joseph S. Wholey, Harry P. Hatry, and Kathryn E. Newcomer eds., *Handbook of Practical Program Evaluation* (3rd ed.) 454. San Francisco: Jossey-Bass.

NEWCOMER, Kathryn E., and Timothy TRIPLETT (2010) "Using Surveys," in Joseph S. Wholey, Harry P. Hatry, and Kathryn E. Newcomer eds., *Handbook of Practical Program Evaluation* (3rd ed.) 262. San Francisco: Jossey-Bass.

NIELSEN, Marianne O. (1998) "A Comparison of Canadian Native Youth Justice Committees and Navajo Peacemakers: A Summary of Research Results," 14 *J. Contemp. Crim. Just.* 6.

NIELSON, Marianne O., and James W. ZION (2005) *Navajo Nation Peacemaking: Living Traditional Justice*. Tucson: University of Arizona Press.

NOLAN, James L., Jr. (2001) *Reinventing Justice: The American Drug Court Movement*. Princeton, NJ: Princeton University Press.

NOLAN-HALEY, Jacqueline (2017) "Dispute System Design: Justice, Accountability, and Impact," 13 *U. St. Thomas L.J.* 315.

445

NORRIS, Amanda L., and Katina E. METZIDAKIS (2010) "Public Protests, Private Contracts: Confidentiality in ICSID Arbitration and the Cochabamba Water War," 15 *Harv. Negot. L. Rev.* 31.

O'CONNOR, Sandra Day (2000) "Foreword," in Richard J. Goldstone, *For Humanity: Reflections of a War Crimes Investigator*. New Haven, CT: Yale University Press.

PAOLINI, Stefania, Miles HEWSTONE, Ed CAIRNS, and Alberto VOCI (2004) "Effects of Direct and Indirect Cross-Group Friendships on Judgments of Catholics and Protestants in Northern Ireland: The Mediating Role of an Anxiety-Reduction Mechanism," 30 *Personality & Soc. Psychol. Bull.* 770.

PARK, William W. (2010) "Arbitrators and Accuracy," 1 *J. Int'l Disp. Settlement* 25.

PARKER, Glenn M., and Robert HOFFMAN (2006) *Meeting Excellence: 33 Tools to Lead Meetings That Get Results*. San Francisco: Jossey-Bass.

PATERNOSTER, Raymond (2010) "How Much Do We Really Know About Criminal Deterrence?," 100(3) *J. Crim. L. & Criminology* 765.

PATTON, Bruce (2005) "Negotiation," in Michael L. Moffitt and Robert C. Bordone eds., *The Handbook of Dispute Resolution* 279. San Francisco: Jossey-Bass.

PBS (2009), Interview with Michael Young, *available at* https://www.youtube.com/watch?v=8-_EP8VI78E (last visited Aug. 15, 2018), and at http://mpt-legacy.wgbhdigital.org/wgbh/masterpiece/endgame/young.html (last visited June 19, 2018).

PEARSON, Jessica, and Nancy THOENNES (1988) "Divorce Mediation Research Results," in Jay Folberg and Ann L. Milne eds., *Divorce Mediation: Theory and Practice* 429. New York: Guilford Press.

PEARSON, Jessica, Nancy THOENNES, and Lois VANDERKOOI (1982) "The Decision to Mediate: Profiles of Individuals Who Accept and Reject the Opportunity to Mediate Contested Child Custody and Visitation Issues," 6 *J. Divorce* 17 (Fall/Winter).

PEPPET, Scott (2008) "The Ethics of Collaborative Law," 2008 *J. Disp. Resol.* 131.

PETERS, Don (2008) "Can We Talk? Overcoming Barriers to Mediating Private Transborder Commercial Disputes in the Americas," 41 *Vand. J. Transnat'l L.* 1251.

PEW RESEARCH CENTER (2014) "Political Polarization and Media Habits," *available at* http://www.journalism.org/2014/10/21/political-polarization-media-habits/.

———————————— (2016a) "Pathways to News," *available at* http://www.journalism.org/2016/07/07/pathways-to-news/.

———————————— (2016b) "Many Americans Believe Fake News Is Sowing Confusion," *available at* http://www.journalism.org/2016/12/15/many-americans-believe-fake-news-is-sowing-confusion/.

———————————— (2018) "News Use Across Social Media Platforms 2017," *available at* http://www.journalism.org/2017/09/07/news-use-across-social-media-platforms-2017/.

PHELPS, Teresa Godwin (2004) *Shattered Voices: Language, Violence, and the Work of the Truth Commissions*. Philadelphia: University of Pennsylvania Press.

POITRAS, Jean (2009) "What Makes Parties Trust Mediators?," 25(3) *Negot. J.* 307 (July).

POTAPCHUK, William R., and Jarle CROCKER (1999) "Implementing Consensus-Based Agreements," in Lawrence Susskind, Sarah McKearnan, and Jennifer Thomas-Larmer eds., *The Consensus Building Handbook: A Comprehensive Guide to Reaching Agreement* 527. Thousand Oaks, CA: Sage Publications.

POU, Charles, Jr. (2004) "Assuring Excellence, or Merely Reassuring? Policy and Practice in Promoting Mediator Quality," 2004 *J. Disp. Resol.* 303.

POVEDA, Tony G. (1994) *Re-Thinking White Collar Crime*. Westport, CT: Praeger Publishers.

PRATT, Travis C., Frances T. CULLEN, Kristie R. BLEVINS, Leah E. DAIGLE, and Tamara D. MADENSEN (2006) "The Empirical Status of Deterrence Theory: A Meta-Analysis," in Frances T. Cullen, John Paul Wright, and Kristie R. Blevins eds., *Taking Stock: The Status of Criminological Theory* 367. New Brunswick, NJ: Transaction Publishers.

PRICE, Vincent (2012) "Playing Politics: The Experience of E-Participation," in Stephen Coleman and Peter M. Shane eds., *Connecting Democracy: Online Consultation and the Flow of Political Communication* 125. Cambridge, MA: The MIT Press.

PRINCEN, Thomas (1994) "Joseph Elder: Quiet Peacemaking in a Civil War," in Deborah M. Kolb and associates eds., *When Talk Works: Profiles of Mediators.* San Francisco: Jossey-Bass.

PUTNAM, Robert D. (2000) *Bowling Alone: The Collapse and Revival of American Community.* New York: Simon & Schuster.

PUTNAM, Robert D., and Lewis M. FELDSTEIN (2003) *Better Together: Restoring the American Community.* New York: Simon & Shuster.

PUTNAM, Robert D., and Thomas H. SANDER (2010) "Still Bowling Along: The Post 9-11 Split," 21 *J. Democracy* 9.

QUIGLEY, John B (2006) *The Genocide Convention: An International Law Analysis.* London: Ashgate Publishing Ltd.

RABINOVICH-EINY, Orna, and Ethan KATSH (2012) "Technology and the Future of Dispute Systems Design," 17 *Harv. Negot. L. Rev.* 141.

RAIFFA, Howard, with John RICHARDSON and David METCALFE (2002) *Negotiation Analysis: The Science and Art of Collaborative Decision-Making.* San Francisco: Jossey-Bass.

RAINEY, Daniel (2015) "Glimmers on the Horizon: Unique Ethical Issues Created by ODR," 21(2) *Disp. Resol. Mag.* 20.

RAPHELSON, Samantha (2018) "Trump Budget Would Eliminate Justice Department's Peacemaking Office," NPR, https://www.npr.org/2018/03/27/597304508/trump-budget-would-eliminate-justice-departments-peacemaking-office, March 18.

REGAN, Paulette (2010) *Unsettling the Settler Within: Indian Residential Schools, Truth Telling, and Reconciliation in Canada.* Vancouver, BC: University of British Columbia Press.

REILLY, Peter (2009) "Was Machiavelli Right? Lying in Negotiation and the Art of Defensive Self-Help," 25 *Ohio St. J. on Disp. Resol.* 481.

REIMER, Gwen, Amy BOMBAY, Lena ELLSWORTH, Sara FRYER, and Tricia LOGARS (2010) *The Indian Residential Schools Settlement Agreement's Common Experience Payment and Healing: A Qualitative Study Exploring Impacts on Recipients.* Ottawa: Aboriginal Healing Foundation.

RELIS, Tamara (2007) "Consequences of Power," 12 *Harv. Negot. L. Rev.* 445.

_____ (2009) *Perceptions in Litigation and Mediation: Lawyers, Defendants, Plaintiffs, and Gendered Parties.* Cambridge, UK: Cambridge University Press.

RENO, Janet (2001) "The Federal Government and Appropriate Dispute Resolution: Promoting Problem Solving and Peacemaking as Enduring Values in Our Society," in Russ Bleemer, Cynthia Blustein, Susan Scott, and Rosemarie Yu eds., *Into the 21st Century: Thought Pieces on Lawyering, Problem Solving and ADR* 16. New York: CPR Institute for Dispute Resolution.

RESNIK, Judith (2018) "2J/A2K: Access to Justice, Access to Knowledge, and Economic Inequalities in Open Courts and Arbitrations," 96 *N.C. L. Rev.* 101.

REUBEN, Richard C. (2004) "Democracy and Dispute Resolution: The Problem of Arbitration," 67 *Law & Contemp. Probs.* 279.

_____ (2005) "Democracy and Dispute Resolution: Systems Design and the New Workplace," 10 *Harv. Negot. L. Rev.* 11.

RISKIN, Leonard L. (1982) "Mediation and Lawyers," 43 *Ohio St. L.J.* 29.

_____ (1996) "Understanding Mediators' Orientations, Strategies, and Techniques: A Grid for the Perplexed," 1 *Harv. Negot. L. Rev.* 7.

RISKIN, Leonard L., and Nancy A. WELSH (2008) "Is That All There Is? 'The Problem' in Court-Connected Mediation," 15 *Geo. Mason L. Rev.* 863.

_____ (2009) "What's It All About? Finding the Appropriate Problem Definition in Mediation," 15 *Disp. Resol. Mag.* 19 (Summer).

RISKIN, Leonard L., James E. WESTBROOK, Chris GUTHRIE, Timothy J. HEINSZ, Richard C. REUBEN, Jennifer K. ROBBENNOLT, and Nancy WELCH (2009) *Dispute Resolution and Lawyers* (4th ed.) St. Paul: West (also published in an abridged 5th ed. in 2014).

RITZ, Philipp (2010) "Privacy and Confidentiality Obligation on Parties in Arbitration Under Swiss Law," 27 *J. Int'l Arb.* 221.

ROBBENNOLT, Jennifer K., and Jean R. STERNLIGHT (2012) *Psychology for Lawyers: Understanding the Human Factors in Negotiation, Litigation, and Decision Making.* Chicago: ABA Publishing.

ROBINSON, Paul H. (2011) "The Ongoing Revolution in Punishment Theory: Doing Justice as Controlling Crime." 42 *Ariz. St. L.J.* 1089.

ROGERS, Nancy H. (2015) "When Conflicts Polarize Communities: Designing Localized Offices That Intervene Collaboratively," 30 *Ohio St. J. on Disp. Resol.* 173.

—————————————————— (2017) "Mediation and the Law," in Stephen B. Goldberg et al., *How Mediation Works: Theory, Research, and Practice* ch. 5. Bingley, UK: Emerald Press.

—————————————————— (2018) "One Idea for Ameliorating Polarization: Reviving Conversations About an American Spirit," 2018 *J. Disp. Resol.* 27.

ROGERS, Nancy H., and Craig A. McEWEN (1998) "Employing the Law to Increase the Use of Mediation and to Encourage Direct and Early Negotiations," 13 *Ohio St. J. Disp. Resol.* 831.

ROSS, Lee (1995) "Reactive Devaluation in Negotiation and Conflict Resolution" in Kenneth J. Arrow et al. eds., *Barriers to Conflict Resolution* 26. New York: W.W. Norton & Co.

—————————————————— (1999) "Reactive Devaluation in Negotiation and Conflict Resolution" in Kenneth J. Arrow et al. eds., *Barriers to Conflict Resolution* 26. Cambridge, MA: PON Books.

ROSS, Marc Howard (1993) *The Culture of Conflict.* New Haven, CT: Yale University Press.

ROSSI, Peter H., Mark W. LIPSEY, and Howard E. FREEMAN (2003) *Evaluation: A Systematic Approach* (7th ed.). Thousand Oaks, CA: Sage Publications.

ROTBERG, Robert I., and Dennis THOMPSON (2000) *Truth v. Justice: The Morality of Truth Commissions.* Princeton, NJ: Princeton University Press.

ROTHMAN, Jay, and Randi LAND (2003-2004) "The Cincinnati Police-Community Collaborative," 18 *Crim. Just.* 35.

ROWE, Mary (2009) "An Organizational Ombuds Office in a System for Dealing with Conflict and Learning from Conflict, or 'Conflict Management System,'" 14 *Harv. Negot. L. Rev.* 279.

RUETE, Edward S. (2000) "Facilitation 101," *in Proceedings of the 6th Annual IAF Conference: Toronto 2000.* St. Paul, MN: International Association of Facilitators.

RULE, Colin (2008) "Making Peace on eBay: Resolving Disputes in the World's Largest Marketplace," *ACResolution* 8 (Fall).

RULE, Colin, and Chittu NAGARAJAN (2010) *Crowdsourcing Dispute Resolution over Mobile Devices* (eBay self-published).

RULE, Colin, Vikki ROGERS, and Louis DEL DUCA (2010) "Designing a Global Consumer Online Dispute Resolution (ODR) System for Cross-Border Small Value-High Volume Claims—OAS Developments," 42 *UCC L.J.* 221.

SALANT, Priscilla, and Don DILLMAN (1994) *How to Conduct Your Own Survey.* San Francisco: John Wiley and Sons.

SALEM, Richard A. (1982) "Community Dispute Resolution Through Outside Intervention," 8(2-3) *Peace & Change* 91.

SANDER, Frank E.A. (2002) "Some Concluding Thoughts," 17 *Ohio St. J. on Disp. Resol.* 705.

—————————————————— (2007) "Developing the MRI (Mediation Receptivity Index)," 22 *Ohio St. J. on Disp. Resol.* 599.

SANDER, Frank E.A., and Stephen B. GOLDBERG (1994) "Fitting the Forum to the Fuss: A User-Friendly Guide to Selecting an ADR Procedure," 10 *Negot. J.* 49 (1994).

SANDER, Frank E.A., and Lukasz ROZDEICZER (2006) "Matching Cases and Dispute Resolution Procedures: Detailed Analysis Leading to a Mediation-Centered Approach," 11 *Harv. Negot. L. Rev.* 1.

SAVAGE, Robert J., and James M. SMITH (2003) "Sexual Abuse and the Irish Church: Crisis and Responses," in *Boston College, The Church in the 21st Century: Occasional Paper #8.*

SCANLON, Kathleen M. (2006) *Drafting Dispute Resolution Clauses.* New York: CPR (*see also* 2008 supplement by Helena Tavares Erickson).

SCHEPARD, Andrew ed. (2010) "Special Issue on Collaborative Law," 38 *Hofstra L. Rev.* 411.

SCHIRCH, Lisa, and David CAMPT (2007) *The Little Book of Dialogue for Difficult Subjects: A Practical, Hands-On Guide.* New York: Good Books.

SCHMITZ, Amy J. (2010a) "'Drive-Thru' Arbitration in the Digital Age: Empowering Consumers Through Binding ODR," 62 *Baylor L. Rev.* 178.

_____ (2010b) "Legislating in the Light: Considering Empirical Data in Crafting Arbitration Reforms," 15 *Harv. Negot. L. Rev.* 115.

_____ (2014) "Secret Consumer Scores and Segmentations: Separating Consumer 'Haves' from the 'Have-Nots,'" 2014 *Mich. St. L. Rev.* 1411.

_____ (2016) "Building Trust in E-commerce Through Online Dispute Resolution," in John A. Rothchild ed., *Research Handbook on Electronic Commerce Law.* Northampton, MA: Edward Elgar Publishing.

_____ (2018) "A Blueprint for Online Dispute Resolution System Design," 21 *J. Internet L.* 3.

SCHMITZ, Amy J., and Colin RULE (2017) "Lessons Learned from eBay," in Amy Schmitz and Colin Rule, *The New Handshake: Online Dispute Resolution and the Future of Consumer Protection.* Washington, DC: ABA Book Publishing.

_____ (2017) *The New Handshake: Online Dispute Resolution and the Future of Consumer Protection.* Chicago: ABA.

SCHNEIDER, Andrea Kupfer (2009) "The Intersection of Dispute Systems Design and Transitional Justice," 14 *Harv. Negot. L. Rev.* 289.

SCHNEIDER, Andrea Kupfer, and Natalie C. FLEURY (2011) "There's No Place Like Home: Applying Dispute Systems Design Theory to Create a Foreclosure Mediation System," 11 *Nev. L.J.* 368.

SCHOENY, Mara, and Wallace WARFIELD (2000) "Reconnecting Systems Maintenance with Social Justice: A Critical Role for Conflict Resolution," 16 *Negot. J.* 253.

SCHÖN, Donald A. (1983) *The Reflective Practitioner: How Professionals Think in Action.* New York: Basic Books.

SCHUMAN, Sandy, ed. (2005) *The IAF Handbook of Group Facilitation: Best Practices from the Leading Organization in Facilitation.* San Francisco: Jossey-Bass.

SCHWAB, William H (2004) "Collaborative Lawyering: A Closer Look at an Emerging Practice," 4 *Pepp. Disp. Resol. L.J.* 351.

SCHWARZ, Roger (2007) *The Skilled Facilitator: A Comprehensive Resource for Consultants, Facilitators, Coaches and Trainers* (3rd ed). San Francisco: Jossey-Bass.

SCHWARZ, Roger, Anne DAVIDSON, Peg CARLSON, and Sue McKINNEY (2005) *The Skilled Facilitator Fieldbook: Tips, Tools, and Tested Methods for Consultants, Facilitators, Managers, Trainers, and Coaches.* San Francisco: Jossey-Bass.

SEBENIUS, James K. (2001) "To Hell with the Future, Let's Get on with the Past: George Mitchell in Northern Ireland," *Harvard Business School Case 9-801-393.* Boston: Harvard Business School Publishing.

SELA, Ayelet (2017) "The Effect of Online Technologies on Dispute Resolution System Design: Antecedents, Current Trends, and Future Directions," 21 *Lewis & Clark L. Rev.* 635.

SHACKELFORD, Scott J., and Anjanette H. RAYMOND (2014) "Building the Virtual Courthouse: Ethical Considerations for Design, Implementation, and Regulation in the World of ODR," 2014 *Wis. L. Rev.* 615.

SHAFFER, Thomas L., and James R. ELKINS (2005) *Legal Interviewing and Counseling.* St. Paul, MN: Thomson West.

SHANE, Peter M. (2012) "Online Consultation and Political Communication in the Era of Obama: An Introduction," in Stephen Coleman and Peter M. Shane eds., *Connecting Democracy: Online Consultation and the Flow of Political Communication* 1. Cambridge, MA: The MIT Press.

SHANE, Peter M., ed. (2008) *Building Democracy Through Online Citizen Deliberation: A Framework for Action.* Columbus, OH: Ohio State University.

SHAPIRO, Daniel L. (2005) "Enemies, Allies, and Emotions: The Power of Positive Emotions in Negotiation," in Michael L. Moffitt and Robert C. Bordone eds., *The Handbook of Dispute Resolution* 66. San Francisco: Jossey-Bass.

SHARIFF, Khalil Z. (2003) "Designing Institutions to Manage Conflict: Principles for the Problem Solving Organization," 8 *Harv. Negot. J.* 133.

SHERIF, Muzafer (1966) *Group Conflict and Cooperation.* London: Routledge & Kegan Paul.

SHESTACK, Jerome J. (2001) "Civility, Mediation and Civitas," in Russ Bleemer, Cynthia Blustein, Susan Scott, and Rosemarie Yu eds., *Into the 21st Century: Thought Pieces on Lawyering, Problem Solving and ADR* 56. New York: CPR Institute for Dispute Resolution.

SILKENAT, James R., Jeffrey M. ARESTY and Jacqueline KLOSEK eds., *The ABA Guide to International Business Negotiations: A Comparison of Cross-Cultural Issues and Successful Approaches* (3rd ed.) Chicago: ABA.

SIMON, William (1985) "Legal Informality and Redistributive Politics," 19 *Clearinghouse Rev.* 385.

SISK, Timothy (2001) "Peacemaking Processes: Forestalling Return to Ethnic Violence," in I. William Zartman ed., *Preventive Negotiation: Avoiding Conflict Escalation* 67. Lanham, MD: Rowman & Littlefield Publishers, Inc.

SKOGAN, Wesley G., Susan M. HARTNETT, Natalie BUMP, and Jill DUBOIS (with the assistance of Ryan Hollon and Danielle Morris) (2008) *Executive Summary, Evaluation of CeaseFire-Chicago.* Evanston, IL: Northwestern University, *available at* https://www.ipr. northwestern.edu/publications/papers/urban-policy-and-community-development/docs/ceasefire-pdfs/executivesummary.pdf, *at* https://www.northwestern.edu/ipr/publications/ceasefire.html, *and at* https://www.ncjrs.gov/pdffiles1/nij/grants/227181.pdf.

SLAIKEU, Karl A., and Ralph H. HASSON (1998) *Controlling the Costs of Conflict: How to Design a System for Your Organization.* San Francisco: Jossey-Bass.

SLUZKI, Carlos E. (2003) "The Process Toward Reconciliation," in Antonia Chayes and Martha Minow eds., *Imagine Coexistence* 21. San Francisco: Jossey-Bass.

SMITH, Stephanie, and Janet MARTINEZ (2009) "An Analytical Framework for Dispute Systems Design," 14 *Harv. Negot. L. Rev.* 123.

SOCIETY OF PROFESSIONALS IN DISPUTE RESOLUTION (SPIDR) (1989) *Report of the SPIDR Commission on Qualifications.* Washington, DC: SPIDR.

———————————————— (1995) "Ensuring Competence and Quality in Dispute Resolution Practice," *Report #2 of the SPIDR Commission on Qualifications.* Washington, DC: SPIDR.

SOSNOV, Maya (2008) "The Adjudication of Genocide: Gacaca and the Road to Reconciliation in Rwanda," 36 *Denv. J. Int'l L. & Pol'y* 125.

SPIEKER, Arne (2018) "Stakeholder Dialogues and Virtual Reality for the German Energiewende," 2018 *J. Disp. Resol.* 75.

STERNBERG, Robert J., ed. (1999) *Handbook of Creativity.* New York: Cambridge University Press.

STERNLIGHT, Jean R. (2010) "Lawyerless Dispute Resolution: Rethinking a Paradigm," 37 *Fordham Urb. L.J.* 381.

STERNLIGHT, Jean, and Jennifer ROBBENNOLT (2012) *Psychology for Lawyers: Understanding the Human Factors in Negotiation, Litigation and Decisionmaking.* Chicago: ABA.

STEWART, David W., Prem N. SHAMDASANI, and Dennis W. ROOK (2007) *Focus Groups: Theory and Practice* (2d ed.). Thousand Oaks, CA: Sage Publications.

STIPANOWICH, Thomas (1996) "Beyond Arbitration: Innovation and Evolution in the United States Construction Industry," 31 *Wake Forest L. Rev.* 65 (1996).

———————————————— (1998) "The Multi-Door Contract and Other Possibilities," 13 *Ohio St. J. on Disp. Resol.* 303.

———————————————— (2009) "Arbitration and Choice: Taking Charge of the 'New Litigation,'" 7 *DePaul Bus. & Com. L.J.* 383.

_____ (2010) "Arbitration: The 'New Litigation,'" 2010 *U. Ill. L. Rev.* 1.

_____ (2012) "The Arbitration Fairness Index: Using a Public Rating System to Skirt the Legal Logjam and Promote Fairer and More Effective Arbitration of Employment and Consumer Disputes," 60 *Kan. L. Rev.* 985.

STIPANOWICH, Thomas J., Curtis E. von KANN and Deborah ROTHMAN eds. (2010) *Protocols for Expeditious, Cost-Effective Commercial Arbitration: Key Action Steps for Business Users, Counsel, Arbitrators and Arbitration Provider Institutions*. Austin, TX: College of Commercial Arbitrators.

STITT, Allan J. (1998) *Alternative Dispute Resolution for Organizations: How to Design a System for Effective Conflict Resolution*. Toronto: John Wiley & Sons Canada.

STONE, Doug, Bruce PATTON, and Sheila HEEN (2010) *Difficult Conversations: How to Discuss What Matters Most*. New York: Penguin Books.

STRAUS, David A. (1999) "Managing Meetings to Build Consensus," in Lawrence Susskind, Sarah McKearnan, and Jennifer Thomas-Larmer eds., *The Consensus Building Handbook: A Comprehensive Guide to Reaching Agreement* 287. Thousand Oaks, CA: Sage Publications.

STULBERG, Joseph (1997) "Facilitative Versus Evaluative Mediator Orientations: Piercing the 'Gridlock,'" 24 *Fla. St. L. Rev.* 985.

STURM, Susan, and Howard GADLIN (2007) "Conflict Resolution and Systemic Change," 2007 *J. Disp. Resol.* 1.

SUN, Jeffrey C. (1999) "University Officials as Administrator and Mediators: The Dual Role Conflict and Confidentiality Problems," 1 *BYU Educ. & L.J.* 19.

SUNSTEIN, Cass R. (2011) "Empirically Informed Regulation," 78 *U. Chi. L. Rev.* 1349.

_____ (2017) *#Republic: Divided Democracy in the Age of Social Media*. Princeton, NJ: Princeton University Press.

SUSSKIND, Lawrence, and Patrick FIELD (1996) *Dealing with an Angry Public: The Mutual Gains Approach to Resolving Disputes*. New York: The Free Press.

SUSSKIND, Lawrence, and Jennifer THOMAS-LARMER (1999) "Conducting a Conflict Assessment," in Lawrence Susskind, Sarah McKearnan, and Jennifer Thomas-Larmer eds., *The Consensus Building Handbook: A Comprehensive Guide to Reaching Agreement* 99. Thousand Oaks, CA: Sage Publications.

SUSSKIND, Lawrence, Sarah McKEARNAN, and Jennifer THOMAS-LARMER eds. (1999) *The Consensus Building Handbook: A Comprehensive Guide to Reaching Agreement*. Thousand Oaks, CA: Sage Publications.

_____ (1999) "Introduction," in *The Consensus Building Handbook: A Comprehensive Guide to Reaching Agreement* xvii. Thousand Oaks, CA: Sage Publications.

"Symposium: Dialogues of Transitional Justice" (2014) 32 *Quinnipiac L. Rev.* 579.

"Symposium: Honoring the Contributions of Christina Merchant to the Field of Conflict Resolution" (2015) 33 *Conflict Resol. Q.* S1 (Winter).

"Symposium: Leveraging on Disruption" (2017) 13 *U. St. Thomas L.J.* 159.

"Symposium: Restorative Justice in Action," (2005) 89(2) *Marq. L. Rev.*

TALESH, Shauhin A. (2012) "How Dispute Resolution System Design Matters: An Organizational Analysis of Dispute Resolution Structures and Consumer Lemon Laws," 46 *Law & Soc'y Rev.* 463.

TEITEL, Ruti (2000) *Transitional Justice*. New York: Oxford University Press.

TESLER, Pauline H. (2007) *Collaborative Law: Achieving Effective Resolution Without Litigation* (2d ed.). Chicago: ABA.

_____ (2008) "Collaborative Family Law, the New Lawyer, and Deep Resolution of Divorce-Related Conflicts," 2008 *J. Disp. Resol.* 83.

_____ (2010) Interview at the Ohio State University Moritz College of Law.

TIPPETT, Krista (2017) *Becoming Wise: An Inquiry Into the Mystery and Art of Living*. New York: Penguin Books.

TITTLE, Charles, Ekaterina BOTCHKOVAR, and Olena ANTONACCIO (2011) "Criminal Contemplation, National Context, and Deterrence," 27(2) *J. Quantitative Criminology* 225-249.

TORGERSON, Carole J., David J. TORGERSON, and Celia A. TAYLOR (2010) "Randomized Controlled Trials and Nonrandomized Designs," in Joseph S. Wholey, Harry P. Hatry, and Kathryn E. Newcomer eds., *Handbook of Practical Program Evaluation* (3rd ed.) 144. San Francisco: Jossey-Bass.

TRUTH AND RECONCILIATION COMMISSION OF CANADA (2012a) *Interim Report*. Winnipeg, Manitoba: TRC of Canada.

————————————— (2012b) *Canada, Aboriginal Peoples, and Residential Schools: They Came for the Children*. Winnipeg, Manitoba: TRC of Canada.

————————————— (2015) *Honouring the Truth, Reconciling for the Future: Summary of the Final Report of the Truth and Reconciliation Commission of Canada*. Winnipeg, Manitoba: TRC of Canada.

TUECKE, Patricia (2005) "The Architecture of Participation," in Sandy Schulman ed., *The IAF Handbook of Group Facilitation: Best Practices from the Leading Organization in Facilitation*. San Francisco: Jossey-Bass.

TYLER, Tom R. (1989) "The Psychology of Procedural Justice: A Test of the Group-Value Model," 57 *J. Personality & Soc. Psychol.* 830.

————————————— (2009) "Governing Pluralistic Societies," 72 *Law & Contemp. Probs.* 187 (Spring).

UMBREIT, Mark S., Betty VOS, Robert B. COATES, and Elizabeth LIGHTFOOT (2005) "Restorative Justice in the Twenty-First Century: A Social Movement Full of Opportunities and Pitfalls," 89 *Marq. L. Rev.* 251.

URY, William (1999) *Getting to Peace: Transforming Conflict at Home, at Work, and in the World*. New York: Viking Penguin.

URY, William L., Jeanne M. BRETT, and Stephen B. GOLDBERG (1988) *Getting Disputes Resolved: Designing Systems to Cut the Costs of Conflict*. San Francisco: Jossey-Bass; Cambridge: Harvard Program on Negotiation, http://www.pon.harvard.edu/shop/getting-disputes-resolveddesigning-systems-to-cut-the-costs-of-conflict/.

U.S. AID (2008) "Judge Walks Eight Days for Rule of Law Training" (U.S. AID, archived).

VAN NESS, Daniel W., and Karen Heetderks STRONG (2002) *Restoring Justice* (2d ed.). Cincinnati, OH: Anderson Publishing Co.

VERDONSCHOT, Jin Ho (2015) "In the Netherlands, Online Application Helps Divorcing Couples in Their Own Words, on Their Own Time," 21(2) Disp. Resol. Mag. 19.

VICK, Wayne J. (2015) *Process-Based Facilitation: Facilitating for Meeting Leaders, Constituents, and Group Facilitators*. Bloomington, IN: iUniverse.

VINING, Richard L. Jr., Amy STEIGERWALT, and Susan Navarro SMELCER (2009) *Bias and the Bar: Evaluating the ABA Ratings of Federal Judicial Nominees*. Atlanta: Emory University SSRN.

VOLPE, Maria R (1998) "Using Town Meetings to Foster Peaceful Coexistence," in Eugene Weiner ed., *The Handbook of Interethnic Coexistence* 382. New York: Continuum.

VOSOUGHI, Soroush, Deb ROY, and Sinan ARAL (2018) "The Spread of True and False News Online," 2018 *Science* 359.

WAGNER, Rodd, and James K. HARTER (2006) *12: The Elements of Great Managing*. New York: Gallup Press.

WAHAB, Mohamed S. Abdel, Ethan KATSH, and Daniel RAINEY eds. (2012) *Online Dispute Resolution: Theory and Practice*. The Hague, The Netherlands: Eleven International Publishing.

WALKER, Laurens (1988) "Perfecting Federal Civil Rules: A Proposal for Restricted Field Experiments," 51 *Law & Contemp. Probs.* 67.

WALL, Victor D., Jr. and Marcia L. DEWHIRST (1991) "Mediator Gender: Communication Differences in Resolved and Unresolved Mediations," 9 *Conflict Resol. Q.* 63.

WANGSNESS, Lisa, and Susan MILLIGAN (2010). "Health Care Summit Underscores Divisions; Democrats Lay Path to Pass Bill in Majority Vote." *Boston Globe*, Feb. 26, p.A1.

WARE, Stephen J. (2016) *Principles of Alternative Dispute Resolution*. St. Paul: West.

WARFIELD, Wallace (1996) "Building Consensus for Racial Harmony in American Cities: Case Model Approach," 1996 *J. Disp. Resol.* 151.

WEBB, Stuart G., and Ronald D. OUSKY (2006) *The Collaborative Way to Divorce: The Revolutionary Method That Results in Less Stress, Lower Costs and Happier Kids—Without Going to Court*. London: Penguin Books.

WEINSTEIN, Jack B. (2009) "Comments on Owen M. Fiss, Against Settlement (1984)," 78 *Fordham L. Rev.* 1265.

WEISS, Carol H. (1999) *Evaluation* (2d ed.). Englewood Cliffs, NJ: Prentice-Hall.

WEISS, Robert S. (1994) *Learning from Strangers: The Art and Method of Qualitative Interview Studies*. New York: Free Press.

—————————————————— (1995) *Learning from Strangers: The Art and Method of Qualitative Interview Studies*. New York: Simon and Schuster.

WELSH, Nancy A. (2001) "The Thinning Vision of Self-Determination in Court-Connected Mediation: The Inevitable Price of Institutionalization?," 6 *Harv. Negot. L. Rev.* 1.

—————————————————— (2008) "Looking Down the Road Less Traveled: Challenges to Persuading the Legal Profession to Define Problems More Humanistically," 2008 *J. Disp. Resol.* 45.

WELSH, Nancy A., and Barbara GRAY (2002) "Searching for a Sense of Control: The Challenge Presented by Community Conflicts over Concentrated Animal Feeding Operations," 10 *Penn St. Envtl. L. Rev.* 295.

WELSH, Nancy A., and David B. LIPSKY (2013) "'Moving the Ball Forward' in Consumer and Employment Dispute Resolution: What Can Planning, Talking, Listening and Breaking Bread Together Accomplish?," 19(3) *Disp. Resol. Mag.* 14.

WESTON, Maureen A., Kristen M. BLANKLEY, Jill I. GROSS, and Stephen HUBER (2018) *Arbitration: Law, Policy, and Practice*. Durham, NC: Carolina Academic Press.

WETLAUFER, Gerald B. (1990) "The Ethics of Lying in Negotiations," 75 *Iowa L. Rev.* 1219.

WHOLEY, Joseph S., Harry P. HATRY, and Kathryn E. NEWCOMER eds. (2010) *Handbook of Practical Program Evaluation* (3rd ed.). San Francisco: Jossey-Bass.

WILKINS, David B. (1994) "Book Review: Practical Wisdom for Practicing Lawyers: Separating Ideals from Ideology in Legal Ethics," 108 *Harv. L. Rev.* 458.

WILKINSON, Michael (2004) *The Secrets of Facilitation: The S.M.A.R.T. Guide to Getting Results with Groups*. San Francisco: Jossey-Bass.

WILLIAMS, Jill E. (2009) "Legitimacy and Effectiveness of a Grassroots Truth and Reconciliation Commission," 72 *Law & Contemp. Probs.* 143 (Spring).

WILLIAMS, Sue K. (2002) "Who Is Calling?," in John Paul Lederach and Janice Moomaw Jenner eds., *A Handbook of International Peacebuilding: Into the Eye of the Storm* 3. San Francisco: Jossey-Bass.

WISSLER, Roselle L. (1996) *Ohio Attorneys' Experience with and Views of Alternative Dispute Resolution Procedures*. Columbus: Supreme Court of Ohio Committee on Dispute Resolution.

—————————————————— (2002) "Court-Connected Mediation in General Civil Cases: What We Know from Empirical Research," 17 *Ohio St. J. on Disp. Resol.* 641.

—————————————————— (2004) "Barriers to Attorneys' Discussion and Use of ADR," 19 *Ohio St. J. on Disp. Resol.* 459.

—————————————————— (2004) "The Effectiveness of Court-Connected Dispute Resolution in Civil Cases," 22 *Conflict Resol. Q.* 55.

—————————————————— (2011a) "Court-Connected Settlement Procedures: Mediation and Judicial Settlement Conferences," 26 *Ohio St. J. on Disp. Resol.* 271.

—————————————————— (2011b) "Judicial Settlement Conferences and Staff Mediation," 17(4) *Disp. Resol. Mag.* 18.

WISSLER, Roselle L., and Bob DAUBER (2005) "Leading Horses to Water: The Impact of an ADR 'Confer and Report' Rule," 26 *Just. Sys. J.* 253.

WISSLER, Roselle L., and Art HINSHAW (2005) "How Do We Know That Mediation Training Works?," 12 *Disp. Resol. Mag.* 21 (Fall).

WONG, Paul T.P., "Creating a Positive Participatory Climate: A Meaning-Centered Counseling Perspective," in Sandy Schuman ed., *The IAF Handbook of Group Facilitation: Best Practices from the Leading Organization in Facilitation* 186. San Francisco: Jossey-Bass.

WOODROW, Peter, and Christopher MOORE (2002) "What Do I Need to Know About Culture? Practitioners Suggest . . . ," in John Paul Lederach and Janice Moomaw Jenner eds., *A Handbook of International Peacebuilding: Into the Eye of the Storm* 89. San Francisco: Jossey-Bass.

YOOST, Stephen M. (2006) "The National Hockey League and Salary Arbitration: Time for a Line Change," 21 *Ohio St. J. on Disp. Resol.* 485.

YOUNG, Michael (2009) "The South African Talks: A Template for Peace," *Huffington Post*, October 20, at http://www.huffingtonpost.com/michael-young/the-south-african-talks-a_b_327316.html.

ZARTMAN, I. William (2000) "Introduction" in I. William Zartman ed., *Traditional Cures for Modern Conflicts: African Conflict "Medicine."* Boulder, CO: Lynne Rienner Publishers.

ZARTMAN, I. William, ed. (2001) *Preventive Negotiation: Avoiding Conflict Escalation.* Lanham, MD: Rowman & Littlefield Publishers, Inc.

ZARTMAN, I. William, and Victor KREMENYUK eds. (2005) *Peace Versus Justice: Negotiating Forward- and Backward-Looking Outcomes.* Lanham, MD: Rowman & Littlefield Publishers, Inc.

ZEHR, Howard (2002) *The Little Book of Restorative Justice.* Intercourse, PA: Good Books.

ZWIER, Paul J. (2013) *Talking with Evil: Principled Negotiation and Mediation in the International Arena.* Cambridge, UK: Cambridge University Press.

Index